The Telling
of the Act

The Telling
of the Act

Sexuality as Narrative
in Eighteenth-
and Nineteenth-Century France

Peter Cryle

DELAWARE

Newark: University of Delaware Press
London: Associated University Presses

Associated University Presses
440 Forsgate Drive
Cranbury, NJ 08512

Associated University Presses
16 Barter Street
London WC1A 2AH, England

Associated University Presses
P.O. Box 338, Port Credit
Mississauga, Ontario
Canada L5G 4L8

The paper used in this publication meets the requirements of the American National Standard for Permanence of Paper for Printed Library Materials Z39.48-1984.

Library of Congress Cataloging-in-Publication Data

Cryle, P. M. (Peter Maxwell), 1946–
    The telling of the act : sexuality as narrative in eighteenth- and nineteenth-century France / Peter Cryle
        p. cm.
    Includes bibliographical references and index.
    ISBN 0–87413–748–9 (alk. paper)
    1. French fiction—18th century—History and criticism. 2. French fiction—19th century—History and criticism 3. Sex in literature. 4. Erotic stories, French—History and criticism. I. Title.

PQ648 .C79 2001   l b 0 2 9 3 b l 3 l
843´.5093538—dc21

                                                                2001027046

T

Contents

Acknowledgments

I WISH TO THANK MY COLLEAGUE JULIANA DE NOOY FOR HER CAREFUL and constructive reading of my manuscript. Ross Chambers and Jill Forbes provided counsel and encouragement when I needed it. Jeremy Horwood, Andrew Munro, Sarah McCosker, and Anousha Victoire all gave me the benefit of their questions and comments about some key issues. Mandy Macdonald played a whole series of roles with good-humored warmth and subtlety. My sister Erica helped, by her own productive uptake, to make more of my work than I might have imagined. And Diana Jones proved herself to be the best research assistant anyone could hope for.

The Telling
of the Act

Introduction

THIS BOOK UNDERTAKES TWO APPARENTLY DISCRETE TASKS IN PARALLEL, and attempts to show that one cannot properly be carried out without the other. The primary task, or at least the more readily located by discipline, is to contribute to the history of sexuality, focusing on representations of desire, pleasure, and gender in French erotic literature of the eighteenth and nineteenth centuries. The second task is a form of critique: I seek to identify the components of a discourse that organizes sexuality in strictly narrative terms, and to relativize its claims to universality. The point of this introduction is to spell out what I understand by each of these tasks, and to demonstrate their relatedness.

The history of sexuality most often takes as its starting point the work of Michel Foucault, and functions as a quasi-disciplinary space founded on his insights. Its uses of Foucault's work are often rather loose, however, and this can result in a failure to enter properly into the opportunities opened up by *Histoire de la sexualité*. Foucault's work is misread, I suggest, when it is taken as an invitation to go looking for sexuality in all its manifestations, historical or anthropological, as if there were recognizable forms of the same libidinal reality simply waiting to be found in various cultures. There is some such misreading even in Gaëtan Brulotte's wonderfully elaborate thematic study, *Œuvres de chair*, which refers frequently to Foucault, but which holds fast to the certainty that, at some level, "the flesh" named in the title is everywhere the same.[1] Foucault's argument is that the discourse in which and by which we know sexuality is itself a particular historical formation, coming together in its fullness only in the late nineteenth century with the emergence of sexual pathology and psychoanalysis.[2] That is why, as he added some

11

years after the appearance of *La Volonté de savoir*, it is important to keep the quotation marks around "sexuality."[3] Indeed,
while we should be wary of academic preciosity, it seems appropriate to recognize a whole range of common sexual expressions
as discursive quotations. To embark on a historical study of
"homosexuality" in the eighteenth century, for example, is almost
certainly to practice a form of systematic anachronism, since the
term was not at that time part of an established discursive order.
Jeffrey Weeks, Gayle Rubin, Vernon Rosario, and others have
shown this admirably for homosexuality,[4] and I shall attempt a
roughly parallel analysis of such notions as "orgasm," "foreplay,"
and "frigidity"—none of which, I contend, has a proper place in
libertine writing of the *ancien régime*. Whatever the particular
notions considered, it can hardly suffice for scholars to range
over space and time in search of the differing complexions of sexuality, since the very object they seek, and indeed their capacity
to range, are inscribed within the discourse of their own time, as
part of their own, historically specific order of knowledge. Experts
in sexuality are empowered by the assumption that sexuality is
everyone's secret truth, ever the same underneath, whatever local
conditions of repression or permissiveness might have inflected
its visible forms. This is a model of inquiry that Foucault unequivocally rejects.[5]

Investigation of this sort falls victim to an interpretive short
circuit, for the *scientia sexualis* described by Foucault is in fact a
manner of naming, finding, and consolidating a supposed universal called sexuality, a universal that only came to be taken as
such, according to his argument, at the end of the nineteenth
century. Here is Foucault's general point, nicely spelt out by
Arnold Davidson: "Sexuality only became a possible object of
psychological investigation, theorizing and speculation because
of a distinctive form of reasoning that had a historically specific
origin; or to put it another way, statements about sexuality came
to possess a positivity, a being-true-or-false, only when the con-
ceptual space associated with the psychiatric style of reasoning
was first articulated."[6] If we take this consideration seriously, we
must learn to temper the enthusiasm of historical discovery with
a close hermeneutical reflection about our own situated capacity
to know. And that does not just mean rhetorical precautions, or
even general inhibition. We might decide to practice a brand of
suspicion, looking for otherness at every turn, but that would not

safeguard against making excessively strong assumptions about what was fundamental.[7] Indeed, the function of *scientia sexualis* as Foucault describes it is to constitute the fundamental as such, and to arm us with the confident foreknowledge of its half-hidden ubiquity. Terry Castle shows what is at stake here, *a contrario*, when she misunderstands the historical point of Weeks and Rubin, and performs her misunderstanding, so to speak, with some authority through the discourse of quasi-universal sexuality. After a skeptical review of attempts to historicize "lesbianism," Castle states disarmingly that "western civilization has always known at some level about lesbians."[8] The talk of "levels" is precisely what allows her to appeal to the transhistorical presence of a hidden lesbian identity, for it reduces the question of discursive shifts to one of "terminology"—that is, of historically changing surfaces over what is, deep down, always the same thing.

Let us consider more carefully the "fundamental" notion of desire. A history of sexuality that is content to suppose the universality of desire, cataloging its peculiar fixations according to time and place, will fall short of the requirements of discursivist understanding, even as it notes a great variety of historical and ethnographic phenomena. To suppose that desire, in the modern sense retailed by psychoanalysis, is present everywhere as a force, as a drive, waiting to be identified under the surface, is precisely to apply or enact our *scientia sexualis*. That does not of itself constitute critical reflection, and it fails to answer Foucault's strongest challenge to historical scholarship.[9] In an earlier study, *Geometry in the Boudoir: Configurations of French Erotic Narrative*, I sought to establish the constraining discursive regularities of what I called classical or libertine eroticism.[10] I was led then to emphasize the artistic representation of a set of bodily positions, often called the figures of Venus, and the self-conscious teaching and learning of them in the practice of pleasure(s). For a classical *ars erotica* of the kind found most often in French fiction from about 1650 to about 1750, "desire" in the broadly modern sense appears more or less redundant, since pleasure is seen to happen in its place, as a kind of discipline, when one takes up the appropriate attitude. My historical thesis, put most generally, is that desire as we know it, desire as we now expect to find it, only took on its characteristic thematic forms in the course of a long transformation beginning around the middle of the eighteenth century and culminating at the end of the nineteenth. That we are able to talk about desire as a hidden-and-manifest universal depends, I suggest, on our understanding it as disruptive, fluid, and communicable from one body to another. These thematic metaphors are demonstrably not eternal, nor even classical. They came to the fore during the period studied in this book. Those one-and-a-half centuries from the mid-eighteenth to the late nineteenth saw the metaphorical elaboration of "desire" in the production of a discourse that allowed it to appear universal. *The Telling of the Act* is, in some sense, a book about desire, but one that is careful not to take its theme for granted. Taking it for granted is the routine business of *scientia sexualis*, and my book is written against this discursive habit. It is written against the kind of compulsive thematics, or thematics of compulsion, that finds desire to be everywhere fundamentally the same. I write, then, without the theoretical support of psychoanalysis or sexology, and by that fact alone, I am writing against the hegemony of those two disciplines.[11] Historical concerns are not usually to the fore in psychoanalytical writing, and for good cause, since psychoanalytical universalism tends not to be at ease with studies that locate its forms of knowledge in particular historical and discursive moments. John C. O'Neal notes ruefully, and a little naïvely, that "a sustained psychoanalytic analysis of Enlightenment literature still remains to be written."[12] I can only say for my part that I shall attempt nothing that might disturb that happy situation. I take it that a history of desire framed by psychoanalysis or sexology could only confirm their discursive habits in an unhelpfully circular way, and I wish to relativize and contain those disciplines, which I take to be the theoretical antagonists of a careful history of sexuality. I hope to trouble their prescience, and undermine their claims to a secure knowledge of things sexual.

The first three chapters that follow tell the story of general shifts, during the period 1750–1900, in representations of furniture, of flesh and blood, and of aphrodisiacs. In chapter 1, I show that furniture, which served in classical environments as a constraining support for the adoption of appropriate venereal positions, came more and more to be a sounding board for erotic intensity, bouncing and creaking under the strain, and often being tested to the point of collapse. The move from the first thematic to the second marks the diminishing importance of disciplined erotic practice, and the emergence of desire as something spontaneous, disruptive, radically unprecedented. Chapter 2 highlights the development of a material dialectic of marble and fire. Where marble had served primarily as the noble medium of sculpted postural figures, it is now involved in the business of circulation, and drawn into a substantive encounter with fire. Marble, in its gendered coldness, is seen to await a libidinal transfusion of fire, blood, and sperm that will bring about the most dramatic and most typical of erotic events. By this transformation, the supposedly dormant woman is awakened to the life of circulatory desire. Chapter 3 traces a history of aphrodisiacs that foregrounds in a comparable way the role of substances and of circulation. Aphrodisiacs, after having been a mere libertine artifice in most eighteenth-century fiction, are called on in the nineteenth to play a fascinating and paradoxical role as "charming poisons." They come to stand for, indeed metaphorically to be, the very essence of seductive and dangerous desire, somehow both exotic and intimately communicable. These three chapters tell much the same story. Their thematics are parallel and mutually supportive, without being exhaustive of the discursive elements in play. They serve to show, by their range and their relative insistence, that between 1750 and 1900 there was a quite general change in what could be acceptably thought and said about "desire."

The second concern that guides this study, in addition to its historical preoccupation, is, as I have said, a critical one. My aim here is to focus attention on the central function of narrative in standard modern representations of desire and pleasure. Much of what the twentieth century knows about sexuality is cast, after all, in narrative terms. Well-integrated moderns routinely claim to sense the build-up of desire, to heighten and communicate it through foreplay, to experience pleasure in climactic moments, and often to repeat those moments in the multiplication of orgasm. This is the "human sex act" in its programmatic fullness, in the glory of its temporal extension. To practice it is to affirm the happy convergence of biological necessity and social regularity. This act "we" know with confidence to be the act par excellence, the proper articulation of desire and pleasure. But none of this is quite so solid as it may seem. Readers will note that I can hardly summarize these verities of sexology without being ironic, and I fear I shall again find myself yielding to irony from time to time in the course of this study. I am able to be ironic, disposed in fact to be so, as I expect many of my readers are, precisely because these purportedly universal patterns no longer seem so natural, so worthy of respect. For one who has read Luce Irigaray, for example, on the very concept of "making love," there must be a question about how pleasure is to be told, or even whether it should be told at all according to the established narrative pattern. When women touch, says Irigaray, "la norme exigerait qu'elles finissent par faire l'amour. Le font-elles ou non? En tout cas, cela ne sera pas donné en spectacle. Il n'y aura pas de cadrage de scène sexuelle au sens strict. Le sexuel est là *continûment*. Sans tension vers un acte précis, sans focalisation de l'espace-temps, sans avant ni après *coup*" [the norm would require them to finish up making love. Do they do it or not? In any case, it will not be put on show. There will be no framed sex scene, in the strict sense of the word. The sexual is there *continually*. Without tension toward a precise act, without a focus in space-time, without a before and after the *event*].[13] The tension in question is a particular experience of desire as delay, its focus is what we often call climax, and the *coup* (event) of which Irigaray speaks is the iterative singularity of the sex act, in its semiotic distinctness. All of these elements are called into question as standard representations, and narrativity itself surrounded by suspicion in the wake of such critique. Anne-Marie Dardigna confronts the dominant story quite directly, arguing that it has a gendered subject and a gendered object: "le 'faire' en question est invariablement mis en acte par un homme et subi par une femme . . ." [the 'doing' of which they speak is invariably enacted by a man and submitted to by a woman].[14] Other forms of pleasure can be imagined and represented, but the sex act occupies a central place in the cultural production of our time, as a narrative ordering of desire and pleasure. To see this discourse as a powerful norm rather than a simple fact of nature, to see it indeed as a cultural norm that has acquired the prestige of naturalness is perforce to engage in critique, and to open up the possibility of irony.

The form of critique to which I hope to contribute is not the kind of outright dismissal practiced, for example, by Andrea Dworkin. Dworkin affirms that the representation of the sex act and the behavior this representation authorizes are unethical:

Sex, a word potentially so inclusive and evocative, is whittled down by the male so that, in fact, it means penile intromission. Commonly referred to as "it," sex is defined in action only by that which the male does with his penis. . . . "The sex act" means penile intromission followed by penile thrusting, or fucking. The woman is acted on; the man acts and through action expresses sexual power, the power of masculinity.[15]

The point of Dworkin's critique is that the very existence and dissemination of this model are wrongs, and must be everywhere resisted. I make no such judgment. I want merely to argue that there is no law of human necessity requiring "sex" to be translated as "the act." A study of erotic literature reveals that other conceptions of pleasure have existed and continue to exist in competition with this, even in a mainstream Western tradition. The now dominant narrative can and should be situated, in fact, within a quite particular historical context. That is the aim of any irony that might appear in this text, and that is the polemical point of its recurrence. Not to marshal indignation or to call for an end to such things, not to demand a ban on pornography or even to defend it, but to demonstrate simply that the dominant erotic representations of our time cannot serve of themselves to demonstrate the eternal recurrence of desire as we know it, for they have a quite checkered history. It was not ever so, and the standard discourse was only able to conquer its place by a confluence of circumstances. Furthermore, it can only hold that place, as we shall see, by dint of adjustment, concession, and running thematic repairs.

In the second section, I concentrate on the marks of sexual narrativity, showing how nineteenth-century fiction elaborated a poetics of intensity. The nineteenth century made climactic narrative where classical libertine writing most often set out the "gradations" as a series of gently ascending *jouissances*, each of value in its own right. Chapter 4 follows the development of a poetics of exclamation, and notes that producing the utterance of pleasure, especially feminine pleasure, becomes a central task of erotic narrative, and a climactic mark of its success. Chapter 5 shows that the related practice of suspension marks came eventually to signify a necessary ellipsis, a failure of writing under the pressure of the unspeakably intense. Chapter 6 considers a thematic rivalry that went on at length in erotic novels of the late eighteenth and early nineteenth centuries. We find characters considering side by side the virtues, or rather the erotic yield, of two temporal models, that of the classical gradations, and that of more urgent "fucking," with a bare minimum of "preliminaries." In the course of the nineteenth century, this contest tends to be won by the active, "virile" model, to the point where the fin de siècle comes to regard the refinements of libertine pleasure as symptoms of perversity. What were once the elegant arabesques of an art of pleasure have become the marks of deviancy. They reveal a disquieting failure to adhere to the now standard narrative. Representation of the center of pleasure "itself" is the subject of chapter 7, which points to the relatively late emergence, during the nineteenth century, of the notion of orgasm, and considers the semiotic work done by erotic fiction in bringing together such notions as "crisis" and paroxysm, in order to provide bodily metaphors of climax that mediate optimally between the pleasurable and the pathological.

The final section of the book considers a problem inherent in the narrative model, one that bedevilled nineteenth-century erotic fiction: the difficulty of finishing. The problem, put most simply, is that nothing guarantees the decisiveness of the sex act. There is of course a certain pleasure to be had, and indeed a boon for serial narrative, in beginning again. But what, if anything, will allow the story to arrive at its proper denouement, at the end of desire? Erotic narrative shows itself to be haunted by the difficulty of concluding, and this difficulty is often given a woman's name. Messalina becomes one of the great (anti-)heroines of nineteenth-century erotic narrative, in view of her invincible feminine capacity to go on desiring even after men have done their utmost with her. Chapter 8 describes the struggle to deal with Messalina, in the bedroom and in fiction, noting the capital made out of her legend by narrative, but also assessing the grave internal damage done to the main thematic model by the need to accommodate contradiction. Chapter 9 shows how the Messalina problem is extended and compounded by another, that of "Lesbos." Pleasure between women tends to be represented in male-focused texts as fascinating but somehow untellable, having the power to resist or otherwise undo the masculine program. Chapter 10 deals with some of the many stories that rehearse, or try to rehearse, the power of males to finish—to finish off the sex act, to finish off Messalinic women, and to finish off erotic novels. Despite or because of all the hearty affirmations, these stories are still obliged to make room for their half-acknowledged enemy: a feminine principle of resistance. Masculine finishing power has the greatest difficulty in overcoming feminine staying power, even when competing, so to speak, on its own terrain, in erotic fiction written largely by men and for men.

I am conscious that, in writing a history of "erotic fiction," I may be open to the criticism I leveled earlier at many recent historical studies of sexuality. What is it, after all, that allows me to gather under the same generic heading an elegant novel by Crébillon dating from the 1750s, a piece of vulgar 1830s pornography such as *Douze aventures du bossu Mayeux*, and a moralizing fin-de-siècle novel such as Prévost's *Les Demi-Vierges*? Clearly, these texts can belong to the same genre only if the notion of genre is understood very loosely. Denis Hollier does in fact argue cogently that such looseness is, exceptionally, the rule with erotic literature, since the generic properties involved are entirely thematic rather than formal.[16] But I cannot be quite content with that, if only because Hollier's definition depends on taking pleasure and desire as themes, without identifying any discursive articulation of them, any thematic of the sort that might lend itself readily to a particular literary form.

To say that the texts I am analyzing can be understood as part of a single corpus because they are all "about sex" must be considered a problematic and hermeneutically perilous move. There is a sense in which I have already made that move, but there is another in which I will continue to resist it, and refuse to ratify it glibly. I have tried to show, here and in *Geometry in the Boudoir*, that someone looking for novels about sex in Crébillon's time would need, in order to enter into the play of meaning in his texts, to adjust to the fact that the practice of seductive conversation and gently graded pleasures functions as a kind of social norm. Such novels are misread if they are recognized as being about sex, in the modern sense, but they are nonetheless the closest equivalent in classical libertine writing to what we call, although only since the late nineteenth century, "erotic literature." We must recognize the approximate equivalence without foreclosing its significance through universalist discourse.

Similarly, with the notion of natural popular vigor as it emerges in Revolutionary times, one finds a veritable thematics of crudeness, whereby brevity and suddenness of impact are given positive value, by contrast with the over-refined complication attributed to effete aristocrats. I am concerned, of course, to show how different is such pornography from the writing of Crébillon, not just because the one is refined and the other vulgar, but because the very notions of refinement and vulgarity have changed, together with the values attached to them.[17] But I can talk about change only by supposing a modicum of sameness. I take it that libertine fiction and Revolutionary pornography have something in common when I argue that we should not confuse the two or collapse the historical difference between them. And where fin-de-siècle writing is concerned, there are still texts that maintain the assertive vulgarity of the earlier nineteenth century, but these are far outnumbered by a relatively new genre—or is it a subgenre?—of prurient fiction, in which all forms of perversity are narratively indulged, but only when framed by sententious pieces of moral and medical discourse. As with the earlier shifts, I argue that this kind of writing needs to be recognized and not-recognized at the same time: it is what "erotic fiction" has characteristically become at this point in history.[18] Only by knowing that we are looking for something like pleasure or desire can we know that we have found something like them, yet failed to find them in the forms that we know best. Only by thematic fussiness can we forestall the undue triumph of self-confirming expectation without falling into pointless wonderment. Thematic fastidiousness will, I hope, provide the very stuff, and the intellectual style of this study. I must accept that any understanding of the past is necessarily shaped by the present, yet endeavor to limit the effects of over-quick recognition. It is a matter of accepting the circular nature of historical understanding, while guarding against any facile closure of the circle.

This book, like *Geometry in the Boudoir* before it, offers as a kind of slogan the notion of attentive irony, where attentiveness to detail is its guard against transhistorical reductiveness, and irony its defense against the overweight complacency of modern sexology. Yet when understanding is declared to be both circular and ironic, it is impossible to avoid the implacable consequence of a circular irony that makes me not only subject but object. It is inescapably ironic that I should define the "we" of modernity, in this context, by the discursive formation of *scientia sexualis*, but appeal to a readership that is already distanced from such knowledge by its familiarity with feminist or gay and lesbian critique. The discrepancy between interpretive communities[19] that are addressed simultaneously is in fact the space of hermeneutical work to be done in this study. I am able to engage in the history of sexuality by following a century-long discursive triumph leading eventually to the discipline in which I am involved, while at the same time drawing ironic attention to the contradictions that surround and inhabit this discourse. That there should be possibilities for collective understanding outside the knowledge of sexuality so widely abroad in our time is of course no achievement of mine, but I hope nonetheless to increase the ironic discrepancy and to further widen the historical credibility gap. Without such a gap, a study like this could not be written, or read.[20]

Let me be quite clear about the orientation of critique in this study. I am not attempting to produce one of those histories that brandishes modern knowledge as the final product of a compelling evolution, regarding sexual enlightenment and freedom as proud, if partial, recent achievements. That is in fact the standard narrative of libertarian modernism, which loves to tell sexual revolution as an overcoming of the past and a defeat for the forces of repression. The established French version of this story describes the emergence of desire in Revolutionary times through the agency of Sade. Sade is, we are told repeatedly, "la première grande figure de la modernité en un sens précis: il met en place, à sa manière, la tragedie de l'Individu comme sujet du désir. Il est le premier à tenir un discours sur le désir au sens moderne (au sens freudien)" [the first great figure of modernity in a precise sense: he sets up, in his way, the tragedy of the Individual as subject of desire. He is the first one to speak the language of desire in the modern sense (in the Freudian sense)].[21] Note that Sade is declared to leap in one single bound from the French Revolution to the birth of psychoanalysis, as if his writing collapsed the two into one decisive moment. Influential writers like Breton, Bataille, Desnos, Eluard, and Klossowski see in Sade the exemplary figure—not to say the author—of literary modernity as an enterprise committed to the utterance of truth. The divinity of the divine Marquis is deemed to lie precisely in this, that he had the courage to speak the hitherto unspoken truth of human desire. The

story told in these modernist accounts of Sade does not correspond in any way to the history of sexuality now being constructed by scholarly endeavor, but it casts a monumental
shadow over the space of inquiry in which I find myself. Sade,
we are forcefully told, is an agent whose story makes any other
history appear trivial. He is "sans précédent."[22] Before him, no
writer had dared to give voice to the forces that dwell within us
all. Indeed, Sade's very history is itself presented as a kind of
erotic narrative: the power and prestige of his fiction are reflected and mimicked in critical accounts of his vigorous coming
to prominence. His supposed break-out from the dungeons of
repression is read as both a symptom and an exemplum of a
new, modern eroticism that courageously expresses the oldest
and darkest of truths. Sade the man stands like a phallus, says
Bataille, following Swinburne.[23] His tumescent glory compels
our recognition, according to doctrine, as both an affirmation
and an acting out of desire.

A thematic history of desire can hardly proceed without seeking to undo, or at least call into question, the powerful convergence of metaphors produced by such lyrical discourse. The
story of an erotic revolution depends for its dramatic impact on
positing a pre-Sadian world characterized by ignorance and repression, or at least by triviality and faint-heartedness. In this
view, classical eroticism is recognized only incidentally, as an
ancien régime awaiting demolition. The process of canonizing
Sade as a hero of the revolution entails not just glorifying his
work—or rather, his figure—but demeaning and forgetting any
minor predecessors or competitors. Desnos says, for example, of
the seventeenth-century writer Brantôme, that he may have
been of some interest as a writer on eroticism in earlier times,
but has now been "relegated" to the attic by Sade's brilliance.[24]
This is how Sade's name, and the story that it stands in, have
become the fortified place of erotic modernism. As Roger Borderie says, with what has become routine hyperbole, "le nom de
Sade constitue en quelque sorte le lieu géométrique critique le
plus fort de notre culture littéraire" [the name of Sade can be
said to make up the strongest geometrical place of criticism in
our literary culture].[25] It has become widely accepted—at least
within this narrow bastion of French literary judgment—that
Sade's is the most outrageous work of all time. Never, says
Blanchot, in any literature, at any time, was there a work so

scandalous.[26] Demonstrably, such glorification of Sade depends on a slippage between historical and transhistorical discourses, whereby Sade's actions and work become *the* Revolution for all time, standing tall as a kind of archetypal historical monument, and producing masterpieces that belong to the universal canon of splendidly unprecedented works of genius.[27]

The history I am attempting here can serve as a contribution to critique by working against the grain of this narrative of liberation, and putting Sade in his place. This is not to say that no historical stories can be told; I am in fact committed to the view, manifestly that of Foucault, that major discursive shifts do occur from time to time, and that these constitute tellable events. This is what Foucault means when he talks about "événementalisation" [the making of an event] as a "rupture d'évidence" [a break in evidence, a break in the obvious]: a breakdown of scientific evidence, if you like, but more particularly an interruption in what can be taken as obvious.[28] As a consequence of such shifts, the things that we all know, the very expressions whose familiarity allows us to say "we" with confidence, can no longer be relied on. That is when quotation marks bloom, and when historical scholarship faces its most challenging tasks. In this study, I want to use "pleasure" and "desire" without undue trepidation—without what philosophers call "scare quotes," since I will be trying to establish the approximate thematic equivalence, across time, of differing erotic representations. Yet I shall insist that historical diversity not be swallowed up by the lyrical narratives of evolution or revolution, according to which later is almost always better.

I spoke at the outset about the double nature of my project, and I am now in a position to articulate this doubleness more tightly. I will firstly be attempting to restore discursive and thematic understandings that appear to have been rather lost from view, even in the history of sexuality. And at the same time I will be critically resisting libertarian histories and sexological home truths, in the hope that classical representations of "pleasure" and "desire" can find room to compete for attention with those that are more familiar, perhaps too familiar, to us. The very thematic deployment of other representations in a space not entirely dominated by modern discourse should reveal that different orders of pleasure were once valid, and once enjoyed. Understanding that fact, and understanding it in detail, should not

I
Beginnings

1
Furniture

M Y TOPIC IN THIS CHAPTER WILL BE FURNITURE, NOTABLY THOSE ITEMS
referred to variously throughout eighteenth- and nineteenth-
century erotic narratives in French as sofas, or *canapés, avantageuses,* or *fouteuses*. This is not a topic whose coherence is
guaranteed from the outset, but rather a kind of thematic pretext. I shall consider what such furniture becomes, in order to
show that it cannot be taken as a theme in the straightforward
sense of the word, since it is not something that remains identical across one-and-a-half centuries of fictive representation. It is
a matter of following such themes through time in order to show
that they are unstable objects of knowledge. The history to
which I wish to contribute will in fact be a history in which drift
leads to disturbance, and disturbance, at times, to jarring transformation. The argument of this chapter, put most broadly, will
be that furniture has a particular narrative function in earlier
eighteenth-century texts that it seems gradually to lose in the
following decades, only to take on another role as part of a new
discursive order. There is, I shall attempt to show, a historical
overlap during which the two thematic functions coexist, allowing us to perceive both continuity and discontinuity, both drift
and disturbance. This study will endeavor to respect thematic
functionality within a given narrative order while recognizing
the net effect of radical transformation over time.[1]

Furniture is so important to eighteenth-century erotic narrative as to provide an alluring title for a number of works. The
most famous of these is undoubtedly *Le Sopha* (1740), by Crébillon *fils*.[2] Amanzéï, the narrator-hero of this novel, is in fact the
victim of a magic spell that condemns him to reside in sofas
until such time as he happens to witness, from below, the first

erotic yielding of a virtuous woman. In a libertine world where feminine virtue is hardly more than a seductive fiction, Amanzéï's narrative quest is bound to be a protracted one. On the way to the conclusion, as the hero moves experimentally from sofa to sofa, a whole series of erotic encounters takes place. The stuff of narrative in Crébillon's text is thus provided, pre-dictably enough, by dalliance rather than virtue, but it is re-markable that the narrator's soul is always located, so to speak, at the seat of the action. Not that we are treated to a lot of talk about warmth, or contact, or sweat: there is something about such things that is too modern for Crébillon. The sofa is merely a place from which intimate observation occurs. An earlier novel, the anonymous *Le Canapé couleur de feu* (1714), actually tells much the same story, and locates the storyteller in the same way.[3]

Narrators are to be found lurking in sofas for reasons of con-venience. Indeed, the narrator-hero of *Le Canapé couleur de feu* dubs himself Mr. or Sir Convenience: "Ainsi je me nommerai, si vous le trouvez bon, le chevalier Commode, à cause de la commodité que tant d'honnêtes gens, y compris monsieur et madame, ont trouvée chez moi lorsque j'étais fait pour la mol-lesse, le repos, et les plaisirs des deux sexes" [So I shall dub myself, if you will, Sir *Commode*, because of the convenience that so many good people, including Sir and Madame, have found in me. I was made for softness, rest, and the pleasures of both sexes] (5–6). The word *commode*, designating an item of furniture in both French and English, although not of course the same item in each case, is a nicely reflexive reminder of the nar-rator's situation. *Commodité* is part of the very definition of fur-niture, as something made for convenience. This rather banal circularity, the convenience of the commode, is one that deserves close attention, because it is crucial to the functioning of much eighteenth-century eroticism. The sofa is constructed for plea-sure: it is a ready-made site for erotic activity. By its very shape (and texture), it extends an invitation. "Mettons-nous sur ce canapé" [Let us sit on this canapé], says one character to an-other in *Lettres galantes et philosophiques de deux nones* (1797), "vois comme il nous invite à prendre nos plaisirs" [see how it in-vites us to enjoy our pleasures].[4] In other words, there is an erotic use, and an erotic purpose, inscribed in the furniture, as there so often is in the decor surrounding it. There may be paint-

ings on the walls or etchings on display. There may even, on
grand occasions, be live tableaux. All these, it seems, have the
same function: they provide models for erotic behavior.[5] Or, to
put it better, they reveal the notion of behavior to be somewhat
anachronistic, since they position the body in precise ways that
are already present as erotic culture, inscribed on the walls, and
built into the furniture. It is a matter, for the participants, of
taking one's place—*se placer*, to place oneself, is one of the most
favored verbs in this context—and of adopting the proper erotic
attitude.[6]

All this can seem very artificial and inauthentic to a modern
reader used only to notions of eroticism as spontaneous and natural. The questions most obvious to moderns, perhaps—but ones
that I claim are never asked in these eighteenth-century texts—
are "What about the characters' motivation? Are the shapes
made available by the furniture appropriate to their individual
inclinations? That is, do they really feel like it?" The fact is that
this set of questions simply does not arise, because it is thoroughly preempted by the workings of an erotic discipline. The
standard libertine view in the eighteenth century seems to be
that erotic convenience and represented models are precisely
what give rise to, or create the opportunity for, desires—in a
thoroughly convenient, circular fashion. The description of a
boudoir is unlikely to make any distinction between the decorative and the functional, because the function of the decor is precisely to invite one to the erotic actions represented and
inscribed there. *La Nouvelle Académie des dames* (1754) presents a clear example of this: "M. de R . . . , aussi recherché dans
ses plaisirs que voluptueux libertin, avait orné cet appartement
de peintures propres à faire naître des désirs, et avait pratiqué
partout des commodités pour les satisfaire avec volupté" [M. de
R . . . , being as refined in his pleasures as he was voluptuous in
the enjoyment of them, had adorned his apartment with paintings meant to create desires, and had installed conveniences for
their voluptuous satisfaction].[7] "Inviting" furniture is thus produced by an architectural technique of desire as comfort, and can
still be found in Sade's *Histoire de Juliette* (1797): "Des canapés
à la turque environnés de glaces qui se voyaient au-dessus, invi-
taient, par leur mollesse, aux plus voluptueuses jouissances"
[Turkish style canapés, surrounded by mirrors that could be
seen above, invited one by their softness to the most voluptuous

pleasures].[8] By convention, the indwelling mythical architect of such spaces is said to be divine. These are temples of Venus, and the proper way to act in them is to respond to the imperatives of erotic ceremony: "Il faisait une chaleur horrible; nous étions seules, nonchalamment couchés dans un boudoir divin: n'eussions-nous pas été coupables de retarder plus longtemps le sacrifice au dieu qui nous préparait ses autels?" [It was dreadfully hot; we were alone, nonchalantly lying about in a divine boudoir. Would it not have been unpardonable to delay any longer our sacrifice to the god who had been preparing his altar for us?][9] Nerciat's *Le Diable au corps* (1803) describes a space that has the same kind of constraining softness, the same inbuilt tendency to shape desire. The Marquise's bedroom is an "endroit délicieux qu'on peut nommer le temple de la mollesse et du libertinage. Tout y est recherché; les moindres ornements y sont analogues aux goûts sensuels de la divinité qui l'habite, et propre à faire naître des désirs" [a delicious spot that can be named the temple of softness and libertinage. Everything there shows refinement. The slightest ornaments are analogous to the sensual tastes of the divinity that dwells there, and suited to the creation of desires].[10] Furniture, it appears, can be taken as a material analogue of the erotic body.[11] The potential for desire and satisfaction is thus situated in the space itself, precluding even the question: who is the appropriate subject for this desire? The furniture is equally suitable for all worshippers of Venus, not only for the master-builder and boudoir owner-decorator, but also for any young person who might be introduced there.

There are, of course, ethical and political reasons to be suspicious about this divine imperative and this spatial matter-of-factness, but such concerns may well be symptoms of our modernity: there can be no doubt that classical eroticism continues right through the eighteenth century to affirm the same happy coincidence of desire for all who use, and are used by, the boudoir. The possibility of recalcitrance or indifference—or of that relatively modern notion, frigidity—does not arise because the cultural space is both comfortable and efficiently didactic, teaching the forms of comfort that it requires. The point can hardly be made more simply than in *Lucette, ou Les Progrès du libertinage* (1765), where we read: "On introduit notre Héroïne dans un cabinet délicieux; les victoires de l'Amour étaient peintes de mains de Maîtres; tout annonçait le plaisir et le faisait désirer" [Our heroine was led into a delightful room. The victories of Love had been painted there by the hands of masters. Everything announced pleasure, and caused it to be desired].[12] The spatial imperative here does not even require a generalizing pronoun like *on*, merely the double infinitive of *faire désirer*. Desire is simply caused by the space.

None of that can suffice to disarm the suspicion I just alluded to: that the boudoir might—indeed, must—work oppressively. And when Sade's horrendous castle at Silling, in *Les Cent Vingt Journées de Sodome* (1785), is said to have rooms that are "munies de canapés et de tous les autres meubles nécessaires aux impuretés de toute espèce" [provided with canapés and all the other furniture needed for impure things of that kind], there is nothing in the least reassuring about that.[13] Sade's vicious libertines use furniture for "placing" their victims in a radically constraining way. Reference is made during the *Cent Vingt Journées de Sodome* to the use of heavy furniture to attach a young woman: "Les cuisses de ma compagne étaient dans le plus grand écartement possible, et fixées à de gros meubles pour qu'elles ne puissent varier" [My companion's thighs were tied in the most widely spread position possible, and fixed to heavy pieces of furniture so that they could not alter], says one of the storytellers (1:160). Of another victim, Juliette says: "Elle était étendue sur une étroite banquette, des courroies contenaient l'attitude, et sa tête, fortement élevée par un collier de fer, s'offrait aux baisers" [She was stretched out on a narrow bench; straps held her in position, and her head, acutely lifted by an iron collar, stood ready to be kissed].[14]

Nothing in classical erotica lends itself better to a Dworkinian critique of pornography-as-rape than this radical positioning of victims, and the delight it brings to libertines. Mechanical and potentially repetitive violence is built into technological furniture whose function is to impose the most spectacularly exposed and strictly unvarying positions. Juliette encounters one such apparatus in her travels: "elles m'approchèrent d'une banquette où elles me firent incliner sur les genoux et sur les mains. Un ressort part; aussitôt tous mes membres sont pris, et trois lames aiguës menacent à la fois et mes flancs et mon ventre, si je fais le moindre mouvement" [They took me toward a bench on which they made me lean with my knees and hands. A spring went off. Immediately, all my limbs were held fast, and three sharp blades threatened both sides and my belly, should I move even slightly] (*Histoire de Juliette*, 9:228). Restif de la Bretonne, in between scathing references to Sadian brutality, depicts in *L'Anti-Justine* a wondrous invention recently purchased by the hero, the function of which is to trap any woman who sits on it, and position her mechanically in the most favorable position for sexual attack.[15] Yet it is important to note that such delight in constrained body positions does not simply coincide with—although it certainly includes—violence toward women victims. Quite regularly, the adoption of the requisite pose is a delight in itself. In Sade's work, female libertines are wont to espouse the shape of sofas as a kind of seductive bodily arabesque. Juliette describes Clairwil thus: "Courbée sur un sopha, la coquine lui présente [le cul] en femme de l'art" [Bent over a sofa, the little devil was presenting [her ass] like a professional] (*Histoire de Juliette*, 8:384). Juliette herself suffers the same fate, the same shape, and the same pleasure when she is "courbée sur un sofa" [bent over a sofa] by Brisa-Testa, being made more beautiful and more available for penetration in the one movement (9:213). On another occasion, Juliette describes herself and Clairwil as comfortably, conveniently positioned: "nous étions étendues sur des canapés larges, élastiques et profonds, les jambes pendantes, les reins soulevés par de gros carreaux, absolument nues, et c'était le con que dans cette première attaque, nous présentions à nos adversaires" [we were stretched out on sofas that were broad, yielding, and deep, with our legs hanging down, our bottoms raised up by large cushions, and in the first encounter it was our cunts that we presented to our opponents"] (8:505). It cannot be forgotten, however, that Juliette's and Clairwil's intimate delight in furniture is thematically complicitous with the suffering of those women held captive by the giant Minski, for his captives are actually compelled to *be* furniture, serving as the "tables vivantes" [living tables] on which dinner for Juliette and her companions is served (8:600).

A concern with ethical questions should not be allowed to obscure the fact that one cannot reliably distinguish victims and oppressors in classical eroticism by measuring their degree of postural freedom. Sade's master libertines, in particular, are not described as transcending erotic spaces, or moving about in them unconstrainedly. They dwell in boudoirs in the most attentive, the most thoroughly immanent manner. Clairwil is in a masterly role when she makes Francaville's high technology couch work for her pleasure:

> Il résultait de cette mécanique entière, que la femme, placée sur le sofa que faisaient mouvoir les ressorts adaptés, y était d'abord mollement étendue sur le ventre, enfilée par un godemiché, sucée par une fille, branlant un vit de chaque main, présentant son cul au vit bien réel qui viendrait le sodomiser, et suçant alternativement, d'après ses goûts, tantôt un vit, tantôt un con, même un cul. (9:372)

> [As a result of this complete mechanism, the woman, who was placed on a sofa operated by well designed springs, was stretched out on her belly, penetrated by a dildo, sucked by a girl, jerking off a prick with each hand, presenting her ass to the very real prick that was about to sodomize her, and sucking in alternation, according to taste, a prick or a cunt, and sometimes even an ass.]

The extraordinary thing about this attitude, to modern eyes, is likely to be its mechanical stringency, highlighted paradoxically by the minimal exercise of personal "taste" in the choice of organs for sucking. But Clairwil describes it all in terms that recuperate modern technology for classical eroticism: "Je ne crois pas, dit Clairwil en s'adaptant bien nue sur ce siège, qu'il soit possible d'inventer rien de plus extraordinairement lubrique; cette seule position m'irrite . . . je décharge rien qu'en me plaçant" ["I do not believe," said Clairwil as she settled naked into position, "that it would be possible to invent anything more extraordinarily pleasurable. This very position is arousing me. I am discharging just by taking up the pose"] (9:372–73). Clairwil settles into desire and pleasure as functions of the same compelling mechanism, and she does so in what might be termed a feminine variation on Sadian libertinism. Male libertines such as the four friends of Silling are less likely to attach themselves to mechanical sofas, but they settle happily enough into a constraining narrative order, accepting the pact that requires their pleasure to follow seriatim the "tastes" or "passions" recounted by the storytellers. The four are bound together, we are told, by "conformity of tastes" (*Les Cent Vingt Journées de Sodome*, 1:20), and this is remarkably convenient for them, but their conformity is actually achieved, or at least confirmed, in the novel as a shaping-together of desires and practices. A key purpose of classical erotic narrative seems to be to rehearse conformity and convenience in the celebration of perfectly apposite desire.[16] Desire is narrated as something that happens opportunely, on time and in its place. And furniture, acting as both a support and a helpful constraint, is itself a kind of opportunity. In the boudoir, eroticism is seen to be cultural, but it is also, for that very reason, local and "occasional"—in the sense of occasional poetry, and occasional tables. So when Michel Delon character-izes luxury in *La Nouvelle Justine* as total freedom, the capacity to do whatever one wishes by "eroticizing objects," his emphasis is misleading. Sadian subjectivity must answer the imperious call of a built environment.[17]

When, in *L'Anti-Justine*, Restif's narrator-hero refers to "un foutoir commode" [a convenient fucking-sofa] that is hollow and has room for someone to hide in it,[18] he is merely producing a rather crude version of the figure we saw in Crébillon's work. It is crude because the name itself is obscene: *foutre* was for Restif's time the crudest way to refer to copulation. It is also crude because *foutoir commode* is a naïve tautology. Of course it is convenient: it was made for fucking! Furniture is always ac-commodating in these stories and one of the purposes of narra-tive is to work out its convenience in the circularity of postural modeling, as a kind of predictable happy surprise. Nerciat makes the circular point more elegantly in *Les Aphrodites*, as he pre-sents the *fouteuse* with a certain amount of descriptive pomp:

> on nomme *fouteuse* un meuble qui n'est ni un sopha, ni un canapé, ni une ottomane, ni une duchesse, mais un lit très bas, qui n'est non plus un lit de repos (il s'en faut de beaucoup), et qui, long de six pieds, sanglé de cordes de boyaux comme une raquette de paume, n'a qu'un matelas parfaitement moyen entre la mollesse et la dureté, un traversin pour soutenir la tête d'une personne, et un dur bourrelet pour appuyer les pieds de l'autre. On a trouvé bon de nommer *fouteuse* cette espèce de duchesse, d'abord parce que *duchesse* et *fouteuse* sont synonymes, ensuite parce qu'on nomme dormeuse une voiture où l'on peut dormir, causeuse une chaise où l'on cause, etc. . . .

> [people give the name *fouteuse* to an item of furniture that is nei-ther a canapé, an ottoman, or a *duchesse*, but rather a very low bed, not a bed for resting—far from it. Six feet in length, strung with gut like a tennis racket, it has just one mattress that is per-

fectly in between the extremes of softness and hardness, a bolster to support one person's head, and a firm pad to support the other's feet. People have seen fit to call this kind of *duchesse* a *fouteuse*, firstly because *duchesse* and *fouteuse* [fucker] are synonyms, and secondly because one calls a carriage in which one sleeps a sleeper, and a chair on which one sits to chat a "chatterer," and so on.][19]

For all the fussiness, for all the show of subtle distinction-making, the point of this description is finally manifest in its very circularity. At the end of it all, we find the same necessary relation between *foutre* and *fouteuse*, verb and noun, action and material support. Narratorial didacticism thus corresponds, in a neatly confirming way, to the furniture's constraining intimation of desire and pleasure. The *fouteuses* themselves are part of the décor, if you will, but as closely supportive figures of an erotic culture. Canonical and classical functions are performed and conformed through the inscription in space of proper erotic attitudes.

This understanding of the role of furniture persists into the early nineteenth century, but it is forced to coexist, from about the middle of the eighteenth century onwards, with another, less comfortable thematic. Something had started to happen to the furniture. It did not just wear out, nor was it stored in the attic. It actually broke. It broke quite dramatically, because people jumped around on it, so that the breaking of furniture itself became standard fare in erotic narrative. The increasing prominence of this pattern, I am going to argue, marked a historical shift in the thematics of desire.[20] What is more, it did so in a remarkably self-conscious way.

In *Histoire de dom Bougre* (1741), one of the great successes of eighteenth-century French pornography, there occurs a scene in which the narrator-hero, Saturnin, makes love to his friend Suzon for the first time. As a prelude to the scene, the two have been observing an older couple through a hole in the wall, and have thereby conceived both the desire and the way to satisfy it. Yet what follows is not simply the classical execution of the model, but a rather complex event. As Saturnin describes it, he is afflicted by sheer bad luck—apparently the exact opposite of that narrative good fortune often called *commodité*: "O ciel! des mouvements si doux devaient-ils être troublés par le plus cruel des malheurs? Je poussais avec ardeur. Mon lit, ce malheureux lit, ce témoin de mes transports et de mon bonheur nous trahit. Il n'était que sanglé, la cheville manqua, nous tombâmes avec un bruit affreux" [Oh my heaven! Were these sweet movements now to be disturbed by the cruellest of misfortunes? I was pushing ardently. My bed, that unfortunate bed, that witness to my delight and my happiness, betrayed us. It was only a camp bed. The pin gave way, and we fell with a dreadful noise].[21] Betrayed by an inadequate piece of furniture, Saturnin seems condemned to see his first erotic experience collapse into farce. Farce there certainly is in the description, but there is a rather surprising and, as far as I can determine, historically new erotic by-product: the fall actually precipitates and concludes the action: "Cette chute m'eût été favorable puisqu'elle m'avait fait entrer jusqu'où je pouvais aller, quoique avec une extrême douleur pour tous les deux" [This fall would have been to my advantage, because it allowed me to enter as far as I could go, although it was extremely painful for both of us] (3:98). As if to demonstrate that broken beds can now have a place in this kind of narrative, the consequences of the fall are decidedly more erotic than far-cical. An older woman, Saturnin's foster-mother, who was the one he and Suzon had so recently been observing, comes rushing into the room and catches the hero with his lover. Far from being indignant, she responds to the spectacle by (re)conceiving the desire she had initially helped to model, and gives Saturnin a telling look. Soon she is coupled with him in an adjoining room, their improbable union having been precipitated by a breaking bed.

This narrative move, whereby an ostensibly comic breakage is quickly turned to erotic advantage, was clearly a happy invention. It reappears in an anonymous sequel to *Histoire de dom Bougre* entitled *Mémoires de Suzon* (c. 1780).[22] And it is taken up with a slight variation in Choiseul-Meuse's *Amélie de Saint-Far* (1802). There we find a casual encounter in which the dissolute Colonel Charles urges his attentions on a housemaid called Elise. When Elise objects, quite classically, that "il n'y a là ni lit ni sopha" [there is neither a bed nor a sofa in the room], he seems to suggest that furniture does not really matter, or at least that just about any piece will do: "Qu'importe! tout sert de trône à la volupté; et l'on a souvent, sur une chaise, goûté des plaisirs plus vifs que sur l'édredon" [What does that matter? Anything can serve as a throne for voluptuousness, and one can often experience livelier pleasures in a chair than on an eider-down].[23] The chair it has to be then, but the improvised arrangement results in an accident, much as it did in the earlier stories: "l'excès de leur ivresse leur fait enfin perdre la raison; ils redoublent d'efforts: mais, ô funeste accident! le siège se brise sous eux avec fracas; le colonel tombe sur le dos, entraînant Elise, qu'il tient fermement enlacée, et qui s'efforce en vain de se détacher de ses bras" [Drunk with pleasure, they finally lost all reason. They threw themselves into it even more. Oh fateful accident! The chair broke under them with a clatter. The colonel fell on his back, still grasping Elise, who tried vainly to free herself from his embrace] (2:20). To the extent that such accidents are becoming thematically familiar, one might expect that the consequence of this fall will not be discovery and disgrace but the furtherance of pleasure. As it happens, Elise's mistress Alexandrine arrives in response to the noise, but her entry is quickly exploited, as Charles, in the heat of the moment, compels her to make love on the very spot, thus depriving her of the right to express indignation. It is as if the proper erotico-narrative use of furniture were coming to be precisely the breaking of it.

In another novel of the late eighteenth century, we see the breakage and the ensuing fall being explicitly taken as models of desire and pleasure. *Vénus en rut* (c. 1785) actually describes two comparable scenes on the same page. In the first, a young monk has placed his lover on a chair—perhaps the closest thing to a sumptuous ottoman that he can find in his spartan environment. So vigorous is his thrusting that the chair breaks and the lovers fall to the ground with a terrible clatter.[24] By an extension of the event, and as a confirmation of its thematic status, the chair-breaking scene becomes an erotic model for the narrator-heroine and her partner, who copy the position with such vigor that her own chair is in continual danger of breaking:

Alors je joue l'Agnès; je me place sur la chaise avec maladresse, et me voilà corrigée par Francour, qui m'arrange lui-même. Excitée par la réminiscence du premier acte, et constamment occupée de l'objet présent, je m'agitai de manière à rompre une chaise de fer! Celle-ci, sans doute, était enchantée: elle résista.

[So I played the role of an Agnes. I placed myself awkwardly on the chair, and Francour had to adjust me himself. Aroused by my

memory of the first act, and continually occupied with the business at hand, I bounced around in a manner fit to break the iron
chair! This one must have been enchanted, for it held up.] (6:132)

The key erotic point here is that sheer vigor of execution
places great stress on the supporting erotic environment, threatening to break through it in some drastic manner. The narrative
tension produced by a fearful, yet reckless anticipation of collapse is in fact harnessed in the building up of erotic intensity,
so that good fortune now consists in not quite, or not yet falling.
In *Vénus en rut*, the model is supplied, and the promise of the
chair fulfilled, but the pleasure of confirmation and the confirmation of pleasure come only after a certain, quite literal, trembling. In the later eighteenth century and especially the
nineteenth, bouncing up and down, wriggling, twisting, and generally putting pressure on the furniture become the thematic
norm, as if the pressure itself, rather than any bodily positioning
inscribed in the furniture, were now of greater significance. The
Countess in *Le Diable au corps* shows her passion, and reminds
us how passion is to be recognized, when she says: "Je me tré-
mousse sur le personnage à l'assommer, à briser le meuble, à
faire écrouler le plancher" [I leaped about on the gentleman in
such a way as almost to knock him senseless, break the furniture, and cause the floor to collapse].[25] Similarly, the narrator of
L'Anti-Justine (1798) tells how the *foutoir* suffers under the
strain of erotic activity: "Cependant, elle remuait admirable-
ment de la charnière et le foutoir craquait sous nous" [During
this time, she wiggled her ass admirably and the *foutoir* creaked
underneath us].[26] This is how the furniture can be made to resonate in sympathy with frantic copulation: "le lit, de structure
assez délicate, se plaint d'abord, puis gémit; puis, par un craque-
ment fort expressif, semble demander grâce" [The bed, which
was lightly built, creaked and groaned, and then, by the most expressive of noises, seemed to plead for mercy] (*Le Diable au
corps* [1803]).[27] In *Gamiani* (1833), the bed is heard to quiver
and cry out under the strain of some particularly wild moving
and shaking: "Le lit craquait aux secousses furieuses de la
comtesse" [The bed creaked beneath the countess's furious agi-
tation].[28] The canapé and the bed are still playing a role in narrative and they may still have some of the value of the old
canapé couleur de feu [fire-coloured sofa], but the emphasis now

seems to be on impact. It is not so much a matter of being properly disposed, apparently, as of hitting the mattress hard and making the springs creak.

There is a set of verbs, including *se placer, s'installer, s'arranger, se disposer, se présenter*, and *s'exécuter*—what might be called verbs of disposition—found throughout classical erotic narratives. These verbs continue in use, to a lesser extent, in the nineteenth and twentieth centuries. Some of them are definite favorites of Sade. Yet in the course of the historical change I am describing, another set develops, competing with these and tending to displace them. The second set includes *tomber* and other verbs signifying falling, collapse or loss of control, such as *renverser, basculer*, or the more vulgar *culbuter*. Characters in erotic narrative are described as subsiding into pleasure, or even throwing themselves into it (*se lancer, s'élancer, se jeter*) rather than just taking up a position. True erotic behavior now seems to consist in the very fact of being overwhelmed instead of holding a particular venereal shape.

In this context, furniture tends to become, more than anything, an occasion for falling: it is properly used when one falls onto it, through it, or off it onto the floor. And that fall is, so to speak, the clincher. The fullness of pleasure is seen as something beyond postural discipline: it is a precipitate coming-together. In *Les Délices de Coblentz* (1791), there is a quite public performance of copulation that takes just this form, and presumably serves as a model:

> il l'empoigne sur un sopha, l'assaille et la cogne avec tant de roideur, qu'à force de brandiller son croupion elle tombe avec lui du sopha sur le gazon, et cette secousse complétant le plaisir, elle reste quelques secondes sans sortir de l'espèce de délire et de ravissement où tous ses sens sont plongés, et n'en sort que pour rire aux éclats, de sa chute et de l'étonnement des spectateurs qui lui applaudissent.

> [he grabbed her on a sofa, and banged her with such vigor that the wiggling of her ass made her fall with him from the sofa onto the lawn. This sudden movement completed her pleasure, and she remained for several seconds in that sort of delirious joy in which all the senses have collapsed together. She came to with a burst of laughter, when she was aware of her fall, and of the astonishment shown by the applauding spectators.][29]

In *Mon Noviciat, ou les joies de Lolotte* (1792), two people fall onto a sofa and are "thrown" together by the same anatomical and libidinal coincidence: "Une demi-volte nous sauve de la chute dont nous sommes menacés, et sans être séparés, il se trouve jeté sous moi sur l'ottomane, dans le délicieux néant du bonheur" [A half-twist saved us from the fall that threatened, without detaching us one from the other, and he was flung onto the ottoman with me on top, in the delightful void of happiness].[30] Erotic good fortune, once seen as the happy coincidence of desire and decor, inclination and opportunity, is now more often rehearsed as a delightful accident, occurring with remarkable frequency in stories of this sort. Every slip, every fall seems to produce the same, ostensibly surprising but entirely satisfying result: "Au même instant elle perd l'équilibre, tombe sur le tapis, et m'entraîne avec elle dans une situation avantageuse qui devient un nouveau piège pour moi. J'en profite, [etc.]" [At the same moment she lost her balance, and fell onto the carpet, pulling me down with her into an advantageous position that once again became a trap for me. I seized the opportunity [etc.]" (*Mon Noviciat*, 155). In *Gamiani* (1833), falling down is both a dramatic symptom of desire and an uncontrolled form of pleasure. The narrator-hero, for all his erect virility, is stunned, nay dizzied on discovering the truth about Countess Gamiani's lesbianism (tribadism), to the point where he collapses onto a sofa.[31] And later, when he spies on the countess as she comes to grips with her young lover, he tells it as an event that really strains the furniture: "La comtesse, dans son étreinte fougueuse, l'emportait sur son lit, l'y jetait comme une proie à dévorer" [The countess, with a passionate embrace, carried her to the bed and threw her down on it like a prey that she was about to devour] (81). To throw the victim onto a bed is already to possess her, so powerful is the gravitational force that takes everyone down to the certainty of copulation. That outcome is somehow made all the surer by the loss of postural stability.

The transformed role of furniture is never more literally incidental, nor more clearly marked, than in a section of *Décrets des sens sanctionnés par la volupté* (1791) entitled "Les Meubles renversés" [The Upset Furniture]. In this text, it is not a matter of breaking the furniture, or falling onto it, but of knocking it all over: "Au même instant, le voluptueux de la C . . . , renversant tous les meubles qui s'opposaient à son passage, s'élança dans

les bras de la sensuelle M . . ." [At the same moment, the voluptuous de la C . . . , knocking over all the furniture in his path,
threw himself into the embrace of the sensual M . . .].[32] When
the élan is what matters most, rather than the apposite position, precipitate desire expresses itself by treating everything
in the space as an obstacle rather than a possible source of
support.

Collapsing and falling are not just preludes to eroticism of
this kind: they are part of its very dynamics. For this reason,
there is a continual threat not just to the furniture, but to the
durability of copulation. The actual risk of uncoupling attains
thematic status through the use of verbs such as *désarçonner*, to
unseat one's rider, a great favorite of the late eighteenth century.
Unseating one's rider is particularly, but not exclusively, what
vigorous and playful women are wont to do to men. For a truly
classical erotic discipline, such instability would have to count
as a distraction and a failure, perhaps a form of playful absur-
dity, but it is included within the range of late eighteenth- and
nineteenth-century eroticism, and valued indeed as a source of
pleasure. *Histoire de dom Bougre* (1741) talks in these terms
when a woman called Marianne is brought into the monastery.
She has "unseated" the most robust of Saturnin's colleagues, but
he manages to hold his position with her: "Elle était enragée de
trouver un moine qui soutînt ses efforts sans s'ébranler, elle qui
avait desarçonné les plus vigoureux de la bande" [She was stung
by the fact that one monk should hold on during the wild ride
without falling off, for she had managed to unseat the most vigorous ones in the group].[33] Staying in the saddle is of course a
test of virility. In *Les Aphrodites* (1793), we read: "il faut à
Boutavant toute la solidité de son moyen d'agencement pour
n'être pas désarçonné par les haut-le-corps variés de Madame de
Pillengins" [Boutavant needs all the solidity of his connecting
piece to avoid being unseated by the unpredictable leaping
movements of Madame de Pillengins].[34] And in *Les Amours de
garnison* (1831), "ses soubresauts auraient désarçonné le cava-
lier, s'il n'eût pas été ferme sur les étriers" [her bucking would
have unseated the horseman, if he had not kept himself firmly
in the stirrups].[35] But the point is that vigorous movement, as
part of the struggle to maintain a kind of rhythmic stability, actively enhances the quality of pleasure. Even when the Marquise, in *Le Diable au corps* (1803), actually succeeds in

unseating her lover, this does not constitute an end to the event, nor even any sort of delay. It is merely a form of play that allows (and invites) an immediate riposte: "deux fois je l'ai fait dégainer par un haut-le-corps, mais inutilement; il n'y avait pas un temps de perdu: au retour j'étais renfilée, et loin que les choses en allassent plus mal, il semblait, au contraire, que ces contretemps donnassent à mon drille un surcroît de vigueur" [Twice I managed to unseat him by a sudden movement, but to no avail. Not a moment was lost before he was back inside again. Far from putting my companion off, this seemed to give him a new burst of vigor].[36] What might otherwise have been obstacles or interruptions are here integrated into a compelling rhythm of pleasure, as each movement away serves only to increase the amplitude and vigor of the return.

Evidence of a shift can be found in the very construction of some pieces of erotic furniture described in *Les Délices de Coblentz* (1791). Rather than the constraining firmness of the classical sofa, these *lits de repos* have a built-in capacity to respond to movement, amplifying pleasure as they do so:

> dans le cabinet des plaisirs de Condé . . . il s[e] trouva douze lits, appelés bien à tort *lits de repos*, mais de ces lits rares, adroitement inventés par un génie heureux pour seconder la nonchalance de la célèbre Huss, dont les ressorts élastiques servent si joliment la volupté, qu'elle semble doubler son odeur quand elle reçoit l'impression de leurs mouvements.

> [In Condé's boudoir there were twelve beds, improperly called resting beds, for they were of an unusual kind, cleverly invented by a happy person of genius to support the nonchalant body of the famous Huss woman. The beds' elastic springs served pleasure so nicely that they seemed to double its effects on receiving the impact of movement.][37]

Elasticity has become a quality par excellence of radical pleasure, with its rise and fall, its coming and going. It is not surprising that *Ordonnance de police sur les filles de joie* (1790) [Police Order on the Subject of Women of Pleasure] should provide mock-serious advice as to the best technique for remaining coupled to one's lover while traveling in a coach, despite all the jolts coming from the road surface.[38] The art of pleasure, we must now understand, is not just the art of placing oneself, but that of riding the bumps and turning agitation to advantage. The heroine of *Julie philosophe* effectively considers the erotic value of the coach alongside that of the boudoir, and seems to conclude in favor of the former:

> le mouvement, le bruit continuel de la voiture occasionnent dans l'âme un certain désordre et dans l'esprit un certain trouble très favorable aux tentatives amoureuses. . . . Je suis assurée que telle fille a succombé en courant la poste, qui avait su résister même dans le boudoir le plus voluptueux.

> [The movement and the continual noise of the coach lead to a certain disorder in the soul, and a disturbance/arousal of the mind that is favorable to seductive moves. I have no doubt that certain women have given in while traveling in a coach, after holding out in the most voluptuous of boudoirs.][39]

Where movement is itself a value, the boudoir, for all its charming intimations of erotic discipline, may now appear too stable an environment. As if the very notion of a decor were somehow less appropriate than before.[40]

The break-up of the furniture and the breakdown of boudoir geometry are further evidenced by the fact that the sofa comes to be analyzed, so to speak, into a set of cushions. The boudoirs described by Nerciat often contain, in addition to beds or sofas, "une quantité de carreaux épars" [a number of scatter cushions].[41] This is furniture at its most mobile and adaptable, given as scattered, given to be scattered. Cushions can in fact be used as building blocks, being recombined and reshaped according to every passing fancy: "plus d'une vingtaine de coussins et d'oreillers carrés pouvaient être employés à volonté sous les culs, sous les têtes, ou empilés pour composer tel échafaudage que pouvait comporter la jouissance, le caprice de chacun ou la combinaison que plusieurs pourraient avoir projetée" [more than twenty cushions and square pillows could be used at will to support asses or heads, or piled up into any structure according to whim, or whatever combination people had in mind, and thus lead to pleasure].[42] In *Les Aphrodites*, we see the combinatory work actually being done by the ever-helpful Mme. Durut, as she improvises beds out of cushions: "En même temps Durut s'est hâtée de former sur le tapis, avec des coussins des espèces de lits" [Meanwhile Durut had quickly used cushions to make up

beds of a kind on the carpet].[43] This sort of arrangement, the last
word in modular boudoirs, allows for improvisation while still
providing postural support for every position. In *Gamiani*, as
Fanny is reaching the heights and depths of *volupté*, she plunges
into the cushions that lie on and around the sofa, distributing
them about her body as surfaces and volumes of pleasure.[44]
Sade's Juliette and Olympe find themselves, for example, in a
room strewn with cushions, and are soon "couchées toutes deux
à terre, sur les piles de carreaux qui couvraient le sol de ce charmant boudoir" [both lying down on the piles of cushions that
covered the floor of this charming boudoir].[45] This is indeed, for
its flexibility of convenience, the furniture of the orgy. In one
such event narrated by Gamiani, we find that cushions have effectively become the only furniture, because they are better
suited to wild sexual exertions (125). By their readiness for scattering, they serve the purposes of Romantic eroticism better
than some imposing, perhaps immutable sofa. There are still
bodily positions involved, it should be noted, and still minimal
pieces of furniture to support them, but *Gamiani*'s form of eroticism tests the furniture to the utmost, requiring of it not just
elasticity but frenzied mobility. The double function of cushions,
as supports for improvisation and the objects of wanton scattering, is maintained to a degree in the later nineteenth century.
We are invited to read the semiotic eloquence of "les coussins en
déroute" [the cushions put to flight] in *Les Fleurs de la volupté*
(1900),[46] and have occasion to witness the careful construction,
in *Les Amours d'un gentleman* (1889), of an arrangement of
cushions that will facilitate copulation between a young man
and his housemaid.[47]

A further thematic shift, exploiting the possibilities opened
up by these boudoir renovations, can be seen to have occurred
by the end of the nineteenth century. Furniture, while still present in erotic narrative, is no longer defined primarily by its
shape. One might say, in fact, that the sofa and its equivalents
persist not so much as form but as matter. Where once they
aligned bodies for contact and penetration, they now seem to
cradle and envelop them in the very substance of pleasure. The
visual representation of figures or attitudes that served to
model desire has rather given way to a thematics of perfume
and penumbra that compels, so to speak, by suffusion. When I
referred earlier to the lack of material description in *Le Sopha*

or *Le Canapé couleur de feu*, I was concerned that the notion of COMMODITÉ not be misunderstood by collapsing this historical difference.

The materiality of furniture begins to come to the fore in such high Romantic texts as *Gamiani* (1833). The secondary heroine of that novel, Fanny, sets the scene for a description of her masturbation in the following way: "L'étoffe du divan était glacée. Sa fraîcheur me cause une sensation agréable, un frôlement voluptueux par tout le corps. Oh, comme je respirais librement, entourée d'une atmosphère tiède, doucement pénétrante!" [The material on the divan was ice cold. Its coolness gave me a pleasant feeling, as it voluptuously brushed against my whole body. Oh, how freely I breathed, surrounded by the warm, gently pervading air!][48] But it is in fin-de-siècle narrative that this materiality becomes atmospheric and all pervasive. A boudoir can now be characterized not by its plasticity but by its drapery: "un boudoir tendu d'étoffes douces et précieuses" [a boudoir draped with soft and precious textiles] is description enough (*Les Demi-Sexes*, 1897).[49] *L'Orgie moderne* (1905) contains furniture that invites love-making, but not in the manner of the classics: "de grands sophas sollicitaient l'amour, capitonnaient les chutes" [great sofas pleaded for love, and cushioned falls with upholstery].[50] This is an environment that offers entreatingly to break the lovers' fall, whenever that might occur exactly, drawing them downwards with the promise of velvet plushness. *L'Odyssée d'un pantalon* (1889) is very much a novel of its time in that it rewrites the story of *Le Sopha*, replacing an item of furniture with a piece of women's lingerie. The narrator refers to Crébillon's story of metamorphosis as an antecedent of his own, telling us that he has been transformed into a delicate feminine *pantalon*, and will only return to his normal state when two lovers have proved their love for each other three times in succession while the woman is wearing him.[51] Instead of simply overhearing conversations at very close quarters, in the fashion of Crébillon's hero, the fin-de-siècle character finds himself "intimement mêlé" [intimately involved] in the materiality of erotic encounters (7), so that his descriptions are filled with talk of warmth and closeness. This is, one might say, the pleasure of fleshliness, not the art of posture and conversation: "J'éprouve un délicieux plaisir à sentir cette chair chaude et douce se coller à moi dans un embrassement intime" [I experienced delicious pleasure as I felt that warm, soft flesh clasped against me in an intimate embrace] (34).

In the deeply textured world of the fin de siècle, the air itself is often heavy with the substances of eroticism: "L'air de la pièce était chargé de parfums qui l'enivraient et le pénétraient" [The air in the room was laden with perfumes that inebriated and pervaded him], we are told in *Amante cruelle* (1903).[52] And when the furniture is described in more detail, its seductive essence is still to be found, disseminated and absorbed, as the most captious of scents: "la chambre, tendue de vieux rose, au lit de cuivre bas et très large, à la chaise-longue couverte de peluche, aux meubles coquets et où flottait un parfum de musc et d'eau de Cologne" [the bedroom draped in old pink, with its low, very wide bed made of brass, its chaise longue covered in fluffy material, and its pretty furniture over which floated a perfume of musk and eau de cologne] (*La Luxure* [1905]).[53] It is as if the furniture were now being vaporized in response to the thematic and narrative exigencies of a different understanding of desire. In *La Cantharide* (1900), we read: "Il avançait machinalement, comme un halluciné, vers le sopha mystérieux d'où s'exhalaient d'aphrodisiaques parfums" [He walked slowly, as if drugged, toward the mysterious sofa that gave off aphrodisiacal perfumes].[54] "Aphrodisiacal perfume" is almost a tautology, so much does the olfactory now come to dominate the sensory representation of desire.[55] The relation between the body and furniture is not one of postural constraint but of euphoric osmosis. The boudoir is not a space for "placing oneself" but for languishing: "la jeune femme s'alanguissait dans la troublante et tiède atmosphère du boudoir" [the young woman lay languishing in the warm, disturbing atmosphere of the boudoir] (*Joyeuses enfilades* [1895]).[56] *Inassouvie* describes the quintessential boudoir of the period:

> Elle ne vivait plus que dans son boudoir, au milieu d'une atmosphère atrophiante de serre chaude, respirant un air alourdi par les plus capiteux parfums, molle, nonchalante, alanguie.
> Une fumée engourdissante, opiacée, de tabac exotique, de pastilles du sérail, de résines orientales, de musc, flottait paresseusement autour d'elle, noyant d'ombres fantastiques les grandes plantes, les lourdes tapisseries, les murs capitonnés de satin lilas, broché de fleurs roses, les glaces et les tableaux effrontément érotiques.

[She now spent all her time in the boudoir, softly, nonchalantly languishing in a deadening hothouse atmosphere, breathing in air filled with the headiest perfumes.

A numbing, drug-laden smoke made of exotic tobacco, harem pastilles, oriental resins, and musk floated lazily about her, drowning in fantastic shadow the heavy tapestries, the walls lined in lilac satin with pink flowered lace, the mirrors, and the shamelessly erotic paintings.][57]

The "shameless" paintings and mirrors that in former times would have served to model the positions to be adopted can no longer be clearly seen. Their geometry is no more than a blurred image as they bathe in the opiate haze of aphrodisiacs.

The fin-de-siècle boudoir is a dark place, haunted by the half-known ghosts of desire. In *Vendeuse d'amour* (1891), it is "tout imprégné d'effluves voluptueuses" [impregnated with voluptuous odors], its (im)moral saturation maintained and enhanced by the softest of lighting: "[le] boudoir, dont la lumière faible qui transparaissait au travers d'un globe teinté de rose, semblait inviter les amants au plaisir voluptueux dans la demi-obscurité si propre aux révélations dont ne peut s'émouvoir la pudeur" [the boudoir, whose weak light shone through a rose-tinted globe, seemed to invite lovers to voluptuous pleasure, in the twilight so suited to revelations, in the soft light at which modesty cannot take offense].[58] The true space of intimacy is thus a kind of perfumed twilight, what Mendès, in *Méphistophela* (1890), calls "la pénombre aromale du boudoir" [the aromatic twilight of the boudoir],[59] and Péladan, in *La Gynandre* (1891), "le boudoir alourdi d'odeurs" [the boudoir laden with odors].[60] One slips into the boudoir or languishes within it, losing sight of modesty and principles, but also of erotic culture as a set of representations—precisely because the culture is now a culture of obscurity. The decor of drapery and incense serves ultimately to bring about its own disappearance as decor: "Tout sombra du salon mauve, des glaces, des peluches, des fleurs, il ne resta plus qu'un lit d'ombre où se convulse son fantôme à lui avec des injures et des coups pour la chair débile de l'adorée. Vision horrible et brève!" [All of the mauve salon sank from view, the mirrors, the covers, and the flowers. All that remained was a bed on which lay his ghost in convulsions, with only abuse and blows to offer the ailing flesh of his adored one. A brief and awful vision!] (*L'Eternelle Poupée* [1894]).[61] This is patently not the libertine world of charming tableaux and elegant moves: it is that of perversity and sexual pathology. But the shift from the one to the other happens over time, within the range of "erotic literature," and must be negotiated by a history of sexuality.

When one can no longer look back to other times with the old confidence that people and their desires are everywhere the same, it is tempting to give up on a certain kind of thematic understanding. One can proclaim epistemic discontinuity as a first and last article of hermeneutical faith, and insist that each "period" be studied separately, in its own right. History can then appear as a domain of irretrievable otherness. It may indeed seem, moving from Crébillon to the fin de siècle and back, that the very notion of the boudoir, or the sofa, or even of furniture, is no more than a kind of pun. Yet it has been the play on words, the play on things that, by its internal range, has made room for the historical understanding of an aspect of erotic narrative. We have seen the old thematic shapes broken up and dissolved in narrative—broken up by the frantic energy of Revolutionary times, and dissolved in the mists of a fin-de-siècle twilight. We have found the theme and lost it, one might say. Found it, indeed, in its very lostness. More themes of the same kind will need to be examined before a broader picture can become apparent, and the choice of those themes will need to be judiciously opportunistic. But the method, or the *démarche*, will perforce involve the same quality of attention, and the same respect for thematic drift.

2

Marble and Fire

THROUGHOUT THE PERIOD THAT LASTS FROM THE RENAISSANCE UNTIL about the middle of the eighteenth century, erotic representation foregrounds sculpture and the sculptural. Statues, paintings, and engravings of body shapes serve as models in the most precise sense. They tend to demonstrate a particular attitude, allowing it to be held, named, and counted, as one of the sixteen *modi* (Aretino) or of some other finite set of positions. These are, generically, the figures of Venus, to be learned as a set, rehearsed as such in erotic art, and applied severally in the exercise of pleasure. In the mid-eighteenth century, however, this thematic begins to be contested and displaced by one that is recognizably more modern—more congenial to modern pornographers, and more commonplace in the discourse of modern sexologists. I shall focus, in what follows, on this self-conscious rejection of an ostensibly outworn *ars erotica*. The statuesque, we shall see, now comes to be understood in terms of its supposed material inadequacy and lack of sentience rather than as a display of formal perfection. Yet as part of the same discursive shift there emerges, I hope to show, a rich erotic ambivalence toward the substance of the statue. Its very lifelessness is often an object of questioning fascination, because that allows the possibility of dramatic change, from coldness to heat, from frigidity to its passionate opposite.

Before considering some textual examples, let me raise a question about the hermeneutical discipline needed to discuss erotic statues in historical context. Paula Findlen's informative article on pornography in Renaissance Italy gives examples of a quite particular way of relating to them, namely copulation, involving inter alia a statue of Venus joined by a young man, and a

statue with an erect penis, enjoyed by a woman.[1] These erotic
practices are worthy of interest, and may well be historically
distinctive, at least by their frequency at that time, but I find
the discussion of them in Findlen's article rather unsatisfying,
precisely because it tends to suppose an unbroken continuity of
human erotic imagination stretching from that period to the
present. The woman who availed herself of the erect penis, when
giving an account of her action, actually quoted Aretino. The
divine author of *I sedici modi* refers, she recalls, to "a statue of
Venus so true to life and so living that it will fill with lustful
thoughts the mind of anyone who looks at it" (63). The point of
this quotation, as I see it, is not taken up in Findlen's analysis.
According to Findlen, talking about statues in this way reveals
the extraordinary versatility of human desire: to minds like that
of Aretino and the woman who quotes him, "all forms of representation harbored an erotic potential" (60). For someone who
gives full importance to figures of Venus, Aretino's comment
might point to the centrality of the statuesque in erotic representation, but Findlen seems to consider statues as a kind of
limit case, so that if they can provoke desire, all things can. The
same rather distant surprise, and the same reluctance to understand, can be found in Peter Wagner's summary of Shurig's *Gy-
naecologia* (1729), which is said by him to talk "about sex with
maids, or demons, and even with statues."[2] It ought to have been
remembered in both cases that for classical eroticism, statues,
when mentioned, are not to be attended by the word "even,"
since they are often considered perfect exempla of the forms of
pleasure. Erotic literature is typically an "art d'aimer" for which
statues are postural models, as in a 1761 poem by Pierre-Joseph
Bernard bearing that (classical) title:

> Là, figurés par des marbres fidèles,
> Les dieux amants sont offerts pour modèles.
> Sous mille aspects leurs couples amoureux
> De la tendresse expriment tous les jeux.
> . . . .
> Tout est modèle, et pour être imité,
> Fait une loi: tout amant qu'il excite
> Voit et jouit, plein du dieu qu'il imite.
>
> [There, figured by faithful marbles,
> The lover gods are offered as models.

From every side their amorous couples
Express all the games of tenderness.

. . . .

All this is a model, and for imitation
Makes a law: every lover who is aroused by it
Sees and takes pleasure, filled with the god he imitates.][3]

The difficulty here is one of frameworks of interpretation, and it must not be forgotten that theories of representation are themselves shot through with historically contingent discourse. Findlen's key theoretical reference, if I may simply consider the more elaborate and more interesting of my two examples, is to a psycho-phenomenological theory that considers the "potentially erotic image" and the intimate act of its contemplation. "The viewing of provocative imagery" can thus be seen to have an effect on "the gaze of the beholder who could no longer sustain his emotional reaction."[4] This talk of images, I contend, is thematically dissonant with the notion of the figures of Venus so prominent in Aretino's time. To refer to an "effect" or a "reaction," as Findlen does, and as standardly modern talk about sexuality requires, is to miss the fact that an erotic postural discipline, propagated through the teaching and learning of figures, has no need of such metaphors, and no need to construct or imagine the space of psycho-physiological interiority in which they are said to occur.[5] The anachronism of such a reading is further demonstrated by the fact that Findlen refers in this context to a classical myth, but in terms that are characteristic of a later eighteenth-century understanding of it. The issue, as she sees it, is the power of sensory imagination with its "Galatea-like" capacity to turn stone into flesh.[6] But the very preoccupation with flesh as such, and with the material contrast that opposes it to stone, seems to matter much less to Aretino's time than to Rousseau's, even if the fundamental reference is always more or less to Ovid's *Metamorphoses*. For a figural eroticism, stone is likely to have value because it can be shaped into erotic forms, and can hold those forms in enduring, exemplary ways. The statue does not need to be transubstantiated in order to be worthy of desire and pleasure, since the object of desire, or rather the template for the performance of pleasure, is not matter but postural shape. In order to distinguish more clearly between the discourse of figures and that of the image, and thereby to avoid undue anachronism, we need to understand clearly the later eighteenth century's interpretation of the Galatea myth, and the place it occupied in discourse about the erotic.

Rousseau's *Pygmalion* (1762)[7] begins with a hiatus that can be made to serve here as an emblematic moment of historical discontinuity. Pygmalion's story—or the apparent impossibility of a story—turns on the hero's vacillating estrangement from his own art. As a sculptor, he is both enthralled by his statue of Galatea and defeated by the essential otherness of stone. Pygmalion stands looking at his "own" statues and feels alienated from them for the very reason that they are statues. There are finished and unfinished works standing around in the studio, but the artist is visited by a desperate sense of material impossibility. "How can cold marble ever be brought to life?" he asks. He has forgotten—and we know this because for a moment he fleetingly remembers it—that these statues are plastic representations "standing for" the most beautiful forms, some of them divine: "Pygmalion! C'est une pierre; c'est ton ouvrage. Qu'importe? On sert des Dieux dans nos temples qui ne sont pas d'une autre matière et qui n'ont pas été faits d'une autre main" [Pygmalion! It is a stone. It is your own work. What does that matter? There are gods being waited on in our temples who were made by the same hand] (1226). A moment later, however, he lapses again into the same cheerless thought: all that stand before him are blocks of inanimate marble. The knowledge that must have founded Pygmalion's vocation is now only glimpsed by him and can no longer be held enduringly. He cannot retain the classical truth that sculpture has value for the ordered beauty of its representations of form. Instead, he is now preoccupied almost exclusively with substance, heat, and life. He confronts the silent marble with a passionately unsatisfied demand for inner fire.

Pygmalion actually dramatizes a broad thematic disturbance whereby statues lose their value, threatening to become mere stumbling blocks to the apprehension of beauty. This disenchantment, and this difficulty, I want to argue, extend far beyond the bounds of Rousseau's *scène lyrique*: they characterize a moment in the history of literary eroticism. During the second half of the eighteenth century, certain kinds of classical representation are made to appear deficient when confronted or displaced by an exigent passion that sees itself as more natural, more human and perhaps more strictly carnal than the canonical figures. The erotic is now identified with qualities that dwell in matter. Passion, or desire, is now confirmed as something intimately substantial.

Where Rousseau's text produces a hiatus, and can thus be read as an emblem of historical change, other texts of this time enter unreservedly into the emerging version of the Galatea myth. La Mettrie, in *L'Art de jouir* (1751), focuses on the subtly graded stages of love's awakening, as the young man draws his lover from her sleep. He is Pygmalion to her Galatea: "Heureux Pygmalion, vous avez une statue vivante que vous brûlez d'animer!" [Oh happy Pygmalion, you have a living statue that you are burning to bring to life!][8] Note that the statue is felt to be alive from the first. *Déjà* says the text twice in quick succession: her "alabaster breasts" have already been touched by his timid lips; already she seems to be coming to life in response to his warm breath. The temporal adverb is the mark of eager impatience, of seductive delay, and of happily anticipated success: "votre air de volupté a passé dans son âme" [your air of voluptuousness has passed into her soul] (172). Here, by contrast with Rousseau's text, the euphoria of newness leaves no room for weariness or staleness, as both lovers are transformed by what La Mettrie calls "une sorte de circulation nouvelle" [a kind of new circulation] (156). What is new in the narrative is the flow of warm desire within their bodies, passing from the male to the female, although paradoxically it is already circulating in her from the outset. "Circulation nouvelle" may in fact be a kind of tautology, not only because the physiological purpose of circulation is renewal from within, but because the fact of circulation was then taking on new importance in erotic, as in scientific, discourse. It is noteworthy that the invocation of *L'Art de jouir* is not so much a call for inspiration, for the breathing-in of speech, as a call for circulation, expressing the hope that what is already flowing within the writer will pass, by a natural dynamic, from his heart to his work: "Esprits mobiles et déliés qui circulez librement dans mes veines, portez dans mes écrits cette ravissante volupté que vous faites sans cesse voler dans mon cœur" [You mobile, supple spirits circulating freely in my veins, carry into my writing the delightful pleasure that you continually diffuse through my heart] (149).

Philip Stewart, in his fine book, *Engraven Desire*, draws attention to the ways in which Ovid's story was reworked in eighteenth-century engravings:

> The many representations of this subject in the eighteenth century, even those specifically illustrating the Ovid text, all stylize it in certain rather predictable ways. They overlook the detail that the statue was of ivory, not marble, and much more significantly the fact that Galatea comes to life *in Pygmalion's bed* rather than on a pedestal: this explicitly sensuous element is thereby edulcorated.[9]

It is important to note that a particular reading of the myth held sway at this time, but Stewart may be mistaken in concluding that the thematic substitution of marble for ivory contributes to an "edulcoration" of the erotic. My claim is that, by allowing—perhaps even requiring—the dramatic opposition of icy marble and passionate heat, the eighteenth-century version of the Galatea story tends to displace a classical form of eroticism, but in so doing makes way for something more recognizably modern, and no less erotic in its own terms.

If Rousseau's Pygmalion had looked about his studio with a truly classical eye, he might have seen a satisfying diversity of poses. Whether or not he saw himself as an erotic artist, he would doubtless also have known of those sculptural representations that took their orderly place in a traditional *ars erotica*, displaying the range of *positiones* that were available for practitioners of a disciplined eroticism. He would have been familiar, at least by reputation, with the figures of Venus portrayed by Elephantis and associated with Astyanassa. He would have known the etchings of Giulio Romano illustrating the sixteen *modi* of Aretino. Were he blessed with sufficient generic versatility, he might have moved, as a reader of *ars erotica*, from poems to novels to engravings, but he would always have been guided by the prestige of sculpture. This was the art form that, better than any other, displayed the proper attitudes of pleasure. Yet, instead of an impressive paradigm of traditional poses, erotic or otherwise, Pygmalion sees only blocks of marble at various stages of (in)completion. Instead of an array, he sees little more than clutter.

It is of course significant that the setting of Rousseau's drama should be the artist's studio. This is not a boudoir or a *pavillon* decorated with finished representations. It is the artist's place of work, and his work is often a discouraging struggle with the obduracy of stone: "Il n'y a point là d'âme ni de vie; ce n'est que de la pierre. Je ne ferai jamais rien de tout cela" [There is no soul or life there: it is only stone. I will never be able to make anything out of it] (1224). His past success as an artist has depended on the inspiration of genius. Somehow he has succeeded, from time to time, in breathing fire into marble. Now, however, it is the frigidity of stone that appears to have triumphed: "Tout mon feu s'est éteint, mon imagination s'est glacée, le marbre sort froid de mes mains" [All my fire has gone out. My imagination has been chilled. The marble is cold as it leaves my hands] (1224). Will he once again find within himself the qualities needed for success? This is the sculptor's essential question: he is caught up in an uncertain drama of transformation rather than participating classically in a ritual of authoritative transmission.

The most positive sign for Pygmalion is the ardor that dwells in the heart of his coldness: "Mais quelle est donc cette ardeur interne qui me dévore? Qu'ai-je en moi qui semble m'embraser?" [But what is this ardor that consumes me? What do I have in me that seems to burn so strongly?] (1225). Here, opened up by the very distinctness of the marble-fire opposition, is the space of a material dialectic. A kind of desire deep within is precisely what makes him so desperately aware of his coldness. He can yet be saved by an inner fire, and perhaps by the very agitation that takes him back and forth between the poles of opposition: "Quoi! dans la langueur d'un génie éteint, sent-on ces émotions, sent-on ces élans des passions impétueuses, cette inquiétude insurmontable, cette agitation secrète qui me tourmente et dont je ne puis démêler la cause?" [How can it be that genius that has languished and died can still feel these emotions, these surges of impetuous passion, this insurmountable anxiety, this secret torment whose cause I cannot fathom?] (1225). Oscillating between despair and hopeful desire, he thinks anxiously of his most recent and finest creation, the statue of Galatea. If he has done no more than produce a decorative object, then this can only mark the untimely end of his career. But if, as he dares to hope, the statue can speak to him, then it may give him back his genius, somehow yielding up again the fire that must dwell in the stone: "Peut-être cet objet ranimera-t-il mon imagination languissante. Il la faut revoir, l'examiner de nouveau" [Perhaps this new object will revive my languid imagination. I must see her and examine her again] (1226).

Is Galatea suffused with life, or merely cold marble? It is the very asking of this polarized question that sets in motion the dynamics of desire in *Pygmalion*, as the hero oscillates between the eager hope for inner fire and a despondent affirmation of mineral frigidity. It is madness to think that the statue might be alive: "Voilà donc la noble passion qui m'égare! c'est donc pour cet objet inanimé que je n'ose sortir d'ici! . . . un marbre! une pierre! une masse informe et dure, travaillée avec ce fer! . . . Insensé, rentre en toi-même; gémis sur toi, vois ton erreur . . . vois ta folie . . ." [So this is the noble passion that is the cause of my distraction! It is for this inanimate object that I do not dare leave here! . . . A piece of marble! A stone! A shapeless, hard mass, worked on with this iron tool! . . . You madman, come to your senses. You should bemoan your error, and behold your folly . . .] (1227). But it is the madness of this longing that appears to be Pygmalion's genius. His "délire" (1228) leads him momentarily to see "traits de feu" [arrows of fire] coming from Galatea, setting fire to his senses and reaching deep into his soul (1228). This *délire*, we begin to understand, is also a powerful, self-realizing belief, the very belief that "animates" the art of genius: "Je crois, dans mon délire, pouvoir m'élancer hors de moi; je crois pouvoir lui donner ma vie, et l'animer de mon âme" [I believe, in my raving, that I can spring out of myself. I believe I can give her my life and animate her with my soul] (1228). In the end, it is precisely this agitated movement between self and other, soul and stone, that appears to produce the metamorphosis as a triumph of desire over frigidity. As he finally sees Galatea step down from her pedestal, he declares his *délire* to be at its most intense: "Infortuné! c'en est donc fait . . . ton délire est à son dernier terme; ta raison t'abandonne ainsi que ton génie! . . ." [Unfortunate man! This must be the end. Your raving has reached its final point. Your reason is abandoning you, as well as your genius!] (1229–30). There is indeed a kind of *abandon* here, but it appears to be the creative self-abandonment of genius. By going back and forth between his heart and the stone, Pygmalion achieves a miraculous transfer of life, of soul, of fire.

Note that Rousseau's text is more concerned with the dialectic of resistant marble and circulatory fire than with understanding material transformation as such. This is where the eigh-

teenth century's substitution of a marble Galatea for Ovid's
ivory original, pointed out by Philip Stewart, begins to reveal its
full thematic significance. Ivory, it might be said by a Bachelardian reader committed to an imaginative apprehension of substances, is "already" animal in itself, and the references in
Ovid's text to such material symptoms as warmth (*tepere*, *Meta-*
morphoses 10:281) and softness (*mollescit* 10:282) may begin to
establish a material thematic in the classical narrative. No such
thing is to be found in Rousseau's *Pygmalion*, says Paul De
Man, for the drama of selfhood, the business of narcissistic interrogation are such in this text as to reduce any imagination of
materiality to mere topical convenience: "Bachelard's thermody-
namics of the material imagination would find nothing to feed
on in *Pygmalion*."[10] We ought to understand the story as a
drama of I and other, rather than marble and flesh, with what
De Man calls the "traditional polarities" of hot and cold being
pressed into service to narrate this psychic event. De Man is undoubtedly right about the absence of material transformation,
but the very fact that he refers to the antinomy of hot and cold
as "traditional" reveals his insensitivity to the disturbance of
tradition I am trying to highlight. It is true enough that
Rousseau's text fails to achieve Bachelardian thematic richness,
but it is worth noting that "hot" and "cold" are now being understood in substantive terms, and the "polarity" made into a dialectic that can function as the central business of erotic
narrative.[11]

Rousseau's text might leave us to wonder not about the imaginative texture of flesh, but about the psychic substance that
must somehow have been communicated from Pygmalion to
Galatea and back again. It is both manifest and invisible: the
very stuff of life, circulating mysteriously from one hot and cold
body to another cold and hot one. The text often calls it fire, although a myriad of approximate synonyms (ardor, life, soul, passion) testify to both its sweeping importance and its indwelling
mystery. That is why it is justifiable to consider *Pygmalion* as a
form of erotic literature, despite the self-conscious estrangement
from canonical forms of classical erotica: desire here appears
consubstantial with life itself.

The question we are then left to ask is a thoroughly material
one: what is the essence of desire and how does it circulate?
Where classical eroticism is concerned with a figural anatomy,

the bodily thematics of *Pygmalion* foregrounds a physiology of animation. It is not—this is De Man's point again—that we are led by Rousseau to any subtle understanding of the circulation of substances within bodies, but rather that the fact of circulation becomes a thematic issue and a source of excitement. "Ardor" and "heat" are not just rhetorical metaphors for strong feeling: the dynamics of eroticism are now caught up in, and perhaps even coincide with, the circulation of intense heat. Locating the fire within, discerning its visible effects, and understanding how it is communicated will become more and more the business of erotic representation.

I have taken *Pygmalion* as an exemplum here partly because of its (erotic) problematization of the erotic. The hiatus encountered at the outset is not a true *aporia*, but rather the preliminary to a heady oscillation between antinomies that open up a possible narrative of desire. In these moments of extremity, we witness the power of desire as genius: a statue is brought to life, and fire is found to dwell deep in the heart of marble. This helps to understand how the very opposition of heat and frigidity sets up the narrative of a dynamic eroticism. It is not, let me be quite clear, that literature of the mid- to late eighteenth century suddenly discovers fire to be hot, or marble to be cold, or even that the contrast between the two might be made to signify. Earlier references to the two in erotic fiction tend simply to lack the narrative dynamic: they refer to fire and marble, or some equivalent, as characteristics of temperament, and use them to establish a classification of quasi-elemental types. When, in *L'Académie des dames* (1655), Tullia talks about women of fiery temperament, she suggests that they are very much the majority of the species, women of marble or porphyry being the exception: "Toutes les femmes, ma chère enfant, brûlent d'un même feu; et il faudrait être aussi froid que le marbre, et aussi dur que le porphyre, pour demeurer insensible à la vue de ce qu'il y a de plus aimable" [All women, my dear child, burn with the same fire. You would need to be as cold as marble and as hard as porphyry to remain unmoved by the most pleasing sights].[12] Tullia does not suggest, however, that a women may pass from one type to another, or that the transformation itself will be of vital erotic interest.

Observations about temperament, and the making of temperamental contrasts, were routine events in classical erotic fiction, but they always seemed to have a pragmatic conversational function. Sometimes a preference was marked in passing—always the same one, of course, and often rather dismissively, as in the example from *L'Académie des dames*. Sometimes there were more subtle kinds of play. In La Morlière's *Angola* (1746), we find amorous negotiation going on in the presence of statues, and indeed a suggestion that the woman is herself too like a statue, but this is all a kind of semiotic banter. The representative qualities of sculpture are precisely what is in (playful) dispute. Pressed by Angola to yield to his charms, Luzéide runs away, but only so far as to let herself be conveniently pursued: "elle était arrêtée dans le bosquet à considérer un groupe de statues de marbre d'une rare perfection; c'était Apollon et Daphné. Les attitudes étaient parfaites, l'amour était peint sur le visage du dieu et animait sa course" [she had come to a stop in the grove, and was contemplating a quite perfect group of statues. It was Apollo and Daphne. The attitudes were perfect. Love was depicted on the face of the god and quickened his step].[13] Represented here, according to classical tradition, is amorous pursuit, apparently a divine model for the hero and the heroine. But the prince does not appear to see the statues in terms of their attitudinal perfection. Or rather, he pretends to think that the qualities of stone are similar to those of Luzéide herself, that she is drawn to marble for its own sake, as a substantive representation of her unyielding rigor: "Venez-vous chercher de nouveaux exemples d'inhumanité et tâcher de vous affermir dans les sentiments rigoureux que vous m'avez découverts tantôt?" [Have you come to seek further examples of inhumanity, so as to harden the severe feelings you revealed to me earlier?] (454). This is, despite appearances, a forward step in the process of seduction, if a gentle, measured one. The prince pretends not to see the statuesque model that is his promise of success, dwelling instead, if only for a while, on the possibility of defeat. He toys with the idea that Luzéide may be *froide*, but the context reassures us, as it must reassure him. The fact that she stands admiring the statues is proof of her readiness to imitate, even though she attempts to deny the obvious by saying, "Ma façon de penser ne dépend pas de semblables objets" [My way of thinking does not depend on objects of this kind] (454). He pretends momentarily to imprison her in cold rigidity, and she counters by denying that the statues have any meaning for her. Both statements are in fact playfully and ironically inaccurate, and their symmetrical errors help define the space of tacit agreement, of erotic convention in the strong sense. At no point does the comparison of Luzéide with cold marble have the value of a diagnosis.

Crébillon's *La Nuit et le moment*, which dates from 1755, is still thoroughly classical in this regard, as in many others. It plays quite explicitly with the opposition of coldness and warmth, showing distinction-making to be a social activity, and indeed a form of negotiation. The hero, Clitandre, in his seduction of Cidalise, not only refers to a distinction between types of women, those who are *froides*, cold, and those who are *sensibles*, sensitive, but embroiders on the distinction, justifies it, and exploits it to his own end. He even expatiates on the difficulty of recognizing women according to type, and notes that inexperienced observers are likely to misread the signs. There is a great deal at stake for the narrative of *La Nuit et le moment* in the actual business of distinguishing, since Cidalise is concerned to locate herself with respect to Célimène, known by her to have been a recent lover of Clitandre. Célimène is in fact declared by both to be *froide*, but Cidalise is a little concerned that she herself might be judged too much the opposite.[14] Clitandre attempts to soothe her by saying: "Vous avez de singulières idées d'imaginer que je vous reprocherai d'être sensible, moi qui avais toutes les peines du monde à pardonner à Célimène de ne l'être pas" [What a strange notion on your part to think that I might reproach you for being sensitive, given that I had the utmost difficulty in forgiving Célimène for not being so] (79). Yet all of these questions and answers are of less interest for their truth value than for their seductive enunciation. What does it mean, after all, to be at just the right point on the scale? Clitandre and Cidalise will arrive together at a finely tuned understanding about this, the point of which is to induce Cidalise to yield by giving a flattering image of her, positioning her at the optimal place, closer to the *sensible* pole without being extreme, and thereby establishing Célimène as unduly *froide*. The positioning itself, the very fact of classification, is part of a seductive conversational strategy. Célimène, the unfortunate one, is said to suffer from a kind of contradiction, since "la froideur de ses sens n'empêche pas la tête de s'animer" [the coldness of her senses does not prevent the mind from quickening] (80), but her coldness and the sensitivity of Cidalise are finally to be understood as negotiated "facts" of temperament,[15] so that there can be no question of anything so dramatic, so passionate, so frankly inelegant, as metamorphosis.[16] The fundamental concern in Crébillon is not with essential truth, but rather with the playful exploitation of pseudo-essential categories.

In keeping with my stated concern about the danger of anachronism, I want to resist the suggestion that the supposed rigor of Luzéide, the agreed coldness of Célimène, or the quality of other characters used for contrastive effect in such representations is a form of what our sexologists call frigidity. Sheila Jeffreys resists anachronism all too thoroughly when she makes the claim that "frigidity" is a recent invention, put together by 1950s sexologists along with male impotence and premature ejaculation. "For such specifications the illnesses that required treatment in sex therapy were created," she says.[17] I am going to argue that frigidity has a much longer history than Jeffreys allows, but not an agelessly classical one, and that it is cognate with the thematics of marble and fire I am seeking to describe. As long as cold women are simply given in their temperamental coldness, to be adverted to derisively as the forgotten ones of pleasure, as long as coldness is playfully imputed to certain women in the course of gentle seduction, frigidity cannot be the object of therapeutic attention or transforming narrative. But when the opposition between marble and fire comes to be understood in dynamic terms, it is possible to imagine fire deep within the marble. The frigid woman can then become not so much an object of desire, as a fascinating, almost inscrutable locus of its circulation, carrying her fire somewhere deep within, beneath a smooth, resistant surface.

I shall have more to say shortly about the narrative aesthetics of frigidity as it begins to emerge in the late eighteenth and early nineteenth centuries, but the dialectical nature of my topic compels me to attend to the increasingly powerful thematics of fire that supports and defines frigidity by acting as its antithesis. Indications of historical change in this regard can be found, for example, in *Histoire de dom Bougre, portier des Chartreux* (1741) by Gervaise de Latouche, one of the eighteenth century's most widely read erotic novels. The story retains elements of classical *ars erotica*, but adds to them quite striking innovations. At the outset, the hero responds to forms of behavior he encounters, and models himself on them. His modeling is not described, however, as an imitative discipline: he encounters his models by chance, and responds to them "naturally." His "initiation" is thus not ritualistic, but spontaneous: he feels, we are told, "un désir violent de faire avec une femme ce que j'avais vu faire au père Polycarpe avec Toinette" [a violent desire to do with a woman what I had seen Father Polycarpe doing with Toinette].[18]

Of interest to us here are the dynamics of this spontaneous response, for such themes are not foregrounded in classical erotica. Saturnin, the hero, lives in a world of thin walls, and it is not surprising that he should, while still quite young, espy a couple engaged in love making. His response to this sight is not described in the time-honored manner, as a gymnastic alignment of his own body, but is characterized in physiological terms, as a build-up of inner fire: "Un feu inconnu se glissait dans mes veines, j'avais le visage enflammé, mon cœur palpitait, je retenais mon haleine, et la pique de Vénus, que je pris à la main, était d'une force et d'une raideur à abattre le cloison, si j'avais poussé un peu fort" [An unknown fire slid into my veins. My face was alight, my heart was palpitating. I held my breath, and the spear of Venus, which I took in my hand, was strong and stiff enough to knock down the partition if I had pushed a little harder] (34). The thinness of the partition within the house seems to figure the low resistance of any inner membrane to the compelling circulation of fire. Desire manifests itself as force, as something that circulates in the blood, builds up internal pressure, and pushes for release. "Ideas" of erotic representation still have their place, in fact, but they are most significant in narrative for the bodily symptoms they provoke: "Animé par l'ardeur vive et brûlante que ces idées répandaient dans tout mon corps, je sortis, j'allai chercher Suzon" [Animated by the lively, burning ardor that these ideas were spreading throughout my body, I went out in search of Suzon] (3:38). Desire comes thus to be understood, in a way that can appear banal to modern eyes, as a process, with its build-up of inner tension and its necessary conclusion: "J'étais brûlé d'un feu qui ne pouvait s'éteindre que par la jouissance" [I was burning with a fire that could only be put out by pleasure] (3:97). For Saturnin, there is only a minimal narrative space separating the perception of the model from the ready discharge of satisfaction. His story continually makes an easy transition between two forms of eroticism that appear to confront each other—or are at least held apart—in Rousseau's *Pygmalion*. The circumstantial didactic moments of *Histoire de dom Bougre* are melted into a dynamic psycho-physiological narrative of desire and satisfaction.

Fire in the veins expands to become a commonplace of late eighteenth-century erotic narrative. Often, its symptoms are most clearly perceptible when there is some disjunction of heat and coldness. In *Lucette, ou Les Progrès du libertinage* (1765), an old man feels the fire coming back: "Le vieillard sentait un feu nouveau couler dans ses veines; il croyait rajeunir, comme le père de Jason. Brûlant, plein d'ardeur, il allait essayer de goûter une partie de la félicité de ses premiers ans" [The old man felt a new fire flowing in his veins. He thought he was young again, like Jason's father. Alight and full of ardor, he was going to try to enjoy some of the bliss he had known in his youth].[19] On another occasion in the same novel, the heat of love triumphs over the massive resistance of obesity: "Mondor . . . convoitait Lucette. Sa lourde masse était enflammée. Le feu de l'amour avait pénétré la chair et la graisse qui l'accablait; il était parvenu jusqu'à son cœur" [Mondor lusted after Lucette. His heavy bulk was on fire. The fire of love had penetrated the flesh and the fat that weighed it down. It had reached his heart] (1:91). In *Le Degré des âges du plaisir* (1793), an aging writer invokes the muse of sensuality in the same terms: "fais circuler dans mes veines cette même flamme qui m'animait dans les embrassements que je prodiguais à la plus tendre des amantes, dans ce temps fortuné où la nature, moins avare de ses dons, me laissait jouir de toutes mes facultés" [circulate through my veins the same fire that once quickened me as I embraced the tenderest of lovers, in that happy time when nature was less stinting, and allowed me to enjoy all my faculties].[20] On each occasion, the erotic event is expected and recounted as the triumph of circulating heat over resistant, residual coldness.

Eroticism, at this time, is characterized to a progressively greater degree as a phenomenon of intensity. Its fire is not of course a local presence, lodged in some organ or other: it moves about, pervading and ordering the whole body as it flows through every vein: "Mon imagination est tellement échauffée qu'elle porte le feu dans toutes mes veines" [My imagination is so heated that it is bearing fire into all my veins], we read in

Lettres galantes et philosophiques de deux nones (1777).[21] The fullness of passion is experienced precisely through this efficacious carrying of fire, which overcomes any substantive resistance within the body. It is still possible, in 1790, to claim the fine old metaphorical equivalence of beautiful flesh with marble—"cette gorge ferme, dont la blancheur fait honte au plus beau marbre" [those firm breasts, whose whiteness shames the finest marble][22]—but truly erotic flesh, whatever its visible formal properties, is now likely to be traversed by veins that actively diffuse the heat of desire throughout its mass.

In the most Romantic texts, the theme of circulation lends itself to various intensifying modes. *Les Délices de Coblentz* (1791) shows that blood can be rendered more weighty, yet no less mobile, by the figurative presence of quicksilver: "il eût semblé qu'un feu liquide courait chez elle de veine en veine, et que le vif argent le plus subtil fût attaché à ses parties internes" [it might have seemed as if liquid fire ran within her from one vein to another, as if the most subtle quicksilver was attached to her inner parts].[23] The prestige of circulation as such is reflected in the association of blood with the most powerful of substances, for the strength of circulation is of far greater import than any supposed singularity of humor, or any finely-tuned balance of *froideur* and *sensibilité*. It matters little what metaphorical cocktails are produced in the course of description, as long as they involve the most formidable materiality. *Le Degré des âges du plaisir* (1793) mobilizes the hottest of minerals for this purpose: "je brûle, le salpêtre et le bitume circulent dans mes sens, un délire convulsif embrase mon imagination" [I am burning. Saltpeter and pitch are circulating in my senses. Convulsive madness has set fire to my imagination] (6:433). The veins may even be filled with a kind of poison, as in *Eléonore* (1795): "ce poison, jusqu'à cette heure endormi, se réveille, se répand dans tous ses sens, y porte un feu qu'elle a juré d'éteindre" [the poison, which had been dormant until that time, awoke and spread throughout all her senses, carrying into them the fire she had sworn to put out].[24] Indeed, circulation itself may be experienced as a form of violence. The high Romanticism of *Gamiani* (1833) represents a body awash with an inner libidinal flow that pushes up inside the head and breaks upon the eyes from within, making them feel like fragile windows: "L'humeur, échauffée de plus en plus et trop abondante, se portait dans ma

tête, et les parties de feu dont elle était remplie, frappant vive-
ment contre la vitre de mes yeux, y causaient une sorte de
mirage éblouissant" [the humor, more and more heated and
overly abundant, flowed to my head, and the particles of fire it
contained sparked against the glass of my eyes, causing a kind
of dazzling mirage].[25]

When powerful circulation becomes a recurrent image for
eroticism, then the quality of inner substance may be less significant than the intensity of desire, imagined as a symptomatic
fullness of the body. The focus now tends to be on desire as process and product—as euphoric congestion, so to speak. Whereas
Venette, in his earlier *Tableau de l'amour conjugal* (1687), could
describe sperm as something accumulated in, then excreted
from the body,[26] it became possible at the end of the eighteenth
century to see sperm as circulating with the blood, blending
with it, in the manner of those other powerful substances we
have already seen coursing through the veins of desire. A
metaphorical consequence of this is that the qualities of blood
are taken to be more or less interchangeable with those of
sperm. It is not the case that the body is represented in priapic
terms: erectness—that postural figure—seems to matter far less
than the physiology of tumescence. Certainly, the vulgar French
word for sperm, *le foutre*, is called on to do heavy thematic duty
toward the end of the eighteenth century and at the beginning
of the nineteenth. *Foutre* is in fact both verb and noun, designating an action and a substance. The verb has a long history in obscene texts, but it is the interdependent use of noun and verb
that is so striking during this period, affirming as it does a circular relationship between action and substance. Aretino, in the
sixteenth century, described the sixteen *modi* without specifying
any verb that would mark the general action of which these
were "modes." This was presumably because, in his more classical view, it was the paradigm as such, the range of positions,
that constituted erotic knowledge.

However, the late eighteenth century produces a text entitled *Quarante Manières de foutre* (1790),[27] declaring a fundamental sameness to lie at the heart of eroticism: these are
forty different ways of doing what is essentially the same
thing. And what makes this thing "essentially" the same, I suggest, is in part a more physiological conception of eroticism,
one that gauges the intensive activity of substances rather

than focusing on postural distinctions. When two characters in
Décrets des sens sanctionnés par la volupté (1793) blush (turn
red), the substance that makes them do so is said to be, not
blood, but *le foutre*: "La rougeur [me] monta au visage, et ses
joues se colorèrent. Ce fut sans doute le foutre, comme le dit
cet auteur immortel, qui ajouta les roses au lys de son teint"
[Redness went to my face, and her cheeks flushed with color. It
was no doubt *le foutre* that added roses to the lilies of her complexion].[28] The "animal spirits" that had played a central role in
classical accounts of human sensibility, and continued to be
present in Sadian disquisitions, were no longer strictly necessary to an erotic physiology. Or rather, they were swept along
in the tide, dissolved in urgent materiality. Nerciat's Céleste
seems to speak for a whole generation when she says, "j'[ai] le
démon de la fouterie délayé dans mon sang" [I have the demon
of fucking dissolved in my blood] (*Les Aphrodites* [1793]).[29] By
this same easy logic of amalgamation, the circulating substance of life is declared to be sperm itself: "cette liqueur spermatique, ce foutre vivifiant, le principe de notre être" [that
spermatic liquor, that invigorating *foutre*, the principle of our
being] (*Décrets des sens . . .* 6:284). *Foutre* in the veins and fire
in the balls: "[le] feu divin qui circule dans mes couilles" [the
divine fire that circulates in my balls] (6:297). It is the very circulation of metaphors that marks the ever-renewed abundance
of desire.

The narrator-hero of *Histoire de dom Bougre* uses the verb
foutre as an imperative, imbuing it with evangelical fervor: "Et
Saint-Paul, interprète sacré des volontés du ciel, qui connaissait
toute l'étendue des devoirs de la nature, a dit: plutôt que de
brûler, foutez mes enfants, foutez" [And Saint Paul, the sacred
translator of heaven's will, who knew the full extent of nature's
demands, said, "Rather than burning, fuck, my children, fuck"]
(3:181). What lends moral force to this unscriptural verb is the
burning, physical substance that makes of it a natural "duty." A
prior in the same novel rails against the sexual interdictions
that govern religious orders. They are both inhumanly cruel and
doomed to failure, because they cannot ultimately contain the
fire within:

L'imbécillité de nos fondateurs et la cruauté des hommes ont voulu
nous interdire une fonction aussi naturelle, elles n'ont fait qu'ir-

riter nos désirs. Comment donc apaiser ces flammes que la nature
elle-même a allumées dans nos cœurs? . . . Fallait-il, pour nous
conformer à leurs idées tyranniques, brûler continuellement d'un
feu qui ne peut s'éteindre que par la mort?

[The imbecility of our founders and the cruelty of men have attempted to forbid us this natural function, but have only stirred
up our desires. How can we quench these flames that nature has
lit in our hearts? Should we, in order to satisfy their tyrannical
ideas, burn continually with a fire that can only be extinguished
by death?] (3:172)

The abstract rule-making of the institution is answered here by
what we might call a physiological economy of compulsion. This
argument—one that has since become wearyingly familiar
through the discourse of "sexual liberation"—depends in fact for
its power on a thematics of substantive desire. When eroticism
is defined as a need for relief or release, it cannot reliably be
contained by ethical stringency:

je ne crois pas que Dieu puisse faire un grand crime à une pauvre
fille de chercher à se soulager quand elle est pressée: elle ne s'est
pas faite elle-même. Est-ce sa faute si elle a des désirs, si elle est
amoureuse? . . . Elle cherche à apaiser ces désirs qui la dévorent,
ce feu qui la brûle, elle se sert des moyens que la nature lui donne.
Rien n'est moins criminel.

[I do not believe that God can consider it such a great crime for a
girl to give herself some relief when she is under pressure. She did
not make herself as she is. Is it her fault if she desires, or if she is
in love? She tries to calm the desires that consume her, the fire
that burns. She uses the means that nature gives her. Nothing
could be less blameworthy.] (3:73)

When Saturnin refers to the young woman in question as
pressée, he produces a kind of pun. We are presumably to understand that she feels pressure from within, and also that
this pressure creates a sense of narrative urgency. The connection between substantive desire and the action of its release is
thus made in directly narrative terms, for the build-up of tension governs the time of eroticism. Where classical eroticism
moved through the paradigm in quasi-ritual fashion, or observed the gradations of pleasure with finely shaded subtlety,

the "essential" eroticism we are considering here requires a particular act, a rudimentary narrative climax, for its realization.

Sade's work is not so easily situated with respect to a classi-
cal/Romantic divide as many modernist Sadophiles would have
us believe: I have argued elsewhere that his texts are strewn
with the vestiges of a classical *ars erotica*. Nonetheless, there
can be no doubting that he takes up with great vigor the narrative economy of desire as inner substance. "Heating up" bodies
may be carried out in various ways, through the display of
models or philosophical discourse, but the application of heat is
found to produce a reliable outcome. The reader/addressee of *Les
Cent Vingt Journées de Sodome* (1785) is told confidently that
some of the *écarts* portrayed in this text "t'échaufferont au point
de te coûter du foutre" [will heat you up to the point of costing
you *foutre*].[30] Being *échauffé* generally leads, in fact, to a "point"
at which *le foutre* comes spurting out of the body. Ejaculation
can thus be recounted as a necessary consequence of the build-
up that precedes it: "Il y eut en un mot tant de lubricité de faite
que le sperme éjacula" [To put it briefly, there was so much lubricity that sperm was ejaculated] (*Les Cent Vingt Journées . . .*
1:52). *Lubricité* in this context is an attitude, if you like, but it is
primarily an action, the literal expression of sperm as accumulated desiring substance. In keeping with this same logic, discharge can be held up, thus increasing inner tension and
threatening to produce explosive violence: "Le feu sortait des
yeux du prélat, son vit était collé contre son ventre, il écumait,
c'était un foutre contenu qui voulait absolument s'échapper et
qui ne le pouvait que par des moyens violents" [Fire was coming
out of the prelate's eyes. His prick was stuck against his belly.
He was foaming. It was *foutre* held in, absolutely determined to
get out, and able to do so only by violent means] (1:97). Intensity
is produced here not only by the quality of inner substances and
the violence of their circulatory movement, but by the narrative
delay in their release.

Lest it be thought that I am failing here to distinguish between two forms of circulation—within bodies and between
them—it should be noted that such failure to distinguish seems
to flow from the dynamics of substantive eroticism. A propos of
Pygmalion, we were led to ask both questions at once: how it is
that fire can move through the heart of icy marble, and how creative warmth can pass back and forth between Pygmalion and

Galatea. More generally, as Rousseau's text is situated within a broad development in literary eroticism, it appears that the economy of physiological desire opens into that of desire as intercorporal currency. The very fact that sperm, which is both accumulated within the body and communicated to the other, should be functionally equivalent to heat and fire is itself a symptom of this thematic commingling. Not that the two economies can be said to coincide, of course: it is just that they are connected and complicit by the very fact of being economies. For a classical *ars erotica*, eroticism entails representation and modeling: erotic discipline works across ceremonious distance, in the space of reflexivity, and its privileged medium is the look. Substantive eroticism, on the other hand, moves readily from the physiology of inner pressure to the drama of communication as contagion. In Nerciat's *Les Aphrodites* (1793), we read: "Ainsi chacun des quatre acteurs se partage presque également; la volupté circule; le plaisir que la duchesse doit au comte, elle le communique au chevalier, qui le rend à Célestine, qui le ramène enfin à la première source" [In this way each of the four actors shared almost equally. Voluptuousness circulated. The pleasure that the duchess owed to the count she passed on to the knight, who gave it to Célestine, who brought it back eventually to the place where it began] (1:59). What might have been, in a more classical text, a well-composed tableau, marked by postural ingenuity and neatness of fit, is now described as a libidinal circuit.

The frequently used metaphor of the spark allows the communication of fire to take place in one impetuous moment: "ce baiser qui fut donné de la manière la mieux conditionnée, fit sur moi l'effet de l'étincelle sur la poudre; des désirs impétueux s'élevèrent au fond de mon cœur" [this kiss, given in the most proper fashion, had on me the effect of a spark on gunpowder. Impetuous desires arose in the depths of my heart] (*Julie philosophe* [1791]).[31] But such intimate transmission is not usually the work of dry heat: the virtues of electricity are materialized and liquefied, becoming tributary in their turn to the great confluence of such metaphors. "Sparks of fire" are "poured" into the soul of the lover (*Caroline et Saint-Hilaire* [1817]),[32] and a kiss becomes a form of oral coupling: "tendresse, désirs, transports, tout nous devint commun; une bouche étroitement collée sur la sienne lui communiquait mes soupirs; sa langue était un

trait qui faisait passer chez moi tout le feu qui le consumait"
[tenderness, desires, rapture, everything was now shared between us. A mouth tightly glued to his communicated my sighs.
His tongue was an arrow transferring to me all the fire that consumed him] (*La Nouvelle Académie des dames* [c. 1774]).[33] In
Gamiani (1833), a glance can suffice, for the look of a passionate
lover is wet with fire: "Les cœurs combustibles ne brûlent pas
d'eux-mêmes: qu'une étincelle approche, et tout part! Ainsi prit
feu mon cœur aux transports de celui qui m'aimait. . . . La
flamme humide qui sortait des yeux de mon amant pénétrait
dans les miens jusqu'au fond de mon âme, et y portait le trouble,
le délire et la joie" [Combustible hearts do not burn by themselves. If one spark comes near, it all goes up! This is how my
heart caught fire at the rapture of the one who loved me. The
moist flame from the eyes of my lover entered mine to the
depths of my soul, bringing with it disturbance, madness, and
joy].[34] The "flamme humide" refers to moisture on the surface of
the eye, but its wetness holds a narrative promise that tran-
scends any epidermic phenomena. This is what guarantees that
contact will be instantly transformed into deep circulation.

For such intercorporal physiology, there need be no rhetoric of
seduction, merely a forceful intervention whereby desire is communicated. In this regard, Sade is very much an author of his
time. As if to justify his fearful and impatient mistrust of the uncertainties of negotiation,[35] he is fond of describing the encounter of desire with its object as if it were a physical impact.
Faire circuler is an abrupt and rudimentary way of describing
the process of influence, of flowing-in: just as heat circulates in
the desiring body, it can be made to circulate, by simple physical
causality, in the body of others. Thus Augustine, in *Les Cent
Vingt Journées de Sodome* (1785), is said to experience "la
volupté qu'un autre faisait circuler dans ses sens" [the voluptuousness that another was causing to circulate through her
senses] (1:313). The same direct expression occurs in other texts
of the period. In the anonymous *La Messaline française* (1790),
we read: "Nos langues mutuellement dardées entre nos lèvres
font circuler dans nos veines des torrents de feu" [our tongues as
they darted between each other's lips caused torrents of fire to
circulate in our veins] (5:310). And elsewhere in the same text,
once again mingling sperm with fire: "Je fais circuler dans ses
veines le plaisir à grands flots" [I made pleasure flow in great

waves through her veins] (5:315). *Faire circuler* can serve indeed as a metaphor for the content of erotic literature, as something communicated and consumed. In *Décrets des sens sanctionnés par la volupté* (1793), the author's stated goal is to achieve a form of circulatory coupling with his readers: "dessiner quelques actes voluptueux de lubricité et faire passer dans les sens de mes lecteurs cette ardeur de foutre qui circule dans les miens" [to describe some voluptuous acts of lubricity and transfer to my readers' senses this ardor to fuck that circulates in mine] (6: 299). Little wonder, then, that ink should give way, on occasion, to the substance of life itself. *Caroline et Saint-Hilaire*, we are informed at the beginning of the text, has been "tracé avec une plume trempée dans le foutre brûlant" [drawn with a pen steeped in burning *foutre*].[36]

When the circulation of fire and blood, sperm and electricity is understood as the very process of life, then the story of Pygmalion and Galatea is no longer a miraculous exception, but a kind of norm, and a standard representation of erotic vitality. Seduction, instead of being drawn out à la Crébillon in conversational arabesques, can now be directly enacted in the heating up of one body by another. There is finally no great mystery at the heart of it all, merely an exciting physiology, and the sentience of life itself. Given the certainty of this bodily truth, with its underlying guarantee of vital process, there can be changes in agency and direction with no loss of thematic regularity, as long as the flow continues. Félicité de Choiseul-Meuse produces some nice thematic variations without any radical disturbance when she partly reverses the gender roles in *Amélie de Saint-Far* (1802). Let us suppose, says one of her characters, the worldly Alexandrine, as she addresses the less experienced Ernest, that you are looking at a marble statue. You bring her to life to such an extent that she takes hold of your hand "comme je fais là" [as I am doing here], and places it on her breast: "le marbre a perdu sa froideur, mais ces contours gracieux que vous admiriez sont toujours les mêmes!" [the marble has lost its coldness, but those graceful curves that you admired are still the same!]. You range further afield, to find that the rest of her body is just as alive, and you find that "elle communique la plus douce chaleur à tout ce qu'elle touche" [she communicates the sweetest warmth to all she touches].[37] For this most active and aware of Galateas, the thematic evocation is itself a "communication" in both senses, figurative and literal. Alexandrine positions herself metaphorically as the statue, tells the story, and uses the telling to seduce a half-innocent young man. She fully deserves to be called a "nouvelle Galathée" (1:117) for her knowledge of the legend, for her erotic enunciation of it, and for the thematic extension that she produces. So powerful is the theme that it can function just as well at another point in the novel without the same topical awareness on the part of the characters. Amélie, the virtuous but sensual heroine, is determined to remain faithful to her fiancé, Ernest, while he spends time in the colonies accumulating wealth for their marital future. She reckons without the Pygmalion-Galatea dynamic, however, for she falls victim to it when she attempts to revive her friend and oft-rejected suitor, the Duc de Nemours. After he has almost drowned in a boating accident, Amélie is carried away by the idea of bringing the duke back to life, even though she sees that "tous les symptômes de la mort se manifestaient déjà" [all the symptoms of death were already visible] (2:48). "Elle était exaltée par l'idée qu'en communiquant au duc une chaleur vivifiante, elle venait de le rendre à la vie. Afin d'achever son ouvrage, elle le couvrait de mille baisers, elle collait sa joue sur la sienne, puis elle remarquait avec délices la légère teinte de rose que ce contact avait produit" [She was thrilled by the idea that by passing on invigorating warmth to the duke, she had just saved his life. In order to finish the task, she showered him with kisses, glued her cheek to his, then observed in delight the tinge of pink produced by this contact] (2:49). The blush of pink in this cold, white body is the mark of hopeful contact, the object of therapeutic pleasure, and the promise that heat will soon be shared: "La plus vive chaleur ne tarda pas à remplacer le froid mortel dont il avait été saisi" [The liveliest warmth soon replaced the deathly cold that had gripped him] (2:50). Once begun, the dynamic is irresistible, and Amélie's virginal resistance simply melts away in the (physical) process.

Adding a tinge of pink to the description of pale, almost lifeless creatures allows them to have statuesque qualities without being trapped in minerality. It is, in the most precise sense, the vital difference between flesh and marble. In Nerciat's *Le Diable au corps* (1803), one character appears by her lack of animation to be the exact opposite of the two heroines whose erotic vitality gives the novel its title. Mademoiselle de Nimmernein is blonde, Germanic, statuesque, and apparently unresponsive. But this makes of her, in an erotic novel, a likely Galatea, and she is indeed, as her name suggests to polyglot readers, a woman who can't say no. The Comte who tells the story of his tryst with her does not fail to make the standard comparisons: "je la mets nue. . . . Oh! Sans hyperbole, je crois voir respirer Galathée après le dernier coup de ciseau de Pygmalion. Ivre de désir, je la renverse à moitié sur le bord d'un grand lit: à mon approche, elle devient rose de la tête aux pieds" [I laid her bare. Oh! Without exaggeration, I thought I was seeing Galatea come to life after Pygmalion's finishing touch with the chisel. Drunk with desire, I half tilted her backward onto a large bed. When I drew near, she was pink from head to foot].[38] This is not utter transformation, mind. The German woman does not suddenly sit upright or roll about on the floor like some stereotypical Italian countess. She does not go red, in fact. Just a nice shade of pink, striking as she does the most ambiguous of life-in-death poses: "immobile, elle m'attend, me reçoit, me laisse faire sans se donner d'autre peine que celle de déployer en crucifix deux bras d'une proportion divine" [she waited motionless, received me, and let me do as I wished without doing any more than spreading her divinely proportioned arms in the shape of the cross] (6:75). There is pleasure to be had with her, and pleasure to be had in reading the mark of her pleasure, but this means going beyond the initial signs of impassivity. Much the same kind of nuance, and the same reading of it, although in less burlesque mode, can be found in *L'Enfant du bordel* (1800). The first reference here in the description of a beautiful woman, as often, is to the near perfection of whiteness: "Dieux! Quel spectacle pour lui! Une gorge naissante qui aurait su le disputer en blancheur à la neige, sans la légère teinte rosée qui corrigeait ce que les lys avaient de trop blanc et empêchait qu'on ne les prît pour deux blocs de marbre. Un léger bouton de rose effeuillé l'embellissait encore" [Ye gods! What a sight it was for him! Cleaving breasts that might have outdone snow for their whiteness, were it not for the pinkish tinge that corrected the excessive whiteness of the lilies, and prevented them from being taken for two blocks of marble. A light rosebud without its petals made them even more beautiful].[39] Truly erotic beauty has the qualities of marble, with an essential "correction," which is more than an embellishment. Discerning this difference and helping to provoke it as a symptom can often become, as we shall see, the work of passionate attention, brought to bear on the body of the other. Most often, this other is not a half-drowned, middle-aged duke, as in *Amélie de Saint-Far*, but an apparently lifeless, ostensibly frigid young woman. The eroticism of frigidity is in fact a profoundly narrative one, committed to the hope of metamorphosis, and sustained by the knowledge of circulation. Its symptomatology, its bodily semiotics dwell attentively on the faint stirring of life, on the barely perceptible nuance, on the palest roseate tinge.

It is hard to imagine a text more radically committed to the love of frigidity than Theophile Gautier's *La Morte amoureuse* (1836). This story can be read as a complex retelling of the Pygmalion-Galatea myth, pursuing the Rousseauian dialectic of fire and marble, but reading it even more equivocally. Once again, erotic value is attached to fire and blood, but equal value is given to human marble. Romuald and Clarimonde first catch sight of each other on the day when Romuald is being ordained as a priest. In the midst of his ceremonious renunciation of worldly things, and of the love of women in particular, it is love at first sight, for him and for her. Love of a quite material sort, indeed, as the two are spontaneously defined by a kind of dialectical asymmetry. She is not given as frigid from the outset, by some fatality of temperament, but turns white, dramatically, at the sight of Romuald: "Le sang abandonna complètement sa charmante figure, et elle devint d'une blancheur de marbre; ses beaux bras tombèrent le long de son corps, comme si les muscles en avaient été dénoués, et elle s'appuya contre un pilier" [The blood completely left her charming face, and she became as white as marble. Her beautiful arms hung beside her body, as if their muscles had been undone, and she leant against a pillar].[40] Romuald has not hitherto shown himself to be fiery by nature, having led an untroubled existence until the sight of Clarimonde transforms him: "je sentais la vie monter en moi comme un lac intérieur qui s'enfle et qui déborde; mon sang battait avec force dans mes artères; ma jeunesse, si longtemps comprimée, éclatait tout d'un coup" [I felt life rising in me like an inner lake swelling and overflowing. My blood pumped in my arteries. My youth, held in for so long, suddenly burst out] (479). This is how she is drained of blood and heat almost instantaneously, while he is filled with them. This is how the two "communicate" from the first moment, despite all that stands between them. Their look establishes a thrilling antithesis and an intercorporal economy that will determine the events of the story. Her coldness and whiteness are both the symptoms of her love and the finest features of her beauty: his blood-red vigor is provoked by her sight, and its abundance serves to sustain them both.

The second major event in *La Morte amoureuse* occurs when Romuald, having gone ahead nonetheless with his life as a priest, is called some years later to the bedside of the dying Clarimonde. He arrives too late to save her from death (487)—or even from damnation, if the stories about her orgiastic existence are to be believed (492). Falling in love on the day of his ordination was itself too late, of course, but the function of narrative in this story is quite systematically to retrieve that which is apparently beyond its time, to revive passion where it appeared to be dead. Romuald finds himself conducting a lonely vigil, given over to the contemplation of Clarimonde as she lies on her deathbed. She was never more beautiful, he observes: "On eût dit une statue d'albâtre faite par quelque sculpteur habile pour mettre sur un tombeau de reine, ou encore une jeune fille endormie sur qui il aurait neigé" [She looked like an alabaster statue made by an expert sculptor to be placed on a queen's tomb, or indeed like a young girl asleep on whom it had snowed] (487). But is she dead, or merely asleep? The doubt, and the possibility of error, prey on his mind: "cette perfection de formes, quoique purifiée et sanctifiée par l'ombre de la mort, me troublait plus voluptueusement qu'il n'aurait fallu, et ce repos ressemblait tant à un sommeil que l'on s'y serait trompé" [That perfect shape, although purified and sanctified by the shadow of death, disturbed me sensually more than it ought to have, and her rest was so like sleep that one could have mistaken one for the other] (488–89). This ambiguity is itself erotic, as it draws Romuald into the Pygmalion story. Will he, like La Mettrie's young hero in *L'Art de jouir*, awaken a sleeping lover? Will he attempt, like Rousseau's gifted artist, to bring a statue to life? Clarimonde shows, after all, just a faint tinge of pink: "La pâleur de ses joues, le rose moins vif de ses lèvres, les longs cils baissés et découpant leur frange brune sur cette blancheur, lui donnaient une expression de chasteté mélancolique et de souffrance pensive d'une puissance de séduction inexprimable" [the pallor of her cheeks, the less vivid pink of her lips, the long,

lowered eyelashes, appearing as a dark fringe on her whiteness,
all this gave her an expression of melancholy chastity and pensive suffering whose seductive power was inexpressible] (489).
Driven by the force of his own circulation—"mes artères palpi-
taient avec une telle force, que je les sentais siffler dans mes
tempes" [my arteries were thumping with such force that I felt
them whistling through my temples] (489)—Romuald cannot
resist the desire to lift up the shroud that veils the
sleeping/dead woman. He leans over her, touches her, breathes
on her, and embraces her: "on eût dit que le sang commençait à
circuler sous cette matte pâleur; cependant elle était toujours de
la plus parfaite immobilité" [you would have said that blood was
beginning to circulate through that mat pallor. Yet she remained perfectly motionless] (489). Note that Gautier does not
use La Mettrie's favorite adverb, *déjà*, in such description, for he
has his own favorite: *toujours*. The effect of this substitution is
to change the import of the theme. Whereas La Mettrie found
the promise of life and love "already" present in the heart of immobility, Gautier finds, by what must count as the very definition of morbid delectation, the coldness and death that are "still"
present in the beautiful woman after her ostensible awakening.
For Romuald does attempt to "souffler sur sa dépouille glacée la
flamme qui me dévorait" [breathe into her cold remains the
flame that consumed me] (490), and succeeds to a degree in reviving her. But this "degree" is precisely the space of ambivalence in which the story is content to dwell. He touches her arm
as she lies there: it is cold, but no colder than on the day she
touched his hand as he left the church (489). For this very
reason, when she begins to breathe in response to his kiss, it appears to be something less than a miracle. Certainly, it is no
definitive story of metamorphosis. Soon after the event has occurred, Clarimonde is "still" being described as "la belle morte"
(490). She will continue to be so for the rest of the story.

The heroine thus continues to be attended by death, and the
beauty of death. Unlike Nerciat's Mlle. de Nimmernein, she does
not go pink from head to toe, but displays the most subtle
shades of pale color: "Elle portait à la main une petite lampe de
la forme de celles que l'on met dans les tombeaux, dont la lueur
donnait à ses doigts effilés une transparence rose qui se pro-
longeait par une gradation insensible jusque dans la blancheur
opaque et laiteuse de son bras nu" [She had in her hand a little

lamp of the kind placed in tombs. Its glow gave to her fingers a pink transparency that extended in the finest gradation as far as the opaque, milky whiteness of her bare arm] (493). Pinkness here is not the first flush of some future ruddiness, but the most delicate, lingering condition. Whereas in Ovid's story, and even Rousseau's retelling of it, the event of metamorphosis was the central point, what matters most for Gautier is a kind of indefinite equivocation, a subtly graded thematic ambivalence extending from the beauty of life to the beauty of death. Is Clarimonde alive or dead, in fact? It hardly matters: "morte ou vivante, statue ou femme, ombre ou corps, sa beauté était toujours la même; seulement l'éclat vert de ses prunelles était un peu amorti, et sa bouche, si vermeille autrefois, n'était plus teintée que d'un rose faible et tendre presque semblable à celui de ses joues" [dead or alive, statue or woman, her beauty was always the same. The brilliant green of her eyes was simply a little dulled, and her mouth, once so crimson, was now only tinged with a weak, tender pink almost the same as that of her cheeks] (493–94). For the purposes of the story, and in the narrow interests of an aesthetics of frigidity, the most important question is not whether the woman is alive or dead but whether she presents the equivocal symptoms in all their beauty. Romuald sustains his lover with his own blood, which she drinks, vampire-like, in small quantities during his sleep (501), but he sustains her in her very weakness. This we can read quite properly as a figure of the mutual thematic dependence of marble and blood, as the ongoing work of their amorous dialectic. But it must also be noted that this is exactly as Romuald wants it. Clarimonde's coldness and whiteness, her life-in-death are fed by his desire. Wittingly or unwittingly, *La Morte amoureuse* presents a striking example of the production of feminine frigidity, sustained as an object of delectation by a diet of male desire. The possibility of transformation may be evoked, but radical change is indefinitely deferred, and emphasis placed on the qualities that are "still" or always present. There is pleasure to be had in holding up frigidity, holding it up in both senses of the word: making of it an object of attention defined by the need for change, and retarding any complete transformation. It is worth asking whether such pleasure and desire are not still at work in modern sexological discourse, sustaining its therapeutic energy and drawing out its clinical practice.

Gautier's rewriting of the Galatea story enhances what we might call its thematic array, without identifying its features as symptoms. Frigidity is not yet produced, therefore, as a true syndrome, of the kind identified in our century by sexological discourse. Clarimonde, it could well be said, is not sick so much as sickly, and not even that so much as pale and wan. Her condition, not subject to medical diagnosis, is to be half dead and half alive. *La Morte amoureuse* describes in full the marks of Clarimonde's coldness, but the unifying principle of this description is its metaphorics of substance and color. It is aesthetic rather than "scientific." Half a century later, erotic writing of the fin de siècle takes a further, decisive step in the construction of frigidity. While maintaining the aesthetics and continuing to trade in metaphors of marble and fire, it comes to account for extreme bodily phenomena as the symptoms of a psychosexual pathology. This was, it can be said, always a possibility inscribed in the discourse of libidinal flow that developed in the late eighteenth century. For insofar as desire is understood in terms of process, as a compelling symbiosis of blood, fire, and sperm, the flow is always prone to dysfunction. Such metaphors of health imply corresponding forms of illness: there may be some blockage, some diversion, or even some insufficiency of vital substances. Of course, one of the generic properties of pornography at its most banal is sustained euphoria and cheery denial that anything might ever go wrong, but the place of a circulatory pathology is nonetheless opened up by the thematic reconfiguration that occurs in the later eighteenth century, and this place comes to be occupied in its every nook and cranny during the fin de siècle. There is a particular cohabitation, at the end of the nineteenth century, of medical and sexual discourses that between them produce the notion of the "erotic" as an object of prurient fascination and scientific condescension.

Fin-de-siècle writing wants apparently to rehearse the story of Pygmalion and Galatea, and often attempts to do so. But its fictional characters are unable to get the job done, for reasons that are far from accidental. Indeed, the incomplete narratives that result are usually presented as evidence of a more general failure, and as the revelation of various maladies or perversions. The young man who tells his pathetic (non-)story in Adolphe Belot's *Mademoiselle Giraud, ma femme* (1870) talks too soon of the supremely narrative pleasure to be had by a husband in gradually taking a young wife from *froideur* to *animation*:

> Ce qu'on est tenté d'appeler de la froideur chez une jeune fille n'est souvent que de la réserve et de la timidité. On se réjouit de ce qui pourrait effrayer, et les moins infatués de leur personne se promettent, après le mariage, de jouer avec leurs femmes le rôle de Pygmalion avec Galatée. Un tel rôle devait paraître séduisant avec la personne que j'ai essayé de vous peindre, et tout semblait indiquer qu'il suffirait d'un souffle pour animer cette admirable statue.

> [What may be seen as coldness in a girl is often only shyness and timidity. People delight in what might otherwise make them anxious, and even those who are least infatuated with their own bodies look forward, after the wedding, to acting the role of Pygmalion to their wife's Galatea. Such a role was bound to appear attractive with the person I have tried to describe, and there was every indication that one breath would be enough to bring this admirable statue to life.][41]

La Mettrie would have found this program unexceptionable, but it is preempted in Belot's novel by the fact that the woman is already caught up in a lesbian relationship with an old school friend, the signs of which are tactfully but unequivocally shown. Any hope of success for the young man is in fact denied from the outset by the novel's title, which promises the failure of consummation. Adrien has to find out in the course of time that there will be no metamorphosis of marble to flesh, even though he seems unable himself to arrive at a clear explanation of why this is so, often producing no more than an unhappy restatement of his theme: "J'avais cru épouser un être animé, et je m'étais mésallié à une statue" [I had believed that I was marrying a living creature, but I had misallied myself with a statue] (78). His failure to understand leaves room for the knowing reader, specifically addressed in the introduction, to see what the narration shows without exactly saying, for this story is risqué but hardly audacious. The central secret is that the flow of desire is already occurring inside Paule, but that it is "deviated" toward another woman. It is this preoccupation, this preemptive indirectness that prevents her from being the statuesque virgin her husband takes her for, and prevents the straight story from being enacted.

A more drastic version of the same symptomatic non-story occurs in Catulle Mendès's *Méphistophela* (1890). Sophie, who is deeply attached to her school friend Emmeline and quite unattracted to men, is delivered up on her wedding night to the impatient and unsubtle energy of her soldier husband, Jean. She does not struggle or cry out for mercy in her position as victim, but simply freezes up: "Si elle avait proféré une plainte, si elle lui avait dit: 'De grâce,' ah! Comme il l'aurait laissée, . . . Mais non, la résistance d'un marbre, de qui l'immobile insensibilité était faite de haine, voilà ce qu'il avait entre les bras. . . . Et il s'animalisa" [If she had cried out, if she had said, "I beg of you," ah! how he would have let her be. But no, what he had in his arms was the resistance of marble, motionless insensitivity born of hatred. And he turned into an animal].[42] This is not the happy intercorporal economy of Gautier's Clarimonde and Romuald, but a drastic and sterile antithesis. Becoming an animal is something that Jean does only too well, as he reveals himself to be a most inadequate Pygmalion: "Lui, il s'acharnait sur cette muette, sur cette immobile, avec la véhémence, plus éperdue d'être sacrilège, d'un violateur de tombe, qui voudrait obliger une morte à la résurrection du plaisir" [He continued to labor away on this silent, motionless woman with a vehemence that was all the greater for his sense of sacrilege. It was the vehemence of a grave robber determined to compel a dead woman to experience the resurrection of pleasure] (121). This is no *art de jouir*, and his violence serves only to drive Sophie away, back to Emmeline, and eventually to the life of lesbian "perversion" to which she was predisposed.

The historical breakdown of the Pygmalion theme is thus manifested in fiction as the theme of its processual breakdown. We must understand, in order to read such narratives as these, why the old story cannot be told, and learn to produce that explanation as a diagnosis. Even in "Le Rideau cramoisi" (1874) by Barbey d'Aurevilly, where the emphasis is less on dysfunction than on a certain quality of horror, we find the story metaphorically "set" against the happy outcome of La Mettrie's and Rousseau's versions. The narrator-hero makes love to a young woman in the apartment in which he is billeted, while her parents are asleep in the next room. She comes to him in her nightdress, tiptoeing through the parents' room, and is ice cold when she reaches his bed. His standard erotic task is to revive her, but that is no simple matter. In a sense, this woman does not need reviving because she is already burning underneath: "Elle me produisait l'effet d'un épais et dur couvercle de marbre qui brûlait, chauffé par en dessous . . ." [She felt to me just like a thick, hard lid of marble that was burning hot underneath].[43] She must be made of some diabolical alliance of substances, and no diagnosis is even attempted. Whatever the mysterious cause, it is beyond the power of this would-be Pygmalion, for the young woman simply cannot be revived. There is no triumph of fire, even at the ostensible high point of passion: "Je croyais qu'il arriverait un moment où le marbre se fendrait enfin sous la chaleur brûlante, mais le marbre ne perdit jamais sa rigide densité" [I thought that there would soon come a time when the marble cracked with the burning heat, but the marble never lost its rigid density] (47). She remains both a statue and a riddle, a "sphinx" (47). Worse still, as a macabre confirmation of this material resistance to the classical role, she finally dies of cold, frozen stiff in his bed "dans son épouvantable rigidité" [in her dreadful rigidity] (51). The horror of this story is that she should be, so exactly and so definitively, an anti-Galatea. "Le Rideau cramoisi" is erotic and anti-erotic at the same time, finding some pleasure in the horror, and drawing from the now untellable Pygmalion story its darkest necrophiliac possibilities.

When the Galatea myth is invested by psychology, the notion of feminine resistance becomes richer and more ambiguous. As long as the communication of desire and pleasure was represented as an essentially physical process, in the action of *faire circuler*, resistance could be understood quite straightforwardly. $V = iR$, physics tells us: when the resistance (R) is greater, for a given voltage (V) the current (i) that flows is proportionately less. Slowness of response is a material quality, characteristic of such substances as marble, and metaphorically transferable to beautiful objects that may stand or lie about, waiting to be slowly brought to life. But what if there were a psychology and perhaps even a half-conscious politics, of marble? What if women, instead of being born marble, were perversely choosing to be marble-like? What if any slowness, any reluctance, any frigidity were to be read as the work of a certain desire? These are questions that fin-de-siècle fiction begins to entertain, and out of which it begins to make narrative. We have already seen, for example, that *Méphistophela* shows a young woman freezing

up—rather than just being naturally frigid—as a desperate refusal of violation. Other novels of the time, such as *Le Vice
suprême* (1884), tell variations on this story: the woman becomes
thoroughly resistant to men after having fallen victim to their
clumsiness or brutality.[44] This hardly constitutes a feminist
theme in any modern sense, not least because it still positions
the male as the initiator of female sexual life, but it does open
up narrative possibilities that were left out of La Mettrie's euphoric story. Instead of women who are asleep or half-dead at
the outset, it shows women being petrified by sexual trauma.
Andrea Dworkin's honoring of the so-called frigid women of history and literature sees them as having chosen the last form of
defense against male aggression.[45] Yet Dworkin is characteristically unable to observe, given her general condemnation of
pornography, that erotic narratives of the late nineteenth century, at least in France, come to make grudging admission, not
just of certain women's victimhood, but of a feminine power to
resist the transformation habitually enacted in the old Pygmalion story. Galatea's coldness, at the end of the nineteenth
century, tends to become an equivocal sign; it can mark not just
a pathology of circulation, but grim determination—and indeed
something that a nascent psychoanalytical discourse might
begin to think of as pathological willfulness.

Even to speak of the motive for resisting is to bring into play
some rather new assumptions. When Richardson's Pamela and
Clarissa were fighting to keep their virtue intact, it was a
matter for them of being heroically resourceful in repelling each
new attack. The question of psychological motivation hardly
arose, so powerfully self-evident were the requirements of
virtue. When Sade's Julie (*Les Cent Vingt Journées de Sodome*
[1785]) and Léonore (*Aline et Valcour* [1788]) were surrounded
by every kind of menace, they needed all their boldness and duplicity just to stay alive, so that ethical and psychological questions were lost in the preoccupation with survival. When
Choiseul-Meuse's Julie (*Julie, ou j'ai sauvé ma rose* [1807]) de-
vised her erotic tactics, developing an art of erotic dalliance de-
signed to preserve the center by giving up the periphery, she was
doubtless seeking to avoid disgrace. But in none of these cases,
where the narration is provided by the woman character herself,
did the novelistic interest focus on motivation as such. It was
the tactics that mattered, for out of the tactics and their at least

partial success the stuff of intriguing delay was made. The fin de siècle, by contrast, produces a causal relationship between motive and action that tends to eliminate the space of tactical choice. Women resist in certain ways because they are compelled to do so. And it is precisely such narrative causality that lends itself to etiological accounts of frigidity.

In *Mademoiselle Giraud, ma femme*, for example, the reason for Paule's behavior has to be discovered in the course of the telling, and retrieved, as I pointed out earlier, on the far side of the narrator-husband's naïve judgments. Yet this can be done, and the proper diagnosis made, precisely because Paule's acts of resistance are compulsively recurrent. We are not privy, in this male-focused narrative, to any calculations she might make, but the point of fictional pathology is that we do not need to read Paule's words, or even her mind, because we can read her symptoms. Does she in fact "find" her form of resistance? Does she fall into it? Is she simply a victim of it? All of the above, no doubt, and all of them together in such a way that she is neither free nor totally irresponsible. She repels and defeats her husband in precisely the same manner, and at the same time, as she gives bodily expression to her lack of desire for him: simply by being utterly cold. After a brief period of successful defense during which she has used established novelistic tactics worthy of Richardson, including bolting her door, Paule finds herself surprised in the middle of the night by a husband determined to take her by force. Adrien has long since given up on La Mettrie's model of gradual awakening in favor of something more vigorous. But his precipitate action only serves to bring about one of those moments of erotic and anti-erotic truth so characteristic of fiction of this period. His desire for combat is denied the pleasure, and the communicative heat, of struggle: "J'étais préparé à tout, excepté au silence obstiné de ma femme, à son impassibilité glaciale. Je croyais rencontrer un adversaire qui allait se plaindre, m'insulter, combattre; j'étais prêt à la lutte et j'en serais sorti victorieux" [I was ready for anything, except for the obstinate silence and the icy impassiveness of my wife. I expected to encounter an adversary who would cry out, insult me, and fight back. I was ready for a struggle, and I would have emerged victorious].[46] Whereas the hearty pornography of an earlier time had found no difficulty in producing the easy circulation of heat and the quick triumph of copulatory violence, the only heroes who manage this in more distinguished novels late in the century are exceptions for their very brutality, such as Jean in *Méphistophela*. Rather than passing on his heat, Adrien experiences the exact thematic opposite: the enervating contagion of frigidity. Paule wins out, as it happens, by not struggling, by not even desiring to struggle. On another occasion when he attempts to embrace her, her reaction is described more fully:

> elle se montra, cette fois encore, ce qu'elle avait toujours été; sa taille se courba docilement, sa tête s'inclina sous la pression de ma main, sa bouche n'essaya pas de fuir la mienne; toute sa personne devint insensible, inanimée, inerte; elle se galvanisa pour ainsi dire. Au lieu d'une femme, j'avais encore, j'avais toujours un cadavre dans les bras.
>
> Alors toutes mes ardeurs s'éteignirent, et subitement glacé au contact de cette glace, je pris la fuite.

> [she proved on that occasion to be exactly as she always had. Her back curved in submission. Her head tilted in response to the pressure of my hand. Her whole body became insensitive, inanimate, inert. She was, so to speak, galvanized. Instead of a woman, I once again found, as ever, a corpse in my arms.
>
> All my ardor was then extinguished. Suddenly frozen by contact with this ice, I took flight.] (165)

In view of his desire to be Pygmalion, and his need for the awakening of her desire, the very fact that she holds the Galatea position too well, maintaining Galatea's initial temperature indefinitely, is quite disabling for him, and serves to ruin the standard narrative program.

The same thematic breakdown occurs, with an interesting variation, in Belot's *La Femme de glace* (1878). The novel presents a man between two women, his dark-haired Brazilian mistress, Esther, and his blonde fiancée, Henriette. Esther we know to be passionate, both by her actions and the easy evocation of racist stereotypes. Are we therefore to suppose, in the absence of an early narratorial indication, that Henriette, who was raised in the mountains, is to be Esther's antithesis, and thus the ice-woman of the novel's title? When Henri deserts Esther to marry Henriette for mundane reasons of financial interest, it might well be thought that he is embarking on a life of sexual dissatisfaction in the company of a passionless woman, forever to regret the woman of fire he left behind. But this is not how things develop. Henriette allows herself to be awakened to desire in the conventional manner, although very little narrative attention is devoted to her sexual development.[47] It seems for a time that the new couple will live happily, if boringly, ever after, but Esther disturbs this, saving the novel from tedium and verisimilitude by presenting herself, under an assumed name, as Henriette's live-in companion. She has not come, she says to a nonplussed Henri, in order to revive their old affair, but to make him suffer (185). Henri is circumspect, not to say suspicious, but cannot resist for long the temptation of her presence. One hot day, he espies Esther asleep in a hammock: "la toile blanche du hamac, en recouvrant ce beau corps, en dissimulant les vêtements, lui prêtait la blancheur du marbre, la nudité de la statue" [the white canvas of the hammock, as it covered that fine body and hid the clothes from view, gave her the whiteness of marble and the nudity of a statue] (196). Henri responds to this sight with all the unthinking enthusiasm of wild desire, but none of the erotic artistry standardly required by the Pygmalion-Galatea topos. He rushes toward Esther, and tries to clasp her in an embrace. The awkwardness and the undue haste are characteristic of a whole class of dubious fin-de-siècle "heroes." So too, the narration tells us, is Esther's reaction. Whether it is pathological or voluntary, her response constitutes a form of immediate resistance, worthy of description as a general phenomenon:

alors eut lieu un phénomène bizarre, souvent constaté même chez les femmes les plus expansives: soit que la surprise, la colère, l'indignation les paralysent tout à coup, soit qu'elles aient en elles une force de volonté capable de dominer la violence de leur tempérament, elles deviennent, parfois, à leur insu ou de leur plein gré, aussi froides, aussi glaciales que dans un autre moment elles auraient été passionnées.

[then there occurred a bizarre phenomenon, often observed in the most expansive women. Whether it is the case that surprise, anger, and indignation cause sudden paralysis, or whether they have an inner strength of will that enables them to overcome the violence of their temperament, they become, sometimes unthinkingly, sometimes deliberately, as utterly cold as they were once passionate.] (199–200)

Although this first reaction is so immediate as to be perhaps involuntary, frigidity soon becomes for Esther a conscious, if not a deliberate tactic, and a quite precise form of sexual revenge: "la vengeance d'Esther avait pris une nouvelle forme, des plus inattendues. En effet, il n'était jamais venu à l'esprit de Mlle Sandraz qu'elle pût être appelée à jouer les rôles de statue: elle se serait cru absolument inhabile à tenir cet emploi. . . . voilà que tout à coup elle se trouvait en état de résister à toutes les attaques, pourvue d'armes défensives qui la rendaient toute-puissante" [Esther's vengeance had taken on a new, quite unexpected form. It had never occurred to Mlle Sandraz that she might be called on to play statuesque roles: she would have thought of herself as quite unsuited for such work. But now she found herself able to resist every sort of attack, equipped with defensive weapons that made her all powerful" (202–3). The tactic is so successful precisely because it is not freely chosen: it is a compelling bodily expression of her (lack of) desire. On subsequent occasions, when approached by Henri, she maintains her "marmoreal impassiveness" (214). There is no quivering, not even a tinge of pink to her complexion: "aucune rougeur, aucun frisson de désir ne courait sur la peau" [no blush, no shiver of desire ran across her skin] (215). Even when he throws her onto a sofa, she merely topples over, "comme s'écroulerait une Vénus en marbre renversée de son piédestal" [as a marble Venus would fall if it were pushed off its pedestal] (215). She can be pushed around, but she cannot be mollified, and to such resistance Henri has no answer. While consumed by lust, and by the desire to "rendre la vie à cette statue" [bring this statue back to life] (241), he does not have the strength to be Pygmalion in contact with such a resolutely uncooperative (anti-)Galatea, because "cette froideur l'avait glacé lui-même" [this coldness made him go cold himself] (202).

It is noteworthy that the character who comes to be the ice-woman in Belot's novel is not ultimately defined as frigid by temperament or by race. She is in fact the more passionate of the two women by nature. *La Femme de glace* does not identify the temperamental categories "passionate" and "cold," as a classical physiology of humors might have done, but rather tends to demonstrate their psychosexual equivalence through narrative. The story of the blonde Henriette is far less interesting for the novel precisely because Henriette moves through a relatively narrow, undramatic range of emotions and desires. Esther, on the other hand, is fascinating for her drastic oscillation between extremes of fire and marble. Frigidity and nymphomania can be seen as roughly equivalent, and are made so in narrative psychology, so that the most seductively perverse women partake of both. It is not entirely clear whether the heroine of *Méphistophela* is wildly agitated or profoundly unmoved, and this very unclarity is a central mystery of the novel: "même dans l'extrême enragement des concupiscences, elle se contient, ou, véritablement calme, n'a pas besoin de se contenir, furieuse et froide comme la torsion d'une statue de marbre" [even in the extreme frenzy of concupiscence, she restrained herself, or, being genuinely calm, did not need to restrain herself, since she was both wild and cold, like the twisting of a marble statue].[48] Twisted marble is the most concrete mark of her perversion, for there is *furia* at the heart of her stillness. Diagnosis here takes the form of a rather lyrical paradox, but a feminine mystery is apprehended nonetheless, delimited and metaphorized through the coexistence, nay the fusion, of fire and marble. This is not the productive dynamic of earlier stories in the tradition of Rousseau and La Mettrie, so much as an ultimately static oscillation, a kind of agitated immobility.

L'Eternelle Poupée (1894), by Jules Bois, tells the story of movement from one feminine extreme to the other, and demonstrates the reversible polarity, just as *La Femme de glace* did, by enacting a drastic shift from one to the other. In this case, however, the direction of change is the opposite. The heroine, Reine, is defined by the title as both a plaything for men and someone essentially unchanging. She is already a mature woman when she becomes the lover of the hero, Marcel, but her sexual "lethargy" appears to be such that he may never be able to arouse her: "Il se courbe, trompeur et caressant, sur les genoux raidis de Reine et sa bouche travaille les lèvres éteintes et ses mains défont la robe, énervées sur la batiste que soulèvent les frigides seins" [he leaned deceptively and caressingly over Reine's stiff knees, as his mouth worked on the lifeless lips and his hands undid the dress, impatiently pulling at the lace that covered her frigid breasts].[49] It is no use, she says in effect as he labors away. With her husband, as with other lovers, she has never been "happy" (81), never known climactic pleasure. But Marcel is not like other lovers, and not like most male characters in fin-de-siècle fiction. He has a quality that nearly all heroes of erotic literature seemed to have in the early part of the century, but that most have now lost, the ability to spark pleasure. In Marcel's case, it is preserved in a peculiarly naturalist form, as a hereditary "afflux de sève" [rising of sap] that actually compels "la contagion sensuelle, qu'il communique aux femmes" [sensual contagion, which he passes on to women] (86). His juice works on Reine—all too well, in fact, as it is somehow bound to do with women of her psychological bent. She crosses over into a "deplorable neurosis" (85) more drastic in its consequences than her earlier unhappy condition: "Une flamme dévorait ce corps à peine formé, l'espoir de connaître une volupté insaisissable. . . . Mais ce ferment d'une jeune passion corrompait son âme, travaillait sourdement ses sens incomplets" [This barely mature body was now consumed by fire, by the hope of knowing an elusive voluptuousness. A newborn ferment of passion was corrupting her soul and working away silently on her incomplete senses] (84). Narrative capital, as we see, can be made out of radical change, just as it was made out of near-total blockage in *Mademoiselle Giraud, ma femme*. These are all narrative pathologies, in both senses of the expression: disturbances of narrative that do not allow the "natural" story to take its course, and constructions of sexual pathology that represent "deviance" or "perversion" in narrative terms.

The twin themes of frigidity and nymphomania are gathered together, with appropriate doses of prurience and scientistic pomp, in a novel by Jean-Claude Dubut de Laforest entitled *Mademoiselle Tantale* (1886), to be found in a multigeneric collection of fictional and erudite works bearing the title *Pathologie sociale*.[50] It may seem surprising that the one whose misfortune it is to be named after a legendary hero of suffering should be a quiet young Englishwoman called Mary Folkestone. But this, we will find, is a way of producing the increasingly familiar paradox about feminine desire and frigidity, for it brings together the myth of Tantalus, as a figure of unquenchable desire, and that of an enduringly resistant Galatea. Tantalus is himself an old favorite of erotic description, being often pressed into service to signify, hyperbolically, the "suffering" of desire. In *Un Eté à la campagne* (1867), his name is used quite routinely in order to signify the frustration, and the excitement, of having an extremely attractive but virtuous young woman sleeping in the next room.[51] In *Lesbia, maîtresse d'école* (1890), the Tantalus reference evokes the mistress's unsatisfied desire for one of her pupils, but this mundane agony is something to which she intends to put an end.[52] In *Mademoiselle Giraud, ma femme*, the erotic suffering is said to be more acute, and more lastingly painful, because it refers to the husband's experience of unrequited desire: "pour vous avoir aimée au point d'être sourd à tous les avertissements, me voici condamné à perpétuité au plus affreux des supplices: celui de Tantale" [loving you to the point of being deaf to all warnings has meant that I am condemned in perpetuity to the most frightful suffering: that of Tantalus].[53] The classical legend of Tantalus, by contrast with that of Galatea, is a non-story in the strict narratological sense. It serves eminently well to mark the blockage of narrative, and the impossibility of change. That is the titular threat hanging over Mary Folkestone from the outset. According to this dire mythical prediction, she is to be forever consumed by unsatisfied desire.

Yet at the same time—this is the paradox that is becoming standard—Mary appears to be the opposite. She is in fact an accomplished sculptor, and we know that sculpture deserves to be regarded, ever since Rousseau, as a demanding and potentially inhuman profession. Other stories of the late nineteenth century show those involved with sculpture to be threatened by the dichotomy between marble and flesh, as they struggle to overcome the distance between the two. They must struggle not just to preserve the space of their art, but to save their own material humanity in the midst of it. *Demi-volupté* (1900) has a hero who cannot bear just to see his lover as a statue, standing naked before him: "Il lui fallait la statue entière, pensante, vibrante, nimbée de ciel, la vie en son essence et en mieux" [He required the whole statue, thinking and living, with a glowing halo, life in its essence, life improved upon].[54] In *Le Vice errant* (1902), it is quite the opposite, and therefore the same thematic. Comte Sternoskof cannot abide the fleshly presence of women, and even has other representations of them destroyed as well. Only statues find favor in his eyes, precisely because of their frigidity: "le froid et la pâleur du marbre rassurent sa défiance, la blanche immobilité des Lédas et des Dianes le satisfait à la manière d'un châtiment; dans les déesses il veut voir des mortes. C'est l'ennemie pétrifiée, raidie et désarmée que ses yeux y veulent voir.

Morte la Bête, *morta la bestia*" [the cold pallor of marble calmed his distrust. The white stillness of the Ledas and Dianas gave him satisfaction because it seemed like a kind of punishment. In these goddesses, he was determined to see only dead women. To his eyes, they showed the enemy petrified, stiffened and disarmed. The beast was dead, *morta la bestia*].[55] All this tends to make of sculpture, from the viewpoint of sexual pathology, something like a professional "neurosis," a stylized practice of resistance to desire. For Mary Folkestone, a young woman, we are certainly meant to regard it as an ominous choice indeed.

As an accomplished practitioner of her art, Mary Folkestone has a fully developed anatomical knowledge of the human body—"l'artiste . . . connaissait les secrets de l'anatomie humaine" [the artist in her knew the secrets of human anatomy] (24)—without yet having experienced erotic contact with a man. When she meets a potential lover, she experiences a painful disjunction between the academic precision of this knowledge, on the one hand, and her virginal intimations of love on the other: the "femme pudique" [modest woman] is "révoltée contre l'artiste" [repelled by the artist] (24). This very discrepancy might have seemed, in some other thematic context, to hold the promise of future reconciliation, but there is no suggestion here that the two poles of Mary's existence can ever be brought together in a narrative of healing or maturation. Their approximate symmetry and their rough equivalence define the space of her oscillation, and of her suffering. This woman's tragedy turns in fact on the ultimate impossibility of reconciling the sculptural and the passionately intimate.

Mary Folkestone is able to see alternately with the look of an "artist" and with that of a "woman," yet there is no fusion of the two. As she contemplates her lover Hector, who has not only a classical name but classically sculptured beauty, she is also responding with unreconciled contradiction to the odor of his flesh: "Mary analysait les beautés de l'académie vivante avec le double regard de la femme et de l'artiste; elle s'enivrait de cette odeur de chair, et admirait les lignes d'harmonie de cette poitrine marmoréenne" [Mary analyzed the beautiful sights of the living academy with the double gaze of a woman and an artist. She was dizzied by the smell of flesh, and admired the harmonious lines of this breast of marble] (25). This is very much the dilemma that confronted Rousseau's Pygmalion, although

Mary's experience of it is unremittingly blocked. No matter how beautiful, or even how *vivante* marmoreal beauty may be to contemplative eyes, it is always fundamentally other than the truly erotic: the sculptor's love of marble can only lead her away from the substantive authenticity of flesh.

It may seem at rare moments in *Mademoiselle Tantale* that the miraculous transformation brought about by Pygmalion is half-realized in Mary's mind: "Elle restait des heures entières devant une reproduction de l'Hercule Farnèse et, peu à peu, il se fit que le marbre vécut pour elle, en chair et en os, dans la prodigieuse puissance de sa musculature" [She stood for hours looking at a reproduction of the Farnese Hercules and gradually the marble came alive for her, in flesh and blood, with all the prodigious strength of its musculature] (50). Yet such euphoric reverie shows itself as fantasy in the face of a cruelly recurring truth: the sculptor's art, so prominent in the classical boudoir, has no place in the late nineteenth-century bedroom inhabited by Mary Folkestone. To put it more stringently still, the pathological failure of Mary's and Hector's sexual relationship is diagnosed as a consequence of the fact that sculpture continues to be present in the space of their intimacy. On one occasion, soon after the two have made love, Mary finds herself with the leisure to draw Hector as he lies sleeping. The ostensible high point of their sexual encounter has had little impact on her, and she is left free to "capture" her lover's pose, in postcoital impotence, when the life has been drained from his body and he has been reduced to stillness: "Ce sourire, qui éclaira ses lèvres, Mary l'avait modelé d'une manière si vivante, l'homme semblait si profondément vaincu, si incapable de batailler encore" [The smile that lit his lips had been modeled by Mary in such a lifelike way. The man seemed so completely submissive, so thoroughly unable to continue the struggle] (37). No matter how "alive" her art might make this smile and this human weakness seem, art in the bedroom does not coincide with the true life of pleasure, dwelling as it does on the aftermath of *la petite mort*. In representing the attitude as such, the artist holds back, or fails to perceive, the flow of life. Worst of all perhaps, Mary finds herself adopting the poses of pleasure without being compelled from within by the substance of desire. Her lover is sadly deceived by this imitative skill, which presumably owes something to her academic knowledge: "Il ne savait pas, lui; il ne pouvait savoir! Elle mentait si bien; elle prenait si bien les attitudes de la femme défaillante, qu'il souriait dans l'accalmie réparatrice des sens" [He did not know. He could not know! She was so good at lying and at striking the poses of the woman fainting away that he smiled during the quiet time of sensual recovery] (28). For a classical *ars erotica*, such positioning of the body would have been itself a technique of pleasure: here, it aggravates the problem by masking it. There is no room for erotic artistry in the world of *Mademoiselle Tantale*: one is either authentically passionate or a sorry poseur.

When appearance is thus habitually disjunct from the inner life of the body, we can expect some uncertainty in the description of physiological processes going on inside the heroine. In fact, the narration indulges in a series of pseudo-analytical metaphors, equivocating about Mary Folkestone's interiority, and doing so in a way that a circulatory thematics might have led us to expect. Mary fails to achieve the inner fullness of desire, we are told, because she is an artist, an academic, and a classicist. She also fails because her lover lacks the necessary qualities to stimulate desire within her: "Joli garçon, Hector, mais trop faible, trop peu terrible; il avait trop de sentimentalité de cœur; il ne vivait pas assez pour le charnel plaisir: ses yeux n'avaient pas ces lueurs fauves et son corps n'avait pas ces soulèvements formidables qui la réveilleraient enfin de sa léthargie!" [Hector was good looking, but too weak, and failed to inspire fear. He was too given to sentimentality, and did not care enough for carnal pleasure. His eyes did not glow with animal passion, and his body did not have the massive surges of power needed to awaken her from lethargy] (51). Hector, it seems, unlike Gautier's Romuald or *L'Eternelle Poupée*'s Marcel, does not have enough erotic fire for the two of them, and Mary can blame him at times for not having the strength to trigger the circulation of desire in her—"la force de faire jaillir en elle l'étincelle de la vie" [the strength to strike in her the spark of life] (52). Yet it is not just a matter of Mary's being an unfulfilled vessel, a feminine space of empty potential, needing desire to be communicated to her. Progressively, she does come to be aware of a problematic presence-and-absence of desire within.

Mary's drama is not, then, a simple lack of desire, for there is a sense in which that would be no drama at all. There would be no pathology, no narrative, and no eroticism. Rather, the desire that exists within her fails to be embodied in substantive form, and therefore fails to circulate as it should. Even as she abstractly imitates the attitudes of pleasure, some more or less concrete desire can be heard within: "ses désirs à elle craquaient au vent de la tempête, comme des arbres morts" [her own desires creaked in the stormy wind like dead trees] (28). The problem is evident in the fact that her experience is not evoked in the standard metaphors of blood and fire. She feels "le souffle d'une brise malsaine" [the breath of an unhealthy breeze] (29) or the weight of a "froid brouillard" [cold fog] (37). She hears the sound of "les effluves terribles qui grondaient dans sa chair" [the dreadful emanations that rumbled within her flesh] (29). Within and without, there is only the raging of a cold wind, and the creaking of dead trees. Instead of being filled with vital substances, she is invaded, pervaded, or simply haunted by a nameless entity that appears to enter her body without properly taking hold:

Mary s'affaissait sur un fauteuil, désespérée, sentant vaguement flotter autour d'elle quelque chose d'incompréhensible et de fatal qu'elle voulait saisir; quelque chose d'impalpable, d'invisible qui papillonnait sur ses yeux, sur sa bouche, qui entrait comme un fluide dans son corps, se promenait sur ses muscles, se mêlait à son sang et s'en allait ensuite, sans jamais se fixer en elle.

[Mary slumped in desperation onto a chair, aware of something vaguely floating around her, something incomprehensible and drastic that she wanted to hold in her grasp. It was something impalpable and invisible that fluttered before her eyes and on her lips, that entered her body like a fluid, moved through her muscles, mingled with her blood, and then left her without ever taking up residence.] (29)

This is what Mary Folkestone, near the moment of her death, describes pathetically to Hector as "mon immatériel amour pour toi" [my immaterial love for you] (102).

The imagery of wind and fog may seem dissonant with that of mineral beauty, but the two sets of metaphors are narratively compatible. Both are distinctively anti-erotic here because they are opposed to the vital substances of true eroticism. So it is that Mary Folkestone's frigidity is also a kind of vaporousness, consisting as it does in being empty of true desire, as well as being inwardly befogged by clouds of torment. The paradox—in keeping with the nondialectical cohabitation of fire and marble—is that she should be coldly "impotent" while revealing in extremis symptoms of "the most fearful nymphomania" (105). When she dies at the end of the story, of an aphrodisiac overdose taken in desperation, there is time for one last (and first) passionate kiss with the lover who has hastened to her side: "la femme baisa la bouche de l'homme; elle la baisa, et avec une rage si violente que leurs lèvres à tous les deux furent meurtries et ensanglantées" [the woman kissed the man's mouth. She kissed him with such violent rage that their lips were bruised and bleeding] (106). At last, blood flows between them, and the spark of passion passes from one to the other. But it is all too late: the physiological symptoms of Mary's passion are also those of her death agony, and her fire turns quickly to its opposite: "Ce baiser si brûlant, devint froid, glacé. . . . Le corps de la victime se raidit. . . . Mary Folkestone était morte" [The kiss that had been so burning hot became ice cold. The victim's body went stiff. Mary Folkestone was dead] (106). Her cruel fate, the exact opposite of Galatea's joyous one, is to experience an icy death, as the ultimate failure to have and to hold the substance of passion.

In following the double thematic that has guided this chapter, I have found myself drifting toward the periphery of "erotic literature," but that in itself reflects a historical movement in the discourse of sexuality. The theme of fiery circulation, as we found it in the texts of the Revolutionary period, helps to define, indeed to constitute, mainstream pornography as uncomplicated narrative. In that context, any resistance to passion is considered only so long as to eroticize the rapid process whereby it melts away. But the full development of a thematics of marble, as in La Morte amoureuse and many later texts, allows erotic literature to include its ostensible opposite. Frigidity, despite Sheila Jeffreys's claim to the contrary, did not need to be invented by 1950s sexologists. It had been present for over a century in literature as a fascinating quality attended by a cluster of metaphors, and occupying a characteristic place in narrative. In the course of a long and unsteady evolution, the woman-object had gone from apparent coolness already inhabited by secret warmth (La Mettrie) to enchanted coldness (Gautier) to a kind of stilted hollowness in which the dialectic of marble and fire was rendered pathetically impossible (Mademoiselle Tantale). This slow reification of frigidity corresponds to an increasingly complex definition of feminine coldness, and to the emergence of pathological representations adjacent to a literature of pleasure. Out of a metaphorical dynamic inherited from Rousseau and others, the nineteenth century eventually produced the rigidity of a sometimes frightening syndrome.

Yet "incurable" frigidity is only the extreme point of the thematic range, for the resilient myth of Pygmalion represents the hope that sleep, stone, even death itself may be "cured" by the passionate agency of fire. The great narrative fancy of so much male-focused erotic literature is that the frigid body can be metamorphosed—and indeed somehow already desires to be—by a generous infusion of heat, blood, and sperm. And even where resistance is said to be pathologically insurmountable, there is no doubt pleasure to be had in the very interrogation of this condition, in the testing of its bodily and psychological quality. "Are you warm, are you real, Mona Lisa?" asks the popular song, contemplating only the drastic alternative, "Or just a cold and lonely, lovely work of art?" We must understand that the answer to this question, if one can ever be given, matters far less than the wishfully seductive asking of it. Rousseau's Pygmalion asked just that question of Galatea, with such passion that the asking produced its own happy outcome. The fin de siècle was far less sure of the outcome, but was accordingly able to dwell longer on the question, adding a full psychological dimension to the material enigma. The asking of this question in our own century continues to rely, for its force, on this long thematic history. The interrogation of frigidity has thus become both an erotic pastime and a pseudo-medical practice.

3

Cantharides

In this chapter, I shall focus on aphrodisiacs and their changing role in what we now call erotic literature. The point will not be just to show that the nineteenth century went beyond the eighteenth in its interest in, and desire for, aphrodisiacs—although it certainly did that—but to suggest that aphrodisiacs came to serve, by the end of the nineteenth century, as the representation par excellence of "desire": desire as a fluid substance circulating within and between bodies. There is a story about aphrodisiacs that was told often in the nineteenth century, at least in broad outline, and continues to be told in the twentieth. I tell it here for the sake of memory. In June 1772, four prostitutes in Marseilles brought what amounted to an official complaint against a young aristocrat from their region.[1] They claimed that he had poisoned them by giving them some *pastilles* before having sex with them. The aristocrat in question was readily identified by the authorities as Donatien-Alphonse-François de Sade, who used the title of Marquis. The "poison" he had administered, on the other hand, could not be identified by the forensic apothecaries. They carefully examined some unused pastilles, and some of the black substance vomited up by one victim, but were able to declare only that it was not arsenic.[2] It is noteworthy that biographers and other commentators on these events, all no doubt familiar with the open secrets of a tradition of eroticism, have had no difficulty whatsoever in identifying the black substance in question. "How could the apothecaries have been so egregiously incompetent?" muses the historian Maurice Lever.[3] Everyone knows that it was cantharides.

Can it be that what is now so familiar was then so utterly arcane? There is no reason to believe that cantharides was un-

96

commonly resistant to chemical analysis. Alice Laborde claims that it had a regular place in eighteenth-century pharmacies and was not considered poisonous,[4] although that seems too broad a generalization. Maurice Lever's quotation of the relevant article from the great *Encyclopédie* (1751) shows that it was the object of great medical suspicion:

> Les cantharides en poudre, appliquées sur l'épiderme, y causent des ulcérations, excitent même des ardeurs d'urine, la strangurie, la soif, la fièvre, le pissement de sang, etc., et rendent l'odeur puante et cadavareuse. Elles causent les mêmes symptômes prises intérieurement. On a observé qu'elles nuisent beaucoup à la vessie.

> [Powdered cantharides applied to the epidermis cause ulceration, and even give rise to urinary burning, strangury, thirst, fever, the passing of blood, etc. They introduce a rotten, cadaverous odor. Taken internally, they produce the same symptoms. It has been observed that they do great harm to the bladder.]

There follows a list of prescribed remedies "against this poison."[5] Modern encyclopedias confirm this, describing cantharides as dried and powdered "Spanish flies"—in fact, beetles of the species *Cantharis vesicatoria*,[6] sometimes given to animals in order to facilitate breeding.[7] Taken internally, "it acts as a powerful irritant on the genito-urinary tract, causing difficulties in urinating, excruciating pain, and bloody urine. As little as 1.5 grams have proved fatal."[8]

My primary interest here is not in the forensic examination as such, but in the talk that surrounds it and finally makes empirical enquiry almost redundant.[9] How does everyone now know that it was cantharides, and how did historians come to be so sure of it in the telling? What kind of recurrent knowledge is shared in the recounting of Sade's life, and of a historical moment? When the young marquis handed out cantharides, as we suppose he did, he must have been intending to use it as an aphrodisiac. By irritating other people's genito-urinary tracts, he sought, no doubt, to introduce his influence into the space of their bodies, to tickle, disturb, and perhaps ignite them from within. *Irriter*, *agacer*, and *piquer*, verbs of teasing and irritation, are in fact some of the words he might have used to describe it, in keeping with the late eighteenth century's standard ways of referring to erotic stimulation. Presumably, cantharides allowed the irritation of outside surfaces, given primacy in the *Encyclopédie* entry, to be carried inside the body as a kind of internal prickly heat. This must have been the imaginative and material dimension of its widely recognized "aphrodisiacal powers."[10] Somewhat like that alchemical substance evoked by Gaston Bachelard as dwelling warmly in the heart of matter,[11] cantharides tablets could function for the imagination as encapsulated erotic fire. Giving them to prostitutes was doubtless meant to serve as a pharmaceutical conferral of desire.

Note that I tell this story, and will continue to refer to it, without questioning its empirical basis or even its thematic coherence. In so doing, I am recounting and further propagating Sade's mythical biography. My focus here is not Sade's life as it really was—whatever that might mean, and however it might be known—nor even the movement whereby the (supposed) reality of a life yields to fantasy, but the construction of Sade's biography as a key, heroic element in standard nineteenth-century histories of sexuality. Michel Delon, in his introduction to the Pléiade edition of works by Sade, offers a careful analysis of what he calls "mythical drift" in contemporary accounts of the Marseilles incident: "Alors que Sade n'est encore que l'acteur d'un fait divers, son histoire est déjà littéraire. Les fantasmes collectifs investissent son nom, gonflent les anecdotes, leur donnent la dimension du mythe. . . . La dérive mythique prend appui sur les pastilles à la cantharide proposées par le marquis à ses partenaires sexuels" [While Sade is as yet only a character in a news item, his story is already literary. Collective phantasms surround his name, inflate the anecdotes, and give them the dimension of myth. Mythical drift is supported by the cantharides pastilles offered by the Marquis to his sexual partners].[12] Just where this drift might finally lead is beyond the scope of Delon's introduction, and doubtless beyond the scope of author studies in general, but my contention is that the cantharides theme comes to take on emblematic significance. So timely is it, indeed, that the mythical story is able to go on "drifting" throughout the nineteenth century, moving as though with a purpose, borne by the most fluent of discursive currents.

It must be said that the flow is not without eddies, but these are the marks of its depth and power. The story of Sade's actions in Marseilles can in fact be told in two quite different ways, according to the teller's purpose. The first variation is, one might say, a story about confectionery: it is self-consciously rational and urbanely apologetic. The second is about poison, and is filled with morbid fascination. The richness of the cantharides theme lies in this very ambivalence, in the fact that the black aphrodisiac gives rise to both kinds of story, ultimately holding them together as parts of a broader discursive economy. Cantharides, we must somehow understand, is both harmless and fatal.

For Sadian apologists, the Marseilles incident provides an exemplum of the great discrepancy between Donatien's real-life peccadillos, and the horrors that were recounted about or projected onto the Marquis de Sade. The court of Aix-en-Provence, we are told, demonstrated its militant bourgeois seriousness in charging Sade with *empoisonnement* and sodomy. It condemned him to decapitation for the first, and burning for the second. All that for a few little bonbons used to spice up a young man's licentious weekend! Madame de Sade herself, says Lever, must have been struck by the lack of proportion between the crime—a banal libertine episode—and the punishment.[13] Raymond Jean suggests that the *affaire* was blown out of all proportion; decapitation was a rather high price to pay for "une histoire de bonbons à la cantharide" [an event involving cantharides candy].[14] How fearful and narrow was the official defense of the body against the supposed poison of outside influences! Such pompousness deserves to be met by libertine banter and circumvented by ingenuity. Once this view is taken, the young marquis' confectionery can then be recognized as one of those quite technical pieces of erotic gimmickry that go to make up the joyful *savoir faire* of classical *voluptueux*. Elsewhere, it might have been a mechanical sofa, or a new ointment to be rubbed on the genitals at times of fatigue, or a new way of joining four people together so that no external organ was protruding and no orifice unoccupied. Alongside these, the standard fare of libertine inventiveness, cantharides can be allowed to take its modest place in a well-organized paradigm, established before Sade's time. In La Morlière's *Angola*, the hero sets out for a foreign land to recapture the woman he loves, armed with a supply of bonbons given to him by a fairy queen, and succeeds in diverting some monsters by offering them "amber pastilles."[15] The point of this joke is a kind of anti-exoticism: the fashion had even spread as far as these people, muses the narrator. Cantharides was never more thoroughly tamed, in fact, than when paired for the purpose of intrigue with its "opposite," opium, as in the erotic play of Grandval *fils*, "Les Deux Biscuits" (1759):

> Par vos ordres, j'avais employé tout mon art
> A faire deux biscuits de trois sols moins un liard.
> L'un était composé de mouches cantharides
> Qui donnent la force aux amants invalides;
> Dans l'autre dominait l'opium et le pavot
> Qui font, par leurs vertus, dormir comme un sabot.

> [By your order, I had employed all my art
> To make two biscuits for two pennies less a farthing.
> One was composed of cantharides flies
> Which give strength to ailing lovers;
> The other was mainly opium and poppy
> Whose property is to make one sleep like a log.][16]

Just like the two sides of a mushroom whose alternate consumption causes Lewis Carroll's Alice to grow or shrink, this pair of substances is here made neatly, quaintly symmetrical.

By contrast, the second version of the Marseilles story, told most often in the nineteenth century, can be called a heroic one, if one allows that Romantic heroes may be both energetic and sinister. According to this account, the handing out of cantharides was a decisive moment in the history of erotic expression. Through the action of Sade, a thrilling, perhaps deadly, power was introduced into the bodies of some prostitutes, into literature, and into the world. Whether Sade's fiction was read in detail by those who made of him such a (monstrous) hero is doubtful, and whether they knew the details of his life is even more so. What is certain is that many knew him as the "author" of cantharides. Jean-Pierre Jacques, in a history of sapphism, is moved to observe: "Au XIXe siècle, l'air bourgeois se surpeuple ainsi d'une nuée de mouches aphrodisiaques venues tout droit de la demeure du 'Vieux'. On est obsédé par les cantharides. On en met partout" [In the nineteenth century, the bourgeois atmosphere is filled with a swarm of aphrodisiacal flies that come directly from the dwelling of the "Old Man" [Flaubert's word for Sade]. People are obsessed with cantharides. They spread it everywhere].[17] The nineteenth century, it has often been remarked, understood history most readily by identifying and glorifying moments of origin. Its recurring temptation, in this instance, was to make of Sade the origin of the most powerful aphrodisiac, seeing him as the one who, in France's plague city, triggered the most seductive of plagues, releasing unprecedented quantities of black desire into the world.[18]

These two versions of the story, the apologetic and the heroic/demonic, cannot coexist without a degree of mutual interference. Certainly, it is possible, according to Foucault's line of argument in *La Volonté de savoir*,[19] to hold the two together in a counterpoint of repression and liberation: Sade's every action, no matter how trivial, becomes heroic by virtue of the extraordinary repression that surrounds him. "Les mystérieuses pastilles . . . par une allitération bien compréhensible le mènent à la Bastille" [The mysterious pastilles, by a fully understandable piece of alliteration, lead him to the Bastille], says André Pieyre de Mandiargues.[20] What Mandiargues understands so readily is that desire leads to prison and vice versa. Something vigorously repressed is thereby highlighted, and Sade comes to stand, by his resistant victimhood, as an incitement to pleasure. Even as he is imprisoned, his revolutionary power is disseminated into the world around him like a volatile black powder. Nonetheless, the *défense* of Sade sits uncomfortably here with the *illustration*, as apologetic trivialization tends to pull apart from Romantic glorification. Sade, we continue to be told in essays and biographies, was a harmless enough man who wrote (relatively) harmless stories about fictional characters doing (sometimes admittedly) harmful, but imaginary things.[21] Yet when cast as hero of the great historical narrative of progressive sexual liberation, he is seen as introducing new themes into a collective erotic imagination. The least that can be said in this case is that causality appears to have been manufactured out of coincidence. Whatever Sade's claims as an innovator in certain areas of erotic endeavor, neither the Marseilles incident nor his literary work in general warrant any account of Sade as a heroic pioneer in the use of aphrodisiacs. There was indeed a change about this time—doubtless more a drift than a revolution—but Sade, although his work played a role, was not in any particular sense the author of the change. Rather, the constitution of his heroic biography by the nineteenth century is both a symptom and a sign: it is one of the ways in which a broader transformation was measured and affirmed. Sade's mythical biography is, in that respect, an example of nineteenth-century historiography, and of nineteenth-century erotic fiction.

If we absolutely must have a pioneer, we can find one elsewhere. More frequently than Sade, Andréa de Nerciat represents in his novels the use of aphrodisiacs, and begins to develop the characteristic ambivalence of the nineteenth-century thematic. In *Mon Noviciat* (1792), an elderly husband is provided with a potion to help him through his wedding night, as he takes the young Lolotte to wife. This is an expedient, used for the purpose of libertine intrigue: it happens that Lolotte is pregnant, and the husband must be persuaded that he is the father of her child.[22] In *Les Aphrodites* (1793), the pièce de résistance of the narrative is a theatrical orgy in which the men are called upon to perform great feats of endurance. As part of their preparation, they take in "des tasses d'un bouillon confortatif" [cups of refreshing broth], as well as "des pâtes et confitures, des fruits échauffants, des diabolini, des bonbons et pastilles à l'ambre" [sweetmeats and jams, spicy fruits, diabolini, and amber sweets and pastilles].[23] The objects they consume are small and apparently trivial, sometimes named with diminutive suffixes (*-ini, -illes*), but consumption of them is narrowly purposeful. Aphrodisiacs are thus integrated, as with carbohydrate loading for modern endurance athletes, into the libertine sporting program. On less ceremonious occasions in Nerciat's novels, the jar of sweets is ready to hand, playing an occasional role—in the sense of occasional furniture—and acting as a means of getting the physiological job done. Such pharmaceutical devices are, however, a resource of limited value, not to be used too often in a given situation. It is, after all, a requirement of taste or tact that no one device be unduly exploited by narrative. The maid in *Les Aphrodites* is mindful of the difficulty: "Célestine, sur les genoux de Sa Grandeur, s'occupe sur le champ de faire redevenir digne du même titre un engin qui a considérablement perdu de sa contenance, quoique déjà deux fois une bonbonnière, dûment fournie de diabolini, ait été appelée à son secours" [Célestine, seated on his Highness's lap, immediately set about doing what she could to make his tool worthy of his title once again, for it had rather lost its proud bearing, even though a candy jar, duly filled with diabolini, had been called on twice already for help] (2:84).

Diabolini, in their diminutive plurality, are said to come from Naples rather than Spain, and it is not clear whether their essential ingredient is cantharides or some other hot Mediterranean substance, but the mode of their consumption and the mode of their availability are clearly recognizable here. Aphrodisiacs are a kind of temporary prosthesis, their effects limited in time by eventual human (male) weakness: they belong within the colorful paradigm of libertine artifices, which is itself like an assortment of sweets in a *bonbonnière*. Here we find described a joyous array of such items, on hand for an orgy in *Le Diable au corps* (1803): "avec la même profusion, les restaurants, les stimulants, comme les pastilles d'ambre, les diabolini de Naples, et autres *boute-feux* de la fabrique de Paphos" [in the same profusion, restoratives and stimulants like amber pastilles, diabolini from Naples, and other igniters manufactured in Paphos].[24] Paphos, the domain of love, contains not just model positions, not just figures of Venus and furniture to accommodate them, but a veritable production line turning out encapsulated fire. Yet by the same token, the very range of products, and the delight in "profusion" itself, suppose that there is no single technique, no singular demonic substance that can stand definitively as the essence of desire and pleasure. Indeed, as if to make fun of such a notion, Nerciat refers teasingly, in *Le Diable au corps*, to an aphrodisiac, aptly named "l'immortalità del cazzo" [immortality of the prick], that is supposed to produce the most powerful and durable of erections (2:54–55). There is ultimately nothing mysterious, indeed nothing of any substance at all, about this wonder drug. The Marquise responds initially by eagerly writing down the name, but later wipes it off when she realises that she has been deceived in the telling (2:57). Such gentle banter, during the next century, would seldom, if ever, attend the magic name of cantharides.

All this belongs well enough to the benign side of our thematic, but the other, malign side can also be glimpsed in Nerciat's fiction from time to time. His systematic preference for euphemism and happy outcomes ensures of itself that any references to danger are only fleeting,[25] but their very presence in a festive libertine context is itself noteworthy. It happens, then, in *Les Aphrodites*, that a man who faces a demanding ordeal prepares himself rather too well: "On lui avait fait manger l'enfer . . . il a sué l'ambre pendant trois jours, et puis ne s'était-il pas empiffré de diabolini sans savoir ce que c'était! Il y avait de quoi en crever" [He had been given hell to eat. He sweated amber for three days. After all, he had stuffed himself with diabolini without knowing what they were! He might have died as a result] (2:23). He does not die, of course, for that would be out of keeping with the genre, but the possibility, however fleeting, is attendant on, indeed included within the theme. Aphrodisiacs, for Nerciat, may not be demonic in any grand sense, but they are diabolically mischievous. In *Le Diable au corps*, the risk is consciously taken, once again by a mature male, in the heart of a semi-public erotic competition, all for the sake of a wager: "L'Anglais ne néglige cependant pas d'avaler, au risque de s'en trouver mal après, un mélange de rhum et de cantarides" [The Englishman took the precaution of swallowing, even though it might make him sick afterward, a mixture of rum and cantharides] (6:153). His delicate companion watches anxiously, perhaps figuring an appropriate concern on the part of sensitive (and knowledgeable) readers: "Dès lors la sensible d'Angemain, non seulement doute du pari, mais tremble pour la vie du parieur" [When she saw what had happened, the sensitive d'Angemain not only doubted the outcome of the wager, but feared for the gambler's life] (6:153). Once again, it happens that the death that was momentarily evoked does not ensue, but the continued evocation must itself have some cumulative weight. Besides, the very title of this novel goes beyond any of Sade's in the importance it accords to the immanence of desire. The devil in the body is experienced by the central women characters as part of their nature, and requires of the men the use of performance-enhancing drugs. Aphrodisiacs provide the supplement needed by many of the male characters to fill the gap between female endurance and male stamina, between desire as a kind of general competence, and pleasure as concrete performance. *Diabolini* and *pastilles* give the males—but only at a potential cost to health—"autant de vigueur que de désir" [as much vigor as desire].[26] No wonder, then, that these substances should be referred to by Nerciat, with a paradoxical blend of frankness and euphemism, as "des poisons voluptueux" [voluptuous poisons] (*Le Diable au corps*, 4:80). This is the material ambivalence of the aphrodisiac, distilled as seductive danger. An anonymous novel that is contemporary with Nerciat's, *Les Délices de Coblentz* (1791), refers generically to stimulating potions as the same thematic concoction, the same mixture of essential erotic qualities. They are, we are told, "des poisons qui charment" [poisons that charm people].[27]

Sade, I repeat, ought not as a matter of historical fact to be considered the inventor of this aphrodisiacal formula, nor the author of its standard representations. Indeed, Sade's libertines occasionally take the opportunity to insist that they have no systematic need of such stimulants to achieve the perfection of desire. When, in *Histoire de Juliette*, Juliette's companion, Durand, suggests that the two go out and perform a particularly licentious act, Juliette responds with congratulatory enthusiasm, saying, "Ah! Putain! Tu es grise" [Oh you whore! You are tipsy]. This is the pretext for a short speech by Durand, a set piece of Sadian erotic didacticism:

Un peu, peut-être; mais n'imagine pourtant pas que les secours de Bacchus me soient nécessaires pour allumer en moi le flambeau du libertinage. Ce que l'on prête à l'autre est divin, je le sais, et je ne me porte jamais si bien aux excès de la luxure, que quand je suis gorgée de mets délicats et de vins capiteux; mais je n'en ai pourtant pas un tel besoin, que je ne puisse, sans ce stimulant, franchir toutes les bornes de la décence et de la pudeur: tu vas le voir.

[A little, perhaps, but you must not imagine that I need the help of Bacchus to light the torch of libertinage in me. His qualities are divine, admittedly, and I am never so given to excesses of lasciviousness as when I am gorged with fine dishes and heady wines. But my need of that stimulant is not so great that I cannot go beyond all limits of decency and modesty without it. I'll show you what I mean.][28]

There is something offensive to the philosophical libertine in the suggestion that alcohol, or any comparable stimulant, could be the origin or explanation of desire. The proper site of desire, as Sade says so often, is *la tête*: "l'âme d'un libertin n'a pas une seule faculté qui ne soit aux ordres de sa tête" [a libertine's soul does not have one faculty that is beyond the control of his head] (*Aline et Valcour*).[29] The head guides and compels systematic erotic behavior by its capacity to "conceive" pleasures, and "imagine" acts of the most extreme kinds. Desires function in Sade as a set of reflective practices, whereby represented images or tableaux are taken up with alacrity as actions to be imitated. It is a matter, for both masters and victims, of bodily discipline. One must be (im)properly disposed, and adopt the right attitude. So when Juliette talks, at one point in her story, about "les stimulants que je venais de recevoir" [the stimulants I had just been given], she means the experience of a particular position (sodomy) as a prelude to more drastic, but formally related pleasures (8:513). For someone who proudly describes herself as "toujours aux ordres de ma tête" [always under the control of my head] (9:61), alcohol or more exotic substances can provide no more than an enhancement of what is already desired, and about to be executed. To make of Sade the great purveyor of cantharides is to read his philosophical libertinism in the deceptive shadow of one of the most powerful metaphors developed by a later eroticism.

By a quite profound irony, the Marseilles incident can be interpreted as an example of libertine imitation at its most classical. Sade may in fact have been using cantharides after reading about it in an erotic novel that antedates any of his own. *Vénus en rut* (1771) contains an episode in which a variety of substances are used as aphrodisiacs.[30] By a fine coincidence—by just that sort of coincidence that so often happens in Sade to provoke and confirm shared desire—the episode in question occurs in Marseilles. This moves Jean-Pierre Dubost, in a preface to *Vénus en rut*, to imagine something that the nineteenth century would have found strictly unthinkable. Could it be that Sade had gone to Marseilles in order to put into practice a scene that he had found in a novel published just a year earlier?

Voilà donc un texte anonyme qui réservera bien des surprises. L'épisode marseillais n'est pas la moindre. Avons-nous bien lu? Cette histoire de "crème à la rose," de "pastilles à l'ambre," et ces "diabolos à la menthe" donnés à ce néophyte amoureux "qui n'en connaissait pas la force" . . . cela ne nous rappelle-t-il pas certain épisode mémorable du 27 juin 1772, son anis et ses bonbons à la cantharide? On se prendrait à rêver. Sade aurait-il décidé ce jour-là de mettre en pratique *Vénus en rut*?

[So here is an anonymous text full of surprises. The Marseilles episode is not the least of them. Have we read correctly? This story about "rose cream," "amber pastilles," and "mint diabolos" given to a neophyte in the field of love who "does not know how strong they are." . . . Does that not remind us of a certain memorable episode on June 27 1772, with its aniseed and cantharides candy? That could set us wondering. Had Sade decided on that day to put *Vénus en rut* into practice?] [31]

If Sade had indeed decided to head for Marseilles armed with aphrodisiacal confectionery, he may not have been acting as the "divine" initiator of erotic modernity, nor even as the audacious and inscrutable experimenter imagined by Pauvert.[32] It is more likely that Sade was simply following the pattern of his own fictional heroes: taking up as his own desire the model, the scenario, the "passion"[33] made available to him through erotic representation.

There is every reason to suppose, certainly, that Sade went to Marseilles in order to hand out cantharides to his victims or accomplices, rather than take them himself. Indeed, on those few occasions in his fiction when aphrodisiacs assume any thematic status at all, it is the distribution rather than the consumption of them that is foregrounded. This is the case, notably, in *Histoire de Juliette* (c. 1797), where the fabrication and distribution of these substances revolves around "la Durand." Durand is a powerful figure, a kind of exotic and dangerous apothecary, who finally triumphs over Juliette's long-time companion, the ruthless, far-sighted Clairwil. Juliette and Clairwil first meet Durand when they go shopping for poisons, and encounter in one part of the boutique a remarkably varied range of aphrodisiacs, including cantharides:

La sorcière, s'emparant alors d'une baguette d'ébène, et descendant à mesure tous les bocaux qui se trouvaient sur les rayons, commença l'explication des aphrodisiaques et des filtres amoureux, ainsi que des emménagogues et des électuaires anti-aphrodisiaques. Nous fîmes mettre de côté une ample provision des premiers, parmi lesquels beaucoup de cantharide, de gens-eng, et quelques fioles de la liqueur de joui, du Japon, que la Durand nous fit payer, à cause de sa rareté et de ses vertus surprenantes, dix louis la fiole.

[The sorceress, taking hold of an ebony wand and working her way through the jars that stood on the shelves, began to explain the aphrodisiacs and love potions, as well as the emmenagogues and anti-aphrodisiacal electuaries. We arranged for her to put aside an ample supply of the first kind, including plenty of cantharides and ginseng, and a few phials of joui liquor, from Japan, for which Durand made us pay ten louis a phial, because of its rarity and its surprising qualities.] (8:548)

This rather gothic set piece of description takes place early in the novel, and seems likely to provide a considerable yield in the course of the story. Prima facie, it appears to be a narrative matrix, a provision of artifices that will allow the two heroines, during their life of erotic adventure, to play manipulative tricks on the bodies of others, and perhaps to manage their own pleasures in well-calculated doses. But if that is the kind of experimentation, and the kind of narrative economy that we expect, then *Histoire de Juliette* cannot fulfil our expectations.[34]

To understand how Sade's novel uses aphrodisiacs, we should note first of all that they are sold by a woman who trades primarily in dark and exotic poisons. In more typical Sadian narrative, including most of *Histoire de Juliette*, erotic behavior is effectively prescribed by theatrical tableaux and quasi-rational disquisitions, but Durand's "prescriptions" have none of that demonstrative quality. With the single exception of the passage I have just quoted, her ingredients and her formulae are not available for examination and imitation. Rather, as the title of *sorcière* given to Durand shows, they belong to the domain of witchcraft. Doubtless for this reason, whatever the alchemical subtleties of Durand's black art, readers of the story witness not its workings but only its consequences, its rather indiscriminate fallout. Juliette never mentions what actual product of Durand she has to hand on those few occasions when she mentions them at all, merely declaring, for example, that she has a pocketful of poisoned sweets (*dragées*) as she walks about. These she hands out indiscriminately (*indifféremment*) in the streets and in brothels (see, for example, 8:540). She behaves rather like Sade in Marseilles, it might be observed.[35] Except that it seemed then to be the grotesque bourgeois and the hysterical plebeian women who failed to distinguish between aphrodisiacs and poisons. Now it appears that failing to distinguish is somehow in itself a source of pleasure for Juliette, even if that pleasure is often trivial or short-lived. At one point during her travels in the south of Italy, she, Clairwil, and Olympe are followed for some time by a group of rough men who wish to have sex with them.

Under her breath Juliette asks Clairwil if she has her sweets (*dragées*). Yes, says Clairwil, "Je ne marche jamais sans cela" [I never go walking without them]. Olympe then explains to the locals that these *dragées* will give them extra desire and strength (*donner le courage*), so that the men agree to swallow the prescription. This actually allows the men to make love once each to Juliette and her friends before dying (9:355). What is offered to them as an aphrodisiac turns out to be also a lethal poison. Sade's fiction at this point confirms and fulfils the narrative of crime begun by the prostitutes of Marseilles and finished off by the judges of Aix.

By a compelling dialectic, it is the indiscriminate distribution of poisons that provokes and intensifies Juliette's pleasure. What is really stimulating for her is to sense the havoc she is causing as she gives poison, at random, to people she meets:

> de mes jours je ne goûtai de plaisirs plus vifs, cette perfide idée de la certitude où je devais être, que, par mes noirceurs, l'homme que je tenais dans mes bras ne s'en arracherait que pour tomber dans ceux de la mort, cette idée barbare mit un sel si piquant à ma jouissance, que je m'évanouis pendant la crise.

> [In all my life, I never knew such keen pleasure as I enjoyed in the perfidious certainty that the man I held in my arms would, because of my treachery, only leave my embrace in order to fall into the arms of death. That inhuman idea added such spice to my pleasure that I fainted during the crisis.] (9:355–56)

The pleasure most acutely felt by Juliette has to do with circulation. Poison is not taken internally, or used in a narrowly domestic way, but put in her pocket as she walks out the door, and handed out as she moves through the world, bringing a form of death that itself circulates destructively through the veins of her victims. The decisive action happens insidiously, in the back streets and dark hovels of the poor, and in the spaces of their bodies. This is indeed a far cry from Sade's philosophical boudoirs, with their highly constrained body shapes and their well-lit demonstrations.

Beyond Sade, and beyond the fiction of Donatien the Candy Man, the thematic convergence of desire and poison reaches a dramatic peak in *Gamiani* (1833). This oft-reprinted erotic novel seems to include both the classical and the Romantic when it describes the decor of an Italian convent and the events that occur there. We find the traditional set of models to be imitated, and well-established rituals governing the performance of erotic positions, but the formal, classical geometry is said to melt away in a newly intense environment heated by the fire within:

> Les mets exquis, les vins chauds irritants étaient enlevés avec un appétit dévorant. Les figures de femmes usées par la débauche, froides, pâles aux rayons du jour, se coloraient, s'échauffaient peu à peu. Les vapeurs bachiques, les apprêts cantharidés portaient le feu dans le corps, le trouble dans la tête.

> [The fine dishes and stimulating mulled wine were soon eagerly devoured. Those faces of women worn out by debauchery, which were cold and pale in the light of day, now gradually took on color and warmth. The vapors of Bacchus and the cantharidal preparations brought fire into the body and desire into the heart.][36]

> J'éprouvais une démangeaison singulière; mon corps frémissait, était en feu. Je m'agitais lubriquement, comme pour satisfaire un désir insatiable.
> Je fondais comme une lave ardente.

> [I felt a strange itch. My body was afire and quivering. I rolled about lustfully, as if to satisfy an insatiable desire.
> I melted like burning lava.] (90)

In the loss of bodily shape, there is a compelling experience of the materiality of desire. Gamiani has fire circulating in her veins (100) to the point where she actually becomes fire, in the very substantiation, the fluid incarnation of desire. It is this state of desire, this quasi-spontaneous inner combustion that becomes a central theme for Romantic eroticism. For Gamiani, cantharides is not a libertine artifice—or rather, it is a transcendent one, because it is the artifice that liberates nature. It is the spark that makes her intensely alive by triggering the revelation of an inner physiological truth. And when in extremis Gamiani poisons herself, she does so, predictably enough, with a "poison ardent." She finds the appropriate way of concluding her story, her life, and that of her lover Fanny. The liquid burns inside her, consumes her entrails and pierces her from within (138). She ends in a wild "rage" of pleasure and pain, a fatal paroxysm of desire (139).

The full thematic consecration of the aphrodisiac does not co-incide historically with the physiological melodrama of *Gamiani*, for all that novel's intensity and popular success. It is the late nineteenth century that develops the theme most ardently and diffuses it to every corner of the field of erotic representation. Having once been an oddity, an adjunct or a *divertissement*, the aphrodisiac finally becomes, it can be said, the very name of the erotic. *Lesbia, maîtresse d'école* (1890) describes the reading of some pornographic texts as alerting Lesbia to the pleasure of whipping: "elle avait retenu que l'application du fouet suggère à celui qui le reçoit, aussi bien qu'à celui qui le donne, des plaisirs voluptueux" [she had retained the fact that the use of a whip suggests voluptuous pleasures to the one who receives it, as well as to the one who administers it].[37] Erotic "retention" is not said to occur here, in the standard eighteenth-century manner, as the visual representation of a model to be self-consciously imitated: desire is retained as a burning fluid. Lesbia and her lover are filled with a fiery substance: "D'ailleurs la simple lecture de ces ouvrages aphrodisiaques allumait en nous une effervescence que nous mettions toute une nuit à éteindre" [Besides, the mere reading of these aphrodisiacal works ignited in us a form of effervescence that took a whole night to dampen down] (140). The relation to erotic art is not understood here via the metaphor of the gaze or as something produced by theatrical demonstration: it is mediated by notions of circulation and contagion. In *Enfilade de perles* (1894), the reader is invited to consume the text as if it were a stimulating potion. One can thus enter into, or be entered into by, "les jouissances inouïes que les personnages recherchent et que le lecteur trouvera indubitablement à la lecture aphrodisiaque de cet unique ouvrage" [the extraordinary pleasures that the characters seek and that the reader will undoubtedly find in the aphrodisiacal reading of this unique work].[38] In this fictive world, a woman's tongue has the same "tiédeurs aphrodisiaques" [aphrodisiacal warmth] (11) as a perfumed boudoir: "une odeur forte . . . remplissait le boudoir de son aphrodisiaque senteur" [a strong smell filled the boudoir with aphrodisiacal perfume] (26). Indeed the epithet circulates so widely in such fiction that its very diffusion serves as the mark of contagious pleasure: the word itself has become a kind of aphrodisiac.

What was historically a transitive and incidental desire for aphrodisiacs has now been so thoroughly transformed and expanded that the aphrodisiac comes to be the very "essence" of desire. Where there was once an occasional connection, we now find a tight thematic circuit. Aphrodisiacs had earlier been present only episodically; now they are invoked in every circumstance and imagined to be present beneath every surface. It was ever the case, no doubt, that the eyes of the beloved were described by erotic texts in terms of their impact on the one who loved. They caused melancholy, immobility, rapture, even death, and they often acted magically in doing so. But the fin de siècle understands this impact, with compelling and compulsive frequency, in pharmaceutical terms: "Tes yeux sont des philtres aphrodisiaques qui déchaînent en moi la plus ardente folie" [Your eyes are aphrodisiacal potions that trigger in me the most ardent madness], we read in *La Volupté féroce* (1905).[39] Aphrodisiacs become a standard figurative reference used to account for the symptoms of desire: "Elle vit rouge, des bouffées de chaleur lui montèrent au visage et, à la fois suffoquée et glacée, un affreux désir la mordit au cœur. Ce fut comme si elle avait bu un philtre" [She saw red. Waves of heat flushed her face. Her breath was taken away and she turned ice cold. A dreadful desire took hold of her heart. It was as if she had drunk a potion] (*Le Vice errant* [1902]).[40] Desire can now be readily understood as a physiological process, and the hypothetical explanation produced as a matter of routine: "Alice lui avait glissé, lui semblait-il, du feu dans les veines . . . il était épris de sa beauté, de son originalité qui ajoutait un piment corsé à ses étreintes et doublait le plaisir de la suprême caresse" [It seemed that Alice must have slipped fire into his veins. He was struck by her beauty and her originality, which added a strong, spicy flavor to her embrace and doubled the pleasure of the supreme caress] (*La Luxure* [1905]).[41] *Glisser* becomes a much-used verb for describing the action of aphrodisiacs, displacing classical favourites like *piquer*, for *glisser* marks both the invasiveness of desire and its irresistible circulation within the body: "Tout cela glissa en son cerveau une griserie plus enivrante que celle d'un vin mêlé d'aphrodisiaques . . ." [All of that slipped into his brain a euphoria more dizzying than if he had drunk wine mixed with aphrodisiacs] (*L'Affolante Illusion* [1906]).[42]

The compound of seduction and poison is never more tightly bound than at this time, never more concentrated than in these metaphorical phials that appear so regularly in erotic description. Moreover, such figurative representations are often accompanied by actual narrative events. Contributing to thematic concentration, one finds the repeated use of aphrodisiacs as objects that drive the narrative and tend to modify its outcome. In libertine fiction of the *ancien régime*, when a man was "enchanted" and unable to fulfil the requirements of erotic circumstance, his momentary inadequacy could be remedied well enough by whatever expedients came to hand. But when, in the later nineteenth century, impotence comes so often to be referred to as a kind of epidemic, an enduring and widespread disorder of the will, this begets a series of erotico-medical narratives whose central preoccupation is a veritable pathology of desire. And when, alongside the morbid lack of libidinal energy, scientistic analysis also finds a pathological excess of it, aphrodisiacs are called into action, so to speak, at both ends of the scale. They represent a form of illness, as a symptom or even a cause, while also serving as a dangerous remedy. The ambivalence of "les poisons qui charment" then seems to reach its zenith as a powerful amalgam of the therapeutic and the deleterious. In *Vingt Ans de la vie d'une jolie femme* (1842), which is in many ways typical of midcentury pornography, one still finds the configuration that took shape in Nerciat's time, with the usual problem, the usual solution, and the standard warning about the dangers of excess. Julie, who is newly married, confides in her maid about the difficulty of arousing her husband. The maid tells of her own troubles, saying that "son mari ne bandait que par artifice, grâce à la boutique de l'apothicaire," and that "le médecin lui avait recommandé de ne plus avoir recours à ce moyen" [her husband only got it up through artifice, thanks to the apothecary's shop. . . . The doctor had recommended that he no longer resort to that method].[43] In fin-de-siècle novels, however, the doctor, whose authoritative voice is heard at almost every point, is likely to have sterner words to say. What was once imprudent or regrettable has now become decidedly sinister. There is, predictably enough, a continual struggle on the part of aging, decadent husbands to penetrate their hapless wives. Sometimes they just manage it, as in *Les Cousines de la colonelle* (1880) or *Deux Amies* (1885).[44] But whether or not they succeed is hardly the point in narratives where physiological process, rather than copulative outcome, is the primary concern. In *Deux Amies*, the young Jeanne discovers a prescribed potion among her husband's things on their wedding night. She does not recognize it, of course—that failure is the mark of her relative innocence—but knowing readers do, because they in their thematic wisdom are always already conscious of the secret that unaccountably eluded the forensic apothecaries of Marseilles in 1772. Jeanne writes to her childhood friend: "j'espère que tu parviendras à savoir à quoi sert cette mixture de cannelle, de genzeng et de 'calumus aromaticus,' qu'il faut prendre, d'après l'ordonnance, 'une heure avant.' Avant quoi?" [I hope that you will manage to find out the use of this mixture of nutmeg, ginseng, and "calamus aromaticus," which must be taken, according to the prescription, "an hour beforehand." Before what?] (80–81). What is most sinister here is that Jeanne should have no understanding of what "we," as the proper readers of this fiction, already know only too well. She has fallen into one of those debilitating fin-de-siècle domestic traps. Her husband is afflicted by a loss of psychosexual energy: the best he can manage is to keep his desire in a container beside the bed.

The excruciating contradiction about such use of aphrodisiacs is that they somehow compound the unnaturalness of it all. Not only do they act as a desperate substitute for what is now a chronic weakness, but they in fact precipitate decay and death by producing powerful symptoms of energy that are not germane to the body itself. *Inassouvie* (1889) describes the use of aphrodisiacs as a kind of perverse therapy, driving the organism to produce signs that might, in an earlier time or in another place, have been natural, but are here sadly unfounded: "de nouveaux verres des boissons les plus excitantes, les plus alcooliques, en refoulant les nausées de la veille, et en fouettant le sang engourdi, rendaient, refaisaient une vie fiévreuse, un entrain factice de machine surmenée" [further drinks of the most stimulating, most alcoholic kind, by suppressing the nausea of the day before and whipping up his sluggish blood, brought him back to febrile activity with the artificial energy of an overloaded machine].[45] Whipping up the blood, driving it along in spite of its century-long fatigue can only serve to aggravate the problem. Aphrodisiacs can make for a dramatic crisis where there might otherwise have been mere torpor, or steady, unremarkable decay.

At a time when impotence is often thought to be endemic, aphrodisiacs are less likely to be called on as casual restoratives than adopted as a general regimen, so that the perils of their use have different narrative effects. In the high Romantic *Gamiani*, the aphrodisiacal poison had nothing to do with diet: it was produced quite suddenly, whatever the thematic support provided by earlier references to inner fire. The heroine ended her life and achieved her proper death in one flamboyant moment. But fin-de-siècle fiction favors slower forms of inner combustion whose symptoms can be examined by doctors and knowledgeable readers. These lead just as surely to death as Gamiani's potion but do so in novelistic time. Narration is in fact so full of stern warnings and confident predictions of the final, deadly outcome that a certain kind of melodramatic surprise cannot occur. Instead, narrative tends to be given over to morbid delectation, which dwells on the inner process in all its debilitating certainty. An authoritative voice in *Mademoiselle Giraud, ma femme* tells us that the process is a lamentable by-product of class refinement: "peasants" eat when they are hungry and express feelings through sex; "dissolute" bourgeois are always in need of new spices to give them an appetite, and of erotic refinements to help them feel love.[46] This is how fin-de-siècle narratives use aphrodisiacs to nourish their plots without losing the certainty that death lies at the end of it all.

It is possible to moderate between crisis and decay by spicing up stories, quite literally, with exotic substances. In *Deux Amies*, after the eventual failure of the marriage, Jeanne returns to her girlhood friend, renewing and confirming their lesbian relationship. This effectively takes her from one use of aphrodisiacs to another, from an inadequate casual tonic to a compelling daily diet that is thoroughly successful in its own, destructive way. Indeed, the "excesses" of lesbianism are parallel to, and apparently dependent on, an intoxicating diet: "Le menu enragé les surchauffait comme ces brouets cantharidés que les garçons d'honneur apportent aux nouveaux mariés, le soir le leurs noces, dans les villages du Languedoc" [The fierce menu overheated them like those cantharidal gruels that best men give to newlyweds on their wedding night in the villages of Provence] (250). With each spicy meal they eat, with each hot drink they consume, the two move one further step down the path to death by desire. Suzanne is described as positively wasting away from the intimate ravages of exotic food: "Cette délicate, qui était faite tout au plus pour sucer de temps en temps un bonbon poivré, pour tremper ses lèvres dans un verre de kümmel, ne mangeait plus que des choses au cary et au poivre rouge, ne buvait plus que des potions cantharidées" [This delicate creature, whose constitution was such that she could barely suck on peppermint candy from time to time, or sip from a glass of kümmel, was now eating only dishes made with curry and red peppers, and drinking only cantharidal potions] (258). The red chilies that she eats in salads come from sun-drenched Spain, just like the black flies that are crushed to make her thoroughly unrefreshing drinks. Suzanne is caught in the slowly narrowing cycle of the aphrodisiac, hungry for curries and yet hollow inside, consumed by desire and consuming ever more of it as her poisonous daily sustenance. So powerful is the narrative program inscribed in this diet that it can represent the (supposed) libidinal danger of all lesbian relationships, and other forms of "perversion," whether by its presence or its absence. In *La Fille de Gamiani* (1906), the heroine devotes herself, rather belatedly, to an angelic ménage with another woman, and defines the angelic qualities of their new life together precisely by the absence of the old demon aphrodisiacs: "Et on n'a pas besoin de cocaïne ou d'éther pour s'émoustiller. Les liqueurs fortes, les cigarettes, les mets au piment, les régimes à la cantharide, j'ai renoncé à tout cela comme elle y a renoncé" [And we do not need cocaine or ether to arouse ourselves. Strong liquor, cigarettes, chili dishes, cantharides diets, I have given them all up, just as she has].[47]

That aphrodisiacs are both natural and unnatural, and indeed defined by the tension in that paradox, is represented by their association with distant places. No matter how long the history of their use, they cannot be recognized as part of a tradition. They must always be introduced. For the foreigners who belong in these exotic places, spicy regimens are natural. But that nature is available only to the French characters in fin-de-siècle stories as a perilously foreign taste. Gamiani was Italian, and shared fully in the Mediterranean qualities that connected her place of origin with Spain and Marseilles, in a geographical order separating dark-haired, hot-blooded people from the un-marked northern European norm.[48] But the racism of the late nineteenth century is more systematic and more radical, as it binds foreignness as such to radical desire, and the dangerously erotic to the wildly exotic. Femmes fatales may come from the Orient, or the Caribbean, they may be Slavic or African or Asian, but all seem to eat hot food and communicate its heat to their lovers. Here, from *Le Journal d'un amant* (1902), is a description of a beautiful Tonkinese woman—or rather, of the taste she left in the narrator-hero's mouth: "J'ai également sur mes lèvres l'âpre goût de ses baisers poivrés, de ses morsures au piment rouge, de ces piments rapportés d'Asie et qu'elle mâchonnait même entre ses repas" [I have too on my lips the sharp taste of her peppery kisses, of her red chili bites, with those chilis she brought back from Asia that she used to nibble between meals].[49] In *Rires, sang, et voluptés* (1901), the lingering memory of such a kiss penetrates the hero and circulates in his veins. It mixes with his own blood like a burning poison that also brings a kind of pleasure.[50] In *Le Journal d'un amant*, the "femme terrible" ac-tually spits out a mouthful of blood in a moment of high passion, splashing the hero's face (40). The fear of contamination through the blood is dramatic, and sadly familiar to those who have known the AIDS panic. The difference is that these foreign women are not actually sick with their own foreignness. They are given over, like Suzanne in *Deux Amies*, to the circularity of consuming desire, but they are, by contrast with her, constitu-tionally able to sustain its fiery circulation. It becomes possible to describe them as being so filled with desire that they become its substantive equivalent, its walking, breathing presence in the world. They actually are aphrodisiacs, in the flesh, so that their beauty is both the sign and the means of a dreadful contagion. Here is a woman from *Rires, sang, et voluptés* (1901), who is desire incarnate:

à l'approche de l'ancienne maîtresse il sentait son corps, comme ses sens, tout imprégné de sa charnelle pâleur et de l'effroyable parfum qui naissait dans sa bouche au plus fort des baisers.
   Oh! Ce parfum!
   Oh! Cette bouche!
   Parfum? Poison; poison de volupté, poison cantharidal qui semait, à travers son sang, la folie du feu.

[as his former mistress drew near, he felt his body and his senses impregnated with her fleshly pallor and with the dreadful perfume that was born in her nostrils at the height of their embrace.

Oh! That perfume!

Oh! That mouth!

Perfume, was it? A voluptuous poison, a cantharidal poison that spread through his veins the madness of fire.] (260)

It is both a consecration and a fixation of the aphrodisiac theme that it should be feminized in this way: not so much inscribed in the bodies of certain women as suffused through their every pore—or better, made cognate and cosubstantive with them. It is unsurprising, then, that there should be two erotic novels entitled *La Cantharide,* one dating from about 1900 and the other from about 1928, in which the title is not just a mark of the genre but the metaphorical name of the central woman character. In the first of these novels, Charlotte, a mixed-race woman from the colonies, seems to have made her life's purpose out of the requirements of the flesh, her vocation out of her very substance:

Car le vice, le vice sans frein ni limites, était le seul dieu, la seule loi de Charlotte. Elle sentait que sa mission sur la terre était de servir ce tout-puissant moteur des plaisirs humains, de faire bouillir le sang dans les veines des mâles, d'exciter leurs passions, de faire raidir leur nerf d'amour . . . d'un regard, d'un sourire, d'un mot. . . . Elle était bien la femme-cantharide, l'Aphrodite des temps modernes, grisant les hommes, éveillant en eux le meilleur de leur être, les appelant, triomphante, aux sacerdoces du Rut.

[For vice, unbridled, unlimited vice, was Charlotte's only law. She felt that her mission on earth was to serve the all-powerful drive of human pleasures, to make the blood of males boil in their veins, to arouse their passions, to stiffen the sinew of love in them . . . with a look, a smile, or a word. . . . She was the cantharides woman, the Aphrodite of modern times, making men drunk, awakening in them the best of their being, calling them, in triumph, to the priesthood of Rutting.][51]

A "modern-day Aphrodite" will not be most striking for her performance of the positional "figures of Venus" but for her ability to stimulate the veins and the sinews of men. Far from being a receptacle for cantharides handed out by a half-distracted libertine, the modern Charlotte of 1900 is the source of material vice as excessively seductive femininity. Her violent death at the end of the novel—for being a femme fatale is once again fatal to the woman herself—is not brought about by poisoning: she is stabbed by a jealous wife. It would hardly be appropriate for Charlotte to die by poisoning, since there is a quite precise sense in which she *is* poison. She does not need to distribute bonbons, or to take them, for she is, like so many late nineteenth-century representations of erotic womanhood, always already saturated with cantharides.

In the second novel of the same title, which is rather beyond the period I am considering, but which reveals the persistence of the theme into the twentieth century, the woman in question is once again presented as a heady racial cocktail. She is disquietingly, nay viciously multicultural, and it follows by some purported rule of nature that she should be a (literal and figurative) poisoner of men.[52] This woman is given the nickname "Cantharide" (9) and her primary mission in life—her desire, her purpose, her bodily need—is to be worthy of that name, to "soutenir la gloire et la dignité de son beau surnom" [uphold the glory and dignity of her fine nickname] (10). Readers who recognize the name and hear its thematic resonance know from the outset that its thrilling promise is inseparable from a terrible threat. What they only half know, perhaps, is that this seductive poison is able to be named via the racist and sexist othering of desire "itself." Desire, as a convergence of the exotic and the erotic, can be contemplated both in its unnatural distinctness and in its fearful natural contagion. It does not belong within the bodies of normal (Northern, Western, European, male) people, but is nonetheless able to be communicated to them by an almost irresistible physiological complicity. Radical desire is both foreign and archaically, substantively familiar.

The figural concentration of aphrodisiacs, their fixation in the body of the femme fatale represents one end of the thematic range to be found in the fin de siècle. At the other, we find the pale impotence of an effeminate, over-refined civilization. Yet it must not be forgotten that these two extremes—what "scientific" sexual pathology was then learning to identify as the nymphomaniac and the impotent—are mutually defining and mutually entailed. The full thematic range, and the full significance of its bipolarity, are exemplified in a novel that I wish to examine briefly in conclusion. That novel is *Mademoiselle Tantale* (1886), which is included in a multigeneric collection of works by Dubut de Laforest entitled *Pathologie sociale*.[53] Mary Folkestone, the heroine, is a young English woman whose fate is compared with that of Tantalus. She resembles the tortured figure of legend only to a degree, however, since her life story is not simply one of unquenchable thirst or enduring sexual unsatisfaction. The metaphorical and narrative focus of the novel is in fact on a pathological failure of desire.

The beginnings of Mary Folkestone's failure, indeed the first two symptoms of it, are to be found in the fact that she is (a) English and (b) a sculptor. That she should be English is itself a clue for those who are familiar with French stereotyping of other nationalities.[54] It suggests that her fatal weakness is likely to be the opposite of the quality found in volatile women of the South and East. That she should be a sculptor is equally significant, since it shows her to be quite literally preoccupied by cold mineral substances and abstract bodily attitudes. Toward the end of the novel, after a protracted and frustrating experience of the insubstantial, of chilling mists and inner emptiness, she attempts to convalesce far from her lover and from sculpture. She chooses to do so in a rented villa in the south of France. Unfortunately, the house proves to be too far from England and too close to Spain. As she sits in her garden one afternoon, she is surrounded by a swarm of small, black flies. This is in fact a sadly familiar metaphor of her experience of sexuality, for she had continually felt as if clouds were floating about her, emphasizing her lack of vital inner substance. On this occasion, however, by the most apposite irony, the insects buzzing around her happen to be Spanish flies. Desperate to transform this taunting volatility into something of substance, she captures some of them and produces for herself a large dose of cantharides, as if to find the ultimate remedy for Englishness and clammy frigidity.

Now cantharides, as many of us know, is a poison. Mary attempts to remedy the lack within her body by drastic pharmaceutical means, but such a radical grab for life condemns her to die. Not only is this, in a cruel sense, the end she desires: it is also the end of her vague desiring. Now, at last, she experiences the spasms enjoyed by the characters of *Gamiani*: "Il se produisait dans ce corps de blonde, des frissonnements, des trépidations musculaires, de soudains courants de vie auxquels succédèrent des douleurs" [There ran through this blonde body shivers and muscular trepidations, surges of life followed by pain] (105). In her white body invaded by black Spanish flies, the spasms of pain are made to coincide momentarily with those of pleasure. Fire now circulates within her: "des ardeurs qu'elle ne pouvait plus contenir l'embrasaient jusque dans son sexe" [ardor that she could not contain set even her sex ablaze] (105). The paroxysm of her death agony thus appears as her narratively necessary climax—the only kind that is to be allowed by sexual pathology: "Par instant, et comme épuisée, la malheureuse demeurait sans mouvement, et bientôt le mal érotique arriva à son paroxysme avec tous les caractères de la plus effrayante nymphomanie" [Momentarily, as if exhausted, the poor woman remained motionless, but soon the erotic illness reached its paroxysm, showing all the characteristics of the most dreadful nymphomania] (105). Mary does not say "Oh!" or "Ah!" like the ejaculatory heroines of so many euphoric sexual narratives of the nineteenth and twentieth centuries. The sounds of pain and physical impact that she utters—"des 'han!' Comme font les pétrins, des 'han!' qui soulevaient le corps" ['huh!' sounds like dough being kneaded, 'huh!' sounds that shook her whole body] (105)—are the approximate symptoms of pleasure produced only in death, after desire has been imbibed as poison.

_ The very opposition of the Mary Folkestones and the exotic femmes fatales is, I suggest, a key structural element in the thematic constitution of feminine desire as continually threatened by illness and by excessive health. Just as dark-haired foreign women can be the incarnation of desire, so excessively blond, excessively Northern women like Mary can fail to hold in their bodies the Mediterranean qualities of substantive eroticism. Femininity can then be resolved, materially and geographically, into thermal and pigmentary opposites, although the eventual outcomes produced in narrative appear to be very much the same for women at either pole. Is it because their bodies are constituted as dramatic sites for the action of desire, marked as they are by dramatic fullness or dramatic emptiness? Women named Cantharides die a violent death, and so does Mary Folkestone.

To conclude, let me revisit the question of method with which I began. I said at the outset that what was required of a history of sexuality was more than routine thematics, and it behoves me

II
The Middle

4
Utterance

In this chapter, I wish to consider one of the thematic and stylistic elements that contributed to the development of climax in erotic narrative: the practice of exclamation. I say "thematic and stylistic" in the one phrase because erotic narrative does not simply refer to exclamatory utterance but often seeks to perform it textually. My contention in this chapter is that exclamations as disparate and disjointed talk, as festive marks of spontaneity and intimacy, came in the later eighteenth century and in the nineteenth to be more clearly focused in narrative as symptomatic of intensity. A stylistic element that had been present in erotic fiction since at least Aretino's *Ragionamenti* (1534–39) was pressed into full thematic duty in order to signify erotic climax as a moment in which the body is compelled to utter the truth of its pleasure. A starting point for my history can be found in a section of Foucault's *Histoire de la sexualité* that has become, as Nancy Miller observes, something of a *locus communis* for critical reflection.[1] I refer to his brief reading of Diderot's erotic novel, *Les Bijoux indiscrets* (1748). While Foucault's analysis in the first volume of his study is largely devoted to the questioning practices informing the Catholic rite of confession, he is able to define his topic quite dramatically by reference to this work of fiction:

> Ce dont il s'agit dans cette série d'études? Transcrire en histoire la fable des *Bijoux indiscrets*.
>
> Au nombre de ses emblèmes, notre société porte celui du sexe qui parle. Du sexe qu'on surprend, qu'on interroge et qui, contraint et volubile à la fois, répond intarissablement.

[What is the object of this series of studies? To transcribe into a
history the fable of *Les Bijoux indiscrets*.

Among its emblems, our society wears that of the sex that
speaks. The sex that is caught in the act, and questioned. Both
constrained and voluble, it replies with inexhaustible chatter.][2]

Foucault's interest is in the utterance of sexuality as it is called
forth and called for by the confessor's questioning. He merely
takes Diderot's fable as an emblem, having nothing in particular
to say about the fictional representation of such utterances. I
shall attempt here to show that so-called erotic fiction tends to
develop both a poetics and a thematics of utterance, finding ways
of performing erotic talk, and concomitant ways of referring to it.
Following Foucault's lead while taking a parallel path, I shall
focus on the representation of confession in these texts, on the
notion of truth as a product of ritual intimacy, and on the modes
of expression that are proper to it. My concern will not be just to
"find" the truth of sexuality. That has been done repeatedly, and
can only take us through an unduly brief circuit of self-confirma-
tion. Rather, I wish to dwell on the thematic opportunities that
such a discourse makes available to narrative, on the local inflections of meaning that it requires. In other words, beginning with
Les Bijoux indiscrets, I shall examine what kinds of *histoire*, in
the sense of "story," have been made in literature out of Foucault's and Diderot's *fable*.

Foucault notes that the power to evince confession is represented thematically in Diderot's novel: it is concentrated with
comical simplicity in a magic ring given to the sultan Mangogul
by a genie. When Mangogul points the ring at a woman and
twists it, her vagina (*bijou*) begins immediately to recount its
past experiences. The magic, Foucault suggests, lies in the direct
articulation of sex with speech, whereby the truth comes flowing
out as a genital avowal that reveals any words uttered by mouth
to have been primly duplicitous. Somewhat beyond the scope of
Foucault's study, however, is the actual quality of spontaneous
storytelling that is produced by forced "indiscretion." Mangogul's
provoking, his calling-forth of the truth, compels his victims to
give voice to their sexual experiences in language over which
they have no control. What kind of writing, what kind of narrative serve to signify spontaneous veracity? What are the characteristics of genital speech? It must be said that Diderot's novel is

more interesting for the fact that it allows these questions to be asked than for any richly complex answers that it may give, although the narrative is briefly troubled by the issue from time to time. When, for example, Mangogul points his ring toward the sleeping Thélis, we read the following account of events: "Je m'en souviens encore, comme si j'y étais, dit incontinent le bijou de Thélis: neuf preuves d'amour en quatre heures. Ah! quels moments! que Zermounzaïd est un homme divin!" ["I remember it as if I were still there," said Thélis's jewel, going on without stopping. "Nine demonstrations of love in four hours. Ah! What moments! What a divine man Zermounzaïd is!"].[3] This could be heard as quite revealing talk, complete with the lover's proper name, but it is not received as such in the novel. The *bijou* is described as speaking "incontinently," in a way that is too immediate or too elliptical for Mangogul's narrative purposes. To his ears, this kind of talk is a failure of eloquence, so that even as it pours forth it serves to hide (*dérober*) something from him. He twiddles his magic ring so as to produce a more finely tuned, more detailed narrative:

> Mangogul, qui désirait s'instruire des particularités du commerce de Thélis avec Zermounzaïd, que le bijou lui dérobait, en ne s'attachant qu'à ce qui frappe le plus un bijou, frotta quelque temps le chaton de sa bague contre sa veste, et l'appliqua sur Thélis, tout étincelant de lumière. L'effet en parvint bientôt jusqu'à son bijou, qui mieux instruit de ce qu'on lui demandait, reprit d'un ton plus historique. . . .

> [Mangogul wanted to know the details of the intercourse between Thélis and Zermounzaïd, which the jewel was keeping from his grasp, for it was only going on about the things that most interest a jewel. He rubbed the setting of his ring against his coat, and applied it to Thélis all sparkling with light. The effect was soon felt on Thélis's jewel. Now with a better a idea of what was required of it, it went on in a more historical tone: [here follows the story as the sultan wanted it].] (126)

Mangogul's requirement that spontaneous talk have a properly recognizable form serves to remind us, as Foucault would have wished, of the exigent nature of confession as a discipline. But the particular narrative discipline chosen is also the mark of Mangogul's classicism. The disjointed language he first hears

appears to him only a *dérobade*, a refusal to respond properly.
He has to insist, via a metaphor of light and clarity, in order to
be told the truth in its proper historico-narrative form.

It is appropriate here to speak of Mangogul's "classicism" because we see him requiring that supposedly non-narrative language be transformed into its worthy opposite. The fact is, of
course, that unruly talk is not banished from the domain of literature, and is actually present in Diderot's text. What is more,
Thélis's vaginal utterance signifies its (quite relative) incoher-
ence in particular, recognizable ways: it contains only short
phrases, with strong punctuation, and includes a number of exclamations. These are presumably the signs of what "strikes" a
bijou most, but they are present here without being valued by
the most authoritative character in the novel. They are practiced episodically, but not owned by any official poetics. The
same kind of discrepancy, the same disturbance of the classical
occurs in Crébillon's *La Nuit et le moment* (1755). When invited
to tell a story by his companion Cidalise, Clitandre declares that
the situation in which they find themselves, in a boudoir, is
generically inappropriate for proper story telling: "Si vous saviez
à quel point je raconte mal dans un lit, vous ne voudriez sûrement pas m'y transformer en historien" [If you knew how poorly
I tell stories in bed, you surely would not want to turn me into a
historian in this place].[4] But the neat opposition between "historical" narration and pillow talk is not maintained throughout
Clitandre's verbal performance. He does tell something of a
story as part of his seductive conversation, and Crébillon's text
follows that seduction to the point where Clitandre finally
achieves his goal. Politely but eloquently, he gives voice to the
impossibility of eloquence at that moment: "Ah! Madame! . . . ma
joie me suffoque; je ne puis parler. [Il tombe, en soupirant, sur la
gorge de Cidalise, et y reste comme anéanti]" [Ah! Madame! . . .
My joy takes my breath away. I cannot speak. [He falls with a
sigh on Cidalise's breast, and lies there as if exhausted]] (9:64).
This we must take to be just the kind of talk that can and ought
to go on in a boudoir, since it is an avowal of pleasure, but we are
required, if we respect the explicit rules of the text, to oppose it
to proper story telling. In that sense, *La Nuit et le moment*, like
Les Bijoux indiscrets, brings together erotic avowal and a form
of poetic disavowal. In the fifty years that follow, erotic fiction
will in fact be less and less disturbed by the supposed discrep-

ancy between civilized talk and sexual babble. It will learn to (re)produce the babble, to organize its representation, and to assert its truth at key moments in narrative.

It could be argued that there is no historical shift of note here, merely the continuance of a tradition going back to Aretino in which exclamatory talk serves as a privileged semiotic vehicle for desire. This is just how Gustave Colline sees it. In fact, he goes so far as to say that erotic literature in general is characterized by "la langue assez décousue, ponctuée d'exclamations et de monosyllabes" [rather disjointed language, punctuated by exclamations and monosyllables]. This was the case in the *Ragionamenti*, according to Colline, and the pattern has hardly varied since.[5] That is too hearty a generalization, if only because it excludes or at best marginalizes a whole class of refined libertine texts, including Diderot's and Crébillon's. Yet there is something in the claim that deserves attention, and that can lead us back to Foucault. At the very least, it can be noted that there is a subgenre of erotic fiction, in fact a quite dominant one in French texts of the seventeenth century, that answers to this broad description. It represents, as in Aretino, intimate conversations between women during which expressions of emotion and sudden changes of direction—interjections, or yielding to other forms of discursive temptation—are said to occur, and occur in the saying. This is the case, notably, in *L'Académie des dames* (1655), *L'Escole des filles* (1660), and *Vénus dans le cloître* (1682). These texts are in fact confessional in an informal sense, confessional partly because of their informality. Their show of unpredictability and their regular indiscipline are the marks of true feminine talk—true, of course, by circular definition. The three French texts can even be said to coincide historically with the emergence of the religious confession studied by Foucault.

At this point, "disjointedness" has its full value as a (conventional) mark of spontaneity. When the language of sex is allowed (and required) to come spilling out, it is likely to be marked by sighs, cries, and exclamations. Producing these vocalizations, drawing them out from women characters in particular, becomes the business of a confessional erotic discipline that is both enacted and recounted in fiction. This talk is undoubtedly a grammatically plain and lexically spare branch of the *dispositif de sexualité,* and as such is neglected by Foucault. Yet it goes on no less volubly than the elaborate discourses of pastoral confession and psychoanalysis. As Foucault's theory, if not his actual analysis, helps us to see, disjointed language may be no less a discursive formation for its relative inarticulacy. Indeed, there is a linguistic practice of "inarticulacy," in which talk keeps on coming in discourse that is breathless and continually interrupted. This discourse is recognizable precisely as one that signifies, by its shape, the loss of shape and the loss of all reticence.

It does not follow from this, however, that the signification of disjointedness is stable throughout four centuries of erotic narrative. To suppose that would be to ignore everything Foucault has to say about the history of sexual discourses. The question is a more subtle, but also a more helpfully immediate one. How, if at all, does exclamatory talk come to be articulated with a thematics of confession, supposing that the two do in fact converge at certain historical points? When and where does exclamatory talk count as the utterance of sexual truth? Not in the *Ragionamenti*, at any rate. In Aretino's text, exclamations are of interest, undeniably, but the primary focus of description is on their extraordinary variety. Here is a passage representing the festive profusion of an orgy as an orchestration of cries:

> all agreed to do it together as choristers sing in unison, or more to the point, as blacksmiths hammer in time, and so, each attentive to his task, all that one heard was: "Oh my God, oh my Christ!" "Hug me!" "Ream me!" "Push out that sweet tongue!" "Give it to me!" "Take it!" "Push harder!" "Wait, I'm coming!" "Oh Christ, drive it into me!" "Holy God!" "Hold me!" and "Help!" Some were whispering, others were moaning loudly—and listening to them one would have thought they were running the scales, *sol, fa, mi, re, do*.[6]

This is both a kind of vulgar symphony and a flamboyant list, in which all the exclamations serve to display the range of sounds produced in pleasure. Yet the range itself, even when exhibited in near-perfect simultaneity, hardly constitutes a moment of confession. This is order made out of disorder, but it is fun rather than truth. "Expression" takes place joyously, in the uttering of instructions, animal noises, and sighs, without any revelation of erotic interiority. Even when, a little later in Aretino's story, the orchestration is more polished, it does not give rise to climactic avowal. There is a collective performance of pleasure in which the eight participants sigh in unison. Their sighs do not signify the triumph of narrative circumstance as the compulsion to speak what lies deep within: they simply come together like a well-disciplined wind ensemble, producing a blast of such force that it could have blown out eight torches (29).

There is a great difference between this and the blurting out of desire, presented as a revelation, and therefore as a narrative event in its own right. We come closer to a Foucaldian narrative moment in *Vénus dans le cloître*, where a priest is drawn despite himself into disturbing the sacramental roles of confession. While listening to a young penitent's account of libertine behavior, he is tempted by the man's beauty into an exclamation of enthusiasm: "Ah, qual gusto! signor."[7] This breaking out of desire, in a foreign tongue indeed, reverses the roles and makes the confessor into the confessee. But for the event to count in full as a moment of truth, it would need to generate further narrative, and that does not happen. The revealing exclamation is only an amusing twist at the end of an anecdote. A later novel, *Les Amours du chevalier de Faublas* (1793) shows how exclamation comes to be put in a strong narrative place, as something decisive yet relatively banal. The young Faublas is indulging in a romp with one of his mistresses but makes the mistake, so often repeated since in popular comedy, of blurting out the wrong name, that of his first, virtuous love:

Mais par une singularité que je n'entreprendrai pas d'expliquer, l'image des vertus les plus pures vint, au sein du libertinage, se présenter à mon esprit troublé; et, ce qui n'est pas moins digne de remarque, je m'avisai de vouloir parler dans un de ces moments, où l'homme plus étourdi, exempt de toutes distractions, ne laisse échapper que de courts monosyllabes ou de longs soupirs étouffés. Ah! Sophie! m'écriai-je! j'aurais dû dire: Ah! Coralie!

[But for some strange reason that I will not attempt to explain, the image of the purest virtues appeared in my troubled mind, right in the midst of a libertine frolic. Furthermore, and this is equally noteworthy, I found myself speaking in one of those moments where the dizziest man, free from all distractions, lets out only short monosyllables or long muffled sighs. "Ah! Sophie!" I exclaimed. I should have said, "Ah! Coralie!"][8]

The dramatic point is, of course, that the superficially wrong name, surrounded by sighs and monosyllables, is the profoundly right one. When "undistracted" by social awareness, Faublas utters the name that is closest to his heart, slipping unguardedly into the exclamation of truth. On such a moment of revelation, the story turns.

Sometimes in the eighteenth century, especially in more pastel-hued texts, the sigh itself takes on thematic status as a timely erotic effusion. This allows the narration to remain quite decorous, partly because the sigh itself is the most nobly insubstantial of bodily emanations, and partly because the language of description need not be interrupted by exclamatory talk. In *Acajou et Zirphile* (1744), for example, a young man and a young woman who have been enclosed in adjoining gardens are drawn into a love story through a dialogue of sighs:

> Un jour que le prince était plongé dans ses réflexions auprès de cette palissade, il laissa échapper un soupir: la jeune princesse, qui était de l'autre côté dans le même état, l'entendit; elle en fut émue; elle recueille toute son attention, elle écoute. Acajou soupire encore. Zirphile, qui n'avait jamais rien compris à ce qu'on lui avait dit, entendit ce soupir avec une pénétration admirable; elle répondit aussitôt par un pareil soupir.
>
> Ces deux amants, car ils le furent dans ce moment, s'entendirent réciproquement.

> [One day when the prince was deep in thought near this fence, he let out a sigh. The young princess, who was on the other side and in the same state of mind, heard it. She was moved. She gathered all her powers of attention and listened. Acajou sighed again. Zirphile, who had never understood anything that had been said to her, understood that sigh with admirable intelligence. She replied with a similar sigh of her own.
>
> These two lovers, for they became so in that instant, heard and understood each other.][9]

Entendirent, in this context, is a pun, and a happy one, signifying both "heard" and "understood." When the two have found a way to communicate face to face, the same kind of language persists between them: "Ils se touchent; ils gardent le silence; ils laissent cependant échapper quelques mots mal articulés" [They touched each other. They remained silent. And yet they let out a few poorly articulated words] (43). They have no need to adjust their language in order to adopt a "more historical tone," as in Diderot. Poor articulation, here, is more richly communicative than any other, and its utterance has been a crucial event in the story. At the same time, however, the narration that refers to inarticulacy remains itself quite "historical," and retains its polish.

In *Kanor* (1750), sighs have comparably dramatic effects. Babillon, the young heroine, appears for a moment to have been killed in a fall. This provokes from her would-be lover, the young Zaaf, a tragic cry that is modulated into a deep sigh: "il s'aperçut qu'elle ne respirait plus; il fit un cri terrible et douloureux et, en s'approchant encore davantage, il ne put retenir un soupir profond" [He noticed that she was no longer breathing. He let out a terrible cry of pain, and drawing closer, could not hold back a deep sigh].[10] That he should go from a cry to a sigh may well be the mark of parody, since it allows the story to move between two registers of effusive language, but it demonstrates nonetheless the power of inarticulate sounds to effect narrative transformation, for the sigh, which is said to come from deep within the prince—"[il] partait du saisissement et de la tendresse de son cœur" [it came from the shock and affection of his heart] (127)—reaches the princess and revives her, bringing about the happiest of erotic confluences:

ce souffle brûlant parut ranimer son amante et lui rendre la vie; ses yeux s'entrouvrirent et, à son tour, elle soupira si juste, que le petit souffle qui partait de son cœur vint se mêler et se confondre avec un second soupir, tout de feu, que le charme de la retrouver vivante tira de l'âme du Prince.

[this burning breath seemed to revive his lover and bring her back to life. Her eyelids fluttered, and she in turn sighed so appropriately that the little breath that came from her heart joined and mixed with a second, fiery sigh that the delight of finding her alive drew from the soul of the prince.] (127)

The careful numbering and the playfully detailed physics, when applied to zephyr-like sighs, account for the production of what we can identify as full-blown effects of love: "Ces souffles si disproportionnés s'unirent, à peu près comme une vapeur légère, comme le plus doux zéphyr s'unirait à un tourbillon impétueux. C'était précisément cette union et ce mélange, qui étaient le talisman décisif" [These disproportionate breaths were united, almost as a light vapor, the slightest of zephyrs, would be united with an impetuous whirlwind. This union and this mixture were exactly what was required as the decisive talisman] (127).

In *Les Nonnes galantes*, which also dates from the mid-eighteenth century, we find the sigh once again revealing the heroine's secret "trouble," the unease of desire, and her lack of self-control. The man who is with her has no trouble interpreting this as a symptom: "Cette tendre émotion de sa jeune maîtresse ne valait-elle pas bien pour lui la plus flatteuse déclaration?" [Was not this tender emotion in his young mistress tantamount for him to the most flattering declaration?].[11] Indeed, in this novel such behavior is given a certain status, and a conventional place, by the existence within the convent of a "room of sighs":

> Et le lecteur remarquera que jamais endroit ne fut mieux nommé: ce cabinet, en effet, qui était au milieu du jardin, ne paraissait destiné qu'à être le secret confident des secrètes peines des jeunes nonnes amoureuses. C'était là où elles allaient se rappeler le souvenir de bien des moments heureux trop rapidement écoulés, ou se plaindre des obstacles que le sort opposait à leurs tendres désirs.

> [The reader will observe that no place was ever better named. This small room in the middle of the garden seemed destined only to be the secret confidant of the secret sufferings of young nuns in love. It was here that they came to recall the memories of happy moments that had been all too fleeting, or to complain of the obstacles that fate put in the way of their tender desires.] (120)

There is thematic room here for that other, parallel form of confession, the erotic sigh, gathered and concentrated in its own topical place.

Théophile Gautier's *La Morte amoureuse* (1836), for all its haunting mystery, performs a remarkably straightforward thematic reprise of the sigh as declaration. The narrator-hero, a priest, is summoned to the bedside of a dying, indeed apparently dead woman whose identity is unknown to him. To his surprise and deep regret, this woman proves to be Clarimonde, the one he had loved and lost, at the moment of his entry into the priesthood. Struck by the "strange event of chance" that has led him to find her once again just as he appears to lose her forever, he expresses his regret in the most natural (or most culturally apposite) bodily manner: "un soupir de regret s'échappa de ma poitrine" [a sigh of regret came from my breast]. This subdued expression of desire, by a further, perhaps more productive, coincidence, is answered by another sigh. Is it, he wonders, just his own sigh echoing around the bedroom, or is this a second sigh, emanating from the "dead" woman in response to his own? The echo itself is again the decisive phenomenon, and the indication that their love has been literally revived.[12]

Erotic fiction that is both more vulgar and more challenging, as it develops at the end of the eighteenth century, includes such narrative effects as those produced by the revealing sigh, while extending the range of bodily expressions and, in particular, representing the impact of such expressions on the writing itself. Gentle sighs may stand euphemistically, in polished fiction, for more forceful utterances and more substantive bodily emissions, but the point to be noted for a thematics and poetics of climax is that they stand in the same narrative place. In more vulgar stories, the sigh is not necessarily exhaled through the noble orifice, as we find in the following episode from Andréa de Nerciat's *Les Aphrodites* (1793): "Déjà le comte, dans un moment de délire assaisonné des exclamations les plus passionnées, est allé jusqu'à déposer un baiser fixe et mouillant sur cette bouche impure de laquelle, en pareil cas, il serait disgracieux d'obtenir un soupir" [Already the Count, in a moment of folly seasoned with the most passionate exclamations, had gone so far as to place a lingering wet kiss on that other, impure mouth from which, in such circumstances, it would have been uncouth to call forth a sigh].[13] Yet this jocose symmetry, parallel to that of *Les Bijoux indiscrets*, reveals in its own way that the narrative force of bodily emissions in late-eighteenth-century erotic stories of a more vulgar sort builds on an established thematic. Nerciat maintains the value of exclamatory expression as one of the marks of *délire*, and of passion. A sigh, as later said in *Casablanca,* is still a sigh. However delicate and playful, however uncontrolled or even obscene, the sigh is equivalent, for its decisiveness, to other forms of ejaculation. When, in *La Nouvelle Academie des dames* (1774?), two lovers are locked together in the most passionate embrace, desire and pleasure pass between them in a mingling of sighs and a liquefaction of breath that give full erotic substance to respiration: "une bouche étroitement collée sur la sienne lui communiquait tous mes soupirs; sa langue était un trait qui faisait passer chez moi tout le feu qui le consumait" [a mouth that was tightly glued to his communicated all my sighs directly to him. His tongue was a dart that passed into me all the fire that burned within him].[14] Sighs and exclamations may be no less profuse here than in the *Ragionamenti*, but they are now no longer countable because they form an erotic flux. The tongue, in this context, is a sexual organ, whose dominant role reflects the directly communicative value that has come to be invested in inarticulate utterance.

The language of sighs and cries is able to function discursively and thematically for the precise reason that it is a language, no matter how spontaneous or unprecedented its manifestations may seem. Indeed, by a paradox I have already alluded to, the written sigh, the written exclamation signifies in this way because it codifies breathing and breathlessness. This point seems to have escaped Michel Camus, even as he was accurately identifying the linguistic patterns. In a preface to *Le Triomphe des religieuses, ou les nones babillardes* (1748), Camus distinguishes the habitually seductive discourse of polite exchange, carried on even in bed, from that which marks "the erotic acme or *raptus*." The latter is characterized by "des petits points spasmodiques" [little spasmodic dots] that disturb the flow of civilized conversation. The cause of this disruption, says Camus, is something profoundly unspeakable: "La langue est impuissante à rendre compte de ce qui, par nature, dans l'intensité même de l'acte d'amour, échappe à toute formulation ou à toute expression adéquate. C'est le feu même de la vie qui est passé sous silence. . . . Le langage de l'esprit doit s'articuler sur le langage du corps pour en arriver à satisfaire la faim sexuelle" [Language is powerless to render that which, by nature, in the very intensity of the act of love, is beyond formulation or expression. The very fire of life is then left unspoken. The language of the mind must be articulated with the language of the body in order to satisfy its sexual hunger].[15] This analysis seems to me not so much wrong as unsubtle, in that it fails to mark a historical distinction between libertine discourse of the eighteenth century and a full-fledged Romantic understanding of Desire. To speak, as Camus does, of the interruption of language under the compulsion of inner fire and sexual hunger is to fail to notice that there is also a language of interruption helping the reader to evoke these secret forces of compulsion. More to the point, it is also almost certainly an overinterpretation of the way ejaculatory language works in *Le Tri-*

omphe des religieuses, or for that matter *La Nuit et le moment*, assimilating them to a later thematics that features (and articulates) unspeakable moments of overwhelming truth. More helpful are the remarks of Jean Marie Goulemot in a preface to *La Messaline française* (1789). Goulemot notes that what he calls "cette difficulté presque ontologique à exprimer la jouissance" [the almost ontological difficulty of expressing pleasure] is partly overcome by the use of an established set of adjectives and nouns that are "strictly coded," and by "les points de suspension . . . comme si la jouissance ne parvenait à s'exprimer que par l'abolition de ce qui avait projet de l'exprimer, le récit lui-même. Les points de suspension, les blancs typographiques sont autant de signes pour désigner ce que les mots sont impuissants à dire" [suspension marks, as if pleasure only managed to express itself through the abolition of that which had aimed to express it, the narrative itself. Suspension marks and typographical blanks are so many signs for designating what words are powerless to say].[16] This is not a definitive failure of language, as Goulemot rightly observes. It is the "constat d'un échec . . . qui finit, par une dialectique propre à l'effet d'écriture, par se donner à lire comme une expression réussie" [recognition of a failure that eventually, by a dialectic proper to the writing effect, offers itself for reading as a successful expression] (291). Gaëtan Brulotte, like Goulemot, insists quite properly on the "as if" when speaking of the marks of inarticulacy. The exclamations, the poorly articulated sounds, and the suspension marks all function "comme pour mimer les balbutiements, les bafouillements, les bégaiements de la conscience évanouissante" [as if to mimic the stuttering and stammering of consciousness losing control].[17] Yet Brulotte speaks somewhat artlessly of the "repercussions" of the *à-dire* on the *dire*—that is, the manner in which the difficulty of expression experienced by the characters impacts on the language of the text (137). This fails to take account of the obverse: in a history seeking to avoid anachronism, we need at least to allow, as the eighteenth century regularly did, that representation is a process whereby the *dire* has repercussions on the *à-dire*. Eighteenth-century libertine writing continually puts forward something modern readers might wish to identify as difficulty of self-expression occasioned by pleasure, but this difficulty is domesticated by semiotic etiquette and reproduced as a set of stylized routines.

A stronger challenge to erotic representation, one that will not be satisfied with classical libertine convention, is pronounced by the narrator of Nerciat's *Le Diable au corps* (1803). What must be written out are not so much the words passing between lovers, as all the subverbal things that characterize amorous exchange at its most passionately vigorous: "Où trouver un historien qui, vraiment digne d'écrire les fastes du *monde foutant*, serait capable de saisir les mots, les demi-mots, les accents, les soupirs, les sanglots mille fois plus éloquents que les plus belles paroles?" [Where can we find a historian who is truly worthy of these festivities of the *fucking society*, and able to capture the words, the half words, the tones of voice, the sighs and the sobs that are a thousand times more eloquent than fine words?].[18] A historian worthy of the task would achieve a "historical tone" by conveying the flow of half-words: unlike Diderot's Sultan, he would render the intermittent flow directly in all its communicative power. Nerciat's reflexivity is, of course, to be read here as a playful rhetorical gesture, setting before his reader and himself the image of eloquent babble as the true language of fucking. There is still something classical in this concern with eloquence and in the debate about poetics that is allowed to go on in the novel. Yet at the same time he begins to glorify the subverbal in ways that would have been unthinkable fifty years earlier, inviting us to focus on the aesthetic qualities (now) inherent in the semi-articulate. Two lovers are described in another of his novels as communicating in a language that is more eloquent than that of the most polished rhetorician: "ils ne peuvent plus proférer que des accents confus, mille fois plus éloquents que les plus beaux tours de force de l'esprit académique" [They can only speak in confused tones, which are a thousand times more eloquent than the figures of academic wit].[19] Not words but *accents*—meaningful sounds or qualities of voice—are the matter, the communicative substance that passes between truly eloquent lovers.

Whether or not there is a drama of profundity at work here, whether we ought to feel anguish at the supposed ontological difficulty of expression is a moot point. Most of the eighteenth century seems generally to regard breathless language in much the same way as it does crumpled skirts or half-laced bodices, fluttering eyelashes or rosy cheeks: all are revealing in the same pleasurable way. They are to be enjoyed as marks of an erotically coded *désordre*. Yet the insistence on eloquence that we find in Nerciat and in some of his early nineteenth-century contemporaries is a step towards a rather different understanding: the notion of a superior erotic language made of something other than, better than words. Pigault-Lebrun's narrator, in *La Folie espagnole* (1801), invites us to imagine a language that is rhetorically beyond all others because it is morphologically and phonetically on the near side of words: "soupirs brûlants sont le seul langage qu'ils emploient: quel autre vaudrait celui-là?" [burning sighs are the only language they use. What other language would be equal to that?].[20] What other, indeed? Presumably not that which we read in *La Folie espagnole*. The nineteenth century will soon be troubled, in its very concern with the literary, by the thrust of this question: how is it to harness for erotic narrative the power of the semi-articulate? It hardly suffices to talk about such language, although it does happen quite often that texts are content to refer to the eloquence of inarticulacy without seeking to perform it in any way. This happens typically in novels of the late nineteenth century that gesture toward such language without "evoking" it in any literal sense. Is that because to write out breathlessness would detract from the generic dignity sought by many fin-de-siècle erotic novels? Instead of an attempt to render an unarticulated bodily truth, they tend to offer lyrical idealizations of the subverbal. *Demi-Volupté* (1900), by Ernest La Jeunesse, glories in the fact that the lovers' cries are freed from signification: "ils ne parlèrent pas: de petits cris pas humains leur montaient aux lèvres, en la saveur des baisers: de petits cris l'un pour l'autre, se répondant en même temps comme des oiseaux et comme des frissons de la foudre" [They did not speak. Little non-human cries came from their lips, among the flavor of kisses: little cries meant for one another, answering each other at the same time like birds or flashes of lightning].[21] In René Saint-Médard's *L'Orgie moderne* (1905), the absence of any comprehensible code allows such (half-)talk to be qualified as celestial: "Leurs bouches étaient unies, nouées dans un baiser sans fin, et ne se séparaient que pour proférer des onomatopées sans signification dans notre langue, mais qui doivent être l'idiome du ciel" [Their mouths were united, bound in an endless kiss, and they separated only to speak onomatopoeias that have no meaning in our language, but must be the language of heaven].[22] Novelistic

writing of this kind seems to have given up all hope of espous-
ing or reflecting erotic language, being content to indulge in a
kind of metalinguistic nostalgia.

Talking about the inarticulate is not the most demanding
task, nor even the most characteristic of erotic narrative.
Beyond the blandly thematic, beneath and around it, a veritable poetics of disjointedness is often at work. We have already
seen that the practice of exclamatory writing, established to
some degree since Aretino, was not authorized, not fully owned
by narratorial discourse in such texts as *Les Bijoux indiscrets*
and *La Nuit et le moment*. The fact is nonetheless that it persisted and became more elaborate. It has to be said that the
formal features of such writing remain uncomplicated, nay
rudimentary: lines of text are punctuated by exclamation and
suspension marks, the alternation of which seems to constitute
a rhythm of emphatic disjointedness. Eighteenth- and nineteenth-century writing often displays these features not to signify undisciplined conversation or festive noise, as in Aretino
and his immediate successors, but to echo the accents or the
voice of pleasure. These formal traits appear well established
by about 1740 and are maintained into the nineteenth century.
Most of them are present in the stylized representations of
spontaneity that occur in Crébillon's novels. Montade, a character in *Tableaux des mœurs du temps dans les différents âges de
la vie* (1750), utters and owns his pleasure in repetitive first
person verbs: "J'achève . . . j'achève . . . je n'en puis plus" [I am
finishing . . . I am finishing . . . I cannot last any longer]. To
which his lover is said to reply, for even extreme pleasure is
conversational in Crébillon: "Je meurs de plaisir! . . ." [I am
dying of pleasure! . . .].[23] It is as if the sentences were always
dying and finishing, compelled to do so by the circumstances of
their enunciation—as if the force of the exclamation itself
caused the suspension. More complicated and sustained instances can be recounted, and even greater disorder presented,
but it will be rhetorically more of the same.

A degree or two beyond Crébillon's text in this regard is *Le
Triomphe des religieuses* (1748), which is dotted with exclamations, and which actually breaks up the longer words used to
speak pleasure: "Eh! . . . Eh! . . . Eh! . . . tu me tues . . . ar . . . rête,
je me . . . meurs" [Hey! . . . Hey! . . . Hey! . . . You are kil . . . ling
me . . . Stop . . . it, I am dy . . . ing].[24] Disintegration into mono-

syllabic elements is quite widespread in pornographic writing of the later eighteenth century, and is still to be found in modern texts of the same type. In his pornographic writing, Restif de la Bretonne seems to favor full-voiced, open vowels, adding to the usual punctuation a few circumflex accents for wider stretching of the mouth, and greater sonority: "Je pa . . . ars! . . . Je décha . . . arge! . . . Hââh! . . ." [I am goo . . . one! . . . I am discha . . . arging! . . . Hââh! . . .] (*L'Anti-Justine* [1798]).[25] Here, even the monosyllabic *pars* cannot resist the word-rending force of the heart. And in *Lettres galantes et philosophiques de deux nones* (1797), we find a striking utterance about—and performance of—breathing: "Mon cœur . . . Hélas! . . . mon cœur pal . . . pite, et mon . . . ha . . . leine ex . . . pire" [My heart . . . Alas! . . . My heart is pal . . . pitating, and my brea . . . th ex . . . piring].[26] Such breathlessness may have something broadly in common with the racy dialogues of Aretino's Nanna and Pippa, as Gustave Colline pointed out, but it is importantly different from them in at least one respect. The language of desire and pleasure claims to be expiring at its high point, uttering as if with its last breath the death of language—except that this death is repeated endlessly, and repeated in language. When the drama recurs from page to page, and from line to line, what is spoken is no more than a *petite mort* of the most routine kind.

The second half of the eighteenth century understands exclamations and interruptions as signs of an erotic state that it often refers to as *vivacité*. A veritable set of symptoms now makes if possible to identify desire as a (temporary) condition of the whole body: suddenness of movement, quickening of the blood, breathlessness of speech. Indeed, a sudden change of state is itself to be read as a symptom: "Les passages imperceptibles de la tranquillité aux mouvements les plus vifs, de l'indifférence au désir, n'étaient plus des énigmes pour moi" [The imperceptible shifts from stillness to the most lively movement, and from indifference to desire, were no longer riddles to me] (*Histoire de dom Bougre* [1741]).[27] Sometimes, the eyes reveal all: "ses yeux m'avaient déjà prévenue, ils m'avaient peint la vivacité de ses désirs" [his eyes had already enlightened me; they portrayed the liveliness of his desires] (*La Nouvelle Académie des dames* [1774]).[28] At other times the inner circulation of fire shows itself on the outside in a whole range of ways: "son teint était animé, ses yeux me lançaient des regards perçants, qui m'obligeaient de perdre contenance chaque fois que ma vue se portait sur la sienne; et la rapidité de ses gestes, de ses mouvements, ne laissait que trop apercevoir le feu dont il était dévoré" [his complexion was bright; his eyes cast piercing looks at me, making me lose my self-control each time I saw him looking at me; and the rapidity of his gestures and movements made it only too clear that a fire was consuming him from within] (*Amélie, ou Les Ecarts de ma jeunesse*).[29] When this state is evoked in first person narration, the description itself tends to be symptomatically disjointed: "mes genoux fléchirent, ma voix s'éteignit, j'étais absorbée; cependant je brûlais de mille feux" [my knees buckled, and my voice failed me. I was absorbed. At the same time, I was alight with a thousand fires] (*Vénus en rut* [c. 1785]).[30]

With the full development of a Romantic discourse of desire as rapidity of circulation and intense fullness of the body, the *cri* will come to be powerfully expressed in metaphors of substance. Whereas eighteenth-century texts often played with the equivalence of sighs and other kinds of emission, allowing for their succession and alternation, Romantic narrative makes all expressions coincide in time as symptoms of the body in climax. The materialization is spoken as a claim and claimed to be spoken in Nogaret's *L'Arétin français* (1787):

> . . . Ah! la liqueur divine
> Circule à grands flots, s'achemine . . .
> Es-tu prêt? . . . Je décharge . . . Ah! mon
> Dieu! que c'est bon!

> [Ah! the divine liquor
> Is circulating in great waves, and making its way . . .
> Are you ready? . . . I am unloading . . . Ah! My
> God! How sweet it is!][31]

When circulation reaches its point of greatest activity, erotic physiology is said to compel the utterance, "I discharge." The economy that builds up sperm within the body is connected in narrative with the very capacity to speak, allowing (and requiring) oral outpouring to coincide with genital emission. This is never more clear or more strongly overdetermined than in the favorite exclamation of Revolutionary eroticism, *"foutre!"*[32] Through the word's double sense, as an obscene verb meaning to copulate and a vulgar name for sperm, *"foutre!"* celebrates the fulfilment of desire while naming the substance that is its most direct physiological expression. The term is not a new exclamation, and is in fact mentioned, although not properly uttered, in *Tableaux des mœurs du temps dans les différents âges de la vie* (1750), as a mark of masculine conversation,[33] but it is only at the end of the century that it commands a place in narrative as a sign of discharge.

Whereas writers such as Crébillon talked about such forceful enunciation and even alluded to obscenity without actually performing it, writing at the turn of the century goes a step further. Nerciat manages to produce the obscenity of *"foutre!"* as the most telling verbal symptom, all the while surrounding it with protocols of tact. On one occasion, he seems to respect the old libertine etiquette, referring to the double meaning without actually writing out the exclamation, although the reference and its narrative significance are unmistakable: "[Hilarion] tombe sans connaissance après avoir mâlement articulé (soit plaisir, soit douleur) le *mot* grenadier de ce dont il vient de si bien réaliser la chose" [Hilarion fell unconscious, after pronouncing the grenadiers' word that corresponds to the thing he had just carried out with such success].[34] Whether he feels pleasure or pain matters infinitely less for narrative than the intensity of his experience. And in expressing what he feels, he utters "the word" that all true males come to utter in that extreme circumstance, whether they be soldiers or, like Hilarion himself, men of the cloth. Indeed, such is the natural compulsion at work here that the same manly expression is heard to come spilling out of the mouths of Nerciat's most vigorous female characters. The Marquise, in *Les Aphrodites*, is about to engage with a young nobleman who has made his way into her apartment disguised as a servant. Here is the imperative of desire with which she summons him to action: "Foutre! s'écrie-t-elle, mets-le donc" ["Fuck!" she exclaimed. "Just put it in"]. After this has been blurted out, Nerciat's narratorial tact comes belatedly into play, so that the unbridled directness of the Marquise's talk is followed by a lengthily apologetic "editorial" note, in which the narrator invites his readers to a kind of brainstorming session, pretending to hope that they will contribute more seemly expressions that might satisfy the double exigencies of truthful vigor and sociable refinement:

Je déteste (comme sans doute tous les lecteurs délicats) ces malheureux moments où des femmes dont on a la meilleure opinion, et
qui ont été bien élevées, s'abaissent aux indécences, à la brutalité du
plus ignoble vulgaire. . . . Je prie les gens d'esprit et ceux qui auront
l'expérience de ces sortes de conjonctures de m'adresser quelques
tournures de bon ton, quelques jolies phrases qui, sans affaiblir les
situations, puissent suppléer à des obscénités, véritables taches
dans cet historique et très moral ouvrage. Nous avons essayé de *tri-
omphez donc . . . d'achevez ma défaite . . .* de *faites-moi mourir . . .* ,
etc. Tout cela ne nous a pas paru valoir cette énergique *foutre! mets-
le donc!* . . . Quel dommage qu'on ne puisse accommoder la bien-
séance qu'aux dépens de l'expression ou de la vérité! . . .

[I hate (like all delicate readers, no doubt) these unfortunate moments where women of whom one has the highest opinion, and
who are well mannered, stoop to indecency, to vulgar brutishness
at its most ignoble. . . . I beg people of intelligence and those who
have experienced this kind of circumstance to send me some distinguished expressions, some pretty phrases that will not weaken
these situations, but will take the place of obscenities, for they are
very much a stain on this historical and highly moral work. We
tried "Wreak your will . . . ," "Complete your triumph . . . ," "Bring
me to my end . . . ," etc. None of them seemed to be equal in value
to that energetic "Fuck! Just put it in! . . ." What a pity that propriety can only be satisfied at the expense of expressiveness or
truth! . . .][35]

We can note in passing that the direct expression of climactic
pleasure is deemed to be grossly unfeminine, thereby indicating
the extent to which the value of exclamation has narrowed and
intensified since Aretino. The main point to note, however, is
that the long-windedness of Nerciat's editorial comment does no
more than demonstrate, and apologize for, the superiority of
short-winded language in the representation of desire. He feigns
unease at the stain made on "historical" narrative by this exclamation, but that is merely a polite way of negotiating change,
and insisting that ejaculation have its place in the heart of the
story. It is no surprise to find the same woman and others exhal-
ing their "*foutre!*" at other times in these novels. The Comtesse is
heard to say "quite loudly": "Ah foutre! . . . fou . . . ou . . . tre! voilà
du plaisir . . ." [Ah Fuck! . . . Fu . . . u . . . uck! There's pleasure for
you . . .].[36] Such phrases are climactically overdetermined. They
are cries of pleasure in every sense: both immediate symptoms

of what is occurring within, and instantaneously reflexive celebrations of its occurrence.

In keeping with this materialization of voice, utterances can
assume all the qualities of bodily fluids. Sade's libertines, who
are eager consumers of the substances emanating from their
victims, can be seen to drink in sighs just as they might absorb
base forms of excreta.[37] Here is an example from *La Nouvelle
Justine* (1797), involving the monk Clément: "osant mêler
l'amour à ces moments d'effroi, sa bouche se colle sur celle de
Justine et veut respirer les soupirs qu'arrache la douleur" [he
dares to mix love with moments of fright, and his mouth adheres
to Justine's as he seeks to breathe in the sighs provoked from
her by pain].[38] Another scene from the same novel actually dramatizes the equivalence of tears and sperm, showing the two to
be produced at the same time, and in response to the same stimulus. Justine and Juliette have just learnt the tragic news of
their father's death, to which Justine responds, as is her wont,
by bursting into tears. Juliette shows what she is made of, quite
literally, by bursting into another substance. She brings herself
to a climax of pleasure in front of her weeping sister, sighing as
she "ejaculates": "Poursuivant ensuite son opération, la putain
soupira; et son jeune foutre, éjaculé sous les yeux baissés de la
vertu, tarit la source des larmes que, sans cette opération, elle
eût peut-être versées comme sa sœur" [Going on with her exercise, the whore sighed, and her young *foutre*, ejaculated before
the downcast eyes of virtue, dried up the source of the tears that
she might have otherwise shed like her sister] (*La Nouvelle Justine* 6:34).[39] Juliette has found something stronger to do than to
weep: she mingles sighs with "sperm," and gives vent to both
grief and pleasure in the same action. The "mixing" of love and
terror that occurs in Clément's encounter with Justine and the
coincidence of tears and sperm in the contrastive sisterhood of
Justine and Juliette can both be read as examples of a practice
of narrative intensity that develops at the very end of the eighteenth century. We see the coming together of narrative interest
and physiological substance in ejaculatory moments. This is
what one might call the qualitative dimension of intensity: the
fact that sexual discharge is loaded with other kinds of significance than the merely physiological.

A further contribution to intensity, dialectically related to this
one, is the production of "spontaneous" blasphemy at moments

of extreme pleasure. In this domain, Sade's libertine heroes are unrivalled virtuosi, although the range of variations is rather limited. Dolmancé uses the classically impious "sacredieu!" (*La Philosophie dans le boudoir* 3:437), but adds to it more richly offensive couplings of the sexual and the divine, such as the following: "Sacré-foutu dieu, comme j'ai du plaisir! . . ." [Holy fucking God, what pleasure this is! . . .] (3:439). His densest and most concentrated ejaculation is the quintessentially obscene "foutredieu!" (3:437), which constitutes a metaphysical counteraffirmation at, and as, the point of greatest intensity. Blasphemy, in this instance, is both a source and a symptom of pleasure.

One of the functions of exclamation in Sade is to produce intensity as climactic coincidence by calling for it imperiously. Not for his master libertines the insidious subtlety of the confessor's art, nor the whimsical short-circuit of Mangogul's borrowed magic. What they require and achieve is a proper timing of discharge somewhat akin to the sighing in unison described by Aretino's Nanna. But whereas in the *Ragionamenti* this event was a happy coincidence, preceded and followed by less successful ones, in *La Philosophie dans le boudoir* it reliably occurs on time, in response to orders that are themselves powerful ejaculations. Dolmancé exhorts his colleagues to discharge all at the same moment: "Chevalier, tu t'emportes, je le sens. . . . Attends-moi! . . . attends-nous! . . . O mes amis, ne déchargeons qu'ensemble: c'est le seul bonheur de la vie! . . ." [Chevalier, you are getting carried away, I can feel it. . . . Wait for me! . . . Wait for us! . . . Oh my friends, let's make sure we unload together: it's life's only happiness! . . .] (*La Philosophie dans le boudoir* 3:468). And when such a moment is about to arrive, the desire for unison spills forth, this time from the Chevalier, as an urgent command: "Déchargez! . . . déchargez toutes deux, mon foutre va s'y joindre! . . . Il coule! . . . Ah! sacredieu! . . ." [Unload! . . . Unload both of you. My *foutre* will soon join yours! . . . It's flowing! . . . Ah! Sacredieu! . . .] (3:458). As the first person singular, "je décharge!" appropriates the second person and expands compellingly into the plural—"déchargez! déchargeons!"—the utterance of pleasure comes out as the call for a particular form of narrative. In much the same way, the heroine of Gamiani longs for, indeed cries out for, the pleasure of crying out: "se toucher, se mêler, s'exhaler corps et âme dans un soupir, un seul cri, un cri d'amour!

Fanny! Fanny! c'est le ciel!" [To touch each other, to mingle, to feel body and soul expiring in a sigh, a single cry, a cry of love! Fanny! Fanny! It's heaven!].[40] What is expressed thus is not just the climax of desire but the desire for climax.

As part of the developing thematics of intensity, in which Sade's work plays a key role, the sheer quantity of ejaculation is deemed to be an object of interest. Loud exclamations are no more absent from earlier erotic narrative than gentle sighs, but loudness appears now to take on new value. In *Thérèse philosophe* (1748), which remains in touch with a classical narrative tradition, a former prostitute who is recounting various incidents and eccentricities from her career tells a story about a particularly vociferous bishop with whom she had had dealings:

> Imagine-toi que, soit par un goût de prédilection, soit par un défaut d'organisation, dès que sa Grandeur sentait les approches du plaisir, elle mugissait, et criait à haute voix *haï! haï! haï!* en forçant le ton à proportion de la vivacité du plaisir dont il était affecté, de sorte qu'on aurait pu calculer les gradations du chatouillement que ressentait le gros et ample prélat, par les degrés de force qu'il employait à mugir *haï! haï! haï!* Tapage qui, lors de la décharge de Monseigneur, aurait pu être entendu à mille pas à la ronde, sans la précaution que son valet de chambre prenait de matelasser les portes et les fenêtres de l'appartement épiscopal.

> [Well, either because it was his preferred taste or because of something in his make-up, as soon as His Grace felt the onset of pleasure, he bellowed, and cried out at the top of his voice, "Aye! Aye! Aye!" increasing the volume in proportion to the strength of pleasure he was feeling, in such a way that one could have calculated the gradation of stimulation experienced by the stout prelate, according to the degree of loudness with which he bellowed, "Aye! Aye! Aye!" This noise would have been heard a mile away during Monsignor's discharge, were it not for the fact that his valet took the precaution of padding the doors and windows of the episcopal apartment.][41]

All this is a *goût*, a *manie*, a diverting eccentricity told as one of a series, and providing the possibility of playful mensuration. It makes of the bishop a potentially laughable object of scandal rather than a champion of desire.

It is amusing and instructive to observe that several sentences from *Thérèse philosophe* are reproduced almost verbatim in *Gamiani* eighty-five years later. To talk of plagiarism here is hardly relevant since the thematic significance of the description has changed in a quite fundamental way. This has now become a description of Gamiani's outstanding erotic performance—in this particular scene, with animals—in which the voice of desire takes on superlative qualities, reaching new heights of frenzied utterance: "La comtesse criait à haute voix: Hai! hai! hai! forçant toujours le ton à proportion de la vivacité du plaisir. On arrait pu calculer les gradations du chatouillement que ressentait cette effrénée Calymanthe" [The Countess cried out at the top of her voice, "Aye! Aye! Aye!" increasing the volume in proportion to the strength of pleasure she was feeling. You could have calculated the gradations of stimulation felt by this frenzied Calymantha].[42] Of another young woman in the same novel, it is said: "Sa joie, ses transports éclatent en une gamme de oh! et de ah! mais sur un ton si élevé que la mère entend" [Her joy and delight burst out in a scale of "oh"s and "ah"s so loud that her mother heard them] (123). The true voice of pleasure in this context is loud, high-pitched, and spectacularly "indiscreet," and the range of exclamations is the thrilling scale of an individual vocal performance rather than the din of carnival.

Between the time of *Thérèse philosophe* and that of *Gamiani*, Sade's fiction had helped add thematic value to the sheer quantity of ejaculation. His heroes distinguish themselves by their stentorian utterances of pleasure. Here is Juliette's description of the unparalleled "crises" of Durand:

> Rien n'égalait les crises voluptueuses de la Durand. De mes jours je n'avais vu de femme décharger ainsi: non seulement elle élançait son foutre comme un homme, mais elle accompagnait cette éjaculation de cris si furieux, de blasphèmes tellement énergiques, et de spasmes si violents, qu'on eût cru qu'elle tombait en épilepsie.

> [Nothing could compare with the voluptuous crises of Durand. In all my life I had never seen a woman discharge like that. Not only did she shoot out *foutre* like a man, but she accompanied her ejaculation with such furious cries, such energetic blasphemy, and such violent spasms, that one would have thought she was having an epileptic fit.] (*Histoire de Juliette* 9:428)

We should not believe, of course, that nothing equals the force of Durand's discharge: it is matched quite regularly by almost every other Sadian master libertine. Certainly, Gernande's dramatic performances, in the different versions of Justine's story, are described in lavish detail, but most of the others are also accorded the honor of quantitative hyperbole. In *Les Cent Vingt Journées de Sodome*, the Duc de Blangis comes down to breakfast expressing astonishment at the sound emitted by his partner in crime Curval: "Peut-on brailler, peut-on hurler comme tu le fais en déchargeant! dit le duc à Curval, en le revoyant le vingt-trois au matin." . . . "—Ah! parbleu, dit Curval, c'est bien à toi qu'on entend d'une lieue à m'adresser un pareil reproche!" ["How can anyone bray and shout the way you do when unloading?!" said the Duke, when he saw him again on the morning of the twenty-third. "By damn!" said Curval, "it is hardly up to you who can be heard from a league away to reproach me with such a thing!"] (1:292).

This last example displays yet another way in which the confluence of exclamations contributes to the thematics of intensity. Blangis and Curval practice what might be called second-order ejaculation, marveling at each others' utterances. They comment on, draw attention to, and echo (quite literally) the vocal power of each other's climax. Exclamations of this sort, in the form of narratorial cries of wonder, occur from time to time in earlier literature, and *Kanor* (1750) provides a nicely lyrical example: "Quel aimable désordre dans les discours! Quel trouble enchanteur dans les sens!" [What charming disorder in their talk! What enchanting disturbance in their senses!].[43] But this is a gently reflexive account of disorder, passed on in the narration itself. It is quite another matter when novelistic characters utter cries of admiration that surround and enhance great moments of intensity. In that sense, Mme. de Saint-Ange plays to perfection the role of the subordinate libertine when she says to Dolmancé, just after he has uttered a string of libidinal exclamations: "Comme tu blasphèmes, mon ami!" [How you blaspheme, my friend!] (*La Philosophie dans le boudoir* 3:437). She is provoked by the force of his utterance into her own, tributary exclamation just as the hypothetical admiring reader is doubtless supposed to be. "How he exclaims!" we should all exclaim, as we follow this model, echoing in chorus with the intensity of climactic pleasure.[44]

Such intensity leaves an opportunity for irony, and that opportunity is nicely exploited, in a way that defines and mocks the theme, in Gautier's *Mademoiselle de Maupin* (1835). The climax of this story is in fact just the kind of powerful convergence of narrative and erotic interest that we have been considering. The hero, d'Albert, discovers finally that the beautiful young man to whom he has been disturbingly attracted for some time is in fact a young woman in disguise. He finds out the truth about Mademoiselle de Maupin, and fulfills his desire for her, when she obligingly comes to visit him in his room, dressed in all her feminine splendor. Now this event provokes absolutely no cries of wonder on the part of the narrator. Indeed the reader is reminded that such a reaction would be quite out of place since the truth has long since been made apparent in the telling. The practice of secondary ejaculation is inverted, in a display of narratorial composure: "qui fut étonné? —ce n'est ni moi ni vous, car vous et moi nous étions préparés de longue main à cette visite; ce fut d'Albert qui ne s'y attendait pas le moins du monde" [Who was surprised? Not me or you, for we have been prepared for this visit. It was d'Albert, who was not expecting it in the least].[45] "Our" comfortable distance from the hero makes it possible to attend closely to his utterance of surprise—and presumably desire and pleasure—"Il fit un petit cri de surprise tenant le milieu entre oh! et ah! Cependant j'ai les meilleures raisons de croire qu'il tenait plus de ah! que de oh!" [He uttered a little cry of surprise situated about halfway between "Oh!" and "Ah!" Nonetheless, I have every reason to believe that it was more like an "Ah!" than an "Oh!"] (408). Not only is this *petit cri* at the opposite end of the scale from the shrieks of Gamiani or the bellowing of Gernande: the very fussiness with which it is described signifies irony, by leaving room for thoughtful attention to the exact phonetic qualities of the utterance. Such fine discrimination is foreign to, and subversive of, the discourse of spontaneous intensity.

Fin-de-siècle erotic narratives do not develop the poetics of inarticulacy to any degree, but they do heighten the thematic seriousness of exclamation by surrounding it with knowing medical discourse. Beyond Sade, beyond *Gamiani*, and sadly beyond irony, they tend to spell out the significance of erotic utterance as the revelation of sexual truth. *Le Roman de Violette* (1883) allows us to measure this thematic development with some precision because it has so many other features in common with the most classical erotic fiction, as I showed in *Geometry in the Boudoir*.[46] There is a drawn-out process of initiation in which the hero, a professor of medicine, supervises the sexual awakening of a beautiful child-woman who has come into his care by chance. He takes advantage of her infatuation with him in order to play the role of teacher and, eventually, of lover. For all its self-conscious gentleness, this process leads to an intense climax for Violette, and the climax is heard by a practiced, analytical ear. When the young woman cries out in pleasure, he hears the voice of the soul, hears the immanence of the soul in a bodily convulsion, and hears the true meaning of inarticulacy: "A partir de ce moment, ce ne fut plus de sa part que des cris inarticulés qui se terminèrent par un de [c]es longs spasmes où passe l'âme entière" [From that moment onward, she produced only inarticulate cries that ended in one of those long spasms in which the soul is fully expressed].[47] The profound truth comes spilling out in an avowal of illness, fire, and death: "C'est de la rage! c'est du feu! . . . Oh! . . . Oh! . . . je meurs . . . prends mon âme . . . tiens . . ." [It is rabies! It is fire! . . . Oh! . . . Oh! . . . I'm dying . . . Take my soul . . . Here it is . . .] (534). The narrator-hero has waited patiently for this moment. He has prepared the climax by ensuring that his pupil is sufficiently mature to experience the fullness of pleasure and to confess its fullness in the audible language of the psyche. Later in the novel, the hero displays the same alliance of voyeurism and medical know-how, when he overhears two women at the height of their pleasure. Their words are said to be "unintelligible," but he listens carefully to the "muffled sighs" and the "rattle of love" (*râle d'amour*). It is even possible for him to make out (*distinguer*) the name of a lover (578), for he hears all the key elements in what is uttered so breathlessly. The pleasure of women coincides perfectly with the intellectual satisfaction of the doctor hero, as the revealing sounds come gushing out. Their well-prepared and well-observed utterance makes pleasure and truth happen together.

Erotic narratives of the climactic kind do not just dramatize the utterance of pleasure: they confirm and indulge a particular form of knowledge that permits the confident recognition of symptoms. The symptoms in question are not to be thought of as transhistorical, for they vary considerably even across the eighteenth and nineteenth centuries. In the mid-eighteenth century, there is pleasure to be had in reading the signs of desire and pleasure in others, whether as *vivacité, langueur,* or the movement between them. But when, from about the time of the Revolution, desire is understood and represented as accumulated energy, demanding to be released through discharge, the old codified marks no longer suffice. Recognizing desire and its promise of pleasure in mid-eighteenth-century fiction was a subtle art, if a somewhat stylized one, involving the reading of half-elegant disorder. In contrast, many texts of revolutionary times affirm the task of recognition to be quite straightforward, although this apparent ease masks a fundamental difficulty—a difficulty aggravated, if not produced, by a newly constituted narrative order. Since the moment of pleasure is now taken to be the point about which meaning is organized, that moment must be quite distinctive. There must be no doubt that pleasure is occurring right at this time as the decisive event. But then, the question can be asked: How is the climactic pleasure of women to be discerned with the requisite clarity and certainty?

Brantôme, in *Les Dames galantes* (1666), did not make a problem out of this. He simply marveled at the extraordinary things that women had been said to do at times of great pleasure, providing a remarkably varied list of eccentricities, rather than a coherent description of symptoms:

J'ai ouy dire et conter à plusieurs amans advanturiers et bien fortunés qu'ils ont veu plusieurs dames demeurer ainsy esvanouyes et pasmées estans en ces doux alteres de plaisir; mais assez aysement pourtant retournoient à soy-mesme; que plusieurs, quand elles sont là, elles s'escrient: "Hélas! je me meurs!" Je croy que ceste mort leur est tres-douce. Il y en a d'autres qui contournent les yeux en la teste pour telle delectation, comme si elles devoient mourir de la grande mort, et se laissans aller comme du tout immobiles et insensibles. D'autres ay-je ouy-dire qui roidissent et tendent si violemment leurs nerfs, arteres et membres, qu'ils en engendrent la goute-crampe; comme d'une que j'ay ouy dire, qu'y estoit si subjecte qu'elle n'y pouvoit remedier. D'autres font peter leurs os, comme si on leur rehabilloit de quelque rompure.

[I have heard tell by some adventurous and successful lovers that they saw ladies faint and swoon in the sweet transformations of pleasure. But they came to quite easily after. Some, when they are in that state, exclaim, "Alas! I'm dying!" I believe that death to be a most pleasant one. Others roll their eyes and their heads about during pleasure, as if they were going to die a real death; they become quite still and unfeeling. I have heard of others who go rigid. Their nerves, arteries, and limbs are so taut that they cramp up completely. I have heard of one who was so given to this that she could do nothing to avoid it. Others have bones that crack, as if they were recovering from a fracture.][48]

Rather than telling a story, Brantôme is producing here a paradigmatic inventory whose very range is the main source of interest, and of descriptive pleasure, as in the earlier quote from Aretino. He is not seeking to identify the distinctive pleasure whose appearance will mark a narrative climax. Whatever he has to say about women's pleasure is marked by its extraordinary, perhaps even ludicrous, variety, but this old theme—la donna è mobile, even in this respect—will not serve the purpose of a strictly narrative eroticism of the kind that developed toward the end of the eighteenth century. These manifestations are too diverse and too scattered. What is needed so that climax can be seen to occur is a well-defined set of symptoms. Needing either to solve or deny this problem, texts at the end of the eighteenth century often do both of those things at once by committing to a thematics that is radically opposed to the wondrous diversity evoked by Brantôme and Aretino. They regularly describe women's pleasure as if it were recognizably singular, corresponding in every particular to that of men.

Male desire is never more conveniently visible, nor more truly physiological, than when it manifests itself organically as visible erection. Not for true revolutionaries the mincing subtleties of libertine discernment: republican eroticism responds best to the undeniable evidence of an erect organ. Here is an example in which rustic simplicity is itself endowed with erotic value, precisely for its directness: "Ce rustre frais et gaillard ne voyait point passer Claudinette dans le village qu'aussitôt son vit se redressât. Ce symptôme est aussi compréhensible pour un paysan que pour un citadin" [This green and hearty peasant could not see Claudinette going by in the village without having his prick immediately stand erect. That symptom is as comprehensible to a peasant as it is to a city dweller] (Décrets des sens sanctionnés par la volupté [1791]).[49] A woman can question a man's desire and be given the most literally tangible response: "Bandes-tu bien, mon ami? me dit-elle en appuyant sa bouche sur la mienne. . . . Pour toute réponse je pris sa main, que j'appuyai sur

mon vit" ["Are you nice and hard, my dear?" she asked me, pressing her mouth to mine. My only response was to take hold of her
hand and place it on my dick] (*L'Enfant du bordel* [1800]).[50] With
a symptom as clear as this, there can be no doubt about the business of eroticism. There are, of course, less rustic ways of making
the point that are just as unequivocal. The "declaration" of the
symptom can be described metaphorically, as in the following:
"Alfonse s'enflamme à loisir. Une sédition subite qui s'élève dans
le pantalon l'oblige enfin à prendre quelque arrangement qui
puisse sauver les apparences. Cette déclaration a été, dès le premier moment, saisie par la marquise, qui en a pris une teinte
animée dont l'effet est de la rendre d'une beauté céleste" [Alfonse
was alight. A sudden sedition in his trousers required him to
make some adjustment that might save appearances. The declaration was grasped by the Marquise from the first, and her complexion became so bright as to create in her an effect of celestial
beauty] (*Les Aphrodites*).[51] "Grasping" the symptom—if I may be
allowed an appropriately crude pun—is a perfectly straightforward thing. Even such euphemistic expressions as "désen-
chantement," whereby erection is characterized as the opposite
of ensorceled impotence,[52] do little to reshape the theme or even
take away its directness: this is merely a polite way of referring
to the same, singular, forthright symptom of desire. If women are
to be included in this convenient thematic arrangement, however, and their sexuality seen as leading from a similar strong
beginning to a similar conclusion, their physiology must be represented in such a way that their (ostensibly singular) pleasure
is available for recognition in the same way, at the same time, as
men's.

Applying this rudimentary thematics to the bodies of women
appears to twentieth-century eyes an imaginatively demanding
task—not to say a closely oppressive one.[53] Indeed, it is here
that the "truth" of late-eighteenth-century sexual knowledge appears intolerably perverse to modern readers, for texts of this
time seldom even recognize as problematic the assimilation of
female body to male. The same discourse is simply used, and the
same narrative economy worked out, for both sexes. A woman's
desire is manifest in her erect clitoris, available for examination
in a way that is parallel, if quantitatively inferior, to a man's.
The heroine of *Le Rideau levé, ou l'éducation de Laure* (1786)
describes the state of male and female colleagues in exactly

parallel ways: "Nous bandions tous encore, nos clitoris gonflés le démontraient aussi bien que la fermeté de leurs vits" [We still had a hard on. Our swollen clitorises showed that just as well as the firmness of their dicks].[54] The woman's desire is required to be demonstrable for the sake of narrative, just as her pleasure must eventually come bursting forth in the climactic discharge of female sperm.

This collapsing of sexual difference shocks modern commentators, for good reason, and may well have led many to a sense of historical estrangement. It is unfortunate, however, that the estrangement (and the critique) have often been focused exclusively on Sade, who is thus transformed from modernist hero into misogynist villain in a way that further exaggerates the monumental, canonical status of his work. The attacks on Sade that I am about to quote are telling, coherent ones: they are merely lacking the historical dimension that might have come from acknowledging the extension of this discourse far beyond one author's work. Anne-Marie Dardigna expresses derision at Sade's representation of female pleasure, quoting some of Sade's favored utterances with exclamation marks of her own: "Certes, Juliette, Clairwil, la Dubois, la Durand, Charlotte et Olympe jouissent, mais c'est chaque fois à la manière des hommes: elles 'déchargent,' elles 'éjaculent!'" [It is true that Juliette, Clairwil, Dubois, Durand, Charlotte, and Olympe experience pleasure, but they do so every time in the way that men do: they "unload," they "ejaculate!"].[55] Andrea Dworkin makes the same point succinctly when she says: "even in such a symptomatic detail as ejaculating sperm, which they all do—Sade's libertine women are men. They are, in fact, literary transvestites."[56] The only qualification I would wish to make in agreeing with Dworkin is that it is not "even" in such details, but precisely in such details, and in the thematic need for them, that transvestism is imposed. Pascal Bruckner and Alain Finkielkraut are more specific in relating the andromorphic semiotics of the female body to Sade's practice of climactic sexuality: "Les héroïnes qui sont citées en exemple . . . ne trouvent rien de mieux à faire, une fois parvenues à l'apogée de leur désir, que de décharger" [The heroines who are held up to us as examples can only manage, when they have reached the apogee, to unload].[57] The fact is that there is no apogee of desire in narrative unless they are seen to discharge.

Sade, who is too often defended, is here too narrowly the focus of attack. In making him the bad guy, critics may fail to perceive the general nature of the problem. His systematic blindness to many specificities of the female body is not eccentric, but is well supported discursively by the state of scientific knowledge at the time, as Richard Lewinsohn points out: "As late as the eighteenth century natural historians still wrote of a female semen which was emitted in coitus in the same way as the male."[58] Theories of "generation" in the eighteenth century were highly contested, and experimental evidence inconclusive, although it is doubtless the case that Sade's fictional use of scientific discourse was quite tendentious.[59] Uncertainty about what actually went on in coitus could, in any case, hardly satisfy the requirements of narrative eroticism. Accordingly, Sade, Restif, Mirabeau, and other erotic writers of the time can regularly be seen to affirm the sexuality of erection and discharge as the one true pattern of all desire and pleasure.

There is a powerfully convergent set of reasons, rational and irrational, technical and political, at work in defining these symptoms as those of female pleasure. If climactic pleasure is to function as avowal, it must display the truth of satisfied desire in utterly conclusive ways. In bringing about this moment, narrative will depend on a set of conventions whose very purpose is to deny their conventionality and enforce their claim to corporeal immediacy. This, as Nancy Huston points out apropos of modern pornography, serves the unstated and unstatable purpose of denying the female body any possibility of withholding or counterfeiting its display: "si [les textes pornographiques destinés surtout aux hommes] insistent tant sur les signes extérieurs de ce plaisir (les cris, les yeux révulsés, les vagins inondés de 'foutre'), c'est justement parce qu'ils savent que, à la différence des hommes, les femmes peuvent feindre le plaisir" [pornographic texts destined primarily for men insist so much on the external signs of pleasure (cries, eyes turned upward, vaginas full of "*foutre*") precisely because they know that, by contrast with men, women can fake pleasure].[60] Women may be stereotyped as capricious, but the intensity of pleasure must be such as to deny them room, at high moments, for any further coquettishness. They must be trapped in the radical immanence of their bodily truth. That they might still have room for mobility, for tactics, must be rendered unthinkable. Their silencing-and-confession is the routine achievement of climactic eroticism, from the late eighteenth century to twentieth-century pornography, and it is achieved all the better for not being made an explicit aim.[61] Only very rarely is this furtive purpose even half-acknowledged, as we shall see.

In "aristocratic" libertinism, it might have been acceptable for desire and pleasure to be defined by convention, but the "natural" eroticism of erection and ejaculation requires that its signs be the undisputed outward symptoms of an inner truth. What climactic eroticism needs and desires is proof. It finds this proof readily in the bodies of men, and exacts it in kind from the bodies of women. Ejaculated sperm gives rise to a moment of decision, not to say of judgment: sperm is exhibit A, the substantive evidence of desire. Indeed, at this time, the word *preuves* often serves as a distinguished synonym for ejaculate. In *La Philosophie dans le boudoir,* Dolmancé utters the following command: "il faut que le sein et le visage de votre amie soient inondés des preuves de la virilité de votre frère; il faut qu'il lui décharge ce qui s'appelle au nez" [The breasts and face of your friend must be drenched with the evidence of your brother's virility. He must unload right in her face] (3:456). Ejaculating so close to the woman's face compels her to attend to the demonstration. It makes material contact coincide, in space and time, with the spectacle of pleasure. Insistently, this demonstration is performed in women's faces, and is just as often required from them in approximately symmetrical terms.

At another point in *La Philosophie dans le boudoir*, Dolmancé is conducting a first lesson in sexual physiology for the benefit of his pupil Eugénie: "Eh bien! tu le vois, Eugénie, après une pollution plus ou moins longue, les glandes séminales se gonflent et finissent par exhaler une liqueur dont l'écoulement plonge la femme dans le transport le plus delicieux. Cela s'appelle *décharger*" [So you see, Eugénie, that after a more or less sustained stimulation the seminal glands swell up and finally express a liquor whose flow immerses the woman in the most delightful pleasure. That is called *discharging*] (3:401; original emphasis). Eugénie does indeed see, in a didactic environment, that this is how her pleasure happens and what it is called. As do Sade's admiring readers, who will presumably not fail to see it again whenever it is demonstrated. They can certainly have the satisfaction of seeing it repeatedly if they limit their attention to erotic narrative. And it is still available for "direct" observation in *Les folies amoureuses d'une impératrice* (1865), where the clitoris is seen to ejaculate in exquisite miniature: "Et tout à coup, de ce bouton s'échappait un petit jet que mes lèvres recevaient avec ravissement, comme la rose, le matin, est rafraîchie par la goutte de rosée . . ." [And suddenly, from this little knob, there came a tiny squirt that my lips caught with delight, as the rose in the morning is refreshed by a drop of dew].[62] This is proof positive of the woman's pleasure, delivered right under the man's nose. Mirabeau's *Hic-et-Haec* (1798) could not be more explicit, either in the demonstration or in the conclusion: "A ce mot, elle ferme les yeux, se roidit et, par la plus copieuse éjaculation, me prouve le plaisir qu'elle prenait" [Hearing this, she closed her eyes, stiffened, and by the most copious ejaculation proved to me the pleasure she felt].[63]

More modern pornographic texts, especially those of the twentieth century, have no doubt been inhibited in their demonstrations of female pleasure by the dissemination of biological notions that make such descriptions as these seem absurd, with the result that cries of pleasure, rather than material discharge, are often required to stand alone in the climactic place as the most decisive signs.[64] Bruckner and Finkielkraut discuss the way in which modern sexology claims to identify the orgasmic moment in the absence of clearly visible signs: "à faire entendre ce qui ne se voit pas, l'orgasme féminin accède, par un autre tour, à la lisibilité. Le bruit relaie l'image: au lieu d'émettre de la semence, la femme émet un signe; en tant qu'équivalent auditif de la décharge séminale, le cri permet le retour de la volupté féminine dans le bercail de la représentation" [When that which cannot be seen is rendered audible, the female orgasm becomes readable. Sound supplants sight. Instead of emitting seed, the woman emits a sign. As an auditory equivalent of seminal discharge, the cry allows female pleasure to return to the fold of representation].[65] Late-eighteenth-century erotic narrative was less constrained in both the visible and the audible representation of symptoms, as if to ensure that female pleasure would never slip away—Diderot's Mangogul would have said, *se dérober*—from the field of clearly perceptible and tellable phenomena. Vindication was to be had at those moments when proof came gushing forth as a mixture of cries and sperm. In *Le Rideau levé, ou l'éducation de Laure* (1786), it happens just this way: "dans le même temps que nous mîmes à chercher le plaisir pour le savourer, Rose avait déjà ressenti quatre fois ses attraits; quatre fois ses élancements et ses transports, ses expressions: je me meurs, je décharge, nous en donnèrent des preuves certaines" [While we were still setting about achieving our own pleasure, Rose had already experienced it four times. On four occasions her spurts and her delight, her expressions, "I'm dying," "I'm unloading," gave us certain proof of it].[66]

In Crébillon's *La Nuit et le moment* (1755), there was anecdotal mention of a woman who had displayed great pleasure with the hero, Clitandre. Her behavior was judged to be a "gratuitous" piece of courtesy, tinged with falsehood.[67] That was, in Crébillon's libertine world, simply misplaced politeness rather than a betrayal of imperative sexual truth. Now, the stakes appear to be higher and the anxiety more profound, as doubts often linger, despite the repeated affirmations, about the confessional nature of such ejaculations. There is a slight wavering in Restif's narrator when, in *L'Anti-Justine* (1798), he describes a woman's swoon. This ought to have been a drastic symptom of pleasure, but Cupidonnet somehow feels obliged to allow that what he has seen may not be entirely conclusive: "Pour Madeleine Linguet, elle déchargea sans doute car elle se pâma" [As for Madeleine Linguet, she must have discharged, because she swooned].[68] Perhaps she is faking it; perhaps she has swooned out of distress. The narrator's *sans doute* can only be the mark of hopeful interpretation: it reveals just the kind of doubt that demonstrative symptoms ought to preempt. The same uncertainty is forthrightly admitted by the narrator of Nerciat's *Le Diable au corps*, who apostrophizes a whole class of women in this way: "Comédiennes de Paphos vous frémissez quelquefois, vous vous disloquez, vous haletez, jurez, mordez: tout cela le plus habilement du monde; et, si nous avons la foi, nous devons supposer que vous avez un plaisir invincible . . ." [Actresses of Paphos, sometimes you groan, you thrash about, you pant, swear, and bite. All that you do most skillfully. And if we have faith, we must believe that you experience invincible pleasure].[69] Do "we" have faith, in fact? Maintaining confidence in the reality of women's pleasure when it is performed in stories, despite an awareness of feminine deceptive skills, enacting the certainty of climax in the midst of haunting fears or worldly skepticism: this is one of the self-appointed tasks of male-focused erotic narrative. Whatever certainty is gained here is only a local, short-term victory over its opposite. Surprisingly often, one finds in the midst of a story the grudging recognition that the symptoms of feminine pleasure require interpretation, and that this interpretation is based on a particular hypothesis: "soit que Fanny éprouvât réellement un grand plaisir, soit qu'elle n'en fît que le semblant, elle manifesta certainement, par ses paroles et par ses actes, la plus extrême félicité" [either because Fanny really felt great pleasure or because she only pretended to, she certainly demonstrated, by her words and actions, the most perfect happiness] (*Les Amours d'un gentleman* [1889]).[70] All that is "certain" here is that there is a recognizable display: nothing guarantees its truly symptomatic nature despite a century of thematic insistence.

Erotic narrative is not generally able to ignore or bracket out women's pleasure, despite Sade's occasional call for this to be done.[71] In that sense, contrary to a commonplace of popular feminism, it does not just "treat women as objects" since it exacts from them the marks of a particular subjectivity. In fact, to take it one step further, this kind of story is less concerned ultimately with the precise quality of response than with the directness and reliability of its occurrence. Sade's Saint-Fond appears not to have been entirely convinced by the ostensibly conclusive displays of pleasure performed so often in his presence, for we find him alluding blackly to his doubt about what is really going on inside the women he deals with. He seems to have solved the problem in ways that Restif's, Mirabeau's, or Nerciat's heroes would not consider, by giving up any attempt to provoke expressions of pleasure and seeking to draw out other signs that can be read with greater certainty as true symptoms: "je ne me soucie pas trop de voir les impressions du plaisir sur le visage d'une femme, elles sont si douteuses; je préfère celles de la douleur, on s'y trompe moins" [I am not particularly interested in seeing marks of pleasure on a woman's face. They are too uncertain. I prefer those of pain. They are less likely to deceive] (*Histoire de Juliette* 8:388). If pleasure is to give way to pain, he says, so much the better. The real point of the action is not to serve women in any way but to provoke a crisis that leads to the unmediated utterance of bodily truth.

I have already observed that fin-de-siècle writing adds little to the poetics of exclamation, although it does contribute to the high thematic seriousness of erotic utterance by surrounding it with medical discourse. Fiction of that time is also able, for this very reason, to exploit the approximate coincidence of pleasure and pain by affirming the dialectical relation of the two, and hearing the desperate cry as the echo of both at once. In *Les Cousines de la colonelle* (1880), such a sound is heard, and its significance spelt out:

> Tout à coup un cri, aussitôt réprimé, s'échappa de sa poitrine et se fondit en un soupir étouffé.
> —Ah! je souffre avec bonheur! Ah! mon bien-aimé, ah! ah! c'est le ciel . . . je suis morte, je . . .

> [Suddenly a cry, immediately stifled, burst from her breast and melted into a muffled sigh.
> "Ah! I am in agony with happiness! Ah! My beloved. Ah! Ah! This is heaven . . . I am dead, I . . ."][72]

Suffering pleasurably and finding pain in the heart of pleasure is the summum of narrative experience and leads to the ultimate vocalization of sexuality. In fact, it produces climactic utterance as the voice of death: *le râle*, the death rattle. In *Demi-Volupté* (1897), we hear "le souffle rauque de la volupté" [the hoarse voice of pleasure] as it exhales, not just the standard exclamation, "je meurs" [I am dying], already present in Crébillon, but a narrower articulation of death and eroticism, a passionate longing for death-in-pleasure: "Oh! mourir ainsi! . . ." [Oh! To die like this!. . .].[73] The ultimate exclamation—in both senses of the word "ultimate"—becomes thus the outcome of the requirement that pleasure and pain be conclusively spoken: *le râle* is as frequent in erotic narrative of the late nineteenth century as the sigh was in the middle of the eighteenth. Its extreme nature, the fact that it stands at the threshold of death, serves as a guarantee of truth, as if the death rattle were too intense to be simulated: "Des sanglots et des râles sortent de la gorge . . . le cœur bat dans la poitrine, il bat à briser ses ressorts puissants; les jambes tremblent, usées par l'effort trop grand; la bête se meurt, la bête râle, la bête étouffe, et c'est dans une apothéose" [Sobs and rattles came from her throat. Her heart beat in her breast, fit to break its powerful springs. Her legs trembled, exhausted by an effort that was beyond them. The beast was dying, the beast was in its death rattle, the beast was unable to breathe, and this was its apotheosis].[74] Yet nothing can ensure that *le râle* will count as definitive: nothing can prevent its becoming part of narrative and thematic routine. It cannot be so extreme, nor so decisive, as to be any more (or less) than a conventional representation, happily nestled in clichéd phrases such as the following: "le corps secoué d'un frisson de désir, elle râlait" [her body was wracked by a shiver of desire, as she gave out a death rattle].[75] Even the theme of death cannot guarantee deadly accuracy in the representation of feminine pleasure.

The key thing, and the conventionally "certain" mark of climax, is not that the woman should experience any specific quality of feeling but that she should cry out in extremis, and that her cry should count as confession of, and coincidence with, her bodily nature. Sophie's husband, in *Méphistophela* (1890), knows that this is the narrative model for a successful wedding night, even as he fails to make it happen: "il obligea la vierge à subir l'intromission triomphale de l'époux. Elle ne proféra pas un soupir, n'eut pas une seule plainte. . . . Sa victoire ne s'achèverait que dans l'aveu de la défaite! Mais pas même en un cri d'horreur, pas même en un sanglot, cet aveu, il ne l'obtenait!"[76] [he compelled the virgin to undergo her spouse's triumphal insertion. She did not utter a sigh, not one sound of complaint. His victory would only be complete when she admitted defeat. But he drew from her no such admission, not even a cry of horror, not even a sob!]. It is not enough, for the male's dramatic purpose, that "intromission" should occur, however triumphantly: the proper conclusion will only be reached when his wife is provoked, by a kind of rough symmetry, to a cry of avowal. Even were this to occur, however, there is likely to be doubt as to whether the utterance called forth is really the substance of truth.[77] The whole procedure is in fact disturbed by its own close circularity and troubled by self-defeating irony. Truth may be no more than a thematic convenience, and the language of compulsive pleasure no more than the well-disciplined sound of compulsory satisfaction, produced on cue.

From Crébillon and Diderot to the fin de siècle, there are no great rifts in the history of exclamation, merely a long process of compaction whereby utterances that were already present in erotic fiction came to be more fully owned and integrated. The exclamation was not invented, or eventfully rediscovered, during those 150 years. It merely gained some poetic elaboration and took on much greater thematic density. It became in fact a privileged mark of bodily pleasure-and-pain, taking its place in the heart of narrative as a sign of expressive climax.

5
Ellipsis

IN THE PREVIOUS CHAPTER, BY TAKING UP EXCLAMATION AS ONE OF THE emblems of erotic discourse, I discussed the thematic not as some shapeless content to be poured into texts at will, but as something always already "marked" with its own narrative proclivities, its own formal inertia. I showed that the exclamation mark signified, by a well-domesticated paradox, that which was so compelling as to be beyond articulation and articulacy—signifying indeed a pure erotic "content" pouring out of the bodies of lovers in the self-avowal of passion. I noted in passing that the exclamation mark occurred in rhythmic alternation with what French calls *points de suspension*, so that the intensity of voice produced by exclamation was not just answered but somehow enhanced by its very interruption. I propose now to return to suspension marks, in order to consider further their own emblematic qualities. I hope to show the evolving thematic value of what might be called interruptive narration.

My interest here, as the title of this chapter indicates, is in ellipsis, in the practice of omitting certain events from the narration, or at least of ceasing to provide the detail that other parts of the same text have established as the norm. There is a sense in which no narrative can function without ellipsis, as Georges Perec effectively shows *a contrario* in his extraordinarily detailed and apparently interminable *Station Mabillon*.[1] What deserves our narrower attention here, however, and what allows ellipsis to attain something akin to thematic status, is the more or less systematic omission of particular details or particular classes of event that are identifiable—and sometimes actually named—in the text. Most often, I want to claim, this is an unambiguous, if indirect, manner of referring to erotic activities. It may not be universally the case that ellipsis signifies in this way, but there is a powerful tendency, supported by a strong literary tradition, working in that direction. Within the genre of erotic narrative, certainly, but also well beyond its range, one finds an established practice of reading non-description as something more than oversight or absence: it is the specific mark of a sexual event. Let me be quite clear about this: I do not wish to suggest that sex is lurking everywhere in the unsaid, waiting to be revealed by a certain quality of attention. My point is a more modest one: a veritable thematics of ellipsis comes into play in certain generic contexts, whenever narrative expectations allow non-description to count as allusion or evocation rather than indifference or neglect.

In order to exemplify the practice and indicate its generic range, let me consider three examples, each of which is more clear-cut and more elaborate than the one before. This should allow us, so to speak, to home in on the problem. Raymonde Robert discusses a marginal case of ellipsis in her introduction to the collection, *Contes parodiques et licencieux du dix-huitième siècle*. No eating or drinking goes on in these stories, although there is a lot of sighing. And if "something else," a certain thing of a bodily nature should occur, says Robert in a mimetically discreet fashion, the reader only learns of it by the eventual outcome. For modern readers unused to reading "between such delicate lines," she suggests, this can create problems. They may be disconcerted to learn that the Comtesse de Tende is now pregnant, when all that they had previously known was that she was in love.[2] Another way of putting this, presumably, is to say that modern readers are inadequately trained in the genre or uncertain as to which generic rules might apply. Even when they eventually infer what must have occurred, they might continue in their uncertainty as to what to make of the text's "delicacy." Does it simply amount to discretion, avoiding reference to a sexual encounter because such things are improper, or is it rather a suggestive, if subtle, reference to a passionate event on which the story turns? In some sense, it must be both of those, as if the equivocation between the two readings were itself a product of ellipsis.

An example that is less equivocal, and perhaps for that very reason more clearly within the range of conventional erotic narrative, can be found in Pigault-Lebrun's *La Folie espagnole*

(1801). Here, the narration speaks of a night spent by two characters as a time of sensual delight, but simply omits all detail of what occurred then, out of respect for the reader's modesty. The narrator moves straight to the immediate sequel, beginning his sentence as follows: "A la fin de cette nuit délicieuse dont j'ai supprimé tous les détails par égard pour votre pudeur" [At the end of that delightful night, the details of which have been omitted out of respect for your modesty].[3] The "suppression," in this case, is less elegant and apparently less adroit than in the previous example, but its very visibility serves a purpose. This is local modesty, focused on the events of a particular night rather than a general demeanor that might lead the narrator never to mention such things at all. The reader's attention is thus drawn both to the event of pleasure and to its titillating impropriety.

Ellipsis only begins to achieve thematic status, in fact, when the text finds a way to indicate that it is currently not describing something that has a dedicated place in the story. As practiced in erotic narrative, ellipsis is likely to come very close to telling without doing so directly, while accounting for its nondescription by alluding to the requirements of both decorum and desire. This is, in an important sense, telling by not telling. So elaborate does the practice become in certain erotic texts that we can identify a veritable art of "suspension" and a quite talkative presentation of the unspoken. In some libertine texts of the eighteenth century, this allows unambiguous reference to sensual pleasure without undue loss of decorum. Crébillon's *La Nuit et le moment* (1755), for example, contains elaborate interruptions that are not just rococo flourishes but thematically productive exercises in ostentation. Clitandre, through a set of seductive moves to which the reader is witness, finds himself established in Cidalise's bed, able to spend the night with her in conversation that becomes progressively more amorous. At one point in the dialogue, she declares her affection for him more warmly and clearly than before. To this he is "required" to respond, says the narrator, in a manner that satisfies the rules of courteous exchange: "En cet endroit Clitandre doit à Cidalise les plus tendres remerciements, et les lui fait" [At this point, Clitandre owes Cidalise the tenderest expression of thanks, and provides it]. Just how and where his vote of thanks is delivered the text does not say, and Crébillon's narrator offers an extraordinary range of reasons why it should not do so. Firstly, he supposes that all his readers will already have had opportunity to take part in such conversations, and have no need to be reminded of them:

> Comme on ne peut supposer qu'il y ait parmi nos lecteurs quelqu'un qui n'ait jamais été dans le cas d'en faire, ou d'en recevoir, ou de dire et d'entendre ces choses flatteuses et passionnées que suggère l'amour reconnaissant, ou que dicte quelquefois la nécessité d'être poli, l'on supprimera ce que les deux amants se disent ici.

> [Since we are not entitled to suppose that there is among our readers anyone who has never had occasion to give or receive such thanks, or to say and hear those flattering things that grateful love brings to mind, or the things that politeness sometimes requires, we shall omit what the two lovers said to each other here.]

The first appeal is a social, not to say a sociable one, pointing to shared experiences in a context of polished manners. This is supported by a second reason, akin to what we might have expected from Diderot's Mangogul, in *Les Bijoux indiscrets*: "l'on ose croire que le lecteur a d'autant moins à s'en plaindre, que l'on ne le prive que de quelques propos interrompus" [we daresay that the reader has all the less reason to complain as we are depriving him of a few interrupted phrases]. What we are missing is apparently inarticulate babble, unworthy of polished narration. And in any case, adds the narrator, with a somewhat contradictory third reason, the omission leaves room for the reader to supply her or his own words and actions in the space left blank: "il aura plus de plaisir à composer lui-même d'après ses sentiments, qu'il n'en trouverait à les lire" [He will have more pleasure making them up himself, according to his feelings, than he would have in reading them]. Moreover, he goes on with exhaustive civility, if perchance there are readers unfamiliar with this kind of social intercourse, he would have happily obliged them by providing instruction, if only this could have been done without cost to natural learning: it would, however, take away the pleasant surprise that awaits such people in the future.[4] This extraordinary deployment of reasons causes the ellipsis to take up as much space and time as telling the event might have. The narrator is ostentatiously demonstrating his thoughtfulness, taking account of every possible eventuality, and answering every hypothetical whim on the part of his readerly guests. As he does so, his loquacity cannot fail to draw attention to his discretion in a way that serves an evocative purpose and parodies itself at the same time. This is libertine ellipsis at its seductive best.

When tact assumes such a wonderfully elaborate form, it draws attention to itself as exemplary conversational performance while at the same time demonstrating its capacity to include sexual activities within its range of reference. Narratorial wit is then located in the very multiplication of reasons for not telling, and in the continual invention of yet more reasons for doing the same, convenient thing. In *Les Bijoux indiscrets*, for example, where indiscretion, as always, is a quite relative matter, a reason must be given why the crudest of the stories has been omitted. To say that the story in question is obscene would itself be out of keeping with libertine civility, and we are therefore treated to speculation on the part of the "editor" who is responsible for presenting the text we read. At this point, he makes bold to affirm, there is not an ellipsis, but a lacuna, and the reason for it is unclear. The community of scholars is in fact called upon to undertake research that would restore the missing fragment: "Nous invitons les savants à méditer et à voir si cette lacune ne serait point une omission volontaire de l'auteur, mécontent de ce qu'il aurait dit, et qui ne trouvait rien de mieux à dire" [We invite men of learning to ponder whether this lacuna might not be a deliberate omission on the part of the author, who could have been dissatisfied with all that he had said, and not found anything better].[5] It is unlikely that many scholars have since applied for research grants in response to this invitation, but allowing its interception by more standard readers of erotic narrative is in fact a form of obliquity that is both playful and polite. Whether the invitation is to search for a missing original or to imagine something of one's own production to fill the space, the upshot is approximately the same—the approximation being part of the thematics. Nerciat's narrator, in the later *Les Aphrodites*, appears just as generous toward his reader, if more perfunctorily so, when he offers free reign in place of a description: "Je laisse ici libre carrière à l'imagination du lecteur" [I leave free rein here to the reader's imagination].[6] Yet it must be remembered that the reader's exercise of freedom is already shaped by a tradition of manipulative narratorial civility. Freedom can only be offered so unreservedly when it is to be exercised "here," in a particular place, surrounded by the discursive constraints that characterize the genre. Let us not suppose that we are dealing here with the unspeakable: this is merely something that is politely, charmingly, engagingly unspoken.

Ellipsis is unquestionably thematic when represented metaphorically, in the image of the veil or the curtain. *Les Amours de Sainfroid, jésuite, et d'Eulalie, fille dévote* (1729) reassures the reader in its preface that the curtain has been drawn in the story, at various points, to cover certain excesses: "quand les choses sont allées un peu loin, on a tiré le rideau derrière lequel on a laissé jouer la farce" [When things went a bit far, we drew the curtain and allowed the farce to be played out behind it].[7] Note that this is not just any old curtain but "the" theatrical one, and that we are invited to see it being drawn at certain moments in the text. The agent who does the drawing ("on") is identified as the narratorial subject. This same person says at one point: "Tirons le rideau sur le reste de la scène" [Let us draw the curtain over the rest of the scene] (151), and then continues to refer to the scene or stage that he has hidden from the reader: "nos deux amants n'étaient pas encore bien remis de l'agitation que leur avait causée la scène qui venait de se passer derrière le rideau que nous avons tiré" [our two lovers had not yet properly recovered from the wild emotion caused by the scene that had just gone on behind the curtain that we drew] (151). Even as it is obscured, the object of allusion is brought close to hand, becoming a concealed presence rather than an absence. The curtain functions thus as a particularly showy form of concealment: it is drawn solemnly and playfully to protect and excite the reader.

Some stories make it seem as if the curtain had to struggle to assert itself against the audacity of the stage. *La Secte des anandrynes* (1789) has a central character who acts as the "historian," but her story is subject to interruption by a disapproving voice: "Ici, Milord, j'interromps la narration de l'historienne et j'étends un voile sur les tableaux dégoûtants qu'elle nous présente" [At this point, my lord, I am interrupting the historian's narration and placing a veil over the revolting paintings that she is presenting to us]. The person who interrupts here stands in two places at once: he is both a member of the audience viewing the "paintings," and someone who has the power to remove them from show. It is noteworthy, once again, that the reason given for the veiling, one of taste, is immediately followed by another that could be considered contradictory, in that it invites Milord to let his imagination complete the picture: "Je laisse courir votre imagination qui, certainement, vous les retracera d'un pinceau plus délicat et plus voluptueux" [I let your imagination roam free. It will certainly redraw them with a more elegant brush, and a more voluptuous one].[8] The expectation is clearly that this privileged reader will paint, in his mind, a picture of the very same subject that will be more tasteful and more sensual. That is why, incidentally, it is inappropriate to speak here of censorship. There is finally no change of subject—not even a shift of attention. The veil actively serves the purpose of representation.

At times, narrators find a way to draw attention to ellipsis while avoiding full "personal" responsibility for it. They justify and dignify their practice by referring to illustrious antecedents. The narrator of *Histoire de dom Bougre* (1741), when confronted with the task of describing a scene of great pleasure, casts over it a veil that has been borrowed from the classics:

> Qu'on me permette d'imiter ici ce sage grec qui, peignant le sacrifice d'Iphigénie, après avoir épuisé sur les visages des assistants tous les traits qui caractérisaient la douleur la plus profonde, couvrit celui d'Agamemnon d'un voile, laissant habilement aux spectateurs le plaisir d'imaginer quels traits pouvaient caractériser le désespoir d'un père tendre qui voit répandre son sang, qui voit immoler sa fille.

> [May I be allowed to imitate, at this point, the wise Greek who, depicting Iphigenia's sacrifice, after showing in full on the faces of all present the marks of deepest suffering, covered Agamemnon's with a veil, skillfully leaving for the spectators the pleasure of imagining what features could mark the despair of a tender father who sees his blood spilt, and his daughter immolated?]

The veil stands for, or rather enacts metaphorically, an ancient figure of rhetoric, except that, in the generic context of *Histoire de dom Bougre*, it is not a father's grief that is thematically foreknown and can thus be covered over. At such moments, the pleasure of imagination simply turns back toward the imagination of pleasure: "Je vous laisse, cher lecteur, le plaisir d'imaginer. . . . Rappelez-vous vos plaisirs, poussez votre imagination encore plus loin s'il est possible, elle demeurera toujours au-dessous de

mes délices" [I leave to you, dear reader, the pleasure of imagining. Remember your pleasures, let your imagination go even further if possible. It will always fall short of what I felt].[9] The
narrator of Nerciat's *Mon Noviciat* makes the same deferent
move, taking as his model for eloquent omission a famous alle-
gorical painting, "L'Ingratitude," in which the most extreme
figure is left blank.[10] *Les Amours du chevalier de Faublas* finds
its glorious antecedent closer to home, in Rousseau's *Julie, ou la
nouvelle Héloïse*, making an allusion that is itself an ellipsis:
"moment de la possession, moment de volupté suprême; le plus
éloquent des écrivains a consacré vos délices dans un ouvrage
immortel; il faut vous taire puisqu'on ne peut vous exprimer
aussi bien" [moment of possession, moment of supreme pleasure,
the most eloquent of writers rendered your delights in a work
that will live forever. I must now keep silent about you because I
cannot express you with the same grace].[11] What Rousseau
"said" so well, however, was also signified in great measure by
not saying. His Julie wrote to her confidante Claire, "Je ne puis
ni parler ni me taire" [I can neither speak nor be silent], but she
appears in fact to have done both of these things, referring to a
particular "instant d'égarement" [moment of folly] and allowing
us to see its effects without plunging into a detailed account of
the action.[12] As we see, the "holes" in the text of *Faublas* can be
filled with the holes in *La Nouvelle Héloïse*. Deferring true description to the literary predecessor is not so much a call for in-
tertextual reading, as the first move in a signifying process that
figures the unspoken as always already spoken, hidden and
available, absent and present in literary memory.

Another form of ellipsis, and sometimes of deferral, occurs
when the narrator suffers an occlusion of knowledge at a particular point, and is reduced to conjecture. This happens in *Kanor*
(1750), in association with several of the other thematic elements I have just been examining. At the end of the story, the
final union of the two lovers is covered over by the wings of a
god, to protect them from being seen or heard by lesser creatures. The veil provided by the god, in the form of a cloud, pro-
tects the two so well that it obscures even the narrator's view:
"Lui seul peut apprendre les particularités qui se passèrent
sous son nuage; il ne m'en a point instruite: ainsi ceux qui
voudront un plus grand détail, pourront s'adresser à lui" [He
alone can tell the details of what went on behind his cloud. He

did not inform me of them, so that those who want more detail will have to ask him personally].[13] This is a form of teasing, of course, and as such a source of gentle pleasure in its own right. It also leaves room for humor, and that opportunity is never more nicely taken up in stories of this kind than in Theophile Gautier's *Mademoiselle de Maupin* (1835). At the story's climax and denouement, Mademoiselle de Maupin first visits d'Albert in his room, then goes to spend the rest of the night with Rosette. We are told what happened with d'Albert, but the authorial persona is powerless to relate what follows because he has been unable to find out what transpired between the two women. "The most conscientious research" has revealed nothing in the papers left behind by the main characters, although the chambermaid, when questioned, did say that the sheets were crumpled and bore the imprint of two bodies. That piece of evidence simply leaves the narrator puzzled. He declares himself quite unable to reach a conclusion, and is driven by his contrived failure to take a step that is in fact the standard rhetorical one: "Je livre cette remarque à la sagacité du lecteur, et je le laisse libre d'en tirer toutes les inductions qu'il voudra; quant à moi, j'ai fait là-dessus mille conjectures, toutes plus déraisonnables les unes que les autres, et si saugrenues que je n'ose véritablement les écrire, même dans le style le plus honnêtement périphrasé" [I pass on this remark for the reader's wise deliberation, and I leave him free to draw from it all the inductions he may wish. As for me, I have come up with a thousand conjectures, each more unreasonable than the one before, and so bizarre that I really do not dare write them, even in the most decently periphrastic style].[14] The ironic point is, of course, that the show of ignorance is itself a form of periphrasis, and the play with innumerable hypotheses a singular interpretive joke. How many "inductions" can a truly wise reader possibly make, and how could the author possibly entertain a thousand different theories? The narrator simply pretends to be a model for the incompetent reader. This point has been missed in Lilian Faderman's reading of the final section of the novel. Her literal-minded reading leads her to claim that Gautier believes women to be incapable of figuring out what to do sexually with each other.[15] A reading informed by familiarity with erotic ellipsis suggests that ignorance is being feigned precisely because narrator and reader know very well what happened but share their knowledge without naming its object, just as they take their pleasure in telling without describing. Sexual activity between women may be something of a mystery here, but it is a teasingly familiar one.

The frequency of ellipsis in erotic narrative and the range of variations that elaborate the theme without dispersing it must raise a question about the notion of explicitness. Whether or not a text can be declared "sexually explicit" is often a matter of vital interest in discussions of pornography and censorship,[16] but it should be clear why I mistrust this notion as a way of defining erotic literature as a genre. Our discussion of the libertine tradition seems to suggest that ostentatious interruption, of the sort found from Crébillon to Gautier, is both explicit and implicit at the same time. It could of course be argued, with the support of the theme of exclamatory utterance, that the business of erotic literature is in fact the revelation of a concealed sexual truth; one could point not only to the confessional ear but to the voyeuristic eye. It is certainly the case that exclamations are readily overheard in erotic stories, and that keyholes can normally be relied on to provide a perfect view of the action, but the interruption of cries and sighs or the obscuring of keyhole vision cannot with safety be taken as signs that a narrative is less likely to offend, or even less obscene. When the narrator has difficulty seeing through a keyhole in *Eléonore, ou l'heureuse personne* (1796), it would be quite inappropriate to see him as straining for clearer perception. The lack of clarity is merely a playful way of entertaining doubt as to which orifice has been penetrated: "Il est impossible d'assurer ce qui en était positivement. Ce sont de ces choses dont on ne convient guère, et à travers une serrure il est facile de se tromper sur une si petite distance" [It is impossible to say with certainty what occurred. These are things about which people do not readily agree, and through a keyhole it is easy to make a mistake about such a small distance].[17] Comparably, when Duclos, in Sade's *Les Cent Vingt Journées de Sodome*, is unsure as to what may have happened during one of the incidents she is relating, that should only be taken as carefully measured reticence along the way to bigger and better things of the same order. Duclos is used to observing through a hole in a wall, but is quite unable to see what is happening when her sister has sessions with a particular client: "car jamais ma sœur ne me l'a voulu dire, et ils ne se plaçaient point dans l'endroit où j'aurais pu les voir" [for my sister never would tell me, and they took up their position in a spot where I could not see them]. On one occasion, after leaving the brothel with this client, the sister disappears forever, and Duclos has never been able to find out what became of her. As it happens, by a narrative figure that is repeated regularly throughout the novel, one of the other storytellers, Desgranges, knows the rest of the "anecdote" and promises to complete it when the time comes for her to speak: "cette anecdote-là me re- garde, je leur en rendrai bon compte" [that anecdote is mine to tell, and I will tell it in full].[18] The mystery is only temporary: it is a stage on the way to full description. In the same novel, the "petits cabinets," which are impenetrable to the narrator, appear to cause him irritation and perplexity since he is unable to see what is making the victims cry out. Yet the final section of the novel is destined to show in exquisite detail these same victims being tortured to death.[19] None of these ellipses can be said to reduce the overall explicitness of the texts in question.

There is a metaphor that is apparently almost identical to the veil or curtain but whose deployment relates rather differently to the notion of the explicit. In the writings of Crébillon and his colleagues, veiling is a matter of playful civility, with the draw- ing of veils being itself a source of pleasure. There, veils and cur- tains are theatrical, even if the theater is no larger than a boudoir. In erotic texts of the late eighteenth century and beyond, we find the veil tending more and more to take on a dif- ferent consistency. The predominant image becomes that of *la gaze*—that is, a light veil considered in terms of its materiality as well as its capacity to cover. The partial transparency of gauze allows the pleasure of not seeing to blend with that of seeing. The narrator of Voisenon's *Le Sultan Misapouf* (1746) claims to have got it just right, and there is no reason to disbe- lieve him: "tout est voilé mais la gaze est si légère que les plus faibles vues ne perdront rien du tableau" [everything is veiled but the gauze is so fine that even those with the weakest eye- sight will be able to see all of the tableau].[20] La Mettrie had been a great advocate of such veiling. He made much of the distinc- tion between voluptuous literature that practiced "veiled aes- thetics," as Jean-Christophe Abramovici calls them, and naked obscenity.[21] The purveyors of obscenity make the mistake, says La Mettrie, of "lever le rideau sur les orgies des Bacchantes, de

révéler les mystères les plus impudiques du dieu des jardins"
[raising the veil on the orgies of the Bacchantes and revealing
the most immodest mysteries of the god of gardens].[22] True
voluptuaries know the seductive pleasures of the veil, which
lends itself admirably to gradations of knowledge and subtleties
of description: "Il faut donc sentir soi-même par quelle inimitable adresse on dit mieux les choses en les supprimant; comment on invite les désirs en aiguillonnant la curiosité de l'esprit
sur un objet en partie couvert, qu'on ne devine pas encore et
qu'on veut avoir l'honneur de deviner" [One must feel for oneself
with what inimitable skill things can be better said by omitting
them, how desires are invited and mental curiosity sharpened
by pointing to a partly covered object that one does not yet dis-
cern, and that one wishes to have the honor of discerning] (175).
This is not a question of decency but of successful representation. Sade's Saint-Ange knew as much. She actually treats the
veil, in a way that so many stories have done since, as a costume
for erotic drama. She proposes to her fellow actors in *La
Philosophie dans le boudoir*: "revêtons-nous de ces simarres de
gaze: elles ne voileront de nos attraits que ce qu'il faut cacher au
désir" [let us put on these gowns of gauze. They will only hide as
much of our charms as must be hidden from desire].[23] The *il
faut*, the exigency to which she refers, is not a requirement of
decorum but an imperative of desire. But Sade allows such cos-
tumes to coexist with an aesthetics of obscenity. The narrator of
La Nouvelle Justine is not concerned with delicacy or even with
playfulness. His only purpose is to excite the reader's imagination: he quotes the passage from La Mettrie that I have just
quoted, and seems to use it as one point of reference for his al-
ternating practice.[24] It is, at least at certain moments, as if
guessing were the most pleasurable form of knowing, and the
play with ellipsis just a slightly roundabout way of being narratively explicit; but many of Sade's contemporaries reflect in
their writing the need to reconcile the demands of desire with
the traditional requirements of civility. The narrator of *Les
Amours du chevalier de Faublas* (1787–90) names *la gaze* as the
metaphorical solution to this dilemma without quite knowing
what that means in practice. He needs to produce an account of
events that avoids giving offense while also answering the call
of truth. His problem is not when to draw the veil or, as in Crébillon, how to negotiate in conversation with his readers the fact

of presuming to draw it. It is rather a question of how thin the veil should be:

> Où trouver la gaze, en même temps légère et décente à travers laquelle il faut que la vérité se laisse entrevoir presque nue? Je blesse l'oreille la moins délicate, si je dis le mot propre; et si j'adoucis l'expression, je la dénature. Comment donc sans outrager la pudeur de personne, satisfaire la curiosité de tout le monde?

> [Where can one find the gauze, both light and decent, through which truth can be seen almost naked? I shall injure even the most robust ears if I say the exact word; and if I weaken the expression, I distort it. How then can one satisfy everyone's curiosity without offending anyone's sense of decency?][25]

In a more classical world where politeness was taken, politely, as the final standard, even to ask the question of what was true would have been indelicate; but the concern with truth urges itself on erotic narrative of the late eighteenth and early nineteenth centuries, so that reproducing the time-honored rhetoric of civility, when it happens a little later in Gautier's show of naïvety at the end of *Mademoiselle de Maupin*, can only appear as a cultivated literary joke.

The talk of a "problem" in *Faublas* is a sign of change. Crébillon's narrator practiced thoughtfulness as a way of preempting or denying problems, whereas the narrator of *Faublas* and many of his fictive contemporaries draw attention to their predicament in a declaration of their double loyalty. Here is the narrator of *Les Aphrodites* struggling publicly with the same difficulty: "Nous devons des ménagements aux personnes délicates qui, susceptibles d'indulgence pour toutes les folies que la séduction des circonstances peut justifier, s'effarouchent avec raison des cochonneries dont on peut les assaillir à brûle-pourpoint" [We owe consideration to those delicate persons who, while capable of indulgence for extravagant actions that can be justified as a response to seductive circumstance, take fright at the smut that is sometimes hurled point blank at them].[26] The rehearsal of this dilemma is no less rhetorical than Crébillon's loquacious courtesy, but its consequences for narrative are less clear. Nerciat's narrator wants to avoid alienating those readers who might incline to indulgence were they not offended by crude language, but he is also committed to passing on the *cochonneries* in all their meaty solidity. At times, this ambivalence will work itself out in the text as a kind of oscillation between propriety and impropriety: "Madame Durut, sans répondre, conduit Limecœur à portée de la marquise assise sur une . . . (il faut bien trancher le mot) sur une fouteuse." [Madame Durut, without saying a word, led Limecœur to within reach of the Marquise, who was seated on a . . . (the word really has to be uttered) on a *fouteuse*] (1:93). This is, one might say, reluctant obscenity, or at least a show of reluctance, complete with *points de suspension*, before the crude word is uttered. A comparable stutter step precedes the leap into coarseness in *Mylord Arsouille* (1858), where we are offered a description of the same event in two different styles, the first "poetic" and the second crude: "ma jeune amie . . . ressemblait à une rose qui venait de s'épanouir sous les larmes de l'aurore; disons mieux, sous les flots de foutre qui s'étaient échappées de son con et de mes couilles" [my young companion resembled a rose that had just opened beneath the tears of dawn; or to put it better, through the stream of *foutre* that had run out of her cunt and my balls]. The rhetorical point of this doubling is to provoke a comparative evaluation of the two: "C'est peut-être moins poétique, mais c'est plus énergique, et plus analogue à la matière et au sujet que nous traitons" [It may be less poetic, but it is in fact more energetic, and more in keeping with the subject at hand].[27] By this account, the task of erotic representation is to do "better" than periphrastic literary metaphor: it should espouse its objects in the most substantive way possible and find a verbal analogue for energetic sexual contact.

From about the end of the eighteenth century, explicitness thus becomes a concern, and a quite explicit one, for writing that seeks to reflect the vigor of "true" sexuality at the expense of any show of civility. As Chantal Thomas suggests, consciousness of historical change is reflected in the rejection of refined libertinism: "En supprimant toute dimension mentale au plaisir, [ces textes égrillards] se situent en flagrante rupture avec une certaine tradition du roman libertin, celle qui joue avec le non-dit et l'ellipse du passage à l'acte" [By taking away any mental dimension of pleasure, [these ribald texts] break radically with a certain tradition in the libertine novel, one which plays with the unsaid, and with ellipsis of the action proper].[28] In agreeing broadly with Thomas, I am compelled to add that the "rupture" of which she speaks is itself dependent on a new thematic arrangement that makes available, or at least renders more "flagrant," the choice between directness and indirectness. Crébillon found a hundred reasons for justifying his indirectness, but the aggregate weight of those traditional reasons may no longer be enough to resist the pressure for "direct" communication. *Gazer ou non*, to veil or not to veil? That has now become the insistent question. The answers to it still vary, even within one text, as Nerciat's self-conscious vacillation shows, but there is now a tendency to speak as if there were only two kinds, direct and indirect, veiled and naked, instead of the countless nuances produced by variations in libertine ellipsis. The conditions are now in place for truth to be identified with nakedness, and for the rejection of all veils to count, of itself, as an energetic affirmation.

The narrator of Nerciat's *Mon Noviciat* takes us through an early version of this great debate when he imagines a conversation in which the reader calls him to account for failing to speak in properly veiled language:

> "Ici je vous arrête," me dites-vous, "et je vous demande pourquoi du moins vous ne gazez point?" D'abord, je pourrais me tirer de là par une plaisanterie, et vous faire convenir qu'en vain on gazerait un vit bien bandant, puisqu'il aurait à l'instant déchirée son enveloppe; mais je vous répondrai plus raisonnablement.

> ["Here I must stop you," you say, "and ask why you do not add some gauze." My first response could be a glib joke, calling on you to agree that it would be pointless to put gauze over a really erect prick, because it would immediately tear through the cover. But I will answer you more thoughtfully.]

His first, rather flippant reply is to evoke a figurative encounter between two emblematic images: the thin veil and the thrusting prick. This allows him to act out in metaphor the triumphant "rupture" of conventional libertinism by direct sexual expression. But there is a second point to his reply, and it concerns generic appropriateness:

> Un ouvrage où il n'est question que de cons, de culs, de fouterie, de gamahucherie et d'enculade, ne serait-il pas ridicule s'il avait la moindre prétention au bon ton? Peut-on le lire en société? Des

femmes pourraient-elles avouer de l'avoir parcouru? Est-il fait pour qu'on en cite des passages?—Non.—Eh! bien! Qu'importe donc sa nudité! . . . Ceci n'est écrit que pour les personnes qui n'ont point honte de leur vit ou de leur con, et qui ne foutent point sans lumière.

[For a work in which the only subjects are cunts, asses, fucking, sucking, and fucking up the ass, would it not be ridiculous to make any claim to politeness? Can it be read in company? Could women admit to having glanced at it? Is it such that passages from it can be quoted? No. Well then, what does it matter that it should be naked? This book is only written for people who are not ashamed of their prick or their cunt, and never fuck without the light on.][29]

The aggressive manner in which these questions are asked pre-empts the answer to them, and the summary of the essential content of erotic literature shows the narrator to be set against a libertine tradition of polite seduction. This, I suggest, is the mark of Nerciat's modernity: his eloquent advocacy of narration that can be—must be—crude because it is in any case excluded from polite exchange. This is a generic declaration of independence—at an appropriate time in history—on behalf of sexually explicit pornography.

To the extent that Nerciat's distinction is followed by later writers, it might be thought that suspension marks were bound to disappear from vigorous erotic fiction, being retained only in more prudish or prurient texts. But that is to reckon without the other thematic and poetic function of such punctuation, roughly parallel to that of exclamation, which is to signify in writing the interruption of speech. There was, as Michel Delon points out, a "breathless style" that typified sensitive or passionate writing ("le genre sensible") at the end of the eighteenth century. An 1801 essay by J.-B. Pujoulx quoted by Delon deplores the new habit of using suspension marks to depict the "transports" of love.[30] That style had some antecedents in libertine writing, but the difficulty of erotic expression is not seen to be everywhere the same. Crébillon's narrator tells us, in the course of seductive ellipsis, that such things are not easily represented, not so much because language might not be equal to the task as because it makes for ungainly literature and maladroit conversation. The narrator might conceivably yield to the immediate temptation of vivacity, at the cost of taxing his reader:

On ne met pas ici la réponse de Clitandre, quelque vive qu'elle puisse être. On n'ignore point que tout ce que se disent les amants, n'est pas fait pour intéresser, et que souvent les discours, qui les amusent le plus, sont ceux qu'il serait le plus difficile de rendre, et qui valent le moins la peine d'être rendus. On supprime donc ici, comme en quelques autres endroits, les propos interrompus qu'ils se tiennent, et l'on n'y rend les deux interlocuteurs que lorsque le lecteur peut, sans se donner la torture, entendre quelque chose à ce qu'ils se disent.

[We have not included Clitandre's reply, no matter how lively it might have been. We are quite aware that the things lovers say to each other are not of interest to onlookers. Often the talk that appeals most is the hardest to convey, and the least worthy of being conveyed. We will therefore be omitting, here and in a few other places, the interrupted phrases they produced, and will only describe the two discussants when the reader is able, without being tortured, to understand something of what they are saying.][31]

The reader, he reminds us, is not in the position of a lover, and his "interest" is not the same. A narrator whose ostensible concern is firstly with his reader's comfort must therefore refrain at all costs from imposing any sort of burden, whether it be boredom or interpretive effort, on his guest. By this standard, the jerky rhythms of "interrupted" talk can be qualified as "torture," in hyperbolic language that is itself a further show of civility.

There is one text of Crébillon's time, however, that understands the difficulty in rather different terms—terms that will come to predominate in later writing. The narrator-heroine of *Margot la ravaudeuse* (1750) evokes her pleasure by telling us that any description of it will necessarily fall short, not of some antecedent text, but of the experience itself: "Que ne puis-je exprimer les ravissantes convulsions, les charmantes syncopes, les douces extases que j'ai éprouvées alors! Mais notre imagination est toujours trop faible pour peindre ce que nous sentons si fortement" [If only I could express the thrilling convulsions, the charming swoons, the sweet ecstasies that I experienced then! But our imagination is always too weak to paint what we feel so strongly].[32] This is description via an appeal to the indescribable, and its development in later texts tends to move the thematics of ellipsis from the tactfully unspoken to the intensely unspeakable. Repeatedly, in texts of the late eighteenth century and beyond, we will be told, as we are in *Mon Noviciat*, that "Sa félicité, son extase ne sont point susceptibles d'être dépeintes" [her bliss, her ecstasy do not lend themselves to description].[33] The difficulty in question is not one of conversational appositeness: it is a problem of fidelity to the experience itself. Delightful ecstasies, it is affirmed, are much easier to feel than to depict (*Lettres galantes et philosophiques de deux nones* [1797]).[34] "Feeling" the ecstasy is a task for the reader, a task to which she or he is invited or compelled by ellipsis. The "problem" with description, and indeed with representation in general, would now appear to be that they constitute a form of mediation or transfer, in which the original heat of passion is dissipated. Nerciat's *Le Diable au corps* warns us, by a quite typical piece of narratorial self-disparagement, that "Ce qui suit ne peut être jeté sur le papier sans perdre de son extrême chaleur" [What follows cannot be put on paper without losing its extreme heat].[35] The very show of weakness is in fact part of the theme: ellipsis is compelled by the force of the event being described, and the function of narratorial comment is to make the reader, who must share the weakness, feel the force of compulsion. Here is a (non-) description from *Les Aphrodites*: "Madame Durut devient presque furieuse et, faisant d'étonnants haut-le-corps, dit de ces folies que le récit ne peut que refroidir; on les supprime pour passer à la suite de leur entretien" [Madame Durut almost went into a fury. She leapt about astonishingly and said extravagant things that can only be chilled in the telling. We leave those out in order to move on to the rest of their exchange].[36] In this text, there is still a narratorial voice taking personal responsibility for ellipsis, but the brunt of responsibility is to be borne by language itself, and the voice can finally do no more than express astonishment. Its refusal to speak further is an unconfident referential gesture—at best a hopeful tribute to the half-lost original.

Jean Marie Goulemot suggests in effect that signalling the erotic motivation of ellipsis is part of the theme: "L'effacement de la parole descriptive du narrateur n'est pas un accident malheureux: elle correspond à une nécessité de son érotisation même" [The effacing of the narrator's descriptive speech is not an unfortunate accident: it is a necessary part of the eroticization itself].[37] My only difficulty with this generalization is that it speaks as if there were only ever a singular necessity at work, that of desire itself, whereas the achievement of erotic narrative in the late eighteenth century and beyond is to lead us to think of erotic description as an exercise in truthfulness. Desire is represented more and more as the direct cause of suspension, sweeping aside as it does so the more traditional demands, and the codified plural desires, of social propriety. Certainly, the true language of unspeakable intensity is not a perfect absence of language: it is the presence of elliptical talk that signifies the inadequacy of words. This is how the acme of pleasure is described or alluded to in Choiseul-Meuse's *Entre chien et loup* (1809): "l'univers est oublié, anéanti par le bonheur . . . nous n'appartenons plus à la terre . . . Pas un mot, pas un soupir; tout langage est trop faible; ah! tous deux nous avions assez vécu" [the universe was forgotten, reduced to nothing by happiness . . . We no longer belonged to the earth . . . Not a word, not a sigh. Any language was too weak. Ah! We had both known all that there was to know in life].[38] The story of pleasure finishes, exquisitely, at the point where language ceases to function.[39]

Romantic narrative actually exploits a formal variation on suspension marks that further contributes to the representation of the unspeakable: whole lines, whole paragraphs, almost whole pages of dots. The earliest example of this I have found is in Cazotte's *Le Diable amoureux* (1776), where an erotic description culminates thus:

> deux bras dont je ne saurais peindre la blancheur, la douceur et la forme, sont des liens dont il me devient impossible de me dégager . . .

> [two arms indescribable in their whiteness, their softness, their shape, became bonds from which it was impossible to free myself]
> . . . .
> . . . .
> . . . . [40]

Ellipsis is not attended here by other forms of ostentation or reflexivity; it has simply expanded to occupy, and empty, a greater textual space. I can find no evidence that Cazotte's demands on the compositor counted as a revolution in the poetics of ellipsis, but a novel written about fifty years later had a great impact by doing much the same thing. I am referring to Boidin's *Le Monstre* (1824), which, according to Claudine Brécourt-Villars, was considered scandalous for its use of extended suspension. After reminding us that the "few lines of suspension marks" occurring almost at the end of the novel were not produced by censorship but by the author herself, Brécourt-Villars goes on to say: "loin de jeter un voile pudique sur le contenu, l'irruption de ces non-dits semble avoir si bien alimenté l'imagination des lecteurs qu'ils apparurent aussi scandaleux que les descriptions qui précèdent" [far from casting a veil of modesty over the contents, the sudden appearance of these unsaids seems to have so nourished the imagination of readers that they appeared as scandalous as the preceding descriptions].[41] To refer to punctuation marks as *non-dits* seems a rather enthusiastic overstatement of their thematic significance, or at least an undue tribute to the authority of psychoanalytical discourse, but the general point is of great interest and the historical moment no doubt decisive. The text of *Le Monstre* is indeed striking for the way in which it surrounds expanses of dots with narrative markers that leave no doubt as to what is concealed. The narrator-heroine, at the point of climax, is in the hands of a man whose character is perfectly summed up in the novel's title. He is about to assault her sexually, even though he knows her to be his daughter:

J'ose encore lui rappeler que le même sang coule dans nos veines; je le supplie de m'accorder la mort sans me donner l'infamie. Il ne me répond pas, il me rejette sur ma couche . . .

[I dared to remind him again that the same blood flowed in our veins. I begged him to grant me death without dishonor. He did not reply, but threw me onto my bed . . .]

. . . .
. . . .
. . . .
. . . .
. . . .
. . . .

There is no ambiguity here: just unutterable, unwritable monstrosity. As if to measure doses of the unspeakable line by line, the story continues with clear temporal indicators and spaces of interruption that allow the (horrified) reader, if not readily to fill in the blanks as a libertine reader might have done, then at least to see that they might perhaps be filled in by an appropriately monstrous writer, one capable of finding words to match the actions of the villain:

Mais ce n'est point assez d'un crime pour ce monstre affamé de sang;
il perce de mille coups ce corps flétri par ses embrassements . . .
[But that one crime was not enough to satisfy the monster, with
his blood lust. A thousand times over, he stabbed the body that
had been soiled by his embrace]

. . . .
. . . .
. . . .

The deictic "ce" that occurs near the beginning of this last sentence is remarkably unambiguous in a text so full of holes: it points to the act that is right at the centre of the previous suspension marks, while the past participle "flétri" [soiled], supplies a verb to complete the ellipsis. The unspeakable occurs thus in stages, and only reaches an end after a final time marker: "enfin il m'abandonna, en prononçant d'odieux blasphèmes, et je perdis tout à fait connaissance" [At last he left me, uttering hateful blasphemies as he did so, and I completely lost consciousness].[42] Brécourt-Villars is of course right to point out that the suspension marks are produced by the author, but there is a sense in which they represent the loss of control, and therefore of authorial responsibility, while at the same time enacting this loss in a confronting manner. There is no censorship, as Brécourt-Villars says, but the narration balks dramatically at the high point of horror and vice. This is ellipsis being used to save us from, and plunge us into, the "sensation" of eroticism. The events omitted are unspeakable in both senses of the word: ellipsis marks a bodily crisis, pleasure or pain, that compels inarticulacy as well as breathless moral indignation.

Within the thematic space of ellipsis, we find both eroticism and reprehension. The moral (or social) requirement that sexual scenes not be described in full coexists, and often happily cohabits, with the pleasure of suggestive understatement. Most of the texts quoted in this chapter exploit this equivocation in some fashion, whether playfully or sententiously, but the cohabitation tends to become more strained, more tensely contradictory in late-nineteenth-century writing. *Un Eté à la campagne* (1868) still makes of it a game rather than a painful difficulty. This is, after all, a more frankly pornographic text than many, though distinguished enough to include telling-by-not-telling within the range of narrative pleasures. Adèle writes to Albertine, her former lover in boarding school: "Je t'écris précisément aujourd'hui parce que, la nuit passée, j'ai rêvé de toi. Je te donne à deviner ce que j'ai fait en me réveillant" [I am writing to you today because last night I dreamed of you. I leave it to you to guess what I did when I woke up].[43] "I give it to you to guess," says the French literally, and the possibility of guessing, with the unambiguous referent that stands behind its show of tact, is indeed a pleasurable gift. "Si tu devines, fais-en autant, mon cher amour" [If you do guess, do the same thing yourself, my sweet love], concludes the letter (418–19). On the other side of the correspondence, however, Albertine unceasingly demands of Adèle that she provide a detailed account of every erotic event that takes place during the summer holiday. In response to one particular letter, she congratulates Adèle on being an excellent "historiographer": "Rien d'omis, pas un détail perdu!" [Nothing left out, not a single detail missing!] (463). The text congratulates itself by the same token on the accuracy and explicitness of its description. And Adèle is enjoined to continue in the same vein: "Je compte avant peu sur la savante description de quelques *ébats peu gazés*, selon l'expression de ton Lucien" [I am expecting to have from you soon the learned description of some *lightly veiled frolics*, according to your Lucien's expression] (463; original emphasis). The expression *ébats peu gazés* is a quotation from a more or less literary text read aloud by one of the characters in the novel. Albertine knows that, in her call for explicitness, she has the support of a certain tradition. Indeed, the tradition seems largely defined, at this point, by the possibility of varying the thickness of *gaze*. Within the novel, the thickness varies from one moment to another as description ranges between the invitingly implicit and the excitingly explicit.

While it is tempting to say that *points de suspension* are roughly parallel, in their representative function, to exclamation marks, we are obliged to note a degree of divergence between the two that becomes more evident in late-nineteenth- and twentieth-century writing. The use of suspension marks had long been ambiguous, and productively so. They served to signify narratorial restraint on the one hand, and the enunciative difficulty of erotic expression on the other. But insofar as erotic literature comes to thematize utterance as the direct emergence of sexual truth, it becomes disquietingly uncertain whether suspension marks are merely the rhythmic complement of exclamations or their contradictory opposite. Do they bespeak the breathlessness that necessarily follows passionate utterance, or do they mark forbearance from obscenity and the veiling of strong scenes? In classical writing, the problem did not arise with any acuity. Crébillon's ellipses were an occasion for playful verbosity on the part of the narrator, while broken utterances occurred in the characters' dialogue from time to time. Nerciat and some of his contemporaries cut through the difficulty by declaring, politely enough, the end of precious civility and the triumph of forthright sexual representation. But self-styled pornography's rejection of euphemism hardly sufficed to remove the ambiguity from the broader field of erotic fiction. Both elements, the intense and the restrained, are strongly present in the blend of obscenity and indignation that marked the end of Boidin's monstrous story. And their coexistence becomes even more visible in erotic novels of the late nineteenth and early twentieth centuries, as these texts regularly attempt to hold together the pleasure of intimate knowledge and the moral excitement of scandal. This is true of Péladan, Mendès, Barbey, and thirty or so lesser authors cited in this book.

I will give a few examples of the fin-de-siècle pattern, but before doing so I will show how the norm is marked by the self-conscious exception found in certain texts. Some fiction of a libertarian—as distinct from a libertine—kind refuses any thematic indirectness and declares its wholesale opposition to suspension marks as a sign of restraint. Emile Henriot, in his influential twentieth-century definition of books of the "second shelf," speaks for the enemies of ellipsis and takes a remarkably narrow view of the genre. He says that suspension marks have only one role, that of marking the disjointedness of passionate speech:

> La nécessité de tout dire, particulière à la littérature érotique, tient à ceci d'abord que la règle y est d'étonner. . . . [C]omme les estampes qui les ornent, ces livres veulent d'abord être sans voile, et les points de suspension n'y ont jamais droit de cité que pour marquer, non la réticence d'une pudeur qui n'y a que faire, après tout, mais ces soubresauts du discours au moment même où par l'effet de l'émotion, les personnages mis en scène n'ont plus le loisir que d'exprimer leurs sentiments sur un mode bien compréhensiblement entrecoupé.

[The need to say everything, which is particular to erotic literature, arises from the fact that the first rule is to astonish the
reader. Like the etchings that adorn them, these books see themselves as without veils. Suspension marks only have a place in
them because they mark, not reticence or modesty, which really
have no place there, but the sudden disturbance of speech at the
very moment when, under the impact of their emotion, the characters can only manage to express their feelings in an understand-
ably jerky way.][44]

This is a considerable overgeneralization, ignoring the history of
classical civility and understatement on the one hand, and denying later, more ambivalent attempts to confront obscenity on the
other. Some texts are militant exponents of Henriot's view, but
they are, as I have suggested, self-consciously opposed to the
dominant practice. They declare their hand as libertarian by the
outright rejection of ellipsis, which they consider insipid and
conformist. The authorial voice of *Mémorandum galant, ou confession d'une femme légère* (1903) promises that there will be no
points de suspension in the text that follows. We shall witness all
the ecstasy and hear all the exclamations: "je promets . . . aux
zigs qui me liront de ne pas remplacer par des lignes de points
les plus belles extases, les cris de jouissance, les exclamations
nerveuses dues à l'épilepsie momentanée des voluptueux dont je
vais narrer les exploits" [I promise all the guys who are reading
this that in the deeds I am about to relate I will not allow lines
of dots to take the place of great ecstasy, cries of pleasure, and
uncontrolled exclamations produced by the momentary epilepsy
of voluptuous creatures].[45] In this view, *points de suspension*
appear as the enemy of exclamation, and the task of confessional narrative is to expunge them. The "author" of the later
Une Heure de désir (1929) assures us that the very substance of
her story is to be found beneath the deceptive covering of suspension marks: "Les trois points de suspension chers aux
écrivains d'hypocrisie traditionnelle sont précisément la substance du présent livre" [the three suspension dots so dear to the
writers of traditional hypocrisy are exactly the subject of the
book you are reading].[46] We should note, in the face of such disparagement, that angry rejection still does not put an end to the
theme's ambiguity, even if it is now denounced as duplicity. Suspension marks are still seen to designate the heart of erotic activity, although they do so hypocritically. By sloganizing a

dynamic movement that takes erotic narrative from the cravenly implicit to the heroically explicit, such texts work against any rhetoric of suggestiveness, tending to replace it with a polemical thematics of liberation and repression. That, as Foucault points out in *La volonté de savoir*, is a decisive move for modern discourse about the sexual.[47]

Far more numerous at the end of the nineteenth century are texts of a prurient kind that actually work out their prurience, their mixture of pleasure and indignation, through the practice of ellipsis. Sometimes they claim to answer the double exigency of propriety and sexual honesty by avoiding explicit statements, except of course the statement that they are avoiding them, and having the sexual truth work itself out in relentless narrative. The authorial voice in *Mademoiselle Giraud, ma femme* (1870), for example, claims to have manifested the underlying (sexual) causality of the action—a young woman's lesbianism as it happens—without actually speaking it. Since the naïve narrator-hero does not himself understand the cause, his talk is only revealing to a knowing ear, and "we" experienced readers are assured that the central truth is beyond the reach of innocents and ignorants: "L'auteur a préféré souvent pécher par trop d'obscurité que par trop de clarté, et il est persuadé que si ce roman venait à s'égarer au milieu de jeunes esprits, il resterait énigmatique" [The author has seen fit to err on the side of obscurity rather than clarity, and he is persuaded that if his novel were by chance to fall among young minds, it would remain enigmatic].[48] This is an unruffled statement of the theme by comparison with certain other novels. At times, the conflict between repression and freedom becomes a veritable drama, brought to a head in moments of ellipsis. *La Fille de Gamiani* (1906), for example, uses suspension marks to signify a struggle between the urgent truth of sex and a demanding moral constraint on language. The narration makes a great show of its efforts to be truthful while avoiding the offense of undue explicitness, and thereby countering the threat of a lapse into pornography. The generic distinction is hard to maintain, and the struggle to avoid the lapse made all the more difficult by the fact that the novel, through its title, claims to be a direct descendant of the most notorious piece of erotic fiction produced in nineteenth-century France. The point of this rhetorical balancing act is no doubt to exploit the fame of the earlier work without incurring the same moral and legal condemnation, and this can best be accomplished by narrative ellipsis. When Jeanne, the heroine, is described as sinking into debauchery, we are informed that she acquires a dog and begins to drink heavily in the company of a group of women. Given our knowledge of the original *Gamiani*, we should have no difficulty imagining an erotic scenario with these elements, and that is more or less what the novel invites us to do. We are then faced with two-thirds of a page of dots, followed by an authorial footnote that characterizes the missing events in moral terms: "Plusieurs feuillets out été éliminés de cette publication parce qu'ils narrent, avec des détails scabreux, des scènes d'orgies déconcertantes" [Several pages have been eliminated from this publication because they relate, in scabrous detail, disturbing scenes of orgies]. The author is laboring at the generic limit of eroticism and moralization, and he cannot but remind us of this struggle. In fact, his morality faces both ways, condemning both the hypocrisy of veiled language and the directness of pornography: "l'auteur, désireux d'écrire une œuvre d'entière vérité, tait ces passages pénibles, pensant que cela vaut mieux que de les dénaturer en les présentant sous une forme acceptable, mais hypocrite" [the author, who desires to produce a work of complete truth, is omitting these painful passages, in the belief that this is better than distorting them by presenting them in an acceptable, though hypocritical form]. The last part of the note makes a generic claim on behalf of the work, in contradiction with its title and other titillating elements of the work: "Le présent ouvrage vise à une portée morale. Il irait à l'encontre de son but s'il falsifiait la pensée de l'héroïne ou s'il frisait la pornographie" [This work has a moral aim. It would be untrue to its purpose if it falsified the heroine's thought or went close to pornography].[49] The narrative seeks to maintain its prurience by exploiting suspension marks to the full, both as ostentatious reference and as a show of reprobation.

The ambivalence of ellipsis is brought to a kind of thematic crisis in the fiction of Georges Bataille, whose work is rather beyond the historical scope of this study. Bataille elaborates a veritable poetics of obscenity for which the notion of "explicitness" is hardly pertinent. Transgressive acts are evoked and declared at the same time to be unspeakable. Even as they are celebrated, they are surrounded by breathless horror.[50] *Madame Edwarda* (1941) contains lines of dots that are used less for concealment than as a way of intensifying the description of copulation. Here is how the long ellipsis concludes:

. . . .
. . . .
. . . . les glaces qui tapissaient les murs, et dont le plafond lui-même était fait, multipliaient l'image animale d'un accouplement: au plus léger mouvement, nos cœurs s'ouvraient au vide où nous perdait l'infinité de nos reflets.

[the mirrors that lined the walls, and even made up the ceiling, multiplied the animal image of copulation: the slightest movement caused our hearts to open into the void in which our infinite reflections were lost.][51]

All around the room, all about the ellipsis itself, are mirrors that multiply the central image, yet their reflections and their reflexivity only serve to open up an ever-widening gap in the centre of the body of narrative. Far from concealing nudity, they actually aggravate it, producing it in glory, as a kind of empty fullness. Ellipsis has become here the figure of ultimate unspeakability. It transfigures that which must not be seen into something dazzlingly invisible. Ellipsis becomes then the mark of obscenity *stricto sensu*.

6

Climax

It is problematic whether the notion of climax deserves to be considered a technical term in the general description of narrative or simply a particular thematic configuration found in certain stories. In a sense, it is both of those. Everyday discussions of narrative refer regularly to the climax as the central event, the crux of meaning in a story. The climax is routinely taken to be the high point of tension and the moment at which complication turns toward resolution. Yet it is only possible to talk about narrative in this way if meaning is thought of as an event that occurs at particular moments, rather than being worked out, as process, through time. The talk of climax belongs, one might say, to the domain of significance, and not to that of signification. Climactic narrative appears not to value time for its own sake but to consecrate what has gone before as a mere prelude, a preliminary to the main event.

This is where the eroticism of narrative meets the narrative of eroticism. A standard modern thematics of sexuality is wedded to a quite particular understanding of the pleasure to be had in stories, for the climax is readily described as the focus of narrative interest. As such, it is the culmination, not to say the vindication, of desire: the moment at which the possibility of infinite deferral yields to the narrow achievement of purpose. Deposited around the notion of climax one finds, so to speak, the heavy thematic sediment of eroticized narrative, which presents itself as the succession of desire and pleasure, arousal and satisfaction. This is what makes of sexuality something eminently tellable, and of telling something erotic.[1] There is a central act, preceded by tributary action and followed by the collapse of interest. Before the climax, there can only be foreplay: after it, sleep, sadness, or a cigarette.

I want to argue here that climax, while now so mundane a notion as often to appear fundamental, is in fact a specific thematic configuration with a history that is bound up with the broader change I have been outlining in this study. I cannot cite narrative theory in support of this claim, partly because narrative theory tends to be synchronic in its approach, but mainly because narrative theory at its most professional has little to say about climax at all.[2] Yet that fact itself may well be noteworthy: it is as if the notion of climax were not considered sufficiently widespread to be the object of general, theoretical description. Instead of theories of climax, narrative theory has tended to develop theories of delay, in which attention is focussed on the durative quality of narrative time. Roland Barthes, for example, writes in S/Z of the tension between the ongoing movement (*déroulement*) of the text and the requirements of the "hermeneutical code," which, by introducing various delays in the revelation of truth, creates a "dilatory space."[3] This theoretical account supposes a rather different understanding of pleasure—and a different narrative eroticism—whereby play is not just foreplay, a preliminary activity that serves contrastively to define the seriousness of climax, but the very stuff of narrative and the very work of textuality. In this context, the end of the story is not to be seen as a handsome bestowal of meaning: it is simply, for Barthes, something of a let-down, a rather tiresome denouement. The final revelation of truth he sees as the closing down of all that held the reader's interest: "le dévoilement est alors ce coup final, par quoi tout le probable initial passe du côté du nécessaire: le jeu est fini, le drame est 'dénoué,' le sujet justement prédiqué (fixé): le discours ne peut plus que se taire" [The unveiling is then the final move by which all that is initially probable crosses over and becomes necessary: the game is finished, the drama "untied," the subject justly predicated (fixed): discourse can only fall silent] (194). Barthes shifts attention from climax to denouement: he identifies the conclusion, or simply the end, of narrative pleasure as the untying of the hermeneutical knot.

Whether all climax is to be read thus as denouement is a moot point and a source of thematic ambivalence. There are two ways to talk about the question, and both need to be kept in mind here. Climax can be assimilated to denouement, as Barthes seems to suggest in the remark just quoted, or the two can be held apart in theory and in practice. When Aristotle writes in his *Poetics* of the "wholeness" achieved in well-made stories, he defines a whole as "that which has a beginning, a middle, and an end."[4] If we were to locate climax in this pattern, that might itself be an anachronistic move, but the very attempt to do so could be revealing. We might presume to identify as the climax of tragedy the point of reversal and/or recognition identified by Aristotle as the central moment. This would make climax distinct from denouement, as insight is distinct from destiny. Yet any attempt to hold the two notions apart when speaking of modern erotic stories is likely to be defeated by the established habit of assimilating the one to the other. It may even be misleading to say that climax occupies the middle of these stories. When the high point is marked by all the conventional signs of intensity, it can be taken to show that there is no more to be achieved once it has occurred: climax will simply collapse into denouement under the force of its own thematic weight. The middleness of narrative is not then constituted, as in Aristotle, by the radical turn of knowledge, but by the climactic peak, with its concentration of thematic and poetic effects.

Now if the middle is just one glorious moment, there may no longer be anything actually durable to separate the beginning of the story from its end. Narrative is in danger of being without substance for it will lack that temporal quality identified by Barthes, Peter Brooks, and others as the very stuff of which stories are made: "the middle as detour, as struggle toward the end under the compulsion of imposed delay, as arabesque in the dilatory space of the text."[5] Erotic narratives of the nineteenth and twentieth centuries, in their desire for climax, often test this paradox to the full. Just as they mark communicative power by the (coded) breakdown of language, they yearn for fulfilment with little regard for the time of their yearning, striving impatiently for the pleasure of conclusion, and pointing up their impatience as impressive proof of desire. They are driven, it seems, by the need to appear driven, spurred on by the prospect of their own prolapsis.[6] The delay on which they necessarily depend for their very extension becomes the object of uneasy disparagement, as they hold fast to the expectation of conclusive erotic action. Climactic denouement appears thus as a hard-won prize wrested from the uncertainties of deferral, and pleasure as a kind of triumphant relief.

It is more subtle—and perhaps the very definition of subtlety—to speak of pleasure as something quite diffuse. Barthes
shows his (nuanced) colors when he reads pornographic texts in
quiet defiance of their own climactic discourse, preferring to
locate the pleasure they give precisely in the middleness of
delay-as-desire: "Les livres dits 'érotiques' (il faut ajouter: de fac-
ture courante, pour excepter Sade et quelques autres) représen-
tent moins la scène érotique que son attente, sa préparation, sa
montée; et lorsque la scène arrive, il y a naturellement décep-
tion, déflation. Autrement dit, ce sont des livres du Désir, et non
du Plaisir" [So called "erotic" books (one must add, "of the standard kind," in order to make an exception of Sade and a few
others) are less given to representing the erotic scene than the
expectation, preparation, and rise of it. And when the scene
comes along, there is naturally disappointment and deflation. In
other words, these are books of Desire, and not of Pleasure].[7] To
the extent that we are persuaded to Barthes's understanding of
textual pleasure, we must conclude that much erotic narrative is
misguided in the way it invites us to move eagerly toward the
great event. The thematics of climax in the nineteenth century,
by its narrative articulation of preliminary desire and conclusive
pleasure, is committed to the pursuit of satisfaction as a high
point of intensity. To seek and find one's pleasure in dalliance, as
Barthes does, is in fact to divert and subvert that standard erotic
narrative. Barthes and all his modern fellow travellers introduce
a pleasurable wandering into what was purportedly a single-
minded quest for the ultimate pleasure.

It is somewhat ironic that Steven Marcus should in fact have
been accepting of climactic discourse even as he delivered the
most damning of judgments on nineteenth-century erotic narrative in its standard forms. Marcus's oft-quoted definition of
pornography identifies a whole class of texts precisely by their
failure to achieve a certain narrative order. He defines nonliter-
ary erotic stories by the fact that they do not have a proper
middle and therefore a proper end: "Most works of literature
have a beginning, a middle and an end. Most works of pornography do not. A typical piece of pornographic fiction will usually
have some kind of crude excuse for a beginning but, having once
begun, it goes on and on and ends nowhere."[8] This amounts to
saying that such stories are generally unable to arrive at a
proper climax, and would thus appear to contradict my general

point; but there is another way to understand it. Marcus's comment falls clearly enough within the broad ambit of a thematics of climax since the concern with whether or not a satisfying ending can be achieved, I shall argue, whatever the assessment of success or failure in particular cases, is endemic to erotic narrative during this period. The very struggle to arrive at a proper conclusion makes for the mutually defining circularity of desire and climax, and this is regularly taken, often maladroitly, to be the business of narrative. Failure to finish properly is indeed a continual threat, and a frequent enough occurrence, but this contributes dialectically to the value of climax, as I shall attempt to show in a later chapter. The fear of not concluding, I suggest, is the thematic double of the climax. It is a ghost that stands hauntingly behind the apparent assurance of definitive pleasure.

The eroticism of climax is denied the privilege of universality and begins to be locatable in history when it is opposed to more diffuse, multiplicitous forms of pleasure such as those identified and advocated by Barthes. If we consider also that climactic narrative was preceded, during the *ancien régime*, by a rather different thematic order (of which I spoke in *Geometry in the Boudoir*), then it may be possible to define climax historically as a phenomenon of nineteenth-century modernity. This is the hope I expressed in the introduction: to circumscribe the discourse at least, if not to contain or undo it. To say that climax was merely a nineteenth-century theme that has now run its course would be quite wrong. Even to claim that it is in decline would be rash, for it remains alive and well in mainstream pornography, and in sexological discourse. My ambition, as I suggested earlier, is to delimit climactic eroticism, marking it off, in particular, from an older discourse of pleasure. It may be that discourses recently emerging in our century have sufficient historical complicity with that of the eighteenth to make the discourse of climax, which certainly dominated the nineteenth century, now appear in its historical contingency, unsupported by the certainty of naturalness.

The eighteenth-century thematic that I wish to use for contrastive effect is the one described in my earlier book. It involves graded *jouissances*, always in the plural, that are presented and enjoyed in series. Let me recall the earlier pattern by giving just one quite elaborate example that is both narrative and philosophical—indeed, strictly both at once. In *L'Art de jouir* (1751), La Mettrie's rather lyrical exposition of the art of pleasure, we find the following description of the proper manner to awaken a sleeping lover:

> que son réveil exactement gradué, comme aux sons des plus doux instruments, la fasse passer en quelque sorte par toutes les nuances qui séparent ce qu'il y a de plus vif; mais pour cela il faut que vos caresses le soient; il faut n'arriver au comble des faveurs que par d'imperceptibles degrés; il faut que mille jouissances préliminaires vous conduisent à la dernière jouissance.

> [Let her exactly graded awakening, as to the sound of the sweetest instruments, take her through all the nuances that go to make up the keenest pleasure; for that to happen your caresses must be finely graded; you must arrive at the height of favours only by imperceptible degrees; a thousand preliminary pleasures must lead you to the final pleasure.][9]

Note that there is a scale of pleasures, whose every rung is to be stepped upon with care along the way to the "dernière jouissance." The focus is not on the intensity of some transcendental moment but on the long and steady progression that is the very shape, the very art of erotic time. Preceding *la dernière jouissance* are all the other, richly finite *jouissances* whose array makes up the space and time of *l'art de jouir*. They do not constitute the preliminaries as mere delay or trivial diversion but as an orderly procedure for the attainment of the highest, most advanced pleasure. There is a summit of delight, La Mettrie goes on to say, and indeed an experience of ecstasy, but the quality of the summit can only be reached when one advances step by quantitative step: "La volupté a son échelle, comme la Nature; soit qu'elle la monte ou la descende, elle n'en saute pas un degré; mais parvenue au sommet, elle se change en une vraie et longue extase, espèce de catalepsie d'amour qui fuit les débauchés et n'enchaîne que les voluptueux" [Sensual delight has its scale, like Nature; whether ascending or descending, it does not leave out one degree; yet when it reaches the summit, it changes into a true, sustained ecstasy, a kind of catalepsis of love that is not available to the debauched and only takes hold of true lovers of pleasure] (183). In this view, there are no quick and dirty climaxes to be had, neither are there any soaring flights of transcendence. Ecstasy simply has its place—the highest—on the scale of pleasures. Whatever change it brings about does not remove one from the space-time of a graded eroticism.

Climbing the scale of pleasures, as La Mettrie shows, is an art, and not just a response to physiological compulsion. The art has to be learned, and that can take time. Erotic pedagogy is thus represented in fiction, and the difficulty of acquisition sometimes made into a theme. It is a matter, above all, of finding an appropriate tempo. La Mettrie's voice addresses one of the women characters thus: "Vous êtes charmante . . . [m]ais vous êtes trop libidineuse: on n'a pas le temps de désirer avec vous. Déjà . . . pourquoi si vite? J'aime qu'on me résiste et qu'on me prévienne, mais avec art, ni trop, ni trop peu" [You are charming, but you are too libidinous. With you, one does not have the time to desire. Already . . . Why the haste? I like to encounter resistance and be forestalled, but skillfully, neither too much nor too little] (193–94). Getting it right is not primarily a matter of satisfying personal taste, even if individual difference is mentioned from time to time. There is a proper rhythm, defined by its measured position between excessive speed and undue slowness. The young hero of Godard d'Aucour's *Thémidore* (1745) manifests his greenness by the fact that he is rather out of time. He talks brashly about the speed of his conquests and the alacrity of his pleasure,[10] but comes eventually to an understanding that leads him to value a slower rhythm: "Ce monde n'est qu'un pèlerinage; il faut faire durer ses provisions jusqu'au bout de la carrière" [This world is just a pilgrimage. One's provisions must be made to last right to the end of the road] (303). For an art of pleasure, this is the very definition of maturity. As if to demonstrate the symmetrical nature of the difficulty, the young hero of La Morlière's *Angola* (1746) reveals his inexperience by progressing too slowly: "peu fait à ces sortes d'aventures, s'il osa espérer de réussir, ce ne fut qu'en imaginant une multiplicité de gradations, dont un peu plus d'expérience aurait pu lui épargner la meilleure partie" [unused to adventures of this kind, he saw the only way to success as involving a multiplicity of gradations, whereas a little more experience would have spared him most of those].[11] Somewhere between the immature extremes there lies a perfectly measured practice of pleasure, a nicely graded way of passing the time.

To discriminate between this thematic order and the emerging order of climax requires no great hermeneutical subtlety, in view of the fact that this very discrimination appears to have become the business of much erotic narrative in the early nineteenth century. We can find in many texts of the time quite forthright deliberations in which gradation and climax are weighed in the balance as narrative options and compared for their erotic yield. The choice made in a given novel will vary, but the mere perception of the options is, I suggest, a symptom of historical change, and each choice is an incremental moment in that process.

In *Julie philosophe* (1791), to take an early example, we find national differences in erotic practice, a commonplace of erotic fiction since at least Aretino, aligned according to this thematic divide. The heroine's encounter with a Dutch sea captain leads her to appreciate a form of virile directness that is associated not only with Flemishness but also—as it was so often in France— with republicanism[12]: "Il me prit par la main, me conduisit dans sa chambre, et là, sans aucun préliminaire, il me jeta sur son lit, et quittant sa pipe, il commença à déployer une énergie républicaine, à laquelle je ne tardai pas de prendre goût" [He took me by the hand, led me to his room, and there, with no preliminaries at all, threw me on the bed, put down his pipe, and began to display republican energy, which I quickly found to my liking].[13] Julie shows her cross-cultural versatility by readily entering into this energetic activity as she responds without delay to the sudden change of position and the frontal attack. This happy experience does not precipitate a total change of erotic values, however, for when she has dealings with a Frenchman during a later stage of her travels, she finds that her compatriot is able to compensate for his lesser vigor by his practice of erotic refinement:

> il connaissait la volupté dans tous ses raffinements, et il avait une manière délicate, en même temps que très sensuelle, de la faire goûter, qui compensait amplement ce qui lui manquait quant à la force et à la matière: l'art chez lui suppléait à la nature, et avec tant d'adresse qu'on ne s'apercevait point du défaut de celle-ci. Dans nos amoureux ébats, nous épuisions tout ce que le génie humain a pu imaginer de situations, de postures, de caresses pour enflammer les sens et mieux savourer le plaisir. Nos préludes valaient la jouissance même et augmentaient le prix de cette dernière.

[He was familiar with pleasure in all its refinements, and had a delicate manner, which was at the same time very sensual, of arousing it [in others]. That compensated amply for what he lacked in strength and substance: art in his case made up for nature, and did it so skillfully that one failed to notice any natural inadequacy. In our lovers' play, we exhausted everything humankind ever imagined by way of situations, positions, or caresses that serve to arouse the senses and heighten pleasure. Our preludes were worth pleasure itself and increased the value of the latter.] (1:117–18)

Julie's French lover practices something very like the *art de jouir* advocated by La Mettrie, and indeed claimed by him as a widely recognized national characteristic,[14] maintaining also a culture of *ars erotica* in the form of studied postural variation, but Julie's appreciation of it, while enthusiastic, is comparative and concessive. It is admittedly less vigorous, she says, and less naturally virile, but these deficiencies are made up for by a delicate art that renders the preliminaries themselves equivalent in value to any singular, final pleasure. Naturalness, with its advantages and disadvantages, is defined by Julie in narrative terms: "La nature ne connaît guère ces convenances sociales que la délicatesse ou plutôt la société a imaginées pour éveiller un peu les sens émoussés. Elle ne calcule pas les données en plus ou moins de plaisir; elle va droit à son but. Un homme grossier, primitif, s'approche d'une compagne; il sent qu'il existe, qu'il faut épandre une portion de son existence. Le code de ces amants est court" [Nature does not know those social niceties that delicacy, or rather society, has dreamed up to stir dulled senses. Nature does not calculate the given situation in terms of more or less pleasure: it goes straight toward its goal. A crude, primitive man approaches a partner. He feels that he exists, and that he must spread about some of his existence. The code of such lovers is limited] (1:8). Just as their social code is limited (*court*), so it seems must be the story of their erotic activity. But moving from brutality to refinement and back, as Julie herself does, is itself both an erotic adventure and an exercise in the philosophy of pleasure.

The heroine of *Julie philosophe* is a republican sympathizer traveling outside her home country. She has no solidarity with émigré reactionaries, yet her vacillating assessment of erotic values corresponds quite closely to the range of views expressed in *Les Délices de Coblentz* (1791), a novel set and produced in the émigré world. Near the beginning of *Les Délices de Coblentz,* we encounter just the sort of judgment that might have been expected in this context: the plebeian class is less delicate, and those who belong to it "ne jouissent que brutalement, sans connaître les raffinements du plaisir" [only take their pleasure brutally, without knowing its refinements]. Their patrician rivals, "avec un physique moins vigoureux, ont l'avantage de jouir plus réellement et de moins s'énerver" [who are less strong physically, have the advantage of taking pleasure in a way that is more real, and keeps better control].[15] But as the story progresses, we hear voices that dissent strongly from the orthodox conservative view. One marquise praises her aristocrat lover well enough, yet adds that his valets are better (1:28). Another produces a veritable tirade against "nos blasés seigneurs, nos efféminés marquis, et tous les fouteurs de la cour" [our worn out lords, our effeminate marquis, and all the fuckers of the court], saying that their "flaccid dicks" are quite unworthy of comparison with that of her favorite servant (2:51–52). No single narrator-hero holds these contradictions together, as in *Julie philosophe*, but their mere coexistence is characteristic of the time.

Novels at the turn of the eighteenth century maintain the thematic contest, finding ways to represent popular eroticism of the "short" kind that give it some narrative status. This is where the so-called preliminaries or preludes come to be identified as a class of pleasures and take their place in stories. It is, historically, the birth of foreplay, defined as tributary to climax. The preliminaries seem to have been made from the thematic residue of the old gradations, but they also include a manifestation of libidinal symptoms whose role is to provoke climax with a minimum of delay. In *Amélie de Saint-Far* (1802), the preliminaries occur regularly but their status is variable and problematic. Amélie's father is refined enough—is it just stereotypical Frenchness?—not to throw his lover Alexandrine onto a bed. Yet he engages with her in fervid caresses of a sort foreign to La Mettrie:

> son heureux amant dévorait avec ivresse les charmes que lui soumettait l'amour; il baisait tout ce qu'il voyait, puis il admirait de nouveau ce qu'il avait baisé; ses mains inquiètes, avides de saisir, s'égaraient partout et pressaient avec une voluptueuse

fureur ce que ses yeux et sa bouche avaient parcouru; il suçait
avec délices les jolies fraises qui couronnaient son sein, il semblait
y puiser une nouvelle existence.

[her happy lover drunkenly devoured the charms that love delivered up to him; he kissed everything he saw, then admired once
again what he had just kissed; his anxious hands, eager to take
hold, wandered everywhere and pressed in wild sensuality those
things that his mouth and eyes had covered; in delight he sucked
the pretty strawberries that crowned her breasts, and seemed to
draw new life from them.][16]

Such passionate contact lacks the artistic order advocated by
classical libertines, for the lover's hands are everywhere at once,
rather than playing the scale of erotic gradation. We are witness
here to a display of desire that signifies the urgent need to reach
a quite specific and necessary conclusion: "l'excès de désir vint
mettre un terme à ces charmants préliminaires. Alexandrine en
donne le signal par le baiser le plus expressif; son amour, fier de
lui voir demander grâce, s'empressa de la satisfaire, et l'on n'en-
tendit plus que le bruit de leurs soupirs" [the excess of desire
brought about the end of these charming preliminaries. Alexandrine gave the signal with the most expressive of kisses; her
love, proud to see her ready to yield, moved quickly to satisfy
her, and all that could be heard was the sound of their sighing]
(1:56). Saint-Far's caresses have served to provoke the "signal"
that brings about the collapse of desire into satisfaction. The
purpose of his "charming preliminaries" is thus both to signify
impatient desire and bring about the move to climax: Alexandrine's impatience is the product of contagion, aroused by contact with her lover's seductive urgency.

It does seem, indeed, to be almost a general verity in *Amélie
de Saint-Far* that the strongest eroticism should be marked by
the most urgent need to conclude. No character incarnates this
erotico-narrative quality better than Colonel Charles, the lover
of Alexandrine, of Amélie's maid Elise, and the would-be seducer
of Amélie herself. The nature of Charles's desire, and the proof of
its intensity, is revealed in a confessional statement he makes to
Alexandrine:

Je ne vous apprendrai rien en vous disant que j'aime Amélie; mais
ce que vous ne pouvez concevoir, c'est l'impétuosité des désirs

qu'elle m'inspire; je volerais dans ses bras avec la certitude d'être écrasé par la foudre, pourvu qu'elle ne me frappât qu'après l'avoir possédée. Il faut que cette nuit même j'éteigne dans les plaisirs une partie du feu qui me dévore.

[You will not be surprised to learn that I love Amélie; but what you cannot conceive is the impetuosity of desires that she arouses in me; I would rush to her arms even though certain to be struck by lightning, provided I were to be struck only after having possessed her. This very night I must quell in pleasure part of the fire that is consuming me.] (1:91)

The evocation of lightning, and the determination that possession should happen that very night, belong to a different temporal order from that of libertine refinement. Erotic representation, at this point, draws us into the drama of impetuosity. This reckless quality of Charles, with its potential yield for dramatic narrative, is seen to be the symptom, and the style, of desire at its most powerful.

Yet *Amélie de Saint-Far*, for all this attention to the frantically climactic, still makes room for its thematic rival—in a literally arresting way. Charles uses the threat of violence to break into Amélie's apartment while she is still sleeping, but he does not hurl himself upon her in the manner his declaration of only a few minutes earlier might have led us to expect. For Amélie's charm as she lies there asleep is such as to arouse even in Charles a slower form of desire and pleasure. The would-be rapist seems compelled by her appearance to moderate his attack: "Charles, qui avait remarqué combien Amélie dormait tranquillement, voulut jouir quelques instants de son sommeil; il réprima ses transports et modéra ses caresses" [Charles, who had noticed how quietly Amélie was sleeping, wanted to dwell for a moment on the pleasure of her sleep; he held back his passion and moderated his caresses] (1:94). As he decides—and now in fact desires—to find pleasure for a while in contemplating her, he is diverted from the lightning strike he had initially imagined. From the first moment he sees her asleep, Amélie's charm has won him over to gradualness, and to the program of La Mettrie's idyllic narrative: "Il respira son haleine embaumée; ce souffle si pur sembla régénérer son âme. Cet homme, qui le moment d'avant menaçait les jours d'une femme fut, par un miracle de l'amour, métamorphosé en amant délicat et tendre"

[He inhaled her perfumed breath; its pure air seemed to regen-
erate his soul. This man, who only a moment before had been
threatening the life of a woman, was by a miracle of love transformed into a delicate, tender lover] (1:94). Here, Choiseul-
Meuse's narrative holds us at a point of thematic equivocation.
Erotic stories can go either way, since it is still possible to be
charmed by gentle, childlike qualities into giving up the immediate narrative program of high impact virility: "Charles, qui
n'avait jamais su apprécier ces faveurs délicieuses qui sont le
principal ou l'accessoire du plaisir selon celui que les reçoit,
pour la première fois, les savoura avec délices" [Charles, who
had never appreciated these delightful favors, which are essential or secondary, according to who receives them, tasted such
delights for the first time] (1:94–95). Are they, in fact, *le principal* or *l'accessoire*? The narrator gives a rather facile double
answer to her own question, suggesting that it is a matter of individual taste, but we have just witnessed a dramatic contest in
which the force of Charles's violent natural preference is overcome in a trice by the gentle seductive power of the sleeping
child-woman.

Another novel by the same author, *Julie, ou j'ai sauvé ma rose*
(1807),[17] is more adventurous and more concerted, although
finally almost as ambivalent, in confronting this thematic
option. At the outset of a promising career as a respectable
woman of pleasure, Julie is counseled by her friend Adolphe to
adopt the tactic of saving the last stronghold of virtue, her
"rose," by the most engaging kind of forward defense-as-retreat.
She must learn how to yield slowly, step by step, so as finally
not to yield all:

> Livre-toi à l'amour sans chercher à lui opposer une résistance inu-
> tile, goûtes-en tous les plaisirs; perfectionne, si tu le peux, l'art
> d'en prolonger les jouissances, de les rendre plus vives, plus
> enivrantes. Nage dans une mer de délices, mais aie le courage de
> conserver assez de sang-froid, au sein même de la volupté, pour re-
> fuser la dernière faveur.

> [Give yourself over to love without putting up pointless resistance;
> taste all its pleasures; perfect, if you can, the art of prolonging its
> delights, of making them more lively and more dizzying. Bathe in
> a sea of delights, but resolve to keep calm enough, in the very
> heart of pleasure, to deny the last favor.][18]

This is what Beth A. Glessner calls, with undue earnestness, Julie's "strict moral philosophy."[19] The strictness here is in fact at the service of carefully managed pleasure. Insofar as all the intermediary pleasures can be drawn out and given their fullest value, then the "last" pleasure will indeed be held back without being explicitly denied, indefinitely delaying the woman's ultimate capitulation. Julie's sexual politics, when she takes this advice, thus involve a series of pleasantly minor diversions, in slow-handed erotic style, from the more vigorously direct action promised or threatened by her male partners. Such successful "defeats" are only achieved through sustained close combat. One partner, Camille, throws her onto a sofa in an unambiguous declaration of his intention, but she resists charmingly and divertingly: "Si l'attaque fut vive, la défense ne le fut pas moins; l'ennemi s'empara des alentours, mais il ne put parvenir jusqu'à la citadelle" [The attack may have been lively, but the defense was no less so; the enemy captured the surrounds, but was unable to reach the citadel] (219). In this very resistance to what appeared inevitable defeat, there is a kind of political satisfaction to be had, as she observes in passing (219). But beyond that, or rather enfolded within it, are all the gentle subtleties of the old *art de jouir*, worked out in the hard-won space of deferral. Camille, instead of throwing his partner about the room, now has the time to display hidden treasures of erotic refinement: "Ah! combien, sous ce maître habile, je me perfectionnai dans l'art de jouir! Combien Camille était voluptueux! comme il savourait jusqu'à la moindre caresse, et que de prix il savait lui donner!" [Ah! How I perfected the art of pleasure in the hands of this skillful master! How Camille delighted in pleasure! How he enjoyed every little caress, and what value he gave to each!] (221).

It might be thought, in fact, that Choiseul-Meuse's Julie is closer to her eighteenth-century predecessors than her "philosophical" namesake in the anonymous novel of 1791 discussed above. Where the earlier Julie gave equal weight to new Flemish republican vigor and old French aristocratic refinement, the later one marks a clear preference:

> Heureux celui qui sent le prix de ces premières jouissances, qui sait différer le plaisir pour en augmenter la vivacité; c'est là vraiment savoir jouir!

Ce n'est point à celui qui, doué d'une force d'Hercule, répète, sans s'émouvoir, une jouissance qui vous tue, que la palme de la volupté doit être donnée, c'est à celui qui sait prolonger le plaisir.

[Happy the one who feels the value of these first delights, and knows how to defer pleasure so as to increase its liveliness; that really is knowing how to enjoy!

The prize for sensual delight should not be given to the one who, with the strength of a Hercules, unfeelingly repeats a form of enjoyment that exhausts you: it should go to the one who knows how to prolong pleasure.] (222)

The generalizing "you," the person addressed and included here, is feminine. It is not to be doubted that women will know how to choose, within the broad domain of pleasure, between the brutish repetition of short-lived, violent events on the one hand, and lovingly drawn-out *volupté* on the other.[20] Furthermore, Julie knows how to impose her preference. When she comes to deal with the Don Juan of Marseilles, one Versac, she diverts him from impetuosity to slowness, and from urgent climax to its refined other: "au lieu de l'impétuosité que Versac avait montrée d'abord, il savourait avec délices tout ce que je lui abandonnais, et semblait rendre un hommage particulier à chacune de ses conquêtes" [instead of the impetuosity Versac had shown at first, he dwelt lovingly on everything I yielded up to him, and seemed to honour each of his conquests to the full] (272–73). This is both the means of seduction and the form of eroticism to which the formerly impetuous male is now seduced. Little wonder that Julie's later dealings with the beautiful Caroline should go so well, for both lovers espouse these "feminine" rhythms, finding their pleasure in the same, slow tempi: "Caroline, dont les désirs ne connaissaient plus de frein, me fit passer, pour les satisfaire, par toutes les gradations du plaisir" [Caroline, whose desires were now completely unhindered, took me, in order to satisfy them, through all the gradations of pleasure] (293). Pleasure with another woman, this quotation affirms, responds to desire that is just as strong as any other. But its very *furia* is channeled, sustained, and enhanced by the "extraordinary refinement" (293) of graded *jouissances*.

Yet despite all this, and despite the quietly triumphant title of her story, Julie is not always sure that she has chosen the right path. Her choice could hardly be more explicit, but this very explicitness keeps in play that which she wishes to set aside. A mysterious power is attributed to the experience she has denied herself, and the thought of it continues to linger at the back of her mind, at the back of her story. There is a tale that she did not want to be telling, a *jouissance* she was not prepared to live, and yet she cannot rid herself of it completely. At times, for example, she speaks defensively of her *art de jouir*, referring to it as a half-measure: "Ces premières amours avaient pour nous tant d'attraits, que Camille oubliait souvent, dans mes bras, qu'il n'était heureux qu'à moitié" [These first expressions of love held so much charm for us that Camille often forgot, while in my arms, that he was only half successful/happy] (222). The full measure, of course, must be that of the other story, the standard narrative of climactic penetration, but the cruel thing is that Julie cannot properly gauge her "happiness" as a fraction of the whole, caught up as she is in a lifelong series of gradual pleasures. She describes herself, in contradiction of her stated principles and avowed delights, as not properly enjoying her play with Alberti, as "deceiving our senses" (241). When finally overcome by desire for a complete "defeat" (237), she is ironically thwarted by Alberti's mutilated condition, and cries out for the ecstasy she cannot and will not know: "ce bonheur suprême, qui nous met au niveau des dieux, cette jouissance unique que j'avais si souvent refusée, et que j'étais prête à implorer, hélas! je la désirais en vain!" [The supreme happiness that raises us to the level of the gods, the unique pleasure that I had so often rejected and that I was now ready to beg for, alas! I desired it in vain!] (237–38).

A contemporary of Choiseul-Meuse, Andréa de Nerciat, takes his place in this debate as an aggressive spokesperson for the other side, an ardent exponent of impetuosity. For Nerciat, one of the most telling signs of desire-and-pleasure is the very promptness, the wonderful ease with which two lovers melt into each other: "deux verres d'eau ne sont pas plutôt mêlés, confondus, unifiés, que ces lascives et brûlantes créatures" [two glasses of water are not more quickly mixed, dissolved, and unified than these two burning creatures].[21] This speed is the sign of naturalness, whether it be that of fire or water, and the time taken for true desire to achieve its end seems to be always the same: "la paille ne vole pas plus tôt à la flamme que nous à notre objet" [Straw is not drawn more quickly to a flame than we are to the object of our attention].[22] Anything that stands in the way of this

happy fusion is to be dissolved, consumed, or cast aside without
a thought: "tout se consomme sans aucune précaution de part ni
d'autre: ils demeurent quelques moments plongés dans le délire
extatique du souverain bonheur" [all is consumed without any
precaution on either side: for a few moments they are plunged
into the ecstatic delight of supreme happiness] (*Le Diable au
corps* 1:91). Yet even as the gradations are flung aside, they are
glanced at in passing with a kind of impatient irony. In *Les
Aphrodites*, the energetically-named Limefort volunteers for the
task of deflowering a young Violette. He sets about his work in a
way that might be called gallant, even classical, although the
motive behind his method is not entirely clear to the narrator:
"Soit obéissance, soit galanterie, soit raffinement de volupté,
Limefort prélude et veut d'abord baiser la plus fraîche des vir-
ginités . . ." [Whether from obedience, gallantry, or the refinement of sensuality, Limefort begins with a prelude, and makes
to kiss the freshest of virginities]. It may be that Limefort is following an *art de jouir*, but the narrator is uncomprehending and
dismissively vague about this. Certainly, Violette, in her youthful enthusiasm, cuts through all the niceties: "mais Violette,
rugissant au moindre contact, plante ses doigts dans les cheveux
du langayeur et lui donne, en l'attirant violemment, une preuve
presque cruelle du plus impatient désir. Il faut y sacrifier toutes
les gradations délicates" [but Violette, roaring at the slightest
contact, plunges her fingers into the hair of her tongue-lover
and, pulling him towards her, gives him almost cruel proof of the
most impatient desire. All the delicate gradations have to be
done away with] (*Les Aphrodites* 1:93). When virgins roar like
lions and display almost brutal impatience, they speak with the
voice of desire, as if to rebuke experienced libertines, or at least
to remind them of the futility of erotic gradations in moments of
intensity. The kind of action valued here is not the gentle step
but the leap into the other's embrace: "franchir du premier saut
l'amour et tout ce qu'il comporte, me jet[er] à corps perdu dans
les bras de l'impudent" [to jump in one move over love and all
that goes with it, and to throw myself into the arms of the bold
young man].[23] Not just throwing one's partner about, then, not
just scattering one's clothes in all directions and disturbing the
furniture, but leaping in a single, libidinal bound over all those
tired precautions and preliminaries. This is, for Nerciat, the
style of a truly ardent eroticism.

Even as he describes incidents in which crudeness and directness are presented as positive qualities, Nerciat's narrator is refined enough to know that he must seek to reassure his reader
about this lack of refinement. He wonders, indeed, whether the
reader of Le Diable au corps might not be tiring of all the "priapic excesses" that are being recounted. To any objection of this
sort, he can only respond that his chosen subject requires him to
turn away from libertine delicacies:

> Le Diable au corps:—Ce n'est pas l'avoir que de sacrifier molle-
> ment, voluptueusement, aux charmes, aux grâces, à la fraîche et
> séduisante jeunesse; de s'assortir; de régler ses goûts et même ses
> caprices. Lecteur? . . . si vous mettez des bornes au plaisir, au
> caprice lui-même; si vous refusez de croire à leur pouvoir, et doutez
> de leurs moyens excessifs; si les produits extravagants qui peu-
> vent en résulter, n'ont pas de prestige pour vous; bornez-vous aux
> romans de boudoir, à la petite curiosité libertine: ce livre n'est pas
> votre fait.

> [Le Diable au corps:—This does not mean sacrificing languidly
> and voluptuously to charms and graces, to fresh, attractive youth,
> or carefully choosing one's partner, and regulating one's taste, or
> even one's whims. Dear reader, . . . if you put limits on pleasure, on
> caprice itself, if you refuse to believe in their power, and cast doubt
> on their excessive means, if the extravagant outcomes to which
> they can give rise have no standing in your eyes, then just restrict
> yourself to boudoir novels, to trivial libertine curiosity: this book is
> not for you.] (Le Diable au corps 4:226–27; original emphasis)

This is a thoroughly assertive delimitation of genre within a
highly contested field. It is what Anne Freadman would call a
not-statement, marking off this kind of vigorous eroticism from
what it sees as the effete libertinage of the boudoir novel.[24] This
might also be said, by the same token, to mark off the genre that
many modern readers are wont to call "vulgar pornography," as-
serting as it does the erotic value and the immediate authenticity of crude expressions of desire. By this kind of generic
definition, Nerciat lays claim to a particular thematic territory
within the broad domain of "erotic literature" through his depre-
ciation of gradualism and his enthusiastic promotion of urgency
as the mark of true desire. Le Diable au corps locates desire
from the outset as a force that is both diabolical and corporeal,
requiring satisfaction as its almost immediate consequence.

The tendency in novels of the following decades is for the thematic option illustrated by Nerciat to gain ground over the one
defended by Choiseul-Meuse. To the extent that the two parallel
themes remain in competition, there are clear signs that the
struggle for ascendancy has become progressively more unequal. In *Amours, galanteries, et passe-temps des actrices* (1833),
a number of erotically experienced women take the opportunity,
in the absence of their male companions, to describe their favorite forms of pleasure. The first one to speak dwells on the
pleasures of the hors d'œuvre.[25] She tells of a particular encounter in which the "sweet preliminaries" gave her great delight,[26] and then goes on to claim that no position and no
climactic pleasure are equal to those of the prelude: "je crois que
telle posture que l'on prenne pour arriver à la jouissance, elle ne
vaut jamais le doux plaisir que nous goûtons par les préliminaires" [I think that whatever position one adopts for reaching
pleasure, it is never equal to the sweet pleasure we find in pre-
liminaries] (1:24). Her advocacy of these pleasures is somewhat
defensive, since it takes up the trivializing expression *la petite
oie* as a description of the nonclimactic,[27] and affirms—despite
the adjective *petite*, and despite the very terms of the defense—
that the lesser deserves to be considered equal. *La petite oie* provides, she says, more lasting pleasure: "si on était raisonnable,
on se bornerait toujours à *la petite oie*, la jouissance n'en serait
pas moindre, et elle aurait l'avantage d'être plus durable" [If
people were reasonable, they would always restrict themselves
to *la petite oie*. The pleasure would be no less great, and it would
have the advantage of lasting] (1:24; original emphasis). For this
option—which is the first one considered in the text, and is
therefore itself a kind of prelude—the person who speaks next
has nothing but scorn. It is not that such things have no value,
she concedes, but they must be kept in their place and in their
time as preliminaries to the real thing: "la petite oie, fi donc, et
par crainte de la grossesse encore, la petite oie; mais c'est
presque du platonisme, passe encore de l'employer pour se
mettre en train, mais. . . . Jouir est tout, voilà ma maxime et ce
dont vous parlez est tout au plus une demi-jouissance, selon
moi" [*la petite oie*, for heaven's sake! Through fear of pregnancy,
perhaps; but this is almost Platonism. It might be understandable as a way of getting started, but . . . pleasure is all, that's my
motto; what you are talking about is only half-pleasure, in my

view] (1:30). For this second, more authoritative speaker, who is not in fact contradicted by any who follow her, what might once have been called gradations, here poorly defended as *la petite oie*, are simply the half-measure that Choiseul-Meuse's heroine had feared. There is only one *jouissance*, one truly complete pleasure, and all others are trivial by comparison: "le suprême bonheur consiste dans ce doux châtouillement que nous éprouvons lorsque le sperme de l'homme s'élance vigoureusement du réservoir qui le contenait et vient darder jusqu'au plus profond de notre matrice" [supreme happiness consists in the sweet tickling we feel when the man's sperm comes spurting vigorously out of its reservoir and penetrates deep into the womb] (1:30–31). Outside this central, natural pleasure there are only fiddling and fumbling, peripheral slap and tickle, "les bagatelles de la porte" [gateway bagatelles] (1:60).

This message is rammed home, so to speak, in a number of other novels published in the early 1830s. *Vingt ans de la vie d'un jeune homme* (1831), *Les Amours de garnison* (1831), and *Les Amours secrètes de M. Mayeux* (1832) are all swiftly convincing demonstrations of virile desire, and often terse celebrations of its performance. In *Vingt Ans de la vie d'un jeune homme,* manliness is exemplified in the hero's actions and enunciated with monosyllabic vigor in his narration: "je la trousse, je vois son con, je lâche mon vit, et sans plus de cérémonie, je la fous. A peine étais-je entré que d'un coup de cul elle me fait aller jusqu'au fond et, croisant ses jambes sur mes reins et remuant la charnière, elle décharge; j'en fais autant" [I lifted her skirts. I saw her cunt. I let go of my dick. And without any more ado, I fucked her. No sooner was I inside her than with a thrust of her ass she drove me all the way in and, crossing her legs behind my back, she unloaded. I did the same].[28] No waiting, no delay. Not even time for a subordinate clause or a periodic sentence. This is the eroticism of unadorned, almost brutal parataxis. It is no coincidence, of course, that this should be a young man's story: youth appears here as a state of unreflecting natural vigor. Young men know how to get on with the job, and have no need whatsoever to be trained for it: "sans perdre de temps, je l'enfilai" [wasting no time I thrust inside her] (*Vingt Ans de la vie d'un jeune homme,* 18). Soldiers, too, can be relied on for their readiness to spring into action, as *Les Amours de garnison* shows. There is hardly time, in the amorous world that surrounds the garrison, for "les propos d'amour" [amorous talk] and "les fadaises sentimentales" [sentimental trifles]. Just a brief interlude, at most, the "main thing" being "le vit et le foutre" [dicks and *foutre*].[29] Should it happen exceptionally that a soldier lose sight of the main point, failing to act as a prompt and efficient lover, should he even linger for a few moments before putting his victim to the metaphorical sword, we can expect that he will be reminded of the behavioral norm by the woman herself: there is no time for shilly-shallying. This is how *Les Amours de garnison* comes in fact to repeat the ironic thematic reversal enacted in the scene between Limefort and Violette in Nerciat's *Les Aphrodites*. The narrator-hero finds his partner cutting through the seductive talk, interpellating him, so to speak, with forthright obscenity: "Ce que vous avez dit depuis trois quarts d'heure, avec assez d'esprit, j'en conviens, se réduit à cela, vous avez envie de foutre avec moi, je suis de votre avis, et si nous étions dans un lieu convenable, ce serait déjà fait" [What you have been saying for the last quarter hour, quite wittily I admit, comes down to this: you feel like fucking me. I am of the same mind, and if we were in an appropriate place, it would already have happened] (28). The deed ought to be as promptly executed as it is vulgarly named. Boiling down the old art of seductive intercourse, reducing it to straightforward, wholesome fucking: this is the impatient concern, and the usual narrative outcome, of military eroticism. Better still, perhaps, than the young man or the soldier, more neatly suited to climactic purpose, is the legendary-historical Mayeux, a "hunchback" devoid of visible elegance or refinement, whose sexual prowess is located exclusively in his penis. *Les Amours secrètes de M. Mayeux* recounts his doings in a matter-of-fact, not to say impoverished way, accumulating feats of virility in number and at speed. The novel is not concerned with unfolding a story of durative pleasure but with racking up an impressive score of achievements. Here is a banal example, nicely representative in its very banality: "je pris la plus jolie, et une minute après, le foutre qui l'inondait témoignait du plaisir que j'avais eu" [I took hold of the prettiest one, and a minute later, the *foutre* that was flooding into her bore witness to the pleasure I had felt].[30]

These stories, it must be repeated, are heartily and aggressively crude, affirming their vulgarity as a proud triumph of natural immediacy over outmodedly elaborate conventions of erotic conduct. On those few occasions where "preliminaries" are said to happen—that is, when they are "used" by the hero—they are mentioned by their relatively new generic name but not graced with the time of telling. Mayeux says on one occasion: "après les préliminaires d'usage, je la baisai sur le canapé" [after the usual preliminaries, I screwed her on the sofa] (*Les Amours secrètes de M. Mayeux*, 18). An assumption here, made explicit in another novel of the same period, *La Perle* (1833), is that the reader himself is straining at the leash, eager to get on to the part that really matters. The reader is constructed, or at least addressed, as the subject of gendered libidinal impatience: "Quel tourment! c'est ce qui plus tard abrégea les préliminaires; mais n'anticipons point sur l'avenir, et vous lecteurs, modérez votre impatience. Vous voudrez déjà voir nos deux amants aux prises et même être à la place de celui auquel on va donner la pomme" [What a struggle! That is why, later on, the preliminaries were shortened; but let us not get ahead of ourselves; you readers, rein in your impatience. You already want to see our two lovers coming to grips, and you would even like to be in the place of the one who eventually wins the day].[31] "We" readers must be wanting it all to finish as quickly and decisively as possible, whatever the cost to any supposed pleasures of dalliance. This is why we will necessarily applaud when the old codes fail to be observed, and indeed *La Perle* gives us this satisfaction. In an eighteenth-century erotic situation of the kind described, say, in Crébillon or Diderot, when a woman says to a man, "Finissez!" this is interpreted as a gentle request to desist, or rather as a mark of tolerance, but with the reminder that some restraint is expected. In *La Nuit et le moment*, for example, Cidalise says to Clitandre, "Finissez donc! Attendrai-je éternellement? Vous êtes insupportable!" [Please desist! Shall I have to wait for ever? You are insufferable!].[32] Saying that he is unbearable is in fact a way of "bearing" his attentions, and the use of "Finissez!" indicates, in libertine code, that she is prepared to wait for a time. Clitandre shows his *savoir faire* by interpreting the invitation in all its subtlety: "En me priant le plus poliment du monde de finir, elle me laissait continuer avec une patience admirable" [While requesting me most politely to desist, she showed admirable patience in allowing me to continue] (9:23). When the same expression is used in *La Perle*, however, it is hastily misunderstood—although quite properly so, according to the narrator—as an invitation to bring matters to a head, to finish off: "le feu prit aux poudres, on chancela, on tomba doucement sur un canapé, en disant d'une voix douce et à moitié expirante: *Finissez*. Mot charmant que l'on comprit comme il devait l'être, et La Perle fut enfilée ou foutue, comme mieux vous l'aimez" [the gunpowder caught fire; she tottered and fell gently onto the sofa, saying with a soft, half-expiring voice: *Finissez*. This charming word was understood as it had to be, and the Pearl was screwed or fucked, however you like it put] (*La Perle*, 333; original emphasis). The "charm" here is to be found, one supposes, in the energetic ease with which the traditional response is neglected in favor of an immediate, more narrowly desirable outcome.

The triumph of spontaneity continues to be acted out in later novels of the century. *Mylord Arsouille* (1858) maintains the style of crude, impatient parataxis even as the narration runs through a couple of quick preliminaries: "je baisai sa motte, son con, que je lavai moi-même, je la branlai, je la gamahuchai, et loisqu'elle fut bien échauffée je la foutis" [I kissed her pussy and her cunt, which I washed myself. I worked her over, I licked her, and when she was really warmed up I fucked her].[33] *Les Libertins du grand monde* (1880) displays pride at the characters' avoidance of time-consuming, nay distracting erotic refinements: "nous étions tous deux pressés de jouir, et nous n'employâmes aucun raffinement de volupté" [we were both in a hurry to reach pleasure, and we did not use any voluptuous refinements].[34] *Les Tableaux vivants* (1870), in turn, pay special tribute to that kind of brief encounter in which there is not even time for lovers to undress:

Les jouissances impromptues sont les meilleures. Le coup de robe est délicieux, parce qu'il se consomme au moment juste où l'on en a envie. Le désir est dans toute sa force, l'action est prompte comme la foudre. "Mon ami, nous n'avons qu'un moment. . . ." La phrase s'achève dans un baiser. La belle vous jette les bras autour du cou, vous la renversez sur un sofa, vous la troussez, et . . .

[Impromptu pleasure is the best. Doing it with her dress on is delightful, because it is consumated at the exact moment when you most feel like it. Desire is there in all its strength, and the action is lightning quick. "My dearest, we only have a moment. . . ." The sentence ends in a kiss. The beauty throws her arms about you, you tip her backward onto a sofa, you lift up her skirts, and . . .][35]

Reducing the time of graded *jouissances* to that of a singular *coup*, taking as one's model the drastically natural time of the lightning strike, with its attendant weak pun on *foudre* and *foutre*,[36] throwing the woman onto a sofa: these are all marks of the theme of climax in its most narrowly focused and most clearly ascendant form.

From about 1830 onwards, then, the "preliminaries" are constituted not as a procedural art whose unfolding leads eventually to the last pleasure but as an ill-defined set of half-purposeful activities whose very absence, on particular occasions, signifies a happy libidinal precipitance.[37] It is indeed a requirement of this new thematic economy that such pleasures be kept in a subsidiary place, before and beneath the central peak of climax. Accordingly, one often finds the preliminaries referred to in a negligent or condescending fashion. The hero of *Les Amours secrètes de M. Mayeux* is almost disparaging, at best minimally indulgent, when he says abruptly: "nous fîmes mille bêtises qui aboutirent à foutre, encore deux fois" [we did all sorts of foolish little things that led, twice more, to fucking] (18). *Bêtises* is the name of that which he does not deign to recount, retaining only the specific act of *foutre* that follows, and the number of times this act takes place. In *L'Ecole des biches* (1868), sexual activity between women takes up much of the time of telling, and is generally subject to more polite treatment, but there is a recognizable language of condescension. Two women together are said to reach the highest extent of pleasure that "pareils jeux" [such games] can produce (40). Their games are not a fully developed alternative to the standard narrative route, as was affirmed and later denied in *Julie, ou j'ai sauvé ma rose*, but mere "dérivatifs," situated and justified in the long run of narrative by union with a male lover (54). In the same text, one finds not only repeated use of the word *jeu*, but also the equally condescending *badinage* and *bagatelle*, each time referring to practices that are tolerable for their very insignificance but ought not to be overly indulged lest they distract from the final purpose (71–72, 88). Play in this sense is characterized not by the observance of rules but by the very display of randomness or wantonness. This is what we examined earlier in *Amélie de Saint-Far*, when Saint-Far embraced Alexandrine in so many fashions almost at once, and rained caresses on her from every direction (1:56): the very disparateness of this contact served to communicate his passion. We see it again, more intensely still, in Gamiani's attack on her lover Fanny: "d'un bond, elle s'élance sur Fanny, qu'elle touche, qu'elle couvre partout. . . . Les baisers, les tendres morsures volent de la tête aux pieds. . . . Sa tête, ses mains se multiplient. Fanny est baisée, frottée, manipulée dans toutes ses parties; on la pince, on la presse, on la mord" [in a single bound, she pounced on Fanny, whom she touched and embraced all over. Kisses and tender nibbles ranged from her head to her feet. Gamiani's head and hands were everywhere. Fanny was kissed, rubbed, and manipulated on every part of her body. She was pinched, pressed, and bitten].[38] At the latter end of the century, the movement is somewhat less frantic, but the indiscriminate nature of foreplay is so well established as to be a routine part of the theme. Descriptions of it frequently include such expressions of desire as the following: "il . . . l'embrassait sur l'œil, sur le front, au hasard" [he embraced her on the eye, on the forehead, at random].[39] One embraces better, more fervidly, it seems, by showering kisses at random. But chance may only be indulged when it is promised, so to speak, to purposeful redemption. The narrative virtue of climactic eroticism, through a century of novelistic writing, was to achieve this order in its time, as the proper resolution of temporary disorder. The preliminaries derived their value only from what followed. They functioned largely as an expression of impatience and a summarily coded invitation to haste. Climactic narrative could thus dally momentarily with disorder, but only because it located the final pleasure beyond chance and attained narrative seriousness on the far side of play.

One of the logical by-products of this shift is the opening up of a narrative place beyond climax: that of the aftermath. In some abstract sense, the aftermath must be symmetrical with foreplay, although the dynamics of narrative work against symmetry, making what precedes more literally telling than what follows. If the narrative theorists I quoted above are right, as surely they are, the work-and-play of delay is the very stuff of narrative, however much it may be devalued by explicit thematic comment in the climactic stories we have just been considering. So often, as I pointed out earlier, these stories display the collapse of middle into end, of turning point into denouement, yet they do not always collapse so quickly as to extinguish all sense of the aftermath as a particular kind of subsidiary pleasure—

including the very pleasure of collapse itself. Even the turbulent
heroes of Nerciat experience a certain quality of pleasurable silence that is heard after the shouting is over: "un extatique et
long silence caractérise le crépuscule de cette jouissance enfin
couronnée par un sonore et mordant baiser" [a long ecstatic silence marked the twilight of this pleasure, which was finally
crowned by a resounding, sharp kiss] (Les Aphrodites 2:97). In
this lapse from agitation to stillness, from "exaltation" to "calme"
(Histoire d'un godmiché [1886]),[40] there are no coded gradations,
merely the gentle subsidence of trembling aftershocks: "après les
plus amples décharges et les plus multipliées, nos belles
restèrent en extase sans mouvement, serrant les fesses avec de
petits mouvements nerveux et convulsifs, les yeux à moitié en-
tr'ouverts et noyés dans une langueur heureuse" [After the most
copious and oft-repeated discharges, our beauties remained in
motionless ecstasy, their thighs clenched and twitching convul-
sively, their eyes barely open, bathing in languid happiness]
(Mylord Arsouille [1858] 39). The half-opened eyes and the langorousness are not the old marks of libertine refinement but
pleasurable symptoms enjoyed in the course of a slow return to
an unaroused state. For novels at the turn of the twentieth century, there is a special quality of post-climactic stillness that
seems momentarily to suspend life itself: "Et l'étreinte qui suivit
eut pour tous deux une plénitude de sensations qui les laissa ensuite pendant des minutes vaincus, le cœur, la pensée, la vie sus-
pendus . . ." [And the embrace that followed was so full of
sensations that it left them exhausted for some minutes after,
their hearts, their thoughts, their lives brought temporarily to a
stop] (Les Amours perverses de Rosa Scari [1907]).[41] It is as if
these precious minutes allowed the lovers to savor the recency,
the very closeness of ecstatic death. "Le sommeil des amants
lassés . . . ," we read in Rires, sang, et voluptés (1901), "c'est un
peu la mort" [The sleep of tired lovers . . . rather resembles
death].[42]

I want to turn now to a closer examination of the late nineteenth and early twentieth centuries. Erotic writing of this
period, from about 1880 to about 1910, deserves attention here
for a number of reasons, not least because it renews the thematic contest between gradations and directness that was
prominent earlier in the century and gives broad significance, of
a different kind, to the contest itself. Unlike novels before about

1830, which were beset by a (diminishing) sense of equivocation between two options, these later stories tend to produce a more elaborate thematics in which the usually positive value of directness is articulated in complex, even dialectical, ways with the often negative value of gradualness or refinement. It still happens regularly enough that speed is celebrated for its own sake, and that pleasure is taken in the specific absence of "préambules" (e.g., *Rires, sang, et voluptés*, 14). It also continues to be the case, from time to time, that the impatient reader is reassured with a promise of speedy progress toward the main event (e.g., *Voluptés bizarres* [1893]).[43] But the choice between directness and refinement is now seen to be of great sociohistorical moment. Langorousness is no longer simply a quality associated with old, perhaps archaic, libertine practices: it is now in the air—or more accurately, in the blood, since so much of society is seen to be ailing, afflicted in its erotic expression by an epidemic loss of vigor. *Le Journal d'un amant* (1902) uses a phrase that would have been a taxing oxymoron for the eighteenth century when it refers to "langueurs navrantes" [distressing langorousness], observed during a journey made by two lovers,[44] but fin-de-siècle writing almost makes of the phrase a tautology. One wonders whether all *langueurs* are not now to be seen as *navrantes*, insofar as langorousness is not just distressing but literally debilitating, and never more so than in erotic stories. What was for much of the eighteenth century the seductive style of an available body comes to be seen here as a disquieting symptom of impotence infecting the physiology of a whole society.

Such morbid weakness is often envisaged as a challenge to virility: maleness at its most vigorously direct, if it can but stiffen the sinew and summon up the blood, ought perhaps to overcome the problem. In any case, erotic stories and erotic dramas provide a likely battlefield for this potentially decisive contest—although the fin-de-siècle question is not who will win but whether the battle will occur. *Mademoiselle Giraud, ma femme* (1870) sets the tone for a number of later novels when it shows a doting husband in a situation resembling prima facie the classic scene of La Mettrie's *art de jouir* but crucially different in one or two particulars. Having been locked out of the conjugal bedroom by his new wife, and thereby denied the expected climax of the wedding night, he eventually manages, weeks later, to enter the room at night by subterfuge. For a moment, he stands in admiration of the half-draped body that lies before him. Will he now move to bring about her awakening, in the full thematic sense of the word? There is not really time for gradualness, as it happens, or even for the pleasures of contemplation: "dans mon deshabillé galant, debout au milieu de la chambre, exposé aux rhumes de cerveau, le moment était mal choisi pour regarder ma femme s'étendre voluptueusement dans son domaine" [in my bathrobe, standing in the middle of the bedroom, exposed to the danger of a head cold, I was hardly at the right moment to contemplate my wife as she lay stretched out voluptuously in her domain]. The risk of catching cold figures the man's frailty and reminds us of the danger, never considered by La Mettrie, that he might lose the physiological heat of passion—which he later does, in fact. As he looks at her, he wonders whether a more direct approach is required: "Ne devais-je pas conquérir [le domaine] au plus vite et m'y installer en maître avant le réveil de l'usurpatrice?" [Ought I not to conquer the domain as quickly as possible and take over before the usurper awoke?].[45] The very fact that he stands still, asking the question about direct action, unable to decide between the two narrative options, shows to what extent slowness and gentleness, so valued by La Mettrie, have now become equivalent to weakness. When he leaves the room, his wife will still be worthy of the title "mademoiselle," for irresolution and impotence are the lot of this young man, and inaction the dominant subject of his story.

Novels in succeeding decades find similar ways to test the (problematic) hero's resolve in relation to his ostensible sexual partner. *Le Désir: journal d'un mari* (1899) and *Inassouvie* (1889) tell much the same story in this regard, with strong thematic echoes also to be found in *La Volupté féroce* (1905) and *Rires, sang, et volupté* (1901). In the first two of these novels, there is a build-up of frustration and an increasing threat of deadly violence resulting from the non-consummation of an official sexual relationship. This non-consummation has nothing in common with dalliance: it treads no primrose paths and cares not a whit about the saving of precious "roses." Indeed, nothing and no one can hope to be saved in these stories, which recount the destruction that must follow inaction, the dreadful consequences of failure to observe the healthy norms of human behavior, as inscribed in the standard climactic program. The husband of *Le Désir* makes an unpardonable mistake in his first advances to his new, still virginal bride: that of being considerate, and listening to her wishes. Confident of his strong position, sure of his virility, he takes the time to reassure his partner, "pouvant la soumettre d'une étreinte et préférant la rassurer d'un sourire . . ." [being capable of dominating her with an embrace and preferring to reassure her with a smile].[46] He believes at this moment that being a true man consists in having the strength, and the kindness, to forbear from brutal directness: "les vrais mâles sont ainsi, trouvent dans la violence même de leur désir la générosité délicate, ou l'égoïsme raffiné d'en reculer la satisfaction" [true males are like that. Even when driven by violent desire, they manage to find the delicate attentiveness or the refined selfishness needed to put off the moment of satisfaction] (35). This attitude, however, whether it be moral elegance or erotic refinement, is the fatal error, the first step on the long downward path of a pathetically unsatisfied and eventually tragic destiny. The immediate consequence of his tact, disturbing the sexist pattern we are supposed to wish for, is that his wife comes to exercise power over him, the power of aloofness, so that his desire is endlessly exacerbated. By the same token, her desire is not allowed to be born as it should have been according to the established story, for she ought to have been transformed on that first night of marriage, being taken from pain to pleasure, and thus from virginal innocence to womanly maturity. When it all begins to go bad, the husband now comes to ask himself how he can have been so foolish as to hold back: "pourquoi avais-je hésité? Pourquoi m'étais-je renfermé dans cette discrétion d'amant transi? Denise n'était-elle pas une femme comme les autres, n'était-elle pas *ma* femme, celle avec qui j'avais le droit et le devoir d'oser?" [Why had I hesitated? Why had I allowed myself to be locked into the position of an awestruck lover? Was not Denise a woman like any other? Was she not *my* wife, the one with whom it was my right and my duty to make the daring advance?] (58; original emphasis). The very definition of his status as husband lies in this circularity of right and duty: he has a duty to himself, to her, and perhaps to pleasure in general. And the carrying out of that duty must involve daring, for only a vigorous attack could bridge the unnatural distance kept open by her resolute defense. His fundamental strategic error—strategic and not tactical because he had mastery of the terrain—has been to imagine that he might move across this gap, step by gentle step, with seductive elegance, enhancing his own eventual pleasure all the while through the practice of delay: "j'avais surtout voulu ménager son innocence, retarder ce rare plaisir de la faire mienne, pour en mieux jouir" [I had especially wanted to look after her innocence and delay the rare pleasure of making her mine, the better to enjoy it] (59). Refinement here is a dreadful psycho-physiological blunder, what he later refers to as "l'excès de ma délicatesse" [my excessive delicacy] (67). His refusal to give vent to the "grossier" [crude] and "brutal" desire he feels (67) leads eventually, by a relentlessly natural process, to the build-up of anger that drives him to kill his wife. This tragic end, we are invited to believe, is the consequence of an overly refined—that is, unnatural—beginning. It is a failure to keep the preliminaries to a bare minimum, a failure to observe the norms of virile action established in erotic novels fifty years earlier. Comparably, when Suzanne in *Inassouvie* treats her official lover and provider Boris in the same distant way, and when we learn that he has already killed five other people in the course of amassing his fortune, a dark cloud of prediction hangs over the story.[47] We are being taught that a woman must not be allowed to keep her partner at a distance since this can only build the potential for her violent end. In each of these two novels, there is a lack of manly directness: the (non-)hero should have bounded energetically, but not destructively, across the female-dominated space of seduction-and-aloofness. Any refinement he may have practiced now comes to be seen as an error—a mere excuse, perhaps simply another name, for erotic decadence.

La Volupté féroce (1905) does not tell quite the same story, but it works within the same topos. Its heroine, the Comtesse de Rochemare, while conversing with her would-be lover Albert, produces a veritable tirade against the men she sees all around her, condemning them for their lack of daring, or even of basic animality: "Les hommes d'aujourd'hui sont des êtres égoïstes qui aiment par vanité, mais il n'en est pas un qui risquerait la cour d'assises pour conquérir une femme, la posséder à tout prix, la violer même; ils sont inférieurs aux animaux" [Men today are selfish creatures who love out of vanity. Not one of them would risk prison to conquer a woman, to possess her at any price, or even rape her. They are inferior to animals].[48] She abhors "notre siècle de veulerie, de lâcheté, de ramollissement" [our century of weakness, cowardice, and soft thinking] (26). There is no longing for seductive gentleness on the part of this woman, no call for sweet nothings whispered at close hand: for her, all those things must be symptoms of generalized chronic fatigue. As it happens, this energetic complaint, for once, does not fall on deaf ears. Albert is goaded by her scathing remarks into self-examination, and indeed into a profound autocritique of his erotic practices. Until now, he realizes, because he has not wanted to behave brutishly, he has found himself with the Comtesse in the classic position of the languishing suitor:

> Je n'ai pas voulu être celui qu'elle désire, qu'elle attend peut-être: la brute farouche, enragée d'amour, qui se rue, prend, éventre! . . .
> Je lui ai murmuré des tendresses pâles et froides. Je lui ai fait du sentiment, comme un étudiant roucoulant aux pieds d'une modiste . . .

> [I have not been prepared to be the one she perhaps desires and awaits: the wild brute, mad with love, that tramples, possesses, and rips open . . .
> I have whispered sweet nothings to her, in a pale, reserved way. I have been all sentimental, like a student cooing at the feet of a shopgirl.] (15)

All is not lost, however, since Albert now sees the error of his ways and the dangers of moral sensibility. He understands that women, and this woman in particular, secretly desire to be thrown about, trampled, raped, and disembowelled. Being still young, he is able to mend his ways, and does so, in fact, with remarkable success, taking on the identity of le Costeau d'Avignon, a vigorous criminal—if that is not itself a tautology. This transformation involves much more than faking a Provençal accent, since it is an exercise in crudeness by which he transforms his dress, his body, and his language so as to deceive the Comtesse and dominate her by his very presence. As a quasinatural consequence, he is able to possess her, so to speak, in passing, with no visible effort of seduction and no apparent concern for her well being. This, as everybody knows by now, is exactly what she desires: "bientôt elle s'était abandonnée, toute offerte et donnée avec une joie vibrante, secouée d'un spasme voluptueux" [soon she had yielded unreservedly, with violent joy, wracked by a voluptuous spasm] (51). The novel's plot, with its almost courageous disregard for all verisimilitude, enacts in one particular case the general transformation that is purportedly needed to restore vigor to an ailing society of over-refined, over-delicate males whose women, we are told, secretly cry out for rape.

In *Rires, sang, et volupté*, this same cry is to be heard, although the tone on this occasion is less desperate, and the consequence less dramatic. Elisabeth, newly married and bearing the title of Vicomtesse, writes to her former lover Raoul, telling of her insipid relations with her husband, who is so smitten as to be absurdly respectful. Elisabeth reveals her frustration at no longer experiencing the violent sexual embrace that she regularly knew with Raoul:

> D'Almide . . . est sans cesse à genoux devant ma beauté, devant mon corps, devant mes formes. Il se met en extase et crie que je suis la plus parfaite créature humaine. Mais que m'importe tout cela s'il n'a pas l'audace ou les bras pour broyer cette beauté contre lui, meurtrir ces chairs trop fines, trop vierges malgré tout! . . .

> [D'Almide is forever on his knees, admiring my beauty, my body, my shapeliness. He goes into ecstasy and proclaims that I am the most perfect of human creatures. But what use is that to me if he does not have the audacity or the strength to crush my beauty against him, to bruise this overfine flesh, which is still too virginal in spite of everything?] (243)

It seems as if society women are unduly constrained by the delicacy imputed to them, condemned to purity by the anemic adoration of society men. Their true wish—according to these texts written by men—is not to be made finer, not to be refined, but to be crushed in violent embrace and made as coarsely material as possible. And if male characters are to be found on their knees in so many of these stories, it is not because the kneeling position signifies playful submissiveness or allows seductive proximity, as it did a hundred years earlier, but because these men are now reduced to unnatural subservience, and to pseudo-erotic abjection.

Not all such stories focus exclusively on weakness and inaction, however. We have already seen that *La Volupté féroce* has a real Hero, and there are other male characters able to rise up

and strike a blow for masculinity. The aging and distinguished
narrator-hero of *La Suprême Etreinte* (1900) has moments of as-
sertiveness—what one might call fits of virility. When he realizes that his mistress has been unfaithful, and that he faces the
prospect of a slow decline into tolerance of that fact, he suddenly
finds the "energy" to hit her.[49] We are not to be in any doubt, according to the novel, that this is a good thing: it is presented as
both a therapeutic moment for him and a turning point in the
story of the couple. He achieves violence, so to speak, as an unexpected victory over his gentle, civilized nature: "Car, enfin, je
suis sûr de n'avoir aucun de ces instincts de brute que je hais
chez certains hommes; au contraire, j'ai la patience et la douce
tendresse des voluptueux qui considèrent la femme aimée
comme la fleur fragile" [I must say that I do not have any of
those brute instincts that I find detestable in certain men. Quite
the contrary: I have the patience and the sweet tenderness of
voluptuous people who treat the woman they love like a fragile
flower] (101). At this point, we can gain a sense that the opposition between directness and refinement has taken on a dialectical quality. The brutal outburst of energy is only of such value
here because it is somehow included within a civilized context.
Without becoming too much like the beasts he continues to
despise, the hero seems to experience what we might call the
inverted grace of momentary brutality. When, at one time
thereafter, he hurls himself at his mistress in desperate passion, he is revisited for a moment by the same brutal force and
experiences a full nocturnal transformation into animality. He
pounces on the sleeping woman with never a thought for any
art de jouir:

> Je serrai l'étreinte, et, sur l'herbe mouillée, dans une confusion
> [emphatically not a gradation] de toutes sortes de baisers, comme
> un sauvage, ou plutôt, comme ces fous lubriques qui vont la nuit,
> dans les cimetières, déterrer les cadavres pour les violer, je pris ma
> maîtresse, je la possédai, je l'aimai dans un accès de délire, dans
> un véritable rugissement, hurlant presque comme ces fauves dont
> chaque baiser est une morsure . . .

> [I grabbed her tightly and, on the wet grass, in a profusion of
> kisses of every sort, like a savage, or rather like those lustful
> madmen who enter cemeteries at night to dig up corpses and vio-
> late them, I took my mistress, I possessed her, I made love to her

in a state of delirium, roaring just like a lion, almost screaming, like those wild animals that cannot kiss without biting at the same time.] (110–11)

To be sure, this is more than just an ardent display of tooth and claw on the part of the male. It actually succeeds in its communicative purpose, "awakening" the woman to climactic pleasure: "Et enfin, à mes ardeurs folles, à ma désespérée prière charnelle, la chair de Marcelle s'éveilla" [And finally, in response to my mad passion, to the desperate demand of my flesh, Marcelle awoke] (111). Marcelle does not resemble Galatea or La Mettrie's heroine, if only because the one who brings the woman to life behaves without artistry or artifice. The story being told is rather one of violent awakening, with the hero being transformed into a werewolf for just so long as it takes to produce a happy outcome through decisive erotic frenzy.

There is another factor making for thematic complexity at this time, in addition to the requirement that violence be only momentary or intermittent. This becomes apparent when one asks the question: who are the really sick or decadent ones in these stories? Is it Albert in *La Volupté féroce* because he is unduly submissive to a woman, or is it the Comtesse because she desires to be raped? Is it a failure of virility not to dominate like a beast, or a perversion of femininity to desire domination of that sort? Can one, indeed, choose between these two as sexualized accounts of social ills and gendered imputations of responsibility? In *La Volupté féroce*, the woman who decries male limpness is both calling for an end to decadence and somehow aggravating it by her very attitude. Women like the Comtesse can be heroines without being models of behavior: the novel calls them "névrosées" [neurotic] and "détraquées" [out of control] referring to their general attitude as "abjection" (80). Where, then, is natural health—bodily, erotic, social—to be found? If fatigue is sickness unto death, can vigor and promptness of action be relied on as effective remedies for this ill? In other words, is vigor merely the deplorably absent other of decadence, or can it be seen to engage in productive struggle with its natural opposite? To use the technical terms of the Greimassian square of oppositions, vigor and refinement usually appear in these novels as contradictories (defined by their mutual exclusion) rather than as contraries (defined by their antagonism).[50] Yet there is a continual moral call, often pathetically unanswered, for them to engage in narrative combat.

Let us consider the case of Sophor d'Hermelinge, the heroine of *Méphistophela* (1890). Mendès's novel happens to be a far more distinguished piece of literature than most of the others being examined here, but it is taken up just as fully with the thematic agenda we have been considering. Sophor, or Sophie as she is called before she graduates to the fullness of adult perversity, has the apparent good fortune to marry not some pallid gentleman of leisure but a soldier endowed with what the narrator dares to call untrammeled brutality. Brutality, in Jean, is not a narrowly professional trait achieved by some kind of training but the very foundation, the very definition of his health. He is, in his own way, more pure than his virginal bride: "Il était rude et doux, brutal et pur. On sentait que la vie n'avait pas gâté cet homme" [He was coarse and sweet, brutal and pure. One could feel that life had not spoilt this man].[51] Proof that he is thoroughly unspoilt can be found in the speed of his sexual pleasure, which knows no detours or deviations: "à ce soldat, tout ce qui . . . n'est pas le prompt plaisir sans lendemain . . . était resté inconnu" [for this soldier, everything that was not rapid pleasure with no tomorrow was beyond his ken] (109). This man, who is described, quite redundantly, as "simple comme un héros" (110), may at first be considered the ideal partner for a woman whose heredity is already heavily burdened, as naturalist writers were given to saying, with atavistic perversity, but the difference between them is too great to allow a proper narrative resolution.[52] Marriage to Jean turns out, however, to be a *remède de cheval*, an overly drastic prescription for Sophie: Jean provides robust good health in much larger doses than she can possibly assimilate. Their wedding night is momentous, but not in the way that the standard narrative might lead us to expect. During the first part of it, she yields painfully and reluctantly to Jean, who wastes no time on his knees and does not fool around with preliminaries. Feeling trapped and violated, she takes advantage of his sleep—for he continues to follow the climactic program—in order to flee in distress to the home of her adolescent companion and neighbor, Emmeline. Her vague hope is to run away with Emmeline and devote herself to the endless continuation of their schoolgirl friendship, but this hope now begins to be transformed into desire of a muted, pastel-hued kind. Sophie stands silently, in the time-honored position, in Emmeline's bedroom, contemplating her sleeping companion, whose breast is half-exposed. How, she wonders, might she begin to realize the dream now taking shape within her? She must, of course, be infinitely patient with Emmeline's dormant senses. She has not read La Mettrie, it goes without saying, yet she feels the need for some seductive art that would gradually win over her innocent friend to the pleasures of same-sex love. But this is where the husband comes in, with a literally shattering display of strength. He smashes through the window, for he has been observing her, and begins to thrash her with a dog whip, calling her a "chienne" (140–41) and causing pandemonium in the household. While this could not be called a therapeutic intervention—as a way of communicating with Sophie it is breathtakingly inappropriate— Jean could hardly be accused of shirking the issue and lapsing into fin-de-siècle resignation.

For the novel's moralizing narrator, Jean is unequivocally the sane, healthy one here. He is exercising his rights, performing his husbandly duty, doing what comes naturally in a world where so many of his contemporaries, including his wife, are out of touch with nature. Yet his drastic response is edifying only insofar as it further signifies his supposedly admirable "purity." For Sophie, it does nothing more than confront her with an erotic (and narrative) option that threatens the novel's ostensible morality, for it pushes her toward the alternative that the reader is supposed to regard as unhealthy and impure. The choice now facing Sophie has a remarkably familiar look about it for one who is acquainted with erotic writing of a century or so before, although here it is accompanied by a moral charge not generally found earlier: "une espèce de confrontation, la même nuit, de la violatrice nudité de l'homme et de la passive nudité d'une vierge endormie, lui avait révélé, dans une occasion de choisir, son dégoût de l'un, sa convoitise de l'autre" [a kind of confrontation, on the same night, of the man's violating nudity and the passive nudity of the sleeping virgin had displayed to her the possibility of choice, revealing her disgust for the first, and her lust for the other] (157). It is, in a sense, the very option, and the very fact of making the choice that constitute Sophie's unnaturalness, just as it constitutes the impotence of so many over-complicated husbands. Jean is pure precisely because he makes no conscious choices, but Sophie chooses the soft lines and the white virginal breast against the moustache and the dog whip, condemning herself by this single step to four hundred pages of perversion and debauchery ending in a painful death. Even within the world of *Méphistophela*, this consequence, and the attribution of responsibility for it, cannot fail to give pause. By being vigorous without being thoughtfully virtuous, Jean appears to have given his wife a shove down the path of depravation. There is an unwitting complicity between his maleness, with its narratively stylized brutality, and Sophie's eventual commitment to lesbianism, which is worked out, not as any form of consolation or refuge but, *bassesse oblige*, as utter moral ruin.[53]

There is a whole set of novels, as I have indicated, about Men who Want to be Men, men whose mistresses, or the novel's narrator wish were proper men, or even men who wish they knew how to want to be men. On the other hand, there are equally many novels whose primary focus, as in *Méphistophela*, is on women and their desires. Not all of these women are *détraquées* or *névrosées*—at least not at the outset. Many of them have life stories that turn on sexual trauma, on the damage done by violence. In *Les Cousines de la colonelle* (1880), things do not go too badly, even though the young woman Florentine marries the aging Georges. At the end of the nineteenth century, should any reminder be needed, this is not a recipe for Chaucerian or Boccacian comedy but an emblem of society's ills. The focus is initially on the man: will he be up to it after all his years of debauchery? The answer on the first night is a sadly predictable no, but on the second he goes about it in a different manner. The preoccupation here is still with male performance and with how it can be, if not enhanced, for that is a term that belongs to modern athletics and/or sexology, but just minimally guaranteed. Georges prepares for the second take of the wedding night with care, using precautions instead of preliminaries. He swallows some liquid vigor in the form of "aphrodisiacal drops" (46), and then resolves not to let himself be diverted from his goal in any way: "Cette fois Georges ne commit plus l'imprudence de s'arrêter aux charmes du prologue . . . il fit quelques caresses sommaires à sa gentille moitié, et monta à l'assaut, décidé à ne se laisser arrêter dans son élan par aucun atermoiement" [This time Georges did not make the mistake of dwelling on the charms of the prologue. He gave a few simple caresses to his

better half, and then forged ahead, determined not to be interrupted in his charge by any shilly-shallying].[54] The strategy of
avoiding any refinement, which is presumably better aligned
with "nature" as perceived in such stories, results in a happy
conclusion—and not only for Georges. This is Florentine's introduction to pleasure, although we find her discovering in the
course of time that the preliminaries left out by Georges on that
climactic night are in fact more pleasurable for her than the
great event itself. On this basis, their marriage builds a modest
libidinal economy as the young wife finds greater pleasure in
the ersatz required by the husband's partial impotence: "Sa
jeune femme n'appréciait certes point suffisamment ses efforts
et préférait infiniment à leur résultat final les caresses préliminaires qui les accompagnaient; en cela fidèle observateur du pré-
cepte qui dit aux maris, aux amants, de ne point oublier que
toujours, avant d'entrer, un homme poli sonne" [His young wife
did not especially appreciate his efforts, and far preferred the
preliminary caresses to the final result. He was in that regard
faithful to the proverb, always to be remembered, that before entering a polite man knocks] (114).[55] This appears to be a roughly
acceptable fin-de-siècle substitute for domestic passion. There is
no suggestion that such practices will result on this occasion in
advanced depravity. Rather than perverse indirectness, they
seem to represent an acceptable compromise between the aging
masculine and the youthful feminine.

That some such compromise is indeed required, that all desire
and pleasure cannot be accounted for in terms of what men do
to women is also suggested by the novel *Demi-Femme* (1901).
The story there actually reverses that of *Le Désir*, following the
same thematic concerns in the opposite direction. Bertrand
marries Odette believing that she has been unfaithful to her
promise and is no longer a virgin. Accordingly, he takes no care
in sexual contact to protect her sensibility or foster her pleasure. The sad irony, however, is that she is indeed a virgin, and
the harsh manner in which he takes possession of her destroys
their chance of sexual communion: "il avait épousé une vierge,
et, dans sa rage aveugle, il l'avait traitée comme une gourgan-
dine. Ah! s'il avait été patient! S'il avait su réfréner ses ardeurs
charnelles! Odette serait venue à lui, et il n'en serait pas aujourd'hui à déplorer l'irréparable" [He had married a virgin, and
in his blind rage had treated her like a trollop. Ah! If only he

had been patient! If he had only managed to restrain his carnal passion! Odette would have reached out to him, and he would not now find himself deploring the irreparable damage he had done].[56] Whatever the dangers of palely loitering, there is sometimes reason, after all, to fear the damage caused by rabid violence.

As if to respond to the ambiguities and pitfalls inherent in the very notion of a difficult choice between two narrative modes or erotic styles, the expeditious and the languid, certain novels begin to work out an economy of vigor and gentleness, especially in stories that focus on sexual pleasure in and around marriage. Instead of always supposing that brutality is an unequivocal good, making for healthy pleasure, they sometimes attempt to negotiate an arrangement in which both brutality and its opposite have their place within a set of normative behaviors. It is not, of course, a matter of rejecting all violence on principle, as in many forms of twentieth-century moralism. Nor is it a matter of regarding all gentleness as asthenic. The key thing is to define a place for each within a broader system of behaviors that serve as psychological and erotic models. The worldly wise question par excellence, asked by one woman of another when a relationship collapses, allows for excesses or shortcomings on both sides of the ledger: "Enfin, que t'a-t-il fait? A-t-il été trop brutal ou pas assez? A-t-il manqué de délicatesse ou de force?" [So what did he actually do? Was he too brutal or not brutal enough? Was he lacking in delicacy or in strength?].[57]

Aware of this double exigency, well-adjusted, healthy characters such as Jean d'Avray in *L'Orgie moderne* (1905) have developed a repertoire of tactics that includes both precipitate and unhurried action in appropriate measures. This allows such exceptional beings to achieve naturalness without undue simplicity: "Jean était d'un naturel complexe. Il tuait systématiquement ses nerfs, fauchait ses désirs en les satisfaisant avant leur éclosion, pour rester maître de sa volonté et de soi-même" [Jean had a complex nature. He systematically killed off his nerves and cut down his desires by satisfying them before they could blossom, so as to keep mastery of his will and himself]. He gives vent with prophylactic speed to his own libido as a means of heading off any threat of pathological delay. But this speed also has the effect of making room for slowness. It clears his mind for the battles of seduction, "afin d'user de toutes les ressources de son esprit et d'une tactique habile, raisonnée, calme ou fougueuse selon le cas, lorsqu'il entreprenait la conquête d'une femme" [so as to use all his wits, adopting skillful, reasoned tactics. When he set about conquering women, he was calm or fiery according to circumstance].[58] Such variety of rhythm within one single "nature," one set of behaviors, or one relationship, is usually a mark of erotic success, standing out against a general background of thematic indecision or agony. In *L'Affolante Illusion* (1906), the two qualities that one so often sees desperately opposed are held together fleetingly in one caress: "sa taille ployait sous l'étreinte câline et vigoureuse de l'aimé dont le souffle caressait son cou, dont la moustache effleurait son oreille" [she softened in response to the charming, vigorous embrace of the loved one, as his breath caressed her neck and his moustache brushed against her ear].[59] This, when it occurs, appears to be the perfect thematic outcome, the sign of nicely resolved pleasure.

Quite often, standing in the way of this outcome is the distribution of erotic roles for women that opposes the virginal bride, usually requiring some gentleness of treatment, to the whore crying out for rape. To the extent, therefore, that there is to be some resolution of the vigor versus gentleness opposition, it can be greatly abetted by the reconfiguration of sexual roles for women within marriage. This task is undertaken, or at least affirmed to be happily complete, in *Les Demi-Sexes* (1897), where Camille and her husband Georges find a successful economy of pleasures through the doubling of womanly roles played by Camille: "parmi les emportements sensuels de son ivresse, il y avait, tout à la fois, des câlineries ingénues de jeune fille et du libertinage de courtisane: des retenues et des impudeurs" [among the impetuous marks of her sensual passion were both the ingenuous cuddles of a girl and the libertine behavior of a courtesan: reticence and boldness].[60] In *L'Inassouvie* (1900)—not to be confused with *Une Inassouvie* (1897) or with *Inassouvie* (1889)—this doubling of roles is not fully achieved, although it is constructed as a potential solution for sexual difficulties faced by the central characters. The young René, in love with Juliette, makes the mistake of addressing only that which is "noble" in her, ignoring other forms of sensuality that have in fact been awakened by an earlier lover: "Pourquoi observa-t-il cette loi superstitieuse qui défend à une passion noble les plus subtiles et les plus puissantes des caresses? Leur raffinement passe pour un artifice de débauche, alors qu'il semble plutôt la preuve d'une ingénieuse ferveur envers cette argile féminine, tressaillante d'une vie ineffable" [Why did he observe the superstitious law that forbids noble passion from using the most powerful and subtle caresses? Their refinement is talked about as a debauched artifice, whereas it seems rather to be proof of ingenious fervor toward feminine clay, which quivers with ineffable life].[61] Let your fervor be ingenious and your passion subtle, the narrator seems to say, but René is deaf to the message. An eventual consequence of his ill-judged forbearance is that Juliette begins to return to her former lover, oscillating between the two men so as to piece together the fullness of her satisfaction, as a mixture of calculating perversity and passionate candor (136). The problem only comes to be resolved, and its narrative exigency answered, when Juliette teaches these less noble practices to René—thereby fulfilling the standard role of a prostitute—so that they now contribute to "une passion nouvelle, surgie dans l'ancien amour" [a brand new passion that had emerged in their old love] (205). Such happy convergence is not only blocked most often by the distribution of roles for women, but is itself still subject to moral stricture when it does perchance occur. There exists at least one novel in which the making of the synthesis of virgin and whore is recounted as a central event but as an utter moral catastrophe. In *Paris-Gomorrhe* (1894), a perverse husband teaches his wife an unspeakable form of pleasure: "Mon mari m'initia à tous les raffinements de cet art d'aimer . . . défendu . . ." [My husband introduced me to all the refinements of that . . . forbidden . . . art of love]. The particular "refinement" in question appears to be fellatio, but naming it is not the point. The point is that the wife is subjugated by her husband, losing all moral strength, all uprightness as she bows to his will and to her sexual task: "Avec un regard, un sourire, il me jetait à ses pieds . . . et, telle une sangsue, je me collais contre son corps et le dévorais de caresses . . ." [With a look and a smile, he threw me at his feet . . . and like a leech I stuck to his body and devoured him with caresses].[62] We are presumably to conclude that this is not a genuine erotic synthesis, nor even a tolerable arrangement, but the lamentable reduction of the virgin to the status of domestic whore.

Another novel of the period seeks to achieve the resolution of roles, of styles, and of tempi in the uncertain domain of adultery.

In *Demi-Volupté* (1900), Roger and Suzanne are about to embark on an adulterous relationship, or would be if only they could agree about what kind of behavior was appropriate for adulterers. Suzanne considers that it is a fine and subtle art: "l'adultère . . . exige . . . tout un code de précautions, de petites choses, de mesquineries utiles, précieuses, mille détails, enfin: ce n'est que nuances, malices, roueries" [Adultery requires a whole code of precautions, of little things, and precious, self-interested calculations, in fine detail. All one's effort goes into nuances, tricks, and stratagems]. Roger, she fears, cannot learn to play these games since he is anything but subtle: "Vous, vous aimez en gros" [Your love is an overall thing]. Indeed, he cannot and will not learn since in his view adultery is only redeemed by the radical singularity of passion: "L'adultère . . . ne peut s'excuser que par la pire passion: il faut s'oublier, s'abandonner, ne plus songer à rien, qu'à son songe" [Adultery can only be excused by the worst form of passion. You must forget yourself, let yourself go, and think of nothing but your dream].[63] The two parties could hardly be further from agreement, and it is no surprise that this scene should end without a happy erotic conclusion. Nonetheless, the central issues have now been defined, and much of what follows will be taken up with the working out of this duality. Suzanne, who has already shown complexity in her erotic behavior—she was "indécise et passionnée" [hesitant and passionate] when first being courted by Roger (54)—sometimes crosses the divide between society women and *filles de joie*. While making an unannounced visit one night to Roger's apartment, she happens to find him in the company of unworthy people, given up to despair and debauchery after failing to seduce her. Her reaction does not follow the predictable pattern of accentuating the moral and social gap between herself and these people: she is less coquettish and more openly attracted to him. He, on the other hand, is now offended because he has been revealed to her in his more animal aspect: "vous avez eu envie du moi que je ne veux pas être, du mâle que j'ai été pour des filles, d'un mâle en rut, de furie et de fringale. Je me voulais autre pour vous, tout en sentiments, tout en nuances . . ." [you wanted that side of me that I reject: the male who has dealings with loose women, the one who is on heat, driven by wild hunger pangs. I wanted to be different for you, all feeling and subtlety] (124). This is a kind of thematic crossover, if not a moment of genuine dialectic, in their ongoing debate. While Roger did not want the coded subtleties referred to initially by Suzanne, he does not want mere brutishness either; and while she does not yet want the headlong commitment he advocated at first, she does long for forthright animal pleasure. At this point, he invites her to leave, as she did before, but this time she refuses and declares her passion. Having previously defended the niceties of civilized adultery, she now confesses impatience with all those things: "Aimons-nous, puisque nous nous aimons et aimons-nous comme on s'aime quand on est une femme et un homme—et qu'on s'aime. Pourquoi raffiner, pourquoi se torturer, pourquoi?" [Let's love each other—since we do love each other—let's love like a man and a woman. Why complicate things? Why torture each other? Why?] (127). True passion can now happen climactically, as they forsake all refinement, and all concern with social propriety. Roger grabs his "prey," throws her onto the bed like the "fauve" [wild animal] that he has temporarily become, and makes as if to tear her clothes. There will be no fine gradations here, no gentle striptease, just the raw passion of fully naked bodies:

> Il voulait la déshabiller non pas avec les délicatesses infinies qui lui avaient déjà servi mais avec une frénésie nouvelle, spéciale, avec des doigts neufs. . . . Cent fois il eut la tentation d'embrasser à mesure les chairs qu'il découvrait: c'était de la conquête immédiate et si chère! Il se contint. Il en avait usé ainsi avec de moindres conquêtes, avec des conquêtes médiocres. Il la lui fallait toute, toute nue, sans un voile, sans une ombre.

> [He wanted to undress her, not with the infinite care he had shown before, but with a new, quite special frenzy, with new hands. A hundred times he was tempted to embrace each piece of flesh as he discovered it, as if to savor the territory he had just won. That was what he had done with women who mattered less, or who hardly mattered at all. This woman he needed to have in her entirety, completely naked, without a veil, without a shadow.] (129)

We are no doubt meant to admire the great self-discipline shown by Roger in achieving such a display of spontaneity. Yet even as the story triumphs over "adulterating" codes of refinement, the novel's title, *Demi-Volupté*, may begin to appear surprising. We are reminded later, however, that it does not refer to any undue restraint of passion within Roger and Suzanne's relationship, merely to the social constraints that confine their natural ardor to certain specific times and places.[64] At moments of true fervor, it is possible for the couple to overcome the oppositions—rashness versus nuances, bestiality versus gentleness—raised in their early disagreements. The high points of their pleasure are triumphant, if short-lived, resolutions of these binary oppositions.

It is striking that many texts of this period and this genre, whether they focus on male or female characters, whether they deal with the vigor-gentleness binary in trenchantly moralistic or indulgently accommodating ways, refer to *raffinement*, and especially to the plural *raffinements*, as worthy only of condemnation. "Refinements" are seen as twists, turns and perversions, deviations from the straight, short path of natural sexual narrative. This view is made quite explicit in the following passage, which describes the attitude of an upright young man named Gilbert in *Demi-Femme* (1901): "Les raffinements érotiques répugnaient à sa prud'hommie native, sa sensualité n'aspirait qu'aux plaisirs licites et il ne comprenait pas les déviations des excès de désir" [Erotic refinements were repugnant to his native decency; his sensuality sought only licit pleasures, and he did not understand the deviations of desire's excesses] (59). The notion of *raffinement* has reached the nadir of its thematic career, after having enjoyed such prestige at the time of Crébillon. Even in the earlier nineteenth century, refinements had been seen as a set of erotic practices that might conceivably compete, for the pleasure they provided, with climactic fucking. Now, for the fin de siècle, there is hardly a term more contemptuous, its only remaining power being that of a certain morbidity. *Raffinements* are the craven opposite of authentic passion. They are diversions from the vigorous expression and satisfaction of desire. Watching two other people make love, for example, by the very way in which it stands at a distance from the struggle, deserves to be called a "raffinement sénile" (*Demi-Femme*, 235). Indeed, the association of noun and adjective in this last phrase is over-determined by discursive regularity: just as all *langueurs* appear *navrantes* in late-nineteenth-century fiction, so all *raffinements* are historically and psychologically *séniles*. Decadence is thus incarnated—or excarnated, if we could say that—in certain erotic practices. It is nowhere more visible than in the very notion of the *érotique*, since eroticism is identified as a certain culture or an undue complication of nature.

A remark made by Philippe Jacob, in an introduction to *Julie ou j'ai sauvé ma rose*, provides if not exactly a summary, then a quick, even careless overview of the questions I have been considering in this chapter. Speaking of Julie's erotic tactics, Jacob gives them three names, two of which he considers generic, "les préludes voluptueux" and "la flirtation," and one of which he is obliged to consider historically specific since it has now fallen into disuse: "L'auteur a fait, sans s'en douter, une étude morale sur ce qu'on nomme la flirtation en Angleterre, et sur les préludes voluptueux de l'amour que nos pères, les bons Gaulois, avaient compris dans cette expression aujourd'hui inintelligible, bien qu'on la rencontre souvent dans les anciens auteurs français: la *Petite Oie*" [The author has carried out, without realising it, a moral study of what the English call flirtation, and of the delightful preludes of love that our fathers, the good old Gauls, referred to by an expression that is nowadays incomprehensible, even though it often occurs in the French classics: *la petite oie*].[65] I find much to object to in this statement and have mainly quoted it here in order to work through my objections. The point of this chapter has, I hope, been to undo some of the interpretive assurance that allows Jacob, whatever his erudition, to sweep through literary history, identifying as he goes the quasi-universal sameness of "preludes" and "flirtation," no matter what name they may have had at a particular time. I have already dwelt sufficiently, I trust, on the discursive shift involved in replacing "les gradations" by "la petite oie," and I have had something to say about the notion of preludes (or preliminaries, or foreplay), but I have yet to devote any attention to the idea of flirtation. I now wish to do so, by putting forward the claim that *le flirt* can be located quite precisely in the history I have been writing: it can be shown that this expression is distinctive to erotic discourse of the fin de siècle and that its development corresponds to the final thematic shift highlighted in my account. What the earlier nineteenth century tended to consider as trivial, secondary pleasures, of value mainly in the preparation of climax, are now seen as dangerous refinements threatening to result in the infinite deferral or displacement of the natural outcome of desire.

While the word "flirtation" is identified by the *Trésor de la langue française* as having been first used by Mérimée in 1837, the narrowing of its sense, its shortening to *le flirt*, and its definition as coded, socially identifiable erotic practice are the work of writers at the end of the century. The first use of *le flirt* is dated 1889 by the *Trésor de la langue française*, and there is evidence of widespread use in the decade that followed. It is present in texts by Bourget, France, and Barrès,[66] but also, I want to add, in the less distinguished production of *romans passionels* or *romans parisiens* that have already claimed my attention. From about 1890 onwards, the term is habitually employed in such novels, precisely if not always consistently defined, and thematically elaborated in the course of narrative.

One of the texts in which *le flirt* comes to play a quite central role, even as it is hedged about with moralizing discourse, is *Les Demi-Vierges* (1901). The author, in his prefatory remarks, begins by identifying the expression as a foreign word—associated by implication with foreign mores, with the supposedly more permissive societies of Britain and America, in which young women frequently took part in sport, including cycling, horse riding, and tennis, and enjoyed attendant bodily freedoms. *Le flirt*, then, has come to France, but beneath the exotic charm of the word, says the author, lies a disturbing truth: "Le flirt est 'Anglo-Saxon,' et l'on aura beau enguirlander le mot de toute l'innocence et de toute la poésie qu'on voudra, nous savons la vérité sur le *flirt*" ["Le flirt" is "Anglo-Saxon," and even if people surround the word with garlands of innocence and poetry, we know the truth about "le flirt"].[67] Identifying this truth as a particular set of erotic practices, and working out the story of its social consequences will be the business of this novel and a number of others published almost at the same time.

In the notion of "semi-virgins," there is, as we come to see more clearly during the story, a compactly disparaging reference to two forms of compromise: moral and erotic. The most literal-minded reading of the title, applied to women's bodies, would suggest that a young woman of this type is simply giving over one half of her body to the caress of her lover or lovers. That first impression is confirmed well enough in the description of an erotic scene played out by the semi-virgin Maud and her companion Julien. The description actually follows the man's embrace as it moves about the woman's body from her lips to the fabric of her dress, to her corsage, to the side of her breast, and via her armpit back to her lips (19–20). The trajectory is of course far too broad for the sake of virginal innocence, but is nonetheless limited. Another novel whose title has the same grammar, but whose descriptions are perhaps less elegantly tactful, draws the line of demarcation quite clearly for us. This is how we are invited to see the semi-adulterous Baronne de Saverny, in *Demi-Femme* (1901): "Car si elle incitait aux propos galants chuchotés dans l'impudicité de la valse, si elle tolérait les frôlements de doigts fiévreux, les effleurements de chaudes haleines sur sa gorge liliale, elle restait toujours maîtresse de ses sens et savait arrêter le flirt à la hauteur de la ceinture" [For while she encouraged racy talk exchanged in whispers during the indecency of the waltz, and tolerated the feverish brushing of fingers and the feel of warm breath on her lily white breast, she always remained in control, and was able to stop the flirting from going below the waist] (66). All sorts of lewd things go on above the waist, but nothing is allowed to occur below it. Note how this is both like and unlike *Julie, ou j'ai sauvé ma rose*. While Julie feared, in moments of self-doubt, that her eroticism was only a half-measure, she was generally able to follow the practice of gradations in order to enjoy all but the very last pleasure, savoring each step to the full. The world of *le flirt*, on the other hand, is characterized not by this almost infinitesimal practice of the limit, but by what sporting discourse would call its zone defense: it completely closes down one half of the body while allowing all sorts of activity in the other, including whispering, pawing, and groping—a kind of semi-passionate disorder.

It might be thought—indeed, it sometimes is—that flirtation is a makeshift eroticism, comparable to the ersatz worked out in those stories about marital pleasure we looked at a little earlier. *Le flirt* may even appear on occasion, when the moralizing voice heard in novels like *Les Demi-Vierges* is less strident, as hardly more than the modern equivalent of feminine coquettishness. It is defended, if not exactly advocated, by no less a figure than Paul Bourget, and its name, "ce monosyllabe britannique, sec et cinglant comme un coup de fouet" [that dry British monosyllable cracking like the sound of a whip], saved from ugly foreignness by etymological connection with *fleureter* and *conter fleurette*, relating the art of fencing to seductive talk.[68] In *Mortelle Etreinte*

(1891), Luce is said to have been "en flirtation réglée" [engaged in formal flirtation] with Pierre throughout a whole evening spent at a reception.[69] The expression is ironic, since flirtation must involve at least some disorder, but precisely because it is "regulated" there is no evidence of any terrible threat to social order, nor even to virtue, as long as the demands of virtue are taken with a half-measure of indulgence. A woman in *Le Vice errant* (1902) is described both as a "coquette" and as a "flirteuse émérite" [accomplished flirt], with every indication that the two are rough synonyms, the second being the slightly more explicit, perhaps more technical, of the two.[70] In *Les Demi-Sexes* (1897)— yet another novel whose title attaches the divisive prefix to a noun that is supposed to signify organic unity—*le flirt* allows for a working compromise between male ardor and feminine re-servedness. Of Camille, we are told: "les mères la citaient en ex-emple, les jeunes gens tournaient autour d'elle avec un vif intérêt que sa froideur maintenait dans les limites d'un flirt re-spectueux" [mothers held her up as an example, and young men waited on her with a lively eye, while her reserved manner kept them within the bounds of respectful flirtation] (14). Flirtation is compatible here with respect, with a certain distance. It seems to be just the welcoming face of virtue, the gentle surface contact of sociable decency. There is not much harm, and not much deca-dent pathos, in that. In a comparable, though more acute and indeed dramatic form, flirtation can be the name for a general attitude on the part of a woman who appears to be available but simply denies her partners satisfaction. *Madame Flirt* (1902) is a novel that Jacob may have wished to quote in defence of his claim, given that the final outcome(s)—although not the unfold-ing—have something in common with *Julie, ou j'ai sauvé ma rose*. The heroine of *Madame Flirt* is playful in dealing with her suitors, but her play, unlike Julie's, is the mark of her disdain. To those who would seduce her, she replies consistently with "un non-vouloir aimable, enjoué, un tantinet sarcastique" [friendly, bantering, slightly sarcastic refusal].[71] Whereas Choiseul-Meuse's heroine made the seriousness of her pleasure out of re-sourceful erotic play, Madame Flirt plays for the sake of playing, so as to avoid the serious issue of direct contact: "il était clair qu'elle s'amusait au jeu, qu'elle ne prenait pas la partie au sérieux. Elle jouait par passe-temps, pour le plaisir, pour l'amour de l'art" [it was clear that she enjoyed playing, and did not take the game seriously. She played to pass the time, for the fun of it, for the love of art] (4). Games, in fin-de-siècle eroticism, may serve to pass the time, but passing the time is not in itself of any particular erotic moment. When things start to get serious, Madame Flirt just calls an end to it: "elle rompait le charme, cessait le flirt" [she broke off the charm, and interrupted the flirtation] (4). Such activities are merely a distraction or a diversion. But that, as we know, makes them akin to refinement and thus to perversion.

There is a dynamic within *le flirt* that tends to disturb the simple move of drawing a demarcation line across the woman's body and allowing it to serve as a neat, geometrical figure of moral compromise. The problem is that the passion developed in the erotic, even vicious, half threatens continually to encroach on the virtuous half. Or rather, that the nature of passion is such as not to tolerate this fifty-fifty ethic. "Il n'y a pas de demi-pudeurs, ni de demi-impudeurs" [there is no half-modesty, and no half-immodesty], says Bourget.[72] In *Les Demi-Sexes*, two wise gentlemen observe the goings-on between young people in a salon, and one comments to the other: "Ah! les demi-vierges out fait du chemin, dans ces derniers temps, et la fraction de pureté qui leur reste est bien minime!" [Ah! Semi-virgins have really moved along in recent times, and the fraction of purity that remains in them is quite tiny!] (101). Not only are there fewer true virgins but each semi-virgin is less sure in herself. Without the support of gradations and the almost endless delay they made available to the subtle and resourceful Julie, these semi-virgins are continually subject to takeover bids on the part of vice, as they struggle to avoid giving up further fractions of the same, urgently desired "whole," attempting to hold the line where it is currently drawn. Semi-virginity, rather than being a happy compromise, often appears to have the worst of both worlds: it has neither the purity of genuine innocence nor the sometimes pardonable, even redemptive frankness of unbridled sensuality.[73] This is how it is in *Les Demi-Vierges*, where flirtation goes on in an atmosphere of furtive contact that threatens the moral ruin of a whole generation of young women. Maxime, the pure young man from the provinces, looks on in dismay: "Ces gestes de frôlement, qu'on ne se donne pas la peine de dissimuler. . . . Et ce mot odieux qui résonne sans cesse comme un appel de libertinage: 'Mon flirt . . . Elle a flirté . . . Nous avons flirté . . . C'est un flirt

de ma fille . . . '" [The brushing up against others that people do
not even attempt to hide. . . . And that hateful word that echoes
endlessly like a call to libertine behavior: "My flirt . . . She flirted
. . . We flirted . . . He is one of my daughter's flirts . . ."] (69). The
word itself circulates through the crowd like a rather sleazy
caress. And when Maxime refers to "ces chastes frôleuses" [those
chaste women who brush up against you] (77), he no doubt
means to suggest something depraved in the very proximity, the
unhealthy promiscuity of virtuous adjective and vicious verb.
From the point of view of worldly wisdom, *le flirt* is no less disturbing. The sophisticated and thoroughly disabused Hector observes that Maud and her half-lover Julien have "leur mode un
peu animal de s'aimer" [their slightly animalistic way of loving]
(59). But this is an intriguing and unsatisfying way to put it. It
leaves unanswered the question of how the demands of their
sensual "animality" can accommodate the subtle dosage of *un
peu*. Certainly, when Maud and Julien are together in private,
many of the standard metaphors are put to service in describing
their half-encounter: "il montra, du regard, la chambre voisine,
pleine d'ombre. Dans les yeux de la jeune fille il lut le consente-
ment. Il l'emporta comme une proie. Les lèvres jointes, ils défail-
lirent ensemble contre cette couche fermée . . . : lui si vite
anéanti que, cette fois encore, Maud n'eut point à se refuser" [he
glanced toward the nearby bedroom filled with shadow. He read
consent in the girl's eyes. He carried her off like a prey. Their
lips joined together, they subsided onto a made bed. He was so
quickly spent that once again Maud did not have to deny him
full possession] (115). Such behavior must be thought of as
doubly reprehensible—for its neglect of virtue and family duty,
of course, but also for its failure to carry out the great erotic narrative, for its artful selection of certain subsidiary aspects of love
against the rest, and against the whole: "Leurs caresses singulières . . . avaient pour ainsi dire pris au rebours le procédé de
l'amour humain" [Their strange caresses had, so to speak,
turned human love upside down] (242). We should not be surprised, then, to find the narrator of *Méphistophela* referring to
"extreme flirtations" (4), for there are extremes of tension, and a
form of moral extremism, in the ardent practice of these half-
measures. This is how virginity, in its most technical or casuisti-
cal sense, can come to be described as hateful and obscene: "Plus
détestables, ces vierges donneuses de leur bouche et de leur

gorge et de tout leur corps nu, qui, pour la fierté du ventre sans ride ou pour épargner le souci du fœtus coupé en morceaux puis jeté aux latrines, restent vierges en leurs lits obscènes" [More hateful are those virgins who give up their mouths and their bosom and their whole naked bodies, and who, for the sake of keeping an unwrinkled belly or avoiding the trouble of a foetus cut into pieces and thrown into the latrines, remain virgins in their obscene beds] (*Méphistophela* 6).

Méphistophela and other stories like it present characters who are unable, for whatever set of social and psychological reasons, to enact the program of climactic narrative. But that program continues to dominate their stories, functioning thematically as an absent ideal. Thus, fin-de-siècle stories effectively foreclose or otherwise condemn the space of play opened up for plural *jouissances* in such novels as those of Choiseul-Meuse. Any compromise they are likely to see as depravation in disguise. The drastic nature of the dilemma faced by the young heroines of *romans passionnels* is spelled out with binary severity in *Journal d'un amant* (1902). Society, we are told, has now so lost contact with the values of the past that there are no true lovers to be found any more. Modern life is "un combat inégal . . . où la jeune fille succombe. Deux portes: l'amour brutal, répugnant, ou bien alors les caresses incomplètes d'une hystérique vicieuse" [an unequal combat in which the girl is defeated. Two doors are open to her: brutal, repugnant love, or the incomplete caresses of a hysteric given over to vice] (120). If the young woman manages to avoid rape—the brutality agenda at its most direct—it will only be because she allows herself to be drawn into a dangerously subtle world of "caresses," involving the practice of *le flirt* and its "incomplete" program. Eroticism of the latter sort, cut off from the natural outcome, can only result in "hysteria." Refinement, we are being told repeatedly, is not a measured step along the path of dalliance but a way of stumbling into the long and painful detours of madness and depravity. Pathological incompleteness draws its followers further and further away from nature's happily short narrative of quasi-immediate desire and gratification.

The historical development of climax in erotic narrative is not reducible to that simple story of displacement, alluded to often in pornography of Revolutionary times, whereby effete libertinage, with its undue complications, gives way to popular forthrightness. Constructing the thematic opposition between the two is in fact part of the theme, and part of the way in which hearty climax, accompanied by the bare minimum of preliminaries, defines its place in relation to an older and longer tradition of erotic representation. For all the show of simplicity, and indeed the advocacy of brutal frankness, erotic narrative that extols the virtues of directness is usually required to negotiate its thematic position with respect to a more refined, more elaborate art of pleasure. In doing so, it must continue, not just to perform climax, but to assert its erotic value. Only by dint of such insistence can the "naturalness" of climax be maintained.

The more-or-less climactic story of climax, as I have attempted to tell it here, is that of a century-long struggle between two themes, two modes of telling, two ways of talking about narrative within narrative. That it is not, despite appearances, the story of a definitive triumph of climax over gradualism, of promptness, spontaneity and brutality over diversion, distraction and deviation is evidenced by the very fact that I have been able to tell it, at least to some extent, against the grain, seeking to make room in my account for those forms of erotic pleasure that so much nineteenth-century writing tended to sweep aside or disparage. I have been conscious, insofar as I have been able to do this, of my own historicity, and of the support provided here by a quite modern thematic of diffuse or distributed pleasure. I have sought to retrieve what the nineteenth century, after much equivocation, came firstly to weigh in the balance, later to neglect, and eventually to condemn.

7

Orgasm

IN THE PREVIOUS CHAPTER I UNDERTOOK A STUDY OF CLIMAX THROUGH the markers that surround and prepare it, or at least serve to define it, within stories, as the proper goal and outcome of narrative. It might have been thought then that I allowed myself to be distracted from the central issue of climax by an interest in its periphery, that I neglected the peak itself in order to measure the gradient of its slopes. To a sexologist, for example, this could appear an unpardonable disregard for the momentously physiological experience that is the heart, and the true bodily purpose, of human sexual experience. The point of my previous chapter was of course polemical, not so much defiance as deferral. By forestalling the question of climax in itself in favor of the climactic as a certain set of narrative signposts, I meant to suggest that climax is effectively constituted in stories by the very disposition of those supposedly peripheral elements, and that the peak of intensity is largely produced by the anticipation that leads up to it. This amounts to saying that the theme of climax "in itself" can helpfully be considered a secondary phenomenon, radically constrained as it is by the practice of narrative delay, whether that delay be long and voluptuous or just thrillingly short.

Having said that, and having delayed until now the question of sexual climax—what we, in our modernity, are wont to call "orgasm"—I come now to consider how "it" is represented in texts.[1] The first thing I want to say, predictably enough, is that I have no confidence whatsoever in the eternal solidity of this notion. The analysis on which I am embarking will in fact attempt to show that there is a complex, nonlinear history at work here, a history that helps produce the notion of climax, and in fact enables it to appear quite perfectly ahistorical, in the confident erotico-narrative proclamation of climax as orgasm, and orgasm as climax. In order to begin on this history, I shall return once again to the territory that has served as a staging ground throughout this study: that of eighteenth-century erotic writing. I shall examine some libertine texts in search of expressions that might well be deemed forerunners of the modern theme of climax. My first concern here will be to tread lightly, taking care not to recognize too quickly a standard theme of modern sexuality. The point of the exercise will not be to find the equivalence of different terms as a triumph of transhistorical interpretation: it will be rather to practice hermeneutical care in assessing the nonequivalence of proximate notions. I want to call attention to the fact that eighteenth-century literature refers to entities or events that may at first blush be taken to be the instant of climax, but that differ from it in important, quite systematic ways. I shall consider a range of ostensibly similar expressions without supposing that they all stand for the same thing.

Libertine literature of the eighteenth century likes to talk of *plaisirs*, in the plural, just as it talks of *désirs*, but it does contain singular names for pleasure that are clearly marked by their inscription in narrative. These include *la dernière jouissance, le dernier période*,[2] *le comble*, and other, less frequently used expressions. It is tempting to see these as names for sexual climax, and indeed as ways of referring to "orgasm," but that is a temptation I intend to resist, even as I pursue a comparative evaluation of them. I shall claim that these expressions, and others of the same order that we might casually take as ways of talking about climax, are defined in the first instance by their place in narratives of gradation. This is most clearly demonstrable in the case of expressions containing the adjective *dernier*. Let me briefly recall, from the discussion in the previous chapter of La Mettrie's *L'Art de jouir*, the manner in which *la dernière jouissance* stands as the last in a finite series of graded pleasures. The adjective *dernière* serves there to mediate quite perfectly between the scale of pleasures and the time of telling, since it marks the end of the scale as being attained only after each of the other steps, each of the other *jouissances* has been savored in its turn. Similarly, *le comble, le faîte du bonheur, le faîte de la volupté, le sommet*, and *le souverain bonheur* are all defined in the eighteenth century by their place in a temporal order. They are points or places reached only at the end, as the end, of a delightfully long and steady climb.

I shall not redeploy in full my account of eighteenth-century narrative, since I trust that I have already shown the differences between the thematics of gradation and that of climax. The key point here, put most simply, is that "the last pleasure" was not at that time defined by radical contrast with subsidiary activities that may have preceded or followed it. When, however, such expressions continue to be used in stories at the turn of the eighteenth century, alongside new ones that I shall examine in due course, their meaning changes. They are, so to speak, recycled, being used loosely and even lavishly in the development of climax as a theme. Consider, for example, *le dernier période*. It is used quite classically in the midcentury novel, *Les Leçons de la volupté* (1758), where it names an outcome to be attained by expert technique: "Un amant expert les conduit au dernier période du plaisir" [An expert lover guided them to the last stage of pleasure].[3] This is recognizably an economical version of La Mettrie's *art de jouir*, since expert guidance leads up to this point. A few years later, however, in *Vénus en rut* (1771), a narrator-heroine uses the same phrase rather differently, describing the work done by a lover to enhance the quality of her desire-and-pleasure as "porte[r] l'ivresse de mon âme au dernier période" [raising the exhilaration of my soul to the final stage].[4] *Porter*, in this quotation, may appear to be an exact equivalent of *conduire* in the previous one, but the form of displacement is not the same: it need not involve the taking of steps along the way. *Le dernier période* begins to resemble a limit of human possibility rather than the consecrated end of a well-practiced series. Instead of the highest point on the scale, it can serve to mark the ultimate development of a certain quality of experience—a kind of insurpassable fullness. As the shape of erotic narrative changes toward the end of the century, such classical phrases as these are subject to considerable torque as they are turned to the purpose of climactic narrative.

Sade contributes in full measure to this discursive rewriting. Even as he continues to pay solemn tribute to the classical gradations in *Les Cent Vingt Journées de Sodome*, counting out their order as the structural principle of his novel, he is beginning to adapt the old terms to a thematics of intensity. When we are told, for example, that one character's raging desire is "au dernier période,"[5] this does not count as a reference to earlier events in which lesser rages might have been measured. It is not the last in a series but a kind of absolute superlative, an indicator that desire cannot be any greater without becoming murderous, or simply unthinkable. The reference to *le dernier période* serves more as a mark of intensity than as any sort of narrative milestone.

It is quite common to find in Sade the use of *porter* as a verb that marks the action, or the process, by which *le dernier période* is attained. We saw in chapter 2 that *porter* is associated with the circulation of desire, and the fluidity of desire seems here to displace the measured regularity of progression. Sade's most unbridled novels come to use "porter au dernier période" quite frequently, as a mark of excess that refers both to the limit of imaginable horror and to the difficulty of actually saying what occurs at that limit. *La Nouvelle Justine* (1797) invites its reader to go to the limit of his (not her) suspicions when it says: "il est facile de soupçonner qu'à ces sortes de fêtes, les luxures, les lubricités, les horreurs étaient toujours portées au dernier période" [one can readily suspect that in those kinds of festivities lewdness, lubricity, and horrible things were always taken to the final stage] (7:76). The action of *porter* appears to be a kind of ethical and material work done to make circulation and its consequences as fierce as possible. Juliette sees the Pope's temporal power in the same terms, as an opportunity to raise one's desires and one's crimes to the very peak of their potential: "Il suffit d'être sur le trône pour porter ces infamies à leur dernier période" [one only needs to occupy the throne in order to take those dreadful actions to the final stage] (*Histoire de Juliette* [1797], 9:203). Indeed, it seems to become a rule of Sadian villainy that there is no *période* worthy of mention other than the *dernier*, no quality of pleasure or crime deserving of esteem other than the ultimate ones. To be a lesser villain, to practice moderation in any particular can only be an episodic activity, destined to be lost from the story. It is a literal shortcoming, punished by death in the case of Olympe Borghèse, Sbrigani, or even Saint-Fond. The only proper way to do things is to go to the farthest extreme. Justine shows her failure to understand this principle, despite her repeated experience of its effects, when she exclaims in horror at Roland's ferocity: "Oh! monsieur . . . à quel point vous portez la scélératesse!" [Oh Sir! How far do you carry wickedness!]. This is not a statement of admiration so much as a reproachful question, but only one so compulsively naïve as Justine could wonder aloud in the presence of an accomplished Sadian libertine how far advanced he is on the scale of criminality. Roland is happy to take his cue and gives just about the only answer possible, according to Sade's rule of maximal intensity. With something approaching pomposity, and with a full sense of the rightness of his position, he tells Justine just how far he is prepared to go: "Au dernier période" (*La Nouvelle Justine* 7:309). *Au dernier période* is a quality added to every desire and every pleasure. Or at least, the only desires and pleasures worthy of narration are those that can be so modulated. This blend of the quantitatively explicit and the qualitatively unfathomable we can recognize as the very matter of the new theme of climax.

The new, here, still carries with it something of the old. One suspects that it is no longer possible for Sade's Roland to work right through the scale: he would not have the patience to spend the 120 days it would take to count up to the ultimate point of desire and pleasure. But there is a sense in which earlier events and earlier villains in Justine's story have already done this for him, even as they did their utmost. Roland talks, in fact, as if he knew his place in the story and measured that place on a scale of intensity. Indeed, intensity is never so great, even in the later novels, as to abolish the comparative awareness of a range of possible actions. We find inscribed in the discourse of Sade's self-conscious libertines a sense of the time taken to work through the range of pleasures on the way to the highest point. Saint-Fond waxes lyrical about violence, but it is striking that his enthusiasm, while anything but "measured," is thoroughly mensurative. It is a matter, he says, of becoming progressively more violent, more extreme, by moving implacably through all the intermediary stages:

qu'on brise un [frein] de plus, l'irritation deviendra plus violente, et nécessairement ainsi, de gradation en gradation, on ne parviendra réellement au véritable but de ces espèces de plaisirs, qu'en portant l'égarement des sens jusqu'aux dernières bornes des facultés de notre être, en telle sorte que l'irritation de nos nerfs éprouve un degré de violence si prodigieux qu'ils en soient comme renversés, comme crispés dans toute leur étendue.

[If one breaks one more restraint, the irritation will become more violent, and necessarily so, from gradation to gradation, one will really only reach the true end of these kinds of pleasures by carrying distraction of the senses to the far limits of one's faculties, so that the irritation of the nerves attains such a prodigious degree of violence that they are as if turned upside down, in contraction throughout their whole length.] (*Histoire de Juliette* 8:366)

Porter, the action whereby the limit of distraction is reached, is still a kind of work, and its achievement is to cross an intermediary space occupied by lesser pleasures and lesser crimes. Violence, in this case, is no simple explosion: it is attained by degrees, and intensity is only fully achieved through an effort that follows, progressively if not patiently, the Sadian rake's progress.

The expression *le comble* is subject to the same kind of inflection and inflation as *le dernier période*, with only a trace of the earlier sense persisting through it all. In this case, instead of the play on the notion of *dernier* that moves from "last-and-highest" to "extreme or ultimate," there is a certain etymological ambiguity that abets the thematic shift. *Le Grand Robert* points out that *le comble* refers both to an overflow (from the Latin *cumulus*) and to a high point or apogee (from the Latin *culmen*).[6] The *culmen* or culmination belongs properly to the order of gradation since it readily evokes a place in a temporal order, but the *cumulus* lends itself well enough to a processual thematics of inner pressure, intensity, and ejaculation. Climax will eventually be made, in its narrative fullness, out of a productive equivocation between two analogous elements: the peak (the middle as high point) and the overflow (the end as explosive collapse). In *Thérèse philosophe* (1748), so often remarkable for its innovations, we actually find the emphasis moved from one of these senses to the other, in varying uses of the word *comble* within a relatively short space of text. At the outset of Thérèse's story, we are promised just the kind of subtle narrative progression that La Mettrie was to describe and prescribe a few years later. The narrator-heroine tells us, speaking of herself in the third person, that "son âme toute entière va se développer dans les détails des petites aventures qui l'ont conduite, comme malgré elle, pas à pas, au comble de la volupté" [her soul will unfold completely through the detailed [story] of the little adventures that have led her, step by step, to the peak of voluptuousness].[7] This is the broad pattern, and the promise of a well-shaped narrative of graded pleasures, but it also happens that occurrences of *le comble* are found along the way to this final stage. Only a few pages from the beginning of the novel, Thérèse tells how she yielded as a child to the temptation to masturbate: "l'enfer en-trouvert sous mes yeux n'aurait pas eu le pouvoir de m'arrêter. Remords impuissants, je mettais le comble à la volupté!" [even hell opening up before my eyes would not have had the power to stop me. Remorse was powerless, as I brought voluptuousness to its peak!] (*Thérèse philosophe* 5:49). The apparent contradiction here is not destructive. Narrative order will be maintained, and the story saved from that inconclusive shapelessness identified by Steven Marcus in his characterization of pornography,[8] as long as the experiences of *le comble de la volupté* that take place along the way are themselves graded in ascending order: from masturbation, to being caressed by a man, to sleeping with a woman, to a relationship with a man. The key notion is one of progressive refinement or increasing complexity rather than of some leap into intensity, but that does not exclude marking the different pleasures to be found along the way with the sign of completeness. As long as the various "overflows" are presented in a series, they do not yet undo the shape of culmination.

When *le comble* and *porter au comble* occur in texts of the nine-teenth century, they tend to lose this ambiguity, highlighting in-tensity at the expense of any sense of progression. In *Gamiani* (1833), for example, *le comble de la volupté* is a point of arrival not always preceded by any particular kind of departure, or by any measured journey. Gamiani and Fanny, as well as the mas-turbating voyeur-narrator, Alcide, are described as arriving there together, in a moment whose intensity is marked and produced by that very coincidence in time: "je suivais leurs élans, leurs soupirs; j'arrivai comme elles au comble de la volupté!" [I fol-lowed their wild movements and their sighs. I arrived as they did at the peak of voluptuousness].[9] Gamiani has no doubt that she can carry (*porter*) Fanny with her in the charge toward violent pleasure, and says as much in her urgent seduction of the young woman. She promises not serial pleasures but the foreplay and the climax: "Je vais m'emparer de toi, je vais te réchauffer, te ranimer peu à peu; je vais te mettre en feu, te porter au comble de la vie sensuelle" [I am going to warm you up and revive you gradually. I will set you alight, and take you to the peak of sensual life] (136). By the end of the century, talk of *le comble* becomes a quite routine way of referring to the effort needed to bring pleasure to its highest point. In *Enfilade de perles* (1894), we read: "[Emma] portait à son comble la jouissance de Minna..." [Emma took Minna's pleasure to its peak].[10] And in *Voluptés bizarres* (1893), "Hélène... résolut de porter à son comble l'inflammation des sens du rhétoricien" [Hélène resolved to bring to a peak the inflammation of the rhetorician's senses].[11] These are intensifying operations, carried out decisively at certain moments, rather than signposts in a long narrative.

A further development of the word's etymological possibilities occurs when *le comble*, or the plural *les combles*, is used to refer to the most distant point of penetration reached within the other's body, thereby providing a spatial representation of the extreme point of pleasure, to be found "fouillant jusqu'aux combles" [exploring right to the top] (*L'Odyssée d'un pantalon* [1889]).[12] It would be a mistake, I contend, to regard this merely as a piece of anatomical description: the fullness of penetration responds to a narrative requirement. It helps to evoke a domain within the penetrated body that fires the imagination but resists observation and description. *Le comble* (or *les combles*) is represented, desired, and strained for as a space that is heroically distant and intimately present. It is the very space of intensity: "ce n'est qu'en sondant le fond de l'abîme, que la volupté atteint le comble de l'intensité" [it is only by sounding the bottom of the abyss that pleasure reaches the height of intensity] (*Lesbia, maîtresse d'école* [1890]).[13]

Not all discursive elements used to affirm intense pleasure are recycled from writing of the *ancien régime*. The adjective *dernier* is sometimes displaced in the nineteenth century by others that are approximate synonyms, yet mark a decisive shift toward climax in its thematic plenitude. Nerciat, that early champion of the climactic, makes a substitution that was eventually to become a dominant usage. He replaces *dernier* with *suprême* and may in fact be the first to do so. Here is an example from *Mon Noviciat* (1792): "il est bientôt frappé de la tête aux pieds par l'éclair du suprême bonheur..." [he was soon struck from head to foot by a lightning flash of supreme happiness].[14] *Suprême* marks an order of significance without counting. It is an affirmation of dominance with no particular sense of scale. And the *suprême* is likely to be attended, as in the example just quoted, by the metaphor of the lightning strike, or joined to the notion of ecstasy, as different nouns are qualified by the same telling adjective: "l'extase de la suprême volupté" [the ecstasy of supreme voluptuousness] (21). *Suprême* comes thus to displace *dernier* while performing quite another function: the pleasure it describes is somehow beyond the *dernier*, while continuing to resemble it, standing at an ecstatic remove from all that may have gone before. This particular adjective was to have a long and successful career. By the latter part of the nineteenth century, to call a pleasure "supreme" was not just a clichéd mark of its general significance, but an economical indicator of the theme of climax. One finds reference to "le suprême baiser," the supreme kiss, as the final, orgasmic embrace to be shared by parting lovers (*Rires, sang et voluptés* [1901]).[15] Elsewhere, "la suprême caresse" is said to be what "the flesh" desires above all else (*La Luxure* [1905]).[16] When nouns like *baiser* and *caresse* are used in the singular and joined to the adjective *suprême*, it should be clear how tightly organized the thematics of climax has become. These expressions manage to avoid crudity while remaining referentially specific, since there is now known to be only one supreme caress, one ultimate erotic practice, just as there is only one true erotic narrative. It should be noted also that the fin de siècle attaches great value to "lastness," not for the seriality that once served to define it but because it stands at the farthest point of life, so that affirmations of intensity are attended by the immediate promise of denouement. That is largely why we find orgasm described as "la suprême agonie des amoureux spasmes" [the supreme death agony of love's spasms], or referred to as "les ultimes pâmoisons" [the final swooning] (*Croquis du vice* [1905]).[17] The ultimate experience has more to do with violent illness than with any high point attained by a progressive art of pleasure: it affirms the intensity of life by the quasi-dialectical proximity of its dreadful opposite.

As part of the general shift I am describing, one finds the emergence, from the late eighteenth century onward, of terms that are narratively reflexive about climax in just the way that *le dernier période* or *la dernière jouissance* are in regard to gradation. In a play that dates from around 1789, the erotic action occurring on stage is refered to in the text in the following manner: "Arrive l'instant définitif" [The definitive instant arrives].[18] Nerciat uses almost the same expression in *Les*

Aphrodites when he refers to a woman's habit of closing her eyes "dans les instants décisifs" (1:176 n. 3). Such reflexivity is both sophisticated and naïve. It shows within stories a clear awareness of narrative process, but it does so in a way that is baldly declarative rather than richly thematic. The reader is told about the importance of these instants and referred to a whole class of events without being made a party to the quality of experience they might entail. The mention of decisiveness should be read as a hopeful claim put forward in the text on behalf of the narrative power of climactic eroticism. That something of vital significance turns on this event—on these repeated events—is candidly affirmed before it can be fully demonstrated in narrative, and often affirmed instead of being demonstrated. But that very affirmation is part of the thematic work being carried out by Nerciat and his successors, as they invite us to understand and enjoy pleasure in these terms, attending to its nodes rather than its wanderings, its moments rather than its hours. In fact, Nerciat's narration hardly ever fails to define pleasure as instantaneous by naming for the reader the "moment décisif" that is about to occur. He teaches the value of "l'instant de plaisir" [the instant of pleasure] as such (see, for example, *Mon Noviciat* 16; *Le Diable au corps* 1:206). We must anticipate that pleasure will occur in this way since the instant is par excellence the time of intensity: "leurs bonds, leurs accents, leurs petits mots énergiques annoncent l'approche du sublime instant" [their sudden movements, their tone of voice, and their short, energetic words herald the approach of the sublime instant] (*Le Diable au corps* 5:110). This naming is itself an expression of desire, desire for the climax that now bids to displace gradation as the true goal, and the proper form, of pleasurable narrative. An erotic novel dating from 1890 is still able to maintain the same grammar while substituting an adjective more characteristic of its own time. In *La Canonisation de Jeanne d'Arc*, we are told that various couples involved in an orgy have reached "le moment psychologique."[19]

Through reflexivity of this sort, Nerciat and some of those who come after him approximate to the tightly closed thematic circle that, in English, binds "climax" and "orgasm." The high point of pleasure can then be called the denouement, by a reflexively happy assimilation of the two: "La marquise, renversée, . . . endure jusqu'au dénouement, qui n'est pas éloigné, cet hommage sublime" [The Marquise, lying flat on her back, endures this sublime homage until denouement, which is not long coming] (*Les Aphrodites* 1:95). Mme. Durut, also, turns her attention in the experience of pleasure toward "le dénouement de cette besogne où personne ne pense plus qu'à soi" [the denouement of that job in which no one thinks of anyone but themselves] (*Les Aphrodites* 1:95; cf. *Le Diable au corps* 5:107). On another occasion, the completion of the action, the end of a certain narrative tension is referred to in the middle of a story as the "conclusion": "il procède à la conclusion, sans l'ombre d'indécision" [he goes on to the conclusion, without a trace of hesitation] (*Le Diable au corps* 3:64). Excluding "indecision" in this way, and with it any refinements or preliminaries, attributes to the decisive moment an assertive, almost polemical quality. The proof of its importance is utterly, proudly circular. The same usage, which once again satisfies the exigency of polished discourse with no loss of referential precision, continues to be found later, although it is not a particular favorite of the fin de siècle. In *L'Ecole des biches* (1868), we find: "Le comte, par ce surcroît d'excitation inattendu, est bientôt amené au dénouement" [The Count, by this unexpected extra arousal, is soon brought to the denouement].[20] The paradoxical aim of so much erotic narrative, with its frequent reassurance that the "end" is close at hand, is to repeat such denouements ad libitum, moving speedily and often to the desired natural conclusion, without actually bringing to an end the delay that constitutes the very space of narrative. I have alluded to that paradox before, and will return to it at length in chapter 10.

It is noteworthy that this reflexive talk draws support from, and supports in turn, the more general theme of the instant. The notion of the instant has thematic resonance of various kinds prior to this time, as Georges Poulet's work has shown,[21] but its value is both focused and invigorated by the increasing importance given to intensity as the erotic quality par excellence. The earlier eighteenth century tended to count the time of pleasure in units of duration rather than highlighting those unanalyzable nodes of intensity that so fascinated the Romantics. Libertine writing speaks most often of the quarter hour in preference to the instant. Here is how the narrator of *Les Amours de Sainfroid, jésuite, et d'Eulalie, fille dévote* (1729) refers to the lovemaking of the two central characters: "tous les quarts d'heures de plaisir que Sainfroid a eus avec elle" [all the quarter hours of pleasure that Sainfroid had with her].[22] This is the proper temporal unit of such eroticism; it is the space of time needed for delight to rise to the fullness of ecstasy, and for ecstasy to expand happily into ongoing delight: "on passe bien souvent des quarts d'heures qui tiennent du ravissement et de l'extase" [They often spend quarter hours that are made of delight and ecstasy] (23). It is not that instants or moments are unknown here: it is simply that they are always able to be summed up, and quite literally recounted in durative terms. Crébillon gives us to understand, in *La Nuit et le moment*, that the two parts of his title are approximate equivalents: a night spent together is a moment, and a moment can last a whole night.[23] In his world of seductive conversation, time passes in elegant distractions, and to court another is to give him or her one's "moments perdus" [spare moments].[24] The moment, as Pierre Hartmann says quite properly, is a key term in Crébillon's language of *galanterie*, and is not to be confused with the dazzling brilliance of the instant so prominent in Romantic writing.[25] When libertines gather, there is no declared purpose of a climactic sort: they are said to be present by chance, whim, or circumstance, just to spend "some (*quelques*) moments" (*La Nuit et le moment* 9:6). And when in fact a "moment de bonté" [moment of generosity] in which a woman yields to a man's advances is qualified as "pas plus durable que l'éclair" [no more lasting than a lightning strike], the reference to lightning indicates no glorious intensity but a regrettable failure to sustain enjoyment (*La Nuit et le moment* 9:108). In this context, the moment is valued precisely for its extension. *Les Amours de Sainfroid* presents at one point an invitation to spend "quelques instants" [a few moments] that is repeated as a request to "rester encore un quart d'heure" [stay for another quarter of an hour] (31). Between the two expressions, there appears at this time to be no quantitative or qualitative difference.

The quarter hour survives into nineteenth-century stories, even while being displaced from the centre of narrative attention by the instant. It is still the time of dalliance, even for the ebullient Nerciat, who uses it to refer to the whole period of time spent together by two lovers—"ce délicieux quart d'heure" [that delightful quarter hour] (*Les Aphrodites* 2:183)—and describes the pleasures of cunnilingus as "un quart d'heure de *glottinade*" [a quarter of an hour of *tonguery*] (*Les Aphrodites* 1:67; original emphasis). The difference with respect to earlier writing is that time measured in quarter hours is now usually that of the "preliminaries," and only takes on full erotic value insofar as it serves to prepare the instant of climax. It is actually used by Alexandrine in *Amélie de Saint-Far* to mark and to measure the absence of climax, as Colonel Charles watches the sleeping Amélie and whispers sweet nothings to her at such length that two units of dilatory time are allowed to pass: "il faut que la conversation d'Amélie soit bien intéressante, pour que vous, toujours si pressé d'arriver au but, oubliiez, pendant une demi-heure, le motif de votre visite nocturne" [Amélie's conversation must be really interesting to make you, who are always in such a hurry to reach your goal, lose sight for half an hour of your purpose in visiting her at night] (1:108). With a response that bears a vague resemblance to Alexandrine's testiness, and a standard of measurement that is exactly the same, a young woman in *Les Matinées du Palais-Royal* (1815) describes a protracted and uncomfortable session with a paying customer. He subjects her to "caresses" of a new and unwelcome kind before finally coming to the point: "Après une demi-heure de préludes de ce genre, il parut se disposer à finir ainsi qu'on le doit" [after a half hour of preludes of that kind, he seemed inclined to finish off in the way one is supposed to].[26] If the quarter hour is the proper measure of dalliance, it may be that the half hour is coming to be that of undue delay.

When durative preliminaries, and sometimes a durative aftermath,[27] are arranged on either side of the instantaneous climax, that allows for both kinds of time to play a role in narrative, even as the hierarchical difference between them is affirmed. In Nerciat's *Mon Noviciat*, a young man who is visiting Félicité proposes a novel erotic position, claiming that it will be an enjoyable way to pass the time. The measure of time that they are invited to pass is the classical one: "vous pourrez, aimables enfants, être toutes deux agréablement occupés pendant un quart d'heure" [you will find yourselves, dear children, pleasantly occupied for a quarter of an hour]. They take up the suggestion eagerly but do not, so to speak, dwell in the pose, or dwell on the pleasure it gives. They simply take it as a novel means for reaching climax, spending the necessary quarter hour in order to attain the instant that really matters. Accordingly, by a paradox inherent in the description of intensity, it is the evocation of this

instant that occupies most textual time, and not the techniques
or practices that give rise to it: "Quel instant que celui où l'une
et l'autre, électrisées jusqu'à la moelle des os, nous confondions
les accents de notre luxurieuse agonie! . . ." [What an instant it
was when the two of us, electrified to the marrow, mingled the
tones of our lascivious death agony!] (66–67). The quarter hour
tends, in fact, to be not only a way to measure the preliminaries
but an expression whose very use is part of preliminary talk, no
doubt as an echo of the old rhetoric of seduction. In *Julie, ou j'ai
sauvé ma rose*, Versac speaks of quarter hours—"Je n'ai d'autre
dessein que de causer un quart d'heure avec vous" [my only aim
is to spend a quarter of an hour chatting with you]—whereas he
is really thinking and desiring in terms of instants: "Versac,
maîtrisé par la violence de ses désirs, . . . bientôt . . . se lance sur
moi avec la rapidité de l'éclair" [Versac, overcome by the violence
of his desires, threw himself at me with the quickness of a lightning strike] (274).

Sade, his modernity so powerfully constrained by his classicism, seems to find a closer way to mediate between the two
kinds of time. After using the quarter hour with remarkable, not
to say obsessive, frequency in *Les Cent Vingt Journées de
Sodome* as a unit of graded time and a source of narrative
order,[28] he actually finds a striking way to apply it, in some of his
later novels, to the description of climax: "Près d'un quart
d'heure entier le paillard était en extase . . . et quelle extase,
grand Dieu!" [For nearly a quarter of an hour the libertine was
in ecstasy, and, ye gods, what ecstasy!] (*La Nouvelle Justine*
7:127). By a nice irony that is not exactly Sade's own, but rather
the irony of his position between two kinds of eroticism, the intensity of the instant is signified by its being expanded into the
durative. This character's ecstatic pleasure is so great that it actually lasts the "whole" quarter hour that others might spend on
mere erotic trifles. This move is often repeated in Sade's descriptions. It translates the qualitative into the quantitative, giving
rhetorical exchange value to the otherwise indescribable instant, and helps produce the overweening quantification, the extraordinarily precise exaggeration that characterize Sade's
material accounts of intensity. Not just the titanic penis mea-
surements, not just the pounds of ejaculate or the many feet it
may travel at the moment of its emergence, but the very quality
of climax are spelled out in a way that allows them to be

counted, assessed, and recounted. Juliette is thus able to describe her "discharge" as an event of great magnitude, both constituted and enhanced by an impressive number of sub-events:
"je déchargeai six fois sous ses doigts savants, ou plutôt ce ne fut
qu'une seule éjaculation qui se prolongea pendant deux grandes
heures" [I unloaded six times in response to his expert hands, or
rather, it was just one ejaculation that went on for two whole
hours] (*Histoire de Juliette* 9:499).

It may seem, on rare occasions early in the century, that there
is to be a genuine competition, or some continuing thematic
option, between the two kinds of time. *Caroline et Saint-Hilaire*
(1817) describes a particular erotic position in terms of its yield
for both, firstly as duration, and secondly as intense climax:

> Par ce moyen, il excite ou arrête le chatouillement mutuel, et l'on
> peut ainsi, par une manœuvre habile, jouir un quart d'heure, sans
> exciter la libation; mais si alors on lui donne un libre cours, elle est
> si abondante que l'on se pâme tous deux et que l'excès du plaisir
> semble nous confondre et nous anéantir ensemble.
>
> [By this means, he maintains or interrupts the mutual stimula-
> tion, and one can, by skillful maneuvering, take pleasure for a
> quarter of an hour, without provoking the libation. But if you then
> allow it to happen freely, it is so abundant that both of you swoon,
> and the excess of pleasures seems to melt you into one another.][29]

Yet even here the order of presentation is significant. It is rare
for enjoyment measured in quarter hours to do anything more,
in fine, than enhance the transcendent delight of the instant.
When the fiction of a choice between the two does appear, it
takes the form of an unreal hypothesis and a rhetorical gesture.
Nineteenth-century erotic narrative is filled with ostensibly
evaluative moments, in which the instant of passion is weighed
against a whole lifetime, or even an eternity of duration. The
outcome is always the same, and the evaluation a kind of theatrical flourish: "qu'elle m'appartienne un instant sur la terre, et
que le ciel m'écrase pendant l'éternité" [let her be mine for an instant on earth, and let heaven punish me for eternity] (*Claire
d'Albe* [1798]).[30] It is invariably the case that the instantaneous
is preferred to the durative. Even one of Choiseul-Meuse's heroines is prepared to wager her life on the value of the instant:
"Oui, oui, Eugène, rappelle-moi la colère de mon père, le sacrifice
de ma réputation, la vengeance du ciel, s'il le faut; voilà ce que je

veux risquer, ce que je veux échanger contre un instant de ta félicité" [Yes, yes. Remind me of my father's anger, the sacrifice of my reputation, heaven's vengeance, if you must. All that I want to risk. I want to exchange it for an instant of your happiness] (*Entre chien et loup* [1809]).[31] According to this uncalculating calculation, the exchange value of the instant of passion is greater than any quality that may endure. The same declaration will be heard repeatedly in later novels, as characters proclaim their readiness to trade "the whole life of a man" for "the incomparable feeling of happiness" that lovemaking brings,[32] to pay "an eternity of expiation" for "the memory of an hour,"[33] "an eternity of darkness" for "a minute of sunny joy,"[34] "eternal martyrdom" for "this moment of pleasure,"[35] to give up "my blood, my life, my soul" for "a minute's voluptuousness."[36] When all these conventional virtues and pleasures, all these durative forms of suffering are placed in one great quantitative pile on the scales, they cannot tip the balance against the infinitely powerful concentration of feeling to be found within a single passionate instant.

A quite precise focus on the instant as a narrative turning point is developed through the remarkably successful notion of the *crise*, or bodily "crisis," which emerges at this time, contributing strongly to the thematic shift I am describing. The historical dictionary *Gesichtliche Grundbegriffe* indicates that the word *Krise* in German, together with its French and English equivalents, was subject to a displacement of meaning toward the end of the eighteenth century. It had until then been largely a medical term, but it now became a byword for revolutionary events of any sort, and began to be used in a range of discourses, including economics, psychology, and theology.[37] Georges Benrekassa, in an article devoted to the French word, mentions some points that are of great interest to my discussion. He notes that *la crise* is used in the language of the theater, in recognition of Aristotle, to designate an event that changes the face of things, and turns the action toward its eventual denouement.[38] This we can recognize as the thematic middle discussed in chapter 6. It is something like "climax" in a technical, poetic sense. At the same time, says Benrekassa, the term signifies a symptomatic event in the course of an illness that will have a decisive consequence, for better or for worse (16–17). Without pursuing the political connotations Benrekassa goes on to discuss, we can see that the discursive versatility of *la crise* lends itself particularly well to the thematic development we have been following. Its great appeal and its thematic promise lie no doubt in the fact of connecting strong bodily symptoms to some change in the course of events, binding physiology and narrative one to the other.

No novelist is more alert to these possibilities than Nerciat. His use of *la crise* takes advantage of this connection in ways that are both inventive and remarkably insistent. On occasion, he simply employs it in the dictionary sense, when talking of illness: "une crise . . . avait annoncé la fin prochaine du malade" [a crisis had pointed to the coming end of the patient] (*Les Aphrodites* 2:32).[39] More commonly, however, he applies it to narrativized description of an erotic kind. In *Les Aphrodites*, Mme. de Montchaud explains how she came to be expelled from a convent. She experienced "des crises, des extases" that were not the moments of high spirituality expected by her superiors but had more immediately "natural" causes (2:9–10). It is the notion of *la crise* that allows this misunderstanding, since it crosses over from the ostensibly spiritual to the physiological. The (re-)reading of symptoms to which we are playfully invited is therefore itself a departure from the world of the convent: it moves ironically from the exalted to the bodily via the symptomatic equivalence of sacred *extase* and erotic *crise*. The temptation, then, happily indulged by Nerciat, is to regard the "crisis" as a particular event, a decisive erotic moment, and to use the expression as an economical way of evoking dramatic changes in the body: "c'est tout juste le moment où le chevalier et la duchesse tombent en crise" [this was the exact point at which the chevalier and the duchess fell into a crisis] (*Les Aphrodites* 1:47). *La crise* is something one falls into, and falling, with the loss of control it entails, with its preclusion of all postural stability, is the proper way to experience climax. Lest it be thought, moreover, that this makes of pleasure something too much like illness, Nerciat is at pains to maintain his usual cheeriness, affirming the drastic nature of the event, its utterly precipitate quality, while denying any sinister overtones. He reminds us that these are good, happy *crises*, in which intensity is unaccompanied by affliction, speaking of "this delicious crisis" (*Le Diable au corps* 6:29) or of "happy crises" (*Mon Noviciat* 133). There is, for the vigorous, the possibility of a more glorious epithet: "Nicole, d'un tempérament bouillant, et d'une vigueur peu commune, éprouve, jusqu'au délire, la crise du plaisir connu pour être le plus sublime" [Nicole, with her ebullient temperament and her uncommon vigor, experienced to the point of delirium the crisis of pleasure that is known to be the most sublime] (*Le Diable au corps* 2:202–3). This appears to be pleasure rising above, or falling below, the very possibility of self-expression, into a sublime state of erotic delirium. Yet Nerciat's actual writing is not delirious. While appearing to suggest that language itself may be thrown into crisis when pleasure is at its most acute, he still finds the language in which to do so. Unlike the textual demonstrations of this to be found much later in the work of Georges Bataille and others, his writing simply contributes to the theme of climax at its most dramatically assertive. This leads Nerciat not to enact a crisis of narrative but to talk about the indescribable in a quite urbane manner, using the notion of crisis as a descriptive term marking the impossibility of further description. In the following passage, tongues are silent, but that is because they are otherwise happily engaged: "[La langue] qui l'avait cherchée ferraille avec elle pendant l'indescriptible crise de leur jouissance. Ils ne parlent plus, ils sont foudroyés de plaisir" [the tongue that had sought hers crossed swords with it during the indescribable crisis of their pleasure. They no longer spoke. They were struck dumb with pleasure] (*Le Diable au corps* 5:12). *La crise*, it seems, is not to be read as a bodily pose, an "attitude" in the classical sense, but the dramatic symptom, the instantaneously appearing syndrome, of a body transformed by the lightning strike of radical pleasure.

An indication of just how much the notion of *la crise* prospers at this time can be found in the fact that it is also present in the work of the novelist that I have described as Nerciat's strongest thematic opponent, Félicité de Choiseul-Meuse. Choiseul-Meuse does not use the term nearly so often as Nerciat, nor does she surround it with such enthusiasm, but the range of meaning she gives to it, with a correspondence being established between the instantaneous, the symptomatic, and the pleasurable, is very much the same. Even while resisting views like those of Nerciat, her novels are helping to accommodate the expression within erotic discourse. At one point, Julie uses the word, conventionally enough, to describe a sudden change in the condition of her ailing father: "une crise heureuse vint rendre mon père à la vie" [a happy crisis brought my father back from death's door] (*Julie, ou j'ai sauvé ma rose* 231), while at another she employs it to describe the climactic pleasure that she has chosen to forego in her own life: "Cette crise heureuse, qui éteint les désirs en les comblant, ne venait point à mon secours" [The happy crisis that extinguishes desires by satisfying them did not come to my aid] (*Julie, ou j'ai sauvé ma rose* 178).

The polyvalence of the notion of *crise*, with its capacity to circulate from one context to another, contributes to a discursive merger that helps constitute the thematic space of climax in the nineteenth century. *La crise* brings together narrative talk and medical terminology, associating a reflexive mark of the turning point with symptomatic description of the body. Not surprisingly, it continues to be part of the thematics of climax throughout the century, undergoing change not as a simple drift of meaning but as a veritable intensification, with its central elements being foregrounded and comprehensively exploited. The blandly euphemistic *la crise heureuse* [the happy crisis] still lingers in certain texts,[40] but there is a widespread and increasing tendency to dwell on the crisis itself for its sheer concentration of bodily violence in space and time, so that any difference between "happiness" and "unhappiness" comes to appear inconsequential. To understand this evolution better, it is helpful to attend to the predication, *la crise de nerfs* [the nerve crisis]. This phrase is found as early as 1825, being used in medical discourse by Brillat-Savarin,[41] and enjoys a career in erotic novels throughout the century as the name of a set of drastic symptoms that are instantaneous in their manifestation, dramatically unpredictable, and peculiarly feminine. It is hardly surprising, then, that fin-de-siècle novels should have come to use the term freely given their fondness for conceiving the erotic as pathological as they take their pleasure in the examination of its symptoms. *Gamiani* (1833) had already presented the *attaque de nerfs* as a manifestation of desire and pleasure at their most acute, making it a sensational object of voyeuristic attention. Alcide says of Gamiani: "Les dents de la comtesse claquaient avec force; ses yeux roulaient, effrayants, dans leur orbite; tout en elle s'agitait, se tordait. . . . Pour moi, je m'attendais à une attaque de nerfs" [The countess's teeth chattered. Her eyes rolled about dreadfully in their sockets. Every part of her was agitated and twisted. For my part, I was expecting her to have a nervous attack] (102). In the decades that follow, especially as the century draws to a close, the reader should always be prepared for an *attaque* or a *crise de nerfs*, if she or he is to be alert enough to expect the unexpected, for that is precisely how the unexpected is thematized and integrated into stories. No ostensibly unpredictable event is more frequent, more thoroughly requisite than this. It is a kind of morbid expression of desire, breaking out most strongly when the expected outcome has been thwarted. One can say that, where Nerciat and his contemporaries might have produced narratorial chatter about decisive instants without actually demonstrating their decisiveness, the fin de siècle found a way to tell its climaxes better, by punctuating its stories with *crises de nerfs* suffered by the central characters. When Simone, in *Chairs épanouies* (1902), learns that her husband has been arrested, she "falls" into labor, in the most literally hysterical reaction, and gives birth to a stillborn child.[42] Mme. de la Pagerie, in *Rires, sang et voluptés* (1901), learns that her husband has died from a fall and goes instantly into convulsions: "la veuve . . . , prise d'une violente attaque de nerfs, se tordait sur le plancher, en proie à des convulsions épouvantables" [the widow fell victim to a violent nerve attack and twisted about on the floor, in the grip of dreadful convulsions].[43] Camille, in *Les Demi-Sexes* (1897), falls into the same, "naturally feminine" state on receiving bad news: "elle fut prise par une de ces crises d'énervement qui jettent les femmes palpitantes, hurlantes et tordues sur le sol. Elle tremblait de tous ses membres, sentant bien qu'elle allait tomber, se rouler sur le tapis en poussant des cris aigus" [she fell victim to one of those nervous crises that make women fall palpitating, screaming and twisting on the floor. She felt all her limbs tremble, and knew very well that she was about to fall and roll on the carpet uttering shrill cries].[44] The *crise de nerfs* serves, in each of these cases and in many others,[45] as the conventional mark of a dramatic turn of events in its bodily impact, but it is equally a conventional mark—a grossly sexist one—of feminine passion as pathological weakness. Furthermore, its symptoms—cries, convulsions, rolling around the floor—are exactly those of erotic climax at its most (conventionally) frenzied. When the exotic and deadly Lia Tasti [*sic*] learns that the young man she desires in fact loves another, she falls into a similar *crise*, doing so with a nice sense of propriety, on the floor of her boudoir: "En proie à une crise nerveuse effrayante, elle s'affaissa, se laissa tomber sur le tapis qui garnissait son boudoir et se mit à pleurer!" [the victim of a dreadful nerve crisis, she slumped and fell onto the carpet that covered the boudoir floor. There she began to cry!] (*Vendeuse d'amour* [1891]).[46]

Other expressions akin to *la crise de nerfs* come to the fore at the end of the century. *Le paroxysme* is one of the most successful of these, doubtless because it enjoys the prestige of medical connotations. "Paroxysm" has general descriptive force, as the name of a convulsive state that grips the whole body. It is already present, somewhat ahead of its time and of its full development, in *Gamiani*, where it marks the ultimate tendency, the infinitesimal limit of "une sensualité délirante, qui touche au paroxysme de la rage" [mad sensuality that reaches a rabid paroxysm] (105). In the following example, it serves more typically, as an approximate, though quite specific and pseudo-medical, synonym for *la crise*: "Elle . . . se remit à pleurer, à râler presque, à n'être que sanglots et crises. Il la calma de douces paroles: elle repartit dans un paroxysme" [She began to cry again, almost to utter a death rattle. She was all sobs and crises. He calmed her down with gentle words. She went off into a paroxysm again] (*Demi-Volupté* [1900]).[47] The term seems to be applied more freely than *la crise de nerfs* to mature men, as if it stood not for erection in its classical priapic splendor but for some more robust, more heavily muscular convulsion. This is the young hero of *L'Arrière-Boutique* (1898): "L'état d'énervement dans lequel se trouvait Charles était à son paroxysme. Il sentait en sa tête comme un bourdonnement tumultueux qui lui surchauffait le crâne et ses tempes avaient des pulsations" [The state of nervous tension in which Charles found himself reached a paroxysm. He felt inside his head a kind of tumultuous buzzing that overheated his skull and made his temples pulsate].[48]

There is a compelling circularity—or just a compulsive circuit—that connects throbbing desire to the longing for convulsion as the most intense form of sensation, whether it be pleasure or pain. We can see this in the doubled but insistent use of *le spasme*, for it functions both as a striking individual symptom and a metaphor for bodily responsiveness in general. When a young woman is said to experience "l'enivrement du premier spasme" [the euphoria of the first spasm] (*La Fille de Gamiani* [1906]),[49] she enters into the circuit of desire and climax at work in this grammatically ambiguous phrase, for to be drunk on the first spasm is also to conceive for the first time a drunken desire for the spasm that will go on indefinitely. "La nuit et les jours," says the hero of *Journal d'un amant* (1902), describing a spasm and the desire for it in a single phrase: "mes fibres se contractent et j'implore un spasme" [Night and day my fibres contract and I ache for a spasm].[50] Walking at night on the boulevards of Paris, this man finds himself surrounded by creatures, subjects and objects of desire, engaged in the same twitching pursuit: "Des ombres fuyaient, revenaient, fantômes solliciteurs, appeleurs de spasmes épileptiques" [Shadowy figures passed by fleetingly, then returned. They were ghosts begging favors, calling for epileptic spasms] (97). When the spasm aches for the spasm, and the body in "crisis" shivers for a more intense paroxysm, one can say that desire has taken on the properties of climax, or that climax is symptomatically prefigured in desire, in such a way that there can no longer be any graded approach to the last pleasure, merely an urgent, involuntary movement whereby the agent/patient lurches tremblingly toward the full outbreak of the "epileptic" malady that already grips his or her body. This is the pathological truth contained in the fin-de-siècle definition of *la volupté*—"la Volupté, aux spasmes infinis" [Voluptuousness, with its infinite spasms][51]— now so far from its eighteenth-century predecessor of the same name. The "spasms" here are perfectly uncountable because, between the first and the last, there is an infinite echo of sameness, an immeasurable quivering that spreads irresistibly through the circuit of desire and climax.

When these thematic elements come together, they allow the spasm to be understood and valued in narrative, for itself, as a febrile equivocation between pleasure and pain. Climactic sexual pleasure can then take on all the visible features of the most drastic illness: "la chère enfant poussant des cris inarticulés, se pâma et eut un tel spasme de plaisir, qu'un instant nous redoutâmes une violente attaque de nerfs" [the dear child uttered inarticulate cries, swooned, and experienced such a spasm of pleasure that for a moment we feared a violent nerve attack] (*Les Libertins du grand monde* [1880]).[52] Conversely, those violent illnesses that have become the favored objects of narrative attention can be seen to correspond, in the intensity of their symptoms, to the convulsive physiology of the erotic body at the point of climax. The spasm is the symptom of truth. Here is a description of the Comtesse de Rochemare, after years of frustrated existence in an unworthy society, at the point where her erotic story finally reaches its peak: "Alors, tout son corps fut secoué de violents frissons, de spasmes subits; elle se tordit les bras et les larmes avec des sanglots coulèrent en abondance. Elle était glacée, frissonnait, et sa peau si fine était devenue rugueuse par un hérissement de chair de poule" [Then her whole body shook violently with sudden spasms. Her arms twisted and tears came sobbing out of her in floods. She went cold and shivered. Her fine skin became rough with the bristling of goose flesh] (*La Volupté féroce* [1905]).[53] It may be remembered from a discussion of this novel in chapter 6 that the Comtesse de Rochemare is described by the narrator as neurotic ("névrosée"), but this does not disqualify her as a heroine, nor does it detract from the general significance of her "case." Quite the contrary, in fact: the violence of her nerves is what allows her to become not only a heroine of desire but a representative champion, a morbidly fascinating exemplum of orgasm at its most convulsive.

Spasmodic eroticism lends itself to an understanding of shared sensations as a form of contagion. In classical times, shared pleasure was largely a matter of mutually accommodating attitudes and of postural appropriateness. Later, it was represented as a spark of fire passing between bodies. For the fin de siècle, it is often a kind of disturbance imparted by proximity or by example, a raging epidemic of involuntary movement. The following description of "contagion" is relatively modest in its focus, but it already moves significantly beyond what we saw in Nerciat. Where Nerciat was content merely to speak of the decisive instant, this description shows how its symptoms are triggered in one body by the action of another: "Ce surcroît de plaisir raffiné, auquel notre fouteur ne s'attendait pas, a un effet immédiat, et un jet bouillant, que Marie sent pénétrer jusqu'au fond de ses entrailles, décide aussi de son côté la crise suprême" [This supplement of refined pleasure, which our fucker had not been expecting, had an immediate effect. A boiling stream, which Marie felt as it penetrated to the depth of her entrails, triggered her own supreme crisis] (*L'Ecole des biches* [1868]).[54] This is "decisiveness" in the second sense of *décider*: to trigger or provoke a quasi-automatic response. When the eager but uninformed Adèle, in *Un Eté à la campagne* (1867), witnesses two lovers in action, she describes the height of pleasure in the man as "epileptic" agitation, and notes that the woman, in turn, "est prise d'une violente crise nerveuse" [fell victim to a violent nervous crisis]. "Is it perhaps contagious?" she asks quite reasonably.[55] Erotic spasms do seem to be contagious, in a sense that ties the biological to the mechanical. Indeed, by an enormous inflation of this metaphor that is itself a form of uncontrolled resonance, the erotic spasm can occur simultaneously on a macrocosmic scale. In certain naturalist texts, the bodies of lovers are described as trembling with the rhythm of nature, and nature itself as one vast spasm: "une sorte de mouvement rotatoire l'anime, ce ventre, rythme accommodé au rythme des planètes, à la houle des digestions, à la palpitation de la mer, au spasme de l'amour" [a kind of rotating movement drove this belly, as if aligned with the rhythm of the planets, the swell of digestion, the rise and fall of the sea, the spasm of love] (*L'Eternelle poupée* [1894]).[56] This is not just the high point of narrative but the fullest vindication, the ultimate naturalization of the theme of orgasm. It finds the spasm at the end of the story, in the depths of the body, at the heart of the universe.

Another expression much in favor at the end of the nineteenth century, the last one that I intend to discuss here, contributes to the discursive closure of desire-and-climax. This is the word *étreinte*. The *étreinte* can be said to combine the energy of the hug with the closeness of the lovers' embrace. At this time, it takes on a quite virulent form, being described often as an uncontrollable mutual seizure, a convulsion for two. Performed as the most drastically intimate contact, it is capable, all at once, of expressing brutality ("une étreinte brutale"),[57] wild passion ("une fougueuse étreinte"),[58] and madness ("une étreinte folle").[59] Between such embrace and the morbid qualities of the individual *crise de nerfs*, there is no great difference. The violent embrace can lead, by compulsion or contagion, to a "critical" condition, as the following passage shows: "Son joli petit corps amaigri se convulse après chaque amoureuse étreinte dans des attaques de nerfs pitoyables ..." [her attractive little thin body was convulsed after each amorous embrace by pitiful nerve attacks] (*Journal d'un amant* [1902]).[60] In its wildest, yet most concentrated forms, the *étreinte* achieves a kind of violent fixity: "Aucune femme jamais ne m'avait fait connaître ainsi l'immense joie de s'étreindre et de se nouer l'un à l'autre, de toutes ses

forces, avec le désir de se broyer, pour mieux se mélanger! . . ."
[No woman ever had given me that immense joy of embracing
and entwining, with all our strength, with the desire to crush
each other, the better to be mingled! . . .] (*La Volupté féroce*
[1905]).[61] This mixing of two persons is emphatically not the
easy running together of two liquids, as evoked by Nerciat in his
descriptions of instantaneous pleasure: it is the insistent blending of two solid bodies, compelled by their trembling immobility
to the crushing fullness of erotic embrace. In the perfection of
seizure, the *étreinte* becomes the tightest possible exchange, the
closest of close libidinal circuits, in which the orgasm resonates
endlessly with itself.

When talking of fin-de-siècle fiction, I no longer hesitate to
use the word "orgasm" because we now find ourselves in a thematic space in which medical discourse intersects powerfully
and productively with the language of pleasure, giving rise, inter
alia, to the notion of eroticism itself. Even if much libertarian affirmation and therapeutic sexology was still required before it
would become possible, in the course of the twentieth century, to
speak of "happy" paroxysms, in the same way as Nerciat spoke
of *crises heureuses*, the timing and the visible manifestations of
orgasm are in place. The euphoric crisis or paroxysm can be expected to occur as a violent climax of the body, a compulsive
movement-as-stasis that impacts decisively on all around it. To
know the orgasm is thus to know it both as a set of symptoms
and as a particular point in a story. This discursive order, we
might say, governs the time of the uncontrolled. For that reason,
it is misleading to regard those expressions used earlier in the
century—*le dernier période, le suprême bonheur, le comble de la
volupté,* and so on—as older names for the same thing. Insofar
as these expressions do not refer to an involuntary psychophysiological response, they do not yet exhibit the full range of thematic elements contained and condensed in the notion of
orgasm—whatever the use made of them, in their time, by the
ebullient thematics of climax.

This chapter has been an avowed exercise in hermeneutical
care, not to say fastidiousness, and I wish to conclude it with
some discussion that I hope will be both an application and a
justification of this attitude. I intend to consider just a few examples of what I claim is loose interpretation on the part of literary critics. This point will be made, as it ought to be, not by

pointing to trivial or unscholarly work but by focusing on critics whose professionalism is unquestionable.

Consider, as a first example, a note provided by Michel Camus in his edition of Mirabeau's *Hic-et-Haec* (1798). Camus glosses *le période* for modern French readers who may well not know the word. Without needing to dwell on the elision whereby *le dernier période* is reduced to *le période*,[62] he goes on to give two "equivalent" terms: "Période au masculin au sens d'apogée ou de paroxysme" [*période*, masculine, in the sense of apogee or paroxysm].[63] Is it historical tact or a sense of literary propriety that leads him to avoid the actual word *orgasme*? The fact is, in any case, that the word itself is absent from erotic literature of both eighteenth and nineteenth centuries, but I wonder, nonetheless, whether the theme is not what allows the explanation of *période* in terms of "synonyms" that belong to different registers and different historical eras. "Apogée" corresponds perfectly well with *le (dernier) période,* if it is understood as the culmination of a long, slow climb rather than of any leap, be it rise or fall, into intensity. "Paroxysme," on the other hand, is anachronistic, since it belongs to a discourse that understands the heart of climax in more narrowly physiological terms. To put it more carefully, it is the very coexistence of registers in Camus's gloss that is anachronistic. The understanding of *le période* to which this note invites us is not strictly incoherent, nor even, in a sense, inaccurate: it is merely a collapse of historical difference and a kind of thematic short circuit.

Certainly, when Angelica Goodden reads Diderot's much earlier *La Religieuse* (1760) for its psychophysiological reference, I feel compelled to object strongly. "That Diderot intended," says Goodden, "the convulsive states the Mother Superior experiences to be interpreted as orgasms in the modern sense of the word there can be no doubt."[64] Just what kind of miraculous synchronicity could have allowed Diderot to intend the modern interpretation, beyond what was available in his context, is anything but clear. Goodden is erudite enough to know, and to state explicitly, that *orgasme* in the eighteenth century did not have its current meaning. She notes that it was "a word often used for convulsive seizures of an unspecific kind,"[65] but completely fails to observe that the mid-eighteenth century was not in the habit of making a thematic connection between "seizure" and pleasure. She seems to consider that the specificity of a modern diagnosis can properly move beyond the apparent un-specificity of earlier usage, and that Diderot's genius has some-how anticipated this. Let me be quite clear about my objection: I do not wish to deny the commonsensical claim that there were processes going on in the bodies of eighteenth-century *Homo sapiens* that still go on today, but my concern is, of course, to show how fiction has made sense of them in different ways, at different times, and to show that there are consistent historical patterns to that sense-making.

The checkered, or at least intermittent, history of the word "orgasm," alluded to by Goodden, is further evidence of the need for care, and a further place in which to apply it.[66] In *Gil Blas* (1727–37), there is actually a fictional debate between two learned doctors about just what Hippocrates means by *orgasme*. One of them believes that it refers to a state in which "les humeurs sont en orgasme, c'est-à-dire en fougue" [the humors are in orgasm, that is, in a fiery state], while the other claims that the word refers to "la coction des humeurs" [the simmering of humors].[67] Whichever of the two may be right within their framework of reference, it is patent that this framework, the sci-ence of humors, is not that of Masters and Johnson.[68] In any case, as the *Encyclopédie* of 1751 shows, *orgasme* was undoubt-edly for the eighteenth century a form of illness, often of a spas-modic kind. *L'orgasme vénérien* is described there as a syndrome occurring differently in men and women, but involving in each case a painful erection: "the erethism of nervous fibres."[69] Nancy Huston points out, quoting *Le Petit Robert*, that the meanings of "orgasm" evolve, or simply shift, from those of anger (cf. "fougue" above) or irritation (cf. "coction") in the seventeenth and eigh-teenth centuries to that of erection in the eighteenth. The first usage in its modern, didactic meaning, she notes, is dated 1837. The terms of this latter definition are utterly familiar to modern readers, in that they focus on climactic sexual reaction, typically in the male: "Le plus haut point du plaisir sexuel qui est son aboutissement et qui coïncide chez l'homme avec l'éjaculation" [The highest point of sexual pleasure, which brings it to an end, and which coincides in men with ejaculation].[70] The *Trésor de la langue française* defines it as the "point culminant de jouissance génésique qui accompagne la relation sexuelle normalement ac-complie" [culminating point of sexual pleasure that accompanies normally conducted sexual relations].[71] The point here, for one who has an interest in the history of narrative, is that this usage emerges just as the climactic sexual story becomes established in its most clearcut form. In the *Petit Robert* definition of orgasm, we find both denouement ("aboutissement") and one of the marks of intensity referred to in chapter 6 ("coïncide"), while in the *Trésor de la langue française* the association of normalcy is also made explicit. Without the actual transfer of the word itself from scientific to literary discourse, we find the thematics of climax doing representative work for the purpose of physiological description. The two, as we had occasion to note at the beginning of the previous chapter, are bound in with each other in a self-confirming circle: orgasm is so powerful because it is the climax of sexual experience, and climax draws its strength from the underlying compulsion of a bodily process.

There is a further notion, alluded to in the title of this study, whose history can be told along the same lines as that of orgasm. Because it is so closely parallel, I shall tell it only in brief outline, with the aim of making a similar critical point. I refer here to the notion of "the sex act," often abbreviated to "the act," by a discursive move that represents it as the most central, most typical form of human behavior. The history of the sex act is not infinitely long, although it is made to seem more ancient by the theological resonance of the expression, or rather the modern renderings of canonical discourse. When medieval theologians talk about *coitus* or *concubitus*, those are terms for sexual congress or intercourse, but the standard translations, "the act of intercourse" or "the sexual act," are, I suspect, anachronistic inflections of their original meaning.[72] On that point, I must concede that I can do no more than invite readers to suspicion since I have not the erudition to pursue the question in more detail. I must concede, too, that key thinkers on whom I am relying in this critique have been less fastidious than I about the term. Irigaray uses it without fuss when summarizing Aristotle,[73] as does Foucault when he summarizes Augustine.[74] Foucault does, however, tend to use the plural "actes sexuels" when speaking of the ancient Greek *aphrodisia*, and that is an important shift of emphasis.[75] It is doubtless a sign of the times that we are coming to be less accepting of this notion as we learn to critique the narrativization of sexuality. Barbara Ehrenreich and her coauthors remind us forcefully of recent history when they put the word "act" between quotation marks.

This is how they characterize the "sexual revolution" of the 1960s and 1970s:

> It is not that women simply had more sex than they had in the past, but they began to transform the notion of heterosexual sex itself: from the irreducible "act" of intercourse to a more open-ended and varied kind of encounter.[76]

Stephen Heath does the same thing, and provides in fact a terse version of the theme—the exact antithesis of my study—when he refers, apropos of the cinema, to "the compulsive repetition of sexuality as a narrative, as 'the sexual act': encounter, preliminaries, penetration, climax."[77]

When Roger Bougard talks about some of the recurring verbs in seventeenth-century erotic texts as referring to "l'acte sexuel," the anachronism seems to me patent. The verbs he mentions are *besoigner*, *bircoler*, and *farfouiller*—all of them, as he notes, words that stand for the action of plowing.[78] Bougard fails to remember that the agricultural metaphor, with its emphasis on work, refers to regular movement rather than to a completed act. This is what French usually calls an *action* since it does not have the narrative distinctness of an *acte*. The failure to distinguish between the two I take as a symptom of the over-ready universalization of modern sexual discourse. As for the historical period on which my analysis is concentrated and my argument founded, I can say with confidence that the term *acte* is rarely present in the *ancien régime* part of my corpus, and even when it is, appears not to have its modern sense. Perhaps that sense developed elsewhere, as in the case of *orgasme* and *spasme*, migrating later into erotic fiction. In medical discourse, the term can be found long before the end of the eighteenth century. Nicolas Venette, for example, writes in his *Tableau de l'amour conjugal* (1687) of the venereal act (*l'acte vénérien*) at a time when fictional texts preferred to speak of venereal figures, or positions, or tableaux, in the plural.[79] It may be that the appearance of *l'acte* in erotic fiction coincides with the disturbance of register whereby medical talk begins to be closely accommodated in fiction, and turned to narrative purpose. It can in any case be shown that the appearance in fiction of "the act" corresponds historically to the full development of climactic stories, and there is every reason to consider them as thematic cognates.

In eighteenth-century writing, the notion of the act, insofar as it is present, owes much to theatrical discourse. A standard procedure in libertine works, as we have had occasion to note earlier, is to present a series of scenes or tableaux, usually numbered, and in ascending order of complication. An "act" can be a group of such scenes, but it is seldom a particular action within one of them. A quotation from Sade helps to remind us of this, precisely because it sounds very modern without actually being so. Sade refers to a "libidinous act" not as a particular thing done by one character to another, but as a dramatic suite: "Trois scènes composaient l'ensemble de cet acte libidineux" [Three scenes made up the whole of this libidinous act].[80] The act is understood to have initially discrete constituent elements: it is not simply "done" but composed and performed in a manner that requires accurate bodily placement and well-executed changes of position. Insofar as the scene or tableau—what Sade also refers to as a "group," an "arrangement," or an "attitude"— functions as the unit of erotic narrative, then it is inappropriate to describe behavior in terms of a singular, central act that is both the focus of attention and the model of nature at work. In order for "the act" to take on a fully modern sense, the theatrical paradigm, with its countable series of tableaux, must be displaced by narration that purports, at least, to tell some decisive sexual event.

Nerciat, for all the eagerness with which he takes up the theme of climax, is far from seeing this (sub)generic transformation through to a conclusion within his own work. He continues to speak of "the act" in a theatrical sense, although the variety of his usage begins to make room for change. On one of the grand occasions of *Les Aphrodites*, a group of outstanding members of the secret libertine society puts on a performance before an audience of colleagues. There are eight divans or *avantageuses* on stage, one for each woman and her partner. This constitutes a spectacular array of "charms" but also marks out a space of competition in which each couple is required to complete a set number of copulations in the time allotted, all to the accompaniment of music. Nerciat's description of this is appropriately theatrical, although perhaps not exclusively so: "Pendant le premier acte, [l'orchestre] a exécuté, comme on sait, un air analogue à l'impétuosité d'une première charge; pour le second acte, on a joué plus voluptueusement, et dans le même genre mais avec variété, pour le troisième" [During the first act, the orchestra played, as you know, an air in keeping with the impetuosity of a first charge. For the second act, it played more voluptuously, and gave a variation of the same genre in the third] (1:185). The whole spectacle is literally orchestrated as a ritual performance, with variations of tempo that call, in a somewhat surprising order, firstly for impetuosity and later for gentle voluptuousness. Accordingly, when there is reference to numbered "acts," we must understand these as formal divisions within the overall production. Yet it would be hard to deny that the reference to each copulation as an "act" serves to remind us of the conclusive nature of each union since the confirmed finishing of each is a requisite part of the performance. Nerciat's account of it all makes two series of numbers coincide: the ordering of scenes and the racking up of copulative scores. Variations of this double usage occur on a minor scale throughout Nerciat's work, when his narrator refers to the characters grouped together for a particular erotic encounter as *acteurs* (*Les Aphrodites* 1:59, 2:60) or speaks of a pause as an "interval" (*Mon Noviciat* 102). We are thus reminded briefly each time of the theatricality produced by their scripting of the action, and of the climactic doing in which they are heartily engaged.

Some of the range of meaning that later constitutes the theme of *l'acte sexuel* at its most powerful appears to be put in place by the various predications attached to *l'acte* by Nerciat, Sade, and their contemporaries. At the end of a quite theatrical series of engagements involving one of his heroines, Nerciat produces both a number and a name for what we have just witnessed: "ces 32 actes de tempérament" [these 32 acts of temperament] (*Le Diable au corps* 6:184 n). The number has all the classical virtues of the foursquare, but the naming of what is counted as "actes de tempérament" goes beyond the classical tendency to count positions, figures, or modes since it identifies each act as a manifestation of temperament (or desire). Whereas a more classical text might have been content to savor the variety for its own sake, as a set of variations, Nerciat provides what we might call a minimal diagnosis, naming the acts in terms of that which they express and pointing briefly to their general underlying cause.

The plural "acts" is found more commonly at this early stage of thematic development, no doubt because it accommodates the

diversity so valued in the eighteenth century even as it puts forward a potentially reductive name for what is common to the
different events. In *Les Délices de Coblentz* (1791), two exhausted lovers are said to be still "animés du désir de renouveler
les actes délicieux de la jouissance" [filled with the desire to
renew the delightful acts of pleasure].[81] They do not wish to do
"it" again, we should note: their desire is to repeat the various
acts that have just given them such pleasure. In this instance,
there appears to be no significant difference between act, action,
and activity. And if the characters are somewhat indiscriminate
in this regard, that very lack of discrimination is presumably to
be read as a mark of their enthusiasm. *L'Enfant du bordel*
(1800) presents a young man whose sexual experience can be
summed up in the following manner: "Théodore a déjà eu sous
les yeux plusieurs actes de priapisme" [Théodore had already
had occasion to see several acts of priapism].[82] The "acts" in
question seem broadly comparable to the *actes de tempérament*,
except that the plural noun at the head of the phrase now has
its meaning inflected more strongly by the singular one at the
end of it. The narrowly androcentric *priapisme* can lead us to
wonder what kind of plural resides in the word *actes*. Are these
genuine variations, or perhaps just different versions, or even
simple repetitions of the same act? There is a potential drift
from the plural to the singular, continued in the very same sentence: "sans avoir lui-même participé à l'acte de virilité, il sait
parfaitement comment s'y prendre" [without having taken part
in the act of virility himself, he knows perfectly well how to go
about it] (*L'Enfant du bordel* 33). This young man will presumably be given no induction into the set of variations that once
made up erotic culture because none is in fact needed. All he has
to learn is the single act that is in any case the natural expression of his virility.

Sade occasionally uses an expression that brings together the
explanatory power of such phrases as *les actes de tempérament*
and the striking singularity of *l'acte de virilité*, doing so in such
a way as to generalize "the act of pleasure." Without confining
himself to the "naturalness" of vaginal penetration, he focuses
on the materiality of pleasure, on the internal dynamic that
makes of this act both something ardently desired, and an experience of passivity. It is a "passion" in the etymological sense as
well: "L'acte de jouissance est une passion qui, j'en conviens, sub-

ordonne à elle toutes les autres, mais qui les réunit en même temps" [The act of pleasure is a passion that, I submit, subordinates all others, but it also brings them together] (*La Philosophie dans le boudoir* 3:541). There are other Sadian passions, of course—*Les Cent Vingt Journées de Sodome*, ten years earlier, had counted six hundred of them—but talk of the act may provide a reductive generalization of their plurality, allowing it to be subordinated to, and effectively included in the singular act. Instead of a paradigmatic range—what *Les Cent Vingt Journées de Sodome* calls a "buffet"[83]—of passions and pleasures, there may be one act par excellence, to be repeated in a variety of ways. So great is Sade's concern with the pleasures of disposition and the dispositions of pleasure, so profound his debt to classical *ars erotica*, that he prefers to manifest the variety rather than insist on the affirmation of underlying singularity, but the term *acte de jouissance*, with its generalizing narrative predication of pleasure, recurs in his work from time to time.[84]

This may be as close as Sade and his contemporaries come to the modern notion of the act. Only in fin-de-siècle writing do we find the repeated lyrical evocation, whether in admiration or in horror, of the act as the erotic theme par excellence, the most powerfully recognizable event of sexual truth: "l'acte sacré" [the sacred act] (*Les Tableaux vivants* [1870]),[85] "l'acte d'amour superbe de voluptés et de joies" [the superb act of love with its pleasures and its joys] (*Chairs épanouies* [1902]).[86] Here is a lyrical celebration of the act taken from *Le Roman de Violette* (1883). It brings together, as marks of climax, all the thematic elements we have identified in this chapter: "l'acte dans lequel Dieu a mis, pour ses créatures favorisées, le suprême bonheur de la vie, le paroxysme momentané de l'exaltation de tous les sens, cette âcre explosion de volupté enfin qui tuerait un géant, si elle durait une minute au lieu de durer cinq secondes" [The act in which God has placed, for his favored creatures, the supreme happiness of life, the momentary paroxysm of all the senses in exaltation, the sharp explosion of pleasure that would kill a giant, were it to last a minute instead of five seconds].[87] Calling it the act and identifying it instantly become the business of literature and provide means of textual closure. The fact that it is qualified as "superb" does not prevent its being called "cet acte bestial d'amour" [that bestial act of love], as we see in *La Suprême Etreinte* (1900), for the act is superbly bestial and bestially superb.[88] It is, of course, "l'acte d'amour à l'aide duquel la race humaine se perpétue" [the act of love with whose help the human race perpetuates itself] (*Le Roman de Violette* 531). Indeed, recognizing the universality of the act with the support of biology, and thus bridging the gap that separates human and animal, working across the range from nobility to degradation, is itself part of the thematics, as if the act could not be spoken of without the resounding evocation of its infinitely recurring generality. There is a dark eroticism to be enjoyed in the very fact of observing, as the narrator does in *Chairs épanouies*, the natural echo of love and brutality: "L'acte d'amour commença de la même façon, presque, qu'avait commencé, quelques semaines plus tôt, le viol" [The act of love began in the same way as the rape had, just a few weeks before].[89]

Reference to the act can thus be integrated into climactic narrative so that particular incidents take their place in stories according to whether they occur before or after the main event, now defined in principle as well as in literary practice. This is the peak of all human and animal behavior, allowing and requiring every form of play or pleasure to be interpreted in terms of the same compulsive and reflexive thematic. All activity can and must stand in relation to the fundamental event. Because of this generality, humans find themselves in close proximity to animals, caught up in a kind of physiological solidarity. It is in fact this very closeness that now defines the space of moral effort in human sexual behavior, as a struggle to avoid assimilation into the compelling pattern of animality. *La Luxure* (1905) speaks of completing the act as part of a quite rudimentary climactic narrative,[90] but the name of the theme is attended hauntingly by the association of bestiality: "L'acte accompli bestialement, il se sentirait ridicule, serait mécontent de lui-même. Il fallait attendre . . ." [If he were to carry out the act bestially, he would feel ridiculous and be displeased with himself. He had to wait].[91] We see that despite the occasional glorious epithet, despite the wonderful narrative assurance of bodily truth, bestiality is not a reliably positive value: the theme of the act is fraught with ambivalence, even as its importance is everywhere affirmed. Is it in fact the energetic event that can change the course of an otherwise ailing existence? Is it not parallel, and sometimes exactly equivalent to the "acte terrible" of murder that puts an end to the suffering of unsatisfied desire? *Une Inassouvie* (1897) suggests that it may be.[92] But is it not also, as in *L'Eternelle Poupée* (1894), the very action whose endless repetition helps to constitute a certain erotic suffering as decadent routine? Reine, in the latter novel, has fled the brutality of her former lovers, who practiced on her "cette immolation de la peau nue" [that immolation of the bare flesh], yet now finds herself no better off, trapped with a partner who does it mechanically: "L'éternel recommencement du même acte—cet acte dont elle fuyait la fougue chez ses anciens amants et qui lui paraît la plus déplorable corvée conjugale—met dans ses gestes une régularité chagrine, la fringale d'en avoir fini au plus tôt" [The eternal recommencement of the same act—the act that had been so fiery with her former lovers—now seemed to be the most deplorable domestic chore. It gave to her movements a sad regularity, and filled her with a desire to finish the thing off as soon as possible].[93] This is "climactic" narrative at its most impoverished and most tiresomely routine. Reine is shut in by the circular generality of the theme. She cannot break out in the direction of adventure without undergoing violence, nor can she seek protection without lapsing into the rehearsal of sameness. Furthermore, her sad awareness of this dilemma is only possible because she recognizes the act in its different forms. There is brutality at one extreme and automaticity at the other, but the act is found right across the range. Indeed, only because she has a strong notion of the act is it possible to see this as a range. To another eye, at another time, they might have appeared quite different, or at least quite varied. But to know the act is always to know its sameness. The products of this habit in critical writing are visible enough. It leads to judgments like that of Geoffrey Gorer: "There can be no real development in pornography. It consists of the same thing happening again and again. The repetition may be more refined or complicated or sensational but intrinsically it is still the same act."[94] This is a clearcut rejection of any *ars erotica*, and shows the thematic perception underlying Steven Marcus's rule of pornographic narrative. If sex is always the same thing, all it can ever do is begin again.

The fin-de-siècle context makes it quite proper, or at least utterly predictable, that Rémy de Gourmont should assign the most central role in human life to the sex act. His essay *Physique de l'amour* (1904) is effectively surrounded by the kind of fiction we have been examining, and by a certain preoccupation with narrative in so-called scientific texts. Here is what

Gourmont has to say about the act: "Entre tous les actes possibles, dans la possibilité que nous pouvons connaître ou imaginer, l'acte sexuel est donc le plus important de tous les actes. Sans lui, la vie s'arrêterait" [Of all possible acts, according to the possibilities that we can know or imagine, the sex act is therefore the most important of all acts. Without it, life would come to a stop].[95] It is a nice intellectual flourish on Gourmont's part to limit his generalization to all the possible acts that "we" can imagine, but he does not achieve—why should he?—the more profound reflexivity that would allow him to see how characteristic of his time is the form of this self-awareness. He defines the options for human behavior, or indeed the set of possible worlds, as a paradigm of "acts." For classical libertines the narrower paradigm, rehearsed and explored in erotic play, consisted of the set of figures of Venus, no one of which could ever take on the transcendent-obsessive singularity of the act. The quality of our historical understanding may depend here on not practicing the generalizing thematic we have inherited from the late nineteenth century. In that respect, a more classical art of pleasure, if we can learn to respect its thematic regularities, may provide us with another model. We might then find a way of distancing ourselves from the overweening assumptions of modern sexual knowledge, with its capacity to find the Act beneath every pleasure. Perhaps this is why I find it all the more regrettable that so accomplished a historian of the eighteenth century as Lester Crocker should fail to question his own position when declaring: "The sexual act, in the eighteenth century, was at the center of art, gastronomy, fashion, and literature."[96] In finding the sexual act at every turn and pointing to its centrality, the critic does no more than perform Gourmont's theme according to its own principle of universal recurrence. But then, Crocker himself was writing before Foucault and before the history of sexuality began to take shape as a discipline. Not the sexual act, I still want to say with unjustified impatience. Not orgasm, perhaps not even eroticism or desire, but *vivacité* and *langueur, badinage* and *égarements, tableaux* and *gradations*. If we were to look for such themes as those in the history of sexuality, we could hope to find a little more than we already knew.

III
Finishing

8

Messalina

MESSALINA, THE DEBAUCHED ROMAN EMPRESS, IS A FAMOUS NAME IN erotic literature, one that we might expect to find throughout the classics. She is, after all, with Venus, Theodora, Cleopatra, and a few others, one of the ancient queens or goddesses of love. All the more striking, then, since it rather goes against the grain of standard literary history, is the fact that her name should occur with far greater frequency in the period 1780–1880 than in the preceding century. Jean Marie Goulemot, focusing on the eighteenth century, observes that Messalina-like heroines are rare in fiction of the time. Instead of "perverse, desiring" women of the Phaedra, Messalina, or Salome type, he says, the eighteenth century presents women who are the victims of vile seducers.[1] Victim heroines do indeed abound during this period, from Richardson's *Clarissa Harlowe* to Sade's Justine. But the pattern is even more general than Goulemot suggests, for pornographic writing of that time presents a whole group of libertine whores, from *Margot la ravaudeuse* to Sade's Juliette, who tell their own stories of adventure, learning, and pleasure, but are seldom compared to Messalina and her kind. As Kathryn Norberg points out, these heroines "are not bacchantes, driven by an unquenchable thirst for sex. They are not a throwback to the ancient, patriarchal myth of the insatiable woman."[2] Literary versions of the "throwback" to which Norberg refers would presumably be a form of classical reference, throwing us back via the famous names in my list or Goulemot's—via that of Messalina in particular. I want to show in this chapter, in confirmation of Goulemot's and Norberg's observations, that it is in fact the nineteenth century that retrieves Messalina and her sisters for the purposes of erotic representation. This is done not so

281

much for the pleasure of rehearsing the ancient legends but as a way of evoking a certain feminine quality and declaring it to be quasi-eternal.

To Messalina, libertine writing of the *ancien régime* tended to prefer her moral and narrative opposite, Lucretia. Of the two, Messalina may seem to modern eyes the more likely subject: she was infamous for her erotic stamina and insatiability, whereas Lucretia was celebrated for her virtue. But Lucretia was, as I showed in *Geometry in the Boudoir*, an important figure for eighteenth-century fiction insofar as she marked a limit: her type of victim story, and the way in which it orders textual time, were to be studiously avoided.[3] Lucretia, it will be recalled, killed herself as soon as she had been raped. Such a radical defense of virtue hardly lends itself to the pleasure of sustained narrative and unsurprisingly becomes a target for libertine irony. Women who display reluctance in yielding to their suitors can be banteringly dubbed "Lucretias," as if to draw playful attention to the vast gap that separates erotic dalliance, with its drawn-out seductive play, from tragic virtue, with its uncompromisingly rapid affirmation of honor in death. Erotic narrative of the eighteenth century makes capital out of virginity and spends that capital slowly, from Richardson and Rousseau to Sade and Choiseul-Meuse. But to achieve its pleasurable ends, and delight in the pleasurable means, it must undo the radical binary of vice and virtue, eschewing the implacable brevity of the Lucretia story. Messalina, as I have suggested, represents not just the moral contrary of Lucretia but her narrative opposite: where Messalina is present, narrative may be indefinitely sustained by continuing desire. In this role, the Roman empress becomes an ongoing preoccupation of the nineteenth century. Her thematic fate is bound up with the narrativization of sexuality and with the distribution of narrow gender roles within the emerging narrative order.

Before I move to examine some Messalina references in climactic narrative, let me utter a word of warning, an echo of earlier caveats. The recurrence of a proper name hardly entitles us to speak freely of the "theme" of Messalina. Joan De Jean has shown in her *Fictions of Sappho* how certain elements of a classical topos can be devalued or forgotten over time, and others take on new importance, to the extent of complete reversal.[4] In the case of Messalina, the eighteenth century may be regarded as a time of relative occlusion, and even at the turn of the century one tends to find impoverished versions of the topos, although in other textual places it was becoming so prominent, and taking on such new significance, as to represent one of the central "problems" of nineteenth-century erotic narrative.

The name of Messalina can simply be used as a commonplace, a trope that provides climactic eroticism with its own form of hyperbole. Whereas *ancien régime* fiction used Lucretia's name ironically, inflating momentary resistance into tragic intransigence, later narrative tends to take Messalina as the *ne plus ultra* of erotic behavior, leaving no room, in its excitement, for irony of any sort. There is nothing particularly classical about such reference, since comparison with the illustrious precedent cannot serve as a model in the attitudinal sense. There never were any "figures of Messalina." Rather, Messalina's name comes to serve as a kind of multiplier, factoring into the poetics of climax great quantities of desire and energy. It serves thus, in a routinely coded way, as a mark of intensity. Quite unadorned versions of this trope, without any particular connection to the old theme of insatiability, are to be found in Sade and Restif. In fact, classical reference is nowhere more perfunctory than in Restif's *L'Anti-Justine* (1798), where Messalina and Cleopatra are taken as the all-time standard of bottom-wriggling: "Elle remua du cul comme Cléopâtre ou Messaline" [She moved her ass like Cleopatra or Messalina].[5] Sade, with more literary distinction but no greater erudition at this point, also refers to Messalina as if she were legendary for her violent movement: "la putain, près de deux heures, se démena comme Messaline" [the whore went on for nearly two hours, flinging herself about like Messalina].[6] In such texts as these, Messalina's name is sprinkled generously, like a pseudo-classical spice. It is likely to be present in descriptions of erotic intensity to mark the fullness of every desirable quality, whether that be the power of discharge—"vous déchargerez comme une Messaline" [you will unload like a Messalina] (*Histoire de Juliette* 9:44)—or the extent of libertine practice: "tout ce que la volupté peut avoir de plus piquant, tout ce que le libertinage a de plus effréné, fut mis en usage par cette Messaline" [the most stimulating kinds of pleasure, the most unbridled forms of libertinage were put into practice by this Messalina] (*Histoire de Juliette* 9:267). Sade even takes Messalina, in outright defiance of the classical story, as the universal benchmark of a woman well-fucked. Dubois, when offering to Justine the services of a virile young man, can give no higher recommendation than this: "Va, je t'assure que quand j'ai cela dans mes entrailles, je me crois mieux foutue que ne le fut jamais Messaline" [I assure you that when I have that thing inside me, I feel better fucked than ever Messalina was] (*La Nouvelle Justine* 6:74). None of these qualities corresponds in any particular to the ancient stories told by Juvenal, Pliny, and others, in which Messalina is (in)famous for the number of her lovers and the endurance of her desire. It is as if reference to her functioned almost indiscriminately, in the absence of any textual precedent, or any properly constraining topos. "Messalina" appears in these examples to be no more than a free-floating addition to the various markers of intensity examined in chapters 4 through 7.

Even when Sade foregrounds classical reference in the most classical fashion, by referring in narrative to artistic representations of the subject, he does so in a way that shows no clear evidence of thematic constraint, and indeed no sense that the theme of insatiability is at work. In *Histoire de Juliette*, the heroine has the opportunity to visit the Vatican's private art collection. There she finds an extraordinary assortment of religious paintings and erotica: "Là, tout se mêlait indistinctement. Près d'une Thérèse en extase, on voyait Messaline enculée, et, sous l'image du Christ, était une Léda . . ." [There, everything was mixed together. Near a painting of Teresa in ecstasy, one found Messalina being fucked up the ass, and beneath the picture of Christ there hung a Leda] (*Histoire de Juliette* 9:148). Messalina is represented in a particular pose—not, it must be said, because the pose is attributed to her by the ancients, but presumably because it is eminently transgressive, and she is transgression incarnate, made contemporary, in a radically indiscriminate move, with Christ and Saint Teresa. Resembling Messalina or following her can therefore be translated via such an intermediary into postural discipline. The reference functions as an accommodation, if not a domestication, of the Messalina theme, placing it alongside others in a gallery of images and making it one of a loose set of postural figures. For Juliette, it is not even a particularly significant narrative moment since she does not immediately give herself over to imitative sodomy. Yet some thematic resonance is heard on a different occasion, when Juliette finds herself in another pose—this time one that has an antecedent in the ancient story. She shows, in fact, a trace of classical postural modeling when she retrieves the past in the present at a moment of passionate erudition. The reference here is to a story told in Juvenal's *Saturae* number 6, in which the empress is said to have paid a visit to the barracks area of Suburra and spent the whole night in serial intercourse with the soldiers there. After an epic number of copulations in a monastery, Juliette and her friend Clairwil can make the comparison with this illustrious precedent, finding the model post hoc, in happy reflexivity: "Nous nous relevâmes, enfin, collées de foutre sur nos sophas, comme Messaline sur le banc des gardes de l'imbécile Claude" [We finally sat up again, stuck to our sofas with sperm, like Messalina to the bench on which she was fucked by the guards of that imbecile Claudius] (*Histoire de Juliette* 8:466). This exemplifies, it must be said, the kind of attitudinal modeling that I discussed in *Geometry in the Boudoir*, although Juliette and her companion do not so much strike the pose as become stuck in it, glued to the furniture by the quantity of ejaculate they have provoked. But more importantly, by understanding Messalina primarily in terms of her (supposed) bodily attitudes, *Histoire de Juliette* fails even here to exploit an element of the Messalina story, present in Juvenal's text—"Et lassata viris nec dum satiata recessit" (*Saturae* 6, line 130)—that was being taken up by some of Sade's contemporaries and was to be alluded to almost obsessively by many of his successors. Messalina, it was to be remembered more and more clearly, stopped only because of fatigue, not satiation.

One of the first indications of the emerging thematic usage is the plural form of Messalina's name, used to designate a whole class of women. Sade's Juliette actually includes Messalina with Theodora in the quite exclusive group of "celebrated whores of antiquity" (*Histoire de Juliette* 8:369), but it is in fact a more radical use of Messalina's name, and a closer integration of her story into erotic discourse, to take "Messalina" and "prostitute" as approximate synonyms. This is what happens in *Ordonnance de police sur les filles de joie* (1790), which refers, in what may well be inflated style, to the general class of prostitutes as "toutes Messalines donneuses de douces" [all Messalinas givers of sweetness].[7] The same text pursues the discursive integration I spoke of by transforming the empress's name into an adjective when it refers to "ces prostituées messalines" [these Messalinic prostitutes] (6:464). The element of stylistic parody ought to deter us from taking this as representative usage, but there seems no reason to suppose that the phrase "Messalinic prostitutes," in this context, is anything other than a simple tautology. Messalina, Theodora, and Cleopatra may have attained heroic status, for the purpose of classical reference, by indulging in "prostitution" from a position of wealth and power, but the adjective and the tautology begin to emphasize what empresses and prostitutes might have in common. The imperial reference serves to celebrate the profession but also to affirm that all women of "temperament"[8] belong in this class whatever their social position. Understood thus, Messalinic qualities can be those of a radically feminine eroticism, wherever it may occur.

If we now add to this, as texts of that time began to do, the element of the Messalina story that Sade and Restif manage to forget, a certain threat becomes perceptible. Juvenal, Pliny, and others refer to Messalina as *invicta*, noting that she remained "unconquered" after twenty-five bouts, or after fourteen young men had had their way with her.[9] Erotic capacity, rather than intensity, is measured here in terms of the ability to endure events in great number, exactly counted, rather than, say, producing large quantities of ejaculate or describing wide arcs in the course of bodily oscillation. Comparison with Messalina is not simply indicative but precisely calculated. And this calculation is no mere calibration: it is often dramatized as a challenge. Messalina is not so much the upper limit on some fixed scale as an active rival for anyone who might lay claim to supremacy in the field of erotic endurance. In this regard, she may be better thought of as a reigning champion, undefeated over two millennia, than as a model of perfection.

To be compared with Messalina is often, for a female character, to have one's achievements assessed against this long-standing record performance. The Duchesse de Polignac, heroine of *La Messaline française* (c. 1793), is a worthy contender in these stakes. We hardly need to be reminded that she has "an ardent temperament,"[10] and cannot be surprised to find her referred to as "the prostitute" (5:328) or "a Messalina" (5:323, 328). But what guarantees her titular status as *the* French Messalina is her superlative erotic achievement. She is "une Messaline qui laisse loin derrière elle les courtisanes les plus débordées" [a Messalina who far outdoes the most extravagant courtesans] (5:299). Hyperbole, in many such instances, is not lavishly qualitative but impressively quantitative, as the famous name is attended by numbers—and the numbers, when they are large enough, seem to call for the famous name. Here is how Rosine, the narrator-heroine of *Vénus en rut* (c. 1785) positions herself in relation to the great predecessor. She says to a group of men: "Messaline, plus célébrée que moi, et qui ne valait pas mieux, offrit quatorze couronnes à Priape, après sa victoire sur autant de jeunes gens vigoureux qu'elle avait excédés; vous n'êtes encore que sept, jugez si je compte que vous me déclariez, comme elle, invaincue" [Messalina, who is more celebrated than me but is no more worthy of fame, offered fourteen wreaths to Priapus after her victory over that number of vigorous young men, whom she had worn out. There are only seven of you here. What do you expect of me? I plan to have you declare me, like her, a woman unconquered].[11] The comparison is both confident and modest in its numerical precision. Rosine simply asks how anyone might think that she could fail to achieve a tally only half of the empress's record. Note that this is hardly an elaborate retelling of Messalina's story, but that it does not simply appropriate the name in the rather indiscriminate manner we saw in most of Sade's allusions. The text rehearses the association between the name and the fact of counting, whether that counting be of bouts or male partners. The *invicta* works out her triumph, quite standardly, in numbers. Mme. Durut, the mistress of ceremonies and general procuress of Nerciat's *Les Aphrodites* (1793), has an admiring complaint about one of her clients: "N'ai-je pas fourni à cette Messaline jusqu'à trois cent-suisses en un jour? Elle ne défout pas!" [Have I not provided this woman with up to three Swiss guards a day? She never stops fucking!][12] It is not just the condescension shown by the aristocratic client in choosing common people as partners for intercourse, nor even the fact that the commoners are soldiers, but the very counting of them that makes of her a worthy (rival of) Messalina.

The "threat" that looms here has little to do with any transhistorical struggle between women, even though we hear now and then that someone is a "dangerous rival" for Messalina.[13] The real danger is to images of virility in male-focused literature. For Messalina's strength, as erotic heroine, is likely to be measured to advantage not just against the foot-soldiers of male sexuality but against its greatest champions. Here is a version of the Messalina topos that lacks the empress's name but contains, in lower-case, generalized form, that of a legendary male. It is Comtesse Gamiani's quite numerical "account" of her early career as a part-time prostitute: "je fus exploitée tour à tour par les plus habiles, les plus vigoureux hercules de Florence. Il m'arriva dans une matinée de fournir jusqu'à trente-deux courses et de désirer encore. Six athlètes furent vaincus et abîmés" [I was exploited in turn by the most skillful and vigorous hercules of Florence. Some mornings I provided up to thirty-two bouts and still went on desiring. Six athletes were conquered and spoilt] (*Gamiani* [1833]).[14] Not only is this Messalina figure unconquered in her feminine resistance: she effectively, if not quite actively, conquers all the male Hercules who try their strength against her, leaving them damaged. The heroine of a later novel, *Inassouvie* (1889), succeeds even more dramatically in reducing the famous names of virility to a state of prostration—or certainly would do so if she were ever to engage them in heroic combat: "Dans les bras potelés de cette enchanteresse, . . . les Samsons et les Hercules . . . n'auraient vite été que des êtres débilités, épuisés, demandant grâce, pareils à des enfants pâlis" [In the plump arms of this enchantress, the Samsons and the Hercules would soon have become debilitated, exhausted creatures pleading for mercy, like pale-faced children].[15] *Une Inassouvie* (1897), whose minimally different title evokes the same feminine capacity, presents a young man who devotes himself body and soul to the business of satisfying the heroine only to die an early death from sexual exhaustion: "il rendit le dernier soupir en taisant le nom de celle qui l'avait tué lentement, lui rongeant poumons et mœlle, mais qu'il avait adorée jusqu'au paroxysme" [he uttered his last sigh without speaking the name of the woman who had slowly killed him, eating away at his lungs and his marrow. He had adored her to the point of paroxysm].[16] The name he refuses to utter is proper to the story, but powerful thematic antecedents invite us to identify it as Messalina.

If, as we are seeing, Messalina comes to stand for a whole class of women, then the name of the feminine force that resists any claim to singular masculine triumph might be Everywoman. To the extent that all women have the potential to be Messalinas and to overcome any sexual Hercules, the threat to virility must be thought of as quite general. Here is an early version of the threat, not yet worked out in narrative, but enunciated in debate by an anonymous woman character in *Histoire de dom Bougre* (1741). Speaking on behalf of her sex, she says:

> La nature nous a donné des désirs bien plus vifs, et par conséquent bien plus difficiles à satisfaire que les vôtres: quelques coups suffisent pour abattre un homme et ne font que nous animer. Mettons-en six: une femme ne recule pas après douze. Le sentiment du plaisir est donc au moins une fois aussi vif dans une femme qu'il l'est dans un homme.

> [Nature gave us much keener pleasures than yours, and consequently we are harder to satisfy. Just a few bouts are enough to exhaust a man, but they only stir us up. Let us say six: a woman shows no reluctance after twelve. The feeling of pleasure is therefore twice as strong in a woman as it is in a man.][17]

The very fact of doing these calculations is a menace to standard notions of virility. The heroic male, for all his insistence on possession and even his pride in counting partners, cannot go as many rounds as his female opponent. Hercules' capacity to conquer is not as great as Messalina's capacity to sustain battle while remaining *invicta*.[18]

John Atkins, writing about erotic literature as a whole, states that the genre consistently fails to recognize this truth about gender difference in sexual performance. "Exhaustion," he says, "is unknown in libertine literature." Male characters go on inexhaustibly "proving [their] virility," ejaculating "again and again."[19] There are in fact many pornographic stories that correspond perfectly to Atkins's description, but its value stops short of absolute generality, for there is in fact a systematic exception to the rule and a regular discrepancy in the affirmation of virile stamina. It is particularly true in erotic narratives of the late eighteenth and early nineteenth centuries that men perform extraordinary feats of sexual potency, yet all the while women somehow remain inexhaustibly beyond them in strength. In many stories, the gender difference is referred to only in passing or exploited for the purpose of a single scene rather than being accorded full thematic status. The fact that a woman character in *Histoire de dom Bougre* is allowed to speak of invincible femininity does not prevent the narrator-hero from affirming of himself that he is sexually "infatigable" (3:186). And the fact that the two heroines of *Le Diable au corps* are defined by their extraordinary sexual appetite does not prevent them from having an episodic encounter with a Chevalier of whom it is said that "[il] bande comme un Carme, lime sans relâche et ne finit jamais" [he gets it up like a Carmelite monk, works it in and out without stopping, and is never finished].[20] How much of this, we might wonder, is to be read as epic boasting and how much of it is an accurate assessment of the combat situation? To what extent is this male capacity an uncomplicated, perhaps unthinking response to narrative exigency? It is arguably no more than insistent affirmation, repeated in the face of Messalina, by and on behalf of heroic virility. The issue is left unresolved in *Histoire de dom Bougre* and *Le Diable au corps*—as if the interests of male-focused eroticism were that it should remain so—but the lack of resolution will later become a problem. Because of the feminine power invoked by reference to Messalina, the assertion of masculine strength in her company may seem like misplaced optimism, or unreasonable denial.

The following example fits Atkins's description in a way that is not just unreasonable or unrealistic: it displays a provocative confidence in masculine performance, carrying its affirmation right into the heart of Messalina's thematic territory. In *La Messaline française,* a young man describes how he "handles" the notorious duchess. He uses the same old arithmetic found in the ancients, and referred to by the debater in *Histoire de dom Bougre,* but does not recount it as a defeat for maleness: "Et remarque, mon ami, que chaque coup elle jouit avec moi double contre simple. Quel tempérament de feu! Cinq fois je doublai ses jouissances de cette manière, et six fois comme je l'avais fait sur mes genoux avant de me coucher" [Take note, my friend, that each time her pleasure happened twice for once of mine. What a fiery temperament! Five times I doubled her pleasures in that way, and six more I did what I had done to her on my knees, before I lay down].[21] What is denied here, even as the counting is maintained, and some gender difference literally accounted for, is the element of competition. Weakness there may be, but it only occurs in extremis, as bodily fatigue, and not as failure or ruination of the man. The famous phrase "lassata nec dum satiata," used by Juvenal to describe Messalina, is appropriated by the male as well, being applied to both partners in the epic encounter: "Nous ne cessâmes nos ébats que lorsque nos forces épuisées mirent obstacle à nos désirs. . . . Nos corps étaient *plutôt las que rassasiés.* Oh! pourquoi la nature nous fit-elle si faibles?" [We only ceased our romp when our strength ran out and placed an obstacle in the path of our desires. Our bodies were *tired rather than sated.* Oh! Why did nature make us such weak creatures?] (5:316; emphasis added). We can see that, even as Atkins's generalization appears to be borne out, a noteworthy exception appears, so to speak, in the middle of it. Exhaustion is in fact mentioned, and its mention has an evocative purpose. When the young man describes himself as "vacillant sur mes jambes, affaibli par les excès auxquels je venais de me livrer" [unsteady on my feet, weakened by the excesses in which I had just been indulging] (5:323), he provides this picture of weakness as a contrapuntal indication of the strength he has just displayed throughout a series of intense encounters. The temporary failure of his body signifies the great and continuing demands made on his stamina by a powerful, Messalinic libido in which he fully shares.

Representations of weakness in the male equivocate between this rather indulgent recognition of fatigue as aftermath, with its denial of significant gender difference, and more ironic contrasts of male and female, in which the man's weakness may become an object of amused contemplation. The narrator-heroine of *Eléonore, ou l'heureuse personne* (c. 1796) seems to take special pleasure in describing the transformation that has taken place in her lover after a period of fierce activity: "Cet amant naguère si ardent, si empressé, si soigneux de me plaire, n'était plus en état de me rendre le plus petit service. La plus légère complaisance était au-dessus de ses forces" [The lover who had just a short while ago been so attentive, so keen to please me, was no longer in any state to do me the least little favor. The slightest act of kindness was beyond his capability].[22] This may be just a form of teasing, even of titillation, like the laughter of a chambermaid in Nerciat's *Le Diable au corps*, when she observes the literally downcast state of her partner after coitus: "l'humilité profonde du braquemart naguère si fanfaron" [the profound humility of the weapon that had shortly before been so boastfully proud].[23] But in each case that cruel little temporal adverb "naguère" [only recently] crops up to taunt the man for his lack of endurance. However fleetingly the comparison is made, and whatever the tone in which it is expressed, we can observe that erotic narrative is not so perfect in its vigilance, not so unrelieved in its androcentricity, as to exclude the gaze of the woman who looks down, literally and figuratively, on her exhausted partner.

I find here some justification for dwelling on texts that might otherwise, for ethical or political reasons, have been dismissed from the field of literary history. If we were to follow Andrea Dworkin on this question, we would simply condemn pornography out of hand for its representations of, and incitation to, the oppression of women.[24] Were we to do so, however, we would fail to perceive the ambivalence that actually inhabits these texts and divides them against themselves. By listening to the thematic dissonance that clatters and rumbles throughout them, we come to see how male-focused writing of this sort is compelled to make concessions or admit exceptions for which it must pay dearly in the long run, according to the rules of its own thematic economy. No concession is more dangerous to its presumed oppressive purpose than the increasingly prominent place given to Messalina as the embodiment of erotic endurance. Climactic narrative, as we have seen, is committed to the representation of desire, and indeed to its figurative incarnation, so that only by the covert acknowledgement of male weakness can it see erotic woman as Messalina. When desire at its most intense is said to be carried by women beyond the male-centered norm, it may also be carried beyond the male's capacity to provide satisfaction, and perhaps beyond his capacity to tell the satisfaction as narrative denouement.

One of the features of sexual representation in the Revolutionary period and beyond is that desire is incarnated in this manner. Instead of being seen, according to classical practice, as circumstantial or epiphenomenal, desire is held up to attention as a state or condition of the body. No longer occurring in its place, as a necessary adjunct to disciplined erotic performance, it may now declare itself as a kind of malady. In Mirabeau's *Erotika Biblion* (1783), this condition is exemplified by Messalina, and her syndrome given the pseudoscientific name of nymphomania:

les désirs s'irritent par ce qui semblerait devoir suffire pour les assouvir, et qui suffirait en effet si le simple prurit de la vulve sollicitait le plaisir. Mais quand le foyer du désir est le cerveau, il s'accroît sans cesse. Et Messaline, plutôt lassée que rassasiée, court sans relâche après le plaisir et l'amour qui la fuit [sic] avec horreur.

[desires are stimulated by what ought to have been enough to satisfy them. It would in fact have been enough if the quest for pleasure came only from an itching of the vulvae. But when the center of pleasure is in the mind, it goes on continually increasing. And Messalina, who is more tired than sated, endlessly pursues pleasure and love, which flee from her in horror.][25]

There is no question here of therapy, of course, since the symptoms are themselves the object of attention—not to say of desire. They are so fascinating, so rich in narrative promise that to bring them to an end would be both a contradiction and a disappointment. Messalina's valuable affliction has spread far beyond genital arousal and has come to invade her brain. As an exciting if monstrous consequence, she is compelled to the endless pursuit of pleasure. Her malady is one to which all women are predisposed, we are told in *Le Rideau levé* (1786), by an organic "emptiness" of the flesh that can never be fulfilled: "les femmes portent un vide qu'une nécessité perpétuelle, un appétit indépendant d'elles les porte à remplir" [women have in them a void that they are required to fill, by a perpetual need and appetite beyond their control].[26] Emptiness here is a stimulus to narrative in every sense of the word. The feminine void that cannot be fulfilled is the space of desire calling out continually for something more, still yearning to go on after the male's capacity to fill it has been utterly spent.

Messalina takes on the highest thematic status when she comes thus to *be* desire in all its fearful splendor, held up to contemplation as the embodiment of feminine insatiability. So strong is this attribute that reference can be made quite powerfully in the absence of her name, and even of counting, as long as Juvenal's famous phrase, *lassata nec dum satiata*, is heard to resonate, filling the topical place with its promise of powerful emptiness. *Les Délices de Coblentz* (1791) actually calls up a number of other classical names, including one previously revived by Rousseau, as it divides émigré women into two erotic classes. Those who belong in the first group are "tendres et passionnées comme Héloïse" [tender and passionate like Eloise], while those in the second are "de nouvelles Phrynès, des Lays modernes, qui lassées, fatiguées par le plaisir, n'en sont jamais rassasiées" [latter-day Phrynes, modern Lays who are tired out by pleasure, but never sated by it].[27] This less straightforward usage deserves, I submit, to be considered the most significant and influential version of the topos. It shows that the names of Messalina can be legion, as long as her story—or rather her predisposition to endless narrative—remains the same.

There is a productive circularity here in the relation between desire and time. Desire can be identified, at certain moments, as a kind of narrative residue, visible after sustained activity has resulted in fatigue: "mes désirs survivaient encore à mes forces épuisées" [my desires still survived while my strength had run out].[28] Only when a woman is quite *lassata*, it seems, can it be seen how insatiable she is. On the other hand, desire claims its place at the beginning of narrative, as a call for action. Via the notion of (feminine) temperament, it maintains a bodily presence, taking responsibility for the story's forward movement, and driving it on through a potentially endless series of events. A typical thematic articulation of temporal and libidinal elements can be found in Nerciat's *Le Diable au corps*, where the promise—or the threat—of desire is uttered with appropriate energy by the Messalinic Comtesse: "Hommes, femmes, filles, enfants; qualité, roture; maîtres, valets; beauté, laideur et jusqu'à la vieillesse, mon insatiable tempérament va tout mettre à contribution" [Men, women, girls, children, aristocrats, bourgeois, lords, servants, beauty, ugliness, even old people, my insatiable temperament will put them all to work].[29] Insatiability here has two dimensions: the Comtesse will not be exhausted by partners of any one category nor will she exclude any class from intercourse. This provokes an expression of fear (and excitement) from her friend the Marquise, who suggests, as Mirabeau might have, that such desire is likely to become a pathological condition: "Mais, paix donc, paix donc, insensée! sais-tu bien que tu n'es plus simplement libertine; que bien plutôt tu deviens maniaque, nymphomane; oui, ton état est, j'en tremble, une dangereuse maladie" [But calm down, calm down, you insane woman! You are no longer just a libertine, you know. You are falling more and more into mania, into nymphomania. Yes, I fear that your condition is a dangerous illness] (6:27–28). Just how dangerous is this really, and what particular quality of trembling should it arouse? It is fortunate indeed, for the sake of the story, that the Comtesse does not heed her friend's momentary advice. Far from lapsing into "peace," she goes on calling for more, and does not subside into tranquillity until the end of the final volume has been reached. Ambivalence remains, then, in disquiet accompanied by curiosity, as if the movement between fear and desire were itself an erotic style. Soon after this quivering expression of concern, the Marquise is provoked during erotic activity to utter a word that is a cry of pleasure, as well as an admiring accusation. "Messaline!" she exclaims to her friend, and the two laugh like madwomen (6:32). Messalina's syndrome is the name of their shared madness, and their recognition of it is a kind of fearful delight.

This is why, despite the poverty of detail, the allusions we found in Sade and Restif are not so far in one respect from the mainstream Messalina theme as it takes shape in the nineteenth century. Neglectful of number and of any notion of a contest between the sexes, they nonetheless call on Messalina to stand for desire "itself," as both violent agitation and requirement for action. High Romantic stories like *Gamiani* bring the process of representation to its most dramatic when they offer the Messalina figure in ostentatious frenzy: "Les plus méchants de la bande attachaient une Messaline par les quatre membres et se livraient devant elle à toutes les joies, aux plaisirs les plus expressifs. La malheureuse se tortillait, furieuse, écumante, avide d'un plaisir qui ne pouvait lui arriver" [The meanest of the group tied up a Messalina by her four limbs and then indulged before her eyes in all the most expressive joys and pleasures. The wretched woman twisted and turned in fury, foaming at the mouth, longing for the pleasure she could not experience].[30] Frantic movement here is the highly visible symptom of an unsatisfied libido: the Messalina thrashes about because she cannot reach satisfaction, and her frustration is what allows desire to become a spectacle. When she sees before her acts in which she cannot participate, she suffers from this inability to conclude, and her suffering is itself an erotic revelation. This is not postural discipline, of course, but *furia*. "Cette fureur de jouissance qui tourmente ces Messalines" [the furious desire for pleasure that torments these Messalinas] (*Vingt Ans de la vie d'un jeune homme* [1830])[31] is an erotic style, produced and maintained by the absence of a properly finished story, at a time when the woman is calling out for urgent satisfaction. It is not simply the case that pleasure is perversely withheld here by some sort of intrigue. The precipitate movement provoked by desire, as we see continually in the case of Gamiani herself, is such that any potential event of satisfaction is likely to be swept aside, trampled underfoot, or overshot. Gamiani is frantic to achieve satisfaction, but it is the quality of her frenzy that matters most in the novel. Of the heroine in *La Luxure* (1905), we are told similarly: "Jamais lasse, elle se ruait à l'amour, ivre de passion, toujours inassouvie" [She was never tired, and rushed headlong into love, drunk with passion, and forever unsatisfied].[32] Women who stampede toward pleasure find that their erotic momentum is such that they cannot arrive. The Messalina theme is thus able to occupy a privileged place in nineteenth-century narrative as a specific articulation of style and story. Wildly passionate movement in certain women is causally linked, through the notion of insatiable desire, to an ongoing call for more and more erotic narrative.

We see that Messalina is held up to admiration and fear because she, more than anyone, expresses this insatiable demand for narrative. That an eminent classical figure should play this thematic role is noteworthy in view of the fact that the difficulty of concluding is sometimes said to be endemic to pornography as a genre. Steven Marcus, in a famous remark quoted in chapter 6, characterizes pornography (as distinct from valuable erotic literature) by its very inability to come to an end: "Most works of literature have a beginning, a middle, and an end. Most works of pornography do not. A typical piece of pornographic fiction will usually have some kind of crude excuse for a beginning, but, having once begun, it goes on and on and ends nowhere."[33] In my earlier reflection on this critique, I focused on middleness, on the relation of climax and denouement, but "Messalina" reminds us that the problem has another dimension. The rise and fall of desire and satisfaction, with its ostensibly automatic collapse of narrative interest, will not suffice to guarantee the shape of erotic stories because of the dynamic that continually requires further events of the same kind. In practice, erotic narrative can have the greatest difficulty achieving any satisfying closure, if only because climaxing is likely to be a serial occupation or an operation continually renewed rather than a definitive act. It may be something counted without being properly recounted. The eager pursuit of climax that is so much a part of a certain generic style is likely to send the story stampeding far beyond the aesthetic elegance of that distinctive, doubtlessly singular high point imagined by Marcus (and Aristotle). This, we are supposed to think, is all the fault of women. A certain kind of woman, at least, is thrillingly responsible for the dynamism of erotic narrative, but the insatiability of such characters must somehow be brought to an end if the story they have helped to generate is to achieve a proper conclusion. To the extent that the conclusion is not reached, the Messalina theme will endure not only as a grudging admission of masculine weakness in the face of feminine desire but as a vague acknowledgment of, and an attribution of blame for erotic narrative's inability to complete its own program and take on a finished shape. We may read this as the thematic inscription of a formal inadequacy.

There is no shortage of examples in the corpus of French texts considered here to support Marcus's claim about a general deficiency of this sort, despite the fact that his judgment happens to be based on a reading of Victorian pornography in English. Even novels at the more distinguished end of the range, such as those of Nerciat, tend to collapse with almost no warning into lamentably weak endings. I shall not encumber my text with a wearisome collection of examples, since my interest is in the textual thematization of weakness rather than the critical demonstration of it. Let it suffice to note that so elegant a novelist as Nerciat is unable to do more, at the end of six volumes of *Le Diable au corps*, than subside into a kind of awkward self-consciousness. He says wanly of his principal characters: "ils ont apparemment cessé d'avoir le *Diable au corps*" [they have apparently ceased to have the *Devil in their Body*].[34] "Cessé" is the key reflexive word, for this is stopping as opposed to properly finishing. It marks in the narration what the ostensible translator/mediator of the story rather feared and admitted: "l'ouvrage m'avait paru menacé, vers sa fin, de redites et de monotonie" [the work had seemed to me threatened toward the end by repetition and monotony] (6:207). The end of *Mon Noviciat* is no more satisfying, as it offers to negotiate with the reader but then hastens to preclude any reply that might prolong the conversation: "Reste-t-il, ami lecteur, encore quelque chose d'intéressant à te dire? Non, que je sache. . . . Eh bien! . . . Bonsoir! . . ." [Is there anything interesting left to say, dear reader? Not that I know of . . . Well then! Good night!].[35] Defeat and fatigue, old age and weakness often come suddenly to the fore at the end of novels like these, as if to indicate failing sexual energy and a consequent loss of narrative interest—although we might just as easily imagine that sexual energy is now being allowed to fail because narrative interest has been lost.[36]

There is a sense in which Messalina, as a stereotype of femininity, is established as a kind of familiar, even beloved enemy within male-focused erotic narrative. In this capacity, she may provide a foothold for critique, so that it becomes interesting to observe what feminist writing has done with her story. Andrea Dworkin, as far as I can determine, has done nothing with it at all, and this is very much to be expected, since her representations of sexual conflict between male and female lead her to value coldness toward men and the refusal of penetration as the clearest marks of feminine resistance. To the promiscuous Messalina, Dworkin would undoubtedly prefer the armor-plated Joan of Arc.[37] Simone de Beauvoir, on the other hand, notes the element of struggle included in the Messalina story as she considers Juvenal's sixth Satire in *Le Deuxième Sexe*. Beauvoir observes that the Romans called Messalina *invicta* because none of her lovers had "given her pleasure."[38] This seems to me a somewhat tendentious, or at least defective reading of the theme as it has developed through literature, in that it fails to give full value to insatiability, which ought no doubt to be seen not as the absence of pleasure but as something continuing in the very midst of it. Beauvoir's concern, however, is not so much with hand-to-hand grappling between male and female as with ethical questions. She denounces the very terms of the "combat" and rejects the attitude that sees women as available for conquest, whether that conquest be successful or not. A more discursively apposite use of the Messalina theme and, in my view, a beautifully contrived feminist intervention into the domain of androcentric pornography is found in a text by Luce Irigaray entitled "'Françaises,' ne faites plus un effort."[39] The title of Irigaray's piece is a call to resistance on the part of French women (and others), a call that signifies its revolutionary nature by parodying the title of Sade's political pamphlet, "Français, encore un effort si vous voulez être républicains," read aloud by Dolmancé to the intimate gathering of *La Philosophie dans le boudoir* in 1793, as a reminder that a further effort was needed if the Revolution was to lead properly to a republic. Irigaray does not just address the almost forgotten half of Sade's audience in his place, through a new version of his words: she also addresses the master himself. Or rather, to be more precise, she avoids taking

Sade as the singular Hero of literary eroticism, and addresses a set of questions to the group of unnamed "master-pornographers." The woman who speaks in Irigaray's text does so from the point of view of one who might have survived, perhaps like Julie in *Les Cent Vingt Journées de Sodome*.[40] Survival here, however, is not to be understood merely as a product of good fortune or tactical adroitness. It is claimed, in itself, as a form of resistance: "S'il arrivait que, restant hors de la scène, je résiste, ou subsiste, à l'emprise de cette autorité souveraine, je hasarderais, vis-à-vis du maître libertin, quelques questions" [If by chance, being away from center stage, I should resist, or subsist beyond, the grip of this sovereign authority, I have a few questions that I might dare put to the master libertine] (197). And while survival might appear to be the weakest, most contingent form of resistance, it is, in this context, the one most threatening to her oppressors. She will in fact have resisted not by abstaining from all contact but by subsisting in desire at the very time when she was supposed to be brought to satisfaction, brought to an end by pornographic mastery. For orgasm, defined in narrative, renewed in series, and taken to the point of exhaustion cannot guarantee, says Irigaray, a feminine quality of pleasure: "Que la femme ait un, deux, dix, vingt . . . orgasmes; jusqu'à épuisement complet— lassata sed non satiata?[41]—ne signifie pas qu'elle jouisse de sa jouissance" [Even if the woman has one, two, ten, twenty . . . orgasms, to the point of complete exhaustion—*lassata sed non satiata?*— that does not mean that she is experiencing pleasure on her own terms] (198). At this point, the Messalina theme takes on the critical function unwittingly prepared for it by the equivocations and concessions of pornography. Messalina becomes a figure of feminine erotic resistance in or near the standard "scenes" of male sexual dominance, and is called up by Irigaray to haunt the master-pornographers as an echo in the inner chambers of their own thematic world. The masters do not find themselves confronted with an image of inviolate purity, for that would suit their narrative program only too well,[42] but with a figure they have long been forced to acknowledge in their own terms as an enduring symbol of libidinal defiance.[43] Elsewhere in her work, Irigaray is able to use the standard temporal adverbs *encore* and *toujours plus* as marks of "sexed" (*sexué*) feminine desire. She accepts the characterization and the othering but will not concede that feminine/female desire is a disease:

"Inassouvissable, sans doute, dans la vie quotidienne. Pas pathologique pour autant" [Unable to be satisfied, no doubt, in everyday life. But not pathological for all that].[44]

Erotic narrative is not simply defeated by Messalina, of course. It struggles to finish her off and makes narrative out of its sustained attempts to do so. The challenge for male characters is to take the apparently insatiable female to the point where she will actually voice her own satisfaction and mark the end of the story, by saying "Enough!" Men sometimes make so bold as to promise this outcome to themselves, and to all who may be listening, thus constructing what we might call the span of the story and giving it a precise point of arrival. In the late-eighteenth-century play, "La Nouvelle Messaline," Vitus, whose name is built on "le vit" [the prick], tells us in advance what the final exchange of dialogue is supposed to be, as he thinks of the resistant empress and apostrophizes his penis thus:

> Et puisqu'on ne l'a vue jamais rassasiée,
> Par tes coups redoublés fais si bien qu'épuisée,
> Elle tombe sans force, et me confesse enfin
> Que j'ai seul le pouvoir de lasser son conin!
>
> [And since she has never been known to be sated,
> Multiply your efforts and make her exhausted
> So that she collapses and confesses to me at last
> That I alone have the power to fatigue her little cunt.][45]

The "confessional" outcome here would be the woman's admission that she has had her fill of pleasure, and desires no more. The imagined success of Vitus the Prick will be carried, so to speak, by exclamation, as Messalina "proves" his power by admitting her exhaustion and calling for an end to it all. Promising such an end becomes, in fact, one of the standard assertions of virility, although it is not always done so flamboyantly. In *Histoire de Juliette*, the monk Claude makes the claim directly to the women characters on behalf of his colleagues: "si vous voulez être bien foutues, vous n'avez qu'à venir l'une et l'autre, et je vous réponds qu'on vous forcera d'implorer grâce" [If you want both to be well-fucked, you only need to come with me. I promise you that we will make you beg for mercy] (8:479). Being *bien foutue* here will mark the end of the episode. It is not defined by some quality of pleasure or *jouissance* but by the closure of nar-

rative. The women will confirm that they have been well-fucked
when they are forced to cry out for mercy.

Messalinic women often articulate their defiance—and hold
out the promise of further narrative—in the same terms, assert-
ing that they are keen to utter the expression of satiety but unlikely to do so. Rosine, in *Vénus en rut*, makes it clear that she
has learned in her maturity to say the magic word on occasion,
to protect herself from certain excesses, but says that she was
quite incapable of uttering it during the early years of her
career: "Malgré mes excès amoureux, il n'y a pas longtemps que
je suis maîtresse de moi, et que je demande quartier, par le mot
assez; dans mes premières années de service, il m'eût été impossible de le prononcer" [Despite my amorous excesses, I have recently taken control of myself, and I ask for quarter with the
word "enough." During my first years of service, I would not
have been able to utter that word].[46] The narrative tension is
greatest, no doubt, when the Messalina figure states that she
longs to speak the fatal word but in fact has great difficulty
doing so. This is the case with the Comtesse in *Le Diable au
corps*, who defines herself from the outset as someone who needs
to go on until compelled to cry "enough": "Quant à moi, lorsque
cela me prend (et c'est souvent, tu le sais) l'univers serait là, que
je ne pourrais me contraindre; il faut qu'on m'en donne jusqu'à
ce que je dise *assez*" [As for me, when the mood takes me (and
that is often, as you know) the whole world could be there, and I
still could not restrain myself. I have to be given it until I say
"enough"].[47] After this self-characterization and this promise,
given at the beginning of the novel, the narrative of the
Comtesse's desire as Messalinic "devil in the body" is worked out
through her sustained refusal—or inability, it is the same thing
here—to declare herself satisfied. A key symptom of feminine
erotic endurance is the specific nonutterance of the word, or the
equivalent phrase, that would bring it all to an end. The military
officer who relates events in *Les Amours de garnison* (1831) describes the provincial women frequented by him and his colleagues in terms of what they cannot be brought to say: "les
femmes sont possédées de la rage du con et du cul, et . . . Hercule
lui-même avec ses cinquante travaux, perdrait peut-être sa
vigueur et s'userait la pine, en se mettant les couilles à sec,
avant que de s'entendre dire: Mon ami, c'est assez, je n'en puis
plus, retires ton vit" [the women are possessed by fever in the

cunt and the ass. Hercules himself, with his fifty labors, would perhaps lose his strength and wear out his prick, having his balls run dry, before he heard them say: "My dear, that is enough. I can't take any more. Withdraw your dick"].[48]

With some regularity but no perfection of consistency, erotic narrative achieves its end with such women as they are eventually forced to confess their defeat. In *L'Ecole des biches* (1868), for example, the young Marie utters the requisite phrase and brings one key scene to a close: "Je n'en puis plus! . . . Assez! . . . Assez!" [I can't take any more! . . . Enough! . . . Enough!].[49] Indeed, she is compelled to utter these words again at the end of a later scene (112), while her companion Caroline is also forced to provide the same exclamatory punctuation (171). Only the woman, it seems, has the power to consecrate the man's triumph by marking the end of her libidinal narrative. In *Chairs épanouies, beautés ardentes* (1902), a dastardly villain seeks to manipulate a woman, and this is exactly how he does it: "Avec impatience, Preux attendait que Mme de Fontal fût rassasiée; pour cela, il ne la ménagea point" [Impatiently, Preux waited for Mme. de Fontal to be sated. To achieve that, he did not hold back]. This man's skill is such that he achieves the desired result, which is effectively always the same, whatever complexities of intrigue might surround the enterprise: "Enfin, tout endolorie, la comtesse demanda qu'on lui fît grâce" [Finally, feeling quite sore, the countess asked for mercy].[50]

In a thoroughly mediocre but typical enough story entitled *Les Folies amoureuses d'une impératrice* (1865), the old narrative problem takes on a virulent form when an empress of love terrorizes her husband and disturbs the household by her voracious demand for intercourse. As a final expedient, a virile substitute for the inadequate emperor, a young man called Jonas, is summoned to complete the task: "Et c'est ainsi que Jonas avait pu procurer, tout en se vengeant, une nuit de délices à la belle impératrice . . . qui, vers les cinq heures du matin, prononça ce seul mot, que jamais homme ne lui fit répéter depuis: Assez!" [And that is how Jonas, while gaining his vengeance, gave a night of delicious pleasure to the empress. About five o'clock in the morning, she uttered this one word, a word that no man has ever made her say since: "Enough!"].[51] Masculine triumph is heard not in any sound that might issue from the man but in the woman's spontaneous admission that

she has had enough. The sign of victory here is not just the vocalization of climax but the avowal of denouement. Satisfaction
is mixed with relief that Messalina should at last have been
made to say "Enough!" It is only to be expected, then, that
"Assez!" should be the last word of the novel. How quickly such
narration seizes the moment of fatigue, leaping to its conclusion
about feminine pleasure! Any residual desire that was said to
traverse Messalina's lassitude is now denied, as the last word is
exacted from her by a desperate measure. It seems that any
woman who can be made to appear *lassata* is quickly to be declared *satiata*. Any symptom of fatigue is to be seized upon as
proof of satiety. Otherwise, someone like Irigaray might ask,
where would it all end?

Later nineteenth-century stories sometimes find another way
of solving and denying the problem called Messalina. They produce a veritable psychology of feminine desire, understood as a
process with its own, thoroughly novelistic outcomes. The void
within women is no longer understood merely in its expression,
as a demanding, perhaps debilitating call on men to engage in
endless intercourse: it offers the promise of degradation and
death on the woman's part. The Vicomtesse de Blancu, in *Enfilade de perles* (1894), has a standardly vulgar pornographic
name, but she is promised by the force of desire to a long and
tragic destiny. She has "un cœur tourmenté, torturé comme par
ce vide que certains pauvres êtres y sentent perpétuellement,
vide navrant et jamais comblé, qui tue plus sûrement qu'un
philtre abrutissant" [a heart that is tormented and tortured as if
by the presence of the void that some beings feel endlessly, a distressing void that is forever unfulfilled, and that brings death
with greater certainty than a stupefying potion].[52] What I find
most striking and most typical about this is not the reference to
inner emptiness, which is by now quite familiar, nor even the
mention of death, but the affirmation, so significant for the
course of narrative, that death is the certain end of it all. There
is a newly confident knowledge here that allows desire, in this
radically feminine form, to be diagnosed as a fatal illness. The
span of narrative is produced, then, not by the promise that the
heroine will eventually be made to say "enough!" but by the
pseudomedical prognosis of a narrator whose wisdom enables
him to see the outcome far in advance. Accordingly, Messalina is
less likely to be acknowledged as a champion than referred to—

somewhat in the manner of Oedipus, Electra, and a few other classical figures—as a well-defined syndrome.

There is in fact a double shift in the thematic configuration: more emphasis is placed on the woman's inner world, that of mind or soul, and greater confidence is shown in describing what goes on there. No longer, it seems, does knowledge depend so narrowly on seizing every exclamation at the moment of utterance. The author-narrator of *Le Vice suprême* (1884) announces something like this when he tells us that the focus of Messalina's story is now likely to be relocated and its meaning applied at another level: "Messaline n'est pas toujours à Suburre ou dans les bras de Silius; on peut se souiller plus encore par l'esprit" [Messalina is not always to be found at Suburra or in the arms of Silius. One can defile oneself even more through the mind].[53] The tone here is heavily moral, of course, but ambivalent play across the range from condemnation to indulgence is characteristic of fin-de-siècle fiction about vice, passion, and the flesh. Here is a less prurient version of the same psychological discourse, taken from *Journal d'un amant* (1897). The hero is able to follow in detail the inner thoughts and feelings of his lover, while recognizing that they take her beyond their shared erotic experience. After intercourse, he says, she does not dwell in a state of satiety as he does but keeps on desiring: "C'est que je ne nage pas dans un septième ciel comme toi! Mes sensations sont purement terrestres, ne dépassent pas un certain domaine. Je ne m'envole pas dans des rêves occultes. . . . Mes joies sensuelles finissent après l'étreinte, tandis que les tiennes s'éternisent; alors que ton corps reste inerte comme un cadavre, ton imagination poursuit sa fantaisie, se repaît de sensualités sans fin" [I do not find myself floating in seventh heaven like you! My sensations are purely of the earth: they do not go beyond a certain realm. I do not soar off into occult dreams. . . . My sensual delights end after the embrace, whereas yours go on forever. Even while your body remains as inert as a corpse, your imagination goes on following its fancy, fed by unending sensuality].[54] When the qualities of Messalina are primarily cerebral or psychological, sexual difference need no longer be understood as (unequal) combat. The focus of concern is now a mind filled with endless fantasies, and the drama takes place in the observable space of feminine interiority. The prospect that the male might be defeated by TKO in the fifth round is no longer of any great moment as attention shifts to the theater within, to the play of forces that promise to carry Messalina on toward her death.

Inassouvie (1889) provides a quite elaborate example of this narrative dynamic, exploited to the bitter end. At the outset, desire is not immediately given in the spectacular form found in *Gamiani*. We do not encounter a woman foaming at the mouth or writhing on the floor: simply one who is unfaithful to her husband. After giving birth to twins, Suzanne indulges in all kinds of festivities and flightiness, without ever frequenting the Parisian equivalent of Suburra.[55] Her husband, who lacks the insight characteristic of narrators and doctors, is condemned to victimhood. When he finds out the truth, his reaction is to take his own life. At this, Suzanne swears that she will completely forget him and his dramatic reproach by living in the most outrageous manner (17). She wants to "be mad" (17), and her state is qualified by an authorial voice as that of a "hysterical widow" and a "neurotic mother" (18). She is filled (and emptied) by a veritable project of self-destruction, driven by a desire to kill "la noble créature de vieille race et de pur sang qui demeurait en elle" [the noble thoroughbred who dwelt within her] (27). She may briefly appear to have a change of fortune when she marries a millionaire, but fortune has no enduring influence on this drama. Beyond frivolity and even beyond routine promiscuity, Suzanne now gives herself over to utter depravity in the form of prostitution. At this late stage, her inner torment breaks out, so to speak, in action that follows the classical Messalina story. She happens to be told by one of her new colleagues, who has not read the classics and apparently does not need to, that "il n'y a rien de tel que de passer trois ou quatre heures de la nuit dans une salle de garde" [there is nothing like spending three or four hours of the night in a guards' room] (110). To this new suggestion, Suzanne responds with a display of eagerness: "J'essaierai! Je veux savoir . . . tout savoir!" [I'll try it! I want to know . . . I want to know everything!] (110). She does in fact experience such a scene, in which the soldiers behave like "une bande de chiens qui entourent une chienne folle" [a pack of dogs surrounding a bitch in heat] (112), and her reaction to it is just like that of her now recognizable classical predecessor. She is "plus inassouvie qu'une Messaline" [more insatiable than a Messalina] (114). What takes her further than Messalina, in a sense, is the relentlessly naturalist development of her story. Far from returning home as the empress did, Suzanne now begins to work the streets because she cannot live without the "brutalités" they provide (142). A further short step then seems to take her from the sidewalk to an even lower place, to "ses débauches ignobles de gouge tombée au ruisseau" [the ignoble debauchery of a cheap whore who has landed in the gutter] (146). She keeps on going down, keeps on desiring to go down further, until she reaches the lowest point of depravity, and is in fact strangled by a man she had once betrayed (152). The man's intervention, as presented here, is not a brutal act of domination but simply a punctuation mark: it is the conclusion required by Suzanne's narrative of degradation. Her story is, as the narrator reminds any who might have failed to notice, "[un] cas de passionnante psychologie" [an absorbing psychological case] (252).

It is psychology of this kind that is called on to guarantee excited observation by an inscribed reader and the certainty of an eventual outcome to the story. Any woman who behaves like Messalina must be mad or, as texts of this period are wont to say, détraquée, although being "off the rails" in this way does not signify long-term unpredictability. Alice in La Luxure (1905) is one of these: "elle se donnait avec une rage insensée, une frénésie telle que, très souvent, l'homme qui avait la chance de cette bonne fortune restait apeuré, croyant avoir affaire à une folle, à quelque détraquée dangereuse" [she gave herself with a kind of insane rage, with such frenzy that, very often, the man who had the good fortune to receive her offer remained fearfully defensive, thinking that he was dealing with a mad woman, or some dangerous pervert].[56] Whatever the fears held at such moments by particular men, there is a general androcentric reassurance to be found in the knowledge that such madness is in fact a terrible "danger" to the women themselves. When Suzanne dies, in Inassouvie, it is because "la malheureuse détraquée" [the unfortunate pervert] is given the final push that leads to "une crise décisive,—fatale, du reste,—d'hystérie inguérissable" [a decisive, indeed inevitable, crisis of incurable hysteria] (152). By a surprising inversion of the Messalina dynamic, it is now a boon for narrative that such hysteria can be declared incurable. This allows the heroine-victim to be eliminated from the world of society, polite or impolite, even if the journey to the grave sometimes passes, as with Suzanne, via the asylum of La Salpêtrière, and perhaps a session or two with the famous Dr. Charcot. Radical feminine sexuality of this sort, while affirmed to be *détraquée*, is able to be followed steadily along the downward narrative track of sickness unto death.

Living (and eventually dying) like a Messalina is, for the fin de siècle, only one of a series of options available to women. They can, and do, just as readily choose the opposite path, although it is striking that the virtuous opposite is no longer attended by the moral certainty and the tragic elegance of Lucretia's self-destructive gesture. Fin-de-siècle fiction finds other, much slower ways for virtuous women to die, and these ways bear a remarkable similarity to those followed by Messalinas of the period. Barbey d'Aurevilly, in his preface to *Le Vice suprême* (1884), notes the approximate equivalence when describing the heroine's behavior as a choice between radical options: "La brutalité d'un mari bestial lui avait donné, dès la première nuit de son mariage, le dégoût des voluptés charnelles, et d'une Messaline ou d'une Théodora qu'elle aurait pu être, elle se fit un autre genre de monstre . . . elle fut le monstre métaphysique. L'orgueil et la volupté domptèrent ses sens et elle fut chaste" [the brutality of a bestial husband had aroused in her, right from the first night of marriage, disgust with the pleasures of the flesh, and, rather than the Messalina or the Theodora she might have been, she became another kind of monster . . . a metaphysical one. Pride and voluptuousness tamed her senses, and she became chaste].[57] This is perverse chastity, and the heroine, Leonora, marks it as such, saying that she would not have the strength to follow Messalina's strenuous program: "Je n'aurais pas la santé de refaire Messaline, si j'en avais le goût" [I would not have the energy to copy Messalina if I felt like it] (73). It almost seems as if her chastity is a kind of fin-de-siècle ersatz for Messalina's libido, chosen, at least in part, because generational fatigue now makes the ancient story unrepeatable. It cannot be denied that something has changed in the nature of "nymphomania." Whatever madness may have been abroad in, say, *Le Diable au corps* depended for its enactment on a form of vigor dwelling in the bodies of women. There was no particular paradox here, just an amusing, even laughable conjunction made explicit in the anecdote of the woman who publicly declared herself to be ill so that she could stay inside and devote herself completely to "passionate excesses" that actually required an "excess" of health.[58] In

fin-de-siècle times, it often seems that this option is no longer
available because everyone is always already *lassata*. Camilla,
in *Les Demi-Sexes* (1897), is in end of story mode long before her
time. Worn out with desire, she has slumped into a kind of routine satiety that preempts any major erotic event: "Je suis rassasiée de voluptés, écœurée de vices; si mes nerfs me
tourmentent encore, mes désirs sont éteints! . . . je vis dans une
lassitude morne" [I am sated with pleasures, and nauseated with
vice. My nerves still torment me, but my desires are extinguished! I live in dismal lassitude].[59] Any virtue that might occur
here is circumstantial: it results from a failure to maintain the
energy needed for vice.

The death of the Messalina theme, or its decline into a thematics of death, is evident in *Mademoiselle Tantale* (1884). This
novel makes plot out of the dialectical relation, in Mary Folkestone's "interesting psychology," between nymphomania and
frigidity. Mary suffers terribly, and is finally driven to her death
by the inability to experience the fullness of pleasure in sexual
relations with her lover. This rather tired (in)version of the Messalina theme makes of her not so much a victim of male brutality or even a lingering adolescent in need of a vigorous male
partner but a disturbing "case," needing referral to the eminent
specialist, Dr. Charcot. We are told in an authorial footnote that
Mary is "impotent":

> On a beaucoup étudié l'impuissance chez l'homme, et quand
> j'écrivis ce livre il n'existait aucune étude sur l'impuissance pour-
> tant véridique et nullement rare de la femme, j'entends: "l'impuis-
> sance à éprouver le spasme d'amour." J'arrivais bon premier, et
> c'est une des raisons pour lesquelles l'illustre et regretté maître
> Charcot accepta mon hommage et me donna des conseils.

> [There have been many studies of impotence in the male, and
> when I wrote this book there were no studies of women's impo-
> tence, even though it is an established fact, and not an uncommon
> one. By this I mean "the inability to experience the spasm of love."
> So I was the first on the scene, and that is one of the reasons why
> the illustrious and lamented master, Charcot, accepted my
> homage and gave me advice.][60]

Earlier in the nineteenth century, Messalina had represented a
terrible threat and promise for narrative. By her "subsistence"
in desire, she was always likely to outlast her partners no

matter how great their number, reducing them all in time to a form of impotence. But fin-de-siècle psychosexuality manages to overcome this threat by making feminine resistance into a syndrome. In narratives of pathological sexuality, there is no longer the same need for males to strive for the woman's libidinal denouement, no longer the requirement that she be made to say "enough" since her "case" will now have its own inevitable logic. In discovering, describing and recounting a new illness, the author of *Mademoiselle Tantale* helps to bury the ancient theme of feminine erotic strength as invincible resistance to males. A certain kind of scientific discourse intersects with a thematics of decadence, producing its own, anemic version of the Messalina theme: that of a woman condemned to death by her pathetic inability to arrive.

9

Lesbos

THERE IS AN INCIDENT IN MAUPASSANT'S SHORT STORY "LA FEMME DE Paul" (1881) that functions, perhaps quite consciously, as a significant moment in the history of erotic representation. At a leisure spot on the Seine near Paris, numbers of *demi-mondains*, half-respectable but permissive people, have gathered to spend their Sunday. They observe a boatload of women and call out, "V'là Lesbos" [There's Lesbos]. The collective cry of recognition, we are told, is both an "ovation" and a "vocifération," a mixture of congratulation and persiflage.[1] The women in question are seen as a sexual subculture, and the easy spontaneity with which they are named reflects an established social practice of exclusion-and-inclusion—what we might call their marginal belonging. The name of their group is taken from literature, although it is not of course clear whether the source is acknowledged by all users.

The word "Lesbos" appears to carry the mark of its classical origin more clearly than the adjectival derivative that did exist then, but has only since become the utterly dominant usage. The name and the allusion constitute these women as a figurative island visible on the outskirts of Parisian society, declaring them, quite crassly, to be all in the same boat. The noisy acclamation-and-derision of Lesbos is accompanied in Maupassant's story by another, darker kind of recognition that proves fatal to the central character, but I shall return to that in chapter 10. It will suffice for the present to note that the cry of public acclaim for Lesbos is accompanied sotto voce by stories of passion: "Leur vice était public, officiel, patent. On en parlait comme d'une chose naturelle, qui les rendait presque sympathiques, et l'on chuchotait tout bas des histoires étranges, des drames nés de furieuses

310

jalousies féminines, et des visites secrètes de femmes connues, d'actrices, à la petite maison du bord de l'eau" [Their vice was public, official, and unmistakable. People talked about it as a natural thing that made them almost likable. Strange stories were told in the lowest of whispers, of dramatic scenes brought about by the furious jealousy of women, and the secret visits by well known women, including actresses, to the little house by the water's edge] (297–98). The whispered anecdotes belong no doubt to another genre than Maupassant's more or less respectable *demi-mondain* story, but their thematic place is specifically identified here. All kinds of strange things might go on in this island topos and all kinds of secrets lurk there, giving rise to stories that circulate in clandestinity, but the place has a familiar name, one that springs readily to everyone's lips.[2]

The chorus of recognition represented in "La Femme de Paul" would not have been possible before Maupassant's time: no assembled crowds would have been able to cry "voilà Lesbos" with the same hearty confidence and the same harmonious richness of tone, for Lesbos did not stand out or stand alone. It is true that classical writing spoke of erotic knowledge in general as being held by women and ritually transmitted through them, but this was not local knowledge, and practices between women were seldom distinguished or distinctive. When an older woman initiated a younger one, it was often as preparation for marriage or for a career in prostitution. In any case, this involved the full range of desires and pleasures in all their ceremonious multiplicity rather than a recognizable set of lesbian practices. Only in the course of the nineteenth century, in fact, does Lesbos become patently thematic. It is true that Sade, with his fondness for classification, proposes in a note to *Aline et Valcour* that sexual activity between women be called *saphotisme*,[3] but the term did not recur, and this is no doubt because the practices it attempts to name were insufficiently delimited within the field of pleasures. They became so only in the following century, as various elements were drawn together and relentlessly exploited for their narrative yield.

In Sade's time and before, we find references to Lesbos and lesbianism that ought to forestall any easy recognition of the terms. When characters in an erotic story of the time are described as imitating the inhabitants of Lesbos, it may be that they do not even indulge at all in same-sex love between women. As

Friedrich Carl Forberg points out in his analytical anthology of Greek and Latin erotica, "les lesbiens"—note the masculine or common gender—were considered by the ancient Greeks to be the inventors and leading exponents of fellatio,[4] and this is a tradition of reference that is maintained at least into the early nineteenth century. When a definition of the term happens to be provided in *Le Diable au corps* (1803), it is made explicit that "donner une lesbienne, c'est gamahucher" [to give a lesbian is to lick someone's cunt]. Lesbos is "cette île heureuse" [that happy isle] to which "l'histoire du plaisir accorde l'honneur de cette invention" [the history of pleasure attributes the honor of this invention].[5] To the extent that the people of Lesbos are taken as models, it will often be in this quite classical sense, as exponents of oral sex, although the tendency may be for their positions to be adopted by women.[6] Sade's Juliette must be relying on such classical knowledge when she invokes the most famous inhabitant of Lesbos, describing a circumstance in which "il fallait . . . que mes six compagnes . . . exécutassent . . . les plus voluptueuses attitudes de Sapho" [my six women companions were required to strike the most voluptuous poses of Sappho].[7] There is no occasion here to stand back and say "voilà Sapho," no particular set of behaviors, no *-isme* of the sort that might be identified as Sapphism or lesbianism: it is merely a matter of getting on with the (erotic) job and its prescribed "attitudes."

Quite distinct from this postural discipline, not even articulated with it in the early nineteenth century, is the habit of identifying a certain class of women as anatomically predisposed to particular sexual practices. These are women with an abnormally long clitoris, sometimes accompanied by unusually luxuriant pubic hair. Their body shape lends itself, we are told repeatedly, to the pleasures of "rubbing" that define the tribade (from the Greek *tribein*). Rubbing no doubt marks a contrast with the pleasures of penetration that seem to have characterized most of the Greek *aphrodisia*.[8] Forberg again provides a classical definition, quite distinct from his definition of the lesbian, including in fact both rubbing and lesser penetration: "Les tribades . . . sont des femmes chez qui cette partie de la nature mulièbre, appelée le clitoris, atteint de telles proportions qu'elles peuvent s'en servir comme d'une mentule, soit pour enfiler, soit pour pédiquer" [Tribades are women in whom that part of womanly nature known as the clitoris is of such proportions that they can use it like a male instrument to penetrate either in front or behind].[9] In erotic literature at its crudest, someone will usually be able to confirm by direct observation of the genitals whether a woman belongs properly to this group. In *La Secte des anandrynes: confession de mademoiselle Sapho* (1789) the eponymous heroine, who is being initiated into an adult life of pleasure, is examined by an old procuress and found to be eminently suited, suited indeed by her eminence, to membership of the secret sect: "elle a un clitoris diabolique; elle sera plus propre aux femmes qu'aux hommes; nos tribades renommées doivent nous payer cette acquisition au poids de l'or" [she has a diabolical clitoris. She will be more suited to women than to men. Our renowned tribades will pay the highest price to acquire this].[10] Note that being an anatomical tribade coincides here with bearing the name Sapho, and indeed with the young woman's induction into a sect of *anandrynes*, in which pleasure is enjoyed "without men." Reading Mademoiselle Sapho's peculiar physique even allows the old procuress to say "Voilà!" but this mixture of elements does not yet make a thematic compound likely to recur in other places. The focus here is on a subspecies of women, available for a certain kind of pleasure, and for pleasurable observation, as intriguing sexual freaks. This natural propensity for frictional contact with other women is sometimes measured with precision. Mme. d'Esterval in Sade's *Histoire de Juliette* has a clitoris three inches long (7:95), and Madame Champville in *Les Cent Vingt Journées de Sodome* has one that protrudes more than three inches (1:48). This is, for Sade, a visible gift of nature, a technical bodily advantage enjoyed by tribades allowing them to experience greater or at least more versatile pleasure: "je crois" [I believe], says Juliette with the support of an authorial footnote, "que la nature favorise infiniment davantage les tribades que les autres femmes, et que, comme elle leur accorde une imagination plus sensible, elle leur a prodigué, de même, tous les moyens du plaisir et de la volupté" [that nature gives an enormous advantage to tribades over other women. As they are endowed with more sensitive imagination, they are also gifted with the means of pleasure and voluptuousness] (*Histoire de Juliette* 9:538). The "means" of which Juliette speaks are quite technical. Women of this type are particularly well equipped for coupling and for the adoption of positions.

"Lesbian" practices of oral sex and tribadic predispositions to coupling with other women make up a range of practices out of which lesbianism might have been constituted as the "figures of Sappho," but the late nineteenth century, with its emphasis on the psychosexual, shows no particular interest in body shapes or the possibilities they might provide. A woman character in fiction is sometimes said to have a large clitoris but no performance of mensuration or geometry ensues. *Lesbia, maîtresse d'école* (1890) makes of it one of the traits that mark the heroine as a dominant woman in a feminine world, but it is not exploited by narrative.[11] In *La Canonisation de Jeanne d'Arc* (1890), it is fetching that a woman should have pubic hair reaching up to her navel, and her woman partner is charmed by the sight of "cette petite chose qui avance" [that little thing that protrudes], but these are now symptoms of psychosexual type rather than bodily advantages or endowments.[12] As the hairy woman in this story says, "Je suis un peu homme . . ." [I am a bit of a man] (625). The shift is quite clear in *Le Roman de Violette* (1883), where the examination is carried out by a professor of medicine. This man, who is also the narrator-hero, takes the enlarged clitoris, or rather its specific absence, as conclusive evidence of a psychosexual tendency. After examining the young Violette, he is relieved to find that "la proéminence était à peine sensible chez elle" [the protruberance was barely noticeable in her case].[13] She can therefore be allowed to dally with the experienced (and beautifully hairy) tribade Odette for the hero's voyeuristic delectation, in the confident knowledge that this will not commit her to a life of pleasure without men. When postural dispositions and predispositions are no longer central to the definition of "lesbian" or "tribade," any difference between the two is no longer pertinent. If desire for other women is merely a psychological phenomenon, then the terms can be used synonymously. This occurs, for example, in *La Canonisation de Jeanne d'Arc*: "Bientôt toutes les deux . . . se livrèrent au plus délicieux transports du tribadisme et se lesbianisèrent à l'envi" [Soon both launched into the most delightful ecstasy of tribadism and lesbianized each other to their hearts' content] (630). The style may be execrable, but the thematic convergence now appears complete.

Sometimes associated with the lesbian or the tribadic we find the name of Sappho, but we should be equally wary of taking this name as a key to "sapphic" sexuality. Joan De Jean has shown admirably, in her *Fictions of Sappho*, that representations of the ancient Greek poet are not reliably tied, in every historical circumstance, to what we now call sapphism or lesbianism. The equivalence only becomes established, she argues, at the end of the nineteenth century.[14] Not until that time is it possible to recognize Sappho consistently as a lesbian. I shall not rehearse De Jean's argument nor even take up her conclusions in detail, if only because the object of this chapter is the thematic becoming of lesbianism during the nineteenth century rather than the vicissitudes of Sappho's legend, all the more since Sappho was often taken to be an emblem of tragically unrequited heterosexual passion. It is nonetheless helpful to note that the apparently straightforward connection, made through history and geography, of person and place, Sappho and Lesbos, guarantees no singularity of reference.[15] The hermeneutic danger identified and avoided by De Jean is the one that has preoccupied me from the outset: the risk that we might assimilate earlier discourses to the dominant thematics of our time. Some other histories of Sappho, I fear, have taken the easy downhill path. Jean-Pierre Jacques, in a worthy but unenlightening essay, tells the story of Sappho's appearances and incarnations during the nineteenth century, making of her a recurring character, and indeed a victim-heroine surrounded by uncomprehending villains. Representation of Sappho during the 1800s, says Jacques, amounts to no more than simplistic and oppressive stereotyping. He denounces erotic fiction throughout the whole century for tailoring the lesbian figure to its own androcentric purpose, cutting its sapphic cloth in exact conformity to the patterns of male desire.[16] But this supposes that the cloth is given in its wholeness from the outset, whereas I want to argue that such fiction, for all its reductiveness, actually does its own textual weaving, making it possible to speak in a more detailed or at least more insistent way about lesbianism, perhaps even enabling the adoption of a contrary view. I have great sympathy with Jacques's ethical position, and even with his critical impatience, but I want to maintain the hermeneutic discipline needed to attend closely to the (quite complicated) "stereotype" to which he refers. Only by picking our way over the terrain will we recognize the unwitting richness of these representations. And only then will we understand, in keeping with a Foucaldian analysis of discourse, how such representations can be oppressive and enabling at the same time. The fact is that, at the end of a century of oppression and repression, there occurred the phenomenon of Sappho 1900. As Martha Vicinus points out, "gay and lesbian history has long concentrated on the fin de siècle as a pivotal period during which the extant homosexual male subculture became a visible part of the mainstream world, the modern lesbian identity was delineated, and the word 'homosexual' was coined and medicalized."[17] In France, "Sapho 1900" became the name of an artistic group, of a thematic network, and thus of a literary historical period. It was, if you like, the trademark of an era, the stamp of an intellectual fashion, coined in André Billy's slogan, "Sapho 1900, Sapho cent pour cent" [Sappho 1900, Sappho 100 per cent].[18]

The "Sappho 1900" phenomenon is worthy of attention for its neoclassicism, for its self-conscious mythmaking, and for its feminization of the lyric at the very least. But my history stops short of it, if only because I am following another genre. It is surely no coincidence that Renée Vivien and others turned (back) to lyric poetry in allegiance to Sappho, and that even such prose works as Liane de Pougy's *Idylle saphique* (1901) claimed the genre of the idyll rather than the novel.[19] My primary interest here is of course in narrative fiction, and I want to consider what representations of Lesbos, Sappho, and tribadism contributed to narrative, as well as what narrative did to Lesbos. It may well be, in fact, that Sappho needed in 1900 to be saved from narrative, but it was nonetheless an achievement of narrative that she was there to be recognized and there to be saved.[20]

To understand the place of Lesbos in climactic narrative, and to measure the semiotic work done by erotic fiction, we need to see how much it overlaps with the Messalina thematic.[21] The earliest example I have been able to find of a connection between Messalina and Lesbos occurs right at the historical point where Messalina first takes on her distinctively modern shape. In *Eléonore, ou l'heureuse personne* (1798), two women work themselves into a state of furious desire, made all the more intense by the fact that it is "impossible" for them, as women, to arrive at any definitive satisfaction: "L'impossibilité où sont deux femmes de satisfaire absolument tout à fait leurs désirs mutuels, prolonge presque sans bornes et la durée et la vivacité d'un feu qu'elles attisent de fureur, et que l'extrême lassitude

peut à peine amortir" [The impossibility for two women of absolutely satisfying their mutual desires extends almost endlessly
both the duration and the vigor of their passion, so that extreme
fatigue can barely dampen it].[22] In the absence of a "natural"
conclusion, they appear condemned to an endless experience of
desire, with the only respite being afforded by fatigue: "Lassées,
fatiguées, les deux amies se laissèrent aller, enivrées, anéanties"
[Tired and worn out, the two women friends lay back, drunk and
exhausted with pleasure] (85). The problem for their erotic narrative is said to be a strictly organic one. If one of them were a
man, desire could be brought to an end by the act of penetration:
"Ah! ma jolie amie, pourquoi n'es-tu pas un homme?" [Ah! My
pretty one, why are you not a man?] (85). This is not, I suggest,
penis envy as a psychological condition so much as a longing for
proper narrative. The longing is itself a mark of intensity since
it is precisely the absence of a man, and of the release he would
provide, that has allowed desire to go on increasing indefinitely.
The (supposed) inability of women to achieve climax and denouement without male help is thus bound up with their (supposed) capacity to maintain endless desire in exclusively
feminine company.

Comtesse Gamiani proclaims this version of the Messalina
theme as a rallying cry for militant tribadism. She boasts to her
young lover Fanny: "Dis . . . un homme, un amant, qu'est-ce, près
de moi? Deux ou trois luttes l'abattent, le renversent; à la qua-
trième il râle impuissant, ses reins plient dans le spasme du
plaisir. C'est pitié! Moi, je reste encore forte, frémissante, inassouvie!" [Tell me, what is a male lover by comparison with me?
Two or three bouts exhaust him and leave him flat out. By the
fourth, he is gasping impotently, and his back gives way in the
spasm of pleasure. It is pitiful! I, on the other hand, remain
strong, eager, and insatiable!].[23] The male can be counted out, reduced to temporary impotence by repeating the mechanism of
his climax, but Gamiani, as a tribade, has extraordinary
stamina for giving and taking pleasure—or at least for sustaining desire. She has worn out many male partners during her
youthful career as a prostitute, and only with a female can she
have the opportunity to display her full capacity for endurance.
Yet female staying power of this kind is not merely celebrated
here: it is surrounded with ambivalence, with a mixture of
pathos and horror. The narration does not just marvel at the

heroine's capacity for action but deplores her inability to come to the end of her desire. For the narrator, Alcide, Gamiani's performance is breathtakingly impressive but also distressingly inhuman—or unmanly. Her pleasure is indistinguishable from pain, and her stamina freakish to the point of monstrosity. Tribadism is defined in *Gamiani*, from the moment it is first mentioned, as a dreadful narrative disorder: "Une tribade! Oh! ce mot retentit à l'oreille d'une manière étrange; puis, il élève en vous je ne sais quelles images confuses de voluptés inouïes, lascives à l'excès. C'est la rage luxurieuse, la lubricité forcenée, la jouissance horrible qui reste inachevée!" [A tribade! Oh! That word resounds to the ear in a strange way. It raises in you all manner of confused images of unparalleled pleasures, lewd in the extreme. It is lascivious rage, frantic lubricity, a horrible pleasure that remains unfinished!] (78). Tribadism is excess and inadequacy—excessive indeed because of its very inadequacy—inscribed in an unending circle of narrative and thematic logic. When Gamiani speaks her desire, she does not simply boast of it, but confesses it as interminable agony: "Mais fatiguez-moi donc! Qu'on me presse, qu'on me batte. . . . Oh! ne pas jouir . . . !" [Come on, wear me out! Somebody bear down on me, beat me. . . . Oh! What it is not to feel pleasure! . . .] (102). At the center of her frenzy is a longing for denouement: she seems to desire nothing so ardently as the cessation of her ardor. Yet it always seems, where she is concerned, that the end is not yet. Even when her partner Fanny cries out the fatal word, "Assez! Gamiani, assez!," Gamiani cannot reply in kind. "Non! non!" she says, and goes on to other things that promise to be more of the same kind (114).

This unending frustration, this routinely carnal experience of the eternal is presumably what Baudelaire understands as the "damnation" of Lesbos. He describes the women who inhabit that place as afflicted by the inner emptiness of insatiable desire. The dark hollowness of feminine avidity is said to attain cavernous proportions, as the key words of the Messalina theme return:

> . . . Je sens s'élargir dans mon être
> Un abîme béant; cet abîme est mon cœur!
> Brûlant comme un volcan, profond comme le vide!
> Rien ne rassasiera ce monstre gémissant
> Et ne rafraîchira la soif d'Euménide
> Qui, la torche à la main, le brûle jusqu'au sang.

Que nos rideaux fermés nous séparent du monde,
Et que la lassitude amène le repos!

[I feel, expanding in my being,
A gigantic abyss. That abyss is my heart!
Burning like a volcano, as deep as the void!
Nothing will ever satisfy this groaning monster,
Nothing will slake the thirst of Eumenides
Who, with torch in hand, burns it until he bleeds.

Let our closed drapes separate us from the world
And let lassitude bring with it rest!][24]

Baudelaire's poetry is outside the generic range of my study, but it happens to make an influential contribution to a narrative thematics of tribadism by focusing on temporality, damning tribadic women to hell for their perpetual desire. After Baudelaire, writers and critics are able to refer to tribades generically as "femmes damnées," just as Jean Desthieux and Henri Drouin do in the titles of their respective essays.[25] A consequence of this predication, exploited by the fin de siècle, is that tribadism can now be represented, not as a matter of simple erotic preference or organic predisposition, but as an implacable program of erotic damnation. For those who really know Lesbos in this way, recognition will not consist in calling out the name on sight but in the fearful acknowledgement of its relentless durability.

In stories that might be considered more straightforwardly pornographic, the positive aspect of tribadic endurance is likely to be noted in passing and even exploited episodically. It is convenient for the telling of *Voluptés bizarres* (1893) that two women, having just finished a scene, should be immediately ready to begin the next, "un peu lasses, mais nullement assouvies . . ." [a little weary, but in no way sated].[26] Equally, no terrible emptiness echoes within when we are told of a particular tribade in *Les Callipyges* (1892) that she would hold out against twenty Messalinas: this is just everyday hyperbole.[27] And even when the comparison is made to the disadvantage of men in general, as in *Toute la lyre!*, there is still no general break in relations, no attempt to make Lesbos an island separate from the world of men. The story can simply go on because the women continue to practice variations in technique and position: "Ces messieurs savent bien ce qu'ils valent et que, malgré toute leur

valeur, cinq ou six coups les vident, alors que nos languettes ne
s'épuisent jamais" [These gentlemen well know their own worth,
and they also know that, in spite of it, five or six bouts empty
them out, whereas our little tongues are never exhausted].[28]
Messalina, here, has all the expedient familiarity of a well-used
whore of narrative.

To uncomplicated pornography of this sort, it is tempting to
oppose those more serious and somewhat more respectable fin-
de-siècle works that called themselves *romans passionnels* or
romans de mœurs parisiennes. To obscenity, we might then
oppose prurience, with its amalgam of erotic narrative, medical
discourse, and moral judgment. But the Messalina theme is present across the range of (sub)genres, and indeed more fully exploited in the more complex and pretentious works. Jeanne de
Tilleray, one of the central characters in *Deux amies* (1885), is
described and situated by a quick roll call of (in)glorious prece-
dents, extending from Juvenal's writing to Baudelaire's: "Elle
dépassait Messaline et Sapho et cette comtesse Gamiani, qui
comme une damnée inassouvie, torture sa chair, cherche dans
tous les raffinements, dans toutes les abjections le secret de l'ab-
solue volupté" [She went further than Messalina and Sappho
and that Countess Gamiani, who like an insatiable damned
woman tortured her flesh and sought in all possible refinements
and forms of abjection the secret of absolute voluptuousness].[29]
The quest for impossible pleasure, and thus for damnation, is
never more relentlessly pursued than by the heroine of
Méphistophela (1890), a novel whose title feminizes the infernal
and the diabolical. Sophor d'Hermelinge is said to cross gender
boundaries not by the length of her clitoris—that is not available for measurement in such a distinguished text—but by her
purposeful evildoing, by the unrelieved temporal perfection of
her sinfulness:

> Elle est, dans le mal, sans défaillance; son péché ne fait jamais de
> faute; elle est irréprochable; c'est ce qui produit l'épouvante.
> "Homo sum!" s'écrie la Messaline de Juvénal; avec raison! puisque
> ce sont des mâles qu'elle espère dans la logette des prostituées de
> Suburre. Mais la femme qui se virilise définitivement, se déshu-
> manise.
>
> [She is unrelenting in evildoing. Her sinfulness is unfailing. That
> is what horrifies people. "Homo sum!" says Juvenal's Messalina,

and with reason, because it is males whom she hopes to find in the guard house at Suburra. But the woman who definitively becomes a man becomes inhuman.][30]

Being definitively evil is the business of Méphistophela: not just beating Messalina at her own game but making of the game a lifelong quest and compounding damnation with devilry. The road to hell passes most directly through sexual relations with other women, and this *invicta* triumphs over men by seducing their partners: "Elle affirmait violemment à quelque invisible contradicteur qu'elle serait sans fin la victorieuse des mâles bafoués, la conquérante insatiable des jeunes femmes" [She violently affirmed to some invisible contradictor that she would be unendingly victorious over flouted males, and the insatiable conqueror of young women] (456). She has found a way—perhaps, for the fin de siècle, *the* way—to embody "le désir jamais repu" [forever unsated desire] (392), transforming what might otherwise have been thought of as frustration into a whole life's project, sufficient to fill a long novel. Where earlier Messalinas might have gone on dreaming, in moments of fatigue, of something more than what they had known to date, Méphistophela has managed to turn their fantasies into a sustained erotic program: "Elle fut la diabolique réalisatrice des chimères qu'inventa la satiété des vieux rois et des impératrices lasses" [Diabolically, she turned into reality fantasies invented in satiety by old kings and tired empresses] (502). Her devilishness consists in making the problem of desire into its own (final) solution, producing damnation not as poetic stasis but as a powerful narrative dynamic. That, as we will shortly see in more detail, constitutes a decisive inflection of Gamiani's tribade story to the point of reversing its narrative significance.

When Alphonse Daudet, in his *Sapho* (1884), endows the central character with a classical erotic name, he might just as easily have called her Messalina. Certainly, he does not particularly use Sappho's name, as Joan De Jean points out, in order to refer to sapphism as we now understand it. De Jean highlights, as a kind of thematic *mise en abyme*, the standard reproduction of Sappho, a commercial bronze described in the novel as it stands on a mantelpiece. Sappho is, says De Jean, a thematic object that is disseminated widely and can be readily bought and sold: Daudet's definition of sapphism is "a variant of prostitutional circulation."[31] What De Jean does not say, however, is that Daudet's heroine also acts as an unspectacular Messalina figure. Fanny is given the nickname Sapho for two more or less convergent reasons: for her erotic versatility—that is, the range of lovers and the types of love she has known ("toute la lyre" [the whole gamut])—and for her capacity to endure in desire, in love, in a relationship.[32] It seems, in practice, as if Daudet's story, in its decency, has chosen to exploit the second of these features rather than the first, evacuating any postural or technical content of the Sappho theme in favor of its Messalinic significance for narrative. The whole problem for the central male character, Gaussin, almost from the very outset is how to put an end to his relationship with this woman, endowed as she is with "la brûlure de Sapho" [the burning mark of Sappho] (40) and with a remarkable propensity to linger. The difficulty of reaching a denouement thus becomes the central theme of the novel, discreetly announced in its title. Early, in the first rush of amorous enthusiasm, Gaussin carries Fanny/Sapho up four flights of stairs to his hotel room, yet even this élan is overtaken by the difficulty of arriving. Sapho becomes heavier with each step, weighing on him finally as "quelque chose de lourd, d'horrible" [something heavy and horrible]. These are just flights of stairs and not sexual climaxes, but the arithmetic and the narrative difficulty are the same. By the time they reach his room, he is exhausted, thinking to himself, "At last!" But she has not had enough, and exclaims, "Already!" (16–17). The question for the hero, and for the novel, is: can she ever be made to say "Enough!"? The question is brought into focus by the contrasting story of Gaussin's friend Déchelette, whose relations with women are governed by the motto "pas de lendemain" [no tomorrow] (13, 41–42). His motto is a variant of the title of Vivant Denon's erotic novel, *Point de lendemain* (1777), which emphasized and isolated the delights of a single, intense night of love.[33] Déchelette seeks to make of singular climax his erotic style and his sexual regimen. Fanny/Sapho he identifies at once as not being a woman for one night stands: "Il y a des femmes qu'on ne garde pas qu'une nuit. . . . Celle-là par exemple. . . . C'est une fille, quand elle aime, elle se cramponne . . ." [There are women you don't just keep for one night. . . . That one, for example. She's the kind of girl who, when she is in love, clings on tight . . .] (42).

Sapho's debilitating strength lies in her capacity to hold a man indefinitely, heavily, in her apparently gentle grasp (26). Desire is in her blood like a kind of "marsh fever" (58, 83), and being with her is like wallowing in the mire, gently sinking into the lukewarm stagnation of an interminable embrace (189–91). Only after years of hanging on does Fanny at last admit that her capacity to love has been used up: "Maintenant je n'en peux plus, tu m'as trop fait vivre, trop fait souffrir, je suis à bout" [Now I can't take any more. You've put me through too much, too much suffering, right to the end] (196). These words are found in her final letter to Gaussin and they occur on the last page of the novel. She may not be *satiata* but she is finally, epically *lassata*, and the story can be allowed to end.

But there is more to the Sappho thematic than another name for Messalina. Underlying the rich ambivalence toward Lesbos is a fundamental equivocation about its comparative status with respect to heterosexual activity. There is uncertainty throughout the nineteenth century as to whether sexual relations between women are lesser or greater, according to some measure of intensity, than those between men and women. The only thing that appears constant is that they are not seen as equal or substituted indifferently for one another. To understand this equivocation is to resolve the thematic components that could be heard in Maupassant's "vocifération" and its whispered undercurrents; erotic contact between women is presented, more or less simultaneously, as a mere bagatelle and as a sinister phenomenon. The trivialization occurs readily wherever the activity of women is marked by the lack of that purportedly essential instrument, the penis. Sometimes, this may take the form of active disparagement, as when the narrator-hero, excluded from a female orgy, apostrophizes the group, unheard by them, from without: "Viande creuse, foutre Mesdames, viande creuse, leur criais-je, ces engins-là sont mous ou le diable m'emporte . . ." ["Hollow meat, my fucking ladies, hollow meat," I shouted. "The devil take me if those weapons aren't soft"].[34] *Viande creuse* characterizes women by their organic emptiness and affirms that their pleasure must be just as hollow, although Mirabeau's breezy young hero does not see in such hollowness the damnable abyss sounded by Baudelaire.[35]

The vituperation of sexual relations between women is nonetheless rare in erotic literature, even in Mirabeau's texts, perhaps because abuse does not permit the establishment of a constraining narrative discipline. Most often, the attitude of men, as narrators and heroes, is far more indulgent. When women spend time in intimate contact, this tends to be seen as a charming interlude of no great consequence, a *divertissement* undeserving either of condemnation or of a central place in the story. Most of the examples of early, initiatory encounters considered in *Geometry in the Boudoir*, from Aretino to Sade and beyond, belong in this category. The playful condescension with which they are usually described constitutes no greater recognition, of course, than the peevish disparagement of Mirabeau's hero. As Françoise d'Eaubonne points out, "on [a] trop vite cédé à la tentation de faire de [Lesbos] des gentilles amusettes sans conséquence où les bergères ne font que badiner" [people are too quick to think of [Lesbos] as an uncomplicated amusement in which shepherdesses merely frolic together].[36] The fact is, as Xavière Gauthier remarks, that feminine erotic activity is not deemed to have a proper narrative shape: "l'excitation manuelle ou linguale n'est pas véritablement considérée comme un acte sexuel" [manual or lingual arousal is not really considered to be a sex act].[37] Playing with this inconsequentiality, and using it as a prelude or a flourish to adorn the more central, more decisive acts carried out by males becomes one of the commonplaces of pornography.

The lack of narrative purpose on such occasions is in fact compounded from within, one might say, by the fact that the female participants are often quite unsure as to how to proceed. This is where "innocence," a broadly feminine trait exploited over centuries by pornographic narrative,[38] manifests itself as technical ignorance, leaving the would-be partners charmingly perplexed about how to play the game through to a conclusion. There is no lack of desire, but young women are often unable to guess how it might be implemented. As Angelica Goodden says, "Suzanne Simonin [the heroine of *La Religieuse*] and Queen Victoria were not alone in wondering what could possibly constitute sexual activity between women."[39] They were not alone if only because their company was regularly expanded by the addition of fresh young heroines from erotic narrative.

Wondering about how to behave becomes, then, a characteristic of behavior. This is nowhere more evident, nor foregrounded more provocatively, than in *Mademoiselle de Maupin* (1835), where the heroine's uncertainty stands at the end of the story as a teasing narrative ellipsis. Mademoiselle de Maupin, who has been disguised as a man throughout, recounts a near-climactic adventure with her friend Rosette. Stylized modesty is manifest not just in the manner of telling, but in the incompleteness of the event itself:

> et puis, je l'avouerai à ma honte, cette scène, tout équivoque que le caractère en fût pour moi, ne manquait pas d'un certain charme qui me retenait plus qu'il n'eût fallu; cet ardent désir m'échauffait de sa flamme, et j'étais réellement fâchée de ne le pouvoir satis-faire: je souhaitai même d'être un homme, comme effectivement je le paraissais, afin de couronner cet amour, et je regrettai fort que Rosette se trompât.

> [And I must add, to my shame, that this scene, with its dubious qualities, was not without a certain charm that kept me there longer than it ought to have. Her ardent desire made me grow warm with its heat, and I was genuinely sorry not to be able to satisfy it. I even wished that I had been a man, as indeed I ap-peared to be, so that I could bring this love to a conclusion. I very much regretted the fact that Rosette was mistaken about me.]

At this point they are interrupted, and the heroine is moved to declare: "un quart d'heure plus tard, le diable m'emporte si je sais le dénoûment qu'aurait pu avoir cette aventure,—je n'en vois pas de possible" [A quarter of an hour longer, and the devil take me if I know what sort of denouement this adventure could have had. I can't imagine any possible one].[40] Not knowing what might have happened is the only proper attitude, for the devil might indeed take anyone who could think of a way for two women to bring matters to a conclusion. When, in *Le Roman de Violette* (1883), Violette is with a more mature woman under close voyeuristic supervision, she shows her charming inexperi-ence by being unable to bring her partner to climax, despite the most specific and urgent instructions.[41] In *Deux amies* (1885), Mme. Thiaucourt suffers from no lack of erotic feeling toward Eva Moïnoff, but she is impeded in her half-innocence, and finally defeated by the fact that she cannot see where it might all lead: "elle . . . n'eût pas demandé mieux que d'ouvrir sa porte toute grande, et ce qui la retenait le plus, ce qui la refroidissait, c'était d'ignorer le terme où s'arrêteraient les transports amoureux de Mlle Moïnoff" [she would have been only too happy to open the door wide, but what held her back and made her go cold was that she did not know what conclusion Mlle Moïnoff's amorous passion could lead to].[42] By the nicest of circular ironies, the young heroine of *Le Roman de Violette* reads *Mademoiselle de Maupin*, which has been left for her seductive edification by the narrator-hero. She does not understand what is going on in the "ambiguous scenes" between the two women in Gautier's novel, but her curiosity is aroused.[43] The communication of knowledge seems here to follow a delicate chain of half-innocent intuitions, as Lesbos is characterized thematically by its very imprecision.

Joséphin Péladan takes up this point in *La Gynandre* (1891), raising the tone and the moral stakes. His self-appointed prophetic hero, Tammuz, embarks on a crusade against the kind of acclaim that we saw given to Lesbos in Maupassant's "La Femme de Paul." Tammuz deplores the fact that people speak of Lesbos with such familiarity, and denounces the very thematic extension that spreads its fame from Baudelaire's poems to the popular press and into *demi-mondain* conversation.[44] Having identified the theme as a literary one, "cette aberration . . . qui a ses livres et ses auteurs" [this aberration that has its books and authors], he sets out to nullify its prestige. Taking for himself the role of "inquisitor against sexual heresy," he visits a series of supposedly lesbian places in order to undo their very topicality. His vocation requires that he follow the thematic in order to hunt it down, and it is entirely unsurprising that he should eventually find himself on a boat captained by a woman, that the boat should be named "Sapho," and that it should be referred to by journalists as a "floating Lesbos" (250). Strenuous close investigation by Tammuz compels the captain, Countess Limerick, to confess that there is really no substance to the rumors surrounding her sexual activity, despite the fact that she has been complicitous in the naming-and-recognition. The prophet is finally able then, by a simple enunciative paradox, to apostrophize Lesbos, that "cauchemar des décadentes" [nightmare of decadent women], in order to deny its existence: "Lesbos, tu n'existas jamais!" [Lesbos, you never existed!] (269). This denial is, like any other, a form of recognition, for it affirms the deep moral seriousness of these apparently trivial activities. While in one sense they cannot be found, in another they are ubiquitous, and dangerously so. Far from being inconclusive, we are now told, they can in fact prove fatal. When asked if he denies Lesbos, Tammuz reformulates the paradox by saying that he denies it as love but not as a vice. Women can in fact be so consumed by "cet abominable feu" [that abominable fire] that they die of it (25, 42).

The notion that nothing of erotic consequence can actually take place between women, and that uncertainty and fumbling are endearing feminine qualities is thus called into question in the most dramatically moralizing way. Instead of being a transitional practice between girlhood innocence and adult knowledge, or even a frenzied aberration found in a unique class of women, Lesbos now tends to appear as the standard, if not the ultimate form of feminine debauchery, surrounded and propagated by literary liars. The tendency to speak condescendingly of such things now comes to be seen as a disquieting symptom of moral and sexual blindness. The nuns in *Les Fausses Vierges* (1902) whose duty it is to provide moral guidance to the girls in their convent school fall into exactly this trap. When they happen upon two of their charges locked in an embrace, they take a lenient view of things, noting that this is a lesser evil than heterosexual contact: "elles ne ressentaient point l'indignation qu'elles auraient éprouvée si elles avaient appris une des jeunes filles au bras d'un amant; elles estimaient que le cas présent blessait moins la chasteté" [they did not feel the indignation they would have felt had they found that one of the girls was in the arms of a male lover. They considered that the case at hand was less offensive to chastity].[45] Showing how mistaken it is to think of lesbian attraction in this way, putting forward the indulgent view in order to demonstrate its error, is one of the sustaining preoccupations of prurient fin-de-siècle narrative. In *Deux amies* (1885), Stanislas discovers his wife Jeanne's relations with Eva but makes the unconscionable mistake of tolerating them: "L'imbécile se réjouissait de sa découverte. . . . Les conséquences de ces infidélités ne l'épouvantaient pas. . . . Le mal n'avait aucune gravité." [The imbecile was delighted at his discovery. The consequences of these infidelities did not horrify him. The wrong done was not in any way serious].[46] Jeanne herself is also able to continue thinking for a while that what goes on between her and Eva is not really a sin since she has not allowed herself to be touched by a man (100), but it is simply not true here that the "hollowness" of women's same-sex eroticism makes it inconsequential. The narration reminds us that anyone who holds this view is an "imbecile," and the story gives both characters ample opportunity to regret their foolish indulgence. Perhaps we should also understand the vociferous, if somewhat ironic applause in Maupassant's "La Femme de Paul" in these terms. The fact that Paul eventually drowns himself when his mistress falls victim to lesbian seduction suggests that Lesbos is no laughing matter.

In *Impériales Voluptés* (1905), a young man expresses the view that the sexual fancy ("fantaisie") in question "ne tirait guère à conséquence" [is of hardly any consequence], and is covered by "l'indulgence générale qui entourait les mœurs dissolues de l'époque" [the general indulgence that surrounds the dissolute customs of the time].[47] But this opinion situates the character in his naïveté rather than expressing a truth. It bears little weight alongside the anonymous narratorial voice that describes a young woman's experience thus: "C'était une sorte d'ivresse morbide, un étourdissement de volupté lancinante qui tordaient les nerfs de Colette et la laissaient sans défense contre ces lèvres entreprenantes, ces mains hardies et ces câlineries dangereuses, aux acuités de supplice" [It was a kind of morbid euphoria, an acute, dizzying pleasure that twisted Colette's nerves and left her defenseless against the forward lips, the bold hands, and the dangerous caresses, with their agonizing intensity] (82). Initially, Colette herself does not see the danger of this (104), and she still makes so bold when confronted by her fiancé as to use the standard trivializing defense, suggesting that what has gone on in her relationship with Silvérie is unworthy of the scrutiny of men: "En quoi vous regarde mon intimité avec Silvérie? . . . Est-ce l'affaire des hommes ces petits secrets entre femmes? . . . et quelques pauvres distractions si superficielles doivent-elles vous alarmer à ce point? . . ." [What does my intimacy with Silvérie have to do with you? . . . Is it men's business to bother about these little secrets between women? . . . Why should a few little surface distractions get you so upset?] (289). The fiancé, however, unlike his friend quoted above, is alert to the terrible danger of lesbian intimacy and knows how profoundly threatening to him such "superficial" activity can be. So thoroughly does he resist indulgence that he actually murders Silvérie. Almost everything in the novel supports him in this,

demonstrating the earnestness of his purpose, confirming the
soundness of his judgment, and showing the rightness of the execution that follows from it.

In *Amants féminins* (1902), Claudette seeks intimacy with
Paloma while holding out the clear intention of keeping relations at an epidermic level—and therefore, she supposes, a platonic one. She sees erotic activity between women, much as
earlier erotic fiction tended to, as a kind of extended foreplay
without climax: "J'aime Paloma et si j'osais, j'aspirerais à en être
aimé d'un amour platonique, c'est-à-dire avec toutes les subtil-
ités exquises qu'autorise le flirt: toutes les troublantes caresses
de la voix, du regard et des lèvres" [I love Paloma, and if I dared
I would aspire to be loved by her with a platonic love, with all
the exquisite subtlety permitted by flirtation: all that delightful
stroking done with the voice, the eyes, and the lips].[48] But just as
le flirt often has more drastic consequences in fin-de-siècle narrative than one might have expected, so too does this "platonic"
relationship: it ends in the suicide of Claudette (32). Long before
this salutary event, the authorial preface to the novel has
warned a feminine "you" to mistrust the softly appealing surface
of sapphism:

> L'amour saphique, en dépit de son caractère monstrueux, n'est pas
> laid, morale à part, il est attrayant et gracieux, doux et enjôleur, il
> vous prend par des dehors séduisants et enchanteurs, mais quand
> il vous tient, vous n'êtes qu'une misérable esclave de ses fan-
> taisies, qu'il fait mouvoir au gré de son caprice, comme la mer
> grondante balance une épave sur ses vagues tourmentées.

> [Sapphic love, despite its monstrous nature, is not ugly, except
> from a moral point of view. It is attractive and graceful, soft and
> engaging. It draws you in by its seductive, enchanting appearance,
> but when it has you in its grip, you are only a miserable slave to
> its fancy, moved about according to its whim, as the stormy sea
> tosses a piece of wreckage in its heaving waves.] (viii)

Sapphism, we are warned, is much more than charming play. It
is a dark leviathan threatening to drive its victims relentlessly
by the power of the undercurrent it generates, and likely to
swallow them up in its unforgiving depths.

A quite complete set of these thematic elements, articulated in
narrative succession, can be found in *Méphistophela* (1890). The

authoritative narrator goes so far as to concede that there may be inconsequential forms of erotic behavior between women, involving forlorn prostitutes, carefree women of society, or unabashed sexual omnivores, but Sophor d'Hermelinge is beyond any of these categories.[49] Women who have sexual dealings with her are "déconcertées, même les plus perverses, par quelque chose de terriblement insolite, à quoi elles n'avaient jamais songé. S'amuser, bien; pourquoi pas? où est le mal? au contraire, c'est très innocent, c'est comme à la pension. Mais Sophor était redoutable" [disconcerted, even the most perverse ones, by something terribly strange that they had never dreamed of. To have fun was fine. Why not? Where was the harm in that? It was all very innocent, just like at boarding-school. But Sophor was redoubtable] (344). It might seem like fun for a while to revert to boarding-school erotic play, but Sophor, through powerful contact with her partners, banishes all frivolity. She seems to embody, quite literally, the ultimate seriousness of Lesbos, driving on toward narrative consequences of the most terrible kind. Before marriage to her, Jean makes the standard mistake of underestimating the drastic nature of her passion, seeing only, in any hypothetical relations between women, the organic lack of maleness and the consequent impossibility of action: "Voyons, voyons, disait le baron Jean, ce n'est pas possible que des filles fassent l'amour avec des filles. Et d'abord, pour faire l'amour entre elles, comment s'y prendraient-elles? oui, comment, je vous le demande? Sacrebleu! il leur manque quelque chose!" ["Really," said Baron Jean, "it is not possible for girls to make love with other girls. Firstly, how would they go about making love between themselves? How, I ask you? Damn it! There is something they need that they do not have!"] (145). But the very confidence of this trivialization is a symptom of blindness, and Jean has his eyes cruelly opened on his wedding night when he finds Sophie/Sophor in the bedroom of his sister Emmeline: "Eh bien! il s'était trompé, cette passion-là, cette pente de la femme à la femme, cela existe, oui. Il avait vu la bouche de Sophie sur le sein d'Emmeline!" [Well! He had been mistaken. That passion, the inclination of one woman for another, did exist, after all. He had seen Sophie's mouth in contact with Emmeline's breast!] (145). Yet it is not simply the case that Jean the pure-hearted, unrefined military man fails to see what any sophisticated Parisian would have recognized at a hundred meters. There are shades of

innocence, or at least ignorance, in the perception of all who surround Sophie, and indeed in the initial, uncertain steps that set
her on the path to damnation. With Emmeline, having run away
from husband and family to an island on the Seine, she finds
that she does not know how to bring her young companion to the
point of satisfaction: "ni les baisers, ni les morsures, ni les souffles sur les duvets du bras et du cou, ne réussissaient à faire
vibrer, jusqu'à la délicieuse rupture, la corde, pourtant tendue à
rompre, du désir" [Nothing, not desires, or biting, or breathing on
the down of arms and neck, succeeded in playing the tautly
drawn string of desire and making it vibrate to breaking point]
(185). Her dark fear is that only men are equipped to give "les
définitives caresses" (185). Emmeline thus becomes the victim of
incompleteness, experiencing the full Baudelairian (non-)pro-
gram, the unslaked thirst of an infernal Lesbos: "la vierge si in-
génue naguère et si paisible . . . , séduite, damnée, était devenue
l'avide créancière de l'enfer" [the ingenuous virgin who shortly
before had been so tranquil had now been seduced and damned.
She had become an avid creditor of hell] (186). This state of frustration, we are told quite clearly, is not the necessary outcome of
any attempt by two women to reach the height of pleasure: it results from technical ignorance on the part of the young Sophie.
Emmeline goes back to her family (192) but Sophie now finds
herself, more or less by chance, with a group of women who have
been staying in a house on the same island, and who no doubt go
boating together on the Seine. She realizes, despite her ambivalent reaction to this group, that they have the *savoir faire*, the
ars erotica that she needs to achieve her ends: "Et à présent,
parmi les dégoûts et les hontes et les colères, se glissait en
Sophie, et s'y installait, et s'y développait, une curiosité ardente,
une envie de toute leur science, si voisine . . ." [And now, among
the disgust, the shame, and the anger, there arose in Sophie, establishing itself and growing steadily, an ardent curiosity, a
desire for all their knowledge, which lay so close to hand] (214).
As this science is revealed to her by an experienced inhabitant of
Lesbos, Sophie is renamed Sophor. She is now fully equipped to
exercise the most fearful erotic power over other women, and
will go on to become "la violente et la savante, la donneuse effrénée d'incomparables joies" [the violent and knowledgeable
one, the wild giver of incomparable pleasures] (347). It seems
that she has acquired, in dealings with other women, a capacity

to give and take pleasure that is incomparably greater than the (masculine) norm.

There are two rather different ways for lesbianism to come to an end in male-focused narrative. The first of these is a kind of dialectical consequence of the Messalina theme. It is fully realized in *Gamiani*, for example, where the heroine is provoked to the most drastic action by the very fact that she cannot attain satisfaction in any other way. At the beginning of the second "night of excess," Gamiani promises her lover Fanny that they will attain the "moment suprême où toutes les deux nous lutterons ensemble pour mourir à la fois!" [the supreme moment in which we will struggle together to die at the same time!].[50] The expression "lutter pour mourir" is ambiguous, doubly so in fact, in a way that initially escapes Fanny and the ever-present voyeur-narrator, Alcide. It could mean "struggle in order to die" or "wrestle, then die." Is it a promise of denouement or simply of pleasurable effort? And how ought they to understand the word *mourir*? Given that both have already witnessed Gamiani thrashing about in repeated, unsuccessful attempts to reach satisfaction, they appear to take the reference to death and to the *moment suprême* as standard hyperbolic metaphors for climax. But standard climax is not achievable by Gamiani: that is the definition of her tribadism. She finds herself compelled then, as the story itself is compelled, to give up on figurative death and plunge into its literal form. Gamiani achieves conclusive power with the desperately artificial measure of a "poison ardent" (138), which she urges on Fanny, then swallows herself. Only in this way can she achieve her desired end and that of her lover, "l'agonie d'une femme mêlée à ma propre agonie" [the death agony of a woman mingled with my own] (139). She finds her own dramatic way to say "assez" at the end of the novel, in cries of pleasure and pain: "Je meurs dans la rage du plaisir, dans la rage de la douleur! . . . je n'en puis plus! . . . heu! . . ." [I am dying in a rage of pleasure, in a rage of suffering! . . . I cannot take any more! . . . Hah! . . .] (139). This is how the erotically greater is born out of the lesser, and frenzied excess out of organic inadequacy.

The late nineteenth century finds other ways for tribadic stories to end that amount almost to a total inversion of Gamiani's problematic story.[51] The myth of impossible climax between women, while continuing to be exploited in some pornographic

stories, is now most often revealed to be dangerous in its consequences since it leads tutelary nuns, fiancés, and husbands to
underestimate the power of lesbian seduction. One finds regularly enough in these later stories that women's shared pleasure
is accompanied by all the conventional marks of erotic climax. In
Amants féminins, for example, Rose and Paloma finally go to bed
together when the novel has run seven-eighths of its course, and
that event is marked elliptically by a line of dots.[52] This culminating moment is attended by quantities of moral agony but not
by any technical difficulty. In fact, by its position in the novel following a long period of uncertainty and delay, the scene is necessarily associated with an advanced form of pleasure. The same
revision and revaluing of inconclusive tribadism allows Jeanne,
the heroine of *Deux amies*, to speak of her companion Eva as "la
seule créature du monde qui lui eût encore procuré de complètes
jouissances" [the only person in the world who had as yet
brought her complete pleasures].[53] Such women as these are not
fumbling innocents. They have become so adroit that they provoke widespread fear, in male-focused stories, of lesbian technique and its diabolical efficiency.

The foregrounding of lesbian technique—or rather, its inescapable background presence—is characteristic of fin-de-siècle
narrative. Before this time, erotic literature tended to show
women restricted in their sexual practices by the difficulty of
proper coupling. Organic inadequacy could be palliated by the
use of dildoes or by the involvement of a tribade with a prominent clitoris, but such expedients were always identified as
such: mere subtitutes for the presence of a male. Late in the century, however, the anatomical difficulty no longer seems to arise.
Sophor d'Hermelinge, in *Méphistophela*, suffers initially, as we
saw, from a lack of erotic skill but later perfects her art in the
company of experienced lesbians. From that time onward, she is
able to wield great seductive power over women.

Silvérie, the lesbian seductress in *Impériales Voluptés* (1905),
shows how those gentle surface things that men often call trivial have their own "poetic" force: "ce qu'il me faut, ce sont ces
mots énamourés qui nous chatouillent délicieusement l'oreille,
ces doux serrements de main, dans l'ombre, qui font frissonner
toute notre chair, ces caresses superficielles des lèvres et des
doigts qui nous énervent jusqu'à l'âme d'un désir exacerbé"
[what I need are those enamoured words that tickle our ear in

such a delightful way, those gentle squeezes of the hand in the shadows that make our whole flesh quiver, those surface caresses of lips and fingers that fill our very soul with exacerbated desire].[54] When Silvérie seduces Colette, she does so precisely by passing on "toute sa science" [all her knowledge] (141). This teaching is itself a bodily process of corruption, working all the way through from surface contact to a point where the pupil-victim is "corrompue jusqu'à la moelle des os" [corrupted to the marrow] (142). In *Deux amies* (1885), we find the same transformation of surface contact into deep emotion, as the caress of a woman is seen to offer more, not less, than that of a man: "ces baisers qui lui avaient révélé comme un monde nouveau, qui aussi emportés, aussi brûlants qu'une caresse d'homme se doublaient de la sensibilité pénétrante, de la douceur extrême, de la science des sensations qu'ont des lèvres de femme" [Those kisses had revealed a new world to her. While as impetuous and ardent as a man's caress, they also had the penetrating sensitivity, the extreme softness, the sensual knowledge of a woman's lips].[55] Even the all-knowing Christian, in *Le Roman de Violette*, is forced to recognize the skill of Odette in her practice of cunnilingus with Violette: "cette caresse est en général le triomphe de la femme qui se fait la rivale de l'homme" [this caress is generally a triumph for women who seek to rival men].[56] The continual danger, even as men still take their pleasure in observing what goes on between women, is that the practices involved might carry sexual technique beyond the male's capacity for sensitive touch and carry lesbian pleasure beyond his descriptive reach.

By a remarkable shift, Lesbos can now appear redoubtable and damnable not for its unbearable futility but for its direct capacity to bring about terrible events. Sophor d'Hermelinge is heroically monstrous, and demonstrates her qualities by making purposeful narrative out of what might otherwise have been *divertissements* in the midst of a generally licentious society: "Faire de toute aventure un événement magnifique ou sinistre par le seul fait qu'ils y participèrent, c'est le privilège des héros et des monstres" [Making every adventure into a magnificent or sinister event by the simple fact of taking part in it is the privilege of heroes and monsters].[57] The love of women for women often leads to death, we are now told, not because it goes absolutely nowhere and generates suicidal frustration but by its own full flowering, its own logical development. Instead of being the narrative malady represented by tribadism in *Gamiani*, requiring a drastic, even deadly intervention in order to be resolved, Lesbos comes to be depicted as a sickness unto death with its own pathetically guaranteed long-term outcome. Hélène, in *L'Affolante Illusion* (1906), shows familiarity with erotico-medical narratives of this kind when, having fallen in love with another woman, she utters her own sadly confident prognosis: "Ah! je suis trop sûre du dénouement de mon utopique passion: un asile d'aliénés ou la . . . tombe! . . ." [Ah! I am only too sure of the denouement of my utopian passion: a madhouse or the . . . grave!].[58] In *Impériales Voluptés*, Colette's soldier fiancé, who has been absent, can hardly hope to save her from the process begun at the hands of Silvérie: "La petite n'avait que trop bien profité des leçons et le pauvre commandant aurait fort à faire, à son retour, pour arracher sa fiancée à cette tombe nauséabonde où elle s'enlisait de plus en plus, la sauver de l'abîme redoutable où, de jour en jour, elle dégringolait plus profondément" [The young thing had learnt her lessons only too well, and the poor captain would have to struggle, when he came back, to drag his fiancée out of the sickening grave into which she was sinking more and more, and to save her from the redoubtable abyss into which she was slipping further every day].[59]

Amants féminins allows the full development of these narrative possibilities by telling two stories in one. The initial statement of the theme, occupying about one quarter of the novel, involves the unrequited and unavowed love of Claudette for the beautiful Paloma. Claudette, who is certainly not the kind of person who might have read *Gamiani*, also comes to take poison to put an end to her love, but she does so with a rather different substance and a different quality of pleasure. Rather then thrashing about and being consumed by intestinal fire, she achieves a kind of ecstasy: "Une passion inexprimable restait figée sur le visage comme un mystère, un rayonnement d'amour jaillissait de sa bouche; elle semblait sommeiller dans une extase" [an ineffable passion remained set on her face like a mystery, a radiating force of love streaming from her mouth. She seemed to be in an ecstatic sleep].[60] This undecaying *jouissance*, this now-eternal delight is just what she had desired and predicted for herself: "je mourrai d'extase de voir possible l'union immatérielle de mon inexpugnable amour" [I will die in ecstasy having seen that it is possible to realize the immaterial union of my impregnable love] (60). Note that union is possible and in some sense achieved, if only in extremis, because the obstacle she faces is not really the same as in *Gamiani*. Claudette has indeed come to be, as Paloma later observes, "morte de ne pouvoir la posséder" [dead from being unable to possess her] (124), but the "impossibility" is moral rather than sexually technical. As Claudette remarks in her diary, "seule l'horreur du vice m'a tuée . . ." [only a horror of vice has killed me] (24). It is as if the Messalina theme, still firmly grafted to Lesbos, were now being rewritten in moralizing terms with important consequences for narrative, including a guarantee of denouement. It is dramatically ironic that Claudette's confessional diary, which Paloma comes to read after her friend's death, should have such a powerful seductive effect on the woman Claudette refused to seduce. Paloma is won over to the love of other women not by Claudette's (in)action but by the belated sharing of a dream of desire: "ton rêve m'a convertie" [your dream has converted me], she says (66).

It happens at about this time in the story that Paloma is deserted by her male lover Raymond, who marries a young woman called Rose. Armed with her beauty and with the knowledge of her seductiveness to women, Paloma half-resolves, in a semi-innocent way, to use her power on Rose, and the story of this seduction occupies the rest of the novel. Rose is so thoroughly won over that she comes to suffer terribly from an as-yet-undeclared desire for her new companion. In search of support and advice, she turns to the only person she knows who has expert knowledge on the question: an old acquaintance who attended the same boarding school and was mocked by Rose and others for her sapphic attraction to certain fellow pupils. To this person, Marthe, Rose confesses her terrible secret and receives advice in return. The advice she requires is manifestly not about erotic positions but about how to live with her passion, if at all. Rose's present expectation is vague but remarkably like that of her predecessor, Claudette: "Je ne sais pas . . . me laisser mourir de l'aimer . . ." [I am not prepared to . . . fade and die out of love for her] (174). Marthe begins by replying, in what looks to modern readers like an encouraging note of sanity, that love is not fatal, although she quickly admits that sapphism is indeed the most dangerous form of it, precisely because it gives rise to the most intense pleasure: "Folle, on ne meurt pas d'amour, même d'amour saphique, je t'accorde cependant qu'il est plus terrible que l'autre, qu'il pousse aux pires folies, parce qu'il procure les pires ivresses" [You foolish woman, people do not die of love, even sapphic love. I admit, however, that it is more to be feared than the other, that it drives people to the wildest extremities, and that it leads to the worst kinds of intoxication] (173–74). We can observe that the seasoned sapphist, or lesbian—by now, it appears to be the same thing—is able to make a strong asser- tion about the quality of her erotic experience while also making a terrible concession to Rose's fears and reinforcing the narra- tive prediction set up by Claudette's suicide. Marthe goes so far as to say to Rose that, if her love for Paloma should prove unre- quited, the best course of action would be to kill herself without delay. Otherwise, the suffering will go on without end: "Quand une femme en prend une autre, c'est pour toujours; on échappe à un homme, pas à un femme. Si celle que tu aimes est insensible, tu agiras sagement en te tuant tout de suite pour évader ce qui t'attend" [When one woman takes hold of another, it is for ever. You can get away from a man, but not from a woman. If the one you love is unresponsive, the best thing for you to do is to kill yourself immediately so as to escape what awaits you] (174–75). It happens that Rose's passion is not unrequited, but Rose does not yet know this, and finds herself standing between a kind of prophylactic suicide on the one hand, and the terrible ruin of love with Paloma on the other. In any case, even as she seems to escape the dilemma and avoid Claudette's drastic solution, she still comes to ruin and to death. "Elle me fait mourir" [I die in her arms], she says of Paloma (226), and this becomes true in every sense. Not just the *petite mort* of erotic climax, but the *grande mort*, the terrible conclusion of madness and death: "l'en- gloutissement, la promiscuité effroyable. . . . Enfin la débâcle de l'amour! . . . la mort de la fécondité! . . . la fin de tout! . . ." [being swallowed up in dreadful promiscuity. In the long run, the deba- cle of love! . . . The death of fertility! . . . The end of everything!] (258–59). Had Rose taken a male lover or two, the story might well have gone on indefinitely, but Lesbos has all the conclusive- ness of a moral and psychological disaster.

According to a diagnosis abroad in fin-de-siècle narrative, there is something inherently malignant in the very nature, the very style of lesbian contact. It provokes fatigue, dwells in lassitude, and works out its destiny in anemic decadence. Whereas tiredness is simply mentioned, or hoped for in stories involving males, as an aftermath of climax, it is said to be continually produced at the heart of a Messalinic Lesbos, achieved as a kind of debilitating (non-)purpose that makes its faithful "deliberately tired" (*lasses exprès*).[61] Here is a description, from the early-twentieth-century *Toute la lyre!*, of a young woman's pleasure in the company of another of her sex. We see that *langueur*, so often the clearest visible symptom of desire and pleasure in eighteenth-century fiction, now appears to have profound consequences, precisely by avoiding the natural directness of males: "Colombe roucoulante, amoureuse languissante, elle ressentait à cette énervante volupté sans les à-heurts ni les brutalités mâles une infinie lassitude qui, lui semblait-il, la muait en eau et la laissait sans résistance" [Like a cooing dove, like a langorous suitor, this enduring stimulation [*énervement*] of voluptuousness, free from the wrenching brutality of males, aroused in her an infinite lassitude that seemed to melt her and leave her unable to resist].[62] *Enervement*, a favored expression of the period signifying both loss of energy and fraying of the nerves, is attached here to the very workings of pleasure as a languid experience of the mundanely infinite. The feminine body, the nerves, and the will are not embraced and penetrated as they ought to be according to the standard heterosexual program but absorbed into figurative dissolution. Jeanne, in *Deux amies*, remains in the convent school after her friend Eva's departure, experiencing *énervement* as an effect of lingering, and a lingering effect. This is intimate decay: "La séparation, l'isolement l'asservissaient davantage à l'influence morbide et énervante de Mlle. Moïnoff, décuplaient ses sens, pourrissaient son imagination et son cœur. Le vice l'envahissait, s'infiltrait dans son organisme anémié" [Separation and isolation brought her more directly under the morbid, energy-sapping influence of Mlle. Moïnoff. It increased her sensuality tenfold, and corrupted her heart and imagination. Vice invaded her, infiltrating her anemic organism].[63] Similarly, in *Impériales Voluptés*, the sustained practice of erotic fatigue is said to produce in the women described "l'énervement de leurs sensualités morbides" [the fatiguing stimulation of their morbid sensualities].[64] This can be talked about in moral terms as decadence or morbidity, but it is just as often characterized in medical language as neurosis or hysteria.

What is implied is that the very practice of an exclusively feminine eroticism leads naturally, at the end of a woman's active life, at the end of a century, at the end of a novel, to neurotic decadence that folds back into decadent neurosis. Lesbian relations are seen as both the cause and the symptom of this secular feminine condition as women are worn out, chronically *lassatae* by "tout cet amour à fleur de peau, toute cette luxure, toute cette névrose" [all this skin deep love, this lewdness, this neurosis] (*Imperiales Voluptés* 161).

Henri Drouin provides a sententious account of this putative syndrome in his essay, *Femmes damnées* (1928): "L'irritation sexuelle constante, jamais suivie de cette détente qu'apporte avec elle la satisfaction complète, prédispose ces femmes à toutes les névroses" [The constant sexual stimulus, which is never followed by the release that occurs with complete satisfaction, predisposes these women to every neurosis].[65] The self-confirming truth of this claim, the fundamental androcentric verity that lesbian relations lead to a necessary end by their own morbid dynamic, had already been well established and implacably exploited in erotic fiction. Jeanne in *Deux amies* just fades away, consumed by a figurative poison, by a libidinal malady that eats at her will: "Elle s'en allait peu à peu, minée par une maladie nerveuse, sentant elle-même les progrès de son mal, pareils aux ravages d'un poison lent et incapable cependant de faire acte de volonté, de repousser l'amie qui la tuait, qui l'idiotisait" [She was going down gradually, consumed by a nervous disease, feeling in herself the advance of her illness, like the ravages of a slow poison. Yet she was incapable of an act of will, unable to reject the woman friend who was slowly killing her and turning her into an idiot].[66] The steady development of her erotic illness guarantees the eventual outcome of the story, while its creeping slowness occupies the space of narrative delay. In *Amants féminins*, we find a passing reference to the veritable army of women afflicted by the illness of Lesbos—"le bataillon des Saphos (pauvres malades affolées par la névrose)" [the battalion of Sapphos, poor sick women driven mad by neurosis] (123)—but the focus of attention is the inner torment of Rose, which is not the frenzy of Gamiani but a properly identified syndrome, grimly (and usefully) predictable in its final outcome: "Dévorée par la névrose, elle passa une nuit terrible; devenue une sensitive anormale, elle se laissa dominer par des excitations plus imaginaires que réelles" [Eaten away by neurosis, she spent a dreadful night. She had become abnormally sensitive, and allowed herself to be carried away with stimulating experiences that were more imaginary than real] (163). Rose is soon well on the way to hysteria (166), promised to a form of destruction from within that obviates the need for any deliberate ingestion of toxins.

It could be said, perhaps, that the heroine of *Méphistophela* is the noble exception to this rule because of the strength and consistency of her ethical commitment to evil, but Sophor is also said to carry in her body a pathological inclination to behave as she does. The concluding paragraph of the novel offers two competing diagnoses of her condition (or her career) and refuses to choose between them: "symptôme d'un mal héréditaire, ou bien rire effrayant de Méphistophela" [the symptom of a hereditary illness, or the dreadful laugh of Mephistophela].[67] There is a rudimentary pun here on the word *mal*: it is not clear whether Sophor's sexual orientation is to be read as *un mal*, now sadly beyond treatment because of its hereditary antecedents and circumstantial aggravation, or as *le mal*, the very incarnation of wickedness. Perhaps that is what constitutes her irredeemable damnation, to be forever between and yet beyond the two: "Elle a dépassé l'hypothèse des solitudes et des hystéries. Elle est véritablement la parfaite damnée!" [She has gone beyond the hypothesis of solitude and hysteria. She really is the perfect damned woman!] (18).

The tellability of lesbian sexuality, its use value for narrative, was transformed in the course of the nineteenth century as the theme of Lesbos was focused and singularized. It had long been thought that women together were incapable of a conclusive act: tribadism represented, as in *Gamiani*, a commitment to unending sexual activity and by that very fact to "damnation." Yet as medical discourse occupied the space of erotic fiction, it became possible to understand desire and pleasure between women as a degenerative condition, masked to the unpracticed eye by its superficial charms. Where an older view of postural technique tended to support the idea that nothing of consequence could happen between women and that frustration, even in a frenzied form, would be the only outcome, a newer understanding of the psychosexual now linked surface activity—caresses and whispers—to the depths of the soul.

Lesbos could now be brought to its deplorable end in fiction, and the very deploring of that end expanded to take up much of the fictional space. This is how libertine frivolity could be diagnosed and disavowed in the name of high erotic seriousness. It is also how Messalina and Sappho could both be branded hysterical, and their terrible challenge to men put in its place: by the cooperative efforts of ethical and medical discourses, and by contrastive reference to the standard program of "natural" erotic narrative.

10
Finishing

THERE IS A PLACE FOR SEXUAL RELATIONS BETWEEN WOMEN IN MOST erotic fiction. That place is a boudoir or an alcove, closely scrutinized by the gaze of a male voyeur. Women are allowed, nay required, to have contact with each other during certain prescribed phases of the story, but any immediate erotic purpose they may have is subject to the discipline of broader androcentric interests. Most often, "lesbian" scenes do not just constitute diverting interludes or even thematic flourishes: they play their part in advancing the central cause. This happens typically, as I tried to show throughout *Geometry in the Boudoir*, in fictions of sexual pedagogy. A girl on the threshold of womanhood receives formal instruction in the art of pleasure, usually from a woman a few years older.[1] This prepares her for marriage, for a career as a whore, or for some ingenious mixture of the two. Nancy Huston describes this scenario, quite accurately, as one of the defining traits of classical pornography: "L'homosexualité féminine est un élément omniprésent dans la littérature érotique, à l'exception (significative) des romans à l'eau de rose. Juliette, Fanny Hill et bien d'autres célèbres courtisanes romanesques sont d'abord 'débauchées' par des femmes. C'est une étape nécessaire, une sorte de rite d'initiation" [Female homosexuality is an omnipresent element in erotic literature, with the (significant) exception of sentimental novels. Juliette, Fanny Hill, and many other famous courtesans of the novel are first of all debauched by women. It is a necessary stage. A kind of initiatory rite].[2] The most clear-cut, the most nicely discrete examples of this ritual are to be found in classical libertine writing, although sapphic initiation continues to be present in some residual form during the nineteenth century.

342

The thematic waning of feminine initiation does not signify any loss of interest on the part of early nineteenth-century writers in sexual relations between women. Rather, the interest comes to be redefined, with emphasis now being placed, as I suggested in chapter 9, on the supposed inconclusiveness of lesbian activity. Concomitantly, a shift occurs in the role of the male: while continuing to be that of a voyeur, it also becomes powerfully interventionist. In classical representations of feminine intimacy, such as *L'Escole des filles* (1660) or *Vénus dans le cloître* (1682), there were signs of a supervisory male presence, as if to ensure that the pleasurable learning of young women was tightly bound to its ultimate heterosexual purpose and inscribed in the broader narrative. But the nineteenth century radicalizes the male presence, or at least gives it new dramatic force, by having a man burst into the women's room and surprise them in the midst of their pleasure. This is not just a violation of privacy. In fact, it is not particularly that at all, in spite of Jean-Pierre Jacques's reference to the profanation of sapphic mysteries,[3] since the scene on which the man is horning in, so to speak, has no authentic status: it is set up for the man's purpose and its violation is, in this sense, its fulfillment. Claudine Brécourt-Villars puts it into perspective when she talks about the interrupted scene as a commonplace of erotic fiction after Sade's time: "Et l'on échappe rarement à la scène de lesbianisme—devenue un lieu commun depuis Sade—; le mari ou l'amant vient participer joyeusement aux ébats des saphiques créatures avec l'intention évidente de parachever ce qu'il ne manque jamais de considérer comme des prologomènes . . ." [One is hardly ever spared the lesbian scene, which had become a commonplace since Sade. The husband or the lover comes to join rapturously in the frolics of the sapphic creatures, with the obvious intention of finishing off something that he unfailingly thinks of as a prelude].[4] The point of the demonstration, as Brécourt-Villars implies, is that the man incarnates a power to conclude that women do not have. Lesbian activities are put in their place, and in their time, as preliminaries: they are included and overcome in the achievement of climax. Because in classical fiction scenes between women tended to appear as the first units of a graded succession, they did not need to be brought to denouement in this drastic way. What were then serial modes of pleasure became in the nineteenth century excruciatingly incomplete (non-)events calling out for climactic resolution.

The mere fact that someone should break in on two lovers, even if those two lovers are women, does not of itself constitute the dramatic scene as nineteenth-century climactic narrative loved to present it. After all, so much eighteenth-century narrative that we might call picaresque or adventurous produces exciting incidents of that kind. A typical example of such a moment can be found in *Histoire de dom Bougre* (1741), where Verland believes he is about to surprise his lover Monique in the company of her chambermaid, Javotte. Verland is disposed to be morally and physiologically generous, including Javotte in the embrace of his pardon, but finds to his consternation that Javotte is actually a young man in disguise.[5] Disguise here has something in common with breaking in: each is a theatrical device, and a source of surprise, but each contributes only to complicate the plot rather than bring it to an end. They are peripatetic elements, not climactic ones. As long as surprise can rebound thus on all sides, and on the interloper himself, the drama of decisive interruption is not yet in place. In *Lettres galantes et philosophiques de deux nones* (1797), one finds adventurous disorder of the same kind when the Mother Superior, who has made herself an intimate counsellor to the young Christine, suddenly enters the latter's convent cell to find her with a young man, also well known to the Superior. The Mother is simply "petrified" with shock: she falls down, cracks her head, and dies on the spot.[6] Clearly, this woman interrupting a heterosexual encounter, despite her ritual authority and her personal closeness to both partners, does not have the erotic power to bring the scene to her desired conclusion—whatever that might be exactly.

My first example of a successful interruption scene with the elements that were to become standard is found in *La Messaline française* (1793). The narrator-hero, having used a key given to him by his mistress to enter her apartment at midnight, overhears her in amorous exchange with her chambermaid. From a convenient observation point, he admires their beauty and their combined movement, then hears them exclaim: "Ah! je n'y saurais tenir . . . grand Dieu . . . j'expire . . ." [Ah! I cannot wait any longer . . . Good lord . . . I am expiring . . .]. At this, the young man can no longer restrain himself either. He bursts in on them, finding them in a state of "anéantissement" (fatigue and satisfaction), and forces his quite precise attentions on the two of them, despite the duchess's show of disapproval and the maid's initial reluctance.[7] This is not yet the full-blown version of the theme, however, for there is no sign that these women suffered from any inability to conclude without his help. The Messalinic element, present in the novel's title, is not fully identified as a narrative problem nor associated with tribadism. By the time of *Gamiani* (1833), this further element was in place. When Gamiani and Fanny are first together, watched of course by Alcide, their passionate embrace eventually leads Fanny to speak her pleasure in a thoroughly recognizable fashion: "Vous me tuez . . . Ah! je meurs!" [You are killing me . . . Ah! I'm dying!].[8] But Gamiani herself has not yet experienced the death of desire, and continues to thrash about: "Le plaisir la tuait et ne l'achevait pas" [Pleasure was killing her but did not finish her off] (82). As Fanny lies on the bed and Gamiani rolls about the room in frenzy, Alcide finds himself moved, in the most concretely physiological way, to become involved in the scene. He comes out of the closet, where he has been hiding behind some dresses, and throws himself on Fanny, penetrating her in a trice. Obligingly, if a little repetitively, she exclaims: "Ah! mon Dieu! . . . on me tue! . . ." [Ah! My God! . . . I'm being killed! . . .] (83). Gamiani, meanwhile, hurls herself at Alcide as if to tear him away, but their wrestling turns to something else and, with Fanny's participation, Gamiani is finally brought to a sticky end: "En un instant, la comtesse fut vaincue, achevée" [In a trice the countess was vanquished and finished off] (84). This is the woman who defied whole bands of men and wore them out with Messalina-like endurance. Yet it is now a man who has chosen the moment well, bringing decisive relief when the female partner was unable to, enjoying his triumph in the heartland of feminine erotic resistance.

Throughout the nineteenth century, this glorious victory will be repeated with an insistence that belies the very notion of definitive triumph, as pairs of women are continually penetrated, made to cry out, and figuratively killed. In *Les Tableaux vivants* (1870), two sexually deprived widows are manipulated by the anonymous gift of a dildo, an object that might seem to allow for decisive acts between women. The *godemiché* has in fact been sent by two men, who hide to observe its effects. When the women reach the point of admitting that "ces jeux ne valent point la nature" [these games are inferior to nature], the men merge from hiding to bring about the natural end that is required.[9] In the belatedly classical *L'Ecole des biches* (1868), some of the drama is taken out of the scene when Marie and Luisa do reach a kind of climax together, watched by Martin from behind a curtain. Martin has merely arrived ahead of time for the next session, and effectively gets it under way by taking off his clothes and lying down between the two of them. This promises a more complicated scene to follow, rather than a more decisive or even a more intense one.

The standard nineteenth-century narrative is told with some care, and a modicum of psychological detail, in *Le Roman de Violette* (1883). The plot involves a contest between the classic libertine story of initiation, represented as the desire of Odette, and a more thoroughly male-dominated program, pursued and eventually realized by the narrator, Christian. Odette, the beautiful and experienced lesbian, wants intimacy with Violette before Violette has been possessed by a man, but Christian knows of her plans and is always there ahead of her. He is assured of his reign as the first and the last lover of Violette. No woman, he says, could ever be a successful rival for Violette's affections, given that women can never provide full sexual satisfaction: "D'une femme! Pourquoi serais-je jaloux d'une femme! Elle te laissera toujours sur tes désirs et je n'en serai que mieux reçu quand j'arriverai pour la compléter" [A woman! Why would I be jealous of a woman?! She will always leave you unsatisfied, and I will be all the more welcome when I arrive to finish the task].[10] Nonetheless, as his very statement of confidence reveals, Christian is intrigued and excited by the idea of seeing Violette and Odette together, and of being able to finish them off. He allows a meeting to happen in his own apartment, then hides in order to observe the attempted seduction, noting that Violette seems to express curiosity rather than desire (547). Odette is bitterly disappointed that her plans no longer have the same narrative point to them, since the prized virginity has already gone to the man: "Oh! la petite sotte! . . . donner sa virginité à un homme!" [Oh! You stupid girl! Fancy giving your virginity to a man!] (550). The classical initiation cannot now occur: "Moi qui te croyais innocente, qui voulais t'initier peu à peu à tous les mystères de l'amour" [And I thought you were innocent. I wanted to initiate you gradually into all the mysteries of love] (551). Odette's first inclination is to give up any further struggle and go home, resigned to defeat in the face of male power (552).

When she leaves, Christian emerges from his hiding place to speak to Violette, but victory in this skirmish has fallen short of the full triumph he desires (553). What he longs for is a more protracted, more complete scene, and he is eventually able to make it occur with Violette's full complicity. Odette is invited back by Violette, and now appears resigned to occupying the second spot in the batting order, while still deploring the fact that the man has gone before (564). With the androcentric ground rules clearly established, the lesbian scene is now able to occur, and Odette can bring Violette to full pleasure, delighting in the false belief that this encounter is taking place without Christian's knowledge, and without his consent (566). It does not prove possible, however, for Violette to bring Odette to a climax, because of the young woman's lack of technique, or her feigned lack of it (566), and that is where the man comes in. Unlike some of his uncomplicated predecessors in earlier novels, Christian enters the room with great subtlety. He actually "crawls" from his hiding place to a position by the bed (567). This style of entry is made possible by the fact that Odette is now lying across the bed, with her head flung back. Christian is thus able to take Violette's place, quite literally, as he practices his skill in cunnilingus, provoking Odette to exclaim that she has never experienced such delight (568), and bringing her to a "suprême aspiration" in which her soul flows into him (569). When Odette comes to her senses and sees that it is in fact a man who has aroused her to such pleasure, she is furious. Like the gentle refined creature he is, Christian does not confront or taunt her but runs off to hide in the bathroom, leaving Violette to smooth things out (569). The net result of it all is the drawing up of a three-way pact (569–70) that has the effect of accommodating pleasure between women not as an insular Lesbos but as a well-domesticated space of local indulgence within a male-dominated world.

In the standard narrative, we find affirmed the transforming power of the male, as opposed to a feminine tendency to persist in a given erotic state. Women may in fact have been thoroughly charmed, in their youth, by incidental contact with others of their sex, but penetration by the male at the onset of maturity is said to change their lives and establish a clear hierarchy of pleasures. It is the destiny of the Sapphos of erotic narrative to discover the male somewhat belatedly, but then to put away childish things so that they can devote themselves to the admiration of men. In *La Secte des anandrynes* (1789), this is what happens to Mlle. Sapho when she has her first, inadvertent contact with a seductive male. The man is disguised as a woman, and she is deceived by the disguise, but the demonstration of sexual truth is all the more convincing for that. When he makes love to her, she feels herself "dévorée d'un feu plus violent que tout ce que j'avais éprouvé jusqu'alors" [consumed by fire more violent than anything I had experienced until then]. By comparison, her lesbian activity now appears "insipide et fatigante" [insipid and tiresome].[11] The fatigue provoked by insatiable desire can in fact be turned back against the Messalinas of narrative, becoming a sign of inadequacy, as it is in an anecdote told by Gamiani, where a man suddenly appears in the midst of an orgy involving a group of nuns. The man can hardly play the role of lord and master in a group of this size, but his presence provides relief from the "fatiguing simulacrum" of tribadic practices.[12] What is continually pointed out in narratorial comment, avowed by women characters, and demonstrated through the glorious progress of narrative is that the heterosexual is above and beyond the homosexual.

"The lesbian" can hardly exist as a sexual identity in stories that regularly enact the transformation of immature sapphism into its mature heterosexual opposite. Antonia, the servant in *L'Ecole des biches* (1868), may appear to have made a definitive choice: she clings to her mistress Caroline and eschews the company of men. But when, by chance and by artifice, she does experience contact with a vigorous male, she is a changed woman. As Caroline says theatrically to Marie: "Regarde donc, Marie, c'est à ne pas y croire. Vois comme Antonia caresse avec amour le vit d'un homme, comme elle en prend soin! C'est une transformation complète" [Look, Marie. It's unbelievable. Look at how lovingly Antonia is caressing the dick of a man. How attentively she does it! It's a complete transformation].[13] Turning the recalcitrant woman around and making of her an admirer of the phallus has only been a matter of well-taken narrative opportunity. As an extension of this pattern, and an ordering of history, novelistic rewritings of the classical Sappho legend, of which a number appeared toward the end of the century, tend to present the competing versions of her myth, homosexual and heterosexual, as a reassuring narrative succession. In Richepin's *Sapphô* (1884),

Phaon tells us that it was he who tamed the wild element in Sappho, the lioness who hungered for the love of women.[14] In Casanova's *Sapho* (1905), the pupils in the gyneceum are taught the hierarchy of pleasures: they observe that the affection Sappho shows toward them counts for naught alongside her passion for Phaon.[15] And when, surprisingly late in Casanova's novel, lesbian pleasure occurs among the girls in a bout of drunken indulgence, Sappho is to be found, detached in the midst of it all, speaking wistfully of the absent heterosexual other: "Ah! vous ne le connaissez pas! . . . L'autre! . . . Le vrai! . . . L'immense! . . . L'éternel! . . ." [Ah! You don't know him! . . . The other one! . . . The real one! . . . The immense one! . . . The everlasting one! . . .] (228). Romilly's *Sappho* (1931) shows that this thematic is maintained well into the twentieth century. The story allows desire for other women to be a protracted phase in Sappho's development, but a phase no less. Sappho has loved Erinna "aussi complètement qu'il est possible" [as completely as possible],[16] yet now the goddess Aphrodite calls her to order after her pupil's death, summoning her to a proper, adult sexuality, and marking the temporal limit of heterosexual tolerance: "je tolère longtemps les caresses stériles, mais je ne veux pas qu'elles emplissent tout le cœur, je ne veux pas qu'elles durent toujours" [I am very tolerant of sterile caresses, but I do not wish them to fill the heart entirely. I do not wish them to endure forever] (119). When at last Sappho has a real encounter with a man, its effect is to devalue all her previous erotic experience: "Non, non ce qu'elle avait pris alors pour de l'amour, ce n'en avait été que le simulacre et le reflet" [No, no. What she had taken to be love was only its simulacrum and its reflection] (175–76). In Sappho's edifying conversion, recounted over and over, the avowal of heterosexual passion is accompanied by the disavowal of a supposedly immature and inauthentic lesbianism.

Toward the end of the century, however, the pattern of standard narrative is quite unsteady. There is a sense, of course, in which it was always already troubled, half-admitting its uncertainty about male power and heterosexual superiority by the very iteration of conquest. But the fin de siècle actually begins to recount somewhat different stories, varying the original in ways that not only further undermine its already doubtful claims but actually assert contrary propositions. This is most commonly done by marking the narrative place of virile intervention, then leaving that place sadly unfilled. In *La Luxure* (1905), we meet a character who is very much a type of the period: an aging lover without the strength to break into the space of feminine intimacy. This man creeps in, like Christian in *Le Roman de Violette* but with none of his productive stealth or technical precision. Alice, his mistress, is in bed with her maid—for it seems that the last domestic chore of the day is always the same—and the man takes great pains, as he enters, to avoid disturbing them. He stands in silent admiration, filled with a desire to finish off the scene in the time-honored manner: "Il aurait voulu étreindre ces deux femmes, les posséder toutes deux" [He would have liked to embrace the two women and possess both of them]. Yet desire here is only expressed in the conditional: it is too late in life, and no doubt too late in the figurative century, for him to be capable of carrying out that program. When he utters an involuntary groan, the women are only briefly put out of their rhythm. He quickly reassures them, saying "Ne vous dérangez pas" [Don't let me disturb you].[17] A similar nonevent, with the same, quite explicit significance, is to be found in *Voluptés bizarres* (1893). Two women make love under the gaze of two men, who happen to be their official lovers. As we might expect in such a text, the description of the women is lavish and the men's arousal seems assured. They do in fact rush to join in, but they have been aroused so often that they are now worn out by "de trop fréquents sacrifices" [excessively frequent sacrifices]. They simply are not up to the occasion.[18]

Other fin-de-siècle stories maintain something like the standard pattern with those moralistic overtones so characteristic of the *roman passionnel*. In *L'Heure sexuelle* (1898), the narrator-hero breaks into a room to find his two mistresses in bed together. He has not had the leisure, in the moments leading up to this, of eavesdropping or peering through a hole in the wall, so that finding the two in such an intimate position is a most disagreeable surprise and provokes him to indignation. Unlike the Mother Superior of *Lettres galantes et philosophiques de deux nones*, he does not die from shock, but he nonetheless fails to play his role to the full. His role is not to join in—that would be depraved—but it is to be the avenging master, bringing about the "proper" conclusion of prurience. He has no lack of enthusiasm for the cause, but even as he sets about the women and the room in punitive fury, he is moved to regret that this feminine apartment contains no weapon, no implement of male power, "ni fouet, ni cravache, ni canne" [neither whip nor riding crop nor walking stick].[19] While thrashing about destructively, he finds himself unable to carry out the patriarchal ritual of punishment for the lack of a phallic weapon. The heroes of some other novels of the time are better armed when they burst in but no more able to maintain moral and sexual dominance. Rachilde's *Madame Adonis* (1888) tells a story that has much in common with *Mademoiselle de Maupin* but is not at all disposed to end with the same elliptical lightness and elegant irresolution. In Gautier's story of 1835, the young woman disguised as a man finally yielded to the man who had been attracted to her all along, and on the same night—if we can make so bold as to join up the dots—yielded to the woman who had also been longing for her. These (presumed) events occurred in quick succession, and their parallelism was gently ironic. *Madame Adonis* reveals how much has changed in half a century of erotic narrative, since it takes much the same set of characters and drives on toward a drastic convergence of lust and morality, in the cruellest of melodramatic resolutions. At the end of the novel, Louis, who suspects his wife, Louise, of infidelity, climbs a ladder and observes her through a window in company with her lover, whose name is Marcel. Louis bursts in, armed with steely virility, and stabs the lover, only to find that his victim has a woman's breasts. It is in fact his own lover, Marcelle, in disguise. Denouement is achieved in a rather crowded moment of intensity, as Louise's Marcel is revealed to be Louis's Marcelle.[20] The mirroring of proper names adds moral weight of a tragic or pathetic kind but at the same time, by its very symmetry, deprives the husband of his dominant role as the subject of vengeance. He is allowed to finish off the story, but only in the most clumsy and self-destructive fashion.

In *Amants féminins* (1902), the man is even better armed when he attacks his wife and his former mistress. Raymond does not actually break in: he crouches down, gun in hand, behind a piece of furniture in his wife's bedroom. His purpose is to confirm his dark suspicions about Rose and Paloma, and then put an end to it all: "il lui fallait une solution, si terrible fût-elle" [he had to find a solution, no matter how drastic].[21] The "solution" here is the death of Rose, whom he shoots from behind in a kind of passionate revenge, with none of the organic confrontation, not even the close combat, that would have marked the triumph of conventional virility. Raymond shoots Rose, drops his gun, and runs away from Paloma, who picks it up and fires after him (254–55). Tried for killing his wife, he is acquitted on the grounds of *crime passionnel*, but this is not the absolute end of the lesbian scene in the novel. As if to confirm its haunting resistance, and Raymond's inability to bring about its proper conclusion, he takes up with two "inseparable" young women from Montmartre. This, we are told in the novel's last sentence, is a "triste retour des sentiments humains . . ." [pathetic return of human feelings] (265). It is, more than anything, a sad recurrence of gender roles, and of a story that the nineteenth century could not stop telling.

The variations considered so far show how the standard narrative fails, most often for the lack of male energy, to work out its ostensible purpose. But there are also more radical revisions of the story that point to the existence of other desires, and other possible conclusions, even as they maintain a thematic relation to the old program. This is the case, for example, with novels about Lesbos that reconsider incidental, precocious contact between girls, coming to regard it as a sinister practice, likely to breed a perverse autonomy, with its own long-term outcome. The boarding school, in particular, becomes the site of corruptive promiscuity, throwing pubescent girls together and allowing them to develop habits they may never lose.[22] For every novel that deploys the full range of libertine initiatory activities, such as *Lesbia, maîtresse d'école* (1890), there seem to be several that express prurient disquiet as they scrutinize the furtive goings-on in dormitories and schoolyards. *Lesbia, maîtresse d'école* presents the usual scenes passed on from classical erotica, with explicit pedagogy, the prescription and imitation of positions, and the construction of theatrical tableaux.[23] Novels like *Deux amies* and *Méphistophela*, on the other hand, point to the accumulation, in the midst of what may seem like innocent frolicking, of a depraved and ultimately fatal desire. In *Deux amies*, girlhood innocence is quite imperfect, accompanied as it is by sideways glances in the showers, sudden flushes of affection, and the borrowing of forbidden books from the library.[24] "Bad habits" of this sort are allowed to develop because of parental indifference and lax supervision (9). The narrator knows, as do the sensible homophobic readers addressed in the text, that any pleasure experienced by Eva and Jeanne must be a simulacrum:

an "illusion" or a "comédie" (13). Yet now that the ritual of initiation has been displaced by the psychology of habit, something quite fundamental must change in the outcome. Eva is probably beyond redemption, and perhaps not even in need of it—partly because, in this racist text, she is a cultural hybrid, of Slavic origin and Slavic destiny—but Jeanne, we are led to hope, might still be saved from enduring girlish passion by sexual union with a man. Certainly, the doctor prescribes marriage as the only remedy for her internal corruption (162–63). Yet even that normally telling event, as we saw in the previous chapter, does not save Jeanne from destruction—for she marries one of those aging men, worn out with debauchery, who seem to be the only eligible bachelors of the period. It is becoming manifest in such stories that there are forces in Lesbos so powerful that they cannot be simply brought to an end by the arrival of a man. Indeed, *Impériales Voluptés* (1905) provides the simplest of counter-examples to the old rule when it shows how trivial the male presence can become in contact with earnest lesbianism— as it had finally come to be at this time. A man breaks in several times on two women who are deeply engaged with each other but has no other power than that of interfering. He merely holds up the real erotic event, which goes on anyhow between the two women, eventually resulting in their shared climax.[25]

In *Les Fausses Vierges* (1902), there is a repetition, with a striking variation, of the scene in *L'Heure sexuelle* mentioned above: the husband happens upon his wife and her female lover, who are embracing. This is not just a surprise for Henry, but an instant revelation of his wife's erotic psychology: "le secret de sa femme lui fut soudain révélé" [his wife's secret was instantly revealed to him].[26] He is the one transformed by the discovery, turning into a "fou furieux" [raving madman] as he grabs a chair and makes as if to assault them with it. The two women huddle together, but their naked, bestial huddle is also a position from which to pounce: "Elles sautèrent sur le tapis, et ramassées la croupe au mur, comme deux tigresses acculées dans leur tanière, elles attendirent l'attaque de l'homme" [They leaped onto the carpet and, curled up with their rumps toward the wall, like two tigresses driven into their lair, they waited for the man to attack] (274–75). There are no happy endings to be had here—at least, not for the husband. Jane, who is better prepared for defence than most of her sapphic predecessors, picks up a gun and shoots him. He lies on the floor dead as the two women go on "irresistibly" with the passionate lovemaking that had been so rudely interrupted: "Alors, avec une force irrésistible, elle [Suzanne] la saisit [Jane] de nouveau et la renversa, la couvrant de caresses et de baisers frénétiques—sous le regard vitreux de l'homme mort, qui gisait à leurs pieds" [Then, with irresistible strength, Suzanne grabbed Jane once again and forced her onto her back, showering her with caresses and frenzied kisses—beneath the glassy stare of the dead man who lay at their feet] (277). The male voyeur is still present, in a sense, still rigid indeed, but the subjective force of his look has now been frozen, his eyes turned to glass by a force stronger than him.

Méphistophela displays the angry husband in full cry, but his moralizing violence is disjunct from the erotic narrative as such, resulting in neither pleasure for his wife nor any fundamental revision of her sapphic desires. It may be remembered that Jean and Sophie spend a wedding night that, while not strictly speaking a failure of virility, does not transform the woman's sexuality according to the standard pattern. The cruellest irony is that the painful and humiliating business of penetration helps Sophie to understand lesbian desire, making clear what she does not want, and leaving her free to focus on what really matters to her:

Mais, à présent qu'elle avait grandi et qu'un horrible instinct l'avait faite femme, lui avait révélé le désir mâle, épouvantable—si différent de celui qu'elle éprouvait, avec des ressemblances pourtant,—à présent qu'elle concevait, d'en avoir subi l'impudeur, la passion qui précipite les bouches sur les bouches, les flancs contre les flancs, elle se demandait, avec orgueil parfois, avec tant de trouble aussi, s'il n'y avait pas en elle adorant le sommeil d'Emmeline, quelque chose de presque pas pareil, d'analogue cependant, à l'ardeur de l'époux qui s'était rué sur elle; et c'était comme si elle avait entrevu la chimérique possibilité d'être le mari de son amie. Oui, la concupiscence de Jean, par une étrange transposition, et malgré les naturelles décences féminines, éveillait en elle comme une clairvoyance de sa propre convoitise.

[But now that she had grown up, a horrible instinct had turned her into a woman. It had revealed to her male desire, in all its horror, so different from the one she felt—yet with some similarities. Now that she understood, having been the victim of its obscenity, the passion that drives mouths toward other mouths, and bodies toward bodies, she wondered, sometimes proudly, and some-

times with a kind of thrill, whether she herself did not feel something similar. As she looked in rapture on the sleeping Emmeline,
there was in her something that was hardly the same as, yet comparable to, the ardor of the husband who had hurled himself at
her. It was as if she had glimpsed the distant dream of being her
girlfriend's husband. Yes, Jean's concupiscence, by a strange transposition, in spite of feminine decency, had given her an insight into
her own lust.][27]

The first experience of the male is in fact a revelation, then, but
not in a way that suits his purpose. Accordingly, when Jean
breaks in on Sophie later that same night, as she leans tenderly
over his sleeping sister, Emmeline, the violence of his reaction
leads to insult and injury, without bringing about the standard
transformation to heterosexual womanhood. Armed with a dog
whip, that instrument for taming bestiality, he beats Sophie,
shouting imprecations at her, and displaying his "pure" masculinity in wildly inappropriate violence. Yet the dramatic irony,
disturbing for patriarchal morality, is that this precipitate expression of virility helps to confirm his wife in her lifelong choice
of lesbianism. The wedding night is not really the end of her
girlhood, as the old story would have it: it merely serves to vali-
date the sexual choice that was already being made from the
outset.
    Jean is, one might say, the exception who proves the fin-de-
siècle rule. He maintains the qualities of crash-through virility
in a world where such qualities are rare, and can hardly have a
productive role in any case. He helps to demonstrate, in a society
despairing of lost energy and animality, that his kind of old-
fashioned violence can only compound the problem. It seems,
after all, that the most appropriate variation on the lesbian
scene is now the decadent one in which the man sneaks in,
hoping just to gain a better view, since he is no longer up to the
challenge of bodily contact with two women. To the group of impotent voyeurs and glassy-eyed intruders, however, we must
also add those who are endowed with a more complex psychology, and who are tormented by their role as voyeurs, eventually
becoming the victims of their own unfulfilled desire.
    L'Affolante Illusion (1906), for example, presents a sensitive,
aesthetically-minded voyeur in the person of René. One day,
when he is supposed to be far away, he comes quietly through
the bushes, with no thought of malice, pulling up with a start

when he sees his mistress bathing in a stream with their young friend Reine. His first thought is not to ravish them, like some faun of ages past, but to run away and hide his confusion. Yet he feels so disturbed that he may not even be able to flee without drawing attention.[28] The focus of the narration becomes the psychological quality of his anguish and trepidation. What is he to do? He cannot possibly allow himself to be identified by the naked virgin Reine as having seen her, and so scurries back to the house where they are all staying together. So great is his tact, so literal his self-effacement, that he crouches out of sight behind the double bed, not daring to breathe for fear of being discovered (176–77). But when the two women fall into an embrace, we begin to wonder whether the time has not come for him to stand erect in the standard role. He thinks about doing this, in fact, and moves to a position where he can be clearly seen, with a look of irony and disgust on his face. But Hélène flings herself on Reine at this very moment "avec une vivacité brutale" [with brutal vivacity] (178), and the intervention fails because it has gone unnoticed. This fate could not have befallen the heroes of earlier erotic stories, such was the power of their physical presence and the impact of their entry. René is nonplussed, and decides not to go on with confrontation, returning to his hiding place (180).

His reaction is deeply ambivalent, traversed by a desire that owes much to old, now almost archaic stories of violation: "René voudrait fondre sur l'une de ces deux femmes, tentations vivantes, il ne sait laquelle, et l'emporter fougueusement dans un lieu solitaire pour la posséder en un élan de ses sens exacerbés" [René would have liked to pounce on one of the two women, those living temptations—he did not know which one—and carry her off in one move to a solitary place where he would ravish her in a great rush of exacerbated sensuality] (191). It is as if the theme of violation were itself exacerbated by its nonrealization, condemned to fester within the novel and within the mind of this civilized, sensitive man.

One moment of high drama in *L'Affolante Illusion* occurs when René finds inside Hélène's corset a photograph of her true (female) love. This unveils the desire that she has kept fast in her breast and smuggled through their sexual embrace: it stretches beyond any love she may have for René (208). He is now filled with hatred and vengeful scorn—erotico-moral scorn that supposes the inferiority and perversity of lesbian pleasure, although the story suggests this judgment to be misplaced. As if to refocus interest on a more straightforward erotic narrative, René attempts to deflower Reine, but Hélène breaks in on the two of them, stopping his "grossier désir de mâle" [crude male desire] from stealing away the young woman's virginity (215). It is Hélène who finally makes love to Reine, in fact, as René discovers belatedly. When he finds the decisive evidence, he berates Hélène for her depravity, but she does not yield any ground. She counterattacks with what we might call a thematic reading of the standard lesbian scene and its role in male-centered narrative. René, she claims, would have been perfectly capable of bringing his two women together after he had married Reine "avec l'espoir, naturellement, d'être le héros . . . de l'aventure . . ." [in the hope, naturally, of being the hero of the tale] (246). She denies him the hero's role, denouncing his "hypocrisy" and that of his "brothers." Whatever they may say, they are driven by their "sensuality": "je ne crois guère à l'existence d'une voix assez puissante pour hurler plus fort qu'elle et la dominer. . . . A qui la faute si les femmes sont vicieuses, quels sont leurs initiateurs? . . ." [I don't believe there is any voice that can speak louder than it and be heard above it. Whose fault is it if women are full of vice? Who initiates them into it?] (247). It is male desire, she says, that prepares and abets sapphic "vice," in the expectation of interrupting at its own good pleasure.

Even more like victims than René are the heroes of *Le Journal d'un amant* (1902) and Maupassant's "La Femme de Paul" (1881). The lover who keeps the "journal" is visited during sleepless nights by the image of two women, his mistress and another, wrapped in their "enlacements éperdus" [wild entanglement]. Obsessed and defeated by lesbian betrayal of his devotion, he can do no more than weep throughout the night.[29] Paul, in Maupassant's story, is introduced as a man deeply attached to his mistress.[30] When a boatload of women appears, he feels not scorn or irony, but "une fureur profonde, instinctive, désordonnée" [a profound, instinctive, unchecked fury] (297). They ought to have a millstone put around their necks and be drowned, he says in disgust (297). But this is prescient without being strictly accurate, for that will turn out to be his own fate rather than theirs. Shortly afterward, Paul and Madeleine make love (301), but Madeleine is apparently not sated by this event for she is soon speaking to one of those redoubtable lesbians in a way that makes the other woman equivalent to Paul himself: "Madeleine murmura: 'Pauline!' du même ton passionné qu'elle disait: 'Paul!'" [Madeleine murmured, "Pauline!" in the same passionate tone in which she said, "Paul!"] (301). His worst fears are realized when he comes upon the two women making love in the grass. Another man he might somehow have accepted, and fought as a rival, but not this. He is overwhelmed with jealousy and disgust, filled with thoughts of death (306). Paul drowns himself, without a millstone, dying the death of a virtuous woman, of Rousseau's Julie and Bernardin's Virginie. Yet this is not quite the end of the story, for even his suicide is not allowed to be decisive. It all finishes with Madeleine leaving in the company of Pauline, still sobbing with grief, but showing signs that she is beginning to be consoled (308). She is now "la femme de Pauline," and the transformation brought about in the story has been a confirmation of lesbianism, fatal to the man.

As the end of Maupassant's story suggests, and as later stories already mentioned were to show more expansively, Lesbos had now achieved a cohesiveness that allowed it to be more than an early gradation or a charming preliminary. It could hold a place in narrative after, rather than before, heterosexual "climax." Instead of being a disparate set of inconclusive sexual practices involving nonessential parts of the body, it was now becoming an island, entire unto itself. That constituted no simple progress toward enlightenment or tolerance: it was undoubtedly change for the better *and* for the worse, at once restrictive and enabling. Lesbianism had become a terrible vice but in doing so it had won a concession: the man's claim to finish off erotic stories by bringing events to their proper, natural end was no longer tenable in worldly fiction after a century of libidinal resistance on the part of Messalina and Sappho.

To situate Lesbos after what ought to have been the climax-and-denouement is of course to question the finishing power of men, but it is not necessarily to eliminate any tendency to view lesbianism as an unnatural offshoot or perverse erotic derivate of heterosexuality. Most of the powerful and dangerous lesbians in fin-de-siècle stories are said to have become what they are because of failed relations with men. In that sense, men, in their clumsiness, insensitivity or brutality, are now invested with the power to deflect women from the course of their natural heterosexual development. Odette, in *Le Roman de Violette*, swore on the day her brutal husband died that she would forever maintain "une haine éternelle des hommes" [an undying hatred of men], and this marked a lifelong commitment as the ethical dimension of her sexuality.[31] The heroine of *La Fille de Gamiani* (1906) is not so much a hereditary lesbian, despite the novel's title, as a woman who has suffered at the hands of men during her life as a prostitute. She now wants to experience intimacy with "une camarade désabusée du mâle" [a female companion who has had enough of men].[32] Suzanne, in *Voluptés bizarres* (1893), is a fellow sufferer who feels that making love to men is always the same damn thing: "D'ailleurs, je suis quelque peu dégoûtée des hommes. . . . Au bout du compte, c'est toujours la même chose . . ." [Besides, I'm rather sick of men. . . . In the end, it's always the same thing . . .].[33] The outspoken Hélène, in *L'Affolante Illusion*, takes a view well supported by her story and many others of the time when she says that all women have sapphic possibilities that may be triggered by particular events: "Sapho revit en toute femme, il suffit d'une circonstance, d'une occasion, d'une heure complice" [Sappho lives on in every woman. It only requires a circumstance, an opportunity, an hour of complicity].[34] This may sound as if it is a matter of utter contingency, of a chance flowering, but the "circumstance" appears to be always the same, the initial cause quite unvarying: it is the trauma of unhappy heterosexuality. Hélène refers to any hypothetical lesbian partner as "une amante vraie qui a connu la décevance de l'amour masculin" [a true woman lover who has known the disappointment of masculine love] (70).

Amants féminins, despite appearances to the contrary, provides confirmation of this theme. The role of Marthe in the story is to be the experienced lesbian with advice to give, the one who displayed her proclivities at boarding school and was subject to social sanctions for attempting to seduce her fellow pupils. She has gone on with lesbianism all her life, yet care is taken in the text lest we think of her, or anyone else, as a born lesbian, even a freely self-chosen one. We are reminded that there is only one root cause: "L'amour saphique ne peut naître que de l'infidélité de l'homme, qu'elle soit morale ou physique" [Sapphic love can only be born from the infidelity of men, whether moral or physical].[35] Marthe herself had been betrayed by a fiancé at seventeen, and was only a precocious lesbian because she was a precocious victim of men (182). There may, she concedes, be a few women who are "vicieuses d'instinct" [vicious by instinct] or guided only by debauchery and self-interest, but these few can be set aside as being without any "sincérité" of passion (183). That small group is presumably beyond understanding because such women are not motivated (and justified) by moral and psychological trauma. Exceptional cases notwithstanding, the general truth, enunciated with authority from within Lesbos, is that the blame can be sheeted home to men. This has the effect of conserving the male's sexual initiative: "Une chose certaine, c'est que *tant que les hommes tromperont les femmes et ne les comprendront pas, il y aura des lesbiennes*" [One thing is certain: *as long as men cheat on women and do not understand them, there will be lesbians*] (182; original emphasis). Lesbian women are tired, as we know, but not just because of their Messalinic activity: they are always already worn out beforehand, morally and physically exhausted by the deception and violence of men. Claudette, in the same novel, recognizes and loves in Paloma someone who is "lasse de tout, surtout de l'amour des hommes" [tired of everything, and especially of the love of men] (*Amants féminins* 46–47). This is why it is appropriate that Lesbos as fatiguing pleasure and eroticism of fatigue should be so widespread in a time of decadence, when men no longer have the desire, the strength, or the technique to bring women to satisfaction in "properly" shaped erotic stories.

Women can thus be described as turning away from the world of men, quitting one erotic style for another. Claudette, having been deceived and buffeted by men, moves toward another "sphere" in search of a poetic ideal.[36] How can people consider, asks Sophor in *Méphistophela*, that "les fleurissantes lèvres des femmes, et la fraîcheur des seins" [the blossoming lips of women and the freshness of breasts] are dirty? Dirtiness is in fact the most striking quality of "le brutal et bestial hymen" [the brutal, bestial hymen], with its sweating and straining—"ses acharnements qui suent" [its sweaty persistence]—and its ugly denouement—"ses achèvements où le désir s'écœure" [its completions that sicken desire].[37] Not for Sophor the nausea and the animality; not for her the red faces and the sweat. She dreams of a quieter activity, touched by the poetry of gentleness and bathed in the glow of whiteness. This is the stuff of which Liane de Pougy fashions her sapphic idyll: it is the half-ethereal matter of which the beautiful heroine, Annhine de Lys, is made. The whiteness of the lily is inscribed in the heroine's name, as it is embodied in her flesh. This is less the mark of virginal purity awaiting the fatal red stain than of a happy state to be dwelt in forever, a lyrical world from which the cruel abruptness, the wrenching suddenness of male-driven narrative have been eliminated.[38]

Lesbian women in fin-de-siècle fiction are by definition caught up in a world of narrative, but they know that their love outlasts the love of men. That is now almost the definition of Lesbos. The love of men withers and dies, says Paloma to Rose: "L'amour des hommes n'est jamais durable, il est fatalement destiné à mourir! . . ." [The love of men never endures. It is always bound to die!] (Amants féminins 117), whereas that of women for each other endures forever: "il y a des amours immortelles, ma Rosette . . . des amitiés plus fortes que la mort! . . . Là, pas de tromperies, une fidélité exclusive, ardente au sacrifice, douce à l'abnégation et que rien ne rebute jamais . . ." [there are undying loves, Rosette, friendships stronger than death! For them, there is no cheating, only exclusive fidelity that is eager to make sacrifices, resigned in self-denial, and never discouraged by anything] (118). Silvérie, in Impériales Voluptés, has the same certainty, the same confidence that her love will always outlast that of her male rival: "Elle songea seulement qu'il ne fallait rien brusquer; l'amour de Colette pour le soudard tomberait de lui-même, quelque jour; le tendre enlacement qu'elle lui apprendrait l'éloignerait, mieux que toutes les paroles, de la brutale étreinte du mâle ennemi" [She merely thought that she must avoid haste. Colette's love for the drunkard would one day collapse by itself. The tender entwining that she would teach her friend would lead her away, better than any words, from the brutal embrace of the male enemy].[39] Silvérie knows, as a woman of her day, that both forces, the unshakeable tenderness of feminine embrace and the repulsive brutality of men, can be relied on, each in their own (narrative) time, to further the interests of Lesbos.

In sum, the nineteenth century brought about some remarkable changes in the representation of Lesbos, and of its place in a male-centered world. Classical initiation tended, in the first part of the century, to be displaced by the unfinished tribadic scene, conceived as a made-to-order problem for men to solve. Toward the end of the century, however, much erotic fiction reflected a grave loss of confidence in male finishing power and a concomitant sense that sapphism, now a dangerous sexual perversion, threatened to undo the established narrative (and social) order. The centrality of the man's role could then only be maintained in many instances by locating it in the distant past. There had been, there must have been some drastic event that gave meaning to the rest, either as trauma in the woman's youth or as a primitive memory buried in the mind of an advanced but sexually impotent society. Insofar as the story of conclusive male power persisted as a memory, it maintained traces of the old male victory, but the theme itself was tired, and reflexively so. The ancient memory of animal strength and brutal triumph was, in its very oldness, a symptom of decadence and a grudging recognition that female libidinal resistance, at least as men had imagined and represented it, had slowly worn down men's domination and rather outlasted their capacity to tell that domination in decisively finished stories.

Conclusion

THE STORY TOLD HERE WILL PROVOKE NO HEARTY CHEERS, FOR IT IS NOT a triumph of liberation or of nature. Nor should it give rise to a wave of nostalgia for the supposed freedoms of an age now past. My point, put most broadly, is that there was in eighteenth-century France a discursive order of pleasures and desires other than the one that dominates our time. This order lent itself to the representation of pleasures in tableaux, in sets of figures and graded series. From about 1740, this pattern came to be disturbed in fiction, giving way over the next half-century to an understanding of sexual pleasure as an intense, climactic event. The fiction of pleasure in the nineteenth century narrated sex as something recurrently singular, with an ever-renewed routine of foreplay, climax, and denouement.

My historical analysis is indeed a story but not a simple one. It shares nothing with those comforting sagas of recent decades that evoke our progressive sexual liberation. In fact, what is recounted in this book is patently not progress in the etymological sense, for change, in this case, does not move steadily forward. The metaphors I have favored when characterizing change tend to be geological, although my geology is hardly monumental or catastrophic. I do not see a great chasm opening up around 1789 to separate the old discursive regime from the new: my analysis shows rather how thematic drift led to sedimentation and often to subsidence. For example, metaphors of heat that had served for centuries to signify passion were channeled into a substantive dynamics of bodily circulation and brought into contact with the ancient matter of sculpted beauty: cold, white marble, now conceived as an intriguingly feminine resistance to the heat of pleasure. Aphrodisiacs that had previously been used as plea-

363

surable gimmicks took on new importance as the pharmaceutical essence of desire. The stylistic practice of exclamation, present in erotic fiction since the sixteenth century, did not need to be invented or eventfully rediscovered: it merely underwent some elaboration and took on greater thematic density, as the marks of intensity compacted around the poetics of climax. In comparable fashion, metaphors of illness and bodily agitation now accumulated around the notion of "crisis," lending weight and substance to the emerging theme of climactic pleasure as *comble*, *période*, or *paroxysme*.

At times, the subsidence of old thematic structures actually brought about a complete reorientation. Boudoir furniture, which had served as an inscription of bodily attitudes, was put under pressure and used as a sounding board for wild agitation. Libertine gradations, valued in the mid-eighteenth century as the proper style of pleasure, came to be thought mere bagatelles and eventually, for novelists of the fin de siècle, unhealthy deviations from the natural directness of "the act." Messalina, for eighteenth-century libertine literature a rather unspecific historical celebrity, became for the nineteenth the fascinating and disturbing incarnation of a feminine capacity to go on indefinitely asking for more. Tribades, seen in the early nineteenth century as hauntingly unable to reach the conclusion of pleasure, became half a century later the victims of a terrible erotic malady that reached its own deadly conclusion with implacable regularity. These changes all took place quite slowly, but their cumulative effect is striking. There may be no great rift in this history, but there are jagged cracks in the ground of our sexuality.

I said at the outset that my aims were twofold: to contribute substantively to a history of sexuality and to engage in historically based critique of some of the universalist assumptions at work in sexological talk. The first of these aims led to the genealogical work I have just been outlining, and the second has been the stuff of my "conclusions," whether to round off a textual analysis or to close a chapter. The prime target of these various conclusions has been the habit of thinking that makes of climax the founding moment of human sexuality. It is in the theme of climax, as I have shown, that the eroticism of narrative meets the narrative of eroticism. In stories of the kind favored by the nineteenth century, the climax is the point where the possibility of infinite deferral gives way to concrete eventuality. The final event of pleasure is always the payoff: the fulfillment of expectation, the end of delay. Deposited around the notion of sexual climax one finds, so to speak, all the sedimentary prestige of eroticized narrative. The pleasure of our stories is thus caught up, in a narrowly circular way, with the story of our pleasure. This thematic circuit is one of the great compulsions of the nineteenth and twentieth centuries, for it serves to define the very pattern of compulsion. By locating this habit of thinking at a particular point in history, we can understand that climax is not the inescapable truth of human sexuality. We may then perhaps find other circuits to follow and other ways to shape our pleasures.

I have refused throughout this book to apologize for studying pornography. The first reason for my refusal is that I do not want to confuse analysis with apologetics. Certain of the texts studied here, notably many of Sade's, I consider ethically and politically offensive. Many people might hope that such texts will not be more widely disseminated than they currently are, but the fact confronting serious scholars is that these texts are already abroad and surrounded by critical opinion that often owes nothing to the reading of primary texts. Erotica, pornography, and the names of notorious figures such as Sade serve as rallying points for libertarianism. They are slogans in the struggle against repression and censorship. But these emblems of freedom can be happily maintained only by ignoring the routine textual work of oppression that is represented in them. I have declared my suspicion of the very notion of sexual liberation, and my concern that erotic literature not be taken simply as a good thing. Having said that, I must add immediately that my work is directed more systematically against the would-be censors. Critics such as Dworkin and Jeffreys reflect on pornography for only so long as it takes to condemn it utterly, without seeing the many ways in which pornography is torn by inner thematic strife. They fail to perceive the ambivalence that actually inhabits these texts and divides them against themselves. By listening to thematic dissonance, I have been able to show how male-focused writing is compelled to make concessions or admit exceptions for which it must pay dearly in the long run, according to the rules of its own thematic economy. These stories need women to be cold, but with a secret inner warmth ensuring that they will eventually respond to contact with a male. They need lesbians to be inhabited by exotic and intriguing forms of desire that can be revealed in extremis as unsatisfied desire for a man. They want all women to be Messalinas, and yet concede awkwardly that the sexual capacity of a Messalina is beyond that of any male partner. Discerning these internal tensions and half-admissions has been my contribution to gender studies. It has been made possible by refusing to align myself with either libertarians or censors.

Notes

INTRODUCTION

1. Gaëtan Brulotte, *Œuvres de chair: figures du discours érotique* (Quebec: L'Harmattan, Les Presses de l'Université Laval, 1998).

2. Michel Foucault, *Histoire de la sexualité* (Paris: Gallimard, 1976–1984).

3. Michel Foucault, *Dits et Ecrits* (Paris: Gallimard, 1994), 4:539.

4. See Jeffrey Weeks, *Coming Out: Homosexual Politics in Britain, from the Nineteenth Century to the Present* (London: Quartet, 1977); Gayle Rubin, "Thinking Sex: Notes for a Radical Theory of the Politics of Sexuality," in *Pleasure and Danger: Exploring Female Sexuality*, ed. Carole Vance (London: Routledge and Kegan Paul, 1984), 285–86; and Vernon A. Rosario, *The Erotic Imagination: French Histories of Perversity* (New York and Oxford: Oxford University Press, 1997), especially 70–71.

5. See, for example, Foucault, *Dits et Ecrits,* 4:320.

6. Arnold Davidson, "Sex and the Emergence of Sexuality," *Critical Inquiry* 14 (1987): 23. See also Foucault, *Histoire de la sexualité*, 1:204–8.

7. James Grantham Turner, "Introduction," *Sexuality and Gender in Early Modern Europe*, ed. James Grantham Turner (Cambridge: Cambridge University Press, 1993), 7, identifies two kinds of history of sexuality—the one "suspicious," having a "destructive" vision of Eros and a concern with its victims, and the other "recuperative," integrative, focusing on empowerment. I do not wish to deny that there are indeed such tendencies, but throughout this study I shall be working against Grantham's dichotomy. Apropos of lesbianism, for example, I shall attempt to show that oppression and enablement are part of the same discursive history. I reject, as Foucault surely would, the notion that history can be written merely as an exercise in suspicion, with no integrative dimension.

8. Terry Castle, *The Apparitional Lesbian: Female Homosexuality and Modern Culture* (New York: Columbia University Press, 1993), 9.

9. I am not affirming that there is no such thing as desire or that there is no biological dimension to this question. In that sense, my position is not strictly "constructivist," as Carole Vance defines the term. She says in "Anthropology Rediscovers Sexuality: A Theoretical Comment," *Social Sciences and Medicine* 33 (1991): 878: "The most radical form of constructivist theory is willing to entertain the idea that there is no essential, undifferentiated sexual 'impulse,' 'sex drive,' or 'lust,' which resides in the body due to physiological

functioning and sensation. Sexual desire, then, is itself constructed by culture and history from the energies and capacities of the body." I am not seeking here to position my work as "radical" but rather to avoid making strong assumptions of any kind.

10. Peter Cryle, *Geometry in the Boudoir: Configurations of French Erotic Narrative* (Ithaca: Cornell University Press, 1994).

11. This is not of course the same thing as engaging with them in hand-to-hand polemical combat. For a good example of that kind of critique, see Meryl Altman's work on sex manuals, "Everything They Always Wanted You to Know: The Ideology of Popular Sex Literature," in *Pleasure and Danger: Exploring Female Sexuality*, ed. Carole Vance (London: Routledge and Kegan Paul, 1984), 115–30.

12. John C. O'Neal, "Review Essay: Eighteenth-Century Female Protagonists and the Dialectics of Desire," *Eighteenth Century Life* 10 (1986): 93. J. E. Fowler, "Diderot's Family Romance: *Les Bijoux indiscrets* Reappraised," *Romanic Review* 88 (1997): 89–102, undertakes an earnest close reading of *Les Bijoux indiscrets* using psychoanalytical models, without reflecting on the ironic frame provided for such readings by Foucaldian uses of Diderot's "fable."

13. Luce Irigaray, "Un Autre Art de jouir," in *Les Femmes, la pornographie, l'érotisme*, ed. Marie-Françoise Hans and Gilles Lapouge (Paris: Seuil, 1978), 57.

14. Anne-Marie Dardigna, *Les Châteaux d'Eros, ou les infortunes du sexe des femmes* (Paris: Maspéro, 1980), 81.

15. Andrea Dworkin, *Pornography: Men Possessing Women* (London: Women's Press, 1981), 22–23.

16. See Denis Hollier, *La Prise de la Concorde: Essais sur George Bataille* (Paris: Gallimard, 1974), 251–52.

17. For a discussion of this, see Lynn Hunt, "Introduction: Obscenity and the Origins of Modernity, 1500–1800," in *The Invention of Pornography: Obscenity and the Origins of Modernity, 1500–1800*, ed. Lynn Hunt (New York: Zone, 1993), 9–45. She says notably: "Pornography did not constitute a wholly separate and distinct category of written or visual representation before the early nineteenth century." See also her chapter, "Pornography and the French Revolution," in the same volume, 301–339, where she says: "political pornography . . . became one of the arms of a self-consciously vulgar popular politics" (302).

18. J. Pierrot has a rather different emphasis in his view of fin-de-siècle "erotic literature," but he also draws attention to the generic range. See J. Pierrot, *L'Imaginaire décadent: 1880–1900* (Paris: Presses Universitaires de France, 1977), 168.

19. The term is Stanley Fish's, although he uses it in a more narrowly professional sense than I intend here. See Stanley Fish, *Is There a Text in this Class?: The Authority of Interpretive Communities* (Baltimore: Johns Hopkins University Press, 1980).

20. Linda Williams argues that there was a quite widespread change during the 1970s that "ultimately entailed a redefinition of the heterosexual act itself." To the extent that this is true, such disturbance of established truths makes room for the kind of critique in which her work and mine, and others, are engaged. See her *Hard Core: Power, Pleasure, and the "Frenzy of the Visible"* (Berkeley: University of California Press, 1989), 171–72.

21. Bernard Sichère, "Pour en finir avec le 'Sadisme' et sa haine," *Obliques* 12–13 (1977): 70. Josué Harari discusses this judgment in *Scenarios of the Imaginary: Theorizing the French Enlightenment* (Ithaca: Cornell University Press, 1987), 188–89. He makes the point that Sade does not actually produce a theory of desire: "Sadian narrative is not a discourse about desire, but a discourse with desire."

22. See, for a literal example, Marcel Moreau, "Le Devoir de monstruosité," *Obliques* 12–13 (1977): 15.

23. Georges Bataille, *La Littérature et le mal* (Paris: Gallimard/Idées, 1957), 119.

24. Robert Desnos, *De l'érotisme considéré dans ses manifestations écrites et du point de vue de l'esprit moderne* (Paris: Cercle des arts, n.d.), 37.

25. Roger Borderie, "La Question de Sade," *Obliques* 12–13 (1977): 2.

26. Maurice Blanchot, *Lautréamont et Sade* (Paris: Minuit, 1949), 217.

27. On the construction of Sade's figure, see Georges Van Den Abbeele, "Sade, Foucault, and the Scene of Enlightenment Lucidity," *Stanford French Review* 11 (1987): 7–16. Van Den Abbeele observes: "Clearly, there is a marked historicity to the interest in Sade, even as Sade is cast as the representative, if not instigator, of the historical break between the classical and modern periods" (8).

28. Foucault, *Dits et Ecrits,* 4:23.

CHAPTER 1. FURNITURE

1. Jean M. Goulemot, "Du lit et de la fable dans le roman érotique," *Etudes françaises* 32 (1996): 14, gives a long list of equivalents of the bed, but I hesitate to take the bed as the generic term or as the name of the theme.

2. Crébillon *fils, Le Sopha* (Paris: UGE, 1966).

3. *Le Canapé couleur de feu* (Paris: Bibliothèque des Curieux, 1910). Apollinaire attributes this text to Fougeret de Montbron (BN Rés p. Y2 2605).

4. *L'Enfer de la Bibliothèque Nationale* (Paris: Fayard, 1986), 5:261.

5. La Morlière, in *Angola* [1746], *Romans libertins du XVIIIe siècle*, ed. Raymond Trousson (Paris: Robert Laffont, 1993), 415, describes the furniture found in noble residences as having a "voluptuous character" that is "difficult to describe." The mirrors, the paintings, a *duchesse*, some *bergères*, some chaises longues all seem "tacitly to designate the use for which they were intended."

6. Philippe Perrot, *Le Corps féminin: XVIIIe–XIXe siècle* (Paris: Seuil, 1991), 64, notes that engravings of mythical subjects at this time were not concerned with a clearer description of mythological subjects but with sketching "acrobatic performance" and "combinatory capacity." An essay by Jean-Claude Renard and François Zabaleta, *Le Mobilier amoureux ou la volupté de l'accessoire* (Briare: Chimères, 1991), provides some interesting detail and draws a general conclusion about historical change that is consistent with my own. Renard and Zabaleta note the "flagrant devaluing of the pose" in the nineteenth century by comparison with the eighteenth. I consider nonetheless that their essay falls too easily into anachronism in its discussion of classical fur-

niture, since it regards all furniture as being an accessory used to signify feelings rather than something bound up in a circular way with bodily desire and pleasure. The authors reach the point of noting that "the heart" and furniture are so indissolubly linked that it is hard to know which is in the ascendancy (17), but they regularly draw back from the consequences of this perception, supposing most of the time that the heart has primacy. Furniture is thus characterized by them as "the precarity of feeling inscribed in the eternity of style" (19). They do not consider seriously the possibility that style might often be a quasi-prescriptive model for feeling.

7. *La Nouvelle Académie des dames* (Cythère: 1774) (BN Enfer 675), 13–14.

8. Sade, *Histoire de Juliette,* in *Œuvres complètes* (Paris: Pauvert, 1986–87), 9:278.

9. Ibid., 9:115; see also 9:62.

10. Andréa de Nerciat, *Le Diable au corps* (Paris: n.p., 1803) (BN Enfer 436–441), 1:xi.

11. In *Julie, ou j'ai sauvé ma rose* (1807), by Félicité de Choiseul-Meuse, we find a boudoir in which "on the ceiling were represented mythological subjects analogous to this charming place, in which everything seemed to be an invitation to voluptuousness" (*L'Erotisme du XIXe siècle,* ed. Alexandrian [Paris: Lattès, 1993], 146).

12. *Lucette, ou les progrès du libertinage* (London: Jean Nourse, 1765), 3:14.

13. Sade, *Les Cent Vingt Journées de Sodome,* in *Œuvres complètes* (Paris: Pauvert, 1986–87), 1:64.

14. Sade, *Histoire de Juliette,* 9:58.

15. *L'Enfer de la Bibliothèque Nationale,* 2:497.

16. This is argued at length in Cryle, *Geometry in the Boudoir.* See esp. 206–25.

17. See Michel Delon, "Luxe et luxure: réflexions à partir de Sade," *Nottingham French Studies* 37 (1998): 20, 24.

18. *L'Enfer de la Bibliothèque Nationale,* 2:348.

19. Andréa de Nerciat, *Les Aphrodites* (n.p., 1793–1925) (BN Enfer 944), 1:93n. Original emphasis. See also 1:170–72.

20. Jean Marie Goulemot, *Ces livres qu'on ne lit que d'une main: lectures et lecteurs de livres pornographiques au XVIIIe siècle* (Aix-en-Provence: Alinéa, 1991), 146, talks in a rather facile way about reconciling fixity and movement: "For description aims to reconcile the pose (the term comes up regularly in Sade's texts), which represents the immobility and drugged fixity of the living tableau, and the violent, breathless movement of pleasure sought and attained." My claim is that there is no easy dialectic but rather an uneasy and transitory coexistence.

21. *L'Enfer de la Bibliothèque Nationale,* 3:98.

22. *Mémoires de Suzon, sœur de D . . . B . . . portier des Chartreux* (J'enconne: Aux dépens de la Jourdan, n.d.) (BN Enfer 704), 39.

23. Félicité de Choiseul-Meuse, *Amélie de Saint-Far, ou la fatale erreur* (Brussels: Gay et Doucé, 1882) (BN Enfer 45), 2:20.

24. *L'Enfer de la Bibliothèque Nationale,* 4:132.

25. Nerciat, *Le Diable au corps,* 5:108. For a similar example, see Félicité de Choiseul-Meuse, *Amélie de Saint-Far,* 1:136.

26. *L'Enfer de la Bibliothèque Nationale*, 2:363.

27. Nerciat, *Le Diable au corps,* 5:132.

28. *L'Erotisme romantique* (Paris: Carrere, 1984), 82.

29. *Les Délices de Coblentz, ou anecdotes libertines des émigrés français* (Coblentz: n.p., 1791) (BN Enfer 1428), 1:51.

30. Andréa de Nerciat, *Mon Noviciat, ou les joies de Lolotte* (Paris: n.p., 1932) (BN Enfer 1106), 210. For a comparable incident, see Félicité de Choiseul-Meuse, *Entre chien et loup* (Hamburg and Paris: Les Marchands de Nouveautés, 1809), 1:36.

31. *L'Erotisme romantique* (Paris: Carrere, 1984), 78.

32. *L'Enfer de la Bibliothèque Nationale*, 6:317–22, esp. 320.

33. Ibid., 3:168.

34. Nerciat, *Les Aphrodites,* 1:186.

35. *Les Amours de garnison* (Aux Invalides: chez le gardien du Dôme, 1832), 53. See also *L'Enfant du bordel* (1800) in *L'Erotisme au XIXe siècle*, ed. Alexandrian (Paris: Lattès, 1993), 93: "I was moving my rump with such agility that he was obliged to take a firm grip on my hips to stop me pulling away from the caresses of his delightful tongue."

36. Nerciat, *Le Diable au corps,* 1:52.

37. *Les Délices de Coblentz,* 2:24–25. Original emphasis. In the highly innovative *Margot la ravaudeuse* by Fougeret de Montbron, Margot is compelled by the elasticity of the family bed to follow the movements of her parents' lovemaking. See *Romans libertins du XVIIIe siècle*, ed. Raymond Trousson (Paris: Laffont, 1993), 680. The springs mentioned by Sade and Restif also have some of this quality, although the emphasis there seems to be on mechanical ingenuity in the imposition of constraint.

38. *L'Enfer de la Bibliothèque Nationale*, 6:402.

39. *Julie philosophe, ou le bon patriote* (n.p., 1791) (BN Enfer 686–87), 45–46. For lovemaking on a swing, see *Mémoires de Suzon*, 58. For rocking-horses in a boudoir, see *Mylord Arsouille, ou les bamboches d'un gentleman* (A Bordelopolis: chez Pinard, rue de la Motte, 1789 [c. 1858]), 4:25–26.

40. The more classical *Point de lendemain* by Vivant-Denon (1777) describes a scene in which the narrator-hero is happily thrown up against an attractive woman by the jolting movement of a carriage. The highest pleasures for him will occur later, however, in a succession of boudoirs. See *Romans libertins du XVIIIe siècle*, 1300–1301. Benoît Melançon, "Faire catleya au XVIIIe siècle," *Etudes françaises* 32 (1996): 65–81, mentions the scene in *Point de lendemain* during a discussion of the "mobile love scene" in French fiction of the eighteenth and nineteenth centuries. He gives an impressive list of examples, but does not enter into a discussion of bouncing up and down.

41. Nerciat, *Le Diable au corps,* 4:25–26.

42. Nerciat, *Mon Noviciat,* 172. On page 114 of the same novel, we find a bench (*banquette*) with its cushions: "This item of furniture, which was highly decorated, had in addition to its own upholstery a number of cushions of different sizes and shapes that were able to be combined according to the players' good pleasure."

43. Nerciat, *Les Aphrodites,* 1:82.

44. *L'Erotisme romantique* (Paris: Carrere, 1984), 94.

45. Sade, *Histoire de Juliette*, 9:65.

46. Jane de La Vaudère, *Les Fleurs de la volupté* (Paris: Flammarion, 1900), 49.

47. *Les Amours d'un gentleman* (Brussels: W. Schmidt, n.d.) (BN Enfer 137), 32.

48. *L'Erotisme romantique* (Paris: Carrere, 1984), 93.

49. Jane de La Vaudère, *Les Demi-Sexes* (Paris: Ollendorff, 1897), 11.

50. René Saint-Médard, *L'Orgie moderne* (Paris: Bibliothèque du fin du siècle, 1905), 95.

51. E.D. [Emile Desjardins], *L'Odyssée d'un pantalon* (Paris: Aux dépens de la compagnie, 1889), 6.

52. Roland Brevannes, *Amante cruelle* (Paris: Offenstadt, n.d.), 31.

53. Jean de Merlin, *La Luxure* (Paris: Bibliothèque du fin du siècle, 1905), 102–103.

54. Victor Joze, *La Cantharide* (Paris: Fort, n.d.), 163.

55. On this point, see Antonin Reschal, *Le Journal d'un amant* (Paris: Offenstadt, 1902), 98: "I had never paid so much attention to the obscenity that lurks in women's nostrils. . . . If they sniff the air with a quivering of their little, coral-like, diaphanous noses, they seem to be immediately impregnated with sensual pleasure, as they breathe in a strong odor of rutting animals."

56. Georges de Lesbos, *Joyeuses Enfilades* (Amsterdam: n.p., 1895), 8.

57. Pierre Duo, *Inassouvie* (Paris: Brossier, 1889), 19.

58. Jules Davray and Jean Caujolle, *Vendeuse d'amour* (Paris: Simon, 1891), 134, 123.

59. Catulle Mendès, *Méphistophela* (Paris: Dentu, 1890), 4.

60. Joséphin Péladan, *La Gynandre* (Paris: Dentu, 1891), 184.

61. Jules Bois, *L'Eternelle Poupée* (Paris: Ollendorff, 1894), 46. Cf. Reschal, *Journal d'un amant*, 67, on the bed as archetype: "The bed that is always the same everywhere, a resting place of immorality, the site of so much shameful coupling, containing many secrets, and many stories of moral decay."

Chapter 2. Marble and Fire

1. Paula Findlen, "Humanism, Politics and Pornography in Renaissance Italy," in *The Invention of Pornography: Obscenity and the Origins of Modernity, 1500–1800*, ed. Lynn Hunt (New York: Zone, 1993), 60.

2. Peter Wagner, *Eros Revived: Erotica of the Enlightenment in England and America* (London: Secker and Warburg, 1988), 13.

3. Quoted in John Edwin Jackson, *Le Corps amoureux: essai sur la représentation poétique de l'éros* (Neufchatel: La Baconnière, 1986), 15.

4. Findlen, "Humanism," 63–64.

5. For a further discussion of the famous examples given by Findlen, and an attempt to situate them in stylized Renaissance debates between champions of sculpture and defenders of painting, see Mary Pardo, "Artifice and Seduction in Titian," in *Sexuality and Gender in Early Modern Europe*, ed. James Grantham Turner (Cambridge: Cambridge University Press, 1993), 62–65. Findlen's key theoretical reference is David Freedberg, *The Power of Images: Studies in the History and Theory of Response* (Chicago: University of

Chicago Press, 1989). Freedberg makes careful statements about the need to be historically specific, but is nonetheless committed to a certain universality of response. See, for example, 22: "Nevertheless, we proceed in the belief that however much we intellectualize, . . . there still remains a basic level of reaction that cuts across historical, social, and other contextual boundaries." A similar objection can be made to Peter Brooks's interpretation of Ovid's *Pygmalion*, which emphasizes the importance of touching and the imprint. Brooks says: "it is the story of how the body can be known, animated and possessed by the artist of desire, and of how the body marked, imprinted by desire can enter narrative" (Peter Brooks, *Body Work: Objects of Desire in Modern Narrative* [Cambridge: Harvard University Press, 1993], 25). I am not about to disagree with this in general terms, but I do not wish to accept its theoretical assumptions. Even to speak of "the body" and of "desire" may be somehow preemptive. These things are not always available to representation in the same ways, and I do not wish to suppose that they are transhistorical entities.

6. Findlen, "Humanism," 63.

7. Jean-Jacques Rousseau, "Pygmalion. Scène lyrique," in *Œuvres* (Paris: Gallimard, Pléiade, 1961), 2:1224–31. Subsequent page references to this edition are given in brackets in the text.

8. Julien Offroy de la Mettrie, *L'Homme machine, suivi de L'Art de jouir*, ed. Maurice Solovine (Paris: Bossard, 1921), 172.

9. Philip Stewart, *Engraven Desire: Eros, Imagery and Text in the French Eighteenth Century* (Durham, N.C.: Duke University Press, 1992), 226–27. Original emphasis.

10. Paul de Man, *Allegories of Reading: Figural Language in Rousseau, Rilke, and Proust* (New Haven: Yale University Press, 1979), 178.

11. Diderot, in his *Entretien entre d'Alembert et Diderot*, in *Œuvres philosophiques* (Paris: Garnier, 1964), 903–64, is concerned with the difference between human and statue, flesh and marble, but the focus of philosophical attention in his text is on the degree of difference between the two and whether the distinction can be made with absolute clarity. Rousseau, on the other hand, is preoccupied with ambivalence for its own sake.

12. Nicolas Chorier, *L'Académie des dames*, *L'Enfer de la Bibliothèque Nationale* (Paris: Fayard, 1988), 7:418.

13. La Morlière, *Angola*, 454.

14. Crébillon *fils*, *La Nuit et le moment*, in *Œuvres complètes* (Geneva: Slatkine Reprints, 1968), 9:79–81.

15. Pierre Fauchery, in his reading of Crébillon's work, supposes in fact that there is an ideal point on the scale "doubtless common to Crébillon and his most distinguished contemporaries." See Pierre Fauchery, *La Destinée féminine dans le roman européen du dix-huitième siècle* (Paris: Armand Colin, 1972), 473.

16. Even when the term is actually used by a later libertine writer who owes much to Crébillon, the usage is likely to take the form of ironic hyperbole. In Claude-Joseph Dorat, *Les Malheurs de l'inconstance* (Paris: Desjonquères, 1983) [first published 1772], 109, we find: "Her eyes, which before were only alert, have now become more tender. She seems almost to be staring. You are undeniably the author of this metamorphosis."

17. Sheila Jeffreys, *Anticlimax: A Feminist Perspective on the Sexual Revolution* (London: Women's Press, 1990), 24, 31.

18. *L'Enfer de la Bibliothèque Nationale, Œuvres anonymes du XVIIIᵉ siècle* (Paris: Fayard, 1985–88), 4:35. Subsequent references to this edition are given in brackets in the text.

19. *Lucette, ou Les Progrès du libertinage,* 2:143.

20. *L'Enfer de la Bibliothèque Nationale,* 4:419.

21. Ibid., 5:279.

22. *La Messaline française, L'Enfer de la Bibliothèque Nationale,* 5:308.

23. *Les Délices de Coblentz, ou anecdotes libertines des émigrés français* (Coblentz: n.p., 1791), 1:43.

24. *L'Enfer de la Bibliothèque Nationale,* 6:33.

25. Alfred de Musset, *Gamiani, ou deux nuits d'excès, L'Erotisme romantique,* ed. J.-J. Pauvert (Paris: Carrere, 1984), 96.

26. This is the term used in Nicolas Venette, *Tableau de l'amour conjugal* (Paris: Agence Parisienne de Distribution, 1950) [first published 1687], 26: "the seed being only an excrement, Nature does not long tolerate it in the testicles." It must be said that Venette takes great care to distinguish his book from erotic writing *stricto sensu,* although a history of the uses of his text might cloud the issue somewhat. "I do not pretend to write for evil-minded people," he says, pointing out that his purpose is not to teach the excesses of love (155). For this seventeenth-century physiology of humors, the "spermatic parts" are "naturally cold" (133), being heated in the practice of love by the temporary internal migration of blood.

27. *Quarante Manières de foutre, dédiées au clergé de France* (Cythère: Au Temple de la volupté, 1790).

28. *L'Enfer de la Bibliothèque Nationale,* 6:300.

29. Nerciat, *Les Aphrodites,* 2:67.

30. Sade, *Œuvres complètes,* ed. Annie Le Brun and Jean-Jacques Pauvert (Paris: Pauvert, 1986–87), 1:79.

31. *Julie philosophe,* 1:84. Compare this with the anonymous *Le Degré des âges du plaisir, L'Enfer de la Bibliothèque Nationale* (Paris: Fayard, 1987) [1793], 6:428: "No, the fire that leaps impetuously from two stones rubbed together does not burn as much as the sparks that flew when I kissed Constance's breast."

32. *Caroline et Saint-Hilaire, ou les putains du Palais-Royal* (Paris: Dans un bordel, an 8), 2:3.

33. *La Nouvelle Académie des dames* (Cythère: n.p., 1774), 77–78.

34. Musset, *Gamiani,* 132.

35. See Cryle, *Geometry in the Boudoir,* 105–19.

36. *Caroline et Saint-Hilaire, ou les putains du Palais-Royal* (Paris: Dans un bordel, an 8), i.

37. Choiseul-Meuse, *Amélie de Saint-Far,* 1:117.

38. Nerciat, *Le Diable au corps,* 6:75.

39. Pigault-Lebrun, *L'Enfant du bordel,* in *L'Erotisme au XIXᵉ siècle,* ed. Alexandrian (Paris: Lattès, 1993), 27. One finds the same syntactical concession, and the same aesthetic adjustment, on p. 54, where the narrator-hero speaks of "a sphere that I should have taken for marble, were it not for the

gentle warmth that dwelt in it, and the intermittent palpitation that made it rise."

40. Théophile Gautier, *La Morte amoureuse*, in *La France frénétique de 1830*, ed. Jean-Luc Steinmetz (Paris: Phébus, 1978), 477.

41. Adolphe Belot, *Mademoiselle Giraud, ma femme* (Paris: Dentu, 1870), 48.

42. Mendès, *Méphistophela*, 119.

43. Jules Barbey d'Aurevilly, "Le Rideau cramoisi," in *Les Diaboliques*, *Œuvres romanesques complètes* (Paris: Gallimard/Pléïade, 1964–66), 2:47.

44. Joséphin Péladan, *Le Vice suprême* (Paris: Librairie moderne, 1884), 166: "traumatized on her wedding night by a brutal spouse, she adopted thenceforth the role of perverse frigidity."

45. Andrea Dworkin, *Intercourse* (London: Secker and Warburg, 1987), 107.

46. Belot, *Mademoiselle Giraud, ma femme*, 101–2.

47. Adolphe Belot, *La Femme de glace* (Paris: Dentu, 1878). There is some description of Henriette's change on 132–33.

48. Mendès, *Méphistophela*, 14.

49. Bois, *L'Eternelle Poupée*, 46.

50. Jean-Louis Dubut de Laforest, *Pathologie sociale* (Paris: Dupont, 1897). *Mademoiselle Tantale* is on pp. 3–106.

51. *Un Eté à la campagne*, in *L'Erotisme au XIXe siècle*, ed. Alexandrian (Paris: Lattès, 1993), 469.

52. *Lesbia, maîtresse d'école* (Paris: Aux dépens de la compagnie, 1890), 140.

53. Belot, *Mademoiselle Giraud, ma femme*, 93.

54. Ernest La Jeunesse, *Demi-Volupté* (Paris: Offenstadt, 1900), 129–30.

55. Jean Lorrain, *Le Vice errant* (Paris: Ollendorff, 1902), 100. Henri de Régnier's "La Femme de marbre," *La Revue de Paris* 7 (1900): 225–41, goes rather against this tendency, although it self-consciously locates a story about the seductive qualities of marble in the Italian sixteenth century. There marble stands, somewhat anachronistically, for resistance to historical change and fleshly decay.

Chapter 3. Cantharides

1. Jean-Jacques Pauvert, *Sade vivant* (Paris: Laffont, 1986), 1:262, points out that the complaint was not laid according to proper procedure.

2. See Alice M. Laborde, *Les Infortunes du marquis de Sade* (Paris and Geneva: Champion-Slatkine, 1990), 302–3.

3. Maurice Lever, *Donatien Alphonse François marquis de Sade* (Paris: Fayard, 1991), 207.

4. Alice M. Laborde, *Les Infortunes du Marquis de Sade* (Paris and Geneva: Champion-Slatkine, 1990), 121.

5. Quoted in Maurice Lever, *Donatien Alphonse François marquis de Sade* (Paris: Fayard, 1991), 208. See also Raymond Jean, *Un Portrait de Sade* (Arles: Actes Sud, 1989), 116.

6. *Encyclopedia Americana* (New York: Americana Corporation, 1978), 25:450.

7. *Encyclopedia Britannica* (Chicago: Encyclopedia Britannica Inc., 1986), 1:480.

8. *Encyclopedia Americana,* 2:95.

9. For an informative but historically naïve work of scientific vulgarization on the subject of aphrodisiacs, see Peter V. Taberner, *Aphrodisiacs: The Science and the Myth* (Philadelphia: University of Pennsylvania Press, 1985). Taberner's concern is to dispell the "mythology" that surrounds certain substances and to undo the "reputation" of some "frankly dangerous" ones (6), including cantharides (105). Unfortunately, in his desire to cut through the mythology and banish premodern thinking, Taberner is often quite uncritical about the history of his own topic and finds himself simply recycling some of the old enormities about Sade. We are told, for example, that several of the prostitutes whom Sade poisoned "committed suicide by throwing themselves out of the windows, such was the intolerable pain produced by the drug" (105).

10. Alice M. Laborde, *Les Infortunes du marquis de Sade,* 121.

11. Gaston Bachelard, *La Psychanalyse du feu* (Paris: Gallimard/Idées, 1972).

12. Michel Delon, "Introduction," in Sade, *Œuvres* (Paris: Gallimard/Pléïade, 1990), xiv–xv.

13. Lever, *Donatien Alphonse François marquis de Sade,* 213.

14. Jean, *Un Portrait de Sade,* 123, 125.

15. La Morlière, *Angola,* 471.

16. Grandval *fils,* "Les Deux Biscuits," in *Théâtre érotique français du XVIIIᵉ siècle,* ed. Jean-Jacques Pauvert (Paris: Le Terrain vague, 1993), 187. There is a comparable example in "Le Tempérament" (1756), by the same author and published in the same collection, 164–65.

17. Jean-Pierre Jacques, *Les Malheurs de Sapho* (Paris: Grasset, 1980), 48.

18. Here is Jean Lorrain on the topic in 1904. Sade is called "A terrific guy for filth. They'll never come up with anything worse. He did heaps, cruelty, dirty stuff, and murders. He liked blood to flow in lovemaking. He flayed broads alive and put on parties. He stuffed his guests with cantharides. Some of them died from it." This passage is quoted in Michel Delon, "Un Type épatant pour les saloperies," *Revue des Sciences Humaines* 230 (1993) 164.

19. See Michel Foucault, *Histoire de la sexualité,* vol. 1, *La Volonté de savoir* (Paris: Gallimard, 1976).

20. André Pieyre de Mandiargues, "Irène encore," *L'Erotisme des années folles,* ed. Jean-Jacques Pauvert (Paris: Garnier, 1983), 32.

21. On Sadian apologetics, see Cryle, *Geometry in the Boudoir,* 120–46.

22. Nerciat, *Mon Noviciat,* 299–300.

23. Nerciat, *Les Aphrodites,* 1:189.

24. Nerciat, *Le Diable au corps,* 4:27.

25. On this question, see Cryle, *Geometry in the Boudoir,* 92–105.

26. This phrase is taken from *Le Diable au corps,* 4:53: "two pastilles, which he had just taken to restore his strength, lent him temporarily, at a heavy rate of interest, a certain amount of vigor and desire."

27. *Les Délices de Coblentz,* 1:36.

28. Sade, *Œuvres complètes,* 9:437.

29. Sade, *Œuvres,* 1:482.

30. *Vénus en rut*, in *Œuvres anonymes du XVIIIᵉ siècle, L'Enfer de la Bibliothèque Nationale* (Paris: Fayard, 1987), 6:135.

31. Jean-Pierre Dubost, "Préface. Une Remarquable Carrière," in *L'Enfer de la Bibliothèque Nationale*, 6:105.

32. See Pauvert, *Sade vivant*, 1:265.

33. On Sade's use of this term, and its preferability in this context to such modern expressions as "perversion," see Pierre Klossowski, *Sade mon prochain, précédé de Le Philosophe scélérat* (Paris: Le Seuil, 1967), 28.

34. A few examples of such manipulative pharmacy—not strictly involving aphrodisiacs, but for erotic purposes—occur in *Les Cent Vingt Journées de Sodome*. Duclos recounts how, on one occasion, she was given en emetic to make her vomit (1:158). On another, she is given aniseed and a "balsamic liquor" to make her pass wind (1:163).

35. Jean, *Un Portrait de Sade*, 116, talks rather benignly of the young Sade's "imprudence." Juliette may be said to move beyond criminal negligence to negligent crime. Delon points up a comparable irony when he notes "while the pseudo-memoirs of the nineteenth century drew on Sade's fiction in imagining his biography, the fiction itself seems to have drawn on the legend that took hold of the man during his lifetime and became attached to him" ("Introduction," in Sade, *Œuvres*, xx.

36. Musset, *Gamiani*, 126.

37. [Emile Desjardins], *Lesbia, maîtresse d'école*, 140.

38. Georges de Lesbos, *Enfilade de perles* (Amsterdam: de Lesbos, 1894), 5.

39. René Saint-Médard, *La Volupté féroce* (Paris: Bibliothèque "Fin de siècle," 1905), 166.

40. Lorrain, *Le Vice errant*, 128.

41. Merlin, *La Luxure*, 160.

42. Adrienne Saint-Agen, *Charmeuses de femmes: L'Affolante Illusion* (Paris: Offenstadt, 1906), 212.

43. *Vingt Ans de la vie d'une jolie femme, ou Mémoires de Julia R . . .* (Vito-Cono-Ano-Clytoropolis: chez Bandefort, rue de la Couille, au Fouteur libéral, 1789 [1842]), 40.

44. *Les Cousines de la colonelle* (Lisbon: da Boa-Vista, n.d.), and René Maizeroy, *Deux amies* (Paris: Victor-Havard, 1885).

45. Duo, *Inassouvie*, 119.

46. Belot, *Mademoiselle Giraud*, 475–76.

47. Louis Besse, *La Fille de Gamiani: journal d'une prostituée* (Paris: Albin Michel, 1906), 133.

48. Here is an earlier example, from Felicité de Choiseul-Meuse, *Julie, ou j'ai sauvé ma rose* (1807). The heroine, who is of Italian origin says, "I was born in a climate where women rarely hold out against their passions." *L'Erotisme au XIXᵉ siècle*, ed. Alexandrian (Paris: Lattès, 1993), 128.

49. Reschal, *Le Journal d'un amant*, 39.

50. Victorien du Saussay, *Rires, sang, et voluptés* (Paris: Bibliothèque du fin du siècle, 1901), 475–76.

51. Joze, *La Cantharide*, 148.

52. Renée Dunan, *Cantharide* (Paris: Querelle, 1928), 175, 114.

53. Dubut de Laforest, *Pathologie sociale. Mademoiselle Tantale* is found on pp. 3–106.

54. For another example, see the character Eveline Harrison in Marc de Montifaud, *Celles qui tuent: la baronne de Livry* (Paris: n.p., 1890), esp. 32–36.

Chapter 4. Utterance

1. See Nancy Miller, *French Dressing: Women, Men and Ancien Régime Fiction* (New York: Routledge, 1995), 3–6. Miller refers to work by Linda Williams, Naomi Schor, and Jane Gallop. To this list can be added Janet Beizer, *Ventriloquized Bodies: The Narrative Uses of Hysteria in France (1850–1900)* (Ithaca: Cornell University Press, 1994), 45, 174. Gallop revisits her relation to Foucault's reading of *Les Bijoux indiscrets* in her book, *Thinking Through the Body* (New York: Columbia University Press, 1988), 89.

2. Foucault, *Histoire de la sexualité,* vol. 1, 101.

3. Denis Diderot, *Les Bijoux indiscrets* (Paris: Garnier-Flammarion, 1968), 126.

4. Crébillon *fils, La Nuit et le moment,* 9:64.

5. *Le Roman de mon alcôve. Confessions galantes d'une femme du monde,* préface de Gustave Colline (Paris: A l'enseigne du musée secret, c. 1935), 6.

6. Pietro Aretino, *Dialogues [Ragionamenti],* trans. Raymond Rosenthal (New York: Stein and Day, 1971), 29.

7. *Vénus dans le cloître, ou la religieuse en chemise* (Paris: Lattès, 1979), 122.

8. Jean-Baptiste Louvet de Couvray, *Les Amours du chevalier de Faublas* (Paris: Chez les marchands de nouveautés, c. 1910), 1:239–240.

9. Charles Pinot Duclos, *Acajou et Zirphile,* in *Contes parodiques et licencieux du XVIIIᵉ siècle,* ed. Raymonde Robert (Nancy: Presses universitaires de Nancy, 1987), 42–43.

10. Marie-Antoinette Fagnan, *Kanor,* in *Contes parodiques et licencieux du XVIIIᵉ siècle,* ed. Raymonde Robert (Nancy: Presses universitaires de Nancy, 1987), 127.

11. D'Argens, *Les Nonnes galantes* (Paris: Librairie anti-cléricale, n.d.), 24.

12. Gautier, *La Morte amoureuse,* 487.

13. Nerciat, *Les Aphrodites,* 1:41. See also *Les Libertines du grand monde* (Au Palais-Royal: chez la petite Lolotte, 1890 [1880]), 55: "he inserted his great thing into me and gave me more pleasure, sometimes so great that it made our assholes blow like clarinets." Beizer, *Ventriloquized Bodies,* 45, observes that "metaphoric connections between the voicebox/throat/neck and vagina/uterus/cervix are retained from antiquity well into the nineteenth century."

14. *La Nouvelle Académie des dames* (Cythère: n.p., 1774), 77–78.

15. Michel Camus, "Les Paradoxes du discours amoureux," in *Œuvres anonymes du XVIIIᵉ siècle III, L'Enfer de la Bibliothèque Nationale* (Paris: Fayard, 1986), 5:194–95.

16. Jean Marie Goulemot, "Préface [to *La Messaline Française*]", *L'Enfer de la Bibliothèque Nationale,* 5:290–91.

17. Gaëtan Brulotte, *Œuvres de chair: figures du discours érotique* (Québec: L'Harmattan, Les Presses de l'Université Laval, 1998), 133. For a splendid set of examples of the stylistic features I am describing here, see 133–40.

18. Nerciat, *Le Diable au corps,* 4:30. Original emphasis.

19. Nerciat, *Les Aphrodites,* 2:185.

20. G.-C.-A. Pigault-Lebrun, *La Folie espagnole* (Paris: P. Arnould, 1889), 17–18.

21. La Jeunesse, *Demi-volupté,* 211–12.

22. Saint-Médard, *L'Orgie moderne,* 120.

23. Crébillon *fils, Tableaux des mœurs du temps dans les différents âges de la vie* (Paris: Lattès, 1980), 224.

24. *Le Triomphe des religieuses, ou les nonnes babillardes, L'Enfer de la Bibliothèque Nationale* (Paris: Fayard, 1986), 5:225.

25. Restif de la Bretonne, *L'Anti-Justine,* in *Œuvres érotiques* (Paris: Fayard, 1985), 364.

26. *Lettres galantes et philosophiques de deux nones, L'Enfer de la Bibliothèque Nationale,* 5:244.

27. Jean-Charles Gervaise de Latouche, *Histoire de dom Bougre, portier des Chartreux, L'Enfer de la Bibliothèque Nationale* (Paris: Fayard, 1985), 3:36.

28. *La Nouvelle Académie des dames,* 76–77.

29. *Amélie, ou les écarts de ma jeunesse* (Bruxelles: Gay et Doucé, 1882), 131. The date of first publication of this novel is not known to me. It must belong in the period 1770–1790.

30. *Vénus en rut,* 4:122.

31. Félix Nogaret, *L'Arétin français, suivi des Epices de Vénus,* ed. Louis Perceau (Versailles: Aux dépens des fermiers généraux, n.d.), 23.

32. Patrick Wald Lasowski, "Les Fouteries chantantes de la Révolution," *Le Magazine littéraire* 371 (Dec. 1998): 36, quotes Nogaret, "Foutons! oui, foutons promptement," noting that this imperative is addressed to the whole of France, as a call to civic duty. *Fouterie,* says Lasowski, becomes a major theme of the Revolution.

33. When Mme. Rastard asks whether her disguise as a male is convincing, Mme. Dodo replies: "My word, Madame! Looking like that, all you would need would be to say 'foutre!' and everyone would be fooled" (Crébillon *fils, Tableaux des mœurs du siècle dans les différents âges de la vie,* 224).

34. Nerciat, *Le Diable au corps,* 4:138; original emphasis.

35. Nerciat, *Les Aphrodites,* 1:150; original emphasis.

36. Nerciat, *Le Diable au corps,* 5:112. See also *Les Aphrodites,* 1:189: "Madame de Vaquifout was beneath the illustrious Boutavant, who was able to make her open her eyes twice and give out at the last moment a *foutre!* that echoed throughout the space" (original emphasis).

37. Cf. Marcel Hénaff, *Sade: L'Invention du corps libertin* (Paris: Presses universitaires de France, 1978), 91–92: "the cry is the presymbolic use of the voice, the voice before it is taken over by language, the voice that escapes from the body or is extorted from it in the same way as other secretions: *foutre,* shit, farts, blood. It is voice reduced to material flux."

38. Sade, *Œuvres complètes,* 6:268.

39. Jane Gallop, in *Thinking Through the Body* (New York: Columbia University Press, 1988), 18, observes that "the connection between these two productions of bodily fluids—tears and arousal—points to a similarity between

the sentimental (coded as feminine), and the pornographic (coded as masculine). In Sade, the difference between libertines and victims is that, in one situation, libertines get aroused whereas victims cry."

40. Musset, *Gamiani*, 114.

41. *Thérèse philosophe* (Geneva: Slatkine, 1981), 2:24–25.

42. Musset, *Gamiani*, 123.

43. Fagnan, *Kanor*, 138.

44. This is what Georges Bataille does when he imagines the force of Sade's personal bellowing as an extension of his characters': "Rose Keller, in official testimony, spoke of the abominable cries that pleasure drew from him. This feature at least makes him like Blangis. I do not know whether it is legitimate, when speaking of such frenzy, to speak simply of pleasure. At a certain level, excess takes us beyond common feelings" (*La Littérature et le mal* [Paris: Gallimard, 1967], 139–40).

45. Théophile Gautier, *Mademoiselle de Maupin* (Paris: Charpentier, 1919), 408.

46. See Cryle, *Geometry in the Boudoir,* 9–10, and 30–31.

47. *Le Roman de Violette*, in *L'Erotisme au dix-neuvième siècle*, ed. Alexandrian (Paris: Lattès, 1993), 524.

48. Brantôme, *Les Dames galantes*, ed. Maurice Rat (Paris: Garnier, 1965), 324–25.

49. *Décrets des sens sanctionnés par la volupté, L'Enfer de la Bibliothèque Nationale* (Paris: Fayard, 1987), 6:335.

50. *L'Enfant du bordel*, 68. See also Nerciat, *Le Diable au corps,* 5:93, where the Comtesse asks a similar question and receives the reply "Have no doubt of it . . ." "And I felt at the same time," she relates, "that he was pressing against my hand something that declared the most ebullient desire."

51. Nerciat, *Les Aphrodites,* 1:143.

52. See for example Andréa de Nerciat, *Félicia, ou mes fredaines* (Paris: Livre de Poche Hachette, 1976), 132.

53. Linda Williams, in her fine book, *Hard Core: Power, Pleasure, and the "Frenzy of the Visible,"* points to a comparable problem that arises in another domain, the medium of pornographic cinema. She refers (147) to "hard core's utopian project of offering visual proof of authentic and involuntary spasms of pleasure." A particular problem is posed by the "invisible place" of female pleasure (49), and this tends to be dealt with by "argu[ing] for the fundamental sameness of male and female pleasure" (50). Williams adds that "the articulate and inarticulate sounds of pleasure that dominate in aural hard core are primarily the cries of women" (123).

54. Mirabeau, *Le Rideau levé, ou l'éducation de Laure,* in *Œuvres érotiques* (Paris: Fayard, 1984), 411.

55. Anne-Marie Dardigna, *Les Châteaux d'Eros, ou les infortunes du sexe des femmes* (Paris: Maspero, 1980), 37.

56. Dworkin, *Pornography,* 95. A similar critique is formulated in Nancy Huston, *Mosaïque de la pornographie* (Paris: Denoël /Gonthier, 1982), 63: "No author illustrates better than Sade that [poverty of the vocabulary of female pleasure]: his libertine heroines screw and talk exactly like libertine heroes. They all say that they have 'hard ons' and 'unload,' preferably while torturing other women."

57. Pascal Bruckner and Alain Finkielkraut, *Le Nouveau Désordre amoureux* (Paris: Seuil, 1977), 71.

58. Richard Lewinsohn, *A History of Sexual Customs*, trans. Alexander Mayce (New York: Harper, 1958), 197. See also Thomas Laqueur, *Making Sex: Body and Gender from the Greeks to Freud* (Cambridge: Harvard University Press, 1990), 25–62.

59. On this question, see Lucienne Frappier-Mazur, *Sade et l'écriture de l'orgie* (Paris: Nathan, 1991), 48–59, and the unpublished thesis of Jeremy Horwood, "Sade et la génération" (B.A. honours, University of Queensland, 1994). See also Jean Mainil, *Dans les règles du plaisir . . . Théorie de la différence dans le discours obscène, romanesque et médical de l'Ancien Régime* (Paris: Kimé, 1996), 19: "What people have taken as a provocation on Sade's part was only the translation (admittedly exaggerated in quantity), of a *scientific truth* that was still widespread at the beginning of the nineteenth century." Original emphasis.

60. Huston, *Mosaïque de la pornographie,* 84. Original emphasis.

61. My insistence, following Foucault, on the subjective discipline of confession makes me reluctant to accept the applicability here of Janet Beizer's otherwise valuable metaphor of ventriloquism, of which she says: "I intend it as a metaphor to evoke the narrative process whereby a woman's speech is repressed in order to be expressed as inarticulate body language, which must then be dubbed by a male narrator." *Ventriloquized Bodies,* 9. I am concerned to show, in the context of erotic fiction, that it is not possible to identify separate phases of repression, forced silence, and dubbed expression. An exclamatory discipline, as a particular fictional form of Foucault's *dispositif de sexualité*, exacts certain types of expression, and claims that they come from the woman's soul.

62. *Les Folies amoureuses d'une impératrice,* 26.

63. Mirabeau, *Hic-et-Haec,* in *Œuvres érotiques* (Paris: Fayard, 1984), 209.

64. See Stephen Heath, *Questions of Cinema* (Bloomington: Indiana University Press, 1981), 189, on the attempts made by pornographic cinema to "deal with the immense and catastrophic problem of the invisibility or not of pleasure." Such films use a "whole gamut of pants and cries . . . to guarantee the accomplishment of pleasure."

65. Bruckner and Finkielkraut, *Le Nouveau Désordre amoureux,* 81.

66. Mirabeau, *Le Rideau levé,* 411.

67. Crébillon *fils, La Nuit et le moment,* 9:30.

68. Restif, *L'Anti-Justine,* 294.

69. Nerciat, *Le Diable au corps,* 4:73.

70. *Les Amours d'un gentleman,* 57–58.

71. See Sade, *La Philosophie dans le boudoir,* 3:542.

72. *Les Cousines de la colonelle* (Lisbon: da Boa-Vista, [1880]), 64–65.

73. La Vaudère, *Les Demi-Sexes,* 237.

74. Victorien du Saussay, *Chairs épanouies, beautés ardentes* (Paris: Méricant, 1902), 65.

75. Merlin, *La Luxure,* 152.

76. Mendès, *Méphistophela,* 120–121.

77. In Mendès's story, it does not ever do so because Sophie's energies are directed towards the love of other women. It is she who will later provoke from her lover Céphise "the avowal of happy death" (*Méphistophela*, 446).

CHAPTER 5. ELLIPSIS

1. Georges Perec, "Tentative de description de choses vues au carrefour Mabillon le 19 mai 1978," *Atelier de création radiophonique*, no. 381, February 25, 1979.

2. Raymonde Robert, "Introduction," in *Contes parodiques et licencieux du XVIIIᵉ siècle* (Nancy: Presses universitaires de Nancy, 1987), 14–15.

3. G.-C.-A. Pigault-Lebrun, *La Folie espagnole* (Paris: Arnould, 1889), 76.

4. Crébillon *fils*, *Œuvres complètes*, 9:72.

5. Denis Diderot, *Les Bijoux indiscrets*, ed. Antoine Adam (Paris: Garnier-Flammarion, 1968), 219.

6. Nerciat, *Les Aphrodites*, 2:202.

7. *Les Amours de Sainfroid, jésuite, et d'Eulalie, fille dévote* (The Hague: Van der Kloot, 1729), xiv.

8. Pidansat de Mairobert, *La Secte des anandrynes: confession de Mademoiselle Sapho*, ed. Jean Hervez (Paris: Bibliothèque des curieux, 1920), 40.

9. Jean-Charles Gervaise de Latouche, *Histoire de dom Bougre, portier des chartreux, écrite par lui-même*, L'Enfer de la Bibliothèque Nationale (Paris: Fayard, 1985), 3:231–32.

10. Nerciat, *Mon Noviciat*, 53.

11. Jean-Baptiste Louvet de Couvray, *Les Amours du chevalier de Faublas* (Paris: Les Marchands de nouveautés, n.d.), 1:350.

12. Jean-Jacques Rousseau, *Julie, ou la nouvelle Héloïse*, ed. Michel Launay (Paris: Garnier-Flammarion, 1967), 69–70 (lettre xxix).

13. Fagnan, *Kanor*, 139.

14. Gautier, *Mademoiselle de Maupin*, 417.

15. Lilian Faderman, *Surpassing the Love of Men: Romantic Friendship and Love between Women from the Renaissance to the Present* (New York: Morrow, 1981), 457 n.11.

16. Peter Wagner, *Eros Revived: Erotica of the Enlightenment in England and America* (London: Secker and Warburg, 1988), 216, attempts to define a whole genre by the practice of ellipsis. For him, the "amatory novel," as distinct from pornography, is marked by the drawing of the curtain at the point where explicit sexual scenes have their beginning. My aim in this chapter is to show firstly that the generic distinction is not as clear as he suggests, and secondly that the making of it is a modern discursive habit.

17. *Eléonore, ou l'heureuse personne*, L'Enfer de la Bibliothèque Nationale (Paris: Fayard, 1986), 3:50.

18. Sade, *Les Cent Vingt Journées de Sodome*, 1:173–74.

19. Ibid., 1:197, 249, 315, 324, etc.

20. Voisenon, *Le Sultan Misapouf*, in *Romans libertins du XVIIIᵉ siècle*, ed. Raymond Trousson (Paris: Laffont, 1993), 501.

21. Jean-Christophe Abramovici, *Le Livre interdit: de Théophile de Viau à Sade* (Paris: Payot, 1996), 132.

22. La Mettrie, *L'Ecole de la volupté*, in Jean-Christophe Abramovici, *Le Livre interdit: de Théophile de Viau à Sade* (Paris: Payot, 1996), 169–70.

23. Sade, *La Philosophie dans le boudoir,* 3:394.

24. Sade, *La Nouvelle Justine,* 7:237.

25. Jean-Baptiste Louvet de Couvray, *Les Amours du chevalier de Faublas* (Paris: Les Marchands de nouveautés, n.d.), 2:51.

26. Nerciat, *Les Aphrodites,* 1:168 n.1.

27. *Mylord Arsouille, ou les bamboches d'un gentleman* (A Bordel-opolis: Chez Pinard, rue de la Motte, 1789), 80.

28. Chantal Thomas, "Préface [to *Décrets des sens sanctionnés par le plaisir*]," *L'Enfer de la Bibliothèque Nationale* (Paris: Fayard, 1986), 6:269–271.

29. Nerciat, *Mon Noviciat,* 165.

30. Sade, *Œuvres,* 1:1233.

31. Crébillon *fils, Œuvres complètes,* 9:97.

32. Louis-Charles Fougeret de Montbron, *Margot la ravaudeuse, Dix-neuf baisers, par un amant de vingt-deux ans; suivis de La Jolie Ravaudeuse* (Paris: n.p., n.d.), 95.

33. Nerciat, *Mon Noviciat,* 205.

34. *Lettres galantes et philosophiques de deux nones, L'Enfer de la Bibliothèque Nationale* (Paris: Fayard, 1986), 5:260.

35. Nerciat, *Le Diable au corps,* 3:63.

36. Nerciat, *Les Aphrodites,* 1:17.

37. Jean Marie Goulemot, *Ces livres qu'on ne lit que d'une main: lectures et lecteurs de livres pornographiques au XVIIIᵉ siècle* (Aix-en-Provence: Alinéa, 1991), 144. See also 143: "the descriptive absence translates the loss of consciousness, which is an effect of pleasure itself. And it is not by chance that the verb 'to die' is used constantly in such passages. It represents, with suspension marks and unfinished sentences, the only way of making present, visually and semantically, the total *abandon* of the heroes." For a comparable opinion, see Nancy Huston, *Mosaïque de la pornographie.*

38. Félicité de Choiseul-Meuse, *Entre chien et loup* (Hamburg and Paris: Les Marchands de nouveautés, 1809), 2:38–39.

39. Gaëtan Brulotte, in his *Œuvres de chair,* 256ff, does some careful classificatory work on different forms of *didascalie*, distinguishing between "suppressions" (ellipses), "dévaluations," and "dénudations." He considers them as instances in which the narrator points to his fragile control over the subject matter.

40. Jacques Cazotte, *Le Diable amoureux*, in *Romanciers du XVIIIᵉ siècle*, ed. René Etiemble (Paris: Gallimard, Pléiade, 1960–65), 2:369.

41. Claudine Brécourt-Villars ed., *Ecrire d'amour. Anthologie de textes érotiques féminins (1799–1984)* (Paris: Ramsay, 1985), 87.

42. Camille Boidin, *Le Monstre*, in *Ecrire d'amour*, ed. Claudine Brécourt-Villars (Paris: Ramsay, 1985), 87–90.

43. *Un Eté à la campagne* (n.p., n.d.), [BN Enfer 840] 418.

44. Emile Henriot, *Les Livres du second rayon, irréguliers et libertins* (Paris: Grasset, 1948), 280.

45. Camille Mireille, *Mémorandum galant, ou confession d'une femme légère* (Paphos: Imprimerie du temple de Cythère, 1903), 1:9.

46. Renée Dunan, *Une Heure de désir* (Paris: Prima, 1929), 7.

47. Foucault, *Histoire de la sexualité*, vol. 1.

48. Belot, *Mademoiselle Giraud, ma femme,* unpaginated preface.

49. Besse, *La Fille de Gamiani,* 166.

50. Gaëtan Brulotte, in his *Œuvres de chair,* 139, notes that the line of dots has a history that includes *Gamiani* and *Le Roman de Violette.* He mentions *Madame Edwarda*, observing wrily that critics of Bataille have taken this form of punctuation to be an invention on the part of Bataille and a mark of his originality.

51. Georges Bataille, *Madame Edwarda*, in *Œuvres complètes* (Paris: Gallimard, 1971), 3:22. Nancy Huston, *Mosaïque de la pornographie,* 62–63, makes the following comment: "Georges Bataille goes even further into 'decency': one of his leitmotive is that paroxysms are beyond words and that texts can only suggest them. For this reason, his pages are decorated with the signs of censorship itself (suspension marks, blank spaces). In this way, the author communicates the idea that something so taboo and so transcendental is taking place that he is unable to describe it."

Chapter 6. Climax

1. Nancy Huston, *Mosaïque de la pornographie,* 158, observes the neatness with which the English language maintains this coincidence through the word "climax": "Ejaculation will be the culmination of the story (as the English language knows well, for it gives the two events the same name: *climax*)." This is not to say, of course, that French has no inkling of the crossover. Some of the expressions that help to do this thematic work will be studied in chapter 7.

2. On this point, see Peter Cryle, "Enunciation and Ejaculation: Telling the Erotic Climax," *Style* 24 (Summer 1990): 187–89.

3. Roland Barthes, *S/Z* (Paris: Seuil, 1970), 81–82.

4. Aristotle, *Poetics*, ed. Francis Ferguson (New York: Hill and Wang, 1961), 27.

5. Peter Brooks, *Reading for the Plot: Design and Intention in Narrative* (Oxford: Clarendon Press, 1984), 107–8.

6. I am indebted to Teresa Bridgeman for supplying this most appropriate word.

7. Roland Barthes, *Le Plaisir du texte* (Paris: Seuil, 1973), 92. Original emphasis.

8. Steven Marcus, *The Other Victorians: A Study of Sexuality and Pornography in Mid-nineteenth Century England* (London: Weidenfeld and Nicolson, 1966), 279.

9. Julien Offroy de la Mettrie, *L'Homme machine, suivi de L'Art de jouir*, ed. Maurice Solovine (Paris: Bossard, 1921), 171.

10. Godard d'Aucour, *Thémidore*, in *Romans libertins du XVIIIe siècle*, ed. Raymond Trousson (Paris: Laffont, 1993). See, for example, 281, 289, 295, 296.

11. La Morlière, *Angola*, 416.

12. For a discussion of the imagined potency and fertility of the people, as opposed to the impotence of royalty, see Antoine de Baecque, *Le Corps de l'histoire: métaphores et politique (1770–1800)* (Paris: Calmann-Lévy, 1993).

13. *Julie philosophe,* 1:57.

14. La Mettrie, *L'Ecole de la volupté,* 86.

15. *Les Délices de Coblentz,* 1:10–11.

16. Choiseul-Meuse, *Amélie de Saint-Far,* 1:56.

17. Beth A. Glessner, "The Censored Erotic Works of Félicité de Choiseul-Meuse," *Tulsa Studies in Women's Literature* 16:136, points to convincing internal evidence to refute Claudine Brécourt-Villars's dating of *Amélie de Saint-Far* as earlier than *Julie, ou j'ai sauvé ma rose.*

18. Choiseul-Meuse, *Julie, ou j'ai sauvé ma rose,* 142.

19. Glessner, "The Censored Erotic Works of Félicité de Choiseul-Meuse," 138.

20. This theme is present in a further novel by the same author. See Choiseul-Meuse, *Entre chien et loup,* 1:136: "incendiary caresses gave everyone lively enough pleasure to put off the thought of the final one, which only causes rest and reflection to happen too soon."

21. Nerciat, *Les Aphrodites,* 1:150.

22. Nerciat, *Le Diable au corps,* 5:94.

23. Nerciat, *Mon Noviciat,* 164.

24. See Anne Freadman, "Anyone for Tennis?" in *Genre and the New Rhetoric*, ed. P. Medway and A. Freedman (London: Taylor and Francis), 43–66.

25. The expression is used in Camille Mireille, *Mémorandum galant, ou confession d'une femme légère* (Paphos: Imprimerie du temple de Cythère, 1903), 2:36: "She admitted that she was very keen on fooling around, and especially on what I shall call the hors d'œuvres of love."

26. *Les Amours, galanteries et passe-temps des actrices, ou confessions curieuses et galantes de ces dames* (Couillopolis: 1700), 1:15.

27. This expression is considered a dated one by twentieth-century writers, even if it continues to be used occasionally. See, for example, Camille Mireille, *Mémorandum galant,* 1:40: "the game that our fathers called 'la petite oie.'" For a discussion of the origin of the expression, see Michel Delon's note on it in Sade, *Œuvres,* 1:1159.

28. *Vingt Ans de la vie d'un jeune homme* (Vito-Cuno-Clytoropolis: chez Bandefort, 1789), 13.

29. *Les Amours de garnison,* 52.

30. *Les Amours secrètes de M. Mayeux* (Brussels: Les Marchands de nouveautés, 1832), 12.

31. *La Perle,* in *L'Erotisme au XIXe siècle,* ed. Alexandrian (Paris: Lattès, 1993), 332–33.

32. Crébillon *fils, Œuvres complètes,* 9:3.

33. *Mylord Arsouille, ou les bamboches d'un gentleman* (Bordel-opolis: chez Pinard, 1789), 65.

34. *Les Libertines du grand monde* (Palais-Royal: chez la petite Lolotte, 1890), 116–17.

35. *Les Tableaux vivants, ou mes confessions aux pieds de la duchesse* (Amsterdam: n.p., 1870), 1:77–78.

36. Nancy K. Miller draws attention to the pun when discussing Sade in her book, *The Heroine's Text: Readings in the French and English Novel, 1722–1782* (New York: Columbia University Press, 1980), 152.

37. My argument here, while quite different in its purpose and its purport from that of Henry Abelove, intersects with his claim in "Some Speculations on the History of 'Sexual Intercourse' During the 'Long Eighteenth Century' in England," in *Nationalisms and Sexualities*, ed. Andrew Parker (London: Routledge, 1990), 335–42, that cross-sex sexual behaviors "are reorganized and reconstructed in the late eighteenth century [in England] as foreplay."

38. Musset, *Gamiani*, 137.

39. Gérard d'Houville, *L'Inconstante* (Paris: Calmann-Lévy, 1903), 35.

40. *Histoire d'un godmiché* (London: n.p., 1886), 69.

41. Camille Pert, *Les Amours perverses de Rosa Scari* (Paris: Librairie artistique, 1907), 123.

42. Du Saussay, *Rires, sang et voluptés*, 406.

43. Georges de Lesbos, *Voluptés bizarres* (Amsterdam: n.p., 1893), 105–6.

44. Antonin Reschal, *De la volupté au tombeau: le journal d'un amant* (Paris: Offenstadt, 1902), 113.

45. Belot, *Mademoiselle Giraud, ma femme*, 99–100.

46. Eugène Delard, *Le Désir: journal d'un mari* (Paris: Calmann-Lévy, 1899), 35.

47. Duo, *Inassouvie*.

48. Saint-Médard, *La Volupté féroce*, 14.

49. Victorien du Saussay, *La Suprême Etreinte* (Paris: Offenstadt, 1900), 99.

50. See Algirdas Julien Greimas, *Du sens: essais sémiotiques* (Paris: Seuil, 1970), 135–55.

51. Mendès, *Méphistophela*, 109.

52. The same (non-)encounter is evoked in Joséphin Péladan, *La Gynandre*, 194, when a military officer marries a young woman who has already experienced the "sodomies" of a disorderly boarding school: "Given that, does the husband realize how fraught with difficulty is his role? How will the cavalry officer deal with the virgin worn out with pleasure? How will he play a warped instrument?"

53. A more straightforward, less moralistic version of the same choice can be found in Adrienne Saint-Agen, *L'Affolante Illusion* (Paris: Offenstadt, 1906), 34: "I will never be able to erase from my memory the utter disgust I felt at the bestiality of that rutting male. In spite of myself, I have never been able to overcome that strange feeling, that particular vision, even of the man I loved, as he appeared in the act of love just like a brute beast. . . ."

54. *Les Cousines de la colonelle* (Lisbon: da Boa-Vista, n.d.), 46.

55. There is a play on words here: *polissonner* means to misbehave, to do naughty things, especially to caress sexually, as in *polissonner avec le doigt*.

56. Jacques Yvel, *Demi-Femme* (Paris: Offenstadt, 1901), 224.

57. Péladan, *Le Livre du désir*, 58.

58. Saint-Médard, *L'Orgie moderne*, 29.

59. Saint-Agen, *L'Affolante Illusion*, 212.

60. La Vaudère, *Les Demi-Sexes*, 232–33.

61. Maxime Formont, *L'Inassouvie* (Paris: Lemerre, 1900), 107–8.

62. Victor Joze, *Paris-Gomorrhe* (Paris: Antony, 1894), 8.

63. La Jeunesse, *Demi-Volupté*, 20.

64. See, for example, 202: "That was the fatal sign, the infamous mark of adultery, the sign of reprobation, the punishment, the indication that it was a crime against nature, since the man and his mistress cannot sleep side by side and spend the whole nights of beautiful intimacy that God owes couples. Half-pleasure, and no more!"

65. Philippe Jacob, "Notice," in *L'Erotisme au XIXe siècle*, ed. Alexandrian, 119.

66. *Trésor de la langue française* (Paris: Editions du CNRS, 1971–1994), 8:986–87.

67. Prévost, *Les Demi-Vierges*, iii–iv.

68. Paul Bourget, *Physiologie de l'amour moderne* [1890] (Paris: Crès, 1917), 167.

69. La Vaudère, *Mortelle Etreinte*, 142.

70. Lorrain, *Le Vice errant*, 77.

71. Jacques Yvel, *Madame Flirt* (Paris: Simonis Empis, 1902), 4.

72. Bourget, *Physiologie de l'amour moderne*, 176.

73. Here is Bourget's metaphorical version of that point, *Physiologie de l'amour moderne*, 185: "Certain flirtations soil a woman more than being possessed. A rose that has been cut from the stalk may still remain fresh and pure. A rose, even a bud, even on the rose bush, if it has been handled and played with, is worse than faded."

Chapter 7. Orgasm

1. It should be clear, in view of this historical preoccupation, that my analysis is unlikely to coincide with the beguiling "petite histoire de l'orgasme" recounted by Gaëtan Brulotte in his *Œuvres de chair*, 133.

2. *Le période* is not to be confused with the standard modern word, *la période*. Michel Delon, in Sade, *Œuvres*, 1:1332, quotes Trévoux's dictionary: "This word is feminine in all its acceptations, except when it is used figuratively to mean the highest point that a thing can reach." The *Trésor de la langue française*, 13:94, describes the masculine word as archaic and literary, defining its meaning as "the maximum degree (of something)."

3. *Les Leçons de la volupté, ou confession générale du chevalier de Wilfort* (Brussels: Gay and Doucé, 1882).

4. *Vénus en rut*, 6:129.

5. Sade, *Œuvres complètes*, 1:428.

6. *Le Grand Robert* (Paris: Société du Nouveau Littré, Le Robert, 1974), 1:831–32. The *Trésor de la langue française*, 5:1083, gives its figurative meaning as the highest degree (of a quality, a feeling, a good or an evil), that one can reach, noting that this sometimes amounts to an excess.

7. *Thérèse philosophe*, 5:40.

8. Steven Marcus, *The Other Victorians*, 279.

9. Musset, *Gamiani*, 117.

10. Lesbos, *Enfilade de perles*, 14.

11. Lesbos, *Voluptés bizarres,* 78.

12. [Emile Desjardins], *L'Odyssée d'un pantalon,* 168.

13. *Lesbia, maîtresse d'école,* 85.

14. Nerciat, *Mon Noviciat,* 277.

15. Du Saussay, *Rires, sang et voluptés,* 173.

16. Merlin, *La Luxure,* 80.

17. Georges Brandimbourg, *Croquis du vice* (Paris: Fort, 1897), 124, 57.

18. Bernard de Saint-Just, "L'Esprit des mœurs au XVIIIe siècle," in *Théâtre érotique français du XVIIIe siècle,* ed. Jean-Jacques Pauvert (Paris: Le Terrain Vague, 1993), 344.

19. *La Canonisation de Jeanne d'Arc,* in *L'Erotisme au XIXe siècle,* ed. Alexandrian (Paris: Lattès, 1993), 648.

20. *L'Ecole des biches,* 141.

21. Georges Poulet, *Etudes sur le temps humain* (Paris: Plon, 1950–68).

22. *Les Amours de Sainfroid, jésuite, et d'Eulalie, fille dévote* (The Hague: Van der Kloot, 1729), xiii.

23. Crébillon *fils, La Nuit et le moment.*

24. Ibid., 9:2.

25. Pierre Hartmann, "Le Motif du viol dans la littérature romanesque du XVIIIe siècle," *Travaux de Littérature* 7 (1994): 224.

26. *Les Matinées du Palais-Royal, ou amours secrètes de mademoiselle Julie B^{***}, devenue comtesse de l'empire* (Berne and Paris: Les Marchands de nouveautés, 1815), 62.

27. See, for example, *Mon Noviciat,* 174: "That short moment was savored at length." And *Vingt Ans de la vie d'une jolie femme,* 30: "We spent more than a quarter of an hour without moving or uttering a word."

28. See Cryle, *Geometry in the Boudoir,* 136–37.

29. *Caroline et Saint-Hilaire, ou les putains du Palais-Royal* (Paris: Dans un bordel, an 8 [1817]), 1:84–85.

30. Sophie Cottin, *Claire d'Albe,* in *Ecrire d'amour. Anthologie de textes érotiques féminins (1799–1984),* ed. Claudine Brécourt-Villars (Paris: Ramsay, 1985), 67.

31. Choiseul-Meuse, *Entre chien et loup,* 2:37–38.

32. Du Saussay, *Chairs épanouies, beautés ardentes,* 121.

33. Saint-Médard, *La Volupté féroce,* 185.

34. La Vaudère, *Mortelle Etreinte,* 282.

35. Yvel, *Demi-Femme,* 193.

36. Besse, *La Fille de Gamiani,* 147.

37. Otto Brunner, Werner Conze, and Reinhart Koselleck, eds., *Gesichtliche Grundbegriffe. Historisches Lexicon zur politisch-sozialen Sprache in Deutschland* (Stuttgart: Cotta, 1982), 3:617–50. For an example of its use in medical discourse in English, see Mary Poovey, "'Scenes of an Indelicate Character': The Medical 'Treatment' of Victorian Women," in *The Making of the Modern Body,* ed. Catherine Gallagher and Thomas Laqueur (Berkeley: University of California Press, 1987), 146.

38. Georges Benrekassa, "Lexique médical, vocabulaire dramatique, métaphore politique: la notion de crise au XVIIIe siècle en France," *Textuel* 19

(1987): 11–12. See also the note by Michel Delon in Sade, *Œuvres*, 1:1233, and *Trésor de la langue française*, 6:498–99.

39. Here is a comparable example from Sade, *Aline et Valcour*, in *Œuvres*, 1:744: "A final crisis seemed likely to do away with me completely. Dolcini announced to him that I was dead."

40. See, for example, Du Saussay, *Chairs épanouies, beautés ardentes*, 353: "your pleasure was immense ... your body writhed in a happy crisis."

41. *Trésor de la langue française*, 6:498–99.

42. Du Saussay, *Chairs épanouies, beautés ardents*, 364–65.

43. Du Saussay, *Rires, sang et voluptés*, 20. See also 407.

44. La Vaudère, *Les Demi-Sexes*, 120.

45. See, for example, Saint-Médard, *L'Orgie moderne*, 81: "She was suffocating, breathless with anger, and seemed in danger of falling into a nervous crisis. She slumped down, her arms writhing and all her muscles drawn tight." In Jules Davray and Jean Caujolle, *Vendeuse d'amour* (Paris: Simon, 1891), 47, it even happens to a young man, when he hears that his father has been murdered.

46. Davray and Caujolle, *Vendeuse d'amour*, 411–12.

47. La Jeunesse, *Demi-Volupté*, 224.

48. Georges Brandimbourg, *L'Arrière-Boutique* (Paris: Fort, 1898), 70–71. See also Davray and Caujolle, *Vendeuse d'amour*, 227, for this advice given to a woman about a man: "As soon as you feel he is ripe, that is, at the paroxysm of his passion, you should agree to meet with him."

49. Besse, *La Fille de Gamiani*, 70.

50. Reschal, *Le Journal d'un amant*, 29.

51. Péladan, *Le Livre du désir*, 6.

52. *Les Libertins du grand monde*, 84.

53. Saint-Médard, *La Volupté féroce*, 281.

54. *L'Ecole des biches*, 163.

55. *Un Eté à la campagne*, in *L'Erotisme au XIXᵉ siècle*, ed. Alexandrian (Paris: Lattès, 1993), 442–43.

56. Bois, *L'Eternelle Poupée*, 125.

57. Camille Pert, *Les Amours perverses de Rosa Scari* (Paris: Librairie artistique, 1907), 83.

58. Merlin, *La Luxure*, 160.

59. Ibid., 156.

60. Reschal, *Le Journal d'un amant*, 231.

61. Saint-Médard, *La Volupté féroce*, 124.

62. *La Messaline française*, 5:322.

63. Mirabeau, *Œuvres érotiques, L'Enfer de la Bibliothèque Nationale* (Paris: Fayard, 1984), 1:194 n.12.

64. Angelica Goodden, *The Complete Lover: Eros, Nature and Artifice in the Eighteenth-Century French Novel* (Oxford: Clarendon Press, 1989), 90.

65. Ibid.

66. On the "semantic evolution" of the word "orgasm," see Nancy Huston, *Mosaïque de la pornographie*, 142 n.2. This history hardly intersects with the one presented by Thomas Laqueur, "Orgasm, Generation, and the Politics of

Reproductive Biology," in *The Making of the Modern Body*, ed. Catherine Gallagher and Thomas Laqueur (Berkeley: University of California Press, 1987), 1–41. Laqueur, whose focus is on the notion of climactic physiological pleasure in medical discourse, argues that orgasm, after being integrated into the understanding of generative process, became peripheral to medical thought toward the end of the eighteenth century.

67. Le Sage, *Gil Blas de Santillane*, in *Romanciers du XVIIIe siècle*, ed. René Etiemble (Paris: Gallimard/Pléiade, 1960–65), 1:694–95.

68. See William H. Masters and Virginia E. Johnson, *Human Sexual Response* (Boston: Little, Brown, 1966).

69. "L'Article 'fureur utérine' de *L'Encyclopédie*," in Bienville, *La Nymphomanie, ou traité de la fureur utérine*, ed. Jean Marie Goulemot (Paris: Le Sycomore, 1980), 167.

70. Huston, *Mosaïque de la pornographie*, 142 n.2.

71. *Trésor de la langue française*, 7:622. The *Trésor* has located an earlier scientific usage (1777), that defines "orgasm" as "the highest point of sexual arousal." It is difficult to know, in fact, whether this refers to the most advanced point of desire or to the moment of climactic collapse. But that very equivocation is somehow part of our theme.

72. Evidence of anachronism and some indications of the possibility of critique can be found in Pierre J. Payer, *The Bridling of Desire: Views of Sex in the Later Middle Ages* (Toronto: University of Toronto Press, 1993), 33–34, 179, 204 n.75.

73. Luce Irigaray, *Ethique de la différence sexuelle* (Paris: Minuit, 1984), 55.

74. Foucault, *Dits et écrits*, 4:174–75.

75. Ibid., 4:661.

76. Barbara Ehrenreich, Elizabeth Hess, and Gloria Jacobs, *Re-Making Love: The Feminization of Sex* (New York: Anchor, 1986), 5.

77. Heath, *Questions of Cinema* (Bloomington: Indiana University Press, 1981), 188.

78. Roger Bougard, *Erotisme et amour physique dans la littérature française du XVIIe siècle* (Paris: Lachurié, 1986), 24.

79. Nicolas Venette, *Tableau de l'amour conjugal* (Paris: Agence Parisienne de Distribution, 1950), 337.

80. Sade, *Œuvres complètes*, 7:196.

81. *Les Délices de Coblentz*, 1:34–35.

82. *L'Enfant du bordel*, 33.

83. Sade, *Œuvres complètes*, 1:79.

84. See for example *Aline et Valcour*, in *Œuvres*, 1:555n, 577, and *Histoire de Juliette*, in *Œuvres complètes*, 8:112.

85. *Les Tableaux vivants, ou mes confessions aux pieds de la duchesse* (Amsterdam: n.p., 1870), 1:45.

86. Du Saussay, *Chairs épanouies, beautés ardentes*, 228.

87. *Le Roman de Violette*, 510.

88. Du Saussay, *La Suprême Etreinte*, 116.

89. Du Saussay, *Chairs épanouies, beautés ardentes*, 102.

90. For a more straightforward example, see *Les Deux Sœurs, ou quatre ans de libertinage* (Montréal: Lebaucher, 1906), 24: "a mutual need to carry out the act."

91. Merlin, *La Luxure*, 92.

92. Reschal, *Une Inassouvie*, 251.

93. Bois, *L'Eternelle Poupée*, 79.

94. Quoted in John Alfred Atkins, *Sex in Literature* (London: Calder and Boyars, 1970), 1:79–80.

95. Rémy de Gourmont, *Physique de l'amour* (Paris: Editions 1900, 1989), 15.

96. Lester G. Crocker, *Nature and Culture: Ethical Thought in the French Enlightenment* (Baltimore: Johns Hopkins University Press, 1963), 356.

CHAPTER 8. MESSALINA

1. Jean Marie Goulemot, "Préface," in Bienville, *La Nymphomanie, ou traité de la fureur utérine* (Paris: Le Sycomore, 1980), 10–11.

2. Kathryn Norberg, "The Libertine Whore: Prostitution in French Pornography from Margot to Juliette," in *The Invention of Pornography: Obscenity and the Origins of Modernity, 1500–1800*, ed. Lynn Hunt (New York: Zone, 1993), 235.

3. See Cryle, *Geometry in the Boudoir*, 169–205.

4. Joan De Jean, *Fictions of Sappho 1546–1937* (Chicago: University of Chicago Press, 1989).

5. Restif, *L'Anti-Justine*, 374.

6. Sade, *Œuvres complètes*, 9:44.

7. *Ordonnance de police sur les filles de joie*, *L'Enfer de la Bibliothèque Nationale* (Paris: Fayard, 1987), 6:400.

8. For a discussion of this term, see Cryle, *Geometry in the Boudoir*, 71–91. Sade's Juliette is herself described as having "a Messalina-like temperament" (*Histoire de Juliette*, 8:368).

9. Augustin Carrache, *L'Arétin, ou recueil de postures érotiques*, preface by Philippe Lemarchand (Geneva: Slatkine, 1985), 54–55.

10. *La Messaline française*, 5:325.

11. *Vénus en rut*, 6:221.

12. Nerciat, *Les Aphrodites*, 1:69.

13. *Les Libertins du grand monde*, 112: "Madeleine was an out and out whore, and I suspect Messalina would have recognized her as a dangerous rival."

14. Musset, *Gamiani*, 133.

15. Duo, *Inassouvie*, 25.

16. Reschal, *Une Inassouvie*, 28.

17. *Histoire de dom Bougre, portier des Chartreux*, *L'Enfer de la Bibliothèque Nationale* (Paris: Fayard, 1985), 3:187–88.

18. On this question, see Jeffreys, *Anticlimax*, 229; and Janine Aeply, *Eros Zéro* (Paris: Mercure de France, 1972), 27.

19. John Alfred Atkins, *Sex in Literature,* vol. 1, *The Erotic Impulse in Literature* (London: Calder and Boyars, 1970), 60–61.

20. Nerciat, *Le Diable au corps,* 6:85.

21. *La Messaline française,* 5:321.

22. *Eléonore, ou l'heureuse personne, L'Enfer de la Bibliothèque Nationale* (Paris: Fayard, 1987), 6:82.

23. Nerciat, *Le Diable au corps,* 4:78.

24. See Dworkin, *Pornography.*

25. Mirabeau, *Erotika Biblion,* in *Œuvres érotiques* (Paris: Fayard, 1984), 596–97. Here is his French version of the Juvenal text:

Mais elle s'enferma dans une pièce retirée

Et là, brûlant du rut d'une vulve enflammée

Elle s'allongea et engloutit des poissons,

Lassée de l'homme et se retira encore insatisfaite.

26. Mirabeau, *Le Rideau levé,* 428.

27. *Les Délices de Coblentz,* 1:11.

28. *La Messaline française,* 5:324.

29. Nerciat, *Le Diable au corps,* 6:27.

30. Musset, *Gamiani,* 98.

31. *Vingt ans de la vie d'un jeune homme,* 61.

32. Merlin, *La Luxure,* 116.

33. Marcus, *The Other Victorians,* 279.

34. Nerciat, *Le Diable au corps,* 6:216.

35. Nerciat, *Mon Noviciat,* 311.

36. For some examples of such lameness, see *La Nouvelle Académie des dames,* 107–8, and *Les Délices de Coblentz,* 1:71. Other examples are given in Peter Cryle, "Gendered Time in Erotic Narrative: Finishing Power vs Staying Power," *Romanic Review* 83:132–33.

37. See Dworkin, *Pornography,* 56.

38. Simone de Beauvoir, *Le Deuxième Sexe* (Paris: Gallimard, 1949), 2:134.

39. Luce Irigaray, "'Françaises,' ne faites plus un effort," *Ce sexe qui n'en est pas un* (Paris: Minuit, 1977), 197.

40. See Cryle, *Geometry in the Boudoir,* 147–66, on how not to be murdered in Sadian stories.

41. Irigaray's slight simplification of the Latin seems to respect the rhythm and the sense of Juvenal's original. Beauvoir had already modified the quotation in exactly the same way in *Le Deuxième Sexe.* It is likely that both were influenced by the fact that one of Baudelaire's poems in *Les Fleurs du mal* is entitled "Sed non satiata." See Charles Baudelaire, *Œuvres complètes* (Paris: Gallimard/Pléïade, 1975–76), 1:28.

42. The virgin figure, and notably the woman in armor, is discussed in Philip Stewart, *Engraven Desire: Eros, Imagery and Text in the French Eighteenth Century* (Durham, N.C.: Duke University Press, 1992), 104–22. The woman in armor, says Stewart, is "a favorite (because extreme), form of provocative sexual discrimination" (122).

43. Mary Jane Sherfey, whose work might well have provided a target for Irigaray's critique of sexology, is nonetheless able to speak—in terms that owe much to Masters and Johnson, but perhaps just a little to Messalina—of the

human female's attaining the highest degree of sexual stimulation as a state of "satiation-in-insatiation." See Mary Jane Sherfey, *The Nature and Evolution of Female Sexuality* (New York: Random House, 1972), 112.

44. Luce Irigaray, *Ethique de la différence sexuelle* (Paris: Minuit, 1984), 67.

45. Grandval *fils*, "La Nouvelle Messaline," in *Théâtre érotique français au XVIIIᵉ siècle*, ed. J.-J. Pauvert (Paris: Le Terrain vague, 1993), 228.

46. *Vénus en rut*, 6:119; original emphasis.

47. Nerciat, *Le Diable au corps*, 1:22; original emphasis.

48. *Les Amours de garnison*, 6–7.

49. *L'Ecole des biches*, 79.

50. Du Saussay, *Chairs épanouies, beautés ardentes*, 110.

51. *Les Folies amoureuses d'une impératrice*, in *L'Erotisme Second empire*, ed. J.-J. Pauvert (Paris: Carrere, 1985), 44.

52. Lesbos, *Enfilade de perles*, 7.

53. Péladan, *Le Vice suprême*, 68.

54. Reschal, *Le Journal d'un amant*, 92.

55. Duo, *Inassouvie*, 12–14.

56. Merlin, *La Luxure*, 198.

57. Jules-Amédée Barbey d'Aurevilly, "Préface," in Péladan, *Le Vice suprême*, x.

58. Nerciat, *Le Diable au corps*, 6:65.

59. La Vaudère, *Les Demi-Sexes*, 194.

60. Jean-Louis Dubut de Laforest, *Mademoiselle Tantale, Pathologie sociale* (Paris: Dupont, 1884), 65 n.1.

Chapter 9. Lesbos

1. Guy de Maupassant, "La Femme de Paul," *Contes et nouvelles* (Paris: Gallimard/Pléiade, 1974), 296.

2. Note that a more condemnatory tone, of the kind found in some other texts, changes little, if anything, about the certainty of recognition. Here is how the narrator hero of Antonin Reschal's *Le Journal d'un amant* (Paris: Offenstadt, 1902), describes a group of women "thirsty" with desire who are always to be found in a certain Parisian café: "Ah! Those ravaged faces, those staring, lifeless eyes, those boyish haircuts, those mannish airs, those disgusting manners!" (146).

3. Sade, *Œuvres*, 1:840n.

4. Friedrich Carl Forberg, *Manuel d'érotologie classique* (Paris: Lisieux, 1882), 1:175.

5. Nerciat, *Le Diable au corps*, 4:88 n.1. See also 2:30.

6. For an example of "lesbien" referring to cunnilingus practiced by a man, see Nerciat, *Le Diable au corps*, 2:59.

7. Sade, *Histoire de Juliette*, 8:196–97.

8. On the *aphrodisia*, see Michel Foucault, *Histoire de la sexualité*, vol. 2, *L'Usage des plaisirs* (Paris: Gallimard, 1984).

9. Forberg, *Manuel d'érotologie classique*, 2:101. For an enlightening discussion of the notion of "tribade" and its emergence in medical discourse, see

Katharine Park, "The Rediscovery of the Clitoris: French Medicine and the Tribade, 1570–1620", in *The Body in Parts: Fantasies of Corporeality in Early Modern Europe*, ed. David Hillman and Carla Mazzio (London and New York: Routledge, 1997), 170–93.

10. Pidansat de Mairobert, *La Secte des anandrynes: confession de mademoiselle Sapho* (Paris: Bibliothèque des curieux, 1920), 17–18. Jeffrey Merrick, "The Marquis de Villette and Mademoiselle de Raucourt: Representations of Male and Female Sexual Deviance in Late Eighteenth-Century France," in *Homosexuality in Modern France*, ed. Jeffrey Merrick and Bryant T. Ragan, Jr. (New York, Oxford: Oxford University Press, 1996), 30–53, discusses Mlle. de Raucourt, the "tribade" or "anandryne" who was the explicit model for the leader of this "sect."

11. *Lesbia, maîtresse d'école*, 77.

12. *La Canonisation de Jeanne d'Arc*, in *L'Erotisme au XIXe siècle*, ed. Alexandrian (Paris: Lattès, 1993), 625.

13. *Le Roman de Violette*, 536. Violette is contrasted with those hermaphrodites who bring together the qualities of both sexes "thanks to an extension of the clitoris" (537).

14. Joan De Jean, *Fictions of Sappho 1546–1937*, 263–65.

15. For a discussion of dictionary entries and dates of first documented usage for "saphisme" and "lesbienne," see ibid., 350 n. 51.

16. Jacques, *Les Malheurs de Sapho*, 34.

17. Martha Vicinus, "The Adolescent Boy: Fin de siècle Femme Fatale?" *Journal of the History of Sexuality*, 5 (1994): 92.

18. André Billy, *L'Epoque 1900* (Paris: Tallandier, 1951), 227. See De Jean, *Fictions of Sappho 1546–1937*, 23, 265, on the "Sappho 1900" phenomenon. Rosario, "Pointy Penises, Fashion Crimes, and Hysterical Mollies," 167, insists that such representations were literary rather than medical: "Despite the long recognition of 'sapphic love,' it was a matter of greater interest to novelists and pseudoscientific writers than to physicians, who largely ignored it."

19. See Liane de Pougy, *Idylle saphique*, ed. Jean Chalon (Paris: Des femmes, 1987).

20. "Sapho 1900" can of course be recounted as the heroic overturning of a century of oppression and ignorance. This is the kind of history told by Jean Desthieux in his *Figures méditerranéennes: femmes damnées* (Paris: Orphrys, 1937), where Renée Vivien appears as the decisive agent in the establishment of a sapphic cult. My point is simply that the "repressive" antecedents must have enabled later understandings as well as restricting them.

21. Jacques, in *Les Malheurs de Sapho*, 51, comments that the lesbian, for the nineteenth century, is often the sister of a whore if not a whore herself. He deplores the general looseness of terms whereby the term "bacchante" is used both for lesbians and for Cleopatra, and a "saphiste" is called a "messaline" (172).

22. *Eléonore ou l'heureuse personne*, *L'Enfer de la Bibliothèque Nationale* (Paris: Fayard, 1987), 6:80.

23. Musset, *Gamiani*, 114. An earlier, less assertive version of this claim can be found in *La Confession de Marie-Antoinette ci-devant reine de France*,

au peuple franc. This text is discussed in Elizabeth Colwill, "Pass as a Woman, Act like a Man," in *Homosexuality in Modern France*, ed. Jeffrey Merrick and Bryant T. Ragan, Jr (New York and Oxford: Oxford University Press, 1996), 59, although the theme of inexhaustibility is not taken up. The duchesse de Polignac states in the text quoted that sexual pleasure with women is "one of those rare pleasures that cannot be used up, because it can be repeated as many times as one likes."

24. Charles Baudelaire, "Femmes damnées," in *Œuvres complètes,* 1:154–55.

25. Jean Desthieux, *Figures méditerranéennes: femmes damnées* (Paris: Orphrys, 1937), and Henri Drouin, *Femmes damnées: essai sur les carences sexuelles féminines dans la littérature et dans la vie* (Paris: La Vulgarisation scientifique, 1945). Drouin begins his essay with an epigraph from Baudelaire's text.

26. Lesbos, *Voluptés bizarres,* 39.

27. Emile Desjardins, *Les Callipyges, ou les délices de la verge* (Paris: aux dépens de la compagnie, 1892), 27.

28. *Toute la lyre! Manœuvres de Lucienne* (n.p., n.d.). This text appears to date from the early twentieth century. Louis Perceau's *Bibliographie du roman érotique au XIXe siècle* (Paris: Fourdrinier, 1930), 2:24, lists it with works of the "long" nineteenth century (i.e., before 1914).

29. René Maizeroy, *Deux amies* (Paris: Havard, 1885), 275.

30. Mendès, *Méphistophela,* 10. On the uninterrupted nature of Messalina's activity, see also Alfred Jarry, *Messaline* [1901], in *Œuvres complètes* (Geneva: Slatkine, 1975), 3:22.

31. De Jean, *Fictions of Sappho 1546–1937,* 260–61. Paul Lorenz, in *Sapho 1900* (Paris: Julliard, 1977), 59, simply declares that there is "nothing sapphic" about Daudet's novel, but the text itself refers to Sappho's name as "the label of an illness" (45).

32. Alphonse Daudet, *Sapho* (Morsang-sur-Orge: Safrat, 1990), 40, 53.

33. Vivant Denon, *Point de lendemain* (Paris: Desjonquières, 1987).

34. Mirabeau, *Ma Conversion,* in *Œuvres erotiques* (Paris: Fayard, 1984), 128.

35. The same expression is used to refer to a woman's masturbation in the anonymous *Vingt Ans de la vie d'une jolie femme, ou mémoires de Julia R . . . ,* 76.

36. Françoise d'Eaubonne, *Eros minoritaire* (Paris: Balland, 1970), 17. See also Claudine Brécourt-Villars, *Petit glossaire raisonné de l'érotisme saphique (1880–1930)* (Paris: Pauvert, 1980), 42.

37. Xavière Gauthier, *Surréalisme et sexualité* (Paris: Gallimard, 1971), 242.

38. On this question, see Cryle, *Geometry in the Boudoir,* 169–205.

39. Angelica Goodden, *The Complete Lover: Eros, Nature and Artifice in the Eighteenth-Century French Novel* (Oxford: Clarendon, 1989), 283.

40. Gautier, *Mademoiselle de Maupin,* 338.

41. *Le Roman de Violette,* 566–67.

42. Maizeroy, *Deux amies,* 186.

43. *Le Roman de Violette,* 537.

44. Péladan, *La Gynandre,* 77.

45. Francis Lepage, *Les Fausses Vierges* (Paris: Offenstadt, 1902), 79.
46. Maizeroy, *Deux amies,* 93–94.
47. Guy de Téramond, *Impériales Voluptés* (Paris: Méricant, 1905), 75.
48. Adrienne Saint-Agen, *Amants féminins* (Paris: Offenstadt, 1902), 45.
49. Mendès, *Méphistophela,* 10.
50. Musset, *Gamiani,* 136.
51. Claudine Brécourt-Villars discusses sapphism as a mythical "mortiferous passion" in her *Petit glossaire raisonné de l'érotisme saphique (1880–1930)* (Paris: Pauvert, 1980), 89. An interesting exception to this general rule, the only one that I have found, occurs in Jean de Kellec, *A Lesbos* (Paris: Simon, 1891). This story tells the life of one woman, beginning with a childhood marked by boyishness and rebellion, but, we are told insistently, no "morbidity" (5). Andrée, the heroine, rejects the approaches of decadent, aristocratic women (117). She is attracted and intrigued by lesbian tastes, as she admits to herself, but does not want to fall into "vice" (120). One would have to say that despite the title, this novel hardly deserves to be qualified as erotic literature even of the most prurient kind since the heroine scrupulously avoids libidinal suffering.
52. Saint-Agen, *Amants féminins,* 227.
53. Maizeroy, *Deux amies,* 197.
54. Téramond, *Impériales Voluptés,* 87.
55. Maizeroy, *Deux amies,* 173.
56. *Le Roman de Violette,* 566.
57. Mendès, *Méphistophela,* 449–50.
58. Saint-Agen, *L'Affolante Illusion,* 26–27.
59. Téramond, *Impériales Voluptés,* 182.
60. Saint-Agen, *Amants féminins,* 26.
61. Mendès, *Méphistophela,* 3.
62. *Toute la lyre! Manœuvres de Lucienne,* 7.
63. Maizeroy, *Deux amies,* 20.
64. Téramond, *Impériales Voluptés,* 142.
65. Henri Drouin, *Femmes damnées* (Paris: La Vulgarisation scientifique, 1945), 63.
66. Maizeroy, *Deux amies,* 61.
67. Mendès, *Méphistophela,* 568.

Chapter 10. Finishing

1. See Cryle, *Geometry in the Boudoir,* esp. 1–31.
2. Huston, *Mosaïque de la pornographie,* 83.
3. Jacques, *Les Malheurs de Sapho,* 253.
4. Brécourt-Villars, *Petit glossaire raisonné de l'érotisme saphique,* 56–57. Let me regret, in passing, that Sade should stand here, as ever, to mark the beginning of the nineteenth century, even though there is no textual reason to credit him with initiating this theme. Jean-Pierre Jacques provides an even more sardonic version of the standard plot in *Les Malheurs de Sapho,* 222.
5. Gervaise de Latouche, *Histoire de dom Bougre,* 3:220.

6. *Lettres galantes et philosophiques de deux nones, L'Enfer de la Bibliothèque Nationale* (Paris: Fayard, 1986), 5:261–62.

7. *La Messaline française,* 5:321–22.

8. Musset, *Gamiani,* 82.

9. *Les Tableaux vivants,* 1:72.

10. *Le Roman de Violette,* 542.

11. Pidansat de Mairobert, *La Secte des Anandrynes: confession de mademoiselle Sapho* (Paris: Bibliothèque des curieux, 1920), 49, 52.

12. Musset, *Gamiani,* 131.

13. *L'Ecole des biches,* 172.

14. Jean Richepin, *Sapphô* (Paris: Marpon/Flammarion, 1884), 30.

15. Nonce Casanova, *Sapho* (Paris: Ollendorff, 1905), 254.

16. Edouard Romilly, *Sappho: la passionnante, la passionnée* (Paris: Figuière, 1931), 92.

17. Merlin, *La Luxure,* 244–46.

18. Lesbos, *Voluptés bizarres,* 73.

19. Rachilde, *L'Heure sexuelle* (Paris: Baudinière, 1933), 143.

20. Rachilde, *Madame Adonis* (Paris: Monnier, 1888), 213–14.

21. Saint-Agen, *Amants féminins,* 251.

22. For a "scientific" reference to this phenomenon, see Dubut de Laforest, *Mademoiselle Tantale,* 44.

23. *Lesbia, maîtresse d'école.*

24. Maizeroy, *Deux amies,* 6–7.

25. Téramond, *Impériales Voluptés,* 83.

26. Lepage, *Les Fausses Vierges,* 274.

27. Mendès, *Méphistophela,* 134.

28. Saint-Agen, *Charmeuse de femmes,* 171.

29. Reschal, *Le Journal d'un amant,* 147.

30. Maupassant, "La Femme de Paul," 292.

31. *Le Roman de Violette,* 555.

32. Besse, *La Fille de Gamiani,* 133.

33. Lesbos, *Voluptés bizarres,* 21.

34. Saint-Agen, *Charmeuse de femmes,* 69–70.

35. Saint-Agen, *Amants féminins,* 182.

36. Ibid., 73.

37. Mendès, *Méphistophela,* 392.

38. See Pougy, *Idylle saphique* [1901].

39. Téramond, *Impériales Voluptés,* 110–11.

Bibliography

NOTE: EDITIONS GIVEN ARE THE MOST RECENT AND WIDELY AVAILABLE, wherever more recent editions exist.

Abel, Elizabeth, Marianne Hirsch, and Elizabeth Langland, eds. *The Voyage In: Fictions of Female Development*. Hanover, N.H., and London: University Press of New England, 1983.

Abelove, Henry. "Some Speculations on the History of 'Sexual Intercourse' During the 'Long Eighteenth Century' in England." In *Nationalisms and Sexualities*, edited by Andrew Parker, 335–42. London: Routledge, 1990.

Abramovici, Jean-Christophe. *Le Livre interdit: de Théophile de Viau à Sade*. Paris: Payot, 1996.

Adbul-Haqq Effendi. *Le Livre de volupté*. Erzeroum: chez Qizmich-Aga, n.d. [1880].

Aeply, Janine. *Eros zéro*. Paris: Mercure de France, 1972.

Airaksinen, Timo. *The Philosophy of the Marquis de Sade*. London: Routledge, 1995.

Alexandrian. *Histoire de la littérature érotique*. Paris: Seghers, 1989.

———. *Les Libérateurs de l'amour*. Paris: Le Seuil, 1977.

———, ed. *L'Erotisme au XIXᵉ siècle*. Paris: Lattès, 1993.

Allen, Suzanne. *L'Espace d'un livre*. Paris: Gallimard, 1971.

Allison, David B., Mark S. Roberts, and Allen S. Weiss, eds. *Sade and the Narrative of Transgression*. Cambridge: Cambridge University Press, 1995.

Amélie, ou les écarts de ma jeunesse. Brussels: Gay and Doucé, 1882.

Les Amours de garnison. Aux Invalides: chez le gardien du Dôme, 1832 [1831].

Les Amours de Sainfroid, jésuite, et d'Eulalie, fille dévote. The Hague: Van der Kloot, 1729.

Les Amours des dieux payens. Lampsaque: Chez tous les marchands de nouveautés, 1802.

Les Amours d'un gentleman. Brussels: W. Schmidt, 1895 [1889].

Les Amours, galanteries et passe-temps des actrices, ou confessions curieuses et galantes de ces dames. Couillopolis: 1700 [1833].

Les Amours secrètes de M. Mayeux. Brussels: Les Marchands de nouveautés, 1832.

Angenot, Marc. "Pornographie fin de siècle: le polisson, le leste, le grivois et le pimenté." *Cahiers pour la littérature populaire* 7 (1986): 38–54.

Apollinaire, Guillaume. *La Fin de Babylone*. Paris: Bibliothèque des curieux, 1914.

Aragon, Louis. *Le Libertinage*. Paris: Gallimard, 1977.

L'Arétin d'Augustin Carrache, ou recueil de postures érotiques. Paris: Cercle du livre précieux, 1962.

Aretino, Pietro. *I Ragionamenti*. Rome: Frank, 1911.

———. *Dialogues [Ragionamenti]*. Translated by Raymond Rosenthal. 6 vols. New York: Stein and Day, 1971.

———. *Les Ragionamenti, ou dialogues du divin Pietro Aretino*. Translated by Alcide Bonneau. Paris: Lisieux, 1882.

———. *Les Sonnets luxurieux du divin Pietro Aretino*. [Translated by Alcide Bonneau.] Paris: Lisieux, 1882.

Ariès, Philippe. *L'Enfant et la vie familiale sous l'ancien régime*. Paris: Plon, 1960.

———. *Western Sexuality: Practice and Precept in Past and Present Times*. Translated by Anthony Forster. Oxford: Blackwell, 1985.

Aristotle. *Poetics*. New York: Hill and Wang, 1961.

Aron, Jean-Paul, and Roger Kempf. "Triumphs and Tribulations of the Homosexual Discourse." In *Homosexualities and French Literature: Cultural Contexts / Critical Texts*, edited by G. Stambolian and E. Marks, 141–57. Ithaca: Cornell University Press, 1979.

Ashbee, Henry Spencer. *Bibliography of Prohibited Books (With Bio-Biblio-Iconographical and Critical Notes on Curious, Uncommon and Erotic Books by Pisanus Fraxi)*. New York: Brussel, 1962.

———. *Forbidden Books of the Victorians*. Edited by Peter Fryer. London: Odyssey, 1970.

Atkins, John Alfred. *Sex in Literature*. Vol. 1, *The Erotic Impulse in Literature*. London: Calder and Boyars, 1970.

———. *Sex in Literature*. Vol. 2, *The Classical Experience of the Sexual Impulse*. London: Calder and Boyars, 1973.

Attitudes et postures de l'amour. Paris: Cercle du livre précieux, 1959.

Augustine. *The City of God Against the Pagans*. Cambridge: Harvard University Press, 1966.

Bachelard, Gaston. *La Psychanalyse du feu*. Paris: Gallimard/Idées, 1972.

———. *The Psychoanalysis of Fire*. Translated by Alan C. M. Ross. Boston: Beacon Press, 1964.

Baldassera, Paul. *Lesbos ou Cythère*. Paris: Figuière, 1934.

Balzac, Honoré de. *La Fille aux yeux d'or*. In *La Comédie humaine*. Paris: Gallimard/Pléiade, 1977.

———. *La Peau de chagrin*. In *La Comédie humaine*. Paris: Gallimard/Pléiade, 1977.

Barbey d'Aurevilly, Jules. "Le Rideau cramoisi." In *Les Diaboliques, Œuvres romanesques complètes*. Paris: Gallimard/Pléïade, 1964–66.

Barthes, Roland. *Fragments d'un discours amoureux*. Paris: Le Seuil, 1977.

———. *Le Plaisir du texte*. Paris: Le Seuil, 1973.

———. *The Pleasure of the Text*. Translated by Richard Miller. New York: Hill and Wang, 1975.

———. *Sade, Fourier, Loyola*. Paris: Le Seuil, 1971.

———. *Sade, Fourier, Loyola*. Translated by Richard Miller. New York: Hill and Wang, 1976.

———. *S/Z*. Paris: Le Seuil, 1970.

———. *S/Z*. Translated by Richard Miller. New York: Hill and Wang, 1974.

Bartkowski, Frances. "Toward a Feminist Eros: Readings in Feminist Utopian Fiction." Ph.D. thesis, University of Iowa, 1982.

Bataille, Georges. *La Littérature et le mal*. Paris: Gallimard, 1967.

———. *Literature and Evil*. London: Calder and Boyars, 1973.

———. "Madame Edwarda." In *Œuvres complètes*, vol. 3. Paris: Gallimard, 1970–88.

———. "La Part maudite." In *Œuvres complètes*, vol. 7. Paris: Gallimard, 1970–88.

Battacharyya, Narendra Nath. *A History of Indian Erotic Literature*. New Delhi: Munshiram Manoharlal, 1975.

Baudelaire, Charles. *Œuvres complètes*. Paris: Gallimard/Pléïade, 1975.

Baudrillard, Jean. *De la séduction*. Paris: Galilée, 1979.

———. *Seduction*. Translated by Brian Singer. London: Macmillan, 1990.

Béalu, Marcel, ed. *La Poésie érotique de langue française*. Paris: Seghers, 1971.

Beauvoir, Simone de. *Le Deuxième Sexe*. 2 vols. Paris: Gallimard, 1949.

———. *Faut-il brûler Sade?* Paris: Gallimard, 1955.

———. *Must We Burn De Sade?* Translated by Annette Michelson. London: P. Nevill, 1953.

———. *The Second Sex*. New York: Knopf, 1952.

Becker, Raymond de. *The Other Face of Love*. Translated by Margaret Crosland and Alan Daventry. London: Neville Spearman, 1967.

Beizer, Janet. *Ventriloquized Bodies: The Narrative Uses of Hysteria in France. 1850–1900*. Ithaca: Cornell University Press, 1994.

Belot, Adolphe. *La Femme de feu*. Paris: Dentu, 1878.

———. *La Femme de glace*. Paris: Dentu, 1878.

———. *Mademoiselle Giraud, ma femme*. Paris: Dentu, 1870.

———. *La Sultane parisienne*. Paris: Dentu, 1878.

———. *Une Affolée d'amour*. Paris: Dentu, 1891.

———. *Une Joueuse*. Paris: Dentu, 1879.

Belot, Adolphe, and Emile Daudet. *La Vénus de Gordes*. Paris: Dentu, 1876.

Benrekassa, Georges. "L'Article 'Jouissance' et l'idéologie érotique de Diderot." *Dix-Huitième Siècle* 12 (1980): 9–34.

——. *Le Langage des lumières: concepts et savoir de la langue.* Paris: Presses universitaires de France, 1995.

——. "Lexique médical, vocabulaire dramatique, métaphore politique: la notion de crise au XVIIIe siècle en France." *Textuel* 19 (1987): 9–20.

Berg, Jean de. *L'Image.* Paris: Minuit, 1956.

Berg, Jeanne de. *Cérémonies de femmes.* Paris: Grasset et Fasquelle, 1985.

Bergler, E., and W. S. Kroger. *Kinsey's Myth of Female Sexuality.* New York: Grune and Stratton, 1954.

Bernardin de Saint-Pierre. *Paul et Virginie.* Paris: Livre de poche, 1974.

Bernheimer, Charles. *Figures of Ill Repute: Representing Prostitution in Nineteenth-Century France.* Cambridge: Harvard University Press, 1989.

Bersani, Leo. "Representation and its Discontents." In *Allegory and Representation*, edited by Stephen J. Greenblatt, 145–62. Baltimore and London: Johns Hopkins University Press, 1981.

——. *A Future for Astyanax: Character and Desire in Literature.* London: Marion Boyars, 1978.

Bersani, Leo, and Ulysse Dutoit. "The Forms of Violence." *October* 8 (1979): 17–29.

——. "Merde alors." *October* 13 (1980): 23–35.

Besnard-Coursodon, Micheline. "Monsieur Vénus, Madame Adonis: sexe et discours." *Littérature* 54 (1984): 121–27.

Besse, Louis. *Amour charnel.* Paris: Librairie parisienne, 1898.

——. *La Débauche.* Paris: Librairie parisienne, 1898.

——. *La Fille de Gamiani: journal d'une prostituée.* Paris: Albin Michel, 1906.

——. *La Foule en rut.* Paris: Fort, 1903.

Bienville. *La Nymphomanie, ou traité de la fureur utérine.* Edited by Jean Marie Goulemot. Paris: Le Sycomore, 1980 [1771].

Bigarrures: coiro-pygo-glotto-chiro-phallurgiques. Edited by Béatrice Didier. Geneva and Paris: Slatkine, 1981.

Billy, André. *L'Epoque 1900.* Paris: Tallandier, 1951.

Blanchot, Maurice. *Lautréamont et Sade.* Paris: UGE, 1967.

——. *Sade et Restif de la Bretonne.* Paris: Complexe, 1986.

Bois, Jules. *L'Eternelle Poupée.* Paris: Ollendorff, 1894.

Bold, Alan, ed. *The Sexual Dimension in Literature.* London: Vision, 1982.

Bonnet, Jean-Claude. "La Harangue sadienne." *Poétique* 13 (1982): 31–50.

Bonnet, Marie-Jo. *Un Choix sans equivoque: relations amoureuses entre les femmes, XVIe–XXe siècle.* Paris: Denoël, 1981.

Borderie, Roger. "La Question de Sade." *Obliques* 12–13 (1977): 1–3.

Bos, Mary, and Jill Pack. "Porn, Law, Politics." *Camerawork* 18 (1980): 4–5.

Bouchard, Jean-Jacques. *Les Confessions d'un perverti.* Paris: Cercle du livre précieux, 1960.

Bougard, Roger. *Erotisme et amour physique dans la littérature française du XVIIe siècle.* Paris: Lachurié, 1986.

——. *Physiologie de l'amour moderne*. Paris: Crès, 1917 [1890].

——. *Un Crime d'amour*. Paris: Lemerre, 1898.

Brahimi, D. "Restif féministe? Etude de quelques 'contemporaines,'" *Etudes sur le XVIIIe siècle* 3 (1976): 77–91.

Bramly, Serge. *La Terreur dans le boudoir*. Paris: Grasset, 1994.

Brandimbourg, Georges. *L'Arrière-Boutique*. Paris: Fort, 1898.

——. *Croquis du vice.* Paris: Fort, 1897.

Brantôme, Pierre de Bourdeille, seigneur de. *Les Dames galantes*. Edited by Maurice Rat. Paris: Garnier, 1965.

Brécourt-Villars, Claudine. *Petit Glossaire raisonné de l'érotisme saphique. 1880–1930*. Paris: Pauvert, 1980.

——, ed. *Ecrire d'amour. Anthologie de textes érotiques féminins*. Paris: Ramsay, 1985.

——, ed. *L'Erotisme Directoire*. Paris: Garnier, 1983.

Bremmer, Jan, ed. *From Sappho to Sade: Moments in the History of Sexuality*. London and New York: Routledge, 1989.

Breton, André. *Anthologie de l'humour noir*. Paris: Pauvert, 1972.

Breton, André, and Paul Eluard. *L'Immaculée conception*. Paris: Seghers, 1961.

——. *The Immaculate Conception*. Translated by Jon Graham. London: Atlas, 1990.

Brevannes, Roland. *Amante cruelle*. Paris: Offenstadt, n.d.

Brissenden, Robert F. *Virtue in Distress: Studies in the Novel of Sentiment from Richardson to Sade*. London: Macmillan, 1974.

Brochier, Jean-Jacques. *Le Marquis de Sade et la conquête de l'unique*. Paris: Le Terrain vague, 1966.

Brooks, Peter. *Body Work: Objects of Desire in Modern Narrative*. Cambridge: Harvard University Press, 1993.

——. *Reading for the Plot: Design and Intention in Narrative*. Oxford: Clarendon, 1984.

Brown, Beverley. "A Feminist Interest in Pornography: Some Modest Proposals." *m/f* 5–6 (1981): 5–18.

Bruckner, Pascal, and Alain Finkielkraut. *Le Nouveau Désordre amoureux*. Paris: Le Seuil, 1977.

Brulotte, Gaëtan. *Œuvres de chair: figures du discours érotique*. Quebec: L'Harmattan, Les Presses de l'Université Laval, 1998.

Brunner, Otto, Werner Conze, and Reinhart Koselleck, eds. *Geschichtliche Grundbegriffe: Historisches Lexicon zur politisch-sozialen Sprache in Deutschland*. Stuttgart: Cotta, 1982. [Article "Krise" 3:617–50]

Buchen, Irving, ed. *The Perverse Imagination: Sexuality and Literary Culture*. New York: New York University Press, 1970.

Burnett, Anne Pippin. *Three Archaic Poets: Archilochus, Alcaeus, Sappho*. Cambridge: Harvard University Press, 1983.

Burns, Alan, ed. *To Deprave and Corrupt: Technical Reports of the US Commission on Obscenity and Pornography*. London: Davis-Poynter, 1972.

Le Cabinet satyrique. Edited by Fernand Fleuret and Louis Perceau. 2 vols. Paris: Fort, Librairie du bon vieux temps, 1924.

Calverton, V. F. *Sex Expression in Literature*. New York: Boni and Liveright, 1926.

Calvo-Platero, Danièle. *Sappho, ou la soif de pureté*. Paris: Orban, 1987.

Campion, Léo. *Le Cul à travers les âges*. Paris: SOS Manuscrits, 1981.

Le Canapé couleur de feu. Paris: Bibliothèque des curieux, 1910 [1714?] [attributed to Fougeret de Montbron].

Capellanus, Andreas. *On Love*. Edited by P. G. Walsh. London: Duckworth, 1982.

Caroline et Saint-Hilaire, ou les putains du Palais-Royal. Paris: Dans un bordel, an 8 [1817].

Carraci, Agostino [Augustin Carrache]. *Arétin, ou recueil de postures érotiques*. Geneva: Slatkine, 1985 [1798].

Carter, Angela. *The Sadeian Woman and The Ideology of Pornography*. New York: Harper and Row, 1980.

Casalegno, Giovanni. "Rassegna aretiniana." *Lettere Italiane* 61 (1989): 425–54.

Casanova, Nonce. *Messaline*. Amiens: Malfère, 1922.

———. *Sapho: roman de Grèce antique*. Paris: Ollendorff, 1905.

Castle, Terry. *The Apparitional Lesbian: Female Sexuality and Modern Culture*. New York: Columbia University Press, 1993.

Cazenobe, Colette. "Le Système du libertinage de Crébillon à Laclos." *Studies on Voltaire and the Eighteenth Century* 282 (1991): 1–461.

Centre aixois d'études et de recherches sur le dix-huitième siècle. *Le Marquis de Sade*. Paris: Colin, 1968.

Centre culturel international de Cerisy-la-Salle. *Sade: écrire la crise*. Paris: Belfond, 1983.

Chanter, Tina. *Ethics of Eros: Irigaray's Rewriting of the Philosophers*. New York: Routledge, 1995.

Charney, Maurice. *Sexual Fiction*. London and New York: Methuen, 1981.

Chasseguet-Smirgel, Janine. *Ethique et esthétique de la perversion*. Paris: Champ Vallon, 1984.

Cherveix, Jean de. *Idylle mortelle*. Paris: Offenstadt, 1903.

Choiseul-Meuse, Félicité de. *Amélie de Saint-Far, ou la fatale erreur*. 2 vols. Brussels: Gay and Doucé, 1882.

———. *Julie, ou j'ai sauvé ma rose*. 2 vols. Hamburg and Paris: Les Marchands de nouveautés, 1807.

———. *Entre chien et loup*. 2 vols. Hamburg and Paris: Les Marchands de nouveautés, 1809.

Chorier, Nicolas, *Les Dialogues de Luisa Sigea sur les arcanes de l'amour et de Vénus, ou satire sotadique de Nicolas Chorier [L'Académie des dames]*. Translated by Alcide Bonneau. 4 vols. Paris: Lisieux, 1882.

Cixous, Hélène. "The Laugh of the Medusa." In *New French Feminisms: An Anthology*, edited by Elaine Marks and Isabelle de Courtivron, 245–64. Brighton: Harvester, 1981.

Clément, P. de. *Amours perverses.* Paris: Editions Modernes, 1929.

Colwill, Elizabeth. "Pass as a Woman, Act as a Man: Marie-Antoinette as Tribade in the Pornography of the French Revolution." In *Homosexuality in Modern France,* edited by Jeffrey Merrick and B. T. Ragan, Jr., 54–79. Oxford and New York: Oxford University Press, 1996.

Copp, David and Susan Wendell, eds. *Pornography and Censorship.* Buffalo, N.Y.: Prometheus, 1983.

Corbin, Alain. *Filles de noce: misère sexuelle et prostitution.* Paris: Aubier Montaigne, 1978.

Cornillon, Susan Koppelman. *Images of Women in Fiction: Feminist Perspectives.* Bowling Green, Ohio: Bowling Green University Popular Press, 1973.

Les Cousines de la colonelle. Lisbon: da Boa-Vista, n.d. [1880].

Crébillon *fils. Œuvres complètes.* Geneva: Slatkine, 1968.

———. *Le Sopha.* Paris: UGE, 1966.

———. *The Sofa; A Moral Tale.* Translated by Bonamy Dobrée. London: Folio Society, 1951.

———. *Tableaux des mœurs du temps dans les différents âges de la vie.* Paris: Lattès, 1980.

Creech, James. *Diderot: Thresholds of Representation.* Columbus: Ohio University Press, 1986.

Crocker, Lester C. *Nature and Culture: Ethical Thought in the French Enlightenment.* Baltimore: Johns Hopkins University Press, 1963.

Cryle, Peter. "Enunciation and Ejaculation: Telling the Erotic Climax." *Style* 24 (1990): 187–200.

———. "Gendered Time in Erotic Narrative: Finishing Power vs Staying Power." *Romanic Review* 83 (1992): 131–48.

———. *Geometry in the Boudoir.* Ithaca: Cornell University Press, 1994.

Cusset, Catherine. "'L'Exemple et le raisonnement': desir et raison dans *Therese philosophe.*" *Nottingham French Studies* 37, no. 1 (Spring 1998): 1–15.

Les Dames de maison et les filles d'amour. [Paris]: Cour de la Sainte-Chapelle, n.d. [c.1830].

Dardigna, Anne-Marie. *Les Châteaux d'Eros, ou les infortunes du sexe des femmes.* Paris: Maspero, 1980.

D'Argens. *Les Nonnes galantes.* Paris: Librairie anti-cléricale, n.d.

Darnton, Robert. *Edition et sédition: l'univers de la littérature clandestine au XVIIIe siècle.* Paris: Gallimard, 1991.

Daudet, Alphonse. *Sapho.* Morsang-sur-Orge: Safrat, 1990.

Dauphiné, Claude. *Rachilde.* Paris: Mercure de France, 1991.

Davidson, Arnold. "Sex and the Emergence of Sexuality." *Critical Inquiry* 14 (1987): 16–48.

Davray, Jules, and Jean Caujolle. *Vendeuse d'amour.* Paris: Simon, 1891.

De, Sushil Kumar. *Ancient Indian Erotics and Erotic Literature.* Calcutta: Mukhopadhyay, 1959.

De Baecque, Antoine. *Le Corps de l'histoire: métaphores et politique, 1770–1800*. Paris: Calmann-Lévy, 1993.

De Jean, Joan. *Fictions of Sappho, 1546–1937*. Chicago: University of Chicago Press, 1989.

————. *Literary Fortifications: Rousseau, Laclos, Sade*. Princeton: Princeton University Press, 1984.

De Jean, Joan, and Nancy K. Miller, eds. *Displacements: Women, Tradition, Literatures in French*. Baltimore: Johns Hopkins University Press, 1991.

Delard, Eugène. *Le Désir: journal d'un mari*. Paris: Calmann-Lévy, 1899.

Deleuze, Gilles. *Présentation de Sacher-Masoch: le froid et le cruel, avec le texte intégral de la Vénus à la fourrure*. Paris: Minuit, 1967.

Deleuze, Gilles, and Félix Guattari. *Capitalisme et schizophrénie. Mille plateaux*. Paris: Minuit, 1980.

Les Délices de Coblentz, ou anecdotes libertines des émigrés français. Coblentz: n.p., 1791.

Delon, Michel. "La Copie sadienne." *Littérature* 69 (1988): 87–99.

————. "Luxe et luxure: Réflexions a partir de Sade." *Nottingham French Studies* 37, no. 1 (Spring 1998) 17–25.

————. "Un Type épatant pour les saloperies." *Revue des sciences humaines* 230 (1993): 163–73.

Del Quiaro, Robert. *The Marquis de Sade: A Biography and a Note of Hope*. London: Messidor, 1994.

De Man, Paul. *Allegories of Reading: Figural Language in Rousseau, Rilke, and Proust*. New Haven: Yale University Press, 1979.

Deneys-Tunney, Anne. *Ecritures du corps: de Descartes à Laclos*. Paris: Presses universitaires de France, 1992.

Desai, Devangana. *Erotic Sculpture of India: A Socio-Cultural Study*. New Delhi: Tata McGraw Hill, 1975.

D[esjardins], E[mile]. *Les Callipyges, ou les délices de la verge*. Paris: aux dépens de la compagnie, 1892.

————. *Lèvres de velours*. Paris: n.p., 1932.

————. *L'Odyssée d'un pantalon*. Paris: aux dépens de la compagnie, 1889.

Desnos, Robert. *De l'érotisme considéré dans ses manifestations écrites et du point de vue de l'esprit moderne*. Paris: Cercle des arts, n.d.

————. *La Liberté ou l'amour! suivi de deuil pour deuil*. Paris: Gallimard, 1962.

Des Olbes, Claude. *Emilienne*. Paris: Losfeld, 1968.

Desthieux, Jean. *Figures méditerrannéennes: femmes damnées*. Paris: Orphrys, 1937.

Les Deux sœurs, ou quatre ans de libertinage. Montreal: Lebaucher, 1906.

Diderot, Denis. "Article 'Jouissance.'" In *Encyclopédie, Œuvres complètes*, edited by John Lough and Jacques Proust, vol. 7. Paris: Hermann, 1976.

————. *Les Bijoux indiscrets*. Edited by Antoine Adam. Paris: Garnier-Flammarion, 1968.

———. "Entretien entre d'Alembert et Diderot." In *Œuvres philosophiques*. Paris: Garnier, 1964.

———. *Memoirs of a Nun. La Religieuse*. London: Routledge, 1928.

———. *La Religieuse*. In *Œuvres romanesques*, edited by Henri Bénac. Paris: Garnier, 1962.

———. "Sur les femmes." In *Œuvres philosophiques*. Paris: Garnier, 1964.

Didier, Béatrice. *L'Ecriture-femme*. Paris: Presses universitaires de France, 1981.

———. *Sade: essai*. Paris: Denoël/Gonthier, 1976.

Dijkstra, Bram. *Idols of Perversity: Fantasies of Feminine Evil in Fin-de-Siècle Culture*. New York: Oxford University Press, 1986.

Dix-Huitième Siècle 12 (1980). Special number, "Représentations de la vie sexuelle."

Dobay Rifelj, Carol de. "Cendrillon and the Ogre: Women in Fairy Tales and Sade." *Romanic Review* 81 (1990): 11–24.

Dorat, Claude-Joseph. *Les Malheurs de l'inconstance, ou lettres de la marquise de Syrcé au comte de Mirbelle*. Paris: Desjonquères, 1983 [1772].

Douze Aventures du bossu Mayeux. Paris: Cercle du livre précieux, 1960.

Les Douze Journées érotiques de Mayeux. Paris: n.p., 1830 [1835].

Drouin, Henri. *Femmes damnées: essai sur les carences sexuelles féminines dans la littérature et dans la vie*. Paris: La Vulgarisation scientifique, 1945.

Du Bourdel, P. *Mademoiselle de Mustelle et ses amis*. N.p., n.d. [1913].

Dubut de Laforest, Jean-Louis. *Pathologie sociale*. Paris: Dupont, 1897.

Duby, Georges. *Love and Marriage in the Middle Ages*. Chicago: University of Chicago Press, 1994.

Duehren, Eugen. "Les Aphrodisiaques, les cosmétiques, les abortifs et les arcanes au XVIIIe siècle." *Obliques* 12–13 (1977): 270–74.

Duggan, Lisa, Nan Hunter, and Carole S. Vance. "False Promises: Feminist Antipornography Legislation in the U.S." In *Women Against Censorship*, edited by Varda Burstyn. Vancouver: Douglas and McIntyre, 1985.

Du Loup, Armande. *Sapho et ses vices*. Paris: Vert-Logis, 1939.

Dunan, Renée. *Cantharide*. Paris: Querelle, 1928.

———. *Une Heure de désir*. Paris: Prima, 1929.

Duo, Pierre. *Inassouvie*. Paris: Brossier, 1889.

Du Saussay, Victorien. *Chairs épanouies, beautés ardentes*. Paris: Méricant, 1902.

———. *L'Ecole du vice*. Paris: Antony, 1897.

———. *Rires, sang, et voluptés*. Paris: Bibliothèque du fin du siècle, 1901.

———. *La Suprême Etreinte*. Paris: Offenstadt, 1900.

Dworkin, Andrea. *Intercourse*. London: Secker and Warburg, 1987.

———. *Pornography: Men Possessing Women*. London: Women's Press, 1981.

Eaubonne, Françoise d'. *Eros minoritaire*. Paris: Balland, 1970.

L'Ecole des biches, ou mœurs des petites dames de ce temps. Erzeroum: chez Qizmich-Aga, n.d. [c. 1868].

Edison, G., ed. *Lesbos.* Paris: Morgan, 1970.

Edmiston, William F. "Irony, Unreliability, and the Failure of the Sadean Project: *Les Infortunes de la vertu.*" *French Forum* 12 (1987): 147–56.

Ehrenreich, Barbara, Elizabeth Hess, and Gloria Jacobs. *Re-Making Love: The Feminization of Sex.* New York: Anchor, 1986.

Encyclopedia Americana. New York: Americana Corporation, 1978.

Encyclopedia Britannica. Chicago: Encyclopedia Britannica, 1986.

L'Enfer de la Bibliothèque Nationale. Vols. 3–4, *Œuvres anonymes du XVIIIe siècle;* vol. 7, *Œuvres anonymes du XVIIe siècle.* Paris: Fayard, 1985–1988.

Erotylos. *Trois filles de Sappho.* Paris: Erotylos, 1936.

L'Escole des filles, ou la philosophie des dames. Edited by Pascal Pia. Paris: Cercle du livre précieux, 1959.

L'Esprit créateur 35, no. 2 (Summer 1995). Special number edited by Abby E. Zanger, "Writing about Sex: The Discourses of Eroticism in Seventeenth-Century France."

Etiemble, René. *L'Erotisme et l'amour.* Paris: Arléa, 1987.

———, ed. *Romanciers du XVIIIe siècle.* 2 vols. Paris: Gallimard/Pléïade, 1960–65.

Etudes francaises 32, no. 2 (1996). Special number, "Faire catleya au XVIIIe siecle: lieux et objets du roman libertin."

Evans, Martha Noel. *Fits and Starts: A Genealogy of Hysteria in Modern France.* Ithaca: Cornell University Press, 1991.

———. *Masks of Tradition: Women and the Politics of Writing in Twentieth-Century France.* Ithaca and London: Cornell University Press, 1987.

Faderman, Lilian. *Odd Girls and Twilight Lovers: A History of Lesbian Life in Twentieth-Century America.* New York: Columbia University Press, 1991.

———. *Surpassing the Love of Men: Romantic Friendship and Love Between Women from the Renaissance to the Present.* New York: Morrow, 1981.

Fauchery, Pierre. *La Destinée féminine dans le roman européen du dix-huitième siècle.* Paris: Armand Colin, 1972.

Ferguson, Frances. "Sade and the Pornographic Legacy." *Representations* 36 (1991): 1–21.

Fink, Béatrice. "Ambivalence in the Gynogram: Sade's Utopian Woman." *Women and Literature* 7 (1979): 24–37.

———. "Food as Object, Activity and Symbol in Sade." *Romantic Review* 65 (1974): 96–102.

———. "Sade and Cannibalism." *L'Esprit créateur* 15 (1975): 403–12.

Fiordo, Richard. "*Tales from the Smokehouse:* A Rhetorical Enquiry into Erotic Didactics." *Semiotica* 60 (1986): 1–27.

Fish, Stanley. *Is There a Text in this Class?: The Authority of Interpretive Communities.* Baltimore: Johns Hopkins University Press, 1980.

Flake, Otto. *The Marquis de Sade, with a Postscript on Restif de la Bretonne.* London: Peter Davies, 1931.

Forberg, Friedrich Carl, ed. *Manuel d'érotologie classique [De figuris Veneris].* Translated by Alcide Bonneau. 2 vols. Paris: Lisieux, 1882.

Formont, Maxime. *L'Inassouvie.* Paris: Lemerre, 1900.

Foster, Jeannette H. *Sex Variant Women in Literature: A Historical and Quantitative Survey.* London: Frederick Muller, 1958.

Foucault, Michel. *The Birth of the Clinic: An Archaeology of Medical Perception.* Translated by A. M. Sheridan Smith. New York: Pantheon, 1973.

———. *Dits et écrits.* Edited by Daniel Defert and François Ewald. Paris: Gallimard, 1994.

———. *Histoire de la sexualité I. La Volonté de savoir.* Paris: Gallimard, 1976.

———. *Histoire de la sexualité II. L'Usage des plaisirs.* Paris: Gallimard, 1984.

———. *Histoire de la sexualité III. Le Souci de soi.* Paris: Gallimard, 1984.

———. *The History of Sexuality.* New York: Vintage, 1986.

———. *Les Mots et les choses.* Paris: Gallimard, 1966.

———. *Naissance de la clinique.* Paris: Presses universitaires de France, 1972.

———. *The Order of Things: An Archaeology of the Human Sciences.* New York: Pantheon, 1971.

Fougeret de Montbron, Louis-Charles. *Le Canapé couleur de feu, suivi de la belle sans chemise, ou Eve ressuscitée.* Paris: Bibliothèque des curieux, 1910 [1714?].

———. *Margot la ravaudeuse.* 2 vols. Hamburg: n.p., 1800 [1750].

———. *Dix-Neuf Baisers, par un amant de vingt-deux ans, suivi de la jolie Ravaudeuse.* Paris: n.p., n.d.

Fowler, J. E. "Diderot's Family Romance: *Les Bijoux indiscrets* Reappraised" *Romanic Review* 88, no. 1 (January 1997): 89–102.

Fowlie, Wallace. *The Clown's Grail: A Study of Love in its Literary Expression.* N.p.: Norwood, 1977.

Foxon, David Fairweather. *Libertine Literature in England, 1660–1745.* London: Book Collector, 1964.

Frantz, David O. *Festum Voluptatis: A Study of Renaissance Erotica.* Columbus: Ohio University Press, 1989.

Frappier-Mazur, Lucienne. "L'Obscène, le mot et la chose." *Poétique* 93 (1993): 29–41.

———. *Sade et l'écriture de l'orgie.* Paris: Nathan, 1991.

———. *Writing the Orgy: Power and Parody in Sade.* Translated by Gillian C. Gill. Philadelphia: University of Pennsylvania Press, 1996.

Freadman, Anne. "Anyone For Tennis?" In *Genre and the New Rhetoric*, edited by F. Medway and A. Freedman. London: Taylor and Francis, 1994.

Freedberg, David. *The Power of Images: Studies in the History and Theory of Response.* Chicago: University of Chicago Press, 1989.

Fryer, Peter. *Private Case: Public Scandal.* London: Secker and Warburg, 1966.

Furber, Donald, and Anne Callahan. *Erotic Love in Literature: From Medieval Legend to Romantic Illusion.* Troy, N. Y.: Whitston, 1982.

Gaëtane. *Histoire d'I.* Paris: Filipacchi, 1974.

Galen. *On the Usefulness of the Parts of the Body.* Translated by Margaret Tallmadge May. Ithaca: Cornell University Press, 1968.

Gallagher, Catherine, and Thomas Laqueur, eds. *The Making of the Modern Body: Sexuality and Society in the Nineteenth Century.* Berkeley and Los Angeles: University of California Press, 1987.

Gallais, Alphonse. *Aux griffes de Vénus: amour morbide, mœurs de la décadence parisienne.* Paris: Fort, 1912.

Gallop, Jane. "Beyond the *Jouissance* Principle." *Representations* 7 (1984): 110–15.

———. *Feminism and Psychoanalysis: The Daughter's Seduction.* London: Macmillan, 1982.

———. *Intersections: A Reading of Sade with Bataille, Blanchot, and Klossowski.* Lincoln: University of Nebraska Press, 1981.

———. "Snatches of Conversation." In *Women and Language in Literature and Society,* edited by Sally McConnell-Ginet, Ruth Borker, and Nelly Furman, 274–83. New York: Praeger, 1980.

———. *Thinking Through the Body.* New York: Columbia University Press, 1988.

Gass, William. *A Philosophical Enquiry: On Being Blue.* Boston: Godine, 1975.

Gauthier, Xavière. *Surréalisme et sexualité.* Paris: Gallimard, 1971.

Gautier, Théophile. *Lettre à la présidente. Voyage en Italie, 1850.* Naples: Imprimerie du musée secret du roi de Naples, 1890.

———. *Mademoiselle de Maupin.* Paris: Bibliothèque Charpentier, 1919.

———. *Mademoiselle de Maupin.* Translated by Paul Selver. London: Hamish Hamilton, 1948.

———. "La Morte amoureuse." In *La France frénétique de 1830,* edited by Jean-Luc Steinmetz. Paris: Phébus, 1978.

Gervaise de Latouche, Jean-Charles. *Histoire de dom B . . . portier des Chartreux, écrite par lui-même.* 2 vols. London: n.p., 1788.

Gillett, Charles Ripley. *Burned Books: Neglected Chapters in British History and Literature.* Fort Washington, N. Y.: Kennikat, 1964.

Giraudoux, Jean. *Pour Lucrèce.* Paris: Grasset, 1953.

Giroux de Morency, Suzanne. *Illyrine.* In *L'Erotisme Directoire,* edited by Claudine Brécourt-Villars. Paris: Garnier, 1983.

Glessner, Beth A. "The Censored Erotic Works of Felicité de Choiseul-Meuse" *Tulsa Studies in Women's Literature* 16, no. 1 (Spring 1997): 131–43.

Godard d'Aucour, Claude. *Thémidore, ou mon histoire, et celle de ma maîtresse.* Paris: Offenstadt, 1907.

Goldberg, Rita Bettina. "Female Sexuality and Eighteenth-Century Culture in England and France: Richardson and Diderot." Ph.D. thesis, Princeton University, 1979.

———. *Sex and Enlightenment: Women in Richardson and Diderot.* Cambridge: Cambridge University Press, 1984.

Goldfarb, Russell M. *Sexual Repression and Victorian Literature.* Lewisburg, Pa.: Bucknell University Press, 1970.

Goldhill, Simon. *Foucault's Virginity: Ancient Erotic Fiction and the History of Sexuality.* Cambridge: Cambridge University Press, 1995.

Goodden, Angelica. *The Complete Lover: Eros, Nature and Artifice in the Eighteenth-Century French Novel.* Oxford: Clarendon, 1989.

Goujon, Jean-Paul. "Pierre Louys: Du libertinage à l'érotomanie." *Magazine littéraire* 371 (December 1998): 50–51.

Goulemot, Jean Marie. *Ces livres qu'on ne lit que d'une main: lecture et lecteurs de livres pornographiques au XVIIIe siècle.* Aix en Provence: Alinéa, 1991.

———. "Du lit et de la fable dans le roman érotique." *Etudes françaises* 32, no. 2 (Autumn 1996): 7–17.

———. *Forbidden Texts: Erotic Literature and its Readers in Eighteenth-Century France.* Translated by James Simpson. Philadelphia: University of Pennsylvania Press, 1994.

Gourmont, Rémy de. *Physique de l'amour.* Paris: Editions 1900, 1989.

Le Grand Robert. Paris: Société du Nouveau Littré, Le Robert, 1974.

Greenblatt, Stephen J. *Allegory and Representation.* Baltimore: Johns Hopkins University Press, 1981.

Greimas, Algirdas Julien. *Du sens: essais sémiotiques.* Paris: Seuil, 1970.

———. *On Meaning: Selected Writings in Semiotic Theory.* Translated by Paul J. Perron and Frank H. Collins. Minnesota: University of Minnesota Press, 1987.

Griffin, Susan. *Pornography and Silence: Culture's Revenge against Nature.* London: Women's Press, 1981.

Gubar, Susan, and Joan Hoff, eds. *For Adult Users only: The Dilemma of Violent Pornography.* Bloomington and Indianapolis: Indiana University Press, 1989.

Guiraud, Pierre. *Dictionnaire érotique: dictionnaire historique, stylistique, rhétorique, étymologique de la littérature érotique.* Paris: Payot, 1978.

———. *Les Gros Mots.* Paris: Presses universitaires de France, 1975.

Gyp. *La Fée.* Paris: Flammarion, 1932.

———. *Sœurette.* Paris: Juven, 1910.

Hackel, Robert J. *De Sade's Quantitative Moral Universe: Of Irony, Rhetoric, and Boredom.* The Hague and Paris: Mouton, 1976.

Hagstrum, Jean H. *Sex and Sensibility: Ideal and Erotic Love from Milton to Mozart.* Chicago: University of Chicago Press, 1980.

Haight, Anne Lyon. *Banned Books: Informal Notes on Some Books Banned for Various Reasons at Various Times and in Various Places.* 3rd ed. New York and London: R. R. Bowker, 1970.

Hans, Marie-Françoise, and Gilles Lapouge. *Les Femmes, la pornographie, l'érotisme.* Paris: Le Seuil, 1978.

Hanson, Gillian. *Original Skin: Nudity and Sex in Cinema and Theatre.* London: Stacey, 1970.

Harari, Josué. *Scenarios of the Imaginary. Theorizing the French Enlightenment.* Ithaca: Cornell University Press, 1987.

Hartmann, Pierre. "Education et aliénation dans *Les Egarements du cœur et de l'esprit.*" *Revue d'Histoire Littéraire de la France* 96 (1996): 71–97.

———. "Le Motif du viol dans la littérature romanesque du XVIIIe siècle." *Travaux de littérature* 7 (1994): 223–44.

Heath, Stephen. *Questions of Cinema*. Bloomington: Indiana University Press, 1981.

———. *The Sexual Fix*. London: Macmillan, 1982.

Heine, Maurice. "Préface à l'édition de 1931 [of *Les Cent Vingt Journées de Sodome*]." In *Œuvres complètes,* by Sade. Paris: Cercle du livre précieux, 1967.

Hénaff, Marcel. *Sade: L'Invention du corps libertin*. Paris: Presses universitaires de France, 1978.

Henric, Jacques. "L'Intolérable et l'infâme." *Obliques* 12–13 (1977): 39–45.

Henriot, Emile. *Les Livres du second rayon, irréguliers et libertins*. Paris: Grasset, 1948.

Herman, Jan. "Topologie du désir dans *Point de lendemain* de Vivant-Denon." *Australian Journal of French Studies* 27 (1990): 231–41.

Histoire d'un godmiché. London: n.p., 1886.

Holbrook, David, ed. *The Case against Pornography*. London: Stacey, 1972.

Hollier, Denis. *La Prise de la Concorde. Essais sur Georges Bataille*. Paris: Gallimard, 1974.

Horwood, Jeremy. "Sade et la génération." B.A. honours thesis, University of Queensland, 1994.

Houville, Gérard d'. *L'Inconstante*. Paris: Calmann-Lévy, 1903.

Howard, Heather. "The Contextualized Body: Narrative Event in *La Religieuse*." *Paroles Gelées* 13 (1995): 49–62.

Hughes, Alex, and Kate Ince, eds. *French Erotic Fiction: Women's Desiring Writing, 1880–1990*. Oxford: Berg, 1996.

Hughes, Douglas A., ed. *Perspectives on Pornography*. New York: Macmillan, 1970.

Hunt, Lynn Avery. *The Invention of Pornography: Obscenity and the Origins of Modernity, 1500–1800*. New York: Zone, 1993.

———, ed. *Eroticism and the Body Politic*. Baltimore: Johns Hopkins University Press, 1991.

Hunter, Ian, David Saunders, and Dugald Williamson. *On Pornography: Literature, Sexuality and Obscenity Law*. London: Macmillan, 1993.

Huston, Nancy. *Dire et interdire. Eléments de jurologie*. Paris: Payot, 1980.

———. *Mosaïque de la pornographie*. Paris: Denoël/Gonthier, 1982.

Hyde, Harford Montgomery. *A History of Pornography*. London: Heinemann, 1964.

Irigaray, Luce. *Ce Sexe qui n'en est pas un*. Paris: Minuit, 1977.

———. *Elemental Passions*. Translated by Joanne Collie and Judith Still. London: Athlone Press, 1992.

———. *Ethics of Sexual Difference*. Translated by Carolyn Burke and Gillian C. Gill. Ithaca: Cornell University Press, 1993.

———. *Ethique de la différence sexuelle*. Paris: Minuit, 1984.

———. *Passions élémentaires*. Paris: Minuit, 1982.

———. *Speculum de l'autre femme*. Paris: Minuit, 1974.

———. *Speculum of the Other Woman*. Ithaca: Cornell University Press, 1985.

———. *This Sex Which Is Not One*. Translated by Catherine Porter. Ithaca: Cornell University Press, 1985.

Ivker, Barry. "On the Darker Side of the Enlightenment: A Comparison of the Literary Techniques of Sade and Restif." *Studies on Voltaire and the Eighteenth Century* 79 (1971): 199–218.

———. "The Parameters of a Period-Piece Pornographer, Andréa de Nerciat." *Studies on Voltaire and the Eighteenth Century* 98 (1972): 199–205.

Jackson, John Edwin. *Le Corps amoureux: essai sur la représentation poétique de l'éros.* Neufchâtel: La Baconnière, 1986.

Jacques, Jean-Pierre. *Les Malheurs de Sapho*. Paris: Grasset, 1980.

Jardine, Alice. *Gynesis.* Ithaca: Cornell University Press, 1985.

———. "Pre-Texts for the Transatlantic Feminist." *Yale French Studies* 62 (1981): 220–236.

Jarry, Alfred. *Messaline*. In *Œuvres complètes,* vol. 3. Geneva: Slatkine, 1975 [1901].

Jean, Raymond. *Un Portrait de Sade*. Arles: Actes Sud, 1989.

Jeffreys, Sheila. *Anticlimax: A Feminist Perspective on the Sexual Revolution.* London: Women's Press, 1990.

Jouve, Séverine. *Obsessions et perversions: dans la littérature et les demeures à la fin du dix-neuvième siècle.* Paris: Hermann, 1996.

Joze, Victor. *La Cantharide*. Paris: Fort, n.d. [c.1900].

———. *La Femme à passions.* Paris: Rouff, 1902.

———. *Paris-Gomorrhe.* Paris: Antony, 1894.

Julie philosophe, ou le bon patriote. N.p., 1791.

Juranville, Françoise. "Un Roman d'apprentissage au XVIIIe siècle: écriture et gai savoir dans *Les Egarements du cœur et de l'esprit.*" *Revue d'Histoire Littéraire de la France* 96 (1996): 98–110.

Juvenal. *Sixteen Satires upon the Ancient Harlot*. Translated by Steven Robinson. Manchester: Carcanet New Press, 1983.

Kaite, Berkeley. *Pornography and Difference*. Bloomington: Indiana University Press, 1995.

Kamuf, Peggy. *Fictions of Feminine Desire: Disclosures of Héloïse.* Lincoln: University of Nebraska Press, 1982.

Kappeler, Susanne. *The Pornography of Representation*. Minneapolis: University of Minnesota Press, 1986.

Kearney, Patrick J. *The Private Case: An Annotated Bibliography of the Private Case Erotica Collection from the British Museum Library*. London: Gay Landesman, 1981.

Kellec, Jehan de. *A Lesbos.* Paris: Simon, 1891.

Kendrick, Walter. *The Secret Museum: Pornography in Modern Culture.* New York: Viking, 1987.

Klossowski, Pierre. *Sade mon prochain, suivi du philosophe scélérat.* Paris: Le Seuil, 1967.

———. *Sade My Neighbour*. Translated by Alphonso Lingis. Evanston, Ill.: Northwestern University Press, 1991.

Kopelson, Kevin. *Love's Litany: The Writing of Modern Homoerotics*. Stanford, Calif.: Stanford University Press, 1994.

Kroker, Arthur and Marilouise, eds. *Body Invaders: Sexuality and the Postmodern Condition*. London: Macmillan, 1988.

Kuhn, Annette. *The Power of the Image: Essays on Representation and Sexuality*. London: Routledge and Kegan Paul, 1985.

———. *Women's Pictures: Feminism and Cinema*. London: Routledge and Kegan Paul, 1982.

Laborde, Alice M. "Sade: l'érotisme démystifié." *L'Esprit créateur* 15 (1975): 438–48.

———. *Les Infortunes du marquis de Sade*. Paris and Geneva: Champion-Slatkine, 1990.

———. *Sade romancier*. Neuchâtel: La Baconnière, 1974.

Lacan, Jacques. "Kant avec Sade." In *Ecrits II*. Paris: Le Seuil, 1971.

Lacombe, Anne. "*Les Infortunes de la vertu*, le conte et la philosophie." *L'Esprit créateur* 15 (1975): 425–37.

Lafarge, Catherine. "*Les Délices de l'amour* de Restif de la Bretonne: attaque efficace contre Sade?" *Studies on Voltaire and the Eighteenth Century* 153 (1976): 1245–53.

Lafon, Henri. "Machines à plaisir dans le roman français du XVIIIe siècle." *Revue des sciences humaines* 18 (1982): 111–21.

La Jeunesse, Ernest. *Demi-Volupté*. Paris: Offenstadt, 1900.

La Mettrie, Julien Offroy de. *L'Ecole de la volupté*. Paris: Desjonqueres, 1996.

———. *L'Homme machine, suivi de l'art de jouir*. Edited by Maurice Solovine. Paris: Bossard, 1921.

Laqueur, Thomas. "Credit, Novels, Masturbation." In *Choreographing History*, edited by Susan Leigh Foster, 119–28. Bloomington: Indiana University Press, 1995.

———. *Making Sex: Body and Gender from the Greeks to Freud*. Cambridge: Harvard University Press, 1990.

Larson, Ruth. "From Ovid to Chorier: Philosophy and Confession in the Ur-Text of Classical European Eroticism." *Bulletin de la société américaine de philosophie de langue française* 6 (1994): 76–103.

Lascault, Gilbert. *Alphabets d'Eros*. Paris: Galilée, 1976.

Laugaa-Traut, Françoise, ed. *Lectures de Sade*. Paris: Armand Colin, 1973.

La Vaudère, Jane de. *Les Demi-Sexes*. Paris: Ollendorff, 1897.

———. *Les Fleurs de la volupté*. Paris: Flammarion, 1900.

———. *Mortelle Etreinte*. Paris: Ollendorff, 1891.

Lebrun. *Les Amours de deux jolies femmes, riches et philosophes, faisant la suite et la fin de la femme publique*. Brussels: Joostens, 1860.

———. *Les Amours libertines de religieuses du couvent des Carmélites*. Brussels: Joostens, 1861.

Le Brun, Annie. *A distance*. Paris: Pauvert/Carrere, 1984.

———. *Les Châteaux de la subversion*. Paris: Pauvert/Garnier, 1982.

———. *Sade, aller et détours*. Paris: Plon, 1989.

———. *Soudain un bloc d'abîme*. Paris: Pauvert, 1986.

Leclerc, Yvan. "XIXe siècle: les Enfants de Sade." *Magazine littéraire* 371 (December 1998): 44–47.

Les Leçons de la volupté, ou confession générale du chevalier de Wilfort. Brussels: Gay and Doucé, 1882.

Lederer, Laura, ed. *Take Back the Night: Women on Pornography*. New York: William Morrow, 1980.

Ledwidge, Bernard. *Sappho: la première voix d'une femme*. Paris: Mercure de France, 1987.

Lee, Vera. "The Sade Machine." *Studies on Voltaire and the Eighteenth Century* 98 (1972): 207–18.

Leibacher-Ouvrard, Lise. "Pseudo-féminocentrisme et ordre (dis)simulé: la *Satyra sotadica* (1658–1678) et l'*Académie des dames* (1680)." In *Ordre et contestation au temps des classiques*, edited by Roger Duchene and Pierre Ronzeaud, vol. 1. Paris: Papers on French Seventeenth Century Literature, 1992.

———. "Transtextualité et construction de la sexualité: la *Satyra sotadica* de Chorier." *L'Esprit créateur* 35 (1995): 51–66.

Lély, Gilbert. Introduction to *Les Infortunes de la vertu*, by Sade. Paris: UGE, 1968.

———. "Le Marquis de Sade et Rétif de la Bretonne." *Mercure de France* 331 (1957): 364–66.

———. "Le Marquis de Sade et Rétif de la Bretonne, auteur de *l'Anti-Justine*." In Sade, *Œuvres complètes*, 483–87. Paris: Cercle du livre précieux, 1966–67.

Lemonnier, Camille. *Claudine Lamour*. Paris: Dentu, 1893.

———. *L'Hystérique*. Paris: Charpentier, 1885.

Le Nismois. *Monsieur Julie, maîtresse de pension*. Paris-Brussels, n.p., 1900.

Lepage, Francis. *Les Fausses Vierges*. Paris: Offenstadt, 1902.

Le Pennec, Marie-Françoise. *Petit Glossaire du langage érotique au XVIIe et XVIIIe siècles*. Paris: Borderie, 1979.

Lesbia, maîtresse d'école. Paris: aux dépens de la Compagnie, 1890.

Lesbos, Georges de. *Enfilade de perles*. Amsterdam: de Lesbos, 1894.

———. *Joyeuses Enfilades*. Amsterdam: n.p., 1895.

———. *Voluptés bizarres*. Amsterdam: n.p., 1893.

Lettres amoureuses d'un frère à son élève. Alexandria: n.p., n.d. [1878].

Lever, Maurice. *Donatien Alphonse François marquis de Sade*. Paris: Fayard, 1991.

Lewinsohn, Richard. *A History of Sexual Customs*. Translated by Alexander Mayce. New York: Harper, 1958.

Les Libertines du grand monde. Au Palais-Royal: Chez la petite Lolotte, 1890 [1880].

Liebel, Frieda. *La Vierge affranchie.* Paris: Vert-Logis, 1936.

Lingis, Alphonso. *Excesses: Eros and Culture.* Albany, State University of New York Press, 1983.

Lo Duca, J.-M. *Histoire de l'érotisme.* Paris: Pygmalion, 1979.

Lorenz, Paul. *Sapho 1900, Renée Vivien.* Paris: Julliard, 1977.

Lorrain, Jean. *Monsieur de Phocas. Astarté.* Paris: Le Livre Club du libraire, 1966 [1901].

Lorrain, Jean. *Le Vice errant.* Paris: Ollendorff, 1902.

Loth, David. *The Erotic in Literature: A Historical Survey of Pornography as Delightful as it is Indiscreet.* New York: Julian Messner, 1961.

Louvet de Couvray, Jean-Baptiste. *Les Amours du chevalier de Faublas.* 2 vols. Paris: Les Marchands de nouveautés, n.d.

Lucette, ou les progrès du libertinage. London: Jean Nourse, 1765.

Lucien de Samostate. *Lucius ou l'âne, suivi de dialogues des courtisanes.* Edited by Gilbert Lély. Paris: Lattès, 1979.

Mac Orlan, Pierre. *La Semaine secrète de Sapho.* N.p.: La Chronique des dames, n.d. [c.1929].

———. *La Semaine secrète de Vénus.* Paris: Cotinaud, 1926.

Maffesoli, Michel. *L'Ombre de Dionysos: contribution à une sociologie de l'orgie.* Paris: Méridiens, 1985.

Mainil, Jean. *Dans les règles du plaisir . . . Théorie de la différence dans le discours obscène, romanesque et médical de l'Ancien Régime.* Paris: Kimé, 1996.

Mairobert, Pidansat de. *La Secte des anandrynes: confession de mademoiselle Sapho.* Edited by Jean Hervez. Paris: Bibliothèque des curieux, 1920.

Maizeroy, René. *Deux Amies.* Paris: Havard, 1885.

Marcadé, Jean. *Eros Kalos: Essay on Erotic Elements in Greek Art.* Geneva: Nagel, 1962.

Marcus, Steven. *The Other Victorians: A Study of Sexuality and Pornography in Mid-Nineteenth Century England.* London: Weidenfeld and Nicolson, 1966.

———. "Pornotopia." *Encounter* 27, no. 2 (1966): 9–18.

Marcuse, Ludwig. *Obscene: The History of an Indignation.* Translated by Karen Gershon. London: MacGibbon and Kee, 1965.

Margueritte, Victor. *La Garçonne.* Paris: Flammarion, 1922.

Marks, Elaine. "Lesbian Intertextuality." In *Homosexualities and French Literature: Cultural Contexts / Critical Texts,* edited by G. Stambolian and E. Marks, 353–77. Ithaca: Cornell University Press, 1979.

Masters, William H., and Virginia E. Johnson. *Human Sexual Response.* Boston: Little, Brown, 1966.

Ma tante Geneviève, ou je l'ai échappé belle. Paris: Barba, 1800.

Les Matinées du Palais-Royal, ou amours secrètes de mademoiselle Julie B‴, devenue comtesse de l'empire. Berne, Paris: Les Marchands de nouveautés, 1815.

Maupassant, Guy de. "La Femme de Paul." In *Contes et nouvelles.* Paris: Gallimard/Pléiade, 1974.

Maupertuis, Alexandre. *Le Sexe et le plaisir avant le christianisme: l'érotisme sacré*. Paris: CELT, 1977.

May, Charles E. "Sex, Submission, and the Story of O." *Carleton Miscellany* 16 (1977): 22–32.

Maynard, John. *Victorian Discourses on Sexuality and Religion*. Cambridge: Cambridge University Press, 1993.

McCalman, Iain. *Radical Underworld: Prophets, Revolutionaries, and Pornographers in London, 1795–1840*. Cambridge: Cambridge University Press, 1988.

Melançon, Benoît. "Faire catleya au XVIIIᵉ siècle." *Etudes françaises* 32, no. 2 (1996): 65–81.

Mémoires de Suzon, sœur de D. . . B . . . portier des Chartreux. J'enconne: Aux dépens de la Gourdan, n.d. [c.1780].

Mendès, Catulle. *Méphistophela*. Paris: Dentu, 1890.

Menke, Anne M. "Liaisons savoureuses: Pornography in the Service of Women?" *Papers on French Seventeenth Century Literature* 24, no. 46 (1997): 85–98.

Mercier, Roger. "Sade et le thème des voyages dans *Aline et Valcour*." *Dix-Huitième Siècle* 1 (1969): 337–52.

Merlin, Jean de. *La Débauche à Paris*. Paris: Antony, 1900.

———. *La Luxure*. Paris: Bibliothèque du fin du siècle, 1905.

Merrick, Jeffrey, and B. T. Ragan, eds. *Homosexuality in Modern France*. Oxford and New York: Oxford University Press, 1996.

———. "The Marquis de Villette and Mademoiselle de Raucourt: Representations of Male and Female Sexual Deviance in Late Eighteenth-Century France." In *Homosexuality in Modern France*, edited by Jeffrey Merrick and B. T. Ragan Jr., 30–53. Oxford and New York: Oxford University Press, 1996.

Michael, Colette V. *Sade: His Ethics and Rhetoric*. New York, Berne, Frankfurt, Paris: Peter Lang, 1989.

Michelson, Peter. *The Aesthetics of Pornography*. New York: Herder and Herder, 1971.

Miller, Nancy K. *French Dressing: Women, Men, and Ancien Regime Fiction*. New York: Routledge, 1995.

———. *The Heroine's Text: Readings in the French and English Novel, 1772–1782*. New York: Columbia University Press, 1980.

———. "'I's' in Drag: The Sex of Recollection," *The Eighteenth Century: Theory and Interpretation* 22 (1981) 47–57.

———. "*Juliette* and the Posterity of Prosperity." *L'Esprit créateur* 15 (1975): 413–24.

———, ed. *The Poetics of Gender*. New York: Columbia University Press, 1986.

Millett, Kate. *Sexual Politics*. Garden City, N. Y.: Doubleday, 1970.

Mirabeau. *Œuvres érotiques*. Paris: Fayard, 1984.

Mireille, Camille. *Mémorandum galant, ou confession d'une femme légère*. Paphos: Imprimerie du temple de Cythère, 1903.

Moi, Toril. *Sexual/Textual Politics: Feminist Literary Theory*. London and New York: Methuen, 1985.

Moinet, Paul. *Messaline la calomniée.* Paris: Bossuet, 1930.

Monneyron, Frédéric. *L'Androgyne décadent: mythe, figure, phantasmes.* Grenoble: Ellug, 1996.

Monnier, Henri. *L'Enfer de Joseph Prudhomme.* Paris: A la sixième chambre, n.d.

Montifaud, Marc de. *Celles qui tuent: la baronne de Livry.* Paris: n.p., 1890.

Moreau, Marcel. "Le Devoir de monstruosité." *Obliques* 12–13 (1977): 15–18.

Morin, Violette, and Joseph Majault. *Un Mythe moderne: l'érotisme.* Paris: Casterman, 1964.

Mosaic 2, no. 1 (1968). Special number, "Eros and Literature."

Moureau, François, and Alain-Marc Rieu. *Eros philosophe: discours libertins des lumières.* Paris: Champion, 1984.

Musset, Alfred de. *Gamiani, ou deux nuits d'excès.* In *L'Erotisme romantique,* edited by J.-J. Pauvert. Paris: Carrere, 1984.

Mylord Arsouille, ou les bamboches d'un gentleman. Bordel-opolis: chez Pinard, rue de la Motte, 1789 [c.1858].

Nelli, René. *L'Erotique des troubadours.* Paris: UGE 10/18, 1974.

Nerciat, Andréa de. *Les Aphrodites, ou fragments thali-priapiques pour servir à l'histoire du plaisir.* 2 vols. N.p., 1793–1925.

———. *Le Diable au corps, œuvre posthume du très recommandable docteur Cazzone, membre extraordinaire de la joyeuse faculté phallo-coïto-pygo-glottonomique.* 6 vols. N.p., 1803.

———. *Félicia, ou mes fredaines.* Edited by Pierre Josserand. Paris: Le Livre de Poche Hachette, 1976.

———. *Mon Noviciat, ou les joies de Lolotte.* Paris: n.p., 1932.

Nobile, Philip, ed. *The New Eroticism: Theories, Vogues and Canons.* New York: Random House, 1970.

Nogaret, Félix. *L'Arétin français, suivi des épices de Vénus.* Edited by Louis Perceau. Versailles: aux dépens des fermiers généraux, n.d. [1787].

Nottingham French Studies 37, no. 1 (Spring 1998). Special number edited by Jean Mainil, "French Erotic Fiction: Ideologies of Desire."

La Nouvelle Académie des dames. Cythère: n.p., 1774.

O'Neal, John C. "Review Essay: Eighteenth-Century Female Protagonists and the Dialectics of Desire." *Eighteenth Century Life* 10, no. 2 (May 1986): 87–97.

O'Reilly, Robert. "Desire in Sade's *Les Cent Vingt Journées de Sodome.*" *Studies on Voltaire and the Eighteenth Century* 217 (1983): 249–56.

Ostrovsky, Erika. "A Cosmogony of O." In *Twentieth Century French Fiction: Essays for Germaine Brée,* edited by George Stambolian, 241–51. New Brunswick, N.J.: Rutgers University Press, 1975.

Ovid. *The Art of Love [Ars amatoria] and Other Poems.* Cambridge: Harvard University Press, 1979.

———. *Les Métamorphoses.* Translated and edited by Georges Lafaye. Paris: Les Belles Lettres, 1965.

Palacio, Jean de. *Figures et formes de la décadence.* Paris: Séguier, 1994.

Pallavicino, Ferrante. *Alcibiade fanciullo a scola*. Geneva: n.p., 1642.

———. *Alcibiade enfant à l'école*. Amsterdam: L'Ancien Pierre Marteau, 1866.

———. *La Retorica delle puttane*. Cambrai: n.p., 1642.

Park, Katharine. "The Rediscovery of the Clitoris: French Medicine and the Tribade, 1570–1620." In *The Body in Parts: Fantasies of Corporeality in Early Modern Europe*, edited by David Hillman and Carla Mazzio, 171–93. New York: Routledge, 1997.

Pastre, Geneviève. *Athènes et le péril saphique: homosexualité féminine en Grèce ancienne*. Paris: Les Mots à la bouche, 1987.

Pauvert, Jean-Jacques. *Sade vivant: une innocence sauvage . . . 1740–77*. Paris: Robert Laffont, 1986.

———. *L'Erotisme des années folles*. Paris: Garnier, 1983.

———. *L'Erotisme Second Empire*. Paris: Carrere, 1985.

———. *Théâtre érotique français au XVIIIᵉ siècle*. Paris: Le Terrain vague, 1993.

———, ed. *Anthologie des lectures érotiques*. 3 vols. Paris: Ramsay, 1980–83.

———, ed. *L'Erotisme romantique*. Paris: Carrere, 1984.

Payer, Pierre J. *The Bridling of Desire: Views of Sex in the Later Middle Ages*. Toronto: University of Toronto Press, 1993.

Peckham, Morse. *Art and Pornography: An Experiment in Explanation*. New York: Basic Books, 1969.

Péladan, Joséphin. *La Gynandre*. Paris: Dentu, 1891.

———. *Le Livre du désir*. Paris: Librairie des auteurs modernes, 1885.

———. *Le Vice suprême*. Paris: Librairie moderne, 1884.

Perceau, Louis. *Bibliographie des romans érotiques du XIXᵉ siècle*. 2 vols. Paris: Fourdrinier, 1930.

Perec, Georges. "Tentative de description de choses vues au carrefour Mabillon le 19 mai 1978." Atelier de création radiophonique no. 381, February 25, 1979.

Perkins, Michael. *The Secret Record: Modern Erotic Literature*. New York: Morrow, 1976.

Perrin, Noel. *Dr. Bowdler's Legacy: A History of Expurgated Books in England and America*. London: Macmillan, 1970.

Perrot, Philippe. *Le Corps féminin: XVIIIᵉ–XIXᵉ siècle*. Paris: Seuil, 1991.

Pert, Camille. *Les Amours perverses de Rosa Scari*. Paris: Librairie artistique, 1907.

Phillips, Eileen, ed. *The Left and the Erotic*. London: Lawrence and Wishart, 1983.

Pia, Pascal. *Les Livres de l'enfer: bibliographie critique des ouvrages érotiques dans leurs différentes éditions du XVIᵉ siècle à nos jours*. 2 vols. Paris: Coulet et Faure, 1978.

Pierrot, J. *L'Imaginaire décadent: 1880–1900*. Paris: Presses universitaires de France, 1977.

Pieyre de Mandiargues, André. *L'Anglais décrit dans le château fermé*. Paris: Gallimard, 1979.

———. *Le Désordre de la mémoire. Entretiens avec Francine Mallet*. Paris: Gallimard, 1975.

Pigault-Lebrun, G.-C.-A. *La Folie espagnole*. Paris: Arnould, 1889.

Pillement, Georges, ed. *La Poésie érotique*. Paris: Deforges, 1970.

Pintard, René. *Le Libertinage érudit dans la première moitié du dix-septième siècle*. Paris: Slatkine, 1983.

Pleynet, Marcelin. "Sade, des chiffres, des lettres, du renfermement." *Tel Quel* 86 (1980): 26–37.

Poovey, Mary. "'Scenes of an Indelicate Character': The Medical 'Treatment' of Victorian Women." In *The Making of the Modern Body: Sexuality and Society in the Nineteenth Century*, edited by Catherine Gallagher and Thomas Laqueur. Berkeley: University of California Press, 1987.

Pops, Martin. "The Metamorphosis of Shit." *Salmagundi* 56 (1982): 26–61.

Porter, Roy. "Spreading Carnal Knowledge or Selling Dirt Cheap? Nicolas Venette's *Tableau de l'amour conjugal* in Eighteenth Century England." *Journal of European Studies* (1984): 233–55.

Poster, Marc. "Patriarchy and Sexuality. Restif and the Peasant Family," *The Eighteenth Century: Theory and Interpretation* 35 (1984): 217–40.

Pougy, Liane de. *Idylle saphique*. Edited by Jean Chalon. Paris: Des femmes, 1987.

Poulet, Georges. *Etudes sur le temps humain*. Paris: Plon, 1950–68.

Praz, Mario. *La Chair, la mort et le diable dans la littérature du XIXe siècle: le romantisme noir*. Paris: Denoël, 1977.

Prévost, Marcel. *Chonchette*. Paris: Lemerre, 1888.

———. *Les Demi-Vierges*. Paris: Lemerre, 1901.

La Putain errante, ou dialogue de Madelaine et de Julie. Paris: n.p., n.d.

La Quinzaine littéraire (August 1976). Special number, "La Pornographie et les femmes."

Quinn, Vincent and Mary Peace, "Luxurious Sexualities." *Textual Practice* 11, issue 3 (Winter 1997): 405–16.

Quarante Manières de foutre, dédiées au clergé de France. Cythère: Au Temple de la volupté, 1790.

Rachilde. *L'Heure sexuelle*. Paris: Baudinière, 1933 [1898].

———. *La Jongleuse*. Edited by Claude Dauphiné. Paris: Des femmes, 1982 [1900].

———. *Madame Adonis*. Paris: Monnier, 1888.

———. *La Marquise de Sade*. Paris: Mercure de France, 1981 [1887].

———. *Monsieur Vénus*. Paris: Flammarion, 1977 [1884].

———. *La Mort d'une fille de marbre*. Paris: Du Fourneau, 1985.

———. *Le Premier Amour*. Paris: Du Fourneau, 1984.

———. *Les Voluptés imprévues*. Paris: Ferenczi, 1931.

Ragan, Bryant T. Jr. "The Enlightenment Confronts Homosexuality." In *Homosexuality in Modern France*, edited by Jeffrey Merrick and B. T. Ragan Jr., 8–29. Oxford and New York: Oxford University Press, 1996.

Réage, Pauline. *Histoire d'O*. Paris: Pauvert, 1975.

———. *The Story of O*. Paris: Olympia, 1954.

Rebell, Hugues. *La Câlineuse*. Paris: La Revue Blanche, 1899.

———. *Les Nuits chaudes du Cap français*. Paris: De la Plume, 1902.

Régnier, Henri de. "La Femme de marbre." *La Revue de Paris* 7 (1900): 225–41.

Reichler, Claude. "Le Récit d'initiation dans le roman libertin." *Littérature* 47 (1982): 100–112.

Renard, Jean-Claude, and François Zabaleta. *Le Mobilier amoureux, ou la volupté de l'accessoire*. Briare: Chimères, 1991.

Reschal, Antonin. *Fille ou femme*. Paris: Librairie parisienne, 1898.

———. *Le Journal d'un amant*. Paris: Offenstadt, 1902.

———. *Une Inassouvie*. Paris: Antony, 1897.

Restif de la Bretonne, Nicolas-Edmé. *Œuvres érotiques*. Paris: Fayard, 1985.

———. *Pleasures and Folies of a Good-natured Libertine [L'Anti-Justine]*. Translated by Pieralessandro Casavini. Paris: Olympia, 1955.

Reveroni Saint-Cyr, Jacques-Antoine de. *Pauliska, ou la perversité moderne, mémoires récentes d'une Polonaise*. Paris: Deforges, 1976.

Revue d'esthétique (1978). Special number, "Erotiques."

Revue des sciences humaines 212 (1988). Special number, "Restif de la Bretonne."

Revue des sciences humaines 230 (1993). Special number, "Jean Lorrain: vices en écriture."

Richepin, Jean. *Sapphô*. Paris: Marpon/Flammarion, 1884.

Le Rideau levé, ou l'éducation de Laure. Paris: Lattès, 1980. [Attributed to Mirabeau and included in his *Œuvres érotiques*: see above; also attributed to Sentilly.]

Riffaterre, Michael. "Sade, or Text as Fantasy." *Diacritics* 2, no. 3 (1972): 2–9.

Robert, Raymonde, ed. *Contes parodiques et licencieux du XVIIIe siècle*. Nancy: Presses Universitaires de Nancy, 1987.

Roger, Philippe. "L'Imaginaire libertin et le corps 'spectaculeux.'" *Revue de l'Université de Bruxelles* 3–4 (1987): 53–60.

———. *Sade: La Philosophie dans le pressoir*. Paris: Grasset, 1976.

Le Roman de mon alcôve: confessions galantes d'une femme du monde. Paris: à l'enseigne du musée secret, n.d. [1869].

Le Roman de Violette. Paris: Castermann, 1982. [Attributed to Mannoury.]

Romilly, Edouard. *Sappho: la passionnante, la passionnée*. Paris: Figuière, 1931.

Rosario, Vernon A. *The Erotic Imagination: French Histories of Perversity*. New York and Oxford: Oxford University Press, 1997.

———. "Pointy Penises, Fashion Crimes, and Hysterical Mollies: The Pederasts' Inversions." In *Homosexuality in Modern France,* edited by Jeffrey Merrick and B. T. Ragan Jr., 146–76. Oxford and New York: Oxford University Press, 1996.

Rousseau, Jean-Jacques. *Julie, ou la nouvelle Héloïse*. Edited by Michel Launay. Paris: Garnier-Flammarion, 1967.

———. *Pygmalion*. In *Œuvres*, vol. 2. Paris: Gallimard/Pléïade, 1961.

Rousselle, Aline. *Porneia: de la maîtrise du corps à la privation sensorielle: III*ᵉ *et IV*ᵉ *siècles de l'ère chrétienne*. Paris: Presses universitaires de France, 1983.

———. *Porneia: On Desire and the Body in Antiquity*. Translated by Felicia Pheasant. Oxford and New York: Basil Blackwell, 1988.

Roy, Bruno, ed. *L'Erotisme au moyen âge*. Montreal: Aurore, 1977.

Sade, Marquis de. *The 120 Days of Sodom and Other Writings*. Translated by Austryn Wainhouse and Richard Seaver. New York: Grove Weidenfeld, 1987.

———. *Les Crimes de l'amour: nouvelles héroïques et tragiques; précédées d'une idée sur les romans*. Edited by Eric Le Grandic and presented by Michel Delon. Cadeilhan: Zulma, 1995.

———. *Justine, Philosophy in the Bedroom, and Other Writings*. Compiled and translated by Richard Seaver and Austryn Wainhouse. New York: Grove Weidenfeld, 1990.

———. *Œuvres*. Edited by Michel Delon. 2 vols. Paris: Gallimard/Pléïade, 1990.

———. *Œuvres complètes*. Edited by Annie Le Brun and Jean-Jacques Pauvert. 15 vols. Paris: Pauvert, 1986.

Saint-Agen, Adrienne. *Amants féminins*. Paris: Offenstadt, 1902.

———. *[Charmeuses de femmes] L'Affolante Illusion*. Paris: Offenstadt, 1906.

Saint-Médard, René. *L'Orgie moderne*. Paris: Bibliothèque du fin du siècle, 1905.

———. *La Volupté féroce*. Paris: Bibliothèque "Fin de siècle," 1905.

Sapho ou l'heureuse inconstance, par Madem. . . . The Hague: A. Troyel, 1695.

Scholes, Robert. "Uncoding Mama: The Female Body as Text." In *Semiotics and Interpretation*, edited by R. Scholes, 127–42. New Haven: Yale University Press, 1982.

Schor, Naomi. *Breaking the Chain: Women, Theory, and French Realist Fiction*. New York: Columbia University Press, 1985.

Sedgwick, Eve Kosofsky. *Between Men: English Literature and Male Homosocial Desire*. New York: Columbia University Press, 1985.

———. *Epistemology of the Closet*. Berkeley: University of California Press, 1990.

Sgard, J. "La Notion d'égarement chez Crébillon." *Dix-Huitième Siècle* 1 (1969): 241–49.

Sherfey, Mary Jane. *The Nature and Evolution of Female Sexuality*. New York: Random House, 1972.

———. "A Theory on Female Sexuality." In *Sisterhood Is Powerful*, edited by Robin Morgan, 220–30. New York: Vintage, 1970.

Sibalis, Michael David. "The Regulation of Male Homosexuality in Revolutionary and Napoleonic France, 1789–1815." In *Homosexuality in Modern France,* edited by Jeffrey Merrick and B. T. Ragan Jr., 80–101. Oxford and New York: Oxford University Press, 1996.

Sichère, Bernard. "Pour en finir avec le 'Sadisme' et sa haine." *Obliques* 12–13 (1977): 69–78.

Smet, Ingrid de, and Philip Ford, eds. *Eros et Priapus: erotisme et obscénité dans la littérature néo-latine: études*. Geneva: Droz, 1997.

Smith, F. J., and Erling Eng. *Facets of Eros: Phenomenological Essays*. The Hague: Martinus Nijhoff, 1972.

Snitow, Anne, Christine Stensell, and Sharon Thompson, eds. *Powers of Desire*. New York: Monthly Review Press, 1983.

Soble, Alan. *Pornography: Marxism, Feminism, and the Future of Sexuality*. New Haven: Yale University Press, 1986.

Sollers, Philippe. *Femmes*. Paris: Gallimard/Folio. 1984.

———. *Women*. Translated by Barbara Bray. New York: Colombia University Press, 1990.

———. "Lettre de Sade." *Tel Quel* 61 (1975): 14–20.

———. "Sade dans le texte." *Tel Quel* 28 (1967): 38–50.

———. "Sade, encore." *Le Monde*, 13 Feb. 1987, 20.

Sontag, Susan. *Illness as Metaphor*. New York: Farrar, Straus, and Giroux, 1978.

Staël, Germaine de. *Sappho*. In *Œuvres complètes*. Geneva: Slatkine, 1967.

Stambolian, George, and Elaine Marks, eds. *Homosexualities and French Literature: Cultural Contexts and Critical Texts*. Ithaca: Cornell University Press, 1985.

Stanton, Domna C. "Sexual Pleasure and Sacred Law: Transgression and Complicity in *Vénus dans le cloître*." *L'Esprit créateur* 35 (1995): 67–83.

Steinmetz, Jean-Luc, ed. *La France frénétique de 1830*. Paris: Phébus, 1978.

Stern, Lesley. "The Body as Evidence: A Critical Review of the Pornography Problematic." *Screen* 23 (1982): 38–60.

Stewart, Philip. *Engraven Desire: Eros, Imagery, and Text in the French Eighteenth Century*. Durham, N.C.: Duke University Press, 1992.

Stoehr, Taylor. "Pornography, Masturbation and the Novel." *Salmagundi* 2 (1966): 28–56.

Sturm, Ernest. *Crébillon fils et le libertinage au XVIIIe siècle*. Paris: Nizet, 1970.

Taberner, Peter V. *Aphrodisiacs: The Science and the Myth*. Philadelphia: University of Pennsylvania Press, 1985.

Les Tableaux vivants, ou mes confessions aux pieds de la duchesse. 2 vols. Amsterdam: n.p., 1870.

Le Tartuffe libertin, ou le triomphe du vice. Cythère: chez le gardien du temple, n.d.

Les Tendres Epigrammes de Cydno la lesbienne. Paris: Bibliothèque des curieux, n.d. [c.1910].

Téramond, Guy de. *Impériales Voluptés*. Paris: Méricant, 1905.

Textual Practice 11, no. 3 (Winter 1997). Special number edited by Mary Peace and Vincent Quinn, "Luxurious Sexualities: Effeminacy, Consumption, and the Body Politic in Eighteenth-Century Representation."

Thérèse philosophe. Paris: Slatkine, 1981.

Thomas, Chantal. *Sade, l'œil de la lettre*. Paris: Payot, 1978.

Thompson, Victoria. "Creating Boundaries: Homosexuality and the Changing Social Order in France, 1830–1870." In *Homosexuality in Modern France,* edited by Jeffrey Merrick and B. T. Ragan Jr., 102–27. Oxford and New York: Oxford University Press, 1996.

Thomson, Ann. "L'Art de jouir de La Mettrie à Sade." In *Aimer en France: 1760–1860,* 315–22. Clermont-Ferrand: Association des publications de la Faculté des Lettres et Sciences Humaines de Clermont-7, 1980.

Trésor de la langue française. Paris: Editions du CNRS, 1971–94.

Todd, Janet. *Women's Friendship in Literature.* New York: Columbia University Press, 1980.

La Tourelle de Saint-Etienne, ou le séminaire de Vénus. Cythère: Chez le gardien du Temple, n.d.

Tort, Michel. "L'Effet Sade." *Tel Quel* 28 (1967): 66–83.

Toute la lyre! Manœuvres de Lucienne. N.p., n.d.

Trouille, Mary. "Sexual/Textual Politics in the Enlightenment: Diderot and D'Epinay Respond to Thomas's Essay on Women." *British Journal for Eighteenth-Century Studies* 19, no. 1 (Spring 1996): 1–15.

Trousson, Raymond, ed. *Romans libertins du XVIIIe siècle.* Paris: Laffont, 1993.

Turner, James Grantham, ed. *Sexuality and Gender in Early Modern Europe.* Cambridge: Cambridge University Press, 1993.

Un Eté à la campagne. N.p., n.d. [Bibliothèque Nationale, Enfer 840].

Vance, Carole S. "Anthropology Rediscovers Sexuality: A Theoretical Comment." *Social Science and Medicine* 33 (1991): 875–84.

———. "Misunderstanding Obscenity." *Art in America* (1990): 49–55.

———. "The Pleasures of Looking." In *The Critical Image: Essays in Contemporary Photography*, edited by Carol Savien, 38–58. Seattle: Bay Press, 1990.

———. "Toward a Conversation about Sex in Feminism: A Modest Proposal." *Signs* 10 (1984): 126–35.

———, ed. *Pleasure and Danger: Exploring Female Sexuality.* London: Routledge and Kegan Paul, 1984.

Van den Abbeele, Georges. "Sade, Foucault, and the Scene of Enlightenment Lucidity." *Stanford French Review* 11 (1987): 7–16.

Van Ussel, Jos. *Histoire de la répression sexuelle.* Paris: Laffont, 1972.

Vatsayana. *The Kama Sutra.* Edited by W. G. Archer, translated by Sir Richard Burton and F. F. Arbuthnot. London: Allen and Unwin, 1963.

Venette, Nicolas. *Tableau de l'amour conjugal.* Paris: Agence Parisienne de Distribution, 1950 [1687].

Vénus dans le cloître, ou la religieuse en chemise. Edited by Marcel Béalu. Paris: Lattès, 1979. [Attributed to Barrin, or to Chavigny de la Bretonnière, under the pseudonym of l'abbé du Prat.]

Verlaine, Paul. "Sappho." In *Œuvres poétiques.* Paris: Garnier, 1969.

Vian, Boris. *Ecrits pornographiques, précédés de: utilité d'une littérature érotique.* Paris: Bourgois, 1980.

Vicinus, Martha. "The Adolescent Boy: Fin de Siècle Femme Fatale?" *Journal of the History of Sexuality* 5 (1994): 90–114.

Vingt Ans de la vie d'une jolie femme, ou mémoires de Julia R. . . . . Vito-Cono-Cuno-Clytoropolis: Chez Bandefort, rue de la Couille, au Fouteur Libéral, 1789 [1842].

Vingt Ans de la vie d'un jeune homme. Vito-Cono-Cuno-Clytoropolis: Chez Bandefort, rue de la Couille, au Fouteur Libéral, 1789 [1830].

Vivant Denon. *Point de Lendemain.* Paris: Desjonquères, 1987.

Vivien, Renée. *Une Femme m'apparut.* Paris: Lemerre, 1905.

Wagner, Peter. *Eros Revived: Erotica of the Enlightenment in England and America.* London: Secker and Warburg, 1988.

Wald Lasowski, Patrick. *L'Ardeur et la galanterie.* Paris: Gallimard, 1986.

———. "La Fessée ou l'ultime faveur." *Magazine Litteraire* 357 (September 1998): 30–33.

———. "Les Fouteries chantantes de la révolution." *Magazine littéraire* 371 (December 1998): 35–38.

———. *Libertines.* Paris: Gallimard, 1980.

———. *Syphilis. Essai sur la littérature française du XIXe siècle.* Paris: Gallimard, 1982.

Wald Lasowski, Roman. "Crébillon fils et le libertinage galant." *Littérature* 47 (1982): 83–99.

Wedeck, Harry E. *Dictionary of Erotic Literature.* New York: Citadel, 1962.

Weeks, Jeffrey. *Coming Out: Homosexual Politics in Britain from the Nineteenth Century to the Present.* London: Quartet, 1977.

———. *Sexuality and its Discontents: Meanings, Myths, and Modern Sexualities.* London: Routledge and Kegan Paul, 1985.

Williams, David. "Another Look at the Sadean Heroine: The Prospects for Femininity." *Essays on French Literature* 13 (1976): 28–43.

Williams, Linda. *Hard Core: Power, Pleasure, and the "Frenzy of the Visible."* Berkeley: University of California Press, 1989.

Young, Wayland Hilton, *Eros Denied.* London: Transworld, 1968.

Yvel, Jacques. *Demi-Femme.* Paris: Offenstadt, 1901.

———. *Madame Flirt.* Paris: Simonis Empis, 1902.

Zanger, Abby E. "Writing about Sex and . . ." *L'Esprit créateur* 35 (1995): 3–8.

Index